Child, Adolescent and Family Development

Second Edition

PHILLIP T. SLEE

Flinders University

CAMBRIDGE
UNIVERSITY PRESS

CAMBRIDGE UNIVERSITY PRESS
Cambridge, New York, Melbourne, Madrid, Cape Town, Singapore,
São Paulo, Delhi, Dubai, Tokyo

Cambridge University Press
477 Williamstown Road, Port Melbourne, VIC 3207, Australia

www.cambridge.org
Information on this title: www.cambridge.org/9780521010900

First published in 1993 by Harcourt Brace and Company, Australia
This second edition first published by Cambridge University Press in 2002
Reprinted 2007

A catalogue record for this publication is available from the British Library

National Library of Australia Cataloguing in Publication data
Slee, Phillip T.
Child, adolescent and family development.
Bibliography.
Includes index.
1. Family. 2. Child development. 3. Adolescence. I.
Title
155.4

ISBN 978-0-521-81200-9 Hardback
ISBN 978-0-521-01090-0 Paperback

Additional resources for this publication at www.cambridge.org/9780521010900

Transferred to digital printing 2009

Contents

Part 1 The Study of Human Development   1

Part 3 Infancy 119

6 Physical Development in Infancy 121

7 Cognitive Development in Infancy 140

8 Social and Emotional Development in Infancy 160

Part 4 Toddlerhood 181

9 Physical Development of Toddlers 183

10 Cognitive Development of Toddlers 202

11 Social and Emotional Development of Toddlers 225

Part 5 The Pre-school Years 247

12 Physical Development of Pre-schoolers 249

13 Cognitive Development of Pre-schoolers 264

Part 7 Adolescence   383

Trends and issues

These 'Trends and issues' boxes cover the broad topics of (i) parents; (ii) culture; (iii) health; (iv) teachers; (v) research; (vi) case-studies; (vii) policy.

Family life-cycles

Figures

Tables

To the student

I was heartened by your responses and feedback to the first edition. As a teacher I was encouraged to proceed with the second edition with the singularly important aim of providing an even more readable, accessible and practical text. But if that was all I achieved I would have failed you miserably!

I am hopeful that in the pages of this second edition the 'voices' of children, adolescents and family members will be strongly heard. It is my fervent belief that children and adolescents are marginalised, ignored and largely disenfranchised in many western countries today. While we continue to view children as the 'property' of adults, we continue to oppress and deny them basic rights. Child psychology and the methods of child study have much to be accountable for in maintaining the status quo, viewing children as 'subjects' to be studied. The hierarchical and patriarchal assumptions inherent in the mainsteam methods of child study deserve to be thoroughly challenged. While we continue to view childhood as a 'journey' towards some completion or resolution found in adulthood instead of appreciating childhood for its more immediate vibrancy and freshness we too are contributing to the oppression of children.

The challenge is yours to help redress much of the injustice and inequality adults daily heap upon children and adolescents. I am confident that you will rise to the challenge.

To work with you towards this end you I have provided a number of new features in this second edition.

1   details regarding the latest developments in theoretical thinking
2   a photo journal entry follows the development of selected children over a span of their life-time providing a 'real-life' example of child and adolescent development. For example, the photo journal entry for 'Christopher' follows his development from birth to his current age of 4 years with pictures, highlighting significant features of his story.
3   significant additional material regarding language development
4   a CD-ROM for your use. This extensive resource provides additional new information regarding the conduct of research, practical child and adolescent observation activities and self review tests.
5   the addition of websites information provides a significant resource for you to follow-up points of interest or to pursue information for projects and essays. In particular the website http://wwwed.sturt.flinders.edu.au/DLT/default.htm which lists university student's investigations into various features of child development is a new and innovative feature of the text.
6   video resources provide significant teaching and learning material for teachers and students to access. For example, a video/discussion package is available from the author on the topic of children, families and stress. A written resource called 'The P.E.A.C.E. Pack: A Program for reducing bullying in schools' is also available from the author.

To the instructor

A CD-ROM is provided presenting:

- an introduction to the study of children
- details of methods for conducting research
- ethical guidelines for the conduct of research utilising a range of methods and linked to research/theory in the text
- Review tests and answers covering each chapter.

Reference to websites

The text provides a link to comprehensive websites addressing key issues associated with child, adolescent and family issues. The websites provide further links to facilitate research and report writing. In particular the websites <http://wwwed.sturt.flinders.edu.au/DLT/default.htm> and <http://www.caper.com.au> provide details of several years of university students' research projects into child and adolescent development (reproduced with permission).

How to use the CD-ROM

The following icon: 🖱️ appears in the margin throughout the book in places where the CD-ROM can be used in conjunction with that particular part of the book or as a specific activity.

The CD-ROM is located in the inside back cover of this book, and contains operating instructions.

The CD-ROM contains:

- an introduction to the study of children
- details of methods for conducting research
- ethical guidelines for the conduct of research
- practical research projects utilising a range of methods and linked to research/theory in the text
- review tests and answers covering each chapter.

CD-ROM contents

This publication no longer contains an attached CD-ROM. The full contents of the CD-ROM are available for download from www.cambridge.org/9780521010900.

Acknowledgements

Once again my special thanks go to all who contributed to the book. Photographs, many from family albums, were kindly provided by Elizabeth Downes, Pat McQuin, and Paul Wallace. Thanks to those who gave permission to reproduce copyright material in the book and, of course, I would be happy to hear from those whom I have been unable to contact.

Peter Debus, commissioning editor at Cambridge University Press, deserves special thanks for his expert help and guidance in editing and shaping the text. Last, but certainly not least, I would like to thank Margaret Trudgeon, my copyeditor, and Paul Watt of Cambridge University Press for their support and encouragement in the development of the book.

This book is lovingly dedicated to Elizabeth and our three boys,
Matthew, Nicholas and Christopher.
The book would not have been written without Elizabeth's unstinting support.
The boys have gently helped remind me what really matters in life
when my attention has strayed.

Introduction

As for the first edition, the second edition of *Child, Adolescent and Family Development* is written for all those who entertain an interest in children's and adolescents' lives, and for all those who appreciate the curiosity, strength and resilience of growing children. It is a book about the richness and diversity of children's and adolescents' lives, considered in the context of the family. In turn, the family and its individual members are viewed in the broader historical context of society and culture. This book is also about change. All that it discusses is considered to be in a process of flux and change.

In planning and writing the second edition I have taken note of the feedback I received from tertiary teachers and their students regarding the content of the book. A number of features in the first edition were consistently endorsed by readers including the 'broad sweep' of the book as it placed human development in an historical, philosophical and cultural context. Readers also commented favourably upon the Australasian flavour which considered child development in an international context. Finally, appreciation was expressed for the 'readability' of the text.

In preparing the second edition a number of anonymous reviewers responded to the proposed content and I am particularly grateful for their opinions. Where possible, I have taken into account their suggestions in this second edition but obviously the final responsibility for the content is mine.

The Foundation for the Text

The foundation for this text draws upon a number of inter-related elements.

- the book is embedded in theory and again for this I make no apology. In the book's inception, its theoretical base reflects my prevailing belief that all our dealings with children in whatever role, whether as parent or teacher or in some other capacity, are bounded by theory, either implicit or explicit.
- human development is seen through the lens of philosophy, history and culture. The writings of this text strongly reflect the manner in which the philosophy of science shapes and influences our thinking about children and their development and particularly the nature of research conducted to better understand development. My intent in placing the study of child development in an historical context reflects my own love of history and my pursuit of its study in my undergraduate years at university. It is consistent with my belief that history provides a framework for helping interpret and understand behaviour. My travel and research in other cultures has strongly impressed upon me how deeply our development is steeped in culture and how significantly different and tantalising similar cultures are from one another.
- The text reflects my abiding commitment to a broad-based systemic view of development. In this regard I owe a depth of gratitude for several sabbaticals in Calgary, Canada, where in studying and practising family therapy I had the fortunate opportunity to explore the basic ideas and practice of systems theory.
- Finally, this text reflects my enduring commitment to translating research into knowledge with a strong practical application.

The Text Presentation

The text is presented in chronological order of the life span so as to provide the reader with a clear understanding of the complexity of the individual's developing capacities. The drawback of this approach is that it may compartmentalise child development, but this is not an intended outcome of the book. Indeed, it has been my concern to show the interrelatedness of the child's development wherever possible. An alternative more topical approach is described here.

The book is divided into eight parts, comprising a total of 21 chapters. Parts 1 and 2 deal with the study of human development, while parts 3–7 examine the development of the child from infancy to adolescence. Part 8 considers a life-span perspective.

In part 1, the first three chapters reflect a concern with the theoretical issues underpinning the study of child and adolescent development. Chapter 3 is an overview of theoretical contributions to developmental psychology and can be used either as a 'stand alone' chapter or as a reference for other chapters. Chapters 4 and 5 (part 2) deal with the beginnings of life, taking us through to the newborn period. Part 3 (chapters 6–8) is devoted to infancy, highlighting different components of the infant's development. Part 4 (chapters 9–11) examines the toddler's place in the world, emphasising the active and constructive nature of toddlers' learning and development. In chapters 12–14 (part 5) the pre-schooler's enlarging world, which draws on wider social contact, is discussed. Middle childhood is addressed in chapters 15–17 (part 6), focusing on the child's place in school and society, and on broader issues facing the family, such as the birth of a second child. In part 7 (chapters 18–20) the rich, complex and diverse world of adolescence is explored, together with the adolescent's moves towards independence from the family. In part 8, chapter 21 draws together the themes discussed throughout the text and places child and adolescent development in a life-cycle perspective.

The Family Life-cycle is a series of 21 items, one at the end of each chapter, dealing with different aspects of the family. These may be studied in the context of each chapter, or as a separate topic. Throughout the book, boxed features are devoted to items of special interest related to topics discussed in the main text. These special interest boxes are grouped under headings of (i) parents; (ii) culture; (iii) health; (iv) teachers; (v) research; (vi) case-studies; and (vii) policy. As an aid to study, each chapter concludes with discussion questions and activities. A separate CD-ROM provides (a) details of research methodology (b) 10 practical child observation activities (c) expanded review tests and answers.

For those who wish to teach a topical course on child development, the following chapter sequence will work well:

THE STUDY OF HUMAN DEVELOPMENT
Chapter 1: Seeing Children in Context
Chapter 2: Concepts of Development
Chapter 3: Theoretical Foundations of Child Development
      Family Life-cycles 1–3

THE BEGINNING OF LIFE
Chapter 4: Prenatal Development
Chapter 5: From Conception to Birth
      Family Life-cycles 4–5

PHYSICAL DEVELOPMENT
Chapter 6: Physical Development in Infancy
Chapter 9: Physical Development of Toddlers
Chapter 12: Physical Development of Pre-schoolers
Chapter 15: Physical Development in Middle Childhood
Chapter 18: Adolescent Physical Development and Health Issues
        Family Life-cycles 6–10

COGNITIVE DEVELOPMENT
Chapter 7: Cognitive Development in Infancy
Chapter 10: Cognitive Development in Toddlers
Chapter 16: Cognitive Development in Middle Childhood
Chapter 19: Cognitive Development in Adolescence
        Family Life-cycles 11–14

SOCIAL AND EMOTIONAL DEVELOPMENT
Chapter 8: Social and Emotional Development in Infancy
Chapter 11: Social and Emotional Development of Toddlers
Chapter 14: Social and Emotional Development of Pre-schoolers
Chapter 17: Social and Emotional Development in Middle Childhood
        Family Life-cycles 15–18
Chapter 20: Social and Emotional Development in Adolescence

A LIFE-SPAN PERSPECTIVE
Chapter 21: Towards a Life-span Perspective
        Family Life-cycle 19

Thank you and best wishes for a peaceful journey in appreciating and understanding the nature and richness of others' lives.

The Study of Human Development

Jacquilyn aged 6 months

Jacquilyn aged 2 years

Jacquilyn aged 4½ years

1 Seeing Children in Context

> ... **Still within the little children's eyes**
> I sought no more that after which I strayed
> In face of man or maid;
> But still within the little children's eyes
> Seems something, something that replies,
> They at least are for me, surely for me!
> I turned me to them very wistfully
> But just as their young eyes grew sudden fair
> With dawning answers there
> Their angel plucked them from me by the hair.
>
> *Francis Thompson*, 'The Hound of Heaven'

CHAPTER OUTLINE

KEY TERMS AND CONCEPTS

- Developmental psychology
- 'Gazing at' children
- proprietal
- Postfigurative, configurative, prefigurative
- Paradigm
- Empiricism
- Positivism
- The experiential child
- The iniquitous child
- The virtuous child
- The competent infant
- Mechanistic, organismic, behaviourist, psychodynamic, humanistic, constructivist

Introduction

Since the first edition of this textbook was written and published in 1993 it is readily apparent to me that general and academic interest in the study of child development has increased exponentially. Notwithstanding this, a quick glance in the relevant sections of the local library or bookstore will show that through the ages children have been the subject of description by poets, novelists, philosophers and playwrights. Dietrich Tiedermann is generally acknowledged by historians of child psychology as a pioneer in the field of systematic description in child development. In 1787 Tiedermann published a study of his own child, predicting that it would soon be followed by many others. True to his prediction, the late nineteenth century was witness to a growing interest in child and adolescent development. The latter part of the twentieth century has in many ways produced a veritable harvest of knowledge regarding child, adolescent and family development.

In this chapter consideration is given to the various factors that shape the way we view children and the approaches psychology has taken to the study of children. Some of the many different ways of defining the word 'family' are outlined in the first of The Family Life-cycle series.

The nature of psychology

Psychology is a relatively young discipline, and it would be fair to suggest that some confusion still exists among the general public as to just what it involves. In all likelihood an informal chat to friends or family would elicit a wide range of answers to a question concerning the nature of psychology. The answers would probably include misconceptions (for example, psychology involves reading people's minds), and/or confusion (such as about the difference between psychiatry and psychology).

Psychology basically grew out of the disciplines of philosophy and physiology. Most psychologists would generally agree that psychology includes:

- the study of overt, observable or otherwise measurable behaviour: for example, facial expressions, or physiological changes such as heart rate;
- the study of unseen mental processes, such as thoughts and dreams.

As psychology has emerged as a field of study in its own right in the last 100 years, different branches of the discipline have evolved. Psychologists now work in many areas: teaching in tertiary institutions, counselling in schools, studying animal behaviour, working with the physically and intellectually handicapped, to name but a few. In Australia, the minimum period for basic training in psychology is six years: four years of undergraduate university training and two years of supervision by a qualified psychologist. Many psychologists have additional training at a Masters or PhD level.

Psychologists are now being challenged in this post-modern era to think beyond mainstream empirical ways of researching and understanding child

'Joy is my name' (W. Blake): An image of childhood

development and to be more critical of the theories and assumptions of developmental psychology.

Developmental psychology

A field of study in psychology that is concerned with how the individual grows and changes from conception till death is known as **developmental psychology**. Within this field one special avenue of interest is child development, which is particularly concerned with the study of the individual from conception. This text is essentially a child development text. In focusing on child development, consideration is given to describing the physical, cognitive and socio-emotional changes the individual undergoes. More particularly, the text addresses a number of broad questions:

developmental psychology
the study of the individual from conception.

- How do children change as they develop?
- What factors influence the developmental changes?
- What individual differences exist in children's growth and development?

Cairns (1998, p. 26) has noted that 'developmental psychology has its own distinctive history, which is associated with, but independent of, the history of experimental or general psychology'. It is reasonable to argue that a dominant theme in the field (as verified by an examination of the contents page of significant journals) is that of raising children (e.g. Charles Darwin's research; see chapter 3). This arose from the writings of seventeenth and eighteenth-century philosophers such as John Locke, Jean Jacques Rousseau and religious writers such as John Wesley (see chapter 3).

Numerous questions arise out of home observations, such as those of Charles Darwin in the following section. For example, what are the guidelines for normative development (see Gesell; see chapter 3)?

Another significant theme evident in the field concerns whether there is there some sequence to development such that an orderly progression can be identified. Other significant themes also arise concerning the nature of the factors influencing such development. That is, what respective roles do genetics and environment play in the development of children? Questions such as these are an important part of the subject matter of psychology and, in particular, of child development. (See CD for practical exercises.)

Why study child development?

Child development is a young science and the systematic study of children is a relatively recent phenomenon. Courses in child, adolescent and family development today embrace a range of professions including teaching, psychology, social work, child care and nursing, to name but a few.

The reasons for studying children are as broad and complex as the field itself. In reading the literature one becomes aware of how accurately theorists such as Charles Darwin, Sigmund Freud, Karen Horney, Leila Berg and Jean Piaget observed children. In part, it is recognised that through the study of children's behaviour we may better come to understand adult behaviour. As John Milton commented in *Paradise Lost*:

The childhood shows the man as morning shows the day.

From a somewhat different perspective, Charles Darwin believed that the child was the link between animal and human species. The birth of his son William Erasmus (nicknamed 'Doddy') on 27 December 1839 prompted Charles Darwin to begin a diary description of the development of his son – 'a baby biography'. For example, in *The Expression of the Emotions in Man and Animals* (first published in 1872), Darwin argued that emotional expressivity was basically a physiological matter and that expressive gestures were largely universal and innate.

Everyone who has had much to do with young children must have seen how naturally they take to biting when in a passion. It seems instinctive in them as in young crocodiles, who snap their little jaws as soon as they emerge from the egg (Darwin 1965, pp. 241–2).

Other investigators were less interested in comparing human and animal species than Darwin. Thus, Gabriel Compayre believed that information concerning the child's early years would serve to illuminate later development.

Medinnus (1976) identified four main reasons for studying children:

1   An intellectual curiosity concerning natural phenomena.
2   The need to gain information to guide children's behaviour.
3   Increasing our ability to predict behaviour.
4   The need to understand our own behaviour.

In searching for an answer to the question of why we study the development of children, it is vitally important not to lose sight of the historical and cultural context in which childhood exists. It is a salutary point to consider that the very words 'child' and 'childhood' have changed their meaning within the context of recent Western history and have different meanings in different cultures.

'Gazing at' children

The study of child development does not occur in a historical, cultural or philosophical vacuum. Charles Darwin's observations were designed to explore the links between animal and human species. The infant was essentially depicted as a biological organism, influenced and shaped to a greater or less degree by the environment. The study of children, along with the study of 'primitives', was seen as the key to better understanding the development of 'normal' behaviour. The concept of 'recapitulation', understood as the idea that 'ontogeny recapitulates phylogeny', or that the individual in her/his lifetime demonstrates the patterns and stages exhibited in the development of the species, underpins the writing of many of the early theorists. The surge of interest in the study of children, the identification of their 'stages' of development and the obsession with minutely recording 'normal' growth and development underpinned the motivations of much early research, involving 'gazing at' children.

The conduct of this 'science' went hand in hand with the development of an empirical methodology which clearly separated the 'observer' from the 'observed' in the best interests of the scientific endeavour. The infant/child/adolescent was 'objectified' in the spotlight of this critical 'gaze'. As Burman (1994) notes, this exercise involved a 'gendered division of labor', with men viewed as having the necessary credentials to conduct 'objective, verifiable observations. Women were excluded from the investigative enterprise because they were declared constitutionally incapable of regarding their children with the requisite objectivity' (p. 12).

Gazing at children

Factors shaping views of children and families

Writers have identified a number of factors that have shaped our views of children and families over the centuries (Ariès 1962; Schorsch 1979; Elkind 1987; Wertsch and Youniss 1987; Young 1990; Clarke-Stewart, 1998). Two factors consistently identified are history and culture. As Ariès (1962) has reminded us, little, if anything at all, escapes history and culture, not even the central elements of life itself – women, men and children. A third factor that will also be discussed in this chapter is the philosophy of science.

The child and family in history

In beginning a study of childhood, it is important to appreciate the view expressed by the social historian, Philippe Ariès, that childhood, as it is understood today in Western society, is a relatively recent phenomenon. Following Ariès' (1962) pioneering writings on the history of childhood, a number of writers have supported his views.

Schorsch (1979, p. 11) observes that:

> thinkers of the 16th century, and of the preceding centuries as well, agreed that the child is nothing more than a lower animal – 'the infant mewling and puking in the nurse's arms' as Shakespeare put it baldly but succinctly.

As Schorsch goes on to note, our contemporary beliefs regarding the innocence and importance of the early years may in fact blind us to the frequent heartlessness and cruelty with which children in Western cultures were treated in the past. For example, consider the message preached by the Bishop of Worcester in 1552:

> I exhort you, in God's behalf, to consider the matter, ye parents: suffer not your children to let, or tell false tales. When you hear one of your children to make a lie take him up, and give him three or four good stripes and tell him that it is naught; and when he make another lie, give him six or eight stripes and I am sure when you serve him so, he will leave it (Pinchbeck and Hewitt 1969).

Elkind (1987) has captured some of the complexity of the changing views of childhood from antiquity to the present time. He notes that in ancient Greece the stress was upon educating children into the laws and cultural mores of the time. Children in Babylon went to school at the age of 6, while in Roman times the children attended school around the age of 7 to acquire reading and writing skills. However, according to Elkind, children in mediaeval Europe fared far less well. During this time the prevailing image of children emphasised that the child was a chattel or piece of property of the parent and state. All in all, during the mediaeval period the child did not account for much in the eyes of society, as a sixteenth-century rhyme indicates:

> Of all the months the first behold,
> January two-faced and cold
> Because its eyes two ways are cast
> To face the future and the past.
> Thus the child six summers old
> Is not worth much when all is told.
> *Cited in Schorsch 1979, p. 23.*

Children as property

In Western societies, history shows that for centuries children have been looked upon as property and, more particularly, as the property of their fathers. Paternalism and patriarchy have been significant elements in parent–child relationships for quite some time. Some basis for understanding the contemporary status of children in Western societies is found in the writings of the Greek philosopher, Aristotle. In Bertrand Russell's description of Aristotelian ethics, it is noted that while Aristotle considered human beings as 'ethically equal':

> [T]he justice of a master or a father is a different thing from that of a citizen, for a son or slave is property, and there can be no injustice to one's own property (1974, p. 186).

Law elaborated between AD 1300 and 1800 prescribed the relationship between parent and child in terms of trust. The parent's rights came from the Crown, and the Crown reserved the right to intervene and protect the child's rights and interests. However, as Fraser (1976, p. 322) notes:

> While the court would intervene to protect a child's interests, it did not provide the child with a vehicle to present his grievances to the court, nor did it guarantee the child the right of independent representation.

Apart from the law, some interesting insight is gained into the status of children in Western society from the writings of seventeenth-century philosophers such as Thomas Hobbes and John Locke and nineteenth-century philosopher John Stuart Mill. Hobbes, writing in the seventeenth century, argued that children were cared for solely because they were capable of serving their father and should be assigned a position of complete dependence. 'Like the imbecile, the crazed and the beasts over ... children ... there is no law' (1931, p. 257). The implication of Hobbes' argument is that children have no natural rights and no rights by social contract because they lack the ability to make formal contracts with other members of society and cannot understand the consequences of such contracts.

Later in the same century, John Locke, arguing from a different perspective, considered children to be under the jurisdiction of their parents until they were capable of fending for themselves. Until such time, children were thought to lack understanding and therefore they could not assert their will (Russell 1974). Unlike Hobbes, Locke believed that both adults and children possessed certain natural rights which needed protection. Parental benevolence was believed to be sufficient to ensure that children's rights were protected. Locke's outlook rejected the proprietary aspect of parenthood, replacing it with the concept of children as God's property.

Locke's description of children as lacking in understanding reflected the view that children need to develop adult capacities for reasoning and understanding. Until such time, parents were under a God-given obligation to care for children. By implication, where parents failed to fulfil their obligation to children, the state would be empowered to do so.

The late eighteenth and nineteenth centuries in Europe were witness to the dramatic social and economic changes wrought by the Industrial Revolution. In large part, children fared very poorly in the face of these changes. Schorsch (1979) notes that children as young as 4 years of age worked in the cotton mills of England.

> A child over seven worked from sunrise to sunset six days a week with two and a half days off a year; children between six and sixteen earned slightly more than half a woman's wages and only a fourth of a man's (1979, p. 143).

The eighteenth-century French novelist Emile Zola (1979), in his book *Germinal*, depicts 12-year-old children working alongside their fathers and older brothers and sisters in the mineshafts of France.

Eventually child labour laws were enacted, the first being in Britain in 1833, to protect children from the excesses and exploitation of the Industrial Revolution. The nature of childhood and the way it was viewed by society were beginning to change. New emphasis was given to education and recognising the special needs of young children. Childhood was gradually recognised as a distinct stage in human development.

Most recently, the field of developmental psychology has contributed to the recognition of divisions in the concept of childhood itself. Beyond infancy, at least four stages of child development are commonly recognised in Western societies today: (a) early childhood, (b) middle childhood, (c) late childhood and (d) adolescence.

The family in history

Just as society's view of children has changed over the years, the concept of the family also has an important historical legacy. In a provocative analysis, Schorsch (1979, p. 12) makes the observation that in relation to the family:

> [t]he reality is that until fairly modern times most children were either abandoned by their mothers or farmed out to other women shortly after birth, and that, in fact, both the family and family house as we know them today did not even exist until well into the 17th century.

Around this time the 'family', including mother, father and children began to be depicted together in art. More and more, the family was drawn and painted in the context of the house. It was not until the eighteenth century that houses as we know them today began to be built, involving:

> structures that would not only allow families to withdraw from the outside world but would allow individuals to withdraw from one another – houses with corridors, where people did not have to pass one another each time they left or entered the room, houses with bedrooms and other rooms that had specific functions (Schorsch 1979, p. 75).

In an article on contemporary images of Australian families, Funder has noted that it is still proving very difficult to define just what constitutes a family. She concludes (1989, p. 28) that '[i]mages of Australian families are diverse. Just as families are formed and re-formed, so are our images of them'.

Shifts in emphasis in the status of children

Overall, it is possible to identify a number of shifts in emphasis in the status of children in contemporary Western societies. Certainly, a major aspect of the way society views children concerns the proprietary factor. Children are always seen as a natural part of the family unit. Children are conceived by their parents, are raised by them, and usually inherit whatever belongs to their parents. The historical context makes it quite clear that children were owned in a chattel-like fashion by their parents. Some modification to this outlook has occurred with the emergence of the care-giving concept of parenting. Despite the contribution of developmental psychology to our understanding of the physical, social and emotional development of children, far more work is required to clarify the way in which we view children or their families and their status in society.

Children, family and culture

A second important factor shaping the way we understand children and families is that of culture. Kessen (1979) has gone so far as to speak of children and child psychology as 'cultural inventions', highlighting that we cannot easily separate the influence of culture from any discussion of the nature of children and families. To this end, an examination of the role of children and the family in traditional and contemporary Aboriginal communities may serve as a timely reminder of the relativity inherent in any discussion of child and family issues.

Traditional Aboriginal society

Aboriginal people had lived in Australia for over 40 000 years before the first Europeans reached the continent. Their cultures thus predate by tens of thousands of years the building of the pyramids a mere 4500 years ago. At the coming of the Europeans, it is estimated that Australia was inhabited by some 300 000–750 000 Aborigines (Collard, 2000), who formed about 500 clan groups with varying customs, languages and territory.

Lorna Lippman (1970) has noted that traditional Aboriginal societies were oriented towards hunting and gathering. A strict division of labour according to sex was practised, with women staying near the camp with 'the children while men hunted large game in a cooperative venture. Each family unit was responsible for its own subsistence' (Lippman 1970, p. 95). Members of a tribe held similar customs and beliefs, and occupied a fairly well-defined territory. The tribe was divided into hunting and food-gathering bands. The nucleus of each band was a smaller group or clan whose members had religious ties with a series of sacred sites in their part of the tribal territory (Lippman 1970).

Among traditional Aboriginal communities, the values stressed included sharing, mutual cooperation, kinship obligations and personal relationships (Jenkins 1988). Aboriginal children were largely brought up by their mother and her sisters: 'In the case of boys, education was later taken over by the father, learning by emulating adults rather than by formal instruction' (Lippman 1970, p. 21). As Collard (2000, p. 22) noted: 'Each society and individual had an intimate knowledge of their lands and seasons based on religious spirituality gained from rich oral traditions communicated through the Dreamings of those societies'.

Aboriginality in contemporary Australian society

Collard (2000) has emphasised the role of history in providing people with a sense of belonging. As Collard (2000, p. 22) notes, '[I]n considering the present it is important to look at the past, particularly an Aboriginal account of history, which has either been conveniently ignored or omitted from the official history of Australia'.

Guilder (1991, p. 45) notes that 'Today it is inaccurate and misleading to talk about Aboriginal students as a homogeneous group who all share common and readily identifiable characteristics, and who share a strong affinity to traditional beliefs and practices'. Dudgeon (2000, p. 137), in referring to psychologists, noted that

> [i]t is probable for some practitioners, assumptions about Aboriginal people are likely to be grounded in stereotypes that are probably based on romantic 'traditional' notions learned from school, or negative images that have been developed from early theories such as Social Darwinism.

Both Healey et al. (1985) and Guilder (1991) emphasise that despite the differences in their background, Aborigines will identify with aspects of traditional Aboriginal cultures. This affiliation has been revealed in a study of urban Aborigines living in Adelaide, South Australia. In her study, Malin (1990) found that Aboriginal families socialised their children in significantly different ways from their non-Aboriginal counterparts. Parents in Aboriginal families emphasised:

- autonomy, by encouraging children to be self-reliant, to regulate their own behaviour, to develop observation skills, to be practically competent, to seek help from peers, to approach new tasks cautiously to avoid mistakes and to be emotionally strong;
- affiliation in children through affectionate caring for younger children, altruism and trusting in the help of others.

Enembaru (2000) has identified two principles that need to be kept in mind when considering Aboriginal children and their development, namely that:

- the Aboriginal child's cognitive development occurs in a cultural context presenting elements of traditional and contemporary Western influences;
- contemporary socialisation practices within Aboriginal homes represent '. . . evolved practices which have developed with the deracination (colonisation) of the traditional culture (pp. 178–9)'.

In contrast, non-Aboriginal families were found to socialise their children towards reliance on adults for direction and to emphasise the fulfilment of adult expectations. A number of researchers, including Malin (1990) and Guilder (1991), have addressed the problems faced by Aboriginal children when confronted by the clash in values and attitudes between their own and mainstream cultures.

Margaret Mead: children and culture

The ideas of the American anthropologist, Margaret Mead, help us to appreciate the role played by culture in shaping our views of children and the family. In her book, *Culture and Commitment*, Margaret Mead (1970) calls upon knowledge she gleaned from studying children in Manus, Bali and New Guinea and following their lives into adulthood to identify three different kinds of culture: postfigurative, cofigurative and prefigurative.

1 **Postfigurative.** According to Mead, in this type of culture children learn primarily from the collective experience and history of their forebears.
2 **Cofigurative.** People living in this type of culture learn from their peers.
3 **Prefigurative.** In this type of culture, adults are also capable of learning from their children, as well as vice versa.

postfigurative
Margaret Mead's description of a culture in which children learn from their forebears.

cofigurative
Margaret Mead's description of a culture in which children learn from their peers.

prefigurative
Margaret Mead's description of a culture in which adults learn from their children as well as vice versa.

In her book, Mead mounts a powerful argument, based on years of anthropological research, to suggest that a number of conditions have combined to bring about the revolt of youth around the world. For the first time, there is the emergence of an identifiable world community characterised by the sharing of knowledge and an awareness of the dangers we face of nuclear annihilation. Second, advances in modern technology, while beneficial in some areas such as food production, are seriously challenging the ecology of the planet (for example, the greenhouse effect). Finally, advances in medical knowledge have reduced the pressure for population increase, which in turn has freed women from the necessity of devoting themselves entirely to reproduction, thereby changing women's role in society and influencing the raising of children. In the light of these momentous changes, Mead believes we are living in a present for which our understanding of the past has not prepared us.

> In the past there were always some elders who knew more than any children in terms of their experience of having grown up within a cultural system. Today there are none (Mead 1970, p. 61).

According to Mead, the young generation feels there must be better ways than those offered by the previous generation to deal with society's problems and that they must find it. They recognise the crucial need for immediate action on world problems. Mead (1970, p. 73) writes:

> Now, as I see it, the development of a prefigurative culture will depend on the existence of a continuing dialogue in which the young, free to act on their own initiative, can lead their elders in the direction of the unknown. Then the older generation will have access to new experiential knowledge, without which no meaningful plans can be made. It is only with the direct participation of the young who have that knowledge, that we can build a viable future.

Impact of migration

From an Australian perspective, the mix of the population should be taken into consideration when examining the effect of culture on child development. Since 1947, nearly 3 million migrants have settled in Australia and 56 per cent of those are of non-British origin (Storer 1985). However, while we might have accurate statistics on the number of migrants who have settled in Australia, we have far less knowledge about how being raised in Australia affects children and adolescents from migrant families. Burns and Goodnow (1979), Storer (1985), Aspin (1987), Schurch and Hopson (1989) and Clifton et al. (1991b) have examined various facets of problems encountered by such children. A recent study by Leung (2001) comparing the adaptation of Chinese migrant adolescents in Australia and Canada pointed to the significance of social support in ensuring adaptation. Overall, a summary of the writing suggests that from a social–psychological perspective, problems for children and adolescents can arise in terms of the family.

The Family in Social Context. In an examination of income and employment data, Storer (1985) reports that male migrant workers from Mediterranean countries earn less than Australian-born or English-speaking migrants and have higher unemployment rates. These factors have an obvious impact on the family in terms of access to education and health services. Interestingly, Clifton et al. (1991b) report that academic achievement of Greek and Italian students is limited by their lack of proficiency in English, while their success is facilitated by cultural values that emphasise a good education.

The Family and Intergenerational Conflict. In the process of migration, the extended family is often broken up and some members remain in the home country. The migrating members may experience 'culture shock' when they encounter 'new attitudes, values, customs, ideas and relationships' in their adopted country (Aspin 1979, p. 297). The scene is then set for some conflict between parents and children in terms of values, attitudes and morality (Storer 1985). For example, southern European girls are more restricted and supervised in their activities than their Australian-born counterparts (Storer 1985). Storer (1985) also notes that adolescents (10 years and older) of migrant families settling in Australia are likely to experience 'extreme cultural confusion', exacerbated by a lack of proficiency in either their own or the English language. These adolescents are more at risk of falling victim to delinquency and drug use.

The Family and Cultural Conflict. As reported by Storer (1985), adolescents often become confused about their identity as a result of the conflict that can arise from the family's struggle to maintain its ethnic identity in the face of Australian mainstream culture.

In contemporary child development thinking, it is clear that the role of culture in shaping the way children grow and develop is being increasingly recognised (Bruner 1986; Bruner and Haste 1987). In his article on the development of the individual, Bruner (Bruner and Haste 1987, p. 91) notes that '[I]t can never be the case that there is a "self" independent of one's cultural–historical existence'.

In order to best appreciate the study of children one should step outside the traditional bounds of views offered by the social sciences, education and science. Viewing childhood as a cultural and historical construction helps us to fully appreciate how children function symbolically as messengers – bearers of messages about human nature, about the ultimate meaning of the human, and about human forms of knowledge.

The influence of the philosophy of science

As noted by Teo (1997, p. 195), while developmental psychology has never hesitated to draw upon disciplines such as biology, anthropology and sociology it has been rather reluctant and '. . . neglected to incorporate recent developments in the philosophy of knowledge'. This rather curious omission has occurred despite the fact that influential writers and researchers in the field, such as Piaget, had epistemology as the basis for their work. Teo suggests that the primary reason for the failure to integrate the latest philosophical thinking in developmental psychology has to do with the rise and dominance of empiricism, particularly as reflected in mainstream North American psychology.

Slee (1987) has argued that the philosophy of science has significant ramifications for the theoretical and conceptual foundations of developmental psychology, shaping the very way we view the subject. 'In the broadest sense of the term a world view helps people interpret, understand and bring some order to their lives' (Slee 1987, p. 8). More particularly, a **paradigm** or world view helps to shape how we use terms like 'knowledge', 'information' and 'science'. That is, it helps to specify the types of theories used in research, and identifies problems worthy of study and the methodology to be employed in investigating a problem (Lerner, 1986).

paradigm
a pattern, model or example; a world view.

In reading the developmental psychology literature, one becomes aware of how strongly 'commonsense' initially prompts and informs the interpretation of behaviour, for example, Darwin's observations regarding the emergence of emotions in children cited at the beginning of this chapter or Piaget's careful noting of the behaviour of his children in relation to their use of their senses and motor activity to acquire knowledge about the world (see chapter 7). These scientists then attempted to bring some order and coherence to their observations in a systematic way, for example, by gathering further examples or 'experimenting' in an attempt to reproduce the initial findings. As Overton (1998, p. 155) notes, 'This issue – the route from common sense to science – constitutes the methodology of science'.

Presently, the dominant Western model of 'reality' draws heavily upon a belief in a particular view of the scientific method as the only valid approach to the acquisition and understanding of a systematic body of knowledge. The basis for the prevailing scientific method is drawn from the world view of empiricism. As described later in this chapter, empiricism as a philosophy of science has exerted a powerful influence on scientific practice. In a very direct way, it has shaped the way we have conducted the science of child study. Thus, in modelling itself upon the natural sciences, such as physics and chemistry, the empirical method of child study has placed a great deal of importance in studying children on a search for causes of behaviour, with an emphasis on reducing the complexity of behaviour to its basic components. Bronfenbrenner (1977) notes that a survey of child development research indicated that some 76 per cent of the research was of an experimental laboratory nature, contrasting with only 8 per cent that used naturalistic observation designs. As Bronfenbrenner has also commented:

> much of contemporary developmental psychology is the science of the strange behavior of children in strange situations with strange adults for the briefest possible period of time (1977, p. 513).

While the empirical method eschewed interpretation at the beginning of the twentieth century, psychology struggled with the method of 'Verstehen', or understanding as a methodology. Ultimately, Verstehen drowned in the sea of empiricism that dominated scientific discourse in developmental psychology. Presently, the role of interpretation is undergoing a re-examination in relation to its role in understanding human development. The press for this comes from the contribution that feminist thinking is making to the field along with a reappraisal of the role of philosophy in understanding human behaviour.

Images of children

As outlined in the preceding pages, the factors of history, culture and the philosophy of science play significant roles in shaping how we view children and families. It is possible to draw out a number of 'images' of children influenced by one or more of these factors, including:

1   the experiential child;
2   the iniquitous child;
3   the virtuous child.

These three views are identified in Figure 1.1.

The experiential child

experiential child refers to the concept that children develop solely as a product of their experience.

empiricism the view that knowledge is derived solely from experience.

As shown in Figure 1.1, a mainstream view of children identifiable in the psychological literature might be labelled the **experiential child**. Inherent in this view is the notion that at birth the infant is like a 'blank slate' or *tabula rasa*, a concept that has developed from the world view of **empiricism**.

The English philosopher, John Locke (1632–1704) was the primary force behind the development of empiricism. Empiricism did much to replace scholasticism (a world view of a God-ruled static cosmos) as the prevailing world view. Empiricism advocates that all knowledge is derived from experience. As Locke noted:

> Let us suppose the mind to be, as we say white paper, void of all characters, without any ideas; how comes it to be furnished? Whence comes it by that vast store, which the busy and boundless fancy of man has painted on it with an almost endless variety. Whence has all the materials of reason and knowledge?

To this I answer in one word; from experience: in that all our knowledge is founded, and from that it ultimately derives itself (cited in Russell 1974, p. 589).

The Scottish philosopher David Hume (1711–76) further developed Locke's philosophy. He focused specifically on sensation, advocating that research drawing directly on experience through the senses was the means by which we acquire knowledge of the world.

Empiricism became the building block of science in the nineteenth century. Science triumphed over philosophy as the means for gaining knowledge about the world. As viewed by the French philosopher Auguste Comte (1798–1857), science referred to the natural sciences such as biology, chemistry and physics. However, the implication for the social sciences was that human behaviour could be investigated and studied by applying the methods and principles of the natural sciences. The philosophy of Comte is better known as **positivism**.

Comte had identified three ages of thought, namely (i) early theological; (ii) a metaphysical age that during his time was in his view just finishing; and (iii) an era of positive science (Gadamer, 1993). During the twentieth century, positivism was further refined in relation to the philosophical writings of the Vienna Circle composed of such influential figures as Schlick, Gödel and A. J. Ayer. Logical positivism focused on reduction and induction which complemented causal explanation.

Battye and Slee (1985) argue that empiricism, as reflected in positivism, has firmly established itself as the predominant means of gaining knowledge about the world. Underpinning this world view are four propositions regarding the nature of science which have had significant implications for the development of psychology as a science. These four propositions, developed by Evans (1979), may be labelled under two headings: scientism, and the unity of science thesis.

> **positivism**
> a branch of philosophy advocating the use of the methods and principles of the natural sciences in the study of human behaviour.

Scientism
1 Science gives us the whole truth about the nature of reality.
2 Science gives us the ultimate truth about the realities it deals with.

Unity of science thesis
3 There is one method that all the genuine sciences employ.
4 This one method consists of giving deterministic causal explanations that are empirically testable.

As already noted, in its most basic form, positivism is concerned with establishing causes and with predicting events or behaviours. Science was to be conducted in a neutral, value-free manner. Overton (1998) has noted two features of logical positivism. Firstly, the reduction of all scientific theories and propositions to words whose meaning could be directly observed requiring a '. . . neutral observation language – completely objective, and free from subjective or mind-dependent interpretation (Overton 1998, p. 158). Secondly, '. . . to be scientifically meaningful, any universal propositions (e.g. hypotheses, theories, laws) had to be demonstrably nothing more than summary statements of the pristine observations themselves'.

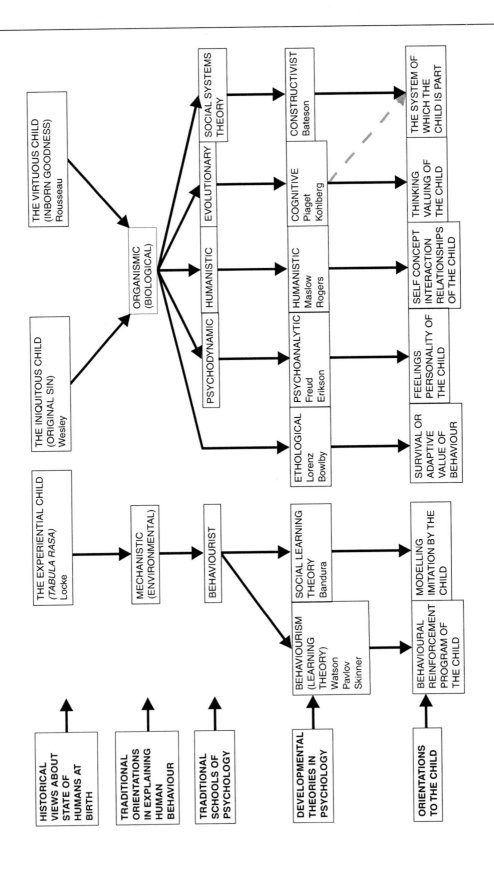

Figure 1.1 Theoretical orientations in psychology
Source: Reproduced courtesy of Ken Hancock, Flinders University of South Australia

The outlook presented humans as passive or inert organisms whose behaviour is directed or shaped by external forces. That is, at birth the infant is a *tabula rasa* and all that the child becomes is determined by the environment. A modern exponent of this view is B. F. Skinner, whose theory of operant conditioning is described in chapter 3. As already noted, this outlook is presently under attack from a variety of sources.

The iniquitous child   – e v i l

The view of children as **iniquitous** accepts the proposition regarding the inherent sinfulness of the human race (Figure 1.1). Because the child is thought to be born into original sin, the task of the parents becomes that of breaking the will of the child. This may be accomplished by teaching the child to submit to the will of parents and God. In the Puritan tradition of seventeenth and eighteenth-century England and the United States, the inherent sinfulness of the child was an accepted outlook of educators and the establishment generally. The English churchman, John Wesley (1703–91) wrote forcefully:

> Break their wills betimes, begin this work before they can run alone, before they can speak plain, perhaps before they can speak at all. Whatever pains it costs, break the will, if you would not damn the child. Let a child from a year old be taught to fear the rod and to cry softly; from that age make him do as he is bid, if you whip him ten times running to effect it. If you spare the rod you spoil the child; if you do not conquer you ruin him (cited in Southey 1925, pp. 304–5).

Wesley's views were incorporated into regulations for running a girls' boarding school. Faint-hearted parents intending to enrol their children at his school were warned off. The girls' daily life included a 4 am rise, an hour of religious instruction followed by public worship, breakfast and then the school day, which ended at 5 pm. All children were supervised, with no time allowed for play (Cleverley and Phillips 1976). A contemporary exploration of the iniquitous view of the child is found in William Golding's portrayal of children's nature in his book *Lord of the Flies*. In this book, a group of children are stranded on a desert island. Free of the restraint of culture and adult supervision, the iniquitous nature of children comes to the fore.

iniquitous child refers to the idea that children are inherently evil.

The virtuous child   – G o o d

An alternative outlook concerning the nature of children to that presented by either the experiential or iniquitous view entails the idea of the **virtuous** child (Figure 1.1). An exponent of the ideal of the virtuous child was the seventeenth-century French philosopher Jean Jacques Rousseau (1712–78). He disputed the prevailing view that the task of parents and educators was to shape and mould an obedient child from an inherently sinful one. Rousseau took issue with Locke's ideas about children, proposing instead the concept of an innocent child whose development was powerfully directed by nature. Rousseau also rejected Locke's notion of the rational child; he argued that the capacity for reasoning does not develop until around 12 years of age.

virtuous child refers to Rousseau's notion that the child is inherently good.

Trends and issues

Children and punishment

There was an old woman, who lived in a shoe
She had so many children she didn't
Know what to do.
She gave them some broth without
Any bread
Then she whipped them all soundly and
Sent them to bed

In Australia, as in other Western countries such as the United States of America, the notion of the iniquitous child as reflected in the use of corporal punishment still continues to elicit controversy as reflected in media reports and the research literature. Sweden became the first country in the world to ban corporal punishment of children and a number of European countries have followed this example, including Denmark, Norway, Finland, Austria, Cyprus, Italy, Croatia and Latvia. In a position paper on the issue of banning corporal punishment, Paintal (1999) noted that in the United States of America corporal punishment in schools is still legal in about half of the states, a situation which has not changed a great deal since Viadero (1988) reported on the matter. In Australia, all states have banned the use of corporal punishment in public schools.

Proponents of the use of corporal punishment, such as Dobson (1970), have argued that excessive permissiveness, both in child-rearing and school punishment, has directly contributed to social problems such as drug taking, delinquency and lack of respect for authorities (e.g. parents and teachers). The position advocated by Dobson is that schools acting in *loco parentis* have the right to maintain control in the classroom '...even if it requires an occasional application of corporal punishment' (Dobson 1970, p.118). The following points have been drawn from Dobson (1970), and Skiba and Deno (1991).

Arguments for corporal punishment

- The administration of corporal punishment is a powerful way of stopping misbehaviour. It is simple and easy to administer.
- Corporal punishment reinforces the idea that some misbehaviour warrants such severity which society has the right to administer. It provides clear guidelines for acceptable behaviour.
- It is consistent with the views of many parents and reinforces continuity between home and school.
- Corporal punishment is less severe than some types of punishment and has less damaging effects than some procedures, such as time out.

Arguments against corporal punishment

- On humanistic grounds corporal punishment is a dehumanising practice outlawed in institutions such as prisons.
- It is an ineffective procedure and simply suppresses behaviour.
- Corporal punishment provides an aggressive role model for children.
- Corporal punishment may be considered to be child abuse and at the very least it is harmful to the self-esteem of the child.

An important summary of the literature regarding the issue is to be found in Paintal's (1999) position paper on banning corporal punishment. Significantly, Durrant (2000), in a study of youth crime trends in Sweden since the abolition of corporal punishment in 1979, reports that the rate of youth involvement in crime, alcohol and drug use, rape and suicide have decreased.

Rousseau denied the idea of original sin and thereby affirmed the notion of the inherent natural goodness of children. In his book *Emile* (1762), Rousseau applied his ideas to education: 'God made all things good; man meddles with them and they become evil' (Rousseau 1914, book 1, p. 5). Rousseau believed that in educating the innocent and amoral child, it made no sense to punish the child for wrongdoing: 'Before the age of reason we do good or ill without knowing it, and there is no morality in our action' (1914, p. 34). If a child committed some wrong action, such as breaking a household object, Rousseau blamed the parents for leaving it within the child's reach.

Rousseau's views are reflected in the more recent thinking of the educator A. S. Neil. Adopting Rousseau's notion of inherent goodness, Neil also rejected the idea of original sin or evil: 'I cannot believe that evil is inborn, that there is original sin' (Neil 1968, p. 12). Neil advocated non-interference in the education of children. He believed in some innate driving force that would lead children to make the best decisions if left to their own devices. Neil became famous for incorporating his philosophy into the education of children.

The competent child   *- born w/ knowledge*
Ig. capacity to learn

David Elkind (1987) presents an arguable case that there exists a fourth contemporary outlook which he labels the 'competent enfant'. This view presents 'infants and young children as having much more capacity to learn academic skills than older children, regardless of background, actually have' (Elkind 1987, p. 8). Elkind argues that this view has been adopted by such educators as Bruner, with his now famous statement in 1962 that it is possible to teach any child any subject matter at any age in an intellectually responsible manner. Elkind believes that Bruner may not have appreciated how sincerely parents and educators would take up this statement as a rallying call. A new optimism was generated regarding the capabilities and competencies of the infant that in Elkind's view overstepped the mark.

Elkind also argued that a second factor contributing to the image of the competent infant concerns Bloom's (1964) idea that one should teach as much as possible to young children because their minds are growing so rapidly. A third influential factor, developed by McVee Hunt (1961), is that intelligence is malleable and not fixed. Finally, Elkind (1987) argues that the historian Ariès, in pointing out that the concept of childhood is largely a social invention, contributed to the idea that we have been ignoring children's true potential. According to Elkind, in over-emphasising the competence of children these four factors have distorted the true nature of young children and how they really grow and learn.

Theoretical orientations

As identified in Figure 1.1, two traditional orientations to behaviour that flow from the experiential, iniquitous and virtuous views of children are the **mechanistic** and **organismic** orientations. The mechanistic orientation emphasises that the environment is all-important in shaping what we become and how we develop. The organismic orientation may draw on the notion of the iniquitous or virtuous child, or competent child or a mixture of all. As later chapters indicate, the organismic view does not consider the infant to be a blank slate or *tabula rasa* at birth. For example, infants may differ at birth in terms of temperament.

The orientations to behaviour described here have in turn given rise to a number of identifiable schools of psychology: **behaviourist**, **psychodynamic**, **humanistic**, and the newly emerging **constructivist** school (see Figure 1.1).

mechanistic emphasising the role of experience and the cause–effect nature of behaviour.

organismic emphasising the contribution individuals make to their own development.

behaviourist focusing on observable behaviour and its causes.

psychodynamic focusing upon the dynamic interaction between the conscious and unconscious in affecting behaviour.

humanistic emphasising individuals, their personal experience and potential for development.

constructivist emphasising the subjectivity of our experience and the role of individuals in actively construing meaning in their world.   *choices*

In Figure 1.1, various mainstream developmental theories in psychology are identified and the nature of a number of these theories is explored in this book. A number of different orientations to the child arise out of developmental theories (see Figure 1.1) and these orientations are explored at some length in this book.

The family life-cycle: 1

The concept of family

Leo Tolstoy, in his novel *Anna Karenina*, observed that while 'all happy families resemble one another, each unhappy family is unhappy in its own way'. In view of the fast changing nature of the 'family' (Krupinski 1974; Callan & Noller 1987; Gilding 1991; Bowes & Watson 1999), some consideration is warranted of how we define what is meant by 'family'. Some historical understanding of the origins of the word will provide a context for a discussion of the term. As noted by Gilding (1991, p. 3), the word emerged in the English language in the fourteenth century, derived from the Latin *familia* (household) and *famulus* (servant). By the seventeenth century, the term was used to refer to 'notions of co-residence (members of a household not necessarily related by ties of blood or marriage) and kinship (persons related by blood or marriage but not necessarily living together).' Gilding noted the term further evolved such that by the nineteenth century it generally referred to a small kin group living under the same roof.

The *Macquarie Dictionary* defines 'family' as:

1. parents and their children, whether dwelling together or not. 2. One's children collectively. 3. Any group of persons closely related by blood as parents, children, aunts and cousins.

Listed below are some common descriptions of families.

1 A set of various roles acquired through marriage and procreation.
2 A group of people who form a household under one head, including parents and children .
3 A set of interacting personalities.
4 Parents and children dwelling together.
5 Any group of people closely related by blood, such as parents, children, uncles or aunts.
6 A group of people who live and communicate with each other continually in a caring and supportive manner.
7 A group of individuals relating to each other out of mutual expectations and obligations, and with common usage of resources.
8 Adults of both sexes, at least two of whom maintain a socially approved sexual relationship, and one or more children living with sexually cohabiting adults.
9 A social group living together in a common residence.

Still other ways to view the family unit have been presented by Don Edgar, in an article in *The Age*, 21 September 1985. He identified three characteristics around which definitions of the family revolve:

a *Political:* This view of the family encompasses the idea that it is a radically active unit that helps mould and shape its members' attitudes and beliefs. Political notions of what constitutes a family have implications for shaping government policy regarding the administration of social security and family support payments.

b *Economic:* Another way to define the family is in economic terms, whereby the commercial world helps to organise adults' and children's lives in relation to work, leisure and shopping hours. As noted by Gilding (1991), during the 1950s, 'working mothers' were seen as a threat to the family. As cited in Gilding (1991), an Australian treatise on growing up in Melbourne society had the author recommending that only 'good homes and family groups' provided the ideal environment for children to attain 'the summit of individual usefulness to the State' (pp. 51–2).

c *Ideological:* In defining the family, the notion of ideology is important. Some views of the family emphasise its oppressive nature and structure. At one extreme, arguments have been put forward in favour of abolishing the family altogether. For example, R. D. Laing, in his book The Politics of Family Life (1971), argued that the hotbed of emotional tangles in family life is the perfect breeding ground for various mental disturbances including schizophrenia. From a different perspective, the feminist author Annie Oakley claimed that the modern nuclear family did not meet the needs of women or children.

Men want their relational needs to be satisfied in a heterosexual connection with women, while women look, throughout their lives, in one way or another, back to the original symbiosis of the mother–child relationship (1986, p. 63).

At the other extreme, any definition that moves away from two married parents with children is rejected. For example, Charles Mackellar (1907), a leading advocate for state intervention in family life in the early twentieth century, argued passionately that:

the most sacred feature in the life of society, the most sacred influence on the social life of the individual, is the family group ... Destroy this influence by breaking up the family, and what is the result? The moral ruin of the individual (1977, p. 55).

It is clear that a range of socio-political factors combine to shape and influence how we define what constitutes a 'family'. It is oversimplifying the matter to prescribe the definition in terms of kinship and household as even the more recent texts attempt to do (Steel & Kidd 2001). However, setting aside various social/political imperatives, a definition provided by a year 7 girl in the video/resource package 'Stressed Out and Coping in Families' (Slee et al. 1997), may be as viable as any definition for prompting discussion of the topic. 'A family is a bunch of people who live together and love one another'.

Chapter summary

In this textbook, I have continued with the general aim of the first edition, that is, to embed child development in a philosophical, historical and cultural context. I firmly believe that how we 'see' children is strongly shaped by these forces and that appreciating these contexts helps inform us of their development. A the same time, since the inception and writing of the first edition some exciting breakthroughs have occurred in our understanding of how children grow and develop. While it is a little like 'chasing butterflies' I hope to capture some of the excitement of this new understanding in the present text.

Discussion questions

1   What are some of the key features of the philosophy of science known as empiricism?
2   How do the characters of the children in Golding's *Lord of the Flies* exemplify the view of the child as iniquitous?
3   Compare and contrast the main features of the 'mechanistic' and 'organismic' orientations to behaviour.
4   Margaret Mead distinguished three different kinds of culture, namely postfigurative, cofigurative and prefigurative. Discuss the identifying features of each and the application of her ideas to understanding the position of children in contemporary Australian society.
5   Identify and discuss the arguments for and against corporal punishment (use a debate format).

	YES	?	NO
1. Common residence			
2. Must have a child or children			
3. Could include servants			
4. Limited to blood relatives			
5. Limited to blood relatives and adopted people			
6. Requires a head of household			
7. Implies sexual relationships			
a. socially approved			
b. not necessarily socially approved			
8. Requires a marriage			
9. Must have a sense of unity			
10. Involves statuses and roles			
11. Could be one parent only			
12. Implies mutual expectations and obligations on the part of members			
13. Involves sharing of resources			
14. There must be mutual support and cooperation			
15. Involves a sense of interdependence			
16. Is indefinable			
17. Other			

Based on the "features" of a family I have identified here I think a family is ....
....
....
....
....
....

Figure 1.2 What do you think are the features of a family?

Activities

1 Form small discussion groups. Each group draws an outline of a child on a large sheet of paper approximately 90 cm x 30 cm. Members of the group write on the outline words that they associate with the word 'child'. Allow 10–15 minutes to fill in the outline.

   1a Each person then explains the words they have contributed and upon what basis they hold such views.

   1b The group then summarises the words under two or three headings and discusses them in relation to Figure 1.1.

2 Using the questionnaire 'What are the features of a family?' (Figure 1.2), share your answers with the group. As individuals or as a group, try to identify key features that might contribute towards defining the concept of a family. Share your answers with a group. As individuals or as a group, try to identify key features that might contribute toward defining the concept of a family.

Selected websites

Child Adolescent Psychological Educational Resources <www.caper.com.au>

Australian Institute Family Studies <www.aifs.org.au>

Readings on the socialisation of the Aboriginal child <www.wn.com.au/abled>

Nippon Hoso Kyokai <www.nhk.or.jp/kosodate/english/index.html>

2 Concepts of Development

'I Never Ask Advice About Growing'

'Seven years and six months!' Humpty Dumpty repeated thoughtfully.
'An uncomfortable sort of age. Now if you'd asked my advice, I'd have said
"Leave off at seven" – but it's too late now.'
'I never ask advice about growing,' Alice said indignantly.
'Too proud?' the other inquired.
Alice felt even more indignant at this suggestion.
'I mean,' she said 'that one can't help growing older'.
'One can't perhaps,' said Humpty Dumpty, 'but two can. With proper
assistance, you might have left off at seven'.

Lewis Carroll, Through the Looking Glass

CHAPTER OUTLINE

KEY TERMS AND CONCEPTS

- Heredity versus environment
- Continuity versus discontinuity
- Similarity versus uniqueness
- Stability versus instability
- Activity versus passivity
- Thinking versus feeling
- Development
- Maturation

- Central tendency
- Mean
- Median
- Mode
- Normal distribution
- Skewed distribution
- Hypothesis
- Correlation

Introduction

In this chapter consideration will be given to understanding the concept of 'development', reasons for studying child development, basic concepts underpinning such study, the conduct of research, and finally the reader will be introduced to some basic statistical terms. The nature of the family in Australia is the topic discussed in The Family Life-cycle: 2.

Child development concepts

Since the beginning of this century significant advances have been made in the study of children in terms of understanding the nature of development. Overton (1998) has identified that one feature of development about which there is general universal understanding is that development implies 'change'. Rather simplistically, this notion has focused psychologists' attention on 'changes in observed behavior across age' (Overton 1998, p. 109). Overton has elaborated on the nature of change, identifying (i) transformational; (ii) variational; (iii) expressive–constitutive; and (iv) instrumental–communicative change.

1 Transformational change is really morphological change which 'involves the emergence of novelty' (Overton 1998, p. 111). The example he gives is that of the single-celled zygote differentiating and emerging into ever more complex forms.
2 Variational change describes the individual differences which occur in development, e.g. the age by which a child walks as it varies from the norm.
3 Expressive–constitutive change focuses on 'the essential features of what changes', e.g. Piaget focuses on the 'schemes' which change.
4 Instrumental–communicative change: here, the focus is on what it is that changes, e.g. Skinner focuses on the operants which change.

The nature of change is now considered in the light of the following frequently debated questions in development. These key concepts are identifiable in various theories of child development presented in chapter 3 and provide a useful heuristic for understanding development. They include:

- heredity versus environment;
- continuity versus discontinuity of development;
- similarity versus uniqueness;
- stability versus instability of behaviour;
- activity versus passivity of behaviour;
- thinking versus feeling.

Heredity versus environment

A major issue not only in psychology, but also in education, sociology, politics and related disciplines concerns the role that heredity and environment play in

A range of factors affect how children develop, even within the same family

shaping the person. Everyday observations reveal similarities and dissimilarities between people. Thus, we may observe that people differ in such diverse ways as physical appearance (for example, tall or short), mental capacity (for example, creativity) or emotional make-up (calm versus excitable). An important question raised by observations such as these concerns the extent to which one is born with particular characteristics. Are the characteristics innate or were they shaped by environmental forces after birth? The debate engendered by this question is often referred to as the nature–nurture debate.

At various times in history, one or another view has held sway. For example, in the twentieth century, fascist thought in Nazi Germany used genetics to justify genocidal acts against people of Jewish origin. At a very different level and from a different viewpoint, television programs such as 'Play School' and 'Sesame Street' emphasise the importance of a stimulating and enriching environment for enhancing children's learning.

The nature–nurture debate has raged inconclusively in social science literature because the issues involved have not been clearly identified, nor have the basic terms been defined. Now it is generally accepted that heredity and environment must interact in order to produce behaviour. The issue, then, is not so much one of how *much* each contributes to an individual's development but rather *how* they combine.

Continuity versus discontinuity

A second important issue in developmental psychology concerns whether an individual's development is gradual (continuous) or sudden (discontinuous).

The continuous viewpoint emphasises slow methodical changes over time. The analogy here would be that of a gum tree growing from a small seedling. That is, growth from the small seedling to sapling and finally mature gum tree is steady and continuous with no 'sudden' transformations or changes into another form. Some psychological theories such as that underlying behaviour therapy draw heavily upon the notion of continuity to explain human growth (see chapter 3).

An alternative viewpoint emphasises the discontinuity of development. The analogy here would be a caterpillar changing into a butterfly. Psychological theories such as those proposed by Sigmund Freud (psychoanalytic theory) or Jean Piaget (cognitive–developmental theory) emphasise a stage-like or discontinuous view of human development (see chapter 3).

Wohlwill (1973, p. 236) has noted that '[t]he usefulness of the stage concept remains an open question today and its potential promise unfulfilled'. The concept of stages in the psychological literature has proved difficult to define, despite the observations made by parents, teachers, social workers, and others who spend time with children, that not all functions are present at birth and that some functions do appear in most children at a particular time in their development.

Moreover, the use of the concept of stages differs from psychological theory to psychological theory. Thus, Meadows (1986, p. 19) notes that in Erik Erikson's psychosocial theory of human development the concept of stages is broad, descriptive and evocative in nature and does not 'refer clearly to anything definite or measurable in behavior'. Meadows observes that the use of the term 'stage' in relation to other psychological theories is more specific.

In Jean Piaget's cognitive–developmental theory, during the child's 'sensorimotor stage' for example, it is generally possible to clearly identify observable aspects of a child's thinking. For example, a favourite toy hidden from a 6-month-old child under a handkerchief will not elicit a search reaction on the part of the child, who acts as though 'out of sight is out of mind'. More particularly, some stages are associated with identifiable, clearly defined behaviours, such as the crawling stage in a 10- to 12-month-old infant. So it appears that the use of the term 'stage' varies along a continuum from less to more specific in terms of associated behaviours.

In reviewing the literature, it appears that in order to enhance the descriptive and explanatory power of stage theories it is desirable to:

1 clearly establish the relationship between structure and behaviour at any one stage (Kagan et al. 1978);
2 account for or explain the factors contributing to the child's movement from one stage to the next (Meadows 1986), such as biological maturation or environmental input;
3 clearly relate the structure of one stage to the succeeding stage (Kagan et al. 1978);
4 specify the behaviours subject to age changes that make up the stages (Meadows 1986).

As discussed in chapter 3, constructivist theories and dynamic systems theory throw new light on the meaning of 'stages'.

Similarity versus uniqueness

One view put forward in developmental psychology is that people are essentially similar despite superficial differences. That is, the search is for general principles that can be applied to everyone. For example, Carl Jung, whose thinking and writing about the human personality have had a profound impact on psychology, has provided important insight into the complex interaction between similarity and uniqueness in human personality. Thus, the Australian writer Peter O'Connor (1985) notes that in his theory of psychological types Jung identified differences in the way people prefer to use their minds. Specifically, these are in the way they (i) perceive (that is, are aware of things); and (ii) make judgments (that is, reach conclusions about what has been perceived). In Jung's theory, the ways in which we perceive the world relate to either (i) sensing or using our five senses of sight, hearing, touch, taste and smell; or (ii) intuition, which involves indirect perception. The ways of judging are (i) thinking or logical reasoning; and (ii) feeling or appreciating things. Underlying the complexity of human behaviour, therefore, there are essentially similar processes common to all people.

An alternative view is that each human being is unique and psychology should be concerned with appreciating the special qualities that distinguish one person from another.

Stability versus instability

Another principle of human development deals with the extent to which we regard human behaviour as stable or unstable. One outlook in psychology emphasises the fixed and unchanging nature of an individual's personality. For example, psychoanalytic theory as expounded by Sigmund Freud (Wollheim 1974) suggests that an individual's personality has largely been shaped and moulded during the early years of childhood.

An alternative outlook is that an individual's characteristics (or personality) are constantly changing. The psychological theory of Erik Erikson (1963) is in accord with this outlook. Erikson proposed that an individual continues to develop throughout the life span. At various times in his or her life, the individual is faced with certain normative crises that must be addressed and dealt with, thereby allowing the person to proceed to the next stage. For example, from the ages of 13 to 19 years, the individual is primarily concerned with establishing an identity or a sense of self, particularly in relation to sexuality and occupation (see chapter 20).

Activity versus passivity

This principle of developmental psychology concerns the extent to which children are initiators (active) as opposed to passive reactive organisms. The former view presents the individual as an agent. An agent is someone who takes responsibility for her or his own behaviour, is understood to be capable of acting for certain purposes or goals, attaches some freedom of choice to his or her acts and may cite reasons for behaviour, reasons that are often guided by values (Battye & Slee 1985). Argument has been mounted that such a view of child development is gaining sway in the psychological literature (Hare & Secord 1972; Gauld & Shotter 1977; Bruner 1986).

Alternatively, individual development can be considered to be shaped by powerful forces that are largely beyond the individual's control. In this view, the individual is seen as essentially a passive/reactive organism. Writers such as Gauld and Shotter (1977) have argued that this view of human behaviour has been promulgated by such lines of thought in psychology as that represented by learning theory.

Thinking versus feeling

In the psychological literature, writers such as Piaget have emphasised the study of children's thinking, while theorists such as Freud and Erikson have focused on the emotional or affective development of the individual. The complex interplay between thinking and feeling in governing behaviour has been revealed by Schacter and Singer (1962). In their experiment, they gave adrenalin injections to individuals, who were told that it was a vitamin compound. These people were then each asked to wait with another individual who was supposed to have received the same 'vitamin' injection but who was in collaboration with the experimenter and had not received the injection. Soon the subject began to experience the physical effects of adrenalin (for example, rapid breathing and hand tremors). The collaborator then began to act in either an angry or aggressive fashion or a playful, euphoric fashion. The subjects who waited with the 'angry' collaborator were observed to become angry, while those who waited with the 'euphoric' collaborator became euphoric. Subjects injected with a placebo of saline solution showed no emotional reaction regardless of how the collaborator behaved, and similarly, subjects who had been forewarned that the 'vitamin' injection had side effects such as rapid breathing or hand tremors showed no emotional reaction regardless of the collaborator's behaviour.

From the experiment it was concluded that emotion consists of more than physiological arousal. A state of physiological arousal for which the individual has no immediate explanation will encourage the person to search his or her environment for an explanation or label, and the choice of a label will determine the emotional response (Schacter & Singer 1962, pp. 379–99).

A critique of the controversies

Overton (1998) has argued that the various 'controversies' presented here suffer from a number of limitations. In the first instance, their 'either/or'-like nature suggests that one or the other represent the 'right' or 'real' nature of

The first three years of life

The significance attached to the early years of life in terms of shaping development has a long history, for example, phrases such as 'As the twig is bent the tree's inclined' (the English poet, Alexander Pope), or 'The child is the father of the man' (the English poet, William Wordsworth). Such common phrases entered folklore regarding child development. However, it was perhaps the writings of Sigmund Freud, based on his clinical observations, which identified that unfortunate experiences early in life can have an irreversible effect on the same individual's subsequent later development. It came to be widely believed that children are highly vulnerable in the first years of life and that they can be permanently affected by their experiences during this critical period. There is a lack of any scientific evidence to support Freudian notions of the impact of early childhood experiences on later development in a simple, direct, causal way.

The emergence of a life-span perspective in human development now casts real doubts on the idea of the first three years being a 'critical period'. It is now better understood that we grow and develop all of our lives. At certain times in our lives across the life span we face important developmental tasks. For example, in infancy acquiring a language is one such task, in early childhood, learning to read and write is important; during adolescence the task is to develop a sense of who one is; while in early adulthood the emergence of a vocation and perhaps finding a partner is an important task, and so on.

During these life stages, certain conditions promote optimal development. For example, in the early years good maternal and infant health, sound nourishment, love and care contribute to later development. Certainly there is scientific evidence that for some children particular problems in early life continue into later years. However, other children are quite resilient in the face of adversity. What this suggests is that a combination of childhood experiences, parenting practices and individual child characteristics probably best account for optimal development.

development. This in turn, suggests that empirical inquiry will soon uncover the correct answer. 'The simple empirical observation that generations of empirical observations have failed to resolve any of these issues demonstrates the inadequacy of this assumption' (Overton 1998, p. 113). For example, see chapter 1 regarding the nature–nurture debate. Instead, Overton argues for shifting the focus away from 'which one' questions to the nature of functioning of each end of the continuum and exploring the relationship between the ends of the continuum.

Personal views of human development

To help understand your own views regarding the major developmental principles presented here, you might like to complete a quiz that has been adapted from a questionnaire presented by Levin (1973) (see activity 1 at the end of this chapter).

In unpublished research (Slee unpub.) conducted with 100 first-year undergraduate students (mean age 21.9 years; 63 females, 37 males) completing their teaching awards, the following results were obtained:

• Heredity versus environment. From a sample of undergraduate students beginning a course in child development, 74 per cent of the students emphasised the role of the individual's environment in shaping development.

- Continuity versus discontinuity. The findings for this sample also highlighted an emphasis on the continuity of development, with 49 per cent strongly advocating this concept.
- Similarity versus uniqueness. In relation to this concept, 72 per cent of students were in favour of the uniqueness and individuality of people.
- Stability versus instability. There was a slight trend favouring the unpredictable nature of development, particularly where chance circumstance and historical events have a role to play in shaping behaviour.
- Activity versus passivity. The tendency was for students to downplay the idea that development is self-initiated, with the individual actively seeking growth and change (18 per cent). Instead, emphasis was given to the passive reactive nature of individuals.
- Thinking versus feeling. Students also downplayed the role of thinking (14 per cent) in human development and instead emphasised the affective nature of development.

Trends and issues

Stimulating children's growth

The question of whether we should go out of our way to stimulate faster development in children, or whether it is better for them to grow at their own pace is one frequently asked by parents and childcare professionals. From the moment a baby is conceived, dramatic changes are occurring in its development. At birth, a baby's brain contains approximately as many neurons as there are stars in the Milky Way (approximately 100 million). The brain also contains virtually all the nerve cells it will ever have. Neural activity prompted in part by sensory experience then begins to shape development. In the first years of life, the baby's brain literally produces an overabundance of connections between neurons – more than it will ever use. Strangely enough, the connections then begin to disappear so that by middle primary school the child is left with roughly its adult quotient.

Observations of humans and experiments with animals clearly indicate that being deprived of a stimulating environment results in less than optimal brain development. But the whole debate about whether the baby comes into the world genetically programmed or whether it is the environment that stimulates development is really not the point of current scientific thinking. A newly emerging idea highlights that even before birth the brain is capable of actively constructing the optimal conditions to promote the development of other parts of the brain. After birth, for example, the infant is known to have a preference for looking at human faces over and above other stimuli. In turn, this preference aids in the development of higher order processes in the brain's development. Now we more clearly understand that the baby plays a very active role in its own development. The baby's own behaviour creates its own environment, which to some extent then encourages or discourages the development of other behaviour. For example, a child with an 'easy' temperament who is a 'joy' to be with 'invites' others to spend more time with it and to be more attentive to it. In turn, this 'cycle of participation' draws forth more 'inviting' behaviour from the baby, and so on.

So, it is not a matter of the more stimulation the better. In fact, it appears that some babies can be over-stimulated. Observant care-givers will note that too much stimulation will have the baby crying or turning away. It is far more important to provide sensitive care-giving attuned to the developing baby's needs at any one time.

The nature of development

development
takes into account
the effect of
experience on an
individual.

maturation
the changes that
occur in an
organism as it fulfils
its genetic potential.

When we talk of human development, just what do we mean and how does **development** differ from maturation? **Maturation** differs from development in that it refers to a genetically determined biological plan that is relatively independent of environmental influence or experience.

> Above all else, development is about change. Whatever disagreements may arise – and they do arise very rapidly – change is our foremost concern . . . Overton 1998, p. 109).
>
> What do we mean when we say that an organism 'develops'? Usually, we see that it gets bigger, but always we mean that it gets more complex (Thelen & Smith 1998, p. 564).

As referred to in chapter 1 and discussed in detail in chapter 3, a recent influential theoretical development is referred to in the literature as dynamic systems (DS). As noted by Lewis (2000, p. 34), according to this theory:

> all developmental outcomes can be explained as the spontaneous emergence of coherent, higher-order forms through recursive interactions among simpler components. This process is called self-organisation, and it accounts for growth and novelty throughout the natural world, from organisms to societies to ecosystems to the biosphere itself.

One conceptualisation of development has it proceeding almost as a straight line at a steady rate, with each new development building on the one before it. This is a gross oversimplification of a complex process. In describing what development means, Kagan et al. (1978) emphasise that:

- it is orderly;
- the emergent process lasts for a reasonable time;
- usually the new state is judged to be more desirable than the previous one;
- as an outcome the organism is healthier, better organised and more efficient.

To quote the summary of Kagan et al. (1978, p. 5), 'Development connotes orderly, organised change toward a hypothetical ideal'.

Lewis (2000) has argued that emergence is the key to understanding developmental change. As noted by Lewis (2000, p. 38), emergence 'refers to the coming-into-existence of new forms or properties through on-going processes intrinsic to the system itself'. Lewis has argued that as a metaphor 'emergence' is common to various theoretical traditions but generally explained in different ways. For example, he notes that mechanistic models of development suggest that 'developmental patterns emerge (spontaneous) without instruction or rules' (e.g. Schulz 1998).

The nature of psychological inquiry

Types of knowledge

The question of what constitutes knowledge is complex (see chapter 1 for an introduction to the debate about the nature of knowledge. The CD also presents in more detail a description of various types of knowledge in relation to child study and so only a summary will be presented here.) Tripodi (1981) has identified four types of knowledge and his ideas can also be applied to the field of developmental psychology.

Hypothetical–developmental

The first of the types of knowledge described by Tripodi, **hypothetical–developmental knowledge**, involves the description of events in a quantitative manner involving the use of general concepts. For example, in parent–child research, a generalised concept is parental over-protectiveness.

hypothetical–developmental knowledge
as identified by Tripodi (1981), the description of events using general concepts.

Quantitative–descriptive

Tripodi suggests that **quantitative–descriptive knowledge** is based on facts that help to describe a relationship between two variables. For example, research on bullying among primary school children might indicate that 11 per cent of boys report being bullied compared with 9 per cent of girls. Here, gender is a variable, and descriptive knowledge helps to elaborate the relationship between bullying and gender.

quantitative–descriptive knowledge
according to Tripodi (1981), a type of knowledge that describes the links between two variables.

Associational knowledge

Associational knowledge draws upon statistical techniques to indicate the degree of the relationship between two variables. For example, research might indicate a statistically significant decline in the amount of bullying from primary to secondary school, thus implicating age as a contributing variable.

associational knowledge
a type of knowledge identified by Tripodi (1981) that indicates the extent of the relationship between two variables.

Cause–effect knowledge

Research conducted with **cause–effect knowledge** in mind 'specifies that changes in the independent or causal variable are directly responsible for producing changes in the dependent variable' (Tripodi 1981, p. 203).

cause–effect knowledge
as defined by Tripodi (1981), a type of knowledge that identifies the cause of an event.

Types of research design

In the field of developmental psychology, a range of different types of research design is evident. Greater detail of the various types is provided in the CD and only a summary will be presented here as a lead into the next section dealing with statistics.

Field studies

A field study is an ex-post-facto, or 'after the fact', investigation directed towards naturally occurring events (Kerlinger 1973). Using this method of research, the researcher does not attempt to deliberately manipulate the situation and every attempt is made to minimise the observer's presence.

Barker and Wright's (1955) classic field study of a mid-western United States town was intended to detail the daily life patterns of people living in a small town. The principal advantages of this research design relate to the immediate and first-hand nature of the data. For example, the field work of Pepler and Craig (1995) into schoolyard bullying among Canadian students utilised video cameras in a field study design. Recent technological advances, such as video equipment, have improved data collection procedures, while recent statistical procedures now permit suggestive causal inferences to be made about behaviour. The disadvantages of field studies relate to the difficulty of controlling for all variables shaping behaviour.

Naturalistic experiments

In a naturalistic experiment, the researcher takes advantage of naturally occurring opportunities to study behaviour. For example, MacFarlane and Raphael (1984) examined the effects of bushfires in south-eastern Australia upon victims' behaviour.

The obvious disadvantage of this type of research design is having to wait for natural events to occur. On the other hand, this type of design provides greater opportunity than natural field studies for isolating causal factors.

Field experiments

A field experiment differs from a field study in that the researcher has control over the independent variable(s) of the events being studied. A field experiment involves the deliberate manipulation of the independent variable(s) in a naturalistic setting. For example, Parke et al. (1977) investigated the impact of exposure to violent and non-violent films on the social behaviour of adolescent boys. The films were shown in the area where the boys lived and the amount and type of aggression shown by the boys in relation to the films was assessed in the same area. Robinson et al. (2000) utilised a field experiment design to examine the effect of television-watching on the aggressive behaviour of primary school students.

The obvious advantage of the field experiment over the field study is that the researcher does not have to wait for suitable event(s) to occur. Ethical problems can arise in assigning individuals to either the experimental or control situation, such as deliberately exposing one group of boys to violent films, as in the example cited above.

Laboratory studies

There is a marked lack of research with children in naturalistic settings, such as school, home or playgroup. Rather, the emphasis thus far has been on laboratory-based research (Bronfenbrenner 1977, p. 513). The attraction of a laboratory study is that it provides the opportunity to hold constant those extraneous variables that might influence behaviour. Hypotheses or predictions can be tested by deliberately manipulating an independent variable and then allowing for observation of any changes in the dependent variable. The intention here is to discover cause and effect.

New paradigm research designs

The philosophy of science influences or shapes the way we conduct science (see chapter 1). The observational research designs described to this point are all firmly rooted in a positivist–empirical tradition. Outside this mainstream empirical tradition there exist other important but widely neglected methods for conducting research. No agreed-upon name exists to describe the methods, although they are variously referred to in the literature as 'new paradigm' research, 'hermeneutic research', 'a priori research' or 'cooperative enquiry' (Hare & Secord 1972; De Maria 1981; Reason 1987).

New paradigm research 'is part of a new world-view which is emerging through systems thinking, ecological concerns and awareness, feminism, education, as well as in the philosophy of human enquiry', and represents a 'discontinuity with previous world-views and methods' (Reason 1987, pp. 3, 9). There are three components to the shift: (i) 'a participatory and wholistic knowing'; (ii) 'critical subjectivity'; and (iii) 'knowledge in action'.

In relation to Reason's first point, participatory and wholistic knowing represents a shift away from the reductionist and fragmentary outlook of Newtonian science towards a more systemic outlook emphasising wholeness, participation and cooperative enquiry (Slee 1987). It is a move away from a natural science outlook emphasising cause and effect towards a more wholistic outlook emphasising the nature of behaviour as it is considered in its context.

A second feature of the new paradigm research, as described by Reason (1987), involves a shift from objective enquiry to critical awareness. In this process, the researcher's own subjective experience is not suppressed but used as part of the process of enquiry. Such an outlook contrasts with the empirical perspective where the observer or experimenter is considered as a neutral, non-participating, objective professional.

The third and final feature of new paradigm research knowledge in action reflects a move away from theory towards practice (Reason 1987).

Reason (1987) argues that these three changes constitute what he and others have identified as a paradigm shift. The implications of this paradigm shift have challenged researchers to develop other means for conducting research apart from those represented by 'mainstream scientific thinking'. For details of research methods using new paradigm designs, see Reason (1987).

Direct observation

The whole task of 'watching and wondering' is one that has occupied the attention of parents, teachers and behavioural scientists for some time now. The strategy of direct observation is an appealing one to many people but it is a complex skill requiring considerable forethought to avoid the pitfalls inherent in the method. Fortunately there is an emerging body of writing to offer some guidelines in the skills (Medinnus 1976; Irwin & Bushnell 1980; Cohen et al. 1983; Slee 1987).

Observation methods

Various methods have been used in the observation of children including:

- baby biographies;
- anecdotal records;
- specimen descriptions;
- event sampling;
- time sampling;
- rating scales;
- participant observation.

Further details of the various methods for observing children are provided on the CD-ROM.

Interviewing children

Successful interviewing is a skill that has the potential to provide important and often unique information about children that cannot be gleaned from other sources. To ensure that the information obtained is as valid and reliable as possible, careful attention must be paid to the instrumentals of interviewing, such as the setting and the process; that is, establishing rapport with the child.

While interviewing is a basic skill in many fields of study involving children, there are remarkably few guidelines available regarding the conduct of interviews. On the CD, different types of interviews are described and guidelines suggested and in this chapter brief mention is made of the nature of interviews.

The *Macquarie Dictionary* defines 'interview' as '1. a meeting of persons face to face; 2. the conversation of a writer or reporter with a person or persons from whom material for a news or feature story or other writing is sought.' There are a number of definitions of an interview in the child development literature, but the general consensus is that it differs from a conversation in that an interview is more narrowly focused on the interviewee's experience.

The CD-ROM provides a great deal of further information regarding the effective conduct of interviews with children and adolescents.

Statistics: a very short course!

To the lay person, the term 'statistics' usually conjures up images of facts and figures or quantitative information. For example, The Australian Bureau of Statistics (ABS) in their publication *Household and Family Projections – Australia 1996–2021* predict that one-parent families will increase from 742 000 in 1996 to between 966 000 and 1.2 million in 2021.

Such facts and figures as these provide us with important information that may help guide policy development, or the implementation of practical intervention strategies.

The methods used to order facts and figures are known as statistical methods. Such methods can be descriptive or inferential.

Descriptive methods

Descriptive methods are used to reduce data to a form that is more manageable and understandable. For example, in measuring the heights of children in her class for a maths lesson, a teacher might record the following heights for 11 children: 166, 160, 165, 175, 169, 172, 166, 166, 163, 171, 173 cm. If each of these heights were represented on a graph, it would look like the histogram shown in Figure 2.1. A histogram provides the teacher with an overall descriptive impression of the height of children in her classroom; that is, how tall or how short each of them is.

Taking descriptive methods one step further, certain arithmetical operations might be performed on the data. However, before describing these operations it is important to understand two key terms: population and sample.

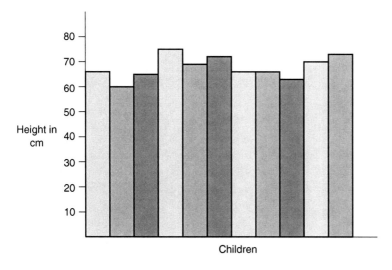

Figure 2.1 A histogram of children's heights

Population. The term 'population' refers to any group of individuals, all of whom have at least one characteristic in common, such as all children in Australia with red hair or all children aged between 7 and 10 years. A population can be large or small.

Sample. It is often difficult to study all members belonging to a certain population, such as all red-haired children in Australia. In the face of such difficulty, researchers will choose a sample that they hope will be representative of the population. Various methods are available to help ensure representativeness, such as randomisation, where all individuals in a population have an equal chance of being chosen in the sample.

The concepts of population and sample are linked to the arithmetical operations of **mean**, **median** and **mode**, which are all measures of central tendency or the middle value of a set of scores. In considering the meaning of the measures of central tendency, it is important to consider the nature of the population and/or the sample drawn from the population. If a sample is used, the key question to consider would be how representative the sample is of the population. For example, in relation to methods for sampling public opinion such as a television phone poll asking the question, 'Who is your preferred Prime Minister?', one might very rightfully consider the validity of the results in terms of how adequate the sample was.

mean
in statistics, the average of a set of scores obtained by summing all scores and dividing the total by the number of scores.

median
in statistics, the value in a series of scores which has as many scores above it as below it.

mode
in statistics, the most frequently occurring value in a set of scores.

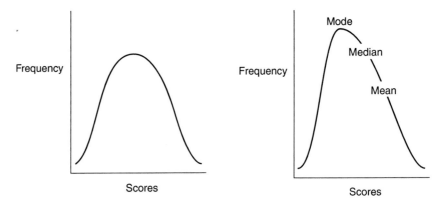

Figure 2.2 Normal distribution or bell-shaped curve

Figure 2.3 Positively skewed curve

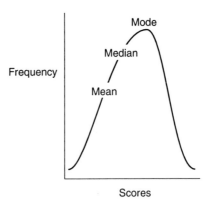

Figure 2.4 Negatively skewed curve

Mean. This is the average of a set of scores calculated by adding all the scores and dividing the result by the total number of scores. The mean height of the school children whose individual heights are shown in Figure 2.1 would be calculated as in Figure 2.2.

Median. The score that falls in the exact middle of a distribution of numbers that are arranged in order from highest to lowest. If the number of cases is even, one may average the two scores either side of the middle scores.

Mode. The mode is the most frequent score in a distribution.

The **normal distribution**, or bell-shaped curve, refers to a symmetrical distribution of scores where the mean, median and mode are equal (see Figure 2.2). In **skewed distribution**, or asymmetrical distributions, a distribution of scores can be skewed either left or right depending upon the dispersion of the measures of **central tendency**.

normal distribution
in statistics, a symmetrical distribution (bell-shaped) of a set of scores, where most values fall around the central area of the curve (the mean) and the frequency of the scores fall off to either side of the mean.

skewed distribution
in statistics, occurs when a set of scores is asymmetrical.

central tendency
in statistics, the typical or central value of a set of scores.

Inference

A second method for organising data calls upon the use of inferential statistics. In psychological research the investigator is frequently interested in making inferences about groups or investigating differences between groups in relation to certain characteristics. When two groups differ in relation to certain characteristics we may want to discover whether the differences are due to some predictable cause or to chance. Whereas descriptive statistics are concerned with organising and describing data, inferential statistics are used to make predictions and draw conclusions about populations based on data obtained from a sample.

Inferential statistics are based on the laws of probability or chance. That is, the question being asked by the researcher is whether the difference between any two scores could be said to be statistically significant or whether the differences have arisen through chance. On the basis of probability and levels of significance, a researcher can calculate whether a particular finding has arisen through chance or whether the probability of such a result is less than 5 in 100 or 1 in 100, expressed statistically as $p<.05$ and $p<.01$ respectively.

Hypothesis

A psychologist will often make a **hypothesis**; that is, a statement about relationships among variables that may be true or false, the probability of which can be calculated through the use of statistical procedures. Hypotheses are usually stated in terms of a *null hypothesis* or statements of no difference between the average scores in two samples. For example, in examining whether girls and boys in primary school differ in the number of stressful life events that they have experienced, a psychologist might propose the null hypothesis that boys and girls do not differ in the number of stressful life events that they have experienced. On the basis of statistical tests that indicate whether or not a particular finding could be expected as a result of chance, the psychologist may reject the null hypothesis of no difference in the number of stressful life events experienced by boys and girls in primary school.

hypothesis
a testable proposition.

Correlation

correlation
in statistics, the relationship between two sets of scores.

A coefficient of **correlation** measures the degree to which two measures, such as stressful life events and adjustment to school, vary together. The measure may be expressed as a positive or negative correlation.

1 A positive correlation means that as one measure gets larger so does the second.
2 A negative correlation means that as one measure gets smaller the second gets larger.

Coefficients of correlation range between +1.00 and −1.00. For example, if a correlation of .00 was found between the number of stressful life events a child had experienced and a measure of school adjustment, it would be concluded that there was no relationship between these two measures. The closer the co-efficient of correlation is to 1.00 (+ or −), the closer is the relationship between the two variables. It is important to appreciate that correlation does not imply causation. For example, one might find a strong positive correlation (such as .80) between the number of incoming overseas flights into Adelaide International Airport and the rate of delinquency in metropolitan Adelaide. It would be erroneous to conclude that an increase in the number of international flights caused an increase in delinquency.

New paradigm research

The statistics described here are part of the prevailing dominant philosophy of science or positivist paradigm, which emphasises 'the "senses" as the factual basis for understanding human behavior' (Slee 1987, p. 8). As discussed in chapter 1, positivism is concerned with establishing causes and predicting events or behaviour. It is to this end that the use of statistics is largely directed.

Currently, there is considerable upheaval occurring in the way the social sciences conceive of and conduct research. New methods are being explored for collecting, analysing and interpreting information in the fields of education (Young 1981), psychology (Manicus & Secord 1983; Reason & Rowan 1981; Reason 1990); and social welfare (De Maria 1981; Battye & Slee 1985), to cite but a few examples. Various writers (Battye & Slee 1985; Viney 1985; Reason 1988) are challenging researchers to adopt a more flexible approach in their research endeavours, an approach that would not be constrained by assumptions inherent in the positivist paradigm.

Researchers are now becoming more keenly interested in developing research methods for providing insight into the 'inner' (subject's) world and its meanings for him or her, as opposed to the observer's constructed view of the world. An example of such research is provided in a study by Carraher et al. (1985), who used a method that they described as a hybrid between the Piagetian clinical method and participant observation in their study of the everyday use of mathematics by Brazilian children in commercial transactions, such as that of children selling vegetables.

The researchers had hypothesised that there might be differences between the way children were taught to solve problems in school and the way they solved problems in familiar working contexts, such as on street corners outside school hours. From their findings, they deduced that mathematics might best be taught by providing real-life examples for children to solve, because it appeared their problem-solving was more often found in the context of real-life settings. From a statistical viewpoint, the authors had to reconsider how best to analyse data that had been collected by methods considered by many to be outside mainstream practice.

The family life-cycle: 2

The family in Australia

As noted in The Family Life-Cycle 1, the task of defining the term 'family' is not as simple as it seems. However, in many ways society still appears to hold the nuclear family as the ideal; that is, consisting of male and female, preferably married with one or more children. As Callan and Noller (1987) observe, there are those who believe that the traditional family is under threat from such forces as the rising divorce rate, the increased incidence of sole parenthood, unemployment and a range of other factors. At the same time it may not be possible (if it ever was!) to identify the 'typical' Australian family. The Australian Bureau of Statistics (ABS) (2000) provides some skeletal outline regarding the nature of contemporary family structure in Australia:

Marriage: As shown in Figure 2.5 the 'crude marriage rate/1000 of population in Australia is on a downwards trend from 7.0 in 1989 to 6.0 in 1999.

Birthrate: In Figure 2.6 the total fertility rate (per woman) in Australia is also on a downwards trend from 1.84 children/woman in 1989 to 1.75 children per woman in 1999.

Types of families
In the ABS publication *Household and Family Projections: Australia 1996 to 2021*, couple families with children are projected to increase slowly over the period 1996–2021, '...reflecting a gradual trend away from this type of family' (ABS 2000, p. 10). As further noted, the explanation for this trend is the '...rapid increase in couple families without children, and the increase in one-parent families, and is driven by ageing, the decline in fertility and increased marital break-up' (p. 10). In Figure 2.7 the projected figures for different family types is presented.

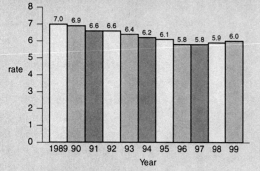

Figure 2.5 Crude marriage rate, Australia per 1000 population   **Source:** ABS 2001

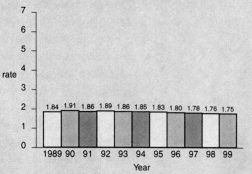

Figure 2.6 Fertility rate per Australian woman
Source: ABS 2001

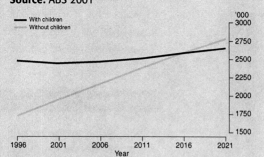

Figure 2.7 Trends in couple families with children and without children
Source: ABS 2001

Women's Labour Force Participation
ABS statistics for the period 1990–2000 indicate an upwards trend in females as part of the total labour force in Australia from 51.8 per cent in 1990 to 54.5 per cent in 2000.

  As noted in the ABS (2000) report, the much higher proportion of Australian women in the part-time labour force is indicative of the traditional roles women fulfill in terms of family and child-care responsibilities.

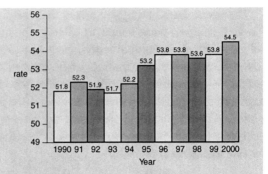

Figure 2.8 Female participation rate in workforce (Australia) per 100 000 people
Source: ABS 2001

Chapter summary

Research can be part of any thoughtful individual's life. In this chapter we have seen that when designing a study to explore one or more identified research questions, various issues must be carefully considered. Initially, before embarking on any such study, the researcher must decide what kind of knowledge and understanding is being sought. This might fall into one of four categories: hypothetical–developmental, quantitative–descriptive, associational and cause–effect. In planning and carrying out the study, the researcher might move through a number of steps in three stages: planning, preliminary study and main study. For the study itself, the researcher may choose to follow an observational research design (a field study, a naturalistic experiment, a field experiment or laboratory study) or a 'new paradigm' method.

  In relation to developmental psychology, the enormous contributions of many researchers initially stemmed from sensitive observations of their own children. Various methods of direct observation have been developed, including event sampling, time sampling and rating scales. Whether interviews with children are standardised or non-standardised, attention should be paid to various criteria to make an interview effective.

  The science of child observation has been refined considerably in the last 50 years and is continuing to develop. Contemporary developments in the philosophy of science, particularly the leaning towards a more systems-oriented view, are of considerable importance for the study of children.

Discussion questions

1 Write down as many reasons as you can why a study of child development is important for your chosen career.
2 How do 'descriptive' and 'inferential' statistics differ from each other?
3 Clarify the differences between the three measures of central tendency.
4 What do the terms 'positive' and 'negative' correlation mean?

Activities

1   Complete the quiz, 'Beliefs about child development' (adapted from Levin 1973) on p. 46. Compare your responses with those of other students in your group and discuss resulting similarities and discrepancies.
2   List various definitions of research and discuss.
3   Discuss Tripodi's four levels of knowledge, focusing on issues such as the most prevalent type of knowledge and the most desirable type of knowledge.
4   Compare and contrast field studies, naturalistic experiments, field experiments, laboratory studies, and new paradigm research designs, considering their advantages and disadvantages.
5   Select any journal in the field of developmental psychology and find an example of a research method described in this chapter. Present details of the study to your class.
6   Apply the major steps in the research design process (see CD-ROM Figure 1) to the examination of an identified research problem; for example, children's cooperative behaviour or a study of parents' views of the facilities available at their local kindergarten, playgroup or school.
7   Conduct mock interviews with both standardised and non-standardised formats, noting the advantages and disadvantages of each method. Which procedures used in your interviews facilitate the conduct of an effective interview? Compare these procedures with those listed in this chapter.

Selected websites

Child Adolescent Educational Resources <www.caper.com.au>

Australian Institute Family Studies <www.aifs.org.au>

Quiz

Circle the number that best represents where you believe is the right balance between each pair of statements. Do not hesitate to use the extreme ends of the scale.

1	Inborn qualities (genetics) determine how we develop our capacities.	1	2	3	4	5	The way a person is raised and the influences of home, school and culture determine our development.
2	We develop and grow older and more mature in the same way that a seedling becomes a tree.	1	2	3	4	5	We undergo development in sudden changes, just as there are distinct stages in the transformation of a caterpillar into a butterfly.
3	People are essentially similar despite surface differences. We must search for general principles that apply to everyone.	1	2	3	4	5	Only after we understand the range of differences that make each human being unique will general trends become apparent.
4	Human development is characterised by stability such that personality and ability are fairly well fixed by a certain age, and certainly by adolescence.	1	2	3	4	5	Human development is unpredictable and dependent upon historical events and chance circumstances.
5	Development is self-initiated. The individual actively seeks growth and change.	1	2	3	4	5	Human development is shaped by powerful forces, such as culture, which are beyond individual control.
6	To understand human development we must start by understanding how a person thinks.	1	2	3	4	5	To understand human development we must start by understanding how a person feels.

Figure 2.9 Beliefs about child development quiz
Source: Adapted from Levin (1973)

3 Theoretical Foundations of Child Development

'...Such a Pleasant Temper'

'You can't think how glad I am to see you again, you dear old thing!' said the Duchess, as she tucked her arm affectionately into Alice's, and they walked off together. Alice was very glad to find her in such a pleasant temper, and thought to herself that perhaps it was only the pepper that had made her so savage when they met in the kitchen.

Lewis Carroll, Through the Looking Glass

KEY TERMS AND CONCEPTS

- Psychoanalysis
- Id
- Ego
- Superego
- Erogenous zones
- Classical conditioning
- Operant conditioning
- Reinforcement
- Punishment

- Humanism
- Existentialism
- Phenomenology
- Self-actualisation
- Sensori-motor period
- Pre-operational period
- Concrete operations period
- Formal operations period
- constructivism

Introduction

This chapter will consider a number of the major theories listed in Figure 1.1 (see chapter 1), including psychoanalytic, psychosocial, behavioural, humanistic, cognitive–developmental and social systems theory. In this second edition, additional information is provided regarding evolutionary, ecological and dynamic systems theory. In discussing the various theories, the work of key writers and researchers will be examined, namely Sigmund Freud, Erik Erikson, Ivan Pavlov, Burrhus Skinner, John Watson, Albert Bandura, Abraham Maslow, Jean Piaget, Eleanor Maccoby and Gregory Bateson. The third item in The Family Life-cycle series introduces the concept of family life-cycle.

VIEWPOINT

What have you heard about the following theorists?

Thirty-four first-year students of education answered as follows (percentage who had heard of the theorist associations):

Sigmund Freud

82%; 'Freudian slip', 'philospher', 'psychoanalyst', and 'famous doctor'.

Erik Erikson

11%; no particular associations

Ivan Pavlov

29%; 'conditioning', and 'experiments with dogs'

Burrhus Skinner

5%; 'behaviourism'

John Watson

No one

Albert Bandura

2%; 'behaviour modification'

Abraham Maslow

5%; 'hierarchy of needs'

Jean Piaget

12%; 'child development'

Eleanor Maccoby

No one

Gregory Bateson

No one

Theoretical development

As defined by the *Macquarie Dictionary*, a fact is 'what has really happened or is the case; truth; reality; something known to have happened'. Research into child development is uncovering facts at a rate that sometimes outstrips our ability to integrate them into a coherent framework. Facts are very important to any science. They have been called the building blocks of science. However, just as a pile of bricks does not make a house, a collection of facts does not make a science.

A theory, in the simplest sense of the term, helps to explain facts, where facts are observations. That is, theory is a way of organising the raw data – the facts – to provide a more complete picture of what the data mean. Such organisation helps the scientist to understand the portion of the world being investigated.

In psychology, theories are used to provide us with future direction to set up further hypotheses. Thus, when motor mechanics wish to fix a mechanical problem they may listen to engine noise and, based upon such an observation, offer an initial 'theory' as to what is wrong. Working from this initial theory, mechanics can then propose and enter upon a course of action for repairing the fault. On the whole, the analogy holds true for a science such as psychology.

There is really very little doubt that the classical developmental theories, such as those of Freud (1933) and Piaget (1983) have provided a sense of the richness and complexity of human beings, in contrast to the oversimplifications that are often evident in more narrowly empirical research'.

Controlling our children

There is an emerging debate in the literature regarding the extent to which children are seen as 'out of control', 'in crisis' and 'at risk'. Fears are held for the safety of children (e.g. in relation to the victimisation of children) and fears are held regarding the 'risk' that children present to others (e.g. in relation to school bullying, and homicide). As an important aside, Wyness (2000) and Scraton (1997) have both raised questions about whether such a 'crisis' is actually taking place. One outcome of the perceived 'crisis' in childhood relates to the manner in which children have become the subject of both overt and covert regulation (James and James, 2000). This can be reflected in the way that adults are now attempting to control and restrict children's use of public space. For example, in my home city of Adelaide, South Australia, in the last year there was considerable public debate about the provision and location of a skate-boarding rink for young people. One point of view held that it should be located in the centre of Adelaide where presumably behaviour could be regulated, controlled and scrutinised. In contrast, it was argued that locating it in the city centre would attract 'undesirables'. It was finally built and located away from the city centre in a disused part of a railyard. Valentine (1996, p. 205) has noted that '... postmodernism's concern with the geographies of "others" has revived interest in children's marginalisation as a social group'.

Sigmund Freud and psychoanalytic theory

In a collection of essays on Freud, Wollheim (1974, p. ix) noted that:

> It is frequently asserted that in our thinking we all nowadays lie in the shadow of Freud: so powerful indeed has his influence been that it is all but impossible for us to imagine ourselves out from under it and to reconstruct the mental habits or attitudes of a pre Freudian age.

As noted by Andrews and Brewin (2000, p. 605), 'The last quarter of the 20th century has seen growing academic criticism of, and public scepticism about, Freudian theory and practice'. Before considering further the criticisms of Freudian theory, some understanding is warranted of the basic tenets of the theory.

Psychoanalytic theory represents a deterministic model of human behaviour. That is, all behaviour is believed to be caused. The symptoms are not the real problem but reflect underlying defects in personality. Treatment consists of a search for the underlying defect; that is, the underlying motive behind the behaviour. The cause of the behaviour is believed to be largely unconscious and not readily available to the person. **Psychoanalysis** is the means by which the underlying defect is rendered conscious. In order to understand the possible nature of such defects it is necessary to understand Freud's view of personality structure.

psychoanalysis
the method for treating mental disorders, developed by Sigmund Freud, in which the underlying defect, the motive behind behaviour, is rendered conscious.

The structure of personality

In psychoanalytic theory, Freud initially placed great emphasis on the division of the mind into the conscious and unconscious. In the latter stage of his life he developed a tripartite structure of personality as represented by the id, ego and superego. According to Freud, each part has identifiable characteristics, but all three parts interact to produce an individual's personality and behaviour.

Id

id
in Freudian theory, that part of the personality containing all of the basic impulses or drives.

In his book *An Outline of Psychoanalysis* (1939, p. 144), Freud wrote that the id contains 'everything that is inherited, that is present at birth, that is laid down in the constitution – above all, therefore, the instincts, which originate from the somatic organisation and which find a first psychical expression here (in the id) in forms unknown to us'. The word **id** is Latin for 'it'. The id represents the source of energy that stimulates the personality. This energy is represented in the form of **drives**. In Freud's view, the true purpose of the individual's life consists of the satisfaction of the instincts. Freud identified two basic **instincts**:

drives
in Freudian theory, powerful instinctive desires, such as hunger or thirst.

1   *eros*, or the life instinct – sexual drive;
2   *thanatos*, or the death or destructive instinct.

instincts
in Freudian theory, forces that exist behind the tensions caused by the needs of the id.

According to Freudian theory, the personality system is most stable when operating at a low level of energy. When energy increases, psychic tension may arise:

> We assume that the forces which drive the mental apparatus into activity are produced in the bodily organs as an expression of the major somatic needs . . . We give these bodily needs, insofar as they represent an instigation to mental activity, the name of Triebe [instincts], a word for which we are envied by many modern languages. Well, these instincts fill the id: all the energy is in the id . . . What, then, do these instincts want? . . . Satisfaction – that is the establishment of situations in which the bodily needs can be extinguished (Freud 1974, p. 122).

Freud proposed that the id operated according to the pleasure principle. As Freud noted (1974, p. 122):

> A lowering of the tension of need is felt by our organ of consciousness as pleasurable: an increase of it is soon felt as unpleasure. From these oscillations arises the series of feelings of pleasure–unpleasure, in accordance with which the whole mental apparatus regulates its activity. In this connexion we speak of a dominance of the pleasure principle.

Ego

ego
in Freudian theory, the conscious self, the realistic rational part of the personality that mediates between the instinctual demands of the id and the superego.

In Freudian theory the **ego** (ich, or I) exists as a:

> kind of facade of the id, as a frontage, like an external cortical layer of it . . . Thus we suppose that the ego is the layer of the mental apparatus (of the id) which has been modified by the influence of the external world (of reality) (Freud 1974, p. 105).

In Freud's own words, 'what you call ego is consciousness' (Freud 1974, p. 107). The ego, once developed, operates according to the reality principle. Thus the ego 'learns that it must inevitably go without immediate satisfaction, postpone gratification, learn to endure a degree of pain, and altogether renounce certain sources of pleasure' (Freud 1963, p. 312). The ego's task is to mediate between the demands of the id for immediate instinctual gratification and the objections of the external world to such gratification.

Superego

The **superego** is the final part of Freud's three-part (tripartite) structure of personality: 'the superego is the vehicle of the phenomenon that we call conscience' (Freud 1974, p. 237). There are two parts to the superego, namely the ego ideal and conscience. The ego ideal is self-created and corresponds to that part 'that incessantly watches, criticises and compares' (Freud 1963, p. 371). The ego ideal therefore represents a set of ideal standards (drawn from identification with one's parents) against which the worth of the self is measured. The conscience represents a judging or punishing agency that leads an individual to experience guilt each time the standards of the ego ideal are violated or broken.

> **superego**
> in Freudian theory, that part of the personality incorporating the internalised values held by the individual and corresponding to the internalised injunctions of the parent.

The development of personality

Freud's work as a neurologist with neurotic patients led him to believe that one's early life is very significant in terms of personality development. Freud's keen observations were based on his patients, recalled accounts of their earliest childhood memories and did not involve direct observation of children (except in the case involving the analysis of a five-year-old boy suffering from anxiety).

Freud's initial writings were considered quite outrageous because he emphasised the sexuality of children. 'A child has its sexual instincts and activities from the first; it comes into the world with them; and after an important course of development passing through many stages, they lead to what is known as the normal sexuality of the adult' (Freud 1974, p. 71). Freud identified parts of the body (**erogenous zones**) that at different ages were susceptible to pleasurable feelings.

> **erogenous zones**
> parts of the body that at different ages are susceptible to pleasurable feelings.

Oral stage

This is the first stage: the infant obtains pleasure first from sucking and later from biting. Thumb-sucking in young infants is an example of auto-erotic satisfaction from an erogenous zone. If the infant should become fixated at the oral level then there is the risk of a dependent personality in adulthood.

Anal stage

As the child develops in the normal course of events the focus of the pleasurable erogenous zone shifts from the mouth to the anus. The two modes of behaviour relevant to this stage relate to holding back and retaining or giving up and expelling.

Phallic stage

During this stage, the child experiences difficulty in bringing masturbation and incestuous feelings for the parents under

During the oral stage the mouth is the primary focus for pleasurable feelings.

control. In his five lectures on psychoanalysis, Freud examined the Greek myth of King Oedipus, who killed his father and took his mother as wife. When the oracle of Delphi prophesied to King Laius of Thebes that he would be killed by his own son, the king ordered the infant to be killed. Rescued by a shepherd, the boy was adopted by King Polybus of Corinth and named Oedipus. As a young man, Oedipus learned from the oracle that he would kill his father and marry his own mother. Later, while on a journey he slew a man who had thrust him from his path, ignorant that he was his father. As Homer writes in *Odyssey*:

> And I saw the mother of Oedipus, fair Epicaste who committed a dreadful deed
> in the ignorance of her mind by marrying her own son; and he married her after
> slaying his own father – deeds the gods immediately made notorious among men.

Odyssey II, line 271ff.

The myth of Oedipus emphasises the elements of parenticide and incest, which were elements of the Oedipus complex in Freudian theory. Freud also considered the personality of Shakespeare's Hamlet to be a manifestation of the Oedipus complex, although better disguised than in the myth of Oedipus.

Latency stage

In Freudian theory, the latency period is one during which sexual instincts lie dormant and repressed. The energies of the child are given over to establishing and incorporating adult values from the family and larger society.

Genital stage

During this final stage of development, the individual's sexuality is maturing. Sexual drives of the earlier phallic stage are reactivated but the individual is now in a better position to satisfy such longings through love relationships outside the family.

Freud's influence

Jerome Bruner called Freud's theory a dramatic theory of personality:

> Freud's is a theory or a prototype theory peopled with actors. The characters are
> from life: the blind, energetic, pleasure-seeking id; the priggish and punitive
> superego; the ego, battling for its being by diverting the energy of others to its
> own use. The drama has an economy and a terseness. The ego develops canny
> mechanisms for dealing with the threat of id impulses; denial, projection and the
> rest. Balances are struck between the actors, and in the balance is character and
> neurosis (Bruner 1956, p. 243).

Certainly Freud's influence on psychology has been immense. His ideas have challenged us to rethink our views of children and alerted us to the importance of the early years in shaping our development. It would be fair to say, however, that many of his ideas are currently being strongly challenged and psychiatry as a profession is under attack from many quarters. Interestingly, some of the more trenchant critics of the theory have been made by non-psychologists (e.g. Crews 1997; Masson 1984).

Andrews and Brewin (2000) have reviewed Freudian theory in terms of modern research. They identify particular criticisms relating to current issues such as 'recovered memory' (Mollon 1998) and more general problems associated with establishing the validity of the theory (Fisher and Greenberg 1996).

Erik Erikson and psychosocial theory

Erikson's book, *Childhood and Society*, was first published in 1950. It is presented in three parts: the clinical method of case study, the influence of culture on development, and Erikson's view of ego development and the evolution of children into adolescence. The magnitude of Erikson's work in this book is often overlooked because greater attention is usually paid to the third part.

In the first part of the book, Erikson details the case-study method as a means of understanding the development of the 'normal' child. He presents his idea of zones of development and modes. For example, the first zone of development in the very young child is the mouth and how we use it is described by the mode. Thus, eating involves the zone of the mouth and taking in or rejecting food represents the mode.

The second part of the book describes Erikson's work with the North American Indian tribes of the Sioux and Yurok. It represents his understanding of anthropology – that primitive societies are neither infantile stages of humanity nor arrested deviations of developed societies. They 'are a complete form of mature human living, often of a homogeneity and simple integrity which we at the time might well envy' (Erikson 1963, p. 107). Erikson argues that Indians have their own way of dealing with the world they know and of raising their children.

In the third part of his book, Erikson is concerned with the growth of the ego. The development of the ego and superego had been well-documented by Freud. The id contains the sum of all instincts, while the superego limits the expression of the id through the demands of the conscience. 'Between the id and the super-ego, there the ego dwells' (Erikson 1963, p. 187). Erikson argues that the ego is hardly passive. It plays the important role of:

> balancing and warding off the extreme ways of the other two; the ego keeps tuned to the reality of the historical day, testing perceptions, selecting memories governing action and otherwise integrating the individual's capacities of orientation and planning (Erikson 1950, p. 187).

In this section, Erikson argues that ego development proceeds through eight **psychosocial** stages (representing the 'eight ages of men'). Erikson proposes that at each stage a different ego capability must occur in order for healthy ego development to proceed. At each of the stages a normative crisis results from the interaction between the biological ground plan of the species and the social

psychosocial
in Erikson's theory, describes the interactions between child and family and between child and culture.

organisation that we call 'culture'. How we meet and cope with these crises depends in part on how we dealt with the crises that we encountered in the previous stages of development.

Although Erikson was originally involved in psychoanalysis, he believed that Freud had placed too much emphasis on pathological and defensive aspects of human nature. Erikson emphasised three dimensions of development: biological, social and individual. The identity of an individual contains three elements:

1 a conscious sense of individual uniqueness;
2 an unconscious striving for continuity of experience;
3 a solidarity with group ideals.

Erikson made many important contributions to psychology, particularly his identification of the eight 'ages' encompassing the life span (see chapter 21).

Table 3.1 A comparison of Freud's and Erikson's stages of personality development

Life Stages	Freud	Erikson
Infancy	Oral	Basic trust versus mistrust
Early childhood	Anal	Autonomy versus shame and doubt
	Phallic	Initiative versus guilt
Middle childhood	Latency	Industry versus inferiority
Adolescence	Genital	Identity versus role confusion
Young adulthood		Intimacy versus isolation
Adulthood		Generativity versus stagnation
Maturity		Integrity versus despair

Behaviourism

Another significant force in psychology and in the understanding of human development is that of behaviourism (see Figure 1.1 in chapter 1). Behaviourism developed in the context of the rise to prominence of Newtonian science in the eighteenth century.

Newtonian science replaced the prevailing contemporary view of the world as a living, organic, spiritual universe with a mechanistic vision of reality. In the Newtonian view of science, the earlier interpretation of the world based upon introspection, revelation, reason and ordinary experience was abandoned in favour of rigid determinism and linear causality. Science delimited knowledge to a world view constrained by statistical probability, value-free research and quantitativity. The presentation of science as the sole arbiter of knowledge has since come to be labelled **scientism** (see also chapter 1).

scientism
the idea that all true knowledge arises from the use of empirical scientific method.

Another underlying factor associated with the development of behaviourism is called materialism. A key feature of materialism was that scientific principles could be applied to the study of living organisms. To this end, physical–chemical laws were the basis of explanation: for example, physiology was reduced to chemistry.

It was in this intellectual climate of scientism and materialism that pioneer psychologists such as Freud and Pavlov were educated.

Ivan Pavlov's scientific thought

Pavlov's interest in physiology was prompted by a curiosity about how such a complicated system as the human body functioned. This curiosity fanned his determination to become an experimental physiologist.

From 1902 until his death in 1936, Pavlov worked on understanding the functions of the highest nervous system. His discovery of **classical conditioning** as a way to view the functioning of the nervous system remains his greatest contribution to psychology. In the course of his experiments, Pavlov noted certain irregularities in the normal functioning of the digestive glands of dogs. Sometimes dogs would start to secrete digestive juices before food was given; that is, as soon as the dog saw the person who customarily fed it. Pavlov's preliminary experiments were conducted by simply showing the dog bread and then giving the dog bread to eat. Eventually the dog would begin to salivate as soon as it saw the bread.

classical conditioning learning in which a neutral stimulus elicits a certain response by repeated association with another stimulus that already elicits the response.

- Salivation when the bread was placed in its mouth was a natural reflex of the digestive system.
- Salivation at the sight of the bread was learned; that is, a conditioned reflex.

Further experimentation clarified the conditioning process. For example, a bell (conditioned stimulus) was repeatedly sounded before food (unconditioned stimulus) was placed in a dog's mouth to produce salivation (unconditioned reflex) until eventually the sound of a bell alone caused salivation (conditioned reflex).

The significance of Pavlov's discovery

Pavlov grasped that the importance of his discovery of the conditioned reflex lay in the potential it provided for reducing complex behaviour to basic elements. Thus, Pavlov's work lay well within the prevailing empirical paradigm of the time. As Pavlov (1970, p. 18) wrote:

> We are becoming better acquainted with the fundamental mode of conduct with which the animal is born – with congenital reflexes, heretofore usually called instincts. We observe and intentionally participate in building new reactions on the fundamental conduct in the form of so called habits and associations, which now increase, enlarge, become complicated and refined. According to our analysis these are also reflexes, but conditioned reflexes.

From a scientific, empirical point of view, the significance of the discovery of the **conditioned reflex** lay in its potential to explain human behaviour, for '[t]he conditioned reflexes which accumulate progressively during the individual life of animals and man are formed within the cerebral hemispheres' (Pavlov 1970, p. 20). Later in his career, Pavlov worked to link the conditioned reflex to an understanding of human neuroses.

conditioned reflex occurs when a previously neutral stimulus acquires the ability to produce a response through association with an unconditioned stimulus (a stimulus that evokes a response that has not been learned).

The psychology of John Watson

The first psychological laboratories set up in Germany and The United States defined psychology as the study of consciousness. Introspection or the consideration of one's own behaviour was the principal method used to discover the content of consciousness. However, in evaluating the methodology, critics quickly identified that subjects could not agree with any reliability on the description of sensation, images and feelings. At the same time, Freud was arguing that important aspects of the mind were not in consciousness.

In brief, Watson's method involved a great deal of emphasis upon objective observation. Drawing upon his experience as a student of animal behaviour, Watson claimed that the subject matter of psychology was not consciousness but the behaviour of the person. Thus, he rejected all subjective methods, relying instead solely on what could be observed or recorded. He emphasised environmental stimuli (such as a loud noise or praise from a teacher) and the response (such as a startled reaction or on-task pupil behaviour). For this reason, Watson's view of behaviour is often called stimulus–response (S–R) psychology.

There are two important aspects to Watson's view of psychology:

1   The belief that the environment is all important. Watson argued that the only inherited features of behaviour were simple physiological reflexes (such as the knee-jerk reflex). Watson credited all else to learning, hence his claim:

> Give me a dozen healthy infants, well formed and my own specified world to bring them up in and I'll guarantee to take anyone at random and train him to become any kind of specialist I might select: doctor, lawyer, artist, merchant-chief, and yes even beggar-man and thief, regardless of his talents, penchants, abilities, vocation and race of his ancestors (Watson 1930, p. 104).

2   Watson was heavily influenced by the work of Pavlov on the conditioned reflex. Watson wanted to explain how all complex behaviours of both animals and humans were the result of conditioning by their environment.

In sum, John Watson's thoughts provided a basis for shaping the nature of psychological thought in the early 1900s, particularly in North America.

B. F. Skinner and operant behaviourism

operant conditioning
behaviour that results from the rewarding or punishment of voluntary behaviour by stimulus consequences.

Behaviourism as developed by Skinner has come to be known as operant behaviourism. One of the most basic differences between **operant conditioning** and classical conditioning is that classical conditioning applies to reflexes while operant conditioning applies to voluntary behaviour. Reflexes are called respondent behaviour, in contrast with voluntary or operant behaviour. Thus, when a dog salivates in response to food in its mouth, the salivation is a reflex or a 'respondent'. Operants, in contrast, are said to occur voluntarily – they are emitted rather than elicited. Thus, operants operate on, or have an effect on, the environment, and are not necessarily associated with any particular stimulus.

The case of little Albert

One of the most frequently cited learning theory experiments in psychological literature is an experiment conducted by John Watson and Rosalie Rayner in 1920. This involved an infant who from birth had been raised in a hospital environment where his mother was a wet-nurse. Watson and Rayner described the baby, Albert, as a healthy, rather unemotional infant, and these qualities led them to believe that little harm could befall him during the planned tests. They had already tested him at 9 months and had found that he did not show any fear reactions when confronted suddenly with a white rat, rabbit, dog, monkey masks, cotton wool and so on. That is, in learning theory terms, the stimuli were neutral.

The unconditioned stimulus was to be a loud sound made by striking a hammer upon a steel bar (see chapter 3 for the methodology). They discovered that when the iron bar was struck behind Albert he would cry. Watson and Rayner proposed to find out if a previously neutral stimulus (a white rat) could be made to elicit the same reflexes as a loud

noise by pairing it with a loud noise. They reported that they had some hesitation about the experiment but comforted themselves with the notion that Albert would encounter and develop such emotional reactions once he left the confines of the hospital.

The experiment proper began when Albert was 11 months and 3 days old. A white rat was presented to him and as he reached for the rat the iron bar was struck immediately behind his head. As Watson and Rayner described it, little Albert jumped and fell forward with his face in the mattress. When he reached for the rat again and his hand touched it, the iron bar was struck and once more he fell forward and began to whimper. The experiment was stopped at this point.

One week later, when the rat was presented he would not reach for it. When the rat was pushed nearer he reached for it very tentatively. Watson and Rayner then provided Albert with blocks which he immediately picked up. The conclusion was that an emotional response had been conditioned. Further testing allowed them to conclude that conditioned emotional responses persist longer than a month.

When you see a bird moving around in its cage, it is not necessarily responding to any stimulus. Similarly the babbling of a young baby is operant behaviour.

A key term relevant to operant conditioning is 'consequences'. In the simplest terms, the consequences that follow a response may either increase (**reinforce**) or decrease (**punish**) the probability of (a) further response(s). If the consequence to a response produces a repetition of the response or an increase in the frequency of responding, the consequence is described as reinforcing or rewarding. Should the consequence to a response result in a suppression or reduction of behaviour, the consequence is described as punishing.

Reinforcement can be either positive or negative:

reinforcement
any stimulus that increases the likelihood of a behaviour recurring.

punishment
any stimulus that results in the suppression or reduction of a behaviour.

1 With positive reinforcement, the frequency of response increases because the response is followed by consequences that the subject finds rewarding. For example, a dog is given a biscuit for running to its owner when it hears a whistle. This increases the likelihood of a repetition of this behaviour when the owner whistles.

2 With negative reinforcement, the frequency of a response increases because the response removes or enables the organism to avoid a negative or painful stimulus. For instance, a child completes a homework assignment to avoid being kept in after school.

a whistle. This increases the likelihood of a repetition of this behaviour
when the owner whistles.

2   With negative reinforcement, the frequency of a response increases because
the response removes or enables the organism to avoid a negative or painful
stimulus. For instance, a child completes a homework assignment to avoid
being kept in after school.

The operantly conditioned response

It has already been noted that operant behaviour is emitted by the organism
rather than elicited by some stimulus. The analysis of operantly conditioned
behaviour has its foundations in laboratory studies of animals such as rats and
pigeons. Most of Skinner's experiments were conducted with animals in a
cage-like apparatus which has come to be known as a Skinner box (Figure 3.1).
At one end of the box is a food dispenser, together with a lever that when
depressed drops a pellet of food into a tray. Above the lever is a light that is
turned on whenever food drops into the tray. The animal is placed in the
Skinner box. In the course of moving around, the animal inadvertently
depresses the lever, which releases food into the tray and turns on the light. The
food serves as a reinforcer to the hungry animal, which will depress the lever
again to obtain more food (reinforcement). The lever-pressing is an operant,
since it does not occur in response to any known stimulus.

Shaping the operantly conditioned response. During operant conditioning,
the experimenter may shape the subject's behaviour. For example, in training a

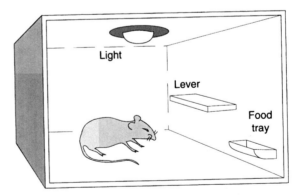

Figure 3.1 A simplified version of the Skinner box

rat to press a lever, the experimenter would not wait until the rat depressed the
lever accidentally, because of the considerable time this might involve. Rather,
the rat might be rewarded for turning to face the lever, for approaching the
lever, for lifting its front feet off the ground, for placing its feet on the lever and
finally for pressing the lever. Shaping uses successive approximations, with
each small step representing a move towards a desired final outcome. If the

2 *Secondary reinforcers* are previously neutral stimuli (such as the light in the Skinner box) that acquire reinforcing properties when paired with primary reinforcers.
3 *Generalised reinforcers* include, for humans at least, praise, social prestige and power.

Operant conditioning depends not only upon the presence or absence of reinforcement but on how the reinforcement is applied (schedules of reinforcement). A number of different schedules are available for conditioning behaviour and each has a different impact on establishing and maintaining the behaviour in question.

Food is a primary reinforcement

1 *Continuous.* This particular schedule involves providing reinforcement for every correct response. It is a particularly useful schedule to adopt in establishing the conditioned response.
2 *Intermittent.* Having established the behaviour in question, perhaps the best way to maintain it involves the use of an intermittent schedule and there are various types of such schedules.

   a *Fixed ratio.* Here the reinforcement is given for a specified number of responses, for example, a reward for 20 lever presses by the rat or the completion of two vehicles on a human car-production line.

   b *Variable ratio.* The reinforcement is provided on average for a certain number of responses, such as for 20 lever presses.

   c *Fixed interval.* This schedule involves rewarding the subject per time interval: for example, a pellet of food is given to the rat every minute regardless of the number of times it presses the lever, or the car-assembly worker is paid by the hour regardless of the number of vehicles produced.

   d *Variable interval.* During this schedule, the subject is rewarded on average per time interval: for example, poker machines operate on such a schedule.

Generally speaking, the variable interval schedules tend to elicit a high response rate from animals or humans (watch individuals playing poker machines) because of the unpredictability of knowing when one will be rewarded.

Parenting Skinner style

B. F. Skinner has reported in some detail the raising of his daughter Deborah in a device he designed and called the baby tender.

> For our second child, Deborah, I built a crib-sized living space that we began to call the 'baby tender'. It had sound absorbing walls and a large picture window. Air entered through filters at the bottom and after being warmed and moistened, moved by convection upward through and around the edges of a tightly stretched canvas, which served as a mattress. [A small fan blew the air if the room was

hot.] A strip of sheeting 10 yards long passed over the canvas, a clean section of which could be cranked into place in a few seconds (Skinner 1979, p. 30).

According to Skinner, Deborah was introduced to the baby tender from the very first weeks of life. He claimed the tender's soundproofing enabled Deborah to sleep well and protected her from infection. Skinner's initial reporting of his invention in *The Ladies Home Journal* in October 1945 generated considerable controversy, including a comparison of the project with the Skinner box. Contrary to rumour, Deborah did not eventually commit suicide but grew up to become a successful artist.

Albert Bandura and social learning theory

In terms of learning theory, we have considered that an individual may learn through classical conditioning (Pavlov) or operant conditioning (Skinner). Throughout their research, learning theorists have attempted to develop a theory to account for all learning, but to date this goal has proved evasive. A third possibility accounting for learning has been described by Albert Bandura and associates, and is known as social learning theory (Bandura 1986).

imitation
copying or reproducing behaviour.

Bandura (1971) and Bandura and Walters (1963) have developed a comprehensive theory to account for learning in terms of **imitation**. They argue that not all learning can be accounted for using explanations derived from classical and operant conditioning. Their research has called attention to the importance of imitation and role models in learning. In what some psychologists have described as a classic study, Bandura et al. (1963) set up a laboratory study where nursery school children watched a woman model play with toys and a life-size plastic doll.

In the experimental condition of the controlled laboratory study, the woman played quietly with the toys for a minute and then approached the doll and began to hit, kick and sit on it along with accompanying vocalisations such as 'Pow' and 'Sock him in the nose'. In the control condition she played quietly with the toys for the entire period. During both conditions neither the model nor the watching children were directly reinforced at any time.

Later, after the model had left the room, each child in turn was left alone with the toys (including the doll). It was discovered that children who had observed the aggressive model were more likely than the control group of children to act aggressively in imitation of the model's aggressive behaviour. These results could not be predicted by operant conditioning theories since there was no apparent reinforcement for the children's behaviour.

Social learning theory has enjoyed wide application to various fields of the social sciences. For example, Bahn (2001) has comprehensively described the application of basic

'Bookworm': Imitation is an important aspect of learning.

tenants of the theory in the field of nursing education. As she concludes '. . . the advantage of social learning theory in nurse education is its focus on the social aspect of learning appropriate to education, which takes place in a social environment, acknowledging the complexity of the environment and the person'.

Humanism

Besides psychoanalytic theory and behavioural theory, a third major force in developmental psychology is **humanism**. The essence of humanism is derived from aspects of existentialism and phenomenology.

Existentialism and phenomenology

Since the Second World War, a complex amalgam of philosophical thought variously labelled under the broad heading of **existentialism** has come to exert a considerable influence on intellectual thought, particularly in Western Europe. Important contributions to the movement have been made by the philosophers Heidegger, Jaspers, Marcel, Sartre and de Beauvoir.

Overshadowing them, though, has been the influence of the Danish philosopher Søren Kierkegaard (1813–1855), who is generally regarded as the first modern existentialist. In his philosophy, Kierkegaard emphasised the supreme importance of the individual, emphasising the individual's personal freedom, responsibility, honesty and commitment. Such a view contrasts with those emphasising the pre-eminence of the environment or one's genetic make-up in determining behaviour. Kierkegaard was a psychologist in as much as he showed deep insight into the nature of the human psyche in his writings. He recognised the immense complexity of the interaction between the individual's cognitive, conative and affective facets. Kierkegaard was the prime exponent of religious existentialism.

Jean-Paul Sartre (1905–1980) was the French writer primarily responsible for the development of atheistic existentialism. In a brilliant career, his work reflected a deep understanding of the thoughts of such influential European philosophers as Hegel, Heidegger and Husserl. Denying the existence of God, Sartre believed that all action we take must be justified in terms of its effects upon people. Without religious values to guide the direction of action, a person is free to make choice. According to Sartre, a person is thus abandoned in this world to fend for himself or herself. Of course, this brief description represents only the barest hint of Sartre's complex view of existentialism. Other writers such as Simone de Beauvoir have made significant contributions to the theory, particularly from a feminist perspective.

Phenomenology was developed by the German mathematician and philosopher Edmund Husserl (1859–1938). In broad outline, phenomenology is concerned with the world of appearance; that is, the world as it appears to the individual. It is the science of the essences of experience and as such comprises

humanism
a school of thought in psychology that emphasises individuals, their personal experience and potential for development.

existentialism
a philosopy emphasising the importance and value of the individual and the role of freedom, responsibility and choice in determining behaviour.

phenomenology
a philosophy that focuses on the world as it appears to the individual.

the study of experiences. From a phenomenological perspective, essence is derived from the belief that no two people see the world in exactly the same way: to understand people, therefore, we must understand their experience of the world.

Existentialism and phenomenology have contributed to humanistic psychology in terms of the emphasis on the individual's experience of the world. Key exponents of humanistic psychology are Abraham Maslow, Carl Rogers and Eric Fromm.

The psychology of Abraham Maslow

Abraham Maslow identified three major influences in psychology:

> First is the behaviouristic, objectivistic, mechanistic, positivistic group. Second is the whole cluster of psychologies that originated in Freud and in psychoanalysis. And third there are the humanistic psychologies or the 'third force' as the group has been called (Maslow 1971, p. 3).

In his writing, Maslow did not reject the views of the psychoanalysts or learning theorists but rather attempted to utilise what was meaningful from such theories and go on from there. However, he was critical of Freud's emphasis on the study of neurotic individuals and argued that mental illness could not be understood until mental health had been understood.

> On the whole I think it is fair to say that human history is a record of the ways in which human nature has been sold short. The highest understanding of human nature has practically always been underrated. Even when 'good' specimens, the saints and sages and great leaders of history, have been available for study, the temptation too often has been to consider them not human but supernaturally endowed (Maslow 1971, p. 7).

Thus, Maslow proposed to focus on what he identified as 'good specimens' as a means for understanding human development. He believed that we would find that psychologically healthy people would be better cognisers and perceivers:

> [T]he study of the crippled, stunted, immature and unhealthy specimens can yield only a cripple psychology and a cripple philosophy. The study of self-actualising people must be the basis for a more universal science of psychology (Maslow 1954, cited in Goble 1974, p. 15).

The study of healthy, functioning people made Maslow's psychology unique.

Self-actualisation

self-actualisation
the individual's full
use of talent,
capacity or
potential.

Self-actualisation is 'the full use and exploitation of talent, capacities, potentialities, etc. Such people seem to be fulfilling themselves and doing the best that they are capable of doing' (Maslow 1971, p. 47). According to Maslow (1971), there are eight ways in which one self-actualises:

1   by experiencing the moment fully, vividly and with full concentration;

2   by choice, which involves a movement towards impulse of choice;

3   by letting one's 'self' emerge – human beings are not a *tabula rasa*;

4   by being honest with oneself and endeavouring not to play games that deceive oneself;

5   by endeavouring at each moment in one's life to make better life-choices and to be courageous rather than afraid with one's choices;

6   by working to do well the thing one wants to do; self-actualisation is a process and not an end-state and so one is concerned with actualising one's potentialities at any time in any amount;

7   by peak experiences, which are transient moments of self-actualisation, although one can set up the situation such that peak experiences are more likely;

8   by exposing oneself to one's weakness, one's pathology and through understanding one's defences having the courage to give them up.

Unique aspects of Maslow's work were the study of mental health (as opposed to mental illness, which was the focus of psychoanalytic theory) and a focus on the individual and her or his potential for development (in contrast to behaviourism, with its focus on averages and statistical method). Maslow believed that a comprehensive theory of human behaviour should take into account both internal/intrinsic aspects of behaviour (as emphasised by Freudians) and environmental determinants (as emphasised by behaviourists).

Jean Piaget and cognitive theory

Piaget's theory of children's cognitive development was at heart an **epistemological** one; that is, a theory of how we know what we know. Elkind (1971) has identified three main phases in Piaget's theory:

> **epistemological development** development of the child's knowledge base.

1   During the first period (1922–1928), Piaget was concerned with the ideas that children held about the physical world. In working with Alfred Binet on routine intelligence testing, Piaget's attention was caught by the incorrect answers children gave on such tests. During this period, Piaget developed and refined his clinical interview technique. As noted by Elkind (1971), Piaget discovered that children reasoned differently from adults and they had literally different philosophies about the nature of the world. Observations that occupied Piaget's attention during this period included young children's 'animistic' beliefs (for example, that sticks and stones are imbued with life and purpose). Piaget was also concerned with the apparent egocentrism of young children and their often observed inability to take in another's perspective.

2   According to Elkind (1971), the second period of Piaget's investigations began in 1929 when he undertook the study of children's mental growth prompted primarily by curiosity about his own children's development. As a result of his acute observations, he published a number of books. Issues

Piaget was initially interested in ideas children held about the physical world.

such as the conservation of the object were addressed by Piaget during this period of his work.

3   The third period of Piaget's studies began during the 1940s when he dealt with the child's understanding of concepts such as number, quantity and speed.

As presented by Honstead (1968), there are two components to Piaget's theory, namely a stage-independent component and a stage-dependent component. In developing his theory incorporating the two components, Piaget emphasised that the child is actively involved in development. In Piagetian theory, the child's mind is not a blank slate (Elkind 1971). On the contrary, the child has a multitude of ideas about the world, which may be quite different from an adult's understanding of it. The child in the course of his or her education is always learning and unlearning ideas about the world such as the concepts of space, time, quantity and number. Finally, 'the child is by nature a knowing creature' and as such 'the child is trying to construct a world view of his own, and is limited only by his abilities and experience' (Elkind 1971, p. 108).

Stage-independent component

In the stage-independent component of his theory, Piaget addresses the issue of how cognitive development proceeds. He lists four factors to account for cognitive development: maturation or organic growth, experience, social transmission and equilibration (Honstead 1968).

1   *Maturation.* From a biological perspective, the developing child is maturing. At birth, the immaturity of the infant's brain is a factor limiting adequate cognition, but brain development (most rapid before birth) proceeds rapidly in the first two years after birth and continues to some extent for much longer. The links between brain development and cognition are only now beginning to be understood (Fischer 1987).

2   *Experience.* Piaget has noted that experience is of two kinds:
    a   direct physical experience, (such as playing with water, and generally using the five senses to experience the world);
    b   mathematical experience, which occurs when the child reflects on the structure of experience and particularly on its logical and mathematical structure. According to Piaget and Inhelder (1969), logico-mathematical experience comes from the child acting on the world rather than from the experience itself.

3   *Social transmission.* The concept of social transmission is the least developed part of Piaget's model: 'Piaget placed his main emphasis on the dialectic between the child and the physical world, but included social interaction as a motivator of development, particularly through conflict of ideas between peers' (Meadows 1986, p. 108). That is, in the process of

interacting with other children or adults, a child is challenged and forced to 'decentre' in order to deal with the multitude of conflicting ideas with which she or he is presented.

4 *Equilibration*. Honstead (1968) has noted that equilibration is probably the most basic of the four factors.

> It is the process of achieving equilibrium, of finding a balance between those things that were previously understood and those that are yet to be understood. A child, encountering something new to him, actively works at relating it to something he knows. As the new object in its turn becomes familiar to him, he reaches a new level of equilibrium. He has thus gone through the process of equilibration of self regulation (Honstead 1968, p. 135).

Stage-dependent component

This component is made up of the four major stages: (1) sensori-motor, (2) pre-operational, (3) concrete operational and (4) formal operations. Each of Piaget's stages is identified in terms of the child's principal method of knowing.

Sensori-motor period (0–2 years)

The child's primary method of knowing during the **sensori-motor period** is through the actions he or she performs on the world. Actions are performed on the world in terms of the five senses. Initially the child's behaviour is governed by simple reflexes but this situation rapidly changes during the next few years.

Pre-operational period (3–7 years)

The emergence of language, modelling and memory are key features of the **pre-operational period**. It is the time when, according McGurk (1975, pp. 36–7), 'the child's internal, cognitive representation of the external world is gradually developing and differentiating but many serious limitations are also in evidence'. As McGurk notes, the child's thinking is dominated by perception rather than concepts. For example, the child makes judgments in terms of how things look to her or him, not how they actually are. If shown two balls of clay of equal size and weight and if one is then squeezed into a sausage shape and the child is asked if there is as much clay in the sausage as the ball, he or she is likely to say that the sausage has more clay because it looks longer. The child's acquisition of language signals the beginning of symbolic thought. Thus, a child sees a hairy animal with four legs, tail, ears and making a barking sound, and calls the animal a dog. The animal is the reality; the word dog is the symbol. Egocentrism is another element of the child's thinking. Thus a girl may tell you she has a sister but deny that her sister has a sister.

Concrete operations period (7–11 years)

During the **concrete operations period**, children's thinking attains greater 'flexibility':

sensori-motor period
Piaget's first cognitive development stage, in which infants use their senses and motor skills to explore their environment.

pre-operational period
Piaget's name for the stage between 2 and 7 years of age, during which children acquire the ability to represent the world using symbols, such as language.

concrete operations period
according to Piaget, the stage between 7 and 11 years of age during which children begin to understand the relationship between things in the world but still cannot think in abstract terms.

He can understand, easily and naturally, the concept of conservation. 'Grouping' of ideas thus comes about; logical deductive reasoning is possible. However, concrete operations are limited in that they are capable of operational groupings only with concrete objects such as blocks, sticks, clay, liquids and marbles. Logical thought does not yet extend to verbal stimuli (Honstead 1968, p. 139).

Formal operations period (11+ years)

formal operations period
Piaget's name for the fourth stage of cognitive development from about 11 years of age onwards, during which individuals acquire the ability to think in abstract terms.

In Piaget's theory, the final period of cognitive development is identified as **formal operations**. McGurk (1975, p. 39) notes that '[t]he hallmark of this stage is the child's ability to reason abstractly without relying upon concrete situations or events'.

Piaget's view of cognitive development is that in the process of development the individual moves from a less to a more mature level of functioning. For Piaget, the child is actively involved in pursuing information and attempting to understand the world (McGurk 1975). Piaget's theory has been labelled 'constructivist' (Gelcer & Schwartzbein 1989), in as much as the child actively constructs the external world in acting upon it. Such a view contrasts with behavioural and Freudian theories which emphasise the passivity of the child who is acted upon and shaped by the external world. From a biological perspective, though, Piaget viewed development as progressive and directional. The invariant feature of his theory emphasised a stage-like development, in which the child's manner of thinking at one level is qualitatively different from the way of thinking at a later stage.

Contemporary cognitive–developmental theory: Eleanor Maccoby

The extensive research interests of Eleanor Maccoby place her at a particular advantage in psychology to integrate the thinking of various theoretical influences and interpret contemporary research findings in child development. In developing her own theoretical beliefs, Maccoby acknowledges the influence of cognitive-developmental theory in shaping her views (Maccoby 1980). However, she has expressed a concern echoed by others, 'that the theory is too "cold" and does not give enough weight to the role of emotions in social development' (1980, p. 31). She has also been critical of stage theory, arguing instead that there are 'decision points' in children's lives and at such points various influences (e.g. family) can lead any two children to follow different developmental patterns.

Maccoby's focus on the complex topic of the socialisation of children draws on a wide range of theory and research. In outlining her views of children's socialisation she acknowledges the influence of behaviourism and the particular contributions that the concepts of reinforcement and contingency have made to our understanding of how children's social behaviour is influenced. According to Maccoby, Freudian theory has also contributed to our understanding of the socialisation process, particularly in relation to sex-role development.

Perhaps most importantly, however, Maccoby has identified those contemporary influences that have shaped children's social development, including:

- research involving trait theory, which has highlighted the inconsistency of children's behaviour in various situations; cognitive-developmental theory, which has alerted us to the manner in which children's thinking shapes their perception of events;
- ethological theory and the associated concept of instincts, which raise the possibility of the predisposition of children to learn certain things, for example, attachment;
- temperament research, which has made us aware of the dissimilarity of infants at birth;
- cross-cultural research, which has alerted us to the influence of social structures such as the nature of the family unit, the economic basis of a society (e.g. agricultural or industrial), the role of men and women, and how a culture educates its members.

Maccoby's view of the socialisation process is particularly far-reaching, drawing as it does on various theoretical influences, and she has made a significant contribution to our current understanding of socialisation. Broadly speaking, though, her views reflect an awareness that the biology of the child should also be taken into account (for example, instinct), that the child actively participates in the socialisation process and also moves through various phases in developing a concept of the social self.

One important feature of Maccoby's thinking concerns the parent's role in aiding the child's social development (Maccoby 1980). She believes that children's social psychological development will be fostered if parents:

Parents play an important role in the child's social development.

- are interested in and responsive to their children's needs;
- have realistic age-appropriate expectations of their children's behaviour;
- provide their children with some structure and predictability in their daily lives;
- are democratic in decision-making within the family;
- listen to their children's views;
- allow their children the opportunity to solve their own problems;
- are warm and affectionate towards their children;
- work at developing a set of values with their children.

Evolutionary psychology

Recent reviews (Caporael 2001; Bjorklund & Pellegrini 1998) have highlighted the increasing attention given to evolutionary psychology for understanding development. Bjorklund and Pellegrini (1998), proffer that the Darwinian theory of evolution '. . . is probably the best and most enduring general explanation we have of the human condition and our adaptation to the world'.

Darwin's theory is composed of essentially two parts. The doctrine of evolution highlighted that different forms of life evolved gradually from some common ancestry.

> During the voyage of the 'Beagle' I had been deeply impressed by discovering in the Pampean formation great fossil animals covered with armour like that on the existing armadillos; secondly by the manner in which closely allied animals replace one another in proceeding southwards over the Continent; and thirdly, by the South American character of most of the productions of the Galapagos archipelago . . . (Darwin 1958, p. 42).

This outlook was not at all new and had been argued by Lamarck and by Darwin's grandfather, Erasmus. However, Darwin's keen eye for observation provided a mass of evidence for the theory.

Stimulated by the writings of the economist Malthus regarding the tendency of population to outgrow resources, Darwin noted that he was:

> . . . well prepared to appreciate the struggle for existence which everywhere goes on from long-continued observation of the habits of animals and plants, it at once struck me that under these circumstances favourable variations would tend to be preserved and unfavourable ones to be destroyed. The result of this would be the formation of new species. Here, then, I had at last got a theory by which to work (Darwin 1958, p. 43).

It is this second part of the theory which has been, and presently still is, hotly disputed.

Bjorklund and Pellegrini (1998) have identified a number of features of Darwinian theory, namely:

1 superfecundity – where animals and plants multiply faster than nature can provide for them;

2   variation – whereby organisms differ slightly in form from
    their parents;
3   heritability – the variation referred to above is heritable;
4   selection – surviving characteristics tend to be selected
    and passed down to ensuing generations

As argued by Bjorklund and Pellegrini (1998), the core
assumption of evolutionary psychology is that psychological
mechanisms have specifically evolved to address specific
problems faced in everyday life. In this regard, Caporael
(2001) has portrayed evolutionary psychology as a continuum. At one extreme is psychological research attempting to
show 'how patterns of everyday life can be explained by adap-
tions to life in the past' (Caporael 2001, p. 627). More centre-
stage is the inter-disciplinary research and mainstream views
encompassing general selection theories. At the other extreme
of the continuum is the more systemic theory.

*In evaluating theory, psychological
mechanisms have evolved to address
everyday life problems.*

Urie Bronfenbrenner's ecological model

Oakley (1984, p. 22) has noted that 'the emphasis on childhood as an individual process unfolded from within has tended to neglect the impact on children
and childhood of social and cultural contexts'. In many ways, a discussion of
Bronfenbrenner's Ecological Model (Bronfenbrenner 1979; 1989; 1993) flows
on from 'Evolutionary Theory', as presented in the previous section, as Bronfenbrenner is attempting to account for development in terms of the environment, while evolutionary theory draws upon nature for its account. In his book
The Ecology of Human Development (1979) Bronfenbrenner explained that:
'The ecology of human development involves the scientific study of the progressive mutual accommodation between an active, growing human being and
the changing properties of the immediate settings in which the developing
person lives, as this process is affected by relations between these settings, and
by the larger contexts in which the settings are embedded' (p. 21).

To account for human development, Bronfenbrenner proposes that we
consider the individual as developing within a series of settings or systems. In
relation to an individual child the systems include:

1   *Microsystem.* This is made up of the individual characteristics of the child
    and the various settings within which the child is embedded – family,
    school, neighbourhood to name but a few.
2   *Exosystem.* These systems do not impinge on the child directly but influ-
    ence the child because they affect one of the microsystems, e.g. extended
    social network of friends, neighbours, the media.
3   *Macrosystem.* These settings refer to the much larger cultural or sub-
    cultural environment in which the child lives. It refers to the values and
    mores which are part of the broader environment, e.g. in Australia being

raised within the context of a particular ethnic group, such as Greek, Italian or Vietnamese.

Two important developments or features of Bronfenbrenner's model need to be taken into account in considering any evaluation or application. Firstly, as it reads here, the child is represented as a rather passive organism shaped and moulded by the environment. The notion of 'developmental niche' was developed according to Bronfenbrenner's belief that the child assumes a very active role in their development. For example, a child who enjoys reading at school will seek out like-minded individuals who share this developmental niche. In turn, in actively seeking out such individuals the child shapes and selects his or her own experiences.

Secondly, Bronfenbrenner has added another system, the 'chronosystem', to take into account history and time which shape development. For example, over time, ideas about ways to discipline children have changed the ways in which parents raise their children.

In reading the literature, there is no doubt that Bronfenbrenner's model has influenced thinking regarding how children grow and development. His model provides grounds for a good deal of rich debate regarding child development theory.

Social systems theory

In the last decade a number of new terms and new ideas have emerged in psychology and generally these ideas are drawn from systems theory. A number of branches of psychology have made an important contribution to the field, namely Gestalt theory and functionalism.

Gestalt psychology

Gestalt
a school of thought in psychology suggesting that the perceived organised whole is more than the sum of its parts.

Prompted by the thinking of the German scientists Köhler (1927) and Koffka (1925), **Gestalt** psychology holds that the whole experience of a person is more than just the sum of its parts: it is itself; that is, it is a phenomenon in its own right. Thus, the colour white is created by an equal mixture of red, green and blue. The Gestaltists point out that the experience of 'white' is more than the sum of its parts. It is composed of red, green and blue, but experiencing the colours red, green and blue is not the same as experiencing white. Using the results of his famous experiments with apes, Köhler (1927) argued that animals and humans learn through 'insight' (and not just through trial and error as the behaviourists advocate). That is, in Köhler's terms there is a tendency to focus on the relationships between parts and not just to pay attention to the parts themselves. Gestaltists argued for the study of relationships, form and pattern.

(a)

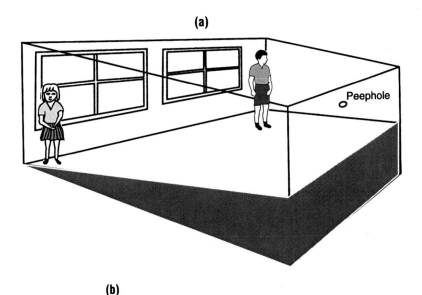

(b)

Because the left-hand corner of the room shown in (a) is almost twice as far away from the viewer as the right-hand corner, the girl standing in the left-hand corner projects a smaller retinal image than the boy in the right even though they are both the same height in reality. When viewing the room through a peephole (diagram b), we assume that we are looking at a normal room and that both children are at the same distance: hence the illusion of the impossibly different relative sizes of the children.

Figure 3.2 The visual illusion of the Ames window

Functionalism

The American, William James (1890), was the founder of the school of thought in psychology known as 'functionalism'. James was severely critical of 'structuralism' (behaviourism) because he considered its outlook on human behaviour to be narrow and artificial. James had been influenced by the thinking of Charles Darwin (Darwin 1959), who emphasised through the mechanism of natural selection the functional nature of the characteristics of animals. Darwin argued that characteristics such as eyes, ears and hands, for example, had a function that through natural selection ensured their survival. In a similar vein, James argued that human consciousness also had a function, namely to enable people to make rational choices.

In the 1940s, the views and research of a number of psychologists belonging to the functionalist school began to gain attention (such as Ames 1951). Ames had been experimenting with striking visual illusions (the best known of which is the Ames window (see Figure 3.2)) that trick the human visual system into misapplying shape and size constancy. From the research of psychologists such as Ames, perception is seen to occur as a result of the relationship between the observing person and the observed object. Context is the critical functional factor in helping us interpret the world around us. Ames and other functionalists argued against the idea that we can ever know anything as it 'really is'. We can know things only in their relationship to us.

General social systems theory

Gregory Bateson

During the 1950s, Bateson began to research schizophrenic families in association with a group of people that included John Weakland, Jay Haley and Don Jackson (known as the Palo Alto group). Adopting many of the ideas associated with general social systems theory, they identified that:

1 families are systems having properties that are more than the sum of the properties of their parts;
2 families are open systems, which none the less are governed by rules;
3 a family is a cybernetic system incorporating the important notion of feedback to family members.

Bateson and his colleagues also identified an important feature of schizophrenic families they called 'the double bind'. The group argued that schizophrenia was not an intrapsychic disturbance (a disturbance within the individual such as a thinking disorder or weak ego function). The essential features of a double bind are that:

1 two or more people are in an intense relationship which has survival value for one or more of them;
2 in this context a message is given such that:
   a it asserts something;
   b it asserts something about its own assertion;
   c the two assertions are mutually exclusive and must be disobeyed to be obeyed;
   d the recipient of the message is unable to escape the message;
   e a double bind can become a long-lasting form of communication not requiring reinforcement;
   f the behaviour of the most overtly disturbed person in the double bind, if seen in isolation, satisfies the clinical criteria for the diagnosis of schizophrenia.

Bateson provides the following example (1972, p. 217):

A young man who had fairly well recovered from an acute schizophrenic episode was visited in the hospital by his mother. He was glad to see her and impulsively put his arm around her shoulders, whereupon she stiffened. He withdrew his arm and she asked 'Don't you love me any more?' He then blushed, and she said, 'Dear, you must not be so easily embarrassed and afraid of your feelings'. The patient was able to stay with her only a few minutes more and following her departure he assaulted an aide and was put in the tubs.

In this example, the son was receiving double messages and these contradictory messages constituted a double bind.

Apart from the concept of double bind, Bateson contributed a number of significant concepts to contemporary systems thinking, including ideas about levels of communication and patterns that connect.

1   *Levels of communication*. As indicated in double bind theory, communication can occur across different levels. Unhealthy communication often involves communication across different levels.

2   *Patterns which connect*. With a consuming interest in biology as well as human behaviour, Bateson was interested in 'patterns which connect'. As he wrote in *Mind and Nature* (1979, p. 16):

> What pattern connects the crab to the lobster and the orchid to the primrose and all four of them to me? And me to you? And all six of us to the amoeba in one direction and to the backward schizophrenic in another?

In the same book, Bateson went on to describe the patterns which connect as meta patterns – a pattern of patterns.

Systems theory based on Batesonian ideas

The ideas expounded by Bateson have been taken up most strongly in the field of family counselling. According to Goolishian and Anderson (1987, p. 529): 'The family could now be described as a system that had characteristics and organising principles that were independent of the psychic structures of the individuals comprising the family'.

A most significant line of family counselling based on Batesonian ideas has been developed by a group of psychologists in Milan, Italy. Known in family counselling circles as the Milan group, the members, comprising Selvini-Palazzoli, Boscolo, Cecchin and Prata, have drawn heavily on the ideas of Bateson in their work with the families of anorexic people (Selvini-Palazzoli et al. 1978). In Adelaide, South Australia, the family counsellor Michael White has developed an approach to counselling based on a unique blend of the ideas drawn from Batesonian theory (Munro 1987).

Recent developments in systems theory

Constructivism

The ideas originally espoused by Bateson have continued to have an important impact on psychologists' understanding of both the individual and the family. The emergence of a line of enquiry known as **constructivism** is testimony to the impact of Bateson's thinking in psychology. Constructivism has its

constructivism
a school of thought in psychology that emphasises the subjectivity of experience and the role of individuals in actively construing their world.

philosophical roots in the European tradition of thinking drawn from the philosophy of Berkley and Kant, who emphasised the subjectivity of our perception. More recently, the links with constructivism have been made with the thinking of Piaget. Gelcer and Schwartzbein (1989) have summarised two important assumptions of Piaget's theory:

- there are different levels of knowing the same experience;
- the higher or greater the level of abstraction, the more flexible is the individual's approach to problem-solving.

Summarising Viaro's ideas (1985), these authors note that 'each organism creatively constructs its world within the limits of whatever biological or environmental context it encounters' (Gelcer & Schwartzbein 1989, p. 440).

Key writers who have contributed to theory relating to constructivism include the Chilean biologist Maturana and his colleague Varela (1988), and the cybernetician von Foerster (1973). The important assertion of constructivism is that reality cannot be revealed to us in only one true way. It is through the process of construing that we come to know reality. Constructivism emphasises a proactive view of the individual, who as an observer participates actively in the process of observation. It is through this process of active participation that the co-creation of meaning occurs. Such a proactive view of the person contrasts with much of mainstream psychology, which views the individual as reactive.

Developmental psychology and systems theory

Patricia Minuchin (1985) has noted the commonalities between developmental psychology and family counselling. 'Both disciplines regard the family as a primary focus for understanding human behaviour and must find some way of conceptualising the relationship between the family and the individual' (p. 289). As Minuchin goes on to note:

> Family therapy is based on systems theory. Although the field is characterised by theoretical argument and a diversity of alternative techniques for creating change the systems view of human functioning is well established. It shapes the nature of clinical work and generates data about children and families from a different perspective than that of developmental psychologists (1985, p. 289).

Minuchin (1985) has summarised the principles of systems theory that are also relevant to developmental psychology.

1   A system (e.g. a family) is an organised whole with each part of the system interdependent with the other parts.
2   Patterns are circular not linear. That is the basic unit is the cycle of interaction, not a search for causation.
3   A system has some stability of patterns.
4   Evolution and change are a part of open systems whereby information is exchanged.
5   Complex systems are made up of subsystems, e.g. mother–father, child–child.

6   There are boundaries between subsystems.

From a systems perspective, the individual is an interdependent, contributing part of the system that controls his or her behaviour. The emphasis is on studying the functioning of the individual as part of the system rather than on internal or intrapsychic processes. Such an approach emphasises understanding the individual's functioning within context (Minuchin 1985).

In a developmental psychology context there is a growing interest in the application of systems theory to the study of children and the family (Scarr 1985; Kaye 1985; Tolan 1990; Wachtel 1990).

Impact of systems theory

Systems theory and related ideas developed by Gregory Bateson are having an impact in the field of psychology. Part of the reason for the slow dissemination of ideas based on systems thinking to child development is that mainstream psychology draws heavily on an empirical positivistic world view, while systems thinking is proposing a radically new way of understanding the world and our behaviour.

Family counselling is providing a testing ground for some exciting developments. Overall, there is an emerging understanding that just as individuals move through developments in their life, so the family passes through various phases or stages. During these 'critical periods' major developmental tasks may need to be addressed.

Dynamic systems theory

In the fifth edition of the *Handbook of Child Psychology* edited by Damon and Lerner (1998), Lerner (p. 1) noted that the current focus in theoretical development was '. . . a burgeoning interest not in structure, function, or content per se, but in change, in the process through which change occurs, and thus in the means through which structures transform and functions evolve over the course of human life'. In many ways, this understanding captures significant features of emergent dynamic systems theory for understanding human development.

As argued by Thelen and Smith (1994, p. 49) in their presentation of principles under-pinning dynamic systems theory, 'What we invoke here are the principles for the global properties of complex systems . . .'. They further note that:

> [t]he new science that can extract common principles in the behaviour of chemical reactions, clouds, forests, and embryos is variously called the study of dynamic, synergetic, dissipative, nonlinear, self-organising, or chaotic theories. (We adopt here dynamic systems as the descriptor to emphasise that these are systems that change continuously over time (p. 50).

As noted in the previous section on systems theory, the strong development of interest in dynamic systems theory has its legacy in broad-based systems thinking through writers and theoreticians embracing a diversity of disciplines (Bertalanffy 1968; Bateson 1984; Prigogine & Stengers 1984; Maturana & Varela 1988).

In the first edition of this text, consideration was given to the development of general systems theory. As Minuchin (1985) has noted, systems theory is a twentieth-century scientific paradigm that has been used in conjunction with physical, biological and social systems. Perhaps one of the foremost thinkers in the field was von Bertalanffy (1968). He was particularly interested in the application of systems theory to biological process. Von Bertalanffy (1968, p. 55) defined a system as a 'complex of interacting elements'. He was particularly interested in the relationship between the parts and the whole. An important contribution that he made to systems theory was to identify 'open' and 'closed' systems. A closed system was defined as one in which there is no interaction with the surrounding environment (such as a chemical reaction in a closed container). An open system is one that interacts with the surrounding environment (such as families).

Another significant contributor to the development of systems thinking was the 1997 Nobel winning Belgian chemist, Ilya Prigogine. His research into dissipative structures arising out of the nonlinear processes in non-equilibrium systems provided a comprehensive theory of change. (See chapter 1 regarding the nature of 'development' as 'change'.) The theory is underpinned by a number of key concepts:

1   *Systems and sub-systems.* All systems are composed of sub-systems which are in a continual state of fluctuation or change. At any one time, the fluctuation may be so strong as to shatter the pre-existing order.
2   *Chaos and order.* At any 'singular moment' or 'bifurcation' the system may descend into 'chaos' or transcend to a higher level of organisation or 'order', known as a 'dissipative structure'. They are called 'dissipative' because they require more energy to sustain them than the previous structure.
3   *Equilibrium.* In Newtonian thermodynamics all systems run down to disorder with energy dissipating over time. In the natural world there are 'closed systems' which do operate like machines. However, many systems are 'open', exchanging energy, matter or information with the environment.

As Thelen and Smith (1998) noted, the implications of Prigonine's theorising is increasingly being recognised, observing 'Adoption of such a systems model, with its assumptions of wholeness, self-stabilization, self-organization, and hierarchical organization, has implications for every aspect of developmental psychology' (p. 575). To illustrate this point, Thelen and Smith cite the need for development to be contextualised because the concept of 'open systems' necessitates an interchange between the organism and the environment. Ideas of non-linearity may be used to explain how apparently small transformations result in significant changes in the organism.

Increasingly, dynamic systems theory is being applied in the field of developmental psychology (Thelen & Smith 1984; Thelen & Smith 1998; Pepler & Craig 2000; Slee 2001).

The family life-cycle: 3

The concept of life-cycle

The concept of the family life-cycle is one that is receiving increasing attention in the psychological literature. Erik Erikson's writings have highlighted the concept of family life-cycle by emphasising the eight ages of the individual. Gail Sheehy (1976) and Daniel Levinson (1978) have also made contributions to our appreciation of life-cycle development. Writers and researchers, such as those referred to here, have emphasised that humans tend to grow and change throughout the life-cycle and are not doomed to live out the effects of early childhood experiences, as suggested by Freudian theory (Slee 1997).

Defining the life-cycle
Neugarten has emphasised that the various turning points in one's life – the completion of school, entry into the workforce, marriage, parenthood and so forth – are significant 'punctuation marks along the life-cycle' (Neugarten 1976. p. 1). Neugarten has noted that these turning points involve changes in the individual's self-concept and sense of identity. They draw forth and result in new social and emotional roles and require new adaptations on the part of the person experiencing the event and those around her or him.

Similarly, just as the individual is seen as passing through various stages (infancy, childhood, adolescence, adulthood), so the family may also be viewed as moving through predictable phases from its formation to its dissolution. A caveat here is that versions of the life-cycle that characterise the traditional nuclear family are not always applicable to alternative forms of families as described in Life-Cycle 2. Hill (1986) has noted that the life-cycle course of the single-parent family differs from the two-parent family, not necessarily in terms of the stages encountered, but in the number, timing and length of the critical transitions experienced.

Schemes for classifying the life-cycle
Various schemes for identifying the nature of the family life-cycles (e.g. Duvall 1971; Carter & McGoldrick 1980; Jenkins 1983) have been put forward. Most have been developed with the concept of the traditional nuclear family in mind (as already noted, this is a misleading concept in most Western countries today). Table 3.2 is based on the writings and research of others but has been adapted to take account of the particular emphasis of this text.

As illustrated in Table 3.2, one way to understand how families grow and change is to appreciate that there are certain universals and rhythms to family life. At each stage, certain tasks present themselves and families find their energies and resources focused on these tasks. As the family develops and grows, certain milestones are passed e.g. the birth of the first child. Where is your family in the life-cycle?
STAGE 1. The beginning family (couples without children)
  MILESTONE e.g. getting to know your partner

Table 3.2 The family life-cycle

Stage	Major Developmental Task
Courtship and marriage	Establishing independence from the parental home and initiating and developing a primary relationship
Pre-parenting	Establishing a couple identity and preparing for parenthood
Birth of first child Birth of subsequent children	Adapting to new roles to include triadic relationships
Children at school	Managing the child's entry to school and dealing with the way the outside world impinges on the family, e.g. school
Adolescence	Managing the adolescent's establishment of identity
The couple identity	Dealing with the 'empty nest'

STAGE 2. The child-bearing Family (oldest child less than 3)
    MILESTONE e.g. enjoying parenthood
STAGE 3. The family with a pre-school child (oldest child less than 5)
    MILESTONE e.g. child starts kindy
STAGE 4. The family with primary school children
    MILESTONE e.g. getting involved in school life
STAGE 5. The family with adolescents
    MILESTONE e.g. coping with study pressure

STAGE 6. The family with one or more children leaving home
    MILESTONE e.g. seeing a child developing a career
STAGE 7. The 'empty nest'
    MILESTONE e.g. enjoying life as a couple
    In considering the idea of family life-cycle, you might examine Table 3.2 and the preceding checklist to consider where your family is in the life-cycle and the nature of the various milestones that are being addressed and/or have been passed.

Chapter summary

As in the first edition of this textbook, in this new edition a good deal of attention is given to the nature of various theories which underpin ideas about child development. One of the significant features of developmental psychology is the richness of its theoretical development. Presently, new and exciting breakthroughs are occurring in this theorising and in this chapter I have attempted to capture some of the vibrancy of the current debate.

Discussion question

Having read about each theory in this chapter, discuss some new understanding with another person.

Activities

Divide the discussion group into four or five small groups. Allocate the name of a theorist to each group. The task of each group is to spend 15–20 minutes in the following activities.

1   Research and write down significant aspects of each theoretical approach to understanding child development. Prepare a summary of this information for presentation to the larger group. Identify new understandings gained and present ideas to the larger group.

See your CD

2   Complete the 'Self Review Quiz' on the CD-ROM to assess your understanding of the content presented in this section. Use your quiz results as a basis for reviewing any chapter content about which you are uncertain.

Selected websites

International Psychoanalytic Society: <www.ipa.org>

Freud Museum London: <www.freud.org>

Conception and Birth

2

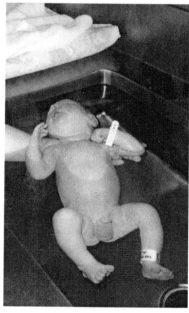

Christopher aged 1 day

Christopher aged 3 days

Christopher aged 4 years

4 Prenatal Development

I Happy Am
I have no name:
I am but two days old.
I happy am
Joy is my name
Sweet joy befall thee!

William Blake, Songs of Innocence

KEY TERMS AND CONCEPTS

- Conception
- Genetics
- Chromosomes
- Genes
- DNA
- Mitosis
- Meiosis
- Dominant and recessive alleles
- Phenotype
- Genotype
- Monozygotic twins
- Dyzygotic twins
- Genetic defects
- Reaction range
- Canalization
- Niche picking
- Genetic counselling
- Preformist
- Empiricist
- Selectionist
- The family as a system

Introduction

Since the first edition of this textbook was published in 1993, considerable development has taken place in our understanding of the influence of genetics on human development. In this second edition, the focus is upon describing the nature of some of these significant gains and highlighting the implications for developmental psychology.

Between the time a baby is conceived and born, she or he has been subjected to nine months of genetic and environmental influence. Medical science has made considerable advances in identifying the likely effects of cigarette smoking, alcohol consumption and stress on the newly conceived child's development and these will be examined in chapter 5. In this chapter, consideration is given to the contribution that heredity and environment make to the foetus's development. In The Family Life-cycle: 4, the view of the family as a 'system' is discussed.

Trends and issues

Traditional Aboriginal views of conception

Hamilton (1981) describes traditional Australian Aboriginal views of conception in some detail. In her study of Arnhem Land Aborigines, she notes three basic explanations for conception:

- Pregnancy is caused by spirit children in different places, such as a waterhole. Certain places are known by Aborigines to be plentiful in spirit children and only a woman who wants a child will approach such a location.
- Pregnancy can be caused by people's daily activities. For example, a man out hunting traps an animal which has chosen his wife as its future mother. The man will refrain from eating it but when the woman eats it the animal allows the spirit of the child to leave the food and enter the woman.
- Pregnancy is caused by copulation.

Such beliefs do not necessarily interfere with Aborigines' understanding of the biology of conception, and may exist alongside this understanding, in just the same way that non-Aboriginal Christians believe that a child is a 'gift from God' while also recognising the biological explanation.

The genetics of conception

Scientists have now determined that some characteristics of the child are determined by genetic make-up, while others are due to environmental influences. As Sternberg and Grigorenko (1999, p. 536) noted: 'It is difficult to pick up a newspaper or magazine without finding a report of some newly discovered gene that is alleged to control such-and-such a trait'. However, many characteristics cannot be attributed solely to either influence. **Genetics** is the name given to the branch of science that studies the mechanics of heredity.

genetics
the scientific study of heredity.

A mature female normally produces a single egg approximately every 28 days. A mature male normally produces billions of sperm every month. Conception occurs when the sperm from the male penetrates the wall of the ovum or egg from the female. The egg, now called the zygote, undergoes a

Genetics and the environment shape the development of the child.

process called mitosis whereby the zygote divides, producing what eventually amounts to millions of cells. Groups of cells take on special functions and become the nervous, skeletal, muscular, circulatory and other systems.

Chromosomes and genes

At the time the small tadpole-shaped sperm penetrates an ovum a fusion process brings together 23 **chromosomes** from the male sperm and 23 chromosomes from the female ovum so that the child begins life with 46 chromosomes (Tortora & Anagnostakos 1987). These include homologous pairs and one pair of sex chromosomes, XX or XY. The Y chromosome determines maleness. The 46 chromosomes contain approximately 10 000 **genes**.

chromosomes
one of 46 small thread-like structures in the nucleus of human cells containing the genetic code in the form of DNA.

genes
biological units of heredity involving a self-reproducing DNA particle located in a particular chromosome.

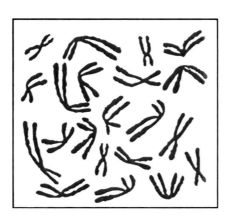

Figure 4.1 An enlargement of some chromosomes

Genes. A gene is a particular nucleic acid sequence within a DNA molecule where the basic building block of the gene is a chemical called **deoxyribonucleic acid (DNA)**. Each gene provides the blueprint for the assembly of a specific protein. The proteins have many functions, including providing some structure to body cells. There are 20 known amino acids that compose proteins and their sequence determines the form and function of each specific protein. That is, the information in the DNA will shape the growth and development of the individual, helping to determine, along with environmental influence to a greater or less degree, such characteristics as eye colour, height and personality. At the outset of the Human Genome Project (see this chapter), it was estimated that there were more than 50 000 genes. Now it is better understood that there are somewhere between 70 000 and 100 000 genes (Rowen, Mahairas & Hood 1997).

> **deoxyribonucleic acid (DNA)**
> a complex chemical containing the genetic code that guides development.

According to the theory originally proposed by James Watson and Francis Crick (1953), DNA is in the shape of a double helix. DNA is a relatively simple structure but has been called the essence of life. It is composed of a phosphate-sugar backbone and four molecules, namely adenine, thymine, guanine and cytosine, which form the cross-links of the DNA molecule (see Figure 4.2).

One feature essential to human development is that the DNA molecule replicates. The original strands first separate to form two separate strands, much like a zipper undoing. The base pairs (adenine (A), thymine (T), guanine (G) and cytosine (C)) separate, leaving single strands with single bases. These units then combine with other single DNA strands produced by the cell – with the bases properly paired (A always joins with T and C with G), so that the new DNA is identical to the original. The significance of this replication is that it makes it possible for the genetic code of each of the parents to be passed on to their offspring, thereby creating a unique individual.

DNA also contains the genetic instruction for making protein. Cells make proteins by translating the genetic information in DNA into specific proteins. Thus, some cells use part of a DNA molecule to specialise as skin cells and others as kidney cells. The DNA molecule synthesises a messenger RNA ribonucleic acid (MRNA) molecule on part of its structure. RNA carries its message from the nucleus out into the cell, where the information is used to produce protein (Tortora & Anagnostakos 1987). The protein produced speeds specific chemical reactions that lead to the manufacture of specialised parts of the cell, such as the production of skin or kidney cells. Some genes have a specific function (regulator genes), which helps account for the timing of development (such as prenatal development; Scarr-Salapatek 1975).

VIEWPOINT
Where do babies come from?
'Mummy's tummy!'
Joanne, 4 years

'It's somewhere where mummy went and paid some money and buyed Daniel and brought him home to me'
Belinda, 4 years

'Dad and Mum make the baby and it is born'
Jack, 7 years

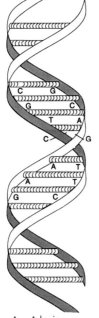

A = Adenine
T = Thymine
C = Cytosine
G = Guanine

Figure 4.2 Part of the DNA molecule illustrating the double helix

Individual differences: Mitosis and meiosis

Why are brothers and sisters so similar in some respects and so different in others, given that they come from the same parents and that each individual has received 23 chromosomes from each parent? The answer to the puzzling question of individual differences lies in large part with the processes called mitosis and meiosis.

Mitosis

One process whereby a new cell develops is called **mitosis** and occurs when an existing cell divides. Before division, the chromosomes are replicated so that upon division the two sets of cells each have the full set of 46 pairs of chromosomes. In their early stages of development, germ cells (sperm and ovum) divide by mitosis just as other cells of the body do.

mitosis
the process of cell division for body cells by which chromosomes in each cell replicate to form a second set of chromosomes, which then separate from the original cell to form a new, identical cell.

Meiosis

In the final stage of development of the sperm/ovum something different occurs. In **meiosis**, the chromosomes replicate as in mitosis, but the cell division that follows results in four cells instead of two. Each cell receives one chromosome from each of the 23 pairs of chromosomes. A sperm cell and an ovum cell therefore each have 23 single chromosomes, half of each parent's 23 pairs of chromosomes. An important feature of meiosis is called crossing over. At one point in the cell division the two chromosomes that make up each pair line up directly opposite each other and some proportion of each chromosome may be exchanged from one member of the pair to another. One of the important effects of crossing over is to increase the number of possible combinations of instructions in each set of 23 chromosomes in sperm and ovum. (Remember that chromosomes are the genetic blueprint carrying the information about the characteristics of the person the fertilised ovum is to become.) It is this process, combined with many other external and internal influences, that contributes to the differences between children born to the same parents. The exception to this is identical twins, who come from the same fertilised ovum. In this case the ovum divides into two distinct identities after it has been fertilised by the sperm.

meiosis
the process of cell division of sex cells, resulting in four new cells.

The science of genetics

What determines the characteristics we may inherit from our parents? To answer this question it is necessary to consider the field of science that has come to be known as genetics.

Ideas regarding heredity can be traced back thousands of years. The Jewish religious book *The Talmud* refers to the existence some 1500 years ago of the inherited bleeding disorder haemophilia. However, it is to the Dutch scientist Reinier de Graaf that we owe the discovery that the union of the sperm and the egg is essential for conception. In the latter part of the seventeenth century, this Dutch scientist described small protuberances in the ovaries of mammals. The protuberances, which have come to be called Graafian follicles, contain the unfertilised egg or ovum. De Graaf established that the sperm alone was not the sole hereditary agent, as was previously believed.

Gregor Mendel's research

The modern science of genetics began with Gregor Mendel (1822–1884). He was born in what is now Czechoslovakia. Entering an Augustinian order at Brunn monastery, Austria (now Brno, Czechoslovakia), he became a priest in 1848. He then studied physics, mathematics, zoology and botany at the University of Vienna, and subsequently became a teacher in a nearby high school. In 1854 he returned to Brunn monastery, where he began his experiments in genetics.

Mendel's research with plants, and in particular garden peas, showed that characteristics of peas such as colour, height and surface features (wrinkled or smooth) disappeared and re-appeared from one generation to the next. He concluded that these traits were handed down through hereditary elements, now called genes. For example, the genes that code for colour are inherited from both parents, so that pea seeds can be either green or yellow.

Alleles. Different genes that can determine characteristics are called **alleles**. For every allelic gene on one chromosome of a pair, its corresponding allele will exist in the same position on the other chromosome of the pair (see Figure 4.3).

Gametes. The union of male and female sex cells (gametes, sperms and eggs) results in the formation of a new individual.

Genotype and phenotype. It is important to distinguish between the appearance, or **phenotype**, of an organism and its underlying genetic make-up (genotype). It is possible to predict phenotype from genotype but not vice versa.

Dominant or recessive. Alleles may be dominant or recessive. In Figure 4.3 the dominant allele is B and the recessive is b. A dominant gene is one whose characteristic will show up when paired with another gene: it produces observable characteristics, such as eye colour (phenotype). A recessive gene is one whose characteristic is not observable when paired with a dominant gene. The actual genetic composition of the organism is known as the genotype.

When the alleles in a pair are identical, such as BB or bb, the pair is defined as homozygous. If the alleles in a pair are different, such as Bb or bB, the pair is called heterozygous.

The recessive trait (such as eye colour) can be expressed only when no dominant allele is present. As an allele for eye colour is inherited from each parent, the recessive trait can be expressed only as a double recessive (bb). For example, in Figure 4.4, B is the allele for brown eyes and b is the allele for blue eyes. The small boxes on the left and at the top of Figure 4.4 indicate the parents' genotypes. In the figure and in this case, only two blue-eyed parents will produce children that all have blue eyes.

Mendel cultivated his plants for two generations and this step was taken to verify the purity of each line; that is, to make sure the phenotype characteristic

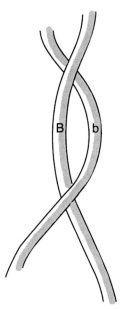

Figure 4.3 Alleles are genes that determine characteristics such as eye colour

alleles
gene factors that determine specific characteristics

genotype
the actual genetic composition of the organism.

phenotype
the physical or behavioural traits in an individual that reflect both genetic and environmental factors.

Parental genotypes

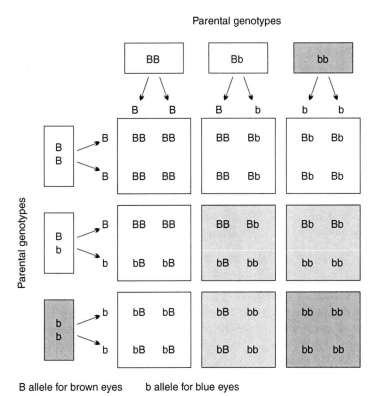

B allele for brown eyes   b allele for blue eyes

Figure 4.4 The role of dominant and recessive alleles and recessive alleles in producing characteristics such as eye colour

of each was indeed inherited by all offspring. With purity established, Mendel then experimented with crosses between individuals of contrasting phenotypes. Mendel designated crosses involving the original parents as P1 crosses. The mature seeds forming were designated as the filial or F1 generation. Mature seeds allowed to self-fertilise produced a second filial or F2 generation.

Sex-linked characteristics. The chromosome that determines sex also carries genes that determine other characteristics, such as colour blindness, eye colour, hair colour and blood type, to name but a few. These genes are found only on the X chromosome, not on the Y. Since the male has only one X chromosome, he consequently always possesses the characteristics produced by these genes, whether they are dominant or recessive. As noted earlier, females have two X chromosomes. As a result, a recessive sex-linked characteristic always shows up in the male, but may be hidden in the female if it is paired with a dominant characteristic.

Colour blindness is an example of a recessive sex-linked characteristic that is carried on the X chromosome. Whenever a male has a recessive gene for colour blindness, he is colour blind. If he marries a woman carrying no genes for colour blindness, his sons will have normal colour vision because they will receive their father's Y chromosome and their mother's X chromosome. His daughters, on the other hand, will be carriers without displaying any colour blindness, given that they will receive a dominant X from their mother and a recessive X from their father. When the carrier mother marries, the possibility of her children being colour blind depends upon whether their father is colour blind and upon which of her X chromosomes, the dominant or recessive one, is passed on to the offspring.

Mendel's First Principle: The Principal of Segregation. In his experiments with peas, Mendel crossed strains of peas that differed from one another in the expression of a single characteristic (e.g. height or colour) and then allowed the F1 offspring to self-fertilise and produce an F2 generation. Classifying each F2 seed according to phenotype, Mendel demonstrated a 3:1 phenotypic ratio in the F2 generation. The underlying 1:2:1 genotypic ratio was verified through seeds arising in the F3 generation. Mendel reasoned that genes occur in pairs and that members of each such pair undergo segregation at gamete formation.

Mendel's Second Principle: The Principle of Independent Assortment. Once Mendel had discovered the method of inheritance for a single pair of contrasting characteristics he applied his first law to the simultaneous inheritance of two and three pairs of characters. Experimenting with colour (e.g. yellow vs green) and appearance (e.g. round vs wrinkled), Mendel reasoned that the segregation of Alleles A and a into separate gametes occurred independently of the segregation of Alleles B and b. Subsequently, the following classes emerge: AB, Ab, aB, and ab. His experiments showed that in the formation of sex cells, the segregation of one pair of alleles (and therefore all gametes containing all possible combinations of alleles) will be produced in equal numbers – independent assortment.

Recognition of Mendel's research. Mendel presented the findings of his research to the Natural History Society of Brunn in 1865 and the results were published in the transactions of the society the following year. However, his findings generated little interest in the scientific community until the turn of the century. In the space of a few months, Mendel's ideas were independently rediscovered by three biologists: Hugo de Vries (University of Amsterdam), Carl Correns (a German botanist at Tubingen) and Erich von Tschermak-Seysenegg (an Austrian worker at an agricultural station near Vienna). All three investigators arrived at the same conclusion as Mendel: chromosomes carry the hereditary factors or genes and the behaviour of the chromosomes at cell division provides the explanation for inheritance. Unfortunately, Gregor Mendel had died 16 years before his research was recognised as one of the most important scientific discoveries of the time.

Human genetics

As already indicated, the study of human genetics, or at least speculation about it, has a long history. The topic generated the interest not only of scientists but also of writers. In a series of novels, *The Rougon-Macquart*, the French writer Emile Zola explored the influence of genetics on generations of a family growing up in nineteenth-century France. Writing against the backdrop of the newly emerging philosophy of materialism and scientific determinism, as reflected in the writings of Auguste Comte, Charles Darwin and Aldous Huxley, Zola set himself the task of using the novel to explore the interplay between heredity and environment. His novels reflect the belief that heredity shapes our fate.

Early studies of human genetics involved the sex-linked characteristics of haemophilia (a blood disorder). Researchers also explored the relationship between heredity and environment. Thus, Charles Darwin, author of *The Origin of Species* (1859), was interested in human genetics from the viewpoint of the effects of in-breeding. The scientist Francis Galton (1869) explored the difference between the effects of nature and nurture. He argued that since identical twins have the same genetic constitution, any difference evident between them must be due to their external environment. That is, identical twins have the same genotype but may have different external environments. Galton was especially interested in the inheritance of physique and special talents, and studied wrestlers in England. Also among Galton's many interests was the advancement of the idea of hereditary improvement of humans and animals by such procedures as genetic selection, for which he coined the term eugenics.

The Human Genome Project

The Human Genome Project is a joint undertaking of The United States Department of Energy (DOE) and the National Institutes of Health (NIH). As reported by Patrinos and Drell (1977) it was motivated by a need to improve methods used to monitor radiation-caused changes in genetic material. In 1986 the DOE gave serious consideration to the mapping of the human genetic sequence, while NIH recognised the significance of genetic information for the prevention of disease. The Human Genome Project officially began in 1990 with a completion date set for 2005 for a total estimated cost of $US3 billion (Munro 1999).

As described by Munro (1999), the project has a number of aims including:

- mapping the 24 human chromosomes;
- map and sequence model organisms (organisms such as the mouse and fruit fly because they are commonly selected to model the human condition);
- improving DNA sequencing technology;
- targeting ethical, legal and social issues and the development of policy related to the project.

The Human Genome Project and health care

The project outcomes obviously have significant implications for general health and well-being. Munro (1997) argues that understandings related to genetic information are likely to effect significant changes in our understanding of disease susceptibility and causation and will be accompanied by significant changes in health care practices. Munro identifies how genetic understanding will lead to different treatment approaches for patients with the same disease, citing the treatment of breast cancer as an example.

Genetics and developmental psychology are closely linked.

Developmental psychology and genetics

As Rifkin (1998) has noted, 'It seems that every week or so a new study is published showing a likely connection between genotype and personality' (p. 649). He cites research claiming a genetic basis for 'novelty seeking', high anxiety' and a gene predisposing girls to better 'social skills' than boys.

Genetics and developmental psychology are inextricably linked. Listen to any conversation of parents describing their offspring:

'The baby has the same colour eyes as the mother.'

'She has her mother's brains.'

'He is such a quiet person – just like his father.'

Three major areas covered by comments such as these concern the link between genetics and physical development, intellectual development and personality.

Physical development

It has already been noted that the genes people inherit (genotype) can influence their physical appearance. Thus, aspects of physical appearance such as eye colour, height, weight and bone structure have been strongly linked to a person's genetic inheritance. In a study of **monozygotic** (MZ) (identical) **twins**, Kallman and Sandler (1949) found that although all those in the study were over 60 years of age, each was remarkably similar to his or her twin in certain aspects of their physical development. For example, the twins tended to show the same kinds of eye and tooth changes and the same extent of the greying of the hair. They became feeble around the same age and in some cases died within weeks of each other.

A number of other physical traits in humans have also been related to genetic inheritance. For instance, the ability to roll the tongue is ascribed to the action of a dominant gene. Other traits related to genetic inheritence include the following:

- the ability to taste the chemical phenylthiocarbamide (PTC);
- red–green colour blindness;
- haemophilia;
- extra fingers or toes;
- astigmatism;
- blood group;
- production of Rhesus antigen or lack of it;
- handedness;
- drooping of eyelids;
- sickle cell disorder;
- ability to produce insulin.

monozygotic twins individuals with identical genes who have developed from the same fertilised egg.

Intellectual development

The study of the influence of heredity on intelligence has generated a great deal of interest and, at times, heated debate. One extreme view is that there is no evidence to date that genetic differences have anything to do with individual or group differences in anything we measure as intelligence (Kamin 1981; Taylor 1980). At the other extreme, writers and researchers claim that the evidence points to a very high degree of genetic determination of differences in intelligence (Jensen 1978; Eysenck 1979). The general consensus would appear to be that about half of the current differences among individuals in European and North American white populations in measured intelligence result from genetic differences among them (Nichols 1978; Plomin & De Fries 1980).

Evidence for the argument of the genetic influence on intelligence has been drawn mainly from studies of twins and foster children. Nichols (1978) compiled 211 studies of intelligence and abilities that compare the resemblance of identical (monozygotic – MZ) and fraternal (**dyzygotic** – DZ) **twins**. An extract from his findings is presented in Table 4.1. From these findings, it can be seen that for general intelligence there is greater similarity in performance for identical twins (correlation .82) than for fraternal twins (correlation .59). From this result it would appear that being genetically related and reared as twins in the same family are two potent determinants of individual differences in measured intelligence.

dyzygotic twins individuals with different genetic blueprints who have developed from two different eggs fertilised at the same time; compare monozygotic twins.

Table 4.1 Correlations on intellectual tasks for fraternal and identical twins

Intellectual Tasks	Fraternal Twins	Identical Twins
General intelligence (IQ)	.59	.82
Verbal comprehension	.59	.78
Number and mathematical ability	.59	.78

Personality development

The effects of heredity on personality have also been explored. The concept of personality is notoriously difficult to define, which makes answering the question of heredity even more of a problem. Basically, however, personality might be considered to be that which helps us understand a person's enduring or predictable behaviour, regardless of time or context. Personality has to do with the typical way each of us interacts with the people and the world around us. If personal consistency develops from a combination of genetics and experience, then biologically related people should have a greater tendency to be similar in personality than biologically unrelated individuals.

One aspect of personality that has received significant attention in the research field is that of temperament. As defined by Thomas and Chess (1977):

Temperament may be best viewed as a general term referring to the how of behaviour. It differs from ability, which is concerned with the what and how well of behaving, and from motivation, which accounts for why a person is doing what he is doing. Temperament, by contrast, concerns the way in which an individual behaves (see Chapter 8).

Thomas et al. (1977) have identified nine dimensions of temperament consisting of:

1	activity	6	intensity of reaction
2	rhythmicity	7	quality of mood
3	approach–withdrawal	8	distractability
4	adaptability	9	persistence
5	threshold of responsiveness.		

Although there is not a lot of evidence for consistency of temperament regardless of age, MZ twin resemblance tends to exceed DZ twin resemblance for most if not all temperamental traits (Torgenson & Kringlen 1978).

How do heredity and environment interact?

As Plomin and Daniels (1987, p. 1) note, 'Ten years ago, in order to redress the imbalance of environmentalism, it was necessary to emphasise the possibility that genetic influence could affect behavioural differences that we observe among individuals'. Today, while scientists acknowledge that both heredity and environment interact for the development of any behaviour, it is no longer sufficient simply to acknowledge this fact. More specific information is needed in order to understand the nature of such interaction.

In the earliest phase of the search to understand the contribution that heredity and environment make to development, the focus was upon how much each factor contributes. Heritability estimates were calculated using various statistical manipulations of data to assess the extent to which variations among individuals, such as in intelligence, could be attributed to heredity or genetic factors. The work of Jensen (1969), was of this nature, hence his claim that up to 80 per cent of the contribution to intelligence came from genetic factors.

Scarr-Salapatek (1975) criticised Jensen's research, referring to the concept as the 'myth of heritability'. She argued that if intelligence was largely determined by heredity, it could not be very malleable. In her view, we inherit a range of reaction or genetic potential for development, which may then be expressed as a result of the interaction of individuals with their environment. Scarr-Salapatek's view has been criticised, but she has alerted us to the dangers of simplifying the issue. Indeed, using more complex statistical techniques, Scarr and Kid (1983) suggest that Jensen significantly overestimated the contribution of genetics to intellectual development. In moving away from how much genetics and environment each contribute to development, the issue becomes more one of how these factors contribute. To this end, reaction range, canalisation and niche-picking have been identified.

1   **Reaction range**. Gottesman (1963) posited the concept of '**reaction range**', whereby each person's genotype (the genes we carry) establishes upper and lower boundaries for development. Each individual's genotype responds uniquely to a given set of environmental conditions. When environments vary, a single genotype may produce different phenotypes, while identical environments can have a differential effect on different genotypes.

reaction range
the broadest possible expression of a genotype.

2   **Canalisation**. This concept, proposed by Waddington (1957), has been discussed in a special edition of *Developmental Psychology* (1991). Waddington likened development to a steel ball (phenotype) rolling down a surface on which there are various hills and valleys and possible paths for the ball to take (see Figure 4.5). Once the steel ball has been channelled into a valley it cannot easily move out. In Waddington's view, some behaviours are strongly canalised; for example, behaviours critical to survival, such as walking and talking. Only significant environmental events such as deprivation will prevent such canalised behaviours from emerging.

canalisation
genetic predisposition towards the development of certain characteristics in the species, such as walking.

3   **Niche-picking**. Scarr and McCartney (1983) have identified two types of genetics–environment interaction.

niche-picking
the selection, as people age, of aspects of their environment to which they will respond in terms of personality, intellect and motivation.

a   *Passive*. When children are very young, it is the parents who largely control the environment for children and hence children are largely passive in their development.

b   *Evocative*. As the children get older they elicit responses from the environment and these responses strengthen predispositions. A quiet, shy child, for example, may elicit less stimulation from parents and friends.

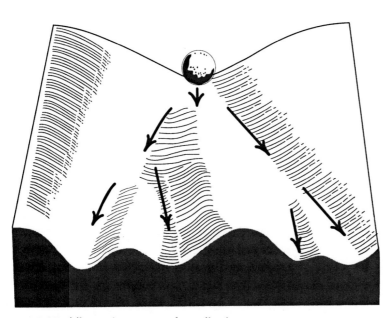

Figure 4.5 Waddington's concept of canalisation

Theories of
gene effects

The current status of genetics – environment debate

The relationship between genetics and environment is a complex and at times controversial one. The significance attached to the field has been highlighted by Crnic and Pennington (1987), Nowakowski (1987) and Bertenthal (1991).

In a discussion of neural development in the central nervous system, Nowakowski (1987) has identified three views that go to the heart of the genetics–environment controversy.

preformist
refers to the view that a miniature adult exists in the egg or sperm.

empiricist
the view that knowledge is derived solely from experience.

selectionist
refers to the view that neuronal networks are modified by environmental influence.

1 In the **preformist** view, experience is not considered to influence the highly ordered anatomy of the brain, and development unfolds according to a pre-set pattern.

2 In the **empiricist** view, experience of learning is emphasised in influencing the 'wiring patterns of the maturing nervous system' (Nowakowski 1987, p. 587).

3 In the **selectionist** view, 'it is considered that the neuronal networks that are initially established are modified by subsequent environmental and experiential influences' (Nowarowski 1987, p. 587). (A neuron is an individual nerve cell or the basic unit of the nervous system.)

The stark positions held on the genetics–environment, nature/nurture debate are highlighted here. A strong genetecist position is reflected in the opinion of Rich and Kim (1978, p. 52) who claim that '. . . the instructions for the assembly and organization of a living system are embodied in he DNA molecules contained within the living cell'. This example of a strongly held genetic viewpoint has reflected a dramatic swing away from nature to nurture now intensified by the findings from the Human Genome Project described earlier. To appreciate how far the pendulum has swung toward the nature position, consider the argument of the editor of *Science*, Daniel Koshland, as reported in Rifkin (1998), indicating that genetics provides the best explanation for 'homelessness' and that social problems are best addressed through the science of genetics.

Research to date would indicate that while the structure of the brain is, to an important degree, specified by genetic and developmental processes, the pattern of interconnections between neurons depends upon experience. It is evident from research that the timing of experience or learning can be a critical element in determining the strength of the connections at a neuronal level. Thus, during development, visual experience in rats activates the gene that codes for tubulin, a protein integral to the axons and dendrites that support the functional connections in the nervous system. This highlights the complex interplay between genetics and the environment.

Gottlieb (1991) suggests that contemporary developmental thinking concerning the nature of genetics–environment interaction is moving towards a systems view of development (see Figure 1.1, chapter 1). The systems view suggests that at the various levels – gene, cell, organ, behaviour, environment – there is some mutual influence that is not hierarchical or linear. The systems view emphasises the interrelatedness, wholeness and integrity of individuals and their development.

Plomin (2001) in a special issue on genetics in *The Psychologist* noted that 'The fundamental accomplishment of genetic research in psychology to date has been to demonstrate the ubiquitous importance of genetics throughout psychology (Plomin 2001, p. 135). He notes that twin studies and adoption studies provide the foundation for understanding the interplay between genetics and development. Maccoby (2000, p. 7) notes that

> In a general sense, the behaviour genetecists have made their case. Children's genetic endowments do clearly affect how individuals will develop – in comparison to other children – to a much greater extent than was thought to be the case during the years of ascendancy of reinforcement learning theories and psychodynamic theories [the middle decades of the twentieth century].

In considering the genetic-environment debate, it is important to keep in mind a number of points.

Heritability. As described by Sternberg and Grigorenko (1999, p. 536) 'Heritability [also called H2] is the ratio of genetic variation to total variation in an attribute within a population'. As the authors go on to note, one should not confuse heritability with genetic influence. To clarify their point they use the example of the heritability of occupational status where there is no gene for 'occupational status'. However, certain factors such as intelligence or personality are under some genetic control, which may in turn lead to differences in occupational status.

Heritability and modifiability. As Sternberg and Grigorenko (1999) have noted, it is important to distinguish between the two concepts as 'genetics is not destiny'. They cite the example of phenylketonuria (PKU) as genetically determined recessive condition. The effects of PKU are highly modifiable by feeding the young infant who has PKU with a diet free from phenylalanine, thus preventing the mental retardation that is an outcome of the condition. As they note, '. . . the genetic endowment does not change: the infant still has a mutant gene causing phenylketonuria. What changes is the manifestation of its associated symptoms in the environment' (p. 541).

Genetic defects

As noted earlier in this chapter, each somatic cell in the human body carries all of our chromosomes, and these reflect our genetic make-up. When chromosomal development is aberrant, abnormalities may appear in the individual's physical or psychological development. Some chromosomal defects are inherited, but others are accidental and occur during the growth of the person. One genetic defect that has been identified brings about a condition in humans known as Down syndrome.

Other conditions known to be caused by genetic defects are the Klinefelter, XYY and Turner syndromes.

1 *Klinefelter syndrome.* This chromosomal aberration linked to the sex chromosomes involves the presence of an extra X chromosome in a male child. It is found in about one in 400 males, and those affected frequently have both male and female secondary sex characteristics.

2 *XYY syndrome.* Males with an extra Y chromosome are characteristically tall and muscular. It was first discovered among prisoners with a history of violence, hence the somewhat tenuous link between XYY and criminality.

3 *Turner syndrome.* In this syndrome, a small number of female children lack one member of the pair of X chromosomes. Many abort spontaneously and those who survive are usually atypically short in stature, and slow in learning.

Down syndrome

In 1866 John Langdon Haydon Down, a physician in England, published the first thorough description of the disorder that was later named after him. He had observed that certain mentally retarded individuals have identifiable characteristics such as flattened facial features, an epicanthic fold of skin over the eyes, short stature and muscular fluidity.

Modern research shows that people with Down syndrome may also suffer from complications such as congenital heart defects, vision impairment, neurological impairment, susceptibility to infection and an increased risk of developing leukaemia. Statistics indicate that in North America Down syndrome occurs with a frequency of one in 700 live births.

In the 1950s it was ascertained that people with Down syndrome had 47 rather than 46 chromosomes. The extra chromosome may result from a malfunction in cell division. According to recent research (Patterson 1987), it appears possible that during meiosis (cell division) non-dysjunction occurs when chromosomes fail to separate properly, producing three instead of two copies of chromosome 21, known as trisomy 21.

The cause of trisomy 21 is obscure, although there is a link with the age of the mother. Women aged 15 to 24 years have a less than one in 1500 chance of bearing a Down syndrome child, but for women older than 45 years the risk increases to one in 45 (Hamerton et al. 1961).

Genetic counselling

The term 'genetic counselling' was coined by Sheldon Reed (1963) to describe how he conscientiously gave careful answers to genetic questions asked by anxious parents about their potential offspring. Although the science of genetic counselling is quite new, the art itself is quite ancient. Over a thousand years ago, a rabbi wrote in *The Talmud* (a Jewish religious book): 'If a woman had a son, and if this woman had a brother or maternal uncle with the bleeding disease, she should not have her son circumcised' (Rosner 1969, p. 834). The bleeding disease referred to by the rabbi is haemophilia, and virtually the same advice would be given to such a woman today, even though much more is known about haemophilia.

Not so long ago, a child was born with whatever defects it had inherited. Now, with the aid of modern genetic science and modern medical science, quite a sophisticated range of techniques are available to assist parents in reducing the risk of disease or abnormality in their child. Genetic disorders occur in nearly 5 per cent of live births in the Western world (Reed 1963). Other genetic abnormalities manifest themselves in later life, such as Huntington's Disease, a disease involving involuntary movements and progressive mental deterioration, the first signs of which typically appear in the fourth or fifth decade of life.

In addition to detailed family histories and physical examinations, a range of screening techniques are available to aid the counselling process, including **amniocentesis**, ultrasound, X-ray and fetoscopy.

Amniocentesis is a medical technique that involves inserting a hollow needle into a woman's abdomen during pregnancy. Through the needle some of the amniotic fluid surrounding the fetus is withdrawn. The procedure can be carried out as early as the first trimester (three months) of pregnancy, although it is usually done between the sixteenth and nineteenth week. Amniocentesis provides a basis for determining the chromosomal constitution of the foetus and for diagnosing problems with metabolism.

amniocentesis
medical procedure for detecting foetal abnormalities by withdrawing a sample of the amniotic fluid and performing chromosomal analyses.

Ultrasound and X-ray screening allow for accurate determination of the date of conception and for the detection of encephaly. Multiple pregnancies can also be detected. A new radiographic technique known as a computerised axial tomography (CAT) scan provides, like ultrasound, a cross-sectional view through tissue. CAT scans aid in the diagnosis of developmental problems in internal organs such as the kidney.

The technology of **foetoscopy** provides for direct viewing of the foetus through an endoscope. Although the field of vision is narrow, favourable circumstances allow malformations in extremities, such as cleft lips, to be identified.

foetoscopy
screening technique in which the foetus is viewed through an endoscope.

The technology for genetic screening is undergoing remarkable developments, but a number of important ethical problems have been raised. Such problems were not evident when death was indisputable and unpostponable. In a survey of Victorian paediatricians, 90.1 per cent said they had faced cases in practice when a decision had to be made whether or not to continue treatment of a defective newborn infant. From the survey, it was concluded that Australian doctors facing morally significant decisions tend to take into account, above all, the expected quality of the infant's life (Singer et al. 1983).

The family life-cycle: 4

The family as a system

Systems theory has made a significant contribution to describing and understanding the nature of the 'family' and what is meant by the term (see chapter 3). Drawing on the work of Robinson (1980) and Combrinck-Graham (1990), it is possible to identify characteristics of an organised system such as a family.

1   The behaviour of one person in the family affects all family members (for example, if a child has a behaviour problem).
2   The behaviour of the whole system or any individual member is consistent with the system to which it belongs. Thus, an adolescent teenager with anorexia may be influenced by the food-watching habits of the family.

3   The family structure is a rule-governed system, whereby rules help determine interactions, such as who talks with whom.
4   The family system is self-regulating. For example, a child's misbehaviour may be seen as an attempt to involve the father more in the family.

The Australian family therapist, Malcolm Robinson (1980, p. 183) notes that the essential point of all systems theory '... is concern for wholeness and organization rather than a reductionist examination of individual parts and isolation; a concern with the exchange of information and energy that acts to maintain an evolving system'. Family systems theory therefore represents a significantly different way of looking at the family, requiring a shift in perspective away from the reductionist and individualistic orientation that has largely dominated child development thinking until recently.

Chapter summary

In many ways, the Human Genome Project and the findings emerging from this project are influencing on an almost daily basis our understanding of the manner in which genetics contributes to our understanding of human development. At the same time, significant ethical dilemmas associated with the findings are being raised. A very useful activity would be to summarise one's understanding of the Human Genome Project, identify some of the current findings and relate these to the various ethical issues which present themselves.

Discussion questions

1   Identify and discuss the main features of DNA.
2   How do mitosis and meiosis differ?
3   What key features of Mendel's discoveries have contributed to our understanding of the science of genetics.
4   How do phenotype and genotype differ?
5   Clarify the nature of dominant and recessive alleles and their relationship to phenotype and genotype.
6   What evidence is there that intellectual development is genetically, rather than environmentally, determined?
7   Identify and describe the different screening techniques available to today's parents to aid genetic counselling.
8   How does a 'systems' view of the family differ from more traditional views?

Activity

In small groups of three or four, describe the family situation in which you grew up: the number of people in the household, changes over time in numbers. In retrospect, what do you now see as the most important thing that your family provided for you as a child?

Selected websites

Child Adolescent Psychological and educational Resources <www.caper.com.au>

The Centre for Brain and Cognitive Development at Birkbeck College, University of London <www.psyc.bbk.ac.uk/cbcd>

Starting Smart – how early experiences affect brain development <www.bcm.tmc.edu/civitas/links/ounce.html>

5 From Conception to Birth

Angels Whispering
Because I feel that, in the heavens above
The angels, whispering to one another,
Can find, among their burning terms of love,
None so devoted as that of 'mother',
Therefore by that dear name I long have called you.

Edgar Allan Poe, To My Mother

KEY TERMS AND CONCEPTS

- Oocyte
- Blastocyst
- Placenta
- Infertility
- Embryo
- Birth
- Apgar test
- Engrossment
- Reflexes

Introduction

From conception to birth a wondrous journey is undertaken. In the last weeks before birth the foetus is fully developed. The baby is about 48 centimetres in length and weighs about 2500 grams. Before birth, she or he will grow up to another 3 centimetres and gain up to 800 grams. This extra weight will help protect the baby upon emerging from the cocooned environment of the womb to the outside world. In the womb the baby drinks up to 3 litres of amniotic fluid per day, thereby preparing to develop the stomach, kidneys and bladder. The amniotic fluid is excreted and the baby's urine (free of toxins) supplies part of the new amniotic fluid. The baby has been practising breathing before birth, may develop hiccups at times and can suck his or her thumb. All the senses are developed and the baby can hear, taste, feel, smell and see. A few weeks before birth the baby moves into a head-down position in the pelvis. The baby is now ready to set out on the next wondrous stage of his or her journey through life.

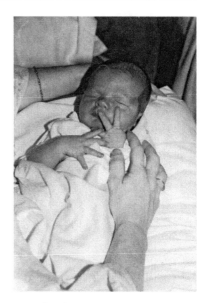

'Angels whispering'.

In this chapter the focus will be on conception, embryonic development, birth and postnatal development. Children's concept of family is discussed in The Family Life-cycle: 5.

Conception

Conception or fertilisation occurs when the father's sperm cell joins with the mother's egg cell, called the ovum. Once released from either of the two ovaries the ovum will enter the Fallopian tube (see Figure 5.1). The ovum moves down the tube towards the uterus assisted by the beating of hair-like cilia that line the end of the oviduct and by smooth muscle contractions (Tortora & Anagnostakos 1987). In all, the ovum may take several days to reach the uterus. Fertilisation normally occurs in the Fallopian tube (Figure 5.1).

The first sperm may arrive at the site of fertilisation in the Fallopian tube about 15 minutes after intercourse. Once in the uterus the sperm are moved towards the ovum principally by upward contractions of the smooth muscles of the uterus and Fallopian tube (Tortora & Anagnostakos 1987). Only approximately 100 to 1000 of several hundred million sperm actually reach the Fallopian tube after the ejaculate has been deposited in the vagina. It is generally assumed that surviving sperm reach the egg by random motion and, while many may reach the ovum, only one sperm successfully penetrates and fertilises the egg cell.

The cell released from the ovary is called an oocyte and when it enters the Fallopian tube it has reached the end of the first of the two meiotic divisions. When the sperm penetrates the **oocyte**, the oocyte nucleus rapidly completes the second meiotic division and develops into the true ovum. If it has been

oocyte
name given to the egg cell when it is released from the ovary.

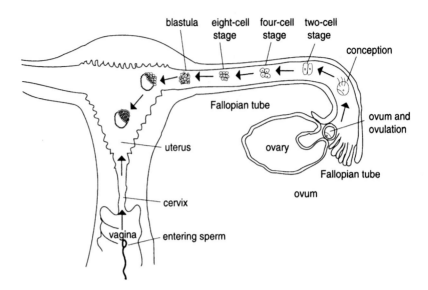

Figure 5.1 Conception

fertilised, the egg continues to travel down the Fallopian tube to the uterus, undergoing developmental changes during its journey.

Implantation

In the journey down the Fallopian tube to the uterus, the cell divides to become two cells, and then divides again and again to become four cells, eight cells and so on until the ball of cells, or blastocyst, enters the uterus. The **blastocyst** consists of approximately 100 cells. It floats free in the uterine fluid for several days, while mitosis and cell division continue. The implantation of the embryo begins approximately six to seven days after fertilisation (Tortora & Anagnostakos 1987). Once it is implanted in the uterine wall, the developing **embryo** receives nutrients by absorption. After two to three weeks, the embryo is receiving nutrients via a developed system of blood vessels. The **placenta** begins to form. This is a uniquely mammalian feature that helps in the exchange of gases and nutrients between the circulatory systems of the mother and foetus. The umbilical cord, containing a complex blood system, differentiates in the embryo at the end of the fifth week. At this stage, the embryonic heart is pumping blood and waste out of the foetus through the placenta. The embryo is usually referred to as the foetus after the end of the second month.

In-vitro fertilisation

The word '**infertility**' is an emotionally charged term associated with other labels such as 'barren' or 'sterile'. The generally accepted definition of 'infertility' is the inability to achieve pregnancy after a year of unprotected intercourse (Clapp 1985). The psychological impact of infertility on those concerned is an issue that is being increasingly addressed. As Clapp (1985, p. 1) notes:

blastocyst
a hollow ball of approximately 100 cells that forms in the very early stages of development following conception.

embryo
the developing human being during the first eight weeks following the implantation of the ovum in the uterine wall.

placenta
a mass of tissue in the uterus through which nutrients are transmitted from mother to foetus and waste products filtered from foetus to mother.

infertility
the inability to conceive.

Couples and individuals facing infertility have to cope with an unanticipated life crisis that results in losses: the hope of pregnancy and parenting a biologic child, self esteem, control over one's life goals, and privacy of one's body and sexual activity.

Figures suggest that between 10 and 15 per cent of the population are confronted with the issue of infertility (Andrew 1984). One recent medical procedure used to deal with infertility is in-vitro fertilisation (IVF). The cost of such programs is high and the probability of successful embryo implantation is only approximately one in 10 (Pace-Owens 1985). None-the-less, such programs are increasingly sought out by couples. As reported by Gibson et al. (2000), approximately 1 per cent of all births in Western societies today involve IVF procedures. In brief, the IVF program involves:

1   assessment and screening of the couple;
2   monitoring the woman during her menstrual cycle;
3   using drugs to produce multiple ovarian follicles;
4   management of the expulsion of the oocyte from the follicle;
5   fertilisation with sperm;
6   incubation of the embryo;
7   embryo transfer;
8   follow-up 10 to 14 days later to see if one or more of the embryos have implanted.

While the medical aspects of IVF have been extensively studied, little is currently known about the psychological effects of the IVF procedure and there are contradictions in some of the research findings.

In a review of the field, Bernstein et al. (1985) observe that a high incidence of psychosexual problems is generally reported for infertile couples. Bernstein et al. (1985) found that infertile couples experienced greater dissatisfaction with themselves and their marriage than fertile couples. Recent research has also focused on the methods for helping couples deal with the issue of infertility (Zion 1988). Resources available to such couples include professional organisations that provide support and counselling. Zion emphasises that the nurse can also play an effective role by helping couples to prepare themselves for infertility treatment, to maintain realistic expectations and to feel in control in a situation where the infertility treatment is directing their sexual activities.

Research on the effect of infertility has been conducted in Adelaide, South Australia by Harris et al. (unpub.) at the Flinders Medical Centre. Harris et al. have reported findings that contrast with those of Bernstein et al. (1985). Harris et al. tested 50 couples who underwent IVF treatment at the fertility clinic between 1985 and 1988. Their results showed that IVF couples in this sample had a 'normal' psychiatric psychological profile and were not seriously psychologically affected by the procedure. In fact, in some areas the men appeared to benefit from the experience.

Six reliable inventories assessing depression, clinical personality traits, psychological and generalised general health problems, and marital satisfaction were administered before and after three cycles of treatment (where treatment was unsuccessful), or after at least one cycle (where a pregnancy occurred). After the experience of IVF, although women were less anxious than men, they showed more somatic symptoms and there was a tendency for women to experience slightly lower marital satisfaction than men. The 'normality' of the sample, in the face of the psychological symptoms expected from reports in the literature, was attributed to the difference in coping and personality variables between couples who opted for IVF treatment and those who did not (Given et al. 1985), and to the fact that the sample covered mainly middle to upper socioeconomic groups.

In this brief review of research it is apparent that, given the current high failure rate in the IVF program, it is important to gain a better understanding of the psychological impact of participating in it.

As the IVF procedure has developed, consideration has now been given as to whether children conceived through the procedure are at any greater risk for developmental or psychosocial problems. Australian researchers (Gibson et al. 1998; Gibson et al. 2000) have reported that IVF children appear at no greater risk in relation to either developmental or psychosocial problems.

Development of the foetus

The following description of the development of the foetus is based on the work of Begley et al. (1980), and Tortora and Anagnostakos (1987).

The embryo: the first eight weeks (first trimester)
- The first cell division occurs some 36 hours after fertilisation.
- Implantation continues during the second week.
- By the third week most of the major organ systems begin to form; that is, the nervous system, brain, spinal cord.
- The eyes are forming by 21 days.
- By the fourth week the embryo has grown from 1.5 to 5.00 millimetres and has increased in mass some 7000 times.
- By the end of the sixth week the heart begins to enlarge and supply blood to the embryo.
- By the seventh week the embryo is 2.5 centimetres long and weighs 1 gram.
- The face is forming during the seventh to eighth week.

The foetus: third to sixth month (second trimester)
- By the third month the foetus has grown to some 8 centimetres in length and weighs about 78 grams.
- The face is more apparent and nails have formed on fingers and toes.
- The kidneys are functioning.
- The foetus can move its arms and legs and has the reflexes of sucking and swallowing.
- By the fourth month the lower pelvis and abdomen of the foetus have developed.

- The long bony skeleton is forming.
- By the fifth month the foetus weighs about 225 grams and measures approximately 18 centimetres.
- The beating heart is audible to the stethoscope.
- Hair has formed on the head and a fuzzy down covers the body.
- A five-month-old foetus can survive outside of the body.
- By the sixth month the foetus weighs approximately 680 grams and is over 30 centimetres in length.

The foetus: sixth to ninth month (third trimester)
- Eyelids open at eight months.
- The foetus can perceive light and taste sweet substances.
- There is rapid brain development.
- By the ninth month the foetus is some 50 centimetres long and weighs approximately 3300 grams.

Abilities of the foetus

Our understanding of the intra-uterine world of the foetus has increased dramatically in the last decade. We are now aware that the foetus is quite responsive to environmental stimuli and after a certain stage of development is quite physically active.

Hearing

It is now understood that the auditory system of the human baby is morphologically mature from approximately 13 weeks before birth. Moreover, there is evidence of a response to sound from the third month before term (Ockleford et al. 1988). In fact, the foetus is surrounded by sound in the uterus: the rhythmical pumping of the mother's heart, the noise of air passing through the mother's intestine. In addition, there is noise from outside the womb, such as music or slamming doors. Research conducted by Ockleford et al. (1988) on responses of neonates to parents' and others' voices showed that infants could discriminate between their own mother's voice and that of a stranger. The infant's heart rate increased more in response to the mother's voice than to that of the stranger. The researchers interpreted their findings to suggest that sounds that are repeatedly experienced before birth (especially the mother's voice) became familiar to the foetus, so that the baby responds selectively by orienting to the mother during the hours immediately after birth.

Vision

Just as the womb is not a quiet place for the foetus, there is no reason to believe that it is a completely dark place either. The muscles of the foetus's eyes develop quite early. Birnholz (1981) has recorded foetal eye movement with ultrasound and has found it to be slow at six weeks, with rapid eye movements at 23 weeks and repetitive movements after 32 weeks. A very premature infant can detect light and shape.

Taste

By around 13–15 weeks a foetus' taste buds closely resemble a mature adult's. It is understood that amniotic fluid can smell of onion, garlic and other features of the mother's diet. While it is not yet understood whether the foetus can taste, it is known that very premature babies will suck harder on a sweet nipple than an unsweetened rubber one.

Movement

The foetus begins to make spontaneous movements at about seven weeks after conception. Between 16 and 21 weeks, the mother begins to feel the movements. The foetus makes a variety of movements (Sorokin & Dierker 1982).

- Squirming movements slowly increase during pregnancy.
- Small, rhythmic kicks continue at a constant rate from five to nine months.
- Sharp kicks increase up to the seventh month, then decrease.

After nine weeks of pregnancy, the hands of the foetus are well enough formed to grasp objects. Early on, the foetus will move away from objects that are touched, while later on the movement is towards objects that are touched. For example, towards the end of pregnancy the foetus can suck fingers or a thumb.

Trends and issues

Foetal learning and soap operas

The notion that the foetus is capable of learning in the womb has been present in Western folklore for many centuries. The ancient Greek philosopher Aristotle proposed that it was during pregnancy that the individual first acquired or experienced sensation. It was not until the twentieth century, however, that empirical research was directed towards answering the question of whether or not the foetus is capable of learning inside the womb. In 1925 Peiper conducted an experiment in which a loud, shrill car horn was sounded within a few feet of a pregnant woman's abdomen. Marked movements were noted in the foetus, but these were not repeated upon repetition of the noise. In classical conditioning (see Pavlov, chapter 3), certain stimuli will elicit reflex responses. Repeated presentation of a neutral stimulus in association with the reflex response will eventually lead the neutral stimulus to elicit the reflex. Foetuses in the last trimester have been successfully conditioned so that after 15 to 20 trials that previously neutral stimulus (such as vibration) alone produces foetal movement.

Other researchers have used the newborn's response to stimuli normally experienced in the womb to show foetal conditioning. De Casper and Fifer (1980) found that newborns would alter their sucking pattern at the sound of their mother's voice. The same researchers also asked mothers to read the children's book *The Cat in the Hat* aloud twice a day for the last six-and-a-half weeks of pregnancy. After the birth of the babies, the sucking test indicated these newborns preferred to hear this story. Hepper (1988) examined the responses of newborns to the theme music of the television 'soapie', 'Neighbours' and found that the infants of the mothers who watched the program would stop crying and become alert when they heard the theme music.

In sum, it appears that by the end of the pregnancy, the foetal nervous system has matured sufficiently such that short-term memory may be operable. This would mean that foetuses might be quite capable of learning in-utero and a kind of Pavlovian conditioning could occur. The far reaching implications of this finding have been explored by Hyde and McCown (1986). They suggest that certain hospital practices – such as exposure of the foetus to high frequency sounds in intensive care nurseries – may bring about learning in the womb that could have undesirable consequences after birth, such as over-sensitivity to sound.

Breathing has been detected as early as the eleventh week. It remains irregular until the last weeks before delivery, when it is slower and more regular (Patrick 1982).

The intra-uterine environment

Evidence to date regarding foetal sensitivities and foetal learning suggests that the womb may not be the impenetrable, protective boundary that it was once thought to be. Further evidence attesting to the vulnerability of the foetus is now emerging in terms of maternal drug abuse.

The foetal alcohol syndrome

There is growing concern among health professionals regarding the effects of alcohol consumption on foetal development. A foetal alcohol syndrome was identified by Jones and Smith (1973). The syndrome was associated with retarded physical growth and mental retardation. It was also noted that infants born to mothers who had abused alcohol could exhibit withdrawal symptoms.

There is also some evidence that moderate drinking (two to three drinks per day) may cause foetal growth retardation and increase the risk of spontaneous abortion. Wekselman et al. (1995, p. 296) have noted that 'Adverse neonatal/pediatric effects of maternal alcohol consumption are potentially devastating'. As the authors noted, the diagnosis indicated contingency depended upon (i) dysmorphology (e.g. midfacial anomalies); (ii) growth retardation including intra-uterine and failure to achieve 'catch-up growth'; and (iii) central nervous system impairment (e.g. learning disabilities). Mills and Graubard (1987, p. 314) conclude from their research that 'the current recommendation of no drinking during pregnancy is the safest'. Waldenstrom et al. (1995) have provided a significant review of the FAS.

Cigarette smoking

Cigarette smoking is probably the most common addiction among pregnant women in Western society and its risks to the developing embryo and foetus are now well documented.

In a large-scale study of 8193 pregnant women, Naeye (1981) concluded that infants of smokers are smaller at birth than those of non-smokers. In fact, the most consistent result of maternal smoking during pregnancy is the reduction of the foetal growth rate. In addition, research indicates that smoking during pregnancy is also associated with an increased risk of pre-term delivery, stillbirth and neonatal death and possibly spontaneous abortion (Naeye 1981). Although an increasing amount of evidence suggests that maternal smoking is detrimental to the mother and foetus, only 20 per cent of pregnant women smokers quit during pregnancy (Prager et al. 1984).

Opiate abuse

Common problems associated with heroin abuse in pregnant women include increased risk of first trimester abortion, premature delivery, maternal–neonatal infection and severe neonatal withdrawal. Findings such as these have been reported in an Australian study (Kelly et al. 1991).

Giving birth

birth
emergence of
young from body
of mother

The *Concise Oxford Dictionary* (1980) defines **birth** as 'Emergence of young from body of mother'. In the book of Genesis, birth is described in the following terms: 'I will intensify the pangs of your childbearing. In pain shall you bring forth children' (Genesis 15:17). In a satirical vein, the comedian Carol Burnett likened the experience of birth to taking your bottom lip and stretching it up and over the top of your head. These descriptions of birth are far removed from the following physiological description of labour and birth.

The initiation of labour

It is still unclear to medical science what brings about the onset of labour in humans, although there is mounting evidence that the cause is hormonal (Oxhorn 1986). The baby's adrenal gland plays an important role in the process by producing cortisone. This results in an increased production of prostaglandin in the mother, which is a hormone that stimulates contractions of the uterus. Oxytocin is another hormone produced by the pituitary gland that stimulates contractions. Prior to the beginning of labour, the foetus has usually turned in the womb and is lying in a head-down position.

The stages of labour

Medical science has identified four basic stages in labour. The description of these four stages has been adapted from Oxhorn (1986).

Stage 1

primipara
a woman giving
birth for the first
time.

In a woman having her first child (**primipara**), the length of the first stage of labour varies from 13 to 28 hours. During this stage the cervix dilates to its fullest. The contractions are intermittent and can be painful and the pains become more frequent and more severe as labour proceeds. The pains are generally experienced in the back and pass to the front of the abdomen and thighs. As labour proceeds, the cervix softens and dilates. When the cervix has opened sufficiently to permit passage of the foetal head, the cervix is described as fully dilated (average dilation for births is 10 centimetres, while average diameter during pregnancy is 2.5 centimetres). The foetus lies within a sac of fluid, known as the amniotic fluid. As labour proceeds, the amniotic sac ruptures. This is known as the 'breaking of the waters'.

Trends and issues

Low-birth-weight infants

Kopp and Parmelee (1979) have reviewed the major studies relating to low-birth-weight infants, distinguishing between those born prematurely and those born at term but classified as small-for-date. It is possible to identify small-for-date infants using reliable criteria, such as birth weights and standard deviations below the mean for a given gestational age. The figure of low birth weight (LBW) is generally accepted as less than 2500 grams. Various aetiologic factors for low birth weight have been identified by Kopp and Parmelee, including foetal oxygen shortage and deficiencies in nutrient transport and/or the exchange of metabolic waste products. Other associated factors include toxaemia, smoking, drug use and viral infections. The structural features of the uterus and placental characteristics have also been implicated.

The matter of low birth weight is of particular concern among Australian Aboriginal infants. As Lancaster (1989) notes, almost 5000 Aboriginal infants are born in Australia each year, which represents about 2 per cent of national births. Lancaster (1989), Roberts et al. (1988) and Thomson (1990) have all noted that Aboriginal infants are prone to pre-term delivery and lower birth weight. In a review of the statistics for South Australia, Western Australia and the Northern Territory Thomson (1990) found that 13.5 per cent of Aboriginal infants were of low birth weight compared to 5.7 per cent of non-Aboriginal children.

The outcomes for low-birth-weight children are well documented. Research by Kuipers-Holwerda (1987) suggests that low birth weight is associated with neurological impairment. Kopp and Parmelee have noted that there may be some intellectual disadvantage in the developing child, with more males than females being at risk. Roberts et al. (1988) note that for Aboriginal children, LBW can have serious long-term effects in terms of Aboriginal children's physical growth potential and can result in permanent growth retardation. Kuipers-Holwerda (1987) assessed LBW children at 4.5 years in terms of language skills, spatial tasks and memory tasks, using a Piagetian framework. The conclusion was that 'LBW children do show a lag in performing Piagetian tasks' (p. 326). The author was optimistic that such a lag could be outgrown although it could hinder development of language skills and spatial and social understanding.

Stage 2

The second stage of labour lasts between 57 minutes and two and a half hours in primiparas women (18 to 50 minutes in multiparas – women who have given birth to two or more children). The second stage begins when the cervix has reached full dilation and finishes with the birth of the baby. During this stage contractions are more frequent and more painful. The clinical indications include:

1 an increase in blood show;
2 the wish of the mother to bear down with each contraction;
3 a pressure on the rectum and desire to defecate;
4 nausea and retching as the cervix fully dilates.

Positions for birth and delivery. A wide variety of positions for delivery are used by women. Basically they can be grouped as follows:

1 *upright* – standing, sitting, squatting and upright kneeling;
2 *horizontal/semi-horizontal* – lateral or prone;
3 *squatting* – a position recorded in the earliest pictures of birth scenes, which has the advantage of enlarging the pelvic outlet.

Stage 3

The third stage involves the expulsion of the placenta which occurs in two phases:

1   separation of the placenta from the uterus wall;
2   expulsion of the placenta from the birth canal.

Stage 4

In the fourth stage, the mother is kept under observation by hospital staff and checked for bleeding, blood pressure and pulse.

The Australian researcher, Waldenstrom and colleagues (1996) surveyed 295 women one day after giving birth. As they reported, during birth '[w]omen usually experienced severe pain and various degrees of anxiety, and most were seized with panic for a short period of time or some part of their labor' (p. 142). As the authors also note, despite the negative feelings '. . . most women felt greatly involved in the birth process, were satisfied with their own achievement, and thought they had coped better than expected' (p. 142).

Baby's first test: Apgar

Apgar
a test routinely
used to assess the
physical condition
of newborn babies.

The obstetrician or midwife often calls out the time when the baby arrives after the last contraction or records the time by pressing a stopwatch. Noting the time enables the **Apgar test** to be carried out directly after birth and repeated at 5 and 10 minutes after the birth. The Apgar test was developed by Virginia Apgar (1953). Her goal in establishing a system for scoring newborns was '. . . to predict survival, to compare several methods of resuscitation which were in use at the time, and through the infant's responsiveness after delivery, to compare perinatal experience in different hospitals' (Apgar 1966, p. 645).

Butterfield and Covey (1962) proposed the acronym APGAR as an aid in recalling the categories:

A: Appearance (color)
P: Pulse (heart rate)
G: Grimace (reflex irritability)
A: Activity (muscle tone)
R: Respiration (respiratory effort)

As noted by Juretschke (2000), problems with the method relate to the ideal of having an independent observer complete the scoring, and the issue of whether the infant is pre- or full term. The author concludes that the method is a useful tool for evaluating resuscitative needs but has limited predictive ability for long-term developmental outcomes.

Results of the Apgar test indicate how well the baby has coped during delivery, and in the immediate post-birth period. In the Apgar test, each of five signs is given a score of 0, 1 or 2 according to the condition of the infant. A total of 8 to 10 points means that the baby is in good to excellent condition;

under 7, that the baby is suffering from a problem, often transient; less than 4, that the baby requires immediate treatment. Apgar et al. (1958) found that in a group of 15 348 infants 1 minute after birth, 6 per cent had scores of 0 to 2, 24 per cent scored 3 to 7, and 70 per cent scored 8 to 10; the infants with the lowest scores had the highest mortality. A number of extraneous factors can influence the score, however, including the type of delivery experienced by the infant (breech delivery had the lowest score and vaginal the highest) and type of anaesthesia, if any, given to the mother.

In addition to the Apgar test, a commonly used test in most Australian hospitals is the examination of blood from the umbilical cord artery. The test indicates whether the newborn's oxygen supply is lacking. Lack of oxygen at birth is a most dangerous complication and can lead to physical and psychological damage. On the basis of this test, the paediatrician can decide whether the newborn needs to be ventilated.

Fathers and the birth process

In a medical textbook (Oxhorn 1986), only one paragraph out of 900 pages is devoted to the role of the family during birth and only one sentence to the role of the father. Oxhorn acknowledges that the attachment of the father to the baby has not been studied as intensively as that of the mother but suggests that the physical presence of the father at the birth does affect his feelings and behaviour towards the child. In the social science field, the role of the father during and subsequent to birth has received a little more attention in the last decade, although, at the time of writing, it remains a vastly under-researched field.

Since the publication of the first edition of this text, interest in the psychology of fatherhood has grown (Marsiglio, Hutchinson & Cohan, 2000). These same authors have drawn attention to the significance of this research in relation to involving males in important policy debates and program interventions addressing issues such as birth control, pregnancy, paternity and fatherhood issues. Fox et al. (2000) have commented on '[c]hanging cultural definitions of the role of father, including changing expectations of the nature and extent of his involvement and intended impact on his offspring . . .' (p. 123).

Engrossment

In a study of the impact of the newborn on fathers, Greenberg and Morris suggest that fathers begin developing a bond to their newborn during the first three days after birth and perhaps even during the pregnancy itself. These authors coined the term '**engrossment**' to describe fathers' 'pre-occupation, absorption and interest in their newborn' (cited in Cath et al. 1982, p. 95). A father's engrossment consists of:

engrossment
a term describing a father's pre-occupation with his newborn child.

1 some visual awareness of the newborn as 'attractive', 'pretty' etc.;
2 a tactile awareness manifested by a desire to touch and hold his child, which is described as pleasurable;
3 an awareness of the distinct features of the child;
4 a view that the newborn is 'perfect';
5 a strong attraction to and focusing of attention on the child;
6 an extreme sense of 'elation' or a 'high' following the birth;
7 an enhanced sense of self-esteem upon first seeing his child.

Fathers' participation at the birth

It is an interesting exercise to consider the way Western society has viewed the role of the father at the birth of his child. In a book on natural childbirth, Benjamin Spock (1955) assumed that there was little that fathers could constructively offer or do at childbirth. However, a little over a decade later, the view had changed somewhat, to the extent that Shapiro (1969) urged fathers to share the experience of birth with the mother.

In the 1990s, it could be argued that the father's role as perceived by the medical profession is still clouded with ambiguity. Although the father's role is now best seen as one of support for the mother, there is little indication of how a father might best carry out this role in hospital. Lacking direction from hospital personnel, fathers often have little idea of how to behave supportively during the birth process. In a review of observations of fathers at birth, Wollett et al. (1982) concluded that lack of direction from hospital personnel to fathers can elicit three types of reactions:

1 Some fathers may feel awed and subdued by the hospital environment and remain uninvolved until they return home with the baby.
2 Others may respond positively in the ward, despite lack of encouragement from hospital staff.
3 Still others may assume the initiative and adopt a pro-active role during the birth and delivery of the baby.

Wollett et al. (1982) conclude that fathers have a clear part to play at delivery in terms of personalising the medical experience and making birth a family concern. As Fox et al. (2000, p. 123) note, 'The popular literature and media reflect the current definition of the good father as co-parent, with special media features routinely focused on the new "nurturant" father'. Importantly, their research questioned whether such cultural expectations crossed race and social class lines. They suggest that emergent ideas about the 'nurturant' father '. . . fosters cleavages among social classes, in part because the accessibility of real-time caregiving participation on the part of men may be a function of having sufficient resources and leisure time to enact this model'.

The hospital experience

Richman (1982) offered an interesting sociological explanation for the difficulties that hospitals and medical personnel often have in accommodating fathers during the birth of their children. He discovered that many fathers recalled their hospital experience – the 'entrance trauma' (especially acute for the first birth) – with anger. They often described their wives as 'being taken away' or 'disappearing'.

Richman (1982) noted that fathers present the hospital organisation with a problem because they represent an anomaly that confronts the hospital's ideologies and organisational routines. That is, hospitals are highly structured ecologically to accommodate certain types of expected behaviour from people. For example, pregnant women are not expected to express pain in antenatal clinics or refuse to see their babies when they are delivered. Women entering hospitals to have babies are subjected to a series of events that are controlled by medical specialists and that often deny women control or individual status. According to Richman,

the powerful impose their dominant timetables on the weaker, even to the extent of determining the time for the baby to be born.

Richman argues that the father represents a potential threat because of unknown qualities. That is, unlike his partner, he has not undergone any of the rites of entry into the hospital organisation (such as meeting the paediatrician). The room where he waits is not called 'The Fathers' Room', and usually he has not brought any private property to the hospital, as his wife has (such as clothes or toiletries), with which to lay claim to some space. Richman argues that the father occupies a status gap between the well defined medical hierarchy (usually high status males), the midwives (usually females) and the mother and the newborn, who are now the hospital's responsibility. While the fathers are accorded some acceptance at the birth, other means operate to exclude the father. For example, on arrival with his partner, the father is often treated as if he were 'invisible'. Being afforded no formal public acknowledgment, his difficulties are intensified should he wish to 'assert himself as a father'.

The later father–child relationship

Immediately after the birth, the father is generally intensely interested in his newborn child (see 'Engrossment'). The research of Wollett et al. (1982) did not clearly identify a link between the extent of the father's involvement with the newborn and his involvement over a longer period of time. They concluded from their studies that the presence of the father at the birth of his child does not necessarily ensure a high level of active involvement by the father some 18 months later.

There is no doubt that in Western countries such as Australia the popular literature points strongly to the 'good' father as one who ideally is a 'co-parent'. The press is for a change in normative expectations regarding how fathers are to be involved with their young infant. Research by Fox et al. (2000, p. 128) indicated '. . . a high level of expectation on the part of the fathers of newborns for participation in and support of their new family member'. As such, the authors went on to note that 'In this sense, the fathers . . . reflect the predominant cultural construction of the "nurturant father"'. The same authors reported that the role of the father was still largely defined in terms of being an 'economic provider'. Interestingly the researchers also found a significant mis-match between the expectations of the mothers and fathers regarding partner expectations in caring for the newborn. Mothers' lower expectations for partners' help was identified as important because '. . . it could portend a lower level of participation than that preferred by fathers of newborns' (p. 128).

The early stages of life

Here we have a baby. It is composed of a bald head and a pair of lungs.

Eugene Field, cited in Lowrey 1986

Dramatic changes have taken place in our understanding of the nature of infant development in the last 20 years. The research of writers such as Jean Piaget (see chapter 3) has begun to have an impact on our understanding of the way children think and how they understand the world. Breakthroughs by Australian, British and US researchers have now effectively dispelled the myth of the incompetent infant (Stone et al. 1973). That is, research has put to rest the view of the helpless infant and a new picture has emerged. This new view encompasses the notion of the infant as 'active, competent, and in some ways, in control, of his/her own learning' (Anastasiou & Stengel 1980, p. 27).

Reflexes at birth

reflexes
involuntary actions of muscles.

Quite apart from any other capabilities at birth, the infant displays an impressive array of **reflexes** or automatic responses (see Table 5.1). A reflex occurs when we react in an involuntary way, and may help us to survive or may protect us. Reflexes also provide important information regarding the infant's neurological development, since there is a timetable for the appearance and disappearance of most reflexes.

Sensory abilities at birth

At birth the way in which the infant experiences the world is initially determined by the abilities of her or his sense organs.

Visual system

It is now understood that within minutes of birth the infant will prefer to orient to a face-like pattern than other patterns of a similar brightness (Carpenter 1974, p. 742). Carpenter also found that, as early as two weeks old, an infant will watch his or her mother's face longer than that of a stranger. The more recent research of Johnson (1988), indicates that one-and-a-half-hour-old neonates will pay attention to a face-like pattern when it moves in and out of their visual field. They prefer to look at face-like features in their natural arrangement in the context of a whole face rather than in other arrangements or without the facial outline. Johnson also discovered that as the infant gets older, a drawing of a face has to be more realistic to evoke interest. Thus, five-month-olds will treat a face-like pattern as a face only if the

VIEWPOINT
What sensory abilities is a baby born with?

178 first-year students of developmental psychology answered as follows:

Vision
Blurry shapes 22%
Everything 10%
Nothing 10%
People 10%

Hearing
Noises 28%
Everything 22%
Voices 10%

Smell
Everything 24%
Mother 14%
Not much 8%

Taste
Milk 40%
Most things 16%

Touch
Smooth/rough 14%
Warmth 8%

Table 5.1 Reflexes at birth

Reflex and Description	Appears	Disappears
1. **Rooting reflex** Sucking and swallowing are present in full-term babies. In the rooting reflex the neonate will orient towards a touch on the cheek which facilitates finding the nipple.	At birth	9 months
2. **Moro reflex** When the neonate's head is dropped back suddenly the hands will be extended. This reflex is usually accompanied by crying, extension of the trunk and movement of legs.	28th foetal week	2–3 months
3. **Grasp reflex** When a finger touches the neonate's palm, the neonate's fingers will flex and close around the finger.	At birth	3–4 months
4. **Walking reflex** When the neonate is held upright over a table so that the sole of the foot presses against the table, the baby will simulate a walking motion.	At birth	8 weeks
5. **Babinski reflex** When the sole of the neonate's foot is stroked, the toes fan out and the foot twists.	38th foetal week	12–16 months
6. **Tonic neck reflex** When the child is laid on his or her back and the head is turned to one side, the child flexes the opposite limbs.	20th foetal week	7–8 months

eyes, nose and mouth are within a face outline. Physically it is now understood that the infant is able to track horizontally at birth and is able to track vertically at four to six weeks (Cole et al. 1984). The newborn's visual system is described in greater detail in chapter 7.

Auditory system

The newborn infant will turn towards sound. In a review of the literature, Appleton et al. (1975) concluded that at birth, the newborn:

- has well-developed auditory skills;
- shows a wide discrimination between auditory signals involving intensity, duration and location of sound;

- finds certain low frequency rhythmical sounds soothing but high frequency sounds distressing.

The child's auditory system is described further in chapter 7.

Olfactory system

Within the first few days of birth the infant's sense of smell has matured to a point where he or she can differentiate a mother's smell from that of a stranger (Mills and Melhaish 1974).

Sensori-motor development

Illingworth (1987) has summarised a number of principles of development:

1 Development is a continuous process from conception to maturity. That is, development occurs in utero and birth is merely an event in the course of development.
2 The sequence of development is the same in all children but individual differences occur in the rate of development: for example, a child always sits before she or he can stand, but some children will learn to sit at an earlier age than others.
3 Development is closely tied to the maturation of the nervous system. This means that no amount of practice can cause a child to walk until the nervous system is ready.
4 Development moves from the general to the discrete. For example, a young baby may literally quiver all over with excitement at the sight of a rattle, while an older child will smile and reach for it.
5 Development is cephalocaudal; that is, it moves from head to foot.
6 Certain primitive reflexes such as the grasping and walking reflexes must be lost before corresponding voluntary movement is acquired by the infant.

The socio-emotional needs of the neonate

It is now better understood that from the birth of the infant, the care-giver and child enter into a complex socio-emotional relationship where the behaviour of each influences and is influenced by that of the other. The understanding that both the parent and child have a role to play in the developing relationship has forced researchers to develop studies and interpret the findings in terms of an evolving interaction. The focus of research has moved away from the traditional socialisation model, which conceived of the relationship in uni-directional terms to an examination of the interactive process. As Parke (1979, p. 17) has noted, '[T]he current zeitgeist . . . has clearly shifted to a study of the reciprocity of interaction and ways that individuals mutually regulate each other during the course of interaction'.

In investigating the emotional dimensions of mother–infant relations, it is clear that the concept of interaction and the expression of feeling are closely

The family life-cycle: 5

Children's concept of family

In the Family Life-Cycle series in chapters 1–4, consideration was given to the nature of families, particularly Australian families, and the concept of 'family'. The children's drawings illustrated in Figure 5.2 highlight some of the different ways in which 9-year-old Australian children see their families. One question that arises concerns that of how children and adolescents see families. In the first edition of this book, a small number of children were asked 'What is a family?' Their answers included the following:

'Someone who looks after you' (Jac, 7 yrs)

'It is somewhere where you are born and grow up' (Katie, 8 yrs)

'A group of people who care for each other' (Sarah, 11 yrs)

Developmental trends

The research of Piaget (1929), Gilbey and Pederson (1982), and Borduin et al. (1990) has identified clear age trends indicating that 'children's understanding of the concept of the family undergoes important developmental changes during the elementary school years' (Borduin et al. 1990, p. 41). That is, younger children use very concrete terms to define the family, such as in terms of the house in which they all live, while older children recognise the importance of genetic relationships in defining a family, whether or not they are all living in the same house.

Sex differences

The findings of Borduin et al. (1990) also suggest that younger girls have a more sophisticated understanding of the family than do younger boys. One interpretation of this finding is that such differences already indicate differing sex-role orientations, (see chapter 18), with girls being socialised differently from boys.

In summary, Borduin et al. (1990, p. 42) make the important point that children's concept of the family '…may influence how they interpret family disruption and resultant changes in family structure'. Thus, the distress children experience during divorce (see chapter 17) may vary with the level of sophistication of the child's understanding of the concept of family.

Figure 5.2 How some 9-year-olds understand the family

intertwined. For example, Trevarthen (1977) has noted that human communication is responsive to information about subjective elements such as feelings – that is, the expression of emotion is closely related to the development of the communicative act itself. Emotional behaviour provides important information to the interactants concerning the nature of the developing relationship. 'Thus surprise, humour, disdain, disbelief, pride, annoyance, approval, sadness, anger and so forth qualify what is taking place in the actual communication' (Trevarthen 1977, p. 233).

Chapter summary

There is no doubt that the birth of a child is a very significant event in the life-course of a family. It represents a significant transition point in the life-cycle impacting on the immediate and extended family. Research presented in this chapter has pointed to the effects of cultural and social class expectations on the behaviour of the parents.

Discussion questions

1   Outline the basic processes involved in conception, describing as you do the terms 'fertilisation', 'blastocyst' and 'placenta'.
2   How safe is the intra-uterine environment?
3   What is meant by the term 'engrossment'?
4   How does the hospital environment welcome or alienate parents?
5   What does 'reflex' mean and what purpose do reflexes serve?

Activities

See your CD

1   Contact a number of groups or classrooms of children and ask them to respond to the question 'What is a family?'. Also ask them to draw a family for you. Discuss the replies in the light of information provided in The Family Life-Cycle: 5 in this chapter.
2   Complete the 'Self Review Quiz' on the CD-ROM to assess your understanding of the content presented in this section. Use your quiz results as a basis for reviewing any chapter content about which you are uncertain.

Selected websites

Child Adolescent Psychological and Educational Resources <www.caper.com.au>
Yale University School of Medicine Center for Child Study <www.info.med.yale.edu/chldstdy>

Infertility <www.ivf.com>

Stillbirth and neonatal death support <sandsnsw.org.au>

Infancy

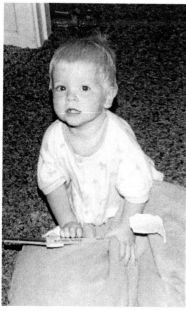

3

Daniel aged 14 months

Daniel aged 4 years

Daniel aged 6 years

6 Physical Development in Infancy

. . . He Sorted Out Those of the Largest Size
'I weep for you', the Walrus said
'I deeply sympathise'.
With sobs and tears he sorted out
Those of the largest size,
Holding his handkerchief
Before his streaming eyes.'

Lewis Carroll, Through the Looking Glass

CHAPTER OUTLINE

KEY TERMS AND CONCEPTS

- Growth
- Development
- Norms
- Low birth weight
- Fine motor development
- Gross motor development
- Maturational theory
- Genogram

Introduction

Everyone understands in a general way what is meant by growth. You only have to walk into a nursery or school and see the wall charts that enable parents or teachers to assess the heights of children. Listening in on any conversation between parents and grandparents about a grandchild will also generally reveal a reference to the child's growth at some point.

The *British Medical Dictionary* defines **growth** as 'The progressive development of a living being or part of an organism from its earliest stage to maturation including the attendant increase in size'. In the same dictionary, the definition of 'development' is: 'The series of changes by which the individual embryo becomes a mature organism'. 'Growth' tends to have the restricted meaning of anatomical and physical change. That is, it refers to an increase in size. Its progression is mainly structural and can be measured or quantified. **Development** refers to an increase in complexity involving both structure and function and, as such, covers the emergence of psychological attributes, ideas and understanding, as well as the acquisition of motor and sensory skills.

In this chapter consideration will be given to the importance of the study of physical growth, and the nature of infant motor development. The Family Life-cycle: 6 outlines the nature of courtship and marriage.

growth
progressive anatomical and physical changes of a living being; compare development.

development
increase in functional complexity of an organism—compare growth; changes that take into account the effect of experience on an individual—compare maturation.

The principles of normal development

Eshkevari is an Adelaide psychiatrist who, following in the steps of writers such as Tiedemann (1787), Darwin (1877) and Piaget (1950), to name but a few, has used a single case study method to trace the development of his own child, Arastoo, born in Iran. In describing the nature of normal development, Eshkevari (1988) and Illingworth (1987) have identified the following principles:

- Development begins at conception, continuing in utero, with birth being just one more developmental step.
- The sequence of development is the same for all children, although the rate can vary from child to child. As Eshkevari (1988, p. 15) notes, 'Arastoo walked a little later than the average, namely at the age of 15 months and 17 days'.
- Development is intimately related to the central nervous system's maturation (for example, a child cannot sit up until the central nervous system is mature enough).
- Development proceeds from the general to the specific (for example, with excitement an infant's whole body moves while an older child may simply smile).
- Development is directional, starting from the head down: such that head control precedes walking.
- Certain reflexes such as walking must disappear before voluntary movement can occur.

In chapter 2 consideration was given to the nature of 'development' and the reader is referred to this section for a review of the concept.

The study of physical growth

One way to appreciate the importance of physical growth for the individual is to consider how different your own life might have been had you been physically different from what you are, however slightly. For example, what difference would it have made to your life if you had been taller or shorter, or fatter or thinner than you are now? How might your life have changed if physically you had matured faster or slower than you did?

There are a number of reasons why the study of physical growth is important.

1   New experience. We have seen in chapter 5 that physical growth occurs in an orderly fashion. As new abilities are acquired, such as the ability to sit up, the opportunity for new experiences arises.
2   Personal experience. The pace and nature of physical growth can have an impact on the sense of self (self-concept). For example, consider the possible impact of being below average height or being 'clumsy' (see chapter 12). In these instances, a child might be the last picked for team sports at school or be subject to comments such as 'He can't help it, he's just clumsy!' How might the self-concept of such a child differ from the self-concept of a child developing more 'normally'?
3   Other experience. A child's physical growth and development helps to shape the reactions of others to them, as is clear from the way parents or teachers talk about children. For example, a well-developed, physically capable child may generate expectations of sporting prowess.

Charting children's growth

In 1835 the Belgian astronomer and statistician Quetelet published the first carefully collected and analysed set of normative data on the heights of children of each sex from birth to 18 years (Eichhorn 1979). The first norms for British children (heights) were published by the Anthropological Committee of the British Association for the Advancement of Science in 1880. By the 1930s. tables and charts relating to **norms** of growth for British and American children were appearing with increasing frequency.

Arnold Gesell (See Trends and Issues) has provided us with a detailed and elegant account of human development. Greatly influenced by the writing of Charles Darwin, Gesell described human development as a unitary process that could be studied using scientific methods and detailed observations, including filming. Thelen (2000, p. 386) has noted:

norms
accepted standards against which individual performance can be compared.

Arnold Gesell and maturational theory

Drawing on the work of the nineteenth century evolutionist, Charles Darwin, who emphasised the maturational component of development (Darwin 1959), Arnold Gesell did much to advance the charting of the growth of children. Working in the United States during the early part of the twentieth century, Gesell embarked on the task of mapping the foetal, infant and early childhood behaviour of thousands of children. In the course of his work, he established and standardised stages of development. His maturational view of development emphasised the natural unfolding of patterns of growth, which he believed were largely predetermined and self-regulated. His theory emphasised the 'lawfulness' of growth and consequently the ability to predict: 'Behaviour is rooted in the brain and in the sensory and motor systems. The timing, smoothness and integration at one stage foretell behaviour at a later age' (Gesell, cited in Knobloch & Pasamanick 1974, p. 3). Gesell was well aware, however, of the multitude of factors impinging on a child that make accurate prediction a risky venture.

Gesell identified four major fields of behaviour:

1 *Adaptive.* The most important field concerns the organisational component of behaviour, such as coordinating eye movements and reaching with the hand. Adaptive behaviour is the forerunner of later 'intelligence'.

2 *Gross and fine motor behaviour.* This includes sitting, standing, walking, using fingers and manipulating objects.

3 *Language.* Gesell maintained that language also assumes distinct behaviour patterns and unfolds in a predetermined fashion. For example, inarticulate vocalisations precede words (see Figure 6.1).

4 *Personal and social behaviour.* This incorporates the reaction of children to the social world in which they live. However, according to Gesell, personal and social behaviour patterns are determined by intrinsic growth patterns. Thus, while toileting is a cultural requirement shaped by social demands, the child's attainment of bladder and bowel control depends upon neuromotor maturation.

According to Gesell, then, 'a child's development proceeds stage by stage in orderly sequence, each stage representing a degree or level of maturity' (cited in Knobloch & Pasamanick 1974, p. 7). However, while the view that body growth is strongly influenced by physical maturation is generally accepted, the assertion that other important aspects of human development, such as personality, are similarly determined has attracted and continues to attract criticism.

The practical importance of Gesell's theory was to act as a counterweight to the popular notions of behaviorism that were fashionable at the time. To parents who were told that infants were totally shaped by their environments, Gesell offered a different view, one of an autonomous unfolding of potential.

Today, quite accurate charts and figures are available tracing an individual's growth from birth to maturity. The foundations for this information were established during the 1920s and '30s. Gesell and colleagues carefully observed and documented age norms for over 500 infants; for example, 41 stages in sitting behaviour were identified using observation techniques including photography (Gesell & Thompson 1934; 1938).

The normal probability curve for charting growth is the bell-shaped curve (see chapter 2 and Figure 2.2). Generally speaking, the assessment of very large numbers of individuals in terms of characteristics such as height, weight or intelligence will find the distribution of scores represented as a normal curve. To draw a normal curve we need to know the mean and standard deviation of a particular population. Properties of the normal curve include:

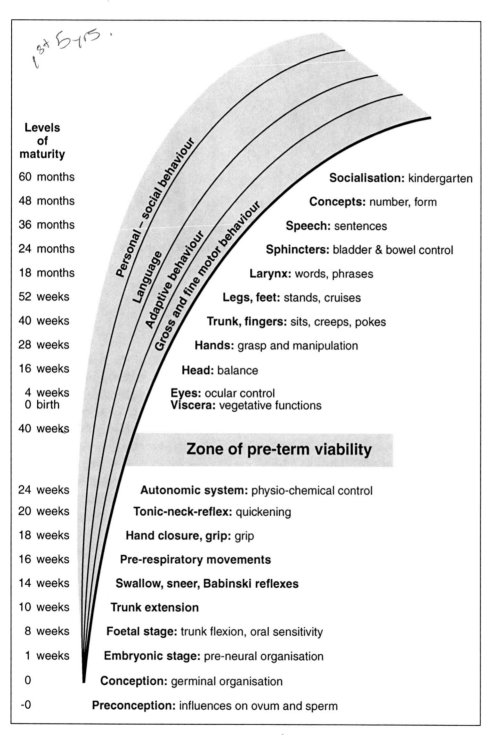

Levels of maturity

60 months	
48 months	
36 months	
24 months	
18 months	
52 weeks	
40 weeks	
28 weeks	
16 weeks	
4 weeks	
0 birth	
40 weeks	

Socialisation: kindergarten
Concepts: number, form
Speech: sentences
Sphincters: bladder & bowel control
Larynx: words, phrases
Legs, feet: stands, cruises
Trunk, fingers: sits, creeps, pokes
Hands: grasp and manipulation
Head: balance
Eyes: ocular control
Viscera: vegetative functions

Zone of pre-term viability

24 weeks	**Autonomic system:** physio-chemical control
20 weeks	**Tonic-neck-reflex:** quickening
18 weeks	**Hand closure, grip:** grip
16 weeks	**Pre-respiratory movements**
14 weeks	**Swallow, sneer, Babinski reflexes**
10 weeks	**Trunk extension**
8 weeks	**Foetal stage:** trunk flexion, oral sensitivity
1 weeks	**Embryonic stage:** pre-neural organisation
0	**Conception:** germinal organisation
-0	**Preconception:** influences on ovum and sperm

Figure 6.1 The development of behaviour
Source: Knobloch and Pasamanick 1974

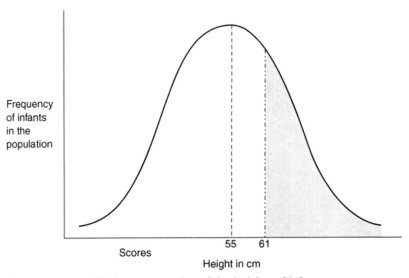

Figure 6.2 A graphical representation of the heights of infants

1   unimodality (one curve);
2   symmetry (one side the same as another);
3   certain mathematical properties.

Using a normal curve we can calculate, for example, the mean height for a specific group of children and the standard deviation. With this information we can calculate what proportion of scores fall within particular limits. Thus, suppose we know the heights of infants in their first year are normally distributed with a mean of 55 centimetres and a standard deviation of 6 centimetres. We can then discover whether a child is tall or short for his or her age and what proportion of children will be 61 centimetres high or taller. Thus, a line one standard deviation above the mean cuts off the top 15.9 per cent of the scores. For any number of standard deviations above the mean it is possible to specify what proportion of scores fall above this value and what proportion falls below it (see Figure 6.2).

Growth in height

The human ovum is just visible to the naked eye. At birth some nine months later, the neonate is about 50 centimetres in length (5000 times the size of the ovum). By adulthood a person may reach a height of up to about 175 centimetres, which is approximately three and a half times the height of a baby.

Growth in height is far from uniform over the life span. In fact, the maximum rate of growth occurs in the fourth month of foetal life, when it is about 1.5 millimetres per day. Thereafter, the pace of growth gradually slows. In the first year after birth, body length increases by about 50 per cent to 75 centimetres and in the following year another 12 to 13 centimetres are added. The child continues to grow at about 5 to 6 centimetres per year, until adolescence when a 'growth spurt' occurs (see chapter 18).

It is not known precisely what stops growth in height. It is generally ascribed to the influence of hormones derived from the gonads. Some cold-blooded animals, such as fish, continue to grow throughout the life span but at a considerably reduced rate after maturity.

Predicting adult height

Sometimes it is desirable to predict the adult height of an individual. For example, height prediction is useful to allow the planning of intervention to avoid psychological stress in children who are excessively small for their age. Many parents know that at the age of 2 years children are approximately half of their future adult height. Unfortunately, this simple method of predicting adult height is often extremely inaccurate when it comes to understanding a particular individual's development.

Size: advantages and drawbacks

The tallest man in the world for whom there are authentic measurements was Robert Wadlow, an American, who at his death at 22 years of age measured 271 centimetres. Most such cases of giantism are due to disorders of the pituitary gland. The most famous dwarf was General Tom Thumb (102 centimetres) who was exploited by Barnum, the American theatre and circus entrepreneur.

Growth in height varies over the life span.

The advantages and disadvantages of height are frequently discussed, particularly in the world of sport. The physical drawback of being excessively tall relates to inertia and momentum, while as a rule, short people are more agile. Nonetheless, the maximum running speed is very similar for both tall and short people, although taller individuals tend to have an advantage in terms of staying power. The psychological effects of size are discussed in chapter 15.

Growth in weight

At birth, a baby weighs on average 3.4 kilograms. This is almost three thousand million times the weight of the ovum. This statistic allows us to appreciate the magnitude of the weight gain of the ovum in just nine months. However, unlike maximum height, maximum weight growth is not achieved until shortly after birth. Thereafter it eases off and, in the 20 or so years from birth to maturity, the individual's weight increases only 20 times, to reach an average adult weight (in Western cultures) of 68 kilograms (Sinclair 1985).

Weight at birth is more variable than height and appears to reflect the maternal environment more than the heredity of the child, that is the phenotype and not the genotype (Sinclair 1985). Small mothers tend to have small babies, irrespective of the size of the father. Mothers from low socioeconomic status (SES) groups have smaller babies than those from higher SES groups. Birth order is reflected in birth weight, with later-born children being heavier than first-borns. As noted in chapter 5, women who smoke tend to have smaller babies than those who do not.

Immediately after birth, a diminished intake of fluid leads to a transient loss of 5 per cent of birth weight, which is recovered in the next 10 days to two weeks. By the end of the first year, birth weight has approximately tripled and by the end of the second year it has quadrupled. The developing child's weight continues to increase annually at about 2.25 to 2.75 kilograms per year until the onset of the adolescent years and the growth spurt (see chapter 18).

Motor development

Holt (1975, p. 1) has commented that '[m]ovement is a fundamental characteristic of all living things. The observation of movement is evidence of life'. Holt goes on to note that, as the organism becomes more complex, simple movements are elaborated into more complex physical skills. For the human infant, movement begins well before birth (see chapter 5). As the foetus grows, movement gradually involves the flexing of limbs and certain automatic or reflex movements such as swallowing. Holt (1975, p. 1) observes that '[a]t birth, babies' movements are usually symmetrical and consist of alternating flexions and extensions. Their pattern, strength and frequency reflect the state of the infant'. In the first days after birth the infant's full behavioural repertoire is evident.

Medical science has made considerable advancements in the assessment of the newborn's behaviour, facilitating the identification of possible developmental abnormalities. Screening tests at birth have been designed to provide a quick and simple method of distinguishing normal infants from exceptional ones who may be in need of special care. Two commonly used screening techniques are the Apgar scoring system (Apgar 1953) (see chapter 5) and the Denver developmental screening test (Frankenburg et al. 1975).

Trends and issues

Toys and young children

In considering the question of whether toys promote children's development, we should begin by understanding something about the nature of children's play. While parents, teachers and psychologists have long studied children's play, it is surprising that we still know very little about it or the purpose that it serves. Generally though, it is broadly agreed that children find play enjoyable and that play, particularly for young children, seems to occur for its own sake.

One view of children's play is that it is an instinct and that it is preparing children for later, more adult, activities. This idea is similar to the view that young kittens in playing with a ball of string are practising their hunting skills. Another view is that children play because they have a lot of excess energy. Various types of children's play have been observed including (i) sensori-motor play, e.g. body rocking or hand-clapping; (ii) symbolic play, where children will take an object, e.g. a stick and pretend it is a rocket; (iii) construction play where children will build blocks or paint or draw; (iv) physical activity play including 'rough and tumble', games of 'chasey' and 'hide and seek'; (v) play with rules, including more organised games such as soccer, tennis.

Children could be considered to play for a number of reasons, including 'having fun', out of curiosity and a desire to know more about their world, to master and control their world and to learn.

Toys then could be considered to be a very useful adjunct to play. The argument for and against the use of toys is something like this. Arguments that toys are bad for children range from the view that the toys encourage consumerism and reinforce gender roles, to the idea that they restrict the child's use of imagination. Alternatively, it is argued that toys provide the child with manipulation skills and that they extend the child's imagination.

When I asked my three boys what kind of toys they liked I received the following responses:

Christopher, our 7-year-old, said he likes Leggo because 'you can build stuff', and he likes collecting model cars. When we watch him play with his model cars we see him counting the cars, playing 'make-believe' games with them and playing cooperative games with his friends and the cars.

Our 10-year-old boy, Nicholas, when asked the question about the kind of toys he most liked said Sony Play Station, Nintendo games, and Game Boy. His choices reflect his passionate interest in computers and his sense of mastery and control from playing computer games.

Our 13-year-old, Matthew, said he likes toys that move, such as remote controlled cars, but said he was less interested in toys than when he was younger and certainly he is now much more interested in skate-boarding and spending time with friends.

There is some consistent research evidence that when parents use toys in their interactions with their children it can benefit the child's language development.

The new generation of 'interactive toys' or 'interactive friends' varies from dolls that talk and sing to building sets which enable the construction of robots that can seek out light sources. One such toy can hear as well as talk, so he can interact with children. When his light-sensitive eyes are covered he asks 'Who has turned the lights out?'. These toys often have the appearance of being 'alive' and are often commercially sold on this basis. Strong arguments against the purchase of such toys include (i) the lack of imagination needed to bring such toys 'to life'; (ii) anxiety among young children when the toy 'dies' (breaks); (iii) reduction in the opportunity for socialisation with other children or parents.

As Thelen (2000, p. 385) has noted: 'The study of how infants and children come to control their bodies is perhaps the oldest topic in scientific developmental psychology. Yet, for many years the study of motor development lay dormant'. Now however, there has been a resurgence of interest in the topic and some very exciting research is throwing new light on how infants develop control over their bodies and is also providing new theoretical insights into child development (Lewis 2000; Thelen & Smith 1994; 1998). Thelen (2000) cites the work of the Soviet physiologist, Bernstein (1967) as providing a significant foundation for a resurgence of interest in the study of motor development.

As argued by Thelen (2000), Bernstein prompted researchers to think differently about how a body composed of hundreds of bones, muscles and joints achieves the act of coordination in order to move. Prior thinking by researchers such as Gesell had linked motor development to the maturation of the nervous system. Bernstein proposed that '. . . movements were organised as synergies, that is, a functional linking of muscles into ensembles that work together' (Thelen 2000, p. 388). As such, the brain was involved in organising relevant patterns to accomplish a motor act, such as reaching for a glass of water, and not directing individual muscles. In a further development of his ideas, Bernstein argued that the motor system is also capable of using the mechanical properties of limbs and muscles such as the '. . . elastic qualities of the muscles and the anatomical configuration of the joints' (Thelen 2000, p. 389). Taken together, Thelen (2000, p. 389) argued that 'in his writing on the development of movement, Bernstein turned the old theories on their heads. It was not he claimed, so much the nervous system instructing the muscles, as the dynamics of the movement instructing the nervous system'.

Movement can be divided into **fine** and **gross** motor activities:

> Motor activities are frequently referred to as fine and gross. The former refers to movements requiring precision and dexterity as in the manipulative tasks, the latter to movements of the entire body or major segments of the entire body as in locomotor activities. Many tasks incorporate both gross and fine motor elements, for example throwing and catching a ball (Malina 1982, p. 211).

Illustrations of the development of fine motor skills may be found in the following situations:

- an infant sitting and turning her head to look at a sound;
- a pre-schooler lacing his own shoes;
- a school-age child learning how to write.

Illustrations of the development of gross motor skills can be found in such achievements as:

- an infant pulling herself up from a lying to sitting position;
- a pre-schooler jumping over a hurdle;
- a school-aged child walking to the school bus.

fine motor
refers to movements requiring precision and dexterity, as in manipulative tasks; compare gross motor.

gross motor
refers to movements of the entire body or of major parts of the body; compare fine motor.

Fine motor development

According to Zuckerman and Frank (1983, p. 88), 'The evolution of fine motor skills increases the infant's capacity to explore and change his/her surroundings'.

First month

At first, the fixed focal length of the eyes limits the newborn's visual exploratory range. Objects far enough away to be seen are too far away to be touched. Objects close enough to be touched cannot be seen clearly. The ideal focusing distance for the newborn infant is around 30 to 45 centimetres.

Second month

The tonic neck reflex disappears. (In the asymmetrical tonic neck reflex, when the child is lying quietly with the head turned to one side, the arm on the same side is usually extended.) This enables infants to look at their hands and touch one hand with the other. The infant is also developing the ability to grasp in a voluntary fashion.

Third month

During the third month the near world comes into focus and infants begin swiping at objects with loosely fisted hands. The primitive grasp reflex of the first two or three months disappears before the voluntary grasp begins. During the first two months the infant has been exploring the world via the senses of taste, touch, smell, sight and sound. Now the groundwork is being laid for another kind of contact with it – physical participation.

Fourth month

The baby's body is now firmer and stronger. The infant can coordinate eye and head movements as well as an adult can, following an object with the eyes. Gradually the baby improves her or his ability to move the head to follow or orient herself or himself towards an object. The perfection of vision and ability to hold the head up allow some appreciation of visual space.

Fifth month

For most infants there is a rapid increase in physical development during the fifth month. At this stage babies can see clearly and can differentiate between parents, and between parents and strangers. Partial thumb opposition develops: the

Coordinating head, hand and eye movements is a real feat.

The 'sitting-up' world opens up many new experiences.

child is able to swap objects from hand to hand and can make a grasping shape with the hands in the horizontal and vertical planes of the desired object immediately before grasping it.

Sixth month

The world of the 6-month-old is a 'sitting-up' world. Now objects such as feeding bottles can be held and infants can turn their hands at the wrist, manipulate objects and reach out with one arm.

Seventh month

By the seventh month, the infant is fast becoming mobile. Thumb opposition is now complete and babies will use thumb and finger to grasp a block. They can hold an object in each hand and coordinate banging them together.

Eighth month

The infant has physically developed to the point of wanting and being able to follow parents around. Crawling is developing and infants may already be standing by holding onto furniture. Fine motor control has developed to the point of being able to use thumb and forefinger in a pincer grasp to pick up thin objects such as string.

Ninth month

By the ninth month a definite crawling style has developed. The mid-line has developed such that objects can be banged together at the mid-line of the body. Fine motor coordination may have developed to the point of being able to place one block on top of another.

Tenth month

As a 'beginning toddler', the infant can carry an object in each hand. Hand preference may appear.

Eleventh month

By this stage, babies are probably standing unsupported. Crayons can be held and used. They may be able to lift a spoon to their mouth, pull up socks or untie shoe laces.

Twelfth month

By the twelfth month the infant is ready to walk. Thumb opposition is complete and in the kitchen the infant is a whiz at taking lids off containers. Hand preference is now detectable and the infant can point with one finger and push objects.

Standing alone is quite an accomplishment.

The merits of size

J. B. S. Haldane (cited in Sinclair 1985) once calculated that the giants described by John Bunyan in *The Pilgrim's Progress* would be about 60 feet (18.2 metres) tall and would weigh about 1000 times as much as the average human being today. However, the cross-section of their bones would be only 100 times greater. Every square centimetre of bone in a giant would therefore have to support 10 times the weight borne by 1 square centimetre of bone in an average person – a level of stress that is just about the breaking point of human bone. Haldane concluded that the giants would break their thigh bones with every step they took.

Gross motor development

In the first 15 months of life, the child is also developing **gross motor** skills. As Zuckerman and Frank (1983, p. 88) note:

> [P]arents anxiously await their child's ability to sit up, crawl and walk. Three processes enable the infant to attain upright posture and the ability to move limbs across the mid-line: (1) balance of flexor and extensor tone, (2) decline of obligatory primary reflexes and (3) evolution of protective and equilibrium responses.

All in all, it is too easy to overlook or forget the effect of the unfamiliar force of gravity on the child after birth. Remember that prior to birth the foetus lives in the relatively weightless world of the mother's amniotic sac.

First month

In the first month virtually all arm, leg and hand movements are reflexive. When babies are on their backs the tonic neck reflex (fencer's position) still predominates. When held in the arms, newborns show an almost complete lack of head control.

Girls superior – yet again!

In a study by Connellan et al. (2000), the oft commented upon notion that girls are superior to boys in relation to sociability was tested with neonates with an average age of 37 hours. The authors cited the research of Hall (1985), in which girls and women show greater eye contact than boys. Research was also cited, indicating the superiority of girls in terms of social understanding (e.g. Baron-Cohen et al. 1999) and their greater facility for understanding social themes in stories (e.g. Willingham & Cole 1997).

The question raised by much of the earlier research concerned whether girls' superiority in many aspects of sociability is due to biological factors or nurturing factors such as styles of parenting. The study by Connellan et al. (2000) utilised young neonates who by definition had not been influenced by social and cultural factors. The study assessed whether there were differences in looking time between boys and girls in response to the stimulus of a face (social object) or a mobile (physical-mechanical object). 'The results showed that the male infants showed a stronger interest in the physical–mechanical mobile while the female infants showed a stronger interest in the face' (Connellan et al. 2000, p. 1130). In concluding their discussion, the authors noted that their findings were consistent with the view that '. . . sex differences cannot readily be attributed to postnatal experience, and are instead consistent with a biological cause, most likely neurogenetic, and/or neuroendocrine in nature'.

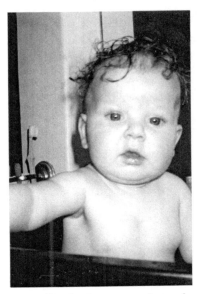

Controlling head movements is a real achievement.

Second month

At 2 months, infants may still startle spontaneously (Moro reflex). Arms and legs may cycle smoothly. When in a prone position on the stomach, infants can hold the head up for a few minutes in the mid-line. When supported while sitting, infants can keep the head erect.

Third month

By the third month, infants have developed more regular patterns of eating, sleeping and being alert. The early reflexes are fast disappearing and voluntary control is more apparent. An infant can keep the head in the mid-position when lying on the back and can hold the head up for 10 seconds or so when on the stomach. The infant can now sit up when supported.

Fourth month

The Moro reflex begins to vanish and the infant can now turn the head in all directions while seated or lying down. The 4-month-old will roll around on a blanket and can sit up with support for 10 to 15 minutes.

Fifth month

This is a very active time in terms of the baby's physical development. When lying on the stomach the infant can lift the head and chest off the floor and can bring the feet to the mouth. The 5-month-old may roll from stomach to back and locomote by rocking or rolling. The infant can sit unsupported (30 minutes) and is able to hold the head upright and steady when pulled up to a sitting position.

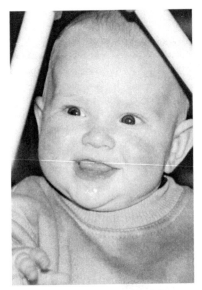

Sitting up opens up new possibilities for exploration.

Sixth month

The ability to sit up opens up new possibilities for exploration. The baby may now be found on all fours in a 'crouch' position, can locomote by creeping, can sit with slight support and stand with substantial support.

Seventh month

During the seventh month, major changes occur in the baby's gross motor development. The baby's creeping improves noticeably with the ability to push up onto the hands and knees and rock back and forth. The baby may coordinate creeping with holding an object and often sits unaided.

Eighth month

The baby is now in almost perpetual motion. Locomotion may be by means of sitting and 'bouncing' backwards or forwards.

Ninth month

The 9-month-old can crawl while carrying an object, can turn around and crawl up stairs. When held by one hand the infant may stand alone briefly. The infant can 'cruise' or side-step along furniture.

Tenth month

At 10 months of age the baby is often crawling on straightened limbs and may stand up by straightening the limbs and pushing up.

Eleventh month

During this month the infant may stand alone and is in control of body when standing upright. The baby may climb upstairs.

Twelfth month

By their first birthday most babies are ready to walk if they are not already doing so. They can stand by flexing the knees and pushing up from the squatting position. They are also able to lower themselves from a standing to a sitting position 'gracefully'.

Physical development – an emerging order

The previous detailed account of infants' gross and fine motor development should sensitise us to a number of features associated with the concept of development elaborated on earlier in this chapter. Certainly, the preceding descriptive account captures the sequential, and directional nature of development. However, in terms of contemporary understanding of the nature of 'development' the description is to be found wanting.

As further elaborated upon in chapter 8, contemporary views of infancy emphasise the active role the child plays in shaping their own development. As noted by Thelen (2000), research by Eleanor Gibson (1969, 1988) and James Gibson (1966) has presented the child as a very active being '... continually coordinating their movements with concurrent perceptual information to learn how to maintain balance, reach for appropriate objects, and locomote across various surfaces and terrains' (Gibson 1988).

Thelen (2000) has identified a number of further significant understandings which have informed our current understanding of a child's physical development.

In the first instance Thelen draws attention to the interaction between the child's perception of the world and their action in it. The idea that there is some entity in the individual's head that provides a representation of the world 'out there' and makes decisions for action, is seriously challenged by current thinking regarding development. As Thelen (2000, p. 390) notes: '[P]erception is essential for movement, but movement also informs perception ... indeed, we can even cast movement as a form of perception, a way of knowing the world by moving in it'. Secondly, research indicates that from the earliest moments following birth the infant appears 'self aware', in terms of the awareness of the relationship between their visual perception of their body (arms and legs) and their sense of them. Finally, Gibson (1988) has drawn our attention to the role of the infant's active exploration of the world for developmental change.

Dynamic systems theory and physical development

As described in chapters 2 and 3, Systems thinking is not 'new', with the systemic ideas of Piaget (1952) and Vygotsky (1965) being readily cited as evidence. In relation to physical and motor development, dynamic systems theory has a number of important implications (Thelen 2000). Firstly, a systems view emphasises that every movement has implications for the 'whole' system such that 'behavior is not "hard-wired" into the brain, but emerges "online" in the light of the person's available structure, energetic resources, and

The family life-cycle: 6

Courtship and marriage

Aravis also had many quarrels (and I'm afraid, even fights) with Cor, but they always made it up again: so that years later when they were grown up, they were so used to quarrelling and making it up again that they got married so as to go on doing it more conveniently.

C. S. Lewis, *The Horse and his Boy* (1954, p. 188)

It is difficult to determine when marriage was formally recognised, but certainly the concept of family is thousands of years old. In Australian Aboriginal tribes, whose culture is well over 40 000 years old, the concept of family has been a powerful force. In the past, each tribe was made up of a number of family groups. A child's most immediate family was made up of mother, father, father's wives and children, and grandparents. As noted by Mattingly and Hampton (1988, p. 148),

In traditional society a marriage was arranged strictly in accordance with kinship groupings. It involved important social and economic responsibilities, which maintained the entity and strength of the group.

Mattingly and Hampton (1988) also write that Goonya marriage tradition was enforced with Aborigines as a means of breaking down traditional patterns of family life among the Nungas. ('Goonya' is the Aboriginal name for original European settlers

derived from the Ngarinyeri word 'grinkari' for corpse or pink skin and the Narungga word 'koonya', meaning excrement. 'Nunga' is derived from Pitjantjatjara and Adynyamathanha words for themselves, Anangu and Yura.)

In Western societies, marriage typically involves some 'free choice' and people usually marry for love. Lieberman (1982) has emphasised that marriage occurs as part of the normal family life-cycle. At this point it is important to note that most Australian children live with both natural parents but in an increasing number of families the parents live in de facto relationships. Generally speaking though, marriage precedes the development of a new nuclear family and the potential expansion into the extended family; that is, the family of the spouse. However, as Lieberman points out in the same article, while marriage may appear to involve complete freedom of choice (marrying for love), the reality is that the choice of marital partner is somewhat limited. Factors that narrow marital choice include social, ethnic, geographic and religious considerations. Thus, it is likely that a person will marry another person who lives within close geographic proximity and from a similar social, religious and ethnic background.

Apart from these immediate factors constraining our choice of partners, research has identified various features that cross generations (we are born and raised in families that may be composed of three to four generations). Lieberman (1982) has suggested that our choice of marital partner may be influenced by a memory or image of a grand-parent, or favourite aunt or uncle. The timing of a marriage may also be influenced by the recent death of a loved relative, for whom the marriage partner acts as a replacement. The choice of a partner may also be affected by parental opinion, whether favourable or not. For example, both families may welcome their respective son- or daughter-in-law into the family, and thus encourage the marriage. On the other hand, parental opposition may only serve to make the couple more determined to marry.

Researchers have identified important life tasks that are accomplished through marriage as part of the life-cycle. Rapoport (1963) has identified three main tasks involved in preparation for marriage:

1 preparing for the role of wife or husband;
2 disengaging from relationships that would compete with the new marital bond: for example, loosening of family ties;
3 integrating aspects of previous lifestyle behaviour into the newly formed marital relationship.

In terms of the interpersonal relationship, Rapoport (1963) believes that in marriage the couple has the following tasks to complete:

1 establishing a couple identity;
2 sexual adjustment during the engagement period;
3 developing a satisfactory communication style;
4 developing a satisfactory relationship with in-laws;
5 developing a satisfactory relationship with friends;
6 developing a satisfactory relationship with work;
7 developing a decision-making process;
8 planning for the wedding, honeymoon and early months of married life.

Mapping family development

One way to represent the development of a family through the generations graphically is with a genogram. This is widely used by clinicians as an assessment tool to study family members and their relationships over several generations, but it is also potentially valuable for researching the characteristics of families (McGoldrick & Gerson 1985).

Basically a genogram provides a simple and graphic format for drawing a family tree that records information about family members and their relationships over at least three generations (McGoldrick & Gerson 1985). There is no generally accepted way

to construct a genogram but the symbols shown in Figure 6.3 are sometimes used.

McGoldrick and Gerson (1985) have identified six categories of information provided by a genogram:

1 *Family structure*. Who is currently in the household.
2 *Life-cycle fit*. Examination of dates and ages enables it to be determined whether life-cycle events are occurring within a normative range.
3 Pattern repetition through several generations. Family events are often repeated from one generation to another, such as divorce. Recognising such patterns may help a family to avoid them.
4 *Life events and family functioning*. The dates of critical life events such as the birth of a child can alert a family to changes in family functioning.
5 *Relational patterns*. A genogram can help to identify patterns in a family such as who is closest to whom.
6 *Family balance and imbalance*. A genogram can help to identify balance or imbalance in family structure, roles and resources: for example, do the oldest children help the youngest?

Genograms have been used to provide some fascinating insights into the lives of psychologists such as Sigmund Freud, Carl Jung, and Harry Stack Sullivan (McGoldrick & Gerson 1985; Reder 1989). Reder (1989, p. 98) writes:

I have outlined significant events in the story of the Freud family which may well have sensitised Sigmund Freud to the creative discoveries that he made. It is also possible to understand how family influences could have produced blind-spots and distortions in his theorising.

In the genogram of the Freud family shown in Figure 6.4, the lines represent the individuals in the family in 1896. As McGoldrick and Gerson note, 1896 was a critical period in the life of the Freud family when Freud's father died and his sister-in-law married into the family. Freud believed that the loss of a father was a significant event in a man's life (McGoldrick & Gerson). Just prior to this time (1895), Freud's last child (Anna, later to become an eminent psychoanalyst in her own right) was born. In the context of the family life-cycle, these critical events are often associated with increased vulnerability. It was around this time that Freud published his first analytic paper and began his time of self-analysis (McGoldrick & Gerson 1985).

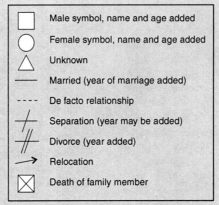

Figure 6.3 Symbols used in a genogram

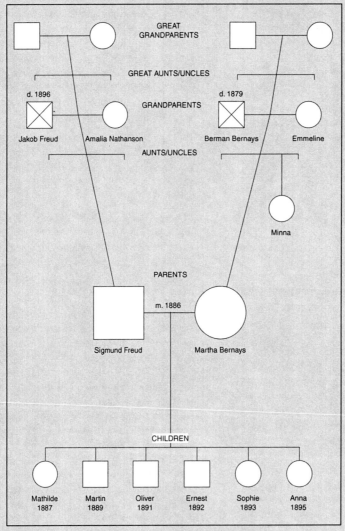

Figure 6.4 A genogram of the Freud family in 1896
Source: Adapted from McGoldrick and Gerson 1985

the nature of the task to be done' (p. 390). Secondly, as Thelen (2000) notes, the approach emphasises change over time rather than taking a 'snapshot' of behaviour at a particular time.

Chapter summary

Since the first edition of this text book was published in 1993 considerable advances have been made in our understanding of what constitutes 'growth' and 'development'. In particular the emergence of 'dynamic systems theory' and its constructs significantly influence how we currently understand infant development.

Discussion questions

1   Identify features of 'growth' and 'development', providing examples of each.
2   Consider how your own life has been influenced by your physical growth and share your thoughts with the group: for example, the effect of physical size on your participation in sport at school.
3   What are the key features of Gesell's maturational theory?
4   What are the implications of Thelen's (2000) for viewing the nature of infant growth and development?

Activities

Make a genogram for your own family, using the symbols shown in Figure 6.3. Working individually or in groups, use the six categories identified by McGoldrick and Gerson (1985) to explore your family's development further.

Selected websites

Child Adolescent Psychological and educational Resources <www.caper.com.au>

Kidslife – Making Parenting Easier <www.kidslife.com.au>

7 Cognitive Development in Infancy

They (grown-ups) always need to have things explained

I showed my masterpiece to the grown-ups, and asked them whether the drawing frightened them.

But they answered: 'Frighten? Why should anyone be frightened by a hat?' My drawing was not a picture of a hat. It was a picture of a boa constrictor digesting an elephant. But since the grown-ups were not able to understand it, I made another drawing: I drew the inside of the boa constrictor, so that the grown-ups could see it clearly. They always need to have things explained.

Antoine de Saint-Exupéry, The Little Prince

KEY TERMS AND CONCEPTS

- Cognition
- Structure
- Equilibrium
- Assimilation
- Accommodation
- Sensori-motor
- Circular reaction

- Object permanence
- Scaffolding
- Enactive representation
- Iconic representation
- Symbolic representation
- Perception

Introduction

In the first 18 months of life, infants are maturing not only physically but cognitively and socially as well. Sometimes their cognitive development is overshadowed by the more readily observable achievements of eye–hand co-ordination, sitting, crawling and walking. But, as noted in chapter 5, children are learning from the moment they are born and perhaps even while they are still inside the womb. After birth this learning continues in ever more complex ways.

In this chapter, consideration is given to children's cognitive development during the first 18 months of life. In a little over half a century, the science of the study of an individual's cognitive development has come a long way. As noted in chapter 1, during the 1930s, psychology was very empirical in its methodology, particularly in North America. Psychology was concerned with the observables. The notion of 'mind' and studying the 'mind' was out of the question. During the 1950s, however, some psychologists began to investigate not only a person's observable behaviour but what a person knew – how that person thought, reasoned and understood the world. In Bruner's words (1986, p. 94), 'The emphasis shifted from performance (what people did) to competence (what people knew). And this inevitably led to the question of how knowledge was represented in the mind'. Broadly speaking, the way people think, reason and perceive the world is labelled cognition.

The focus of the chapter is on two theorists who have contributed to our understanding of children's cognitive development during infancy: Piaget and Bruner. Infant perception is then described and, in The Family Life-cycle: 7, preparation for fatherhood is discussed.

Theoretical foundations: Jean Piaget

The cognitive development theory of the Swiss psychologist Jean Piaget has greatly enriched our understanding of children's development (see chapter 3). Piaget describes the first two years of life as a time of rapid growth in the child's ability to think, reason and understand the world. The picture that emerges from Piaget's description of cognitive development is one of the young infant and toddler as an active participant in the growth process. The child is an initiator and an experimenter, and cognitive growth occurs as the child interacts with the world around him or her. It is from this view of the child that Piaget's theory derives its constructivist label.

Although Piaget's theory has come under critical scrutiny recently, his developmental outline of **cognition** provides a powerful model for teachers, social workers and psychologists. Since Piaget derived much of his knowledge of infancy from watching his own children at home, his observations can be duplicated by parents and those working with children. From Piaget's voluminous writings it is apparent that the success of his work is largely due to the accuracy of his observations.

cognition
the way we know about the world through the use of thinking, reasoning, learning and remembering.

Piaget entered the field of cognitive development while working in Binet's laboratory (see chapter 10). His curiosity was aroused by the incorrect answers children gave to Binet's intelligence test items. Piaget argued that in order to understand the nature of human intelligence one must consider:

- the way people interact with their environment – their performance;
- why people perform as they do, taking into account the cognitive structures underlying their actions.

Structures

structures
in a Piagetian theory, the way a child organises his or her experience of the world.

From his **observations** of infants and children, Piaget came to believe that the coherent logical **structures** underlying children's thought differ from those underlying adult thought. Piaget used the term 'structure' to explain how the infant or child organises the world of objects or events. Each of the major periods of cognitive development – for example, the sensori-motor period – is characterised by different cognitive structures. Children's actions or thoughts are directed by their structures, which determine the extent and limits of their abilities to solve problems.

A structure is not something tangible that can be seen or measured. In Piagetian terms, in younger children (0–2 years) structures involve something children do – some activity such as manipulating, looking, reaching or sucking. In contrast, structures in older children are reflected in mental activity: for example, calling on memory, imagery, or language to plan. Thus, by virtue of memory and past experience, an older child may be able to separate a set of blocks into two piles, those made of wood and those made of plastic, or organise a group of animals into classes, such as warm-blooded and cold-blooded.

Active participation

According to Piaget, the child is an active participant in his or her cognitive development. Intellectual development occurs in invariable stages (see Table 7.1 and chapter 3), with each successive stage incorporating and extending the accomplishments of the preceding stage. Although the rate of development may vary from child to child, the stages and their sequence were considered by Piaget to be universal. Assimilation and accommodation are key elements in cognitive development:

1 **Assimilation** occurs when the child incorporates new information into existing patterns of thought and behaviour. For example, the infant will mouth and feel objects to learn about them and will fit information about them (such as their texture or shape) into ways of organising the information.
2 **Accommodation** occurs when the infant must modify an existing structure to deal with new information. For example, not all objects that are put into the mouth taste pleasant. Bread placed in the mouth may be assimilated into an existing structure of food. But when the child first encounters a carrot, initial attempts to assimilate it into the existing structure of food will

fail and the existing scheme must be modified to include carrot as a food.

Piaget believed that the process of learning is intrinsically satisfying to the infant. Moreover, the first 18 months of life represent enormous gains in the infant's intellectual development.

By actively accommodating and assimilating information from the inanimate and social world, the infant learns that objects exist when they are not perceptually present (object permanence), that events have causes and objects have uses (causality) and that one object can represent another (symbolic play) (Zuckerman & Frank 1983, p. 90).

The Sensori-motor period

During this first stage, infants are using their sensory systems and motor activity to help them acquire knowledge about the world. According to Piaget, children's knowledge about the world results from their interaction with the world. The first stage is divided into six substages.

The young infant relates to the world through the five senses.

Substage 1: Modification of reflexes (0–1 month)

Reflexes are important at this first stage of sensori-motor development. Infants use reflexes such as sucking to assimilate their experience of the world. Through astute observations of his own children, Piaget realised that during the first month of life a reflex, such as sucking, is modified.

Table 7.1 The sensori-motor period is the first of Piaget's stages of cognitive development

Stage	Age	Abilities
Sensori-motor period	0–2 years	Use of five senses to relate to the world
Substage 1	0–1 month	Modification of reflexes
Substage 2	1–4 months	Primary circular reactions
Substage 3	4–8 months	Secondary circular functions
Substage 4	8–12 months	Coordination of secondary reactions: attainment of object permanence
Substage 5	12–18 months	Tertiary circular reactions
Substage 6	18–24 months	Representational thought
Pre-operational period	2–7 years	Language and symbolism
Concrete operations period	7–11 years	Can apply simple logic to solve problems
Formal operations period	11+ years	Abstract reasoning

The day after birth Laurent seized the nipple with his lips without having to have it held in his mouth. He immediately seeks the breast when it escapes him as a result of some movement (Piaget 1952, p. 25).

Thus, to use a Piagetian concept, infants accommodate their behaviour to new situations, enabling them to suck more vigorously for milk while rejecting non-food substances. The reflex becomes more efficient and more voluntary as infants learn by sucking on objects and then choose whether to suck or not.

Not all reflexes change in the sensori-motor period. The constriction of the pupil in the eye to bright light, for instance, remains virtually unchanged throughout life. Piaget believed that the newborn is an active and dynamic individual who reaches out to the environment for sensory experience and gratification. The use of existing structures (such as reflexes) and the accommodation to the world leads to increasingly more complex adaptive behaviour and the next stage of sensori-motor development.

Substage 2: Primary circular reactions (1–4 months)

circular reactions
any behaviour that
the infant repeats.

During this stage, according to Piaget, the infant experiments with repetitive movements, or primary **circular reactions**. For example, a baby finds having her thumb in her mouth a pleasant sensation; if the thumb falls out she will try to put it back in her mouth. The notion of primary is related to the idea that the interesting activity involves only the infant's own body. Repetition is a key element of this stage. When his daughter was 1 month old, Piaget observed:

Lucienne plays with her tongue, passing it over her lower lip and licking her lips increasingly. Observation is made of the existence of a habit acquired a certain number of days previous. The behaviour is extended to sucking the thumb and beyond (Piaget 1952, p. 50).

From the third month on, the infant becomes increasingly curious about the more distant social and physical world. During this time the child will endeavour to repeat pleasurable sounds, such as the sound produced by hitting a rattle suspended over the cot.

Substage 3: Secondary circular reactions (4–8 months)

In this third stage, infants are still repeating primary circular reactions (that is, repeating interesting events occurring by chance), but now the repetitions act on the world external to the child's body.

After reproducing the interesting results discovered by chance on his own body, the child tries sooner or later to conserve also those which he obtains when his actions bear on the external environment (Piaget 1952, p. 164).

One of Piaget's observations of his daughter, Jacqueline, provides an illustration of his argument.

She is presented with a doll suspended from the string which connects the hood to the handle of the bassinet. In grasping this doll she shakes the bassinet hood:

she immediately notices this effect and begins again at least twenty times in succession, more and more violently while watching the shaken hood laughingly (Piaget 1952, p. 164).

Substage 4: Coordination of secondary reactions (8–12 months)

During this stage, infants are coordinating two or more previously acquired schemata to attain a certain goal. The infant is now able to generalise visual, motor and tactile schemata to reach certain objectives. For example, Piaget (1952) described Laurent reaching for a matchbox in front of which Piaget held a pillow. His son pushed the pillow out of the way to grab the matchbox, a movement that needed the coordination of striking and grabbing schemata.

A feature of this stage is the attainment of **object permanence**. Before stage 4, out of sight is out of mind, such that if an object is hidden from view the infant will not continue to look for it. Thus, during earlier months if a toy that the infant has been playing with is then hidden by placing a cloth over it, the infant will not search for the toy, even if it is within reach. In attaining object permanence at stage 4, the infant becomes capable of searching for an object that has disappeared. To illustrate this point, Piaget would hide an object such as his watch behind a screen or under a pillow. To search for the hidden object the infant must be able to conceive of the object even though it cannot be seen. When the child can conceive of an unseen object and coordinate the act of pushing aside a barrier (such as a pillow) to grab for it, then object permanence has been attained. According to Piaget, object permanence is attained in six stages, as described in Table 7.2.

object permanence
the understanding that objects can exist independently of one's interaction with them.

Young infants soon learn to manipulate aspects of their environment.

Psychologists have disagreed with Piaget about how early one can find signs of object permanence (Bower 1971), but the sequence of stages that Piaget identified has been reaffirmed in other research (e.g. Gruber et al. 1971). Perhaps the value of Piaget's discovery was that the child's concept of object permanence undergoes significant developmental changes during the sensori-motor period.

Substage 5: Tertiary circular reactions (12–18 months)

The term 'tertiary circular reactions' denotes that while events are still repeated the toddler has now moved to the point of actively seeking novelty: the child experiments. Tertiary circular reactions are discussed in greater detail in relation to toddler cognitive development in chapter 10.

Substage 6: Representational thought (18–24 months)

According to Piaget, representational thinking involves mental reasoning about a problem before acting. This sixth stage of the sensori-motor period is discussed in chapter 10.

Trends and issues

Parental beliefs about infant development

There is a steadily accumulating body of research regarding parental beliefs about child development (Clarke-Stewart 1998; Granger unpub.; Goodnow et al. 1984, 1985; Ninio 1988; Silverman & Dubow 1991). The Australian research described by Goodnow et al. (1984, 1985) compared the beliefs of mothers of Australian and Lebanese origin. Their findings indicate that mothers' ideas regarding major developmental achievements in infancy and child-hood, such as walking and talking, are largely influenced by cultural factors. The results indicated that, in Western cultures, mothers adopt beliefs emphasis-ing an earlier timetable of development in infancy than mothers from non-Western cultures. Moreover, mothers' beliefs apparently change little with more children and greater experience of child-rearing. A similar finding has been reported in an Australian study of Vietnamese mothers by Rosenthal and Gold (1989). Clarke-Stewart (1998), traced common themes, humans are perfectible through better child-rearing, to the United States of America's earliest establishment as a nation.

Their findings have been replicated across diverse cultures. In Israel, Ninio (1988) reports that fathers have even later expectations regarding the ages for major developmental achievements. Ninio points out that this could account for fathers' tendency to engage infants in rough and tumble play as opposed to more verbal and toy-related play, given that they consistently underestimate infants' abilities. Ninio (1988) concludes from this study that evidence suggests 'that people enter parenthood with a set of preconceived ideas about the cognitive capabilities of infants. These ideas are consolidated sometime during adolescence and later undergo very little change as a consequence of exposure to, and being able to observe closely, the actual behaviour of their own children. Rosenthal and Roer-Strier (2001) have argued that parental socialising practices are based on parents' naïve or ethnotheories of child develop-ment. The naïve theories (i.e. not informed by academic theories) '. . . reflect the culture's beliefs about how children develop towards their social roles, what influences their development, how they acquire different skills, and the roles other people play in this process' (p. 21). In their study of Israeli and Soviet mothers, they concluded that culture does indeed influence the mothers' developmental goals for their children.

Enriching early life – superbabies!

It was noted in chapter 1 that Elkind (1987) has identified 'the competent infant' as one of the contemporary images of childhood. A number of forces have combined to promote such a view. As Elkind (1974) has commented, the thrust of such ideas is to promote the period of early childhood as a critical time for intellectual growth. Such a view contends that should children be left to fun and games we run the risk of failing to help them reach their full potential. As a result, parents now buy toys and games to promote motor skills and cognitive development and to give their competent child 'the edge'. Similarly, the shelves of bookstores are crammed with self-help books designed to promote infants' and toddlers' cognitive skills.

At birth, a baby's brain contains approximately as many neurons as there are stars in our Milky Way (approximately 100 million). The brain contains also virtually all the nerve cells it will ever have. Neural activity prompted in part by sensory experience then begins to shape development. In the first years of life, the baby's brain literally produces an overabundance of connections between neurons – more than it will ever use. Strangely enough, the connections then begin to disappear, so that by middle primary school the child is left with roughly its adult quotient.

Observations of humans and experiments with animals clearly indicate that being deprived of a stimulating environment results in less than optimal brain development. But the whole debate about whether the baby comes into the world genetically programmed or whether it is the environment that stimulates development is really not the point of current scientific thinking. A newly

Table 7.2 Piaget's stages in the development of object permanence

Stage 1 (0–2 months)
Out of sight is out of mind. There is no search for objects removed from the infant's sight.

Stage 2 (2–4 months)
By 2 months the infant will continue to look at a person's empty hand after an object has been dropped from it.

Stage 3 (4–8 months)
The infant will locate a partially hidden object but if it disappears completely the infant will stop reaching for it.

Stage 4 (8–12 months)
The infant can find an object that has been hidden.

Stage 5 (12–18 months)
The toddler can reliably find objects even after multiple displacements.

Stage 6 (18+ months)
The toddler has sufficient ability to infer a hidden object's position from other clues without actually having observed the removal of the object to that position.

emerging idea highlights that even before birth the brain is capable of actively constructing the optimal conditions to promote the development of other parts of the brain. After birth, for example, infants are known to have a preference for looking at human faces over and above other stimuli. In turn, this preference aids in the development of higher-order processes in the brain's development. Now we more clearly understand that babies play a very active role in their own development. The babies' own behaviour creates their own environment, which to some extent then encourages or discourages the development of other behaviour. For example, children with an 'easy' temperament who are a 'joy' to be with 'invite' others to spend more time with them and to be more attentive to them. In turn, this 'cycle of participation' draws forth more 'inviting' behaviour from the babies and so on.

So, it is not a matter of the more stimulation the better. In fact, it appears that babies can be over-stimulated. Observant parents will note that too much stimulation will have the baby crying or turning away. It is far more important to provide sensitive parenting attuned to the developing baby's needs at any one time.

Doman's *How to Teach Your Baby to Read* (1983) is representative of 'the competent infant' image of childhood. It is based on assumptions about the nature of learning and, more particularly, the nature of children. Doman has adopted as his creed Watson's (1930) claim: 'Give me a child for the first six months of life and you can do with him what you will thereafter' (Doman 1983, p. 46). According to Doman, the child is like a computer and the human brain can be filled with knowledge. The earlier one begins the process, the better.

An alternative view to the *tabula rasa* environmental perspective invokes the Piagetian concept of 'stages' of cognitive development. Piaget, as noted in Elkind (1974), refers to what he called the 'American question'. When Piaget visited in the United States he was frequently asked whether a child's progress through the stages could be accelerated. To this query Piaget answered in the affirmative, with the qualification that the movement through stages is determined by experience and biological maturation. The child's active participation in the learning process is required, as is some readiness to move through the stages.

Reading to babies

In Western societies, where literacy is generally highly valued, a number of studies have examined both the nature of parents' reading to their infant and the outcomes of such behaviour – for example, facilitating later reading (Moon & Wells 1979). Around the child's first birthday, parents read to their child more frequently. This apparently simple activity constitutes a rather complex teaching experience for both parent and child. During reading the infant learns first of all that a book is something to look at rather than to chew or manipulate (Werner & Kaplin 1963), that there is a right way to hold the book and to turn the pages, and that (in Western societies) we read from left to right. For the parent, reading to a young child involves a wide interpretation of pictures, and often the words, if there are any, are ignored (De Loache & De Mendoza 1987).

De Loache and De Mendoza (1987) draw on Vygotsky's (1978) concept of **scaffolding** to explain how a mother skilfully acts as a competent teacher during reading. She does this by actively initiating and determining the topic, for example: 'What is Spot doing?'. As the child gets older, greater demands are made by the mother in terms of the child's responses. De Loache and De Mendoza (1987, p. 122) believe that early reading provides a 'crucial part of the social context of early cognitive development'.

scaffolding
Vygotsky's term for the way in which a mature person skilfully encourages a learner to acquire a new skill or understand a concept.

The familiarity with books can be the beginning of a life-time enjoyment of reading.

Matthew (far right) expressed an early interest in reading and had his 'favourite' books.

Matthew has developed a real love for reading over the years.

Early experience

As noted in chapter 3, a number of theorists (e.g. Freud) emphasised or drew attention to the importance of early experience in relation to human development. The significance attached to the early years of life in terms of shaping development has a long history; for example, it can be seen in phrases such as 'As the twig is bent the tree's inclined' (the English poet, Alexander Pope) or 'The child is the father of the man' (the English poet, William Wordsworth). Such common phrases entered folklore regarding child development. However, it was perhaps the writings of Sigmund Freud, based on his clinical observations, which identified that unfortunate experiences early in life can have an irreversible effect on some individuals' subsequent later development. It came to be widely believed that children are highly vulnerable in the first years of life and that they can be permanently affected by their experiences during this critical period. There is a lack of any scientific evidence to support Freudian notions of the impact of early childhood experiences on later development in a simple, direct, causal way.

The emergence of a life-span perspective in human development now casts real doubts on the idea of the first three years being a 'critical period'. It is better understood that we grow and develop all of our lives. At certain times in our lives we face important developmental tasks. For example, in infancy, acquiring a language is one such task; in early childhood learning to read and write is important; during adolescence, the task is to develop a sense of who one is; while in early adulthood, the emergence of a vocation and perhaps finding a partner is an important task; and so on.

During these life stages, certain conditions promote optimal development. For example, in the early years, good maternal and infant health, sound nourishment, love and care contribute to later development. Certainly, there is scientific evidence that for some children particular problems in early life continue into later years. However, other children are quite resilient in the face of adversity. What this suggests is that a combination of childhood experiences, parenting practices and individual child characteristics probably best account for optimal development.

As Schaffer (2000) has noted, common folk sayings such as: 'As the twig is bent the tree's inclined (A. Pope):

> ... express the belief that children at the beginning of life are more malleable than at any period later on, that initially they can absorb whatever experiences they are exposed to and retain their effects indefinitely, and that the clues to later personality formation are therefore to be found primarily in those first encounters of the child with his/her environment (p. 5).

Schaffer has identified a number of insights which recent research has provided into the effects of early childhood experience:

- the simplistic idea that children are moulded like clay is just that – simplistic!
- children are not passive beings in the development process and as such there is no direct relationship between age and the impact of experience on development;
- the effects of early experience are certainly not irreversible;
- early experience alone does not predict developmental outcome.

In summary, Schaffer (2000) has identified three phases in our thinking regarding human development and early experience:

Phase 1: This phase was characterised by 'profound pessimism' in view of the belief that victims of adversity in early life would not recover from their early negative experience. The victim '... was irreversibly marked and beyond help' (Schaffer 2000, p. 12–13).

Phase 2: The pendulum then swung to one of marked optimism and appropriate early intervention was considered to be able to undo the negative effects of early experience.

Phase 3: According to Schaffer, the current phase represents a mid position which acknowledges the impact of early experience on certain individuals while holding out the hope that the reversal of ill-effects is possible.

Infants and adding up

Researchers have noted that young infants are more interested in novel perceptual displays – e.g. blocks that differ in the number of elements present – than they are in familiar displays of elements. Young infants are capable of discriminating between small numbers (less than four elements) in both static and moving displays (e.g. Antell & Keating 1983; van Loosbroek & Smitsman 1990). So apart from discriminating between elements, what evidence is there that infants can add or subtract? Wyn (1992) tested 5-month-old infants on a simple display of dolls where an arithmetic transformation was conducted

(1 + 1 or 2–1). Wyn found that in the subtraction condition their preference was to look at two dolls, looking longer at one or two dolls when they were the incorrect results. In the addition experiment, infants looked longer at three dolls in which both the correct and incorrect results were in the correct direction (1+1=2 or 3). As a result of these experiments, Wyn concluded that young infants calculate the exact result, as well as the ordinal direction of simple arithmetic tasks, suggesting that such abilities have an innate foundation.

Recent research by Wakeley, Rivera and Langer (2000) challenges the simple notion that infants are capable of adding or subtracting. They concluded that infants' reactions to displays of adding and subtracting are variable and that numerical skills develop gradually and continuously in infancy and early childhood.

Jerome Bruner and cognitive development

The North American psychologist Jerome Bruner has written extensively on the nature of children's cognitive development. Like that of Piaget, Bruner's theory involves a series of stages. Bruner has been greatly influenced by the thinking of Piaget and the Russian psychologist, Lev Vygotsky. While Bruner's theory is similar to that of Piaget in many respects, it also differs in crucial aspects. For Bruner, language is intimately related to a child's cognitive growth. In his view, thinking would not be possible without language. Bruner (1987) has also argued that the competencies of children are greater than Piaget's theory leads us to believe. He places great emphasis on the child as a social being whose competencies 'are interwoven with the competencies of others' (Bruner 1987, p. 11).

Bruner (1966) has identified three major themes in understanding cognitive growth and the conditions that shape it.

1   The first theme relates to how humans organise and represent their experience of the world. Bruner argues that as children develop they pass through three stages or three modes of representing their world: enactive, iconic and symbolic. Each of these three modes enables the child to represent the world in unique ways (Bruner 1987).
2   A second theme in his theory relates to the impact of culture on growth. Bruner notes that cognitive growth is shaped as much 'from the outside in as the inside out' (Bruner 1966, p. 13).
3   A third major theme in Bruner's view relates to the evolutionary history of humans. Bruner believes that humans are particularly suited to adapting to their environment by social means rather than by morphological means (Bruner 1986).

enactive representation
the ability to experience the world through actions, or doing.

Enactive representation

According to Bruner (1966), the first way that infants understand their world is through their actions. The stage of **enactive representation** is equivalent to

Piaget's sensori-motor period. Bruner argues, as does Piaget, that the infant gains knowledge about the world not from mental images but rather from action. Comparing his enactive stage with Piaget's sensori-motor stage, Bruner notes that Piaget regards the 'first part in sensori-motor intelligence as one in which things are lived rather than thought' (Bruner 1966, p. 17). Bruner likens this type of intelligence to an irreversible and fixed succession of static images, each connected to an action. The child seems able to 'hold an object in mind by less and less direct manual prehension of it' (Bruner 1966, p. 17). During the enactive stage, infants can perform actions but do not know how they perform them. To this extent, Bruner agrees with Piaget that the infant's intelligence is one in which things are 'lived rather than thought' (Piaget 1954).

Iconic representation

Bruner's second stage of knowing, that of **iconic representation**, involves using a mental image or picture in the mind:

> A second stage in representation emerges when a child is finally able to represent the world to himself by an image or spatial schema that is relatively independent of action (Bruner 1966, p. 21).

The word 'iconic' comes from the word 'icon' (from the ancient Greek word for likeness or image). A mental image is a genuine cognitive representation. It is representative of a body of information but takes a different form from what it represents. Whereas enactive knowledge is knowing through doing, iconic knowledge is knowing through images or pictures.

In Bruner's (1966) view, iconic knowledge has a number of identifiable characteristics.

1   It is 'inflexible'.
2   It focuses upon small details.
3   It is self-centred in relation to having central reference to the child as an observer;
4   It is subject to distortion because of the child's needs or feelings.
5   Perception is closely tied to action or doing.
6   Perception is unsteady in terms of the young child's unsteadiness of concentration.

Bruner and Piaget disagreed about the role of iconic representation in a child's thinking. In Bruner's theory, the role of iconic knowledge is crucial to the explanation of conservation or the ability to understand that the physical attributes of objects (for example, mass) do not vary when the object's shape is changed (see chapter 10).

Symbolic representation

Bruner's third stage of knowing, **symbolic representation**, refers to the ability to represent our experience of the world by using symbols. Bruner (1966, p. 31)

iconic representation
the ability to use mental images or pictures to represent experience.

symbolic representation
ability to represent experience by using symbols.

writes: 'The idea that there is a name that goes with things and that the name is arbitrary is generally taken as the essence of symbolism'. Thus, a written sentence describing a beautiful landscape does not look like a landscape, whereas a picture of a landscape looks like a landscape. The landscape is symbolised in the language describing it. In Bruner's (1966) theory, symbolic representation is enhanced through language acquisition in particular. Without the ability to symbolise, the child will grow into adulthood dependent upon the enactive and iconic modes of representing and organising knowledge of the world.

Perception

Perception is defined (in part) by *The Macquarie Dictionary* as '1. the action or faculty of perceiving; cognition; a taking cognisance, as of a sensible object. 2. an immediate or intuitive recognition, as of a moral or aesthetic quality'. Not so very long ago it was believed that the baby's perceptual world was bare of meaning (see Bower 1977). If this were so, as psychologist William James notes, the baby's world would indeed be a 'blooming, buzzing confusion' (Vernon 1974). Now, it is better understood that the baby enters the world prepared to pay attention to changes using the various sensory modalities such as sight, hearing, taste and smell (Kagan et al. 1978).

The physical senses

Vision

Of all the senses, we understand most about the baby's visual system, possibly because it is the easiest to study. That is, the baby indicates attention by looking at the object, ceasing some other activity or changing the level of intensity of activity. Another procedure for testing visual capabilities is to expose the baby repeatedly to an event. For example, when a child is exposed repeatedly (say, 15 times) to a particular pattern of lines, the child's attention will wane in the course of **habituation**. If the infant is subsequently presented with a slightly different pattern of lines and shows a change in looking pattern (dishabituation), we assume that the infant has detected the events that were altered in the second presentation. The various refinements of these methods have been well described by the Australian researchers Day and McKenzie (1985).

Since Fantz (1963) demonstrated that babies could distinguish between visually presented patterns, a great deal of research on infant visual perception has been undertaken. It is now clearly established that the baby's initial visual experience is three-dimensional (Bower 1977; Day & McKenzie 1985). That is, infants are able to perceive the position of an object in three-dimensional space as well as changes to its position in space. In relation to wave-length, infants apparently perceive the categories of blue, green, yellow and red in the same way as adults do (Kagan et al. 1978). Infants are attracted to curvature and will look longer at curved than linear patterns (Kagan et al. 1978). Schaffer

habituation
the eventual disappearance of a response following repeated presentation of a stimulus.

(1977) has observed that, on the basis of research evidence, if we were to design an object specifically to capture an infant's attention it would be a human being. In particular, infants are fascinated by human faces and the eyes are a special source of attraction (Schaffer 1977).

Hearing

The monitoring of heart rate or sucking on a nipple shows that babies can differentiate sound to an impressive degree. Within the first weeks of life, they can discriminate the loudness and pitch of sound and identify the source of the sound (Schaffer 1977). Wertheimer (1962) studied infants' auditory abilities in the first seconds after birth and found they could distinguish whether a sound source was ahead of them or not. Recent research has served to emphasise the sophisticated nature of infants' hearing abilities (see Clifton et al. 1991a).

Smell

Babies show preferences for certain smells (Bower 1977). They can identify the source of an odour soon after birth and turn towards it or away from it, depending on whether they find it pleasant or not.

Taste

Like most adults, babies prefer sweet substances (Bower 1977).

Sensory coordination

We are only just beginning to appreciate the nature of the sensory capacities of the young baby. As Kagan et al. (1978, p. 63) note:

> The very young infant seems prepared to orient to fundamental dimensions in the external world. Contour, movement, concentricity, curvilinearity, and colour have a claim on his attention, especially when each represents an alteration in the immediate visual field.

Moreover, the perceptual competencies of the very young baby extend to the relatively sophisticated coordination of the various sensory modalities.

In Wertheimer's (1962) study of auditory perception, the significant component was auditory–visual coordination. Bower (1977) described an experiment in which a baby could see his mother through soundproof glass but hear her voice only via two stereo speakers. The sound balance on the stereo was adjusted so that the voice sometimes appeared to come from the mother's mouth and sometimes not. If the heard voice and seen mouth do not coincide, very young infants 'manifest surprise and upset, indicating auditory localisation, auditory–visual coordination and more surprising, an expectation that voices will come from mouths' (Bower 1975, p. 115).

In a recent review of research, Haith (1990) notes that early research into infant sensory capabilities was in response to simple questions such as 'When do babies first see?', 'What are they capable of hearing?' or 'What colours do they prefer?'. Criticising the research into infant sensory capabilities, Haith comments that such simple questions generated rather simple cause-and-effect experimental designs calculated to assess the infant's response to single discrete stimuli, for example, a sound. Such an outlook was quite consistent with the prevailing stimulus response psychology of the time. Psychology and the study of infant sensory capabilities has moved beyond the stimulus–response outlook to a better understanding that 'this creature is actively processing whatever lies within its visual province and even looks for more, rather than simply choosing one stimulus over another' (Haith 1990, p. 15).

The family life-cycle: 7

Preparing for fatherhood

In preparing for parenthood, a couple is about to take on important new roles, which represent a significant step in the family life-cycle. Before becoming parents, many couples may have had some experience of caring for a baby, but this experience in no way compares to the intensity of coping with an infant totally dependent upon them.

In reported South Australian research, interviews with 114 Adelaide couples who became parents for the first time reveal that the 'happy' event is not without its drawbacks, even with a planned baby (Baum 1988). Preliminary findings from the research indicate that becoming a parent for the first time is stressful. Stressors include tiredness, financial strain, less time for oneself and the primary relationship, and less spontaneity in one's life. Interestingly, little attention has been given to the men's views on impending fatherhood.

Reasons for fatherhood

In a study of British men's reasons for wanting to become parents, Owens (1982) found that they believed that:

- wanting to have children was natural;
- children would be a source of companionship; for example, they could be involved in sport with a boy and a daughter would be a companion for their wives.
- having children would give them a greater sense of 'family'.

It is interesting that as late as 1982 men should hold such stereotypic views as reasons for wanting children (see chapter 17 on sex-role stereotyping).

The role of the father

Some idea of the role of the father in parenting can be gleaned from relevant psychological theory and from alternative sources such as child-care literature and surveys.

Psychoanalytic theory. In Freud's description of the Oedipus complex in relation to sex-role development (see chapter 3), the father is a role model, but Freudian theory gives minimal indication of the father's role as a parent.

Post-Freudian theory. Prominent post-Freudian authorities such as J. Bowlby (1951) and W. Winnicott (1957) continued to emphasise the mother's role in parenting. It appears from their writing that parenting was certainly not viewed as a joint venture at the time and that there were clearly delineated sex-roles. Bowlby saw the father to be of no direct importance; rather he played an indirect role by providing economic and emotional support for the mother. Winnicott encouraged mothers to appreciate the father's feelings of responsibility for the welfare of his wife and child but gave little other guidance as to the father's role. Views on the nuclear family, such as those of Bowlby and Winnicott, were well summarised by Rappoport et al. (1977, p. 87), who note that the expectation was that 'normal "mature" men will be economic providers and normal "mature" women will be house-wives and mothers'.

Child-care literature. In his first book, *Common Sense Book of Baby and Child Care* (published in 1946), Benjamin Spock expressed the view that fathers had a supportive and economic role to play but had little else to do in relation to parenting. By 1958, Spock had altered his views somewhat to advocate that the father could be involved in caregiving. He suggested, however, that there was little to be gained from trying to force the reluctant father to look after the child or children if he did not want to. Then, in the 1979 edition of his book, Spock finally recognised the equal responsibility of fathers and mothers in child-rearing.

Table 7.3 Four types of couple

Tasks	Traditional	Honeymoon	Rhetorical Sharing	Genuine Sharing
Child-care				
a. Rhetoric	Woman physiologically suited for child-care, man not	Man's employment constrains sharing	Man willing, woman seen as 'more experienced'	Man wants involvement with child
b. Practice	Woman does nearly all	Man involved with infant of 8 weeks but much less with 1-year-old	Woman's contribution increases in spite of part-time work, man's contribution may increase at 1-year-old stage	Man increases contribution as woman works part-time
c. Conflict	Mutual role acceptance	Initial acceptance; woman dissapointed at 1-year-old stage	Woman feels under stress, increasing conflict	Mutual satisfaction
Money management	Separate accounts, man gives woman housekeeping	Mostly joint accounts	Mostly joint accounts	Mostly joint accounts
Use of child-care	Not used; man ideologically opposed, woman enjoys child-care	May use family members or paid child-care	May use family members or paid child-care	May use family members or paid child-care

Source: Adapted from Baum 1990

Surveys. An Adelaide study of 58 parents (Baum 1990) identified four types of couples, grouped by behaviour and attitudes towards child-care tasks (see Table 7.3). Summarising the research findings, Baum (1990, p. 79) comments 'that the way couples divide up their home and family work is an important contemporary political issue that reflects the wider power relations between men and women'. Australian research by Russell (1983) has indicated that fathers can be competent care-givers, given the opportunity. Cultural and social factors, however, often mitigate their effective participation as parents.

An Australian Institute of Family Studies survey of 1500 Australians aged 27–44 years found that men are now participating more in child-rearing:

About 80 per cent of couples questioned agreed women did most of the housework but, surprisingly, more than half said the workload was fairly distributed because men had taken on extra parenting responsibilities. The baby-boomer generation is happier to see men developing a better relationship with their children, even if they still only take the garbage out once a week.

Men, according to the survey, are more prepared to take time off work if a child is sick.

They are also happier to take annual leave during school holidays while their partner is at work.

The Advertiser, 2 December 1991, p. 3.

Chapter summary

In reading Piaget's theory, one must keep in mind the recent criticisms that have been made and an examination of these points is made in chapter 19. Most recently the rise to prominence of dynamic systems theory (see chapter 3) has focused attention on the adequacy with which Piagetian theory is able to fully account for cognitive development. The reader is strongly referred to texts such as Thelen and Smith (1994), and Lewis (2000) for a critical examination of the central tenants of Piagetian theory. This chapter has also considered points regarding development which are still the subject of fierce debate, e.g. the impact of early experience, and concerns about accelerating children's growth and development.

Discussion questions

1   What do you understand by the term 'cognition'?
2   What is meant by the Piagetian concept of structure?
3   Describe what is meant by 'assimilation' and 'accommodation'.
4   What are the arguments for and against enriching a baby's early life?
5   Identify the main differences between the views of cognitive development of Piaget and Bruner.
6   What does research tell us about infants' perceptual capabilities?

VIEWPOINT

What is a Father?

'A person that's a man and who your mum married' Katie, 8 years

'Someone who cares for you' Sarah, 11 years

Activity

Interview a number of fathers (preferably fathers-to-be or fathers of young infants), asking them such questions as:

a   What does fatherhood mean to men in Australian society?
b   Why do men want to have children?
c   Do their feelings about having a boy differ from those about having a girl?

If you know the interviewees sufficiently well, you might ask them to elaborate on their own reasons for wanting or having a child. Compare your findings with the findings reported in this chapter.

Selected websites

The Jean Piaget Archives <www.unige.ch/piaget/presentg.htm>

Child Adolescent and Psychological Resources <www.caper.com.au>

Kidslife – Making Parenting Easier <www.kidslife.com.au>

8 Social and Emotional Development in Infancy

One Must Look with the Heart

'The men where you live', said the little prince, 'raise five thousand roses in the same garden – and they do not find in it what they are looking for'.

'They do not find it,' I replied.

'And yet what they are looking for could be found in a single rose, or in a little water'.

'Yes, that is true,' I said.

And the little prince added:

'But the eyes are blind. One must look with the heart'.

Antoine de Saint-Exupéry, The Little Prince

CHAPTER OUTLINE

KEY TERMS AND CONCEPTS

- Libido
- Cathexis
- Trust versus mistrust
- Conditioning of emotions

- Nativist
- Cognitive/constructionist
- Attachment
- Temperament

Introduction

Parents have long known, and child development researchers are coming to better understand the rich and complex emotional and social experience of the young child. Historically, researchers' understanding of the parent–infant socio-emotional relationship has undergone considerable transformation in the last century. The major changes that have taken place are:

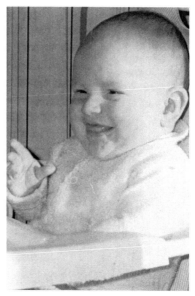

- a greater understanding of the extent of the infant's socio-emotional capabilities;
- the view of the infant as an active participant in the development of his or her capabilities;
- a greater appreciation of individual differences between infants.

In this chapter consideration will be given to various theoretical views of infant socio-emotional development, the nature of emotions, attachment and infant temperament. The Family Life-cycle: 8 discusses a woman's preparation for motherhood.

The emotional life of the young child is rich indeed.

Theoretical foundations

An examination of some basic theoretical perspectives as proposed by Freud and Erikson will provide a foundation for understanding the quantum shifts in thinking which have occurred regarding the nature of social/emotional development in infancy.

Freudian theory

Freud's theory of personality development had a major impact on initial theorising about children's socio-emotional development (see also chapter 3). As a biologist, Freud assumed that at birth infants were equipped with biological instincts that demanded satisfaction. He identified two important drives:

1 the drive for self-preservation;
2 the drive for procreation (that is, for the preservation of the species).

According to Freud, as the child strove for sensory pleasure, this was reflected in the level of psychic energy or **libido**. Freud believed that during the individual's life-span libidinous energy was concentrated in different points of the body – principally the mouth, anus and genitals, in that order (see Table 8.1).

libido
a relatively fixed quantity of energy in each individual that primarily relates to the sexual drive.

The oral stage (0–1½ years)

In Freud's theory, during the first year of life the psychic energy of the infant is focused on the mouth. Events surrounding the reduction of psychic tension and attaining pleasure relate primarily to acts of feeding, such as sucking on a nipple or bottle. In turn, the infant's attention is focused on the person

cathexis
the focusing of mental energy on a particular action or memory.

providing gratification and/or who helps reduce the level of psychic tension. From this process, which Freud named **cathexis**, the attachment between the child and the person develops.

Freud believed that too much or too little gratification of the infant's oral needs would impede progress to the next stage. The infant would then become fixated at the oral stage and the effect of this would manifest itself later in terms of psychological symptoms. Thus, those who have been fixated orally as infants may as adults derive an undue amount of pleasure from the mouth, reflected in activities such as smoking, drinking, eating or kissing. Those whose infant needs were undergratified might as adults be prone to depression, while those who were overgratified might become excessively dependent upon others.

Table 8.1 The oral stage: the first of Freud's psychosexual stages

Ages	Stages
Infancy	Oral
1½–3½ years (approx.)	Anal
3½–5½ years (approx.)	Phallic
5½–12 years (approx.)	Latency
Adolescence	Genital

The importance of Freud's theories

While Freud's theories attracted a storm of attention in his day, and still provoke heated controversy today (see chapter 3), they did serve the vitally

The early years of life are vitally important to growth and development.

important purpose of alerting parents and those working with children to the special importance of the first years of life. His ideas also served to emphasise the rich emotional life of the child in the early years. Later theorists, such as Erikson (1963), Bowlby (1969) and Ainsworth et al. (1978b) chose to build on Freud's central theme of the significance of the early years for the child's later development. However, rather than focusing on specific issues such as eating and toileting, as Freud did, these theorists have emphasised the need for infants to be cared for in a consistent, predictable and gentle manner. The theory of Erik Erikson is of particular importance in this change in emphasis.

Erikson's theory

Erikson was a student of Freud's who later broke away from Freud's view of psychosexual development (see chapter 3). He emphasised that development was a life-long process and focused much more attention than Freud on the development of the ego (psychodynamic theory). Erikson believed that the ego continued to develop throughout the life-span: it was that part of the individual that was in contact with the real world. In Erikson's view, the ego did more than simply ward off the demands of the id and superego, or conscience. It enabled individuals to respond in inventive, creative and resourceful ways to their environment.

Like Freud, however, Erikson was a stage theorist (see Table 8.2). He believed that at each stage of life the individual faced crucial issues, or a central crisis had to be dealt with before moving on to the next stage. In the course of development, individuals might fail to resolve the central issue of a stage satisfactorily and this failure might be reflected later in their adult behaviour.

Basic trust versus mistrust

According to Erikson, the first one and a half years of life essentially form an 'incorporative stage', when the infant takes in food and drink and experiences the world through the five senses. During this time, the chief issue for the infant involves the development of a sense of trust, which Erikson (1968, p. 96) described as 'an essential trustfulness of others as well as a fundamental sense of one's own trustworthiness'. Trust is achieved along a bi-polar continuum, such that the infant develops a sense neither of trust nor mistrust, but rather a feeling somewhere in between the two.

A sense of trust results from consistency and continuity of care: it develops not from the quantity of care a child receives, but from the quality of that care. A sense of trust helps the child to develop a rudimentary sense of ego, providing the foundation for 'a sense of identity which will later combine a sense of being "all right", of being oneself, and of becoming what other people will trust one will become' (Erikson 1963,

According to Erikson, a sense of 'trust' is the foundation for later development.

Table 8.2 'Basic trust versus mistrust': the first of Erikson's psychosocial stages

Ages	Stages
Infancy	Basic trust versus mistrust
1½–3½ years (approx.)	Autonomy versus shame and doubt
3½–5½ years (approx.)	Initiative versus guilt
5½–12 years (approx.)	Industry versus inferiority
Adolescence	Identity versus role confusion
Young adulthood	Intimacy versus isolation
Adulthood	Generativity versus stagnation
Maturity	Ego integrity versus despair

p. 241). A sense of mistrust results from uncertainty and unpredictability of care, and from a feeling of having lost or given up a desirable state.

The conditioning of emotions: classical conditioning

According to behavioural theory, the infant is literally a blank slate (*tabula rasa*) at birth and the environment is all important in shaping what the infant becomes (see also chapter 3). The behaviourists (Pavlov, Watson & Skinner) strongly rejected Freudian notions of personality development and the related concepts of the id, ego and superego, primarily because such concepts cannot be seen or measured. Instead, they emphasised biological drives (such as hunger and thirst). For example, when the biological drive of hunger is reduced by eating, this event becomes a primary reinforcer. A secondary reinforcer is an event such as a smile or the presence of a person associated with a primary reinforcer. A care-giver would therefore quickly acquire secondary reinforcing properties because of her or his presence when the child's biological drives are met. In the words of Mussen et al. (1974, p. 120):

> The idea that an infant's emotional ties to the mother and approach behaviours to her were based on the reduction of biological drives that dominated American theories of infancy from World War I until the early 1960s.

The role of the infant in the socialisation process

Almost a quarter of a century ago Lewis and Rosenblum (1974), in a significant publication, addressed the question of how infants affect their own development.

Early approaches to infant socialisation adopted what has been called a unidirectional model, in which emphasis was given to the parents' influence on the child's development. The child's contribution to his or her own socialisation was rarely acknowledged.

However, in 1978 an important paper by Richard Bell alerted child development researchers to consider infant socialisation as a two-way (bi-directional) process rather than a one-way influence from parent to child. Investigators are now more aware of infants' ability to participate in and influence the outcome of their socialisation. Infants are not simply passive creatures who are moulded and changed by their care-givers, any more than care-givers are unresponsive to infant behaviour. In a review of the infant's social world, Lamb (1977, p. 69) concluded that there is very little support for the belief that infants are passive recipients of socialising stimulation. Not only are there marked individual differences apparent at birth and consistent thereafter; infants are also shown to play an active role in modulating their interaction with the social world.

Recent research into infant neurobiological development has emphasised the links with plasticity in development. Contrasting with other organisms with a lower ratio of association-to-sensory fibres (Hebb 1949) resulting in a higher correlation between sensory input and behavioural output, human behaviour is less stereotyped in nature. As Heckhausen (1999, p. 8) notes '. . . the relative dearth of biologically based predetermination of behavior gives rise to a high regulatory requirement on the part of the human individual and the social system'. Lerner and Stefanis (2000, p. 476) have argued that '. . . the regulation by individuals of their relations with their complex and changing context is the process involved in successful development across life' (Baltes 1997; Baltes & Baltes 1990; Freund & Baltes 1998). As noted in chapter 3, contemporary theoretical thinking in developmental theory is associated with a systemic view which eschews a unidimensional view of the developing individual (e.g. the child seen in terms of cognitive or emotional development).

Summary

Most recent thinking has identified the relationship perspective as a framework for considering the nature of early infant socialisation (Collins & Laursen 1999). From this perspective, the early history of the mother–infant relationship, particularly early sensitivity, harmony and affective positive interactions between mother and infant, play a pivotal role in the course of early socialisation. Thus attachment theory (see this chapter) has emphasised how maternal responsiveness is linked to mutual coordination, cooperativeness and bonding in the dyad. Clark and Mills (1979) and Maccoby (1999) have emphasised the role of strong emotional ties and shared feelings of commitment in the socialisation process. Kochanska (1997) and Kochanska, Forman and Coy (1999) have proposed that mother–child mutual responsiveness is encompassed by two major components: (i) responsiveness to each other's signals and needs; and (ii) shared positive affect.

Schematising infant emotional development

In their early months, babies answer in true meaningful responses the expressive behaviour in their environment. The children's world of toys and funny tales is understandable and appeals to them because it is full of physiognomies. That

VIEWPOINT

What emotions are present at birth?

198 first-year university students enrolled in a developmental psychology answered:

Sadness 18%
Fear 18%
Happiness 16%
Contentment 9%
Frustration 8%
Anger 8%
Other 25%

stones and trees, sun and wind and wolf and rabbit all can talk is not surprising in a world where expressions reign (Strauss 1966, p. 240).

A number of theoretical schemes have been proposed to account for emotional expression and development during infancy. One such scheme was developed by the scientist Charles Darwin (Darwin 1965, first published 1872), who argued that emotional development is innate and not learned. He identified the appearance of the emotional states of anger, fear, amusement and discomfort in the first year of life.

My first child was born on December 27th 1839, and I at once commenced to make notes on the first dawn of the various expressions which he exhibited, for I felt convinced, even at this early period, that the most complex and fine shades of expression must all have a gradual and natural origin (Darwin 1958, p. 50).

From a very different perspective, John Watson (1930), the psychologist, held the view that at birth the infant's primary emotions were love, anger and fear, and that the differentiation of these emotions occurred as a result of learning. Bridges (1932) believed that at birth the infant is capable only of general excitement and that emotions are the product of the gradual differentiation of the state of excitement over time. Table 8.3 sets out Bridges' scheme for infant emotional development.

Considerably more attention is now being given to the nature of infant emotion and development (Sroufe 1979; Slee 1983; Malatesta et al. 1989). However, there is no satisfactory taxonomy of infant emotional expressions and no generally recognised standard procedure specifying the stimulus conditions under which emotions are elicited (Slee 1983). In the research field, there is currently lively debate about the nativist and cognitive/constructivist viewpoints on infant emotional development, but more research is needed to clarify these positions and their findings.

Table 8.3 Infant emotional development according to Bridges (1932)

Age	Emotions										
Birth						EX					
3 months					DI	EX	DE				
6 months	FE	DG	AN		DI	EX	DE				
12 months	FE	DG	AN		DI	EX	DE		EL	AA	
18 months	FE	DG	AN	JE	DI	EX	DE		EL	AA	AC
14 months	FE	DG	AN	JE	DI	EX	DE	JO	EL	AA	AC

Key
AA affection for adults; AC affection for children; AN anger; DE delight; DG disgust; DI distress; EL elation; EX excitement; FE fear; JE jealousy; JO joy

Nativist view

The **nativist** view stresses that certain emotions are present at birth. According to Malatesta et al. (1989, p. 4), 'This approach also maintains an original iso- morphism between expressive behaviour and feeling states'. The work of Izard et al. (1980) reflects Darwin's early formulation of infant emotional develop- ment and the significance of emotions in helping the infant adapt biologically and socially. Izard et al. (1980) have researched and written a great deal in this tradition. The emphasis in their work is on the identification of a limited number of discrete emotions, each with their accompanying verbal and non- verbal identifiers. In the view of Izard et al., the infant's facial and vocal expressions of emotion are of primary importance in helping establish commu- nicative links with the care-giver. As the infant matures physically, the infant's emotions develop. Thus, certain emotions are considered to be present at birth, whereas others require maturation before they appear. In a videotaped study of her infant daughter in the first months of life, Camras (1988) identified almost all the basic adult emotions – happiness, anger, sadness, distress and surprise.

nativist
refers to the idea that emotions are innate, or inborn.

Cognitive/constructivist view

The **cognitive/constructivist** view emphasises that 'emotion and cognition must be studied together' (Sroufe 1979, p. 462). The research of Sroufe advances a differentiation theory of emotion based on Bridges' (1932) observations of early infant emotion: 'Bridges' paper on the ontogenesis of the emotions has been the reference since 1932 and certainly qualifies as a developmental analysis' (Sroufe 1979, p. 471).

cognitive/ constructivist view
emphasising the interrelatedness of cognition and emotion in the developing scheme of emotions.

Like Bridges, Sroufe maintains that specific emotions emerge develop- mentally from global or diffuse distress/non-distress states. Moreover, the emergence of emotions in the first two years of life is paralleled by changes in cognitive development. Thus, he sees in the endogenous smile of the newborn the basis for pleasure, delight and joy. Similarly, the startle response of the newborn is the precursor to wariness, fear, anxiety and shame, and in the distress response lies the basis for rage, anger, defiance and guilt. Referring to Sroufe, Malatesta et al. (1989, p. 11) comment: 'Cognition is an all important variable in his developmental scheme and acts as a central mechanism in the growth, elaboration and differentiation of the emotions'. Sroufe's scheme of infant emo- tional development is closely linked with accompanying cognitive development, so that '[b]y nine months the infant is an emotional being' (Sroufe 1979, p. 488).

Stage 1

Sroufe discounts the existence of discrete emotions at birth. At around 2 to 3 months of age the differentiation of 'affects', or feeling states, from diffuse distress/non-distress states begins.

Stage 2

The emergence of the social smile at about 2 to 3 months ushers in a period of positive affect (3 to 6 months). The infant begins to experience disappointment and frustration, so that in addition to pleasure, negative emotions such as rage and wariness may develop. If this emotional development is linked with Piaget's secondary circular reactions period (chapter 7), it can be seen that the infant can begin to experiment with the effect that such emotions have on the external world (for example, the effect on care-givers).

Stage 3

Infants continue to develop as social beings from 7 to 9 months of age. At this stage, they begin to initiate interactions with care-givers and enjoy social games.

Stage 4

At about 9 months of age, infants become aware of their emotions – joy, fear, anger and surprise.

Stage 5

From around 9 to 12 months, children become preoccupied with their care-givers (see 'Infant attachment'). During this period, they show subdued affect and a fear reaction to strangers. The care-giver becomes a source of security. The emotional expression of infants at this stage is refined; more finely tuned emotions are displayed and there is a clear communication of emotion.

Stage 6

During the 12-to-18-month period infants are actively exploring and mastering their environment. Discrete emotions continue to be refined.

Stage 7

At this stage of the infant's life (from 18 months) a self-concept is developing, together with a sense of separateness from the care-giver. The infant is now capable of expressing a wide range of emotions

Attachment

attachment
the primary social bond between one individual and another.

An important feature related to infant emotional development is that of **attachment**. The essential argument put forward regarding attachment is that the emotional bonds established in infancy form the basis of attitudes and behaviour patterns in later adult life, particularly in terms of their relationship with others. As noted by Feeney and Noller (1991, p. 187), an 'attachment relationship is an "affectional bond" by which one individual seeks to maintain closeness with another'. The essential goal of such relationships is the maintenance of intimacy

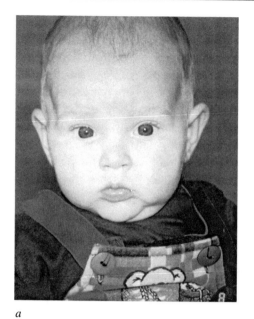

a

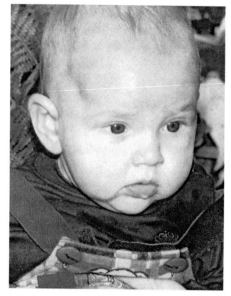

b

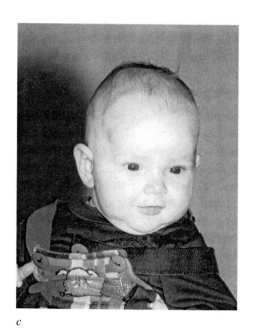

c

d

Referring to Table 8.3, can you classify the emotion expressed by this 8-month-old child?

via emotional and physical closeness. Forming strong bonds with significant others enhances the survival possibilities for the infant and young child. Drielsma (2000) has linked the capacity to attach to the creation of social capital and the development of a civil society. In relating the development of **social capital** to the strength and nature of the relationship between children and parents and family and community, attachment and the promotion of healthy early childhood experiences are a crucial components in the formation of social capital. The concept of attachment has important policy and service delivery implications. Various theories have been put forward to account for the process by which infants become attached or show a preference for their care-givers.

social capital
refers to networks which provide a basis for trust, cooperation and perception of safety.

Psychoanalytic theory

According to psychoanalytic theory, as proposed by Anna Freud (1946), infant social bonding is based on the child's dependency needs. For example, the child 'loves' that person who feeds him or her (the cupboard-love theory of mother-love!).

Behavioural (learning) theory

Behavioural theory, as proposed by Dollard and Miller (1950), proposes that there are countless opportunities during the first year of life when the care-giver's behaviour is positively associated with the alleviation of an uncomfort-able state (for example, changing a wet nappy). When the care-giver responds to such primary needs, his or her actions take on secondary reinforcing value. The infant then learns to engage in attachment behaviour (for example, crying) to gain closeness to the care-giver who will then fulfill the infant's needs.

Bowlby–Ainsworth ethological theory

Perhaps the prime exponent of attachment theory is the British psychiatrist, John Bowlby (1969), who called upon fields of study such as ethology and psychoanalytic theory to describe the **attachment behaviour** of young children to their parents. Bowlby proposes that every human being is genetically pro-grammed to show attachment towards one or more care-givers. That is, infants are genetically programmed to engage in behaviours that ensure the proximity of the care-giver, such as crying, clinging, smiling or babbling. In a reciprocal fashion, care-givers are innately predisposed to respond to such signals. It is in the context of these reciprocal behaviours on the part of the mother and infant that the infant comes to develop an attachment bond to the care-giver. Malatesta et al. (1989, p. 13) note:

attachment behaviour
behaviour that promotes contact and/or proximity of an infant to the care-giver.

> At the emotional level attachment connotes felt security: the child discriminates the care-giver from others and prefers to be in this person's presence, especially under conditions of threat.

Sroufe (1979) argues that attachment is not just the exhibition of attachment behaviours, such as crying or smiling, but is an 'affective bond', citing the research of Ainsworth (1973) in this regard.

Trends and issues

Attachment

As noted in this chapter, attachment theory is essentially a concept which begins with the nature of the early infant–caregiver relationship and which is postulated to influence the way an individual deals with future relationships. Bowlby (1969) argued that attachment behaviour demonstrated at 6 months of age and which comprises various instinctual responses serves the function of binding the child to the mother. Behaviours such as clinging, crying and smiling, among others, signal that the infant is discriminating between the mother or mother figure and 'others'. Bowlby (1988) further argued that where the

mother/mother figure failed to meet the child's needs for comfort and protection, was inconsistent in their behaviour to the child or actively rejected the child, the risk was that normal development would be compromised. West et al. (1998, p. 662) argue that '[a]ttachment relationships beyond childhood have an important functional role in the overall adjustment of the individual (Aisworth 1985; Weiss 1991; West & Sheldon-Keller 1994). The study of attachment and later development has been linked to adjustment in early primary school (e.g. Moss et al. 1998); adolescent functioning (e.g. Allen et al. 1998) and school bullying (e.g. Myron-Wilson & Smith 1999).

The development of attachment

As described by Bowlby (1973), attachment does not start to become organised until some time during the second six months of the first year. Certainly, attachment is gradually developed as a result of behaviours shown from birth (such as crying, looking, smiling) that appear designed to encourage the care-giver to interact and come into closer proximity with the infant. As the infant gets older, these behaviours become organised and directed more explicitly to a particular person, such as the mother, in preference to others, such as strangers.

The quality of attachment

The research of Ainsworth (1969, 1973) has been instrumental in clarifying the notion of attachment and its emergence at about 9 months of age. Her work with Ugandan children and later with North American infants led her to propose that the quality of attachment amongst mother–infant pairs can differ. Ainsworth et al. (1974) developed three scales to measure differences they had observed in the quality of mothers' responses to their infants, namely:

1 maternal sensitivity;
2 maternal cooperation;
3 maternal acceptance.

The most comprehensive of these scales, a nine-point maternal sensitivity scale, assessed 'whether a mother perceived her infant's signals at all; whether she interpreted them correctly and whether she responded to them appropriately and promptly' (Grossman & Grossman 1990, p. 32).

Attachment to a particular person develops over time.

The 'strange situation' assessment

Ainsworth et al. (1974) assessed infant attachment with a standardised 'strange situation' assessment method whereby infants' behaviour was observed following two brief separations from their care-givers in a familiar but pleasant room. Maternal sensitivity was defined as the mother's ability to read and respond appropriately to her infant's non-verbal behaviour. Three types of attachment behaviour were identified:

Type A, avoidant,
Type B, secure,
Type C, ambivalent,

Types A and C reflect insecure attachment. In type A, the most conspicuous behaviour of the infant when the mother returned to the room after the brief separation was avoidance of contact or interaction. The infant typically turned away, looked away, pulled away or ignored the mother. In type C, the infant showed some ambivalence by seeking proximity to the mother by engaging in avoidance behaviour. Sroufe (1979, p. 497) believes that the maladaptive attachment patterns are 'maladaptive because the infant's feelings [we presume anger; cf. Ainsworth et al. 1978(a); Main (unpub.] interfere with seeking and maintaining contact'.

Implications of attachment

Sroufe (1979) has outlined the implications of attachment for the child's later development. He suggests that the quality of attachment is related to the extent to which children will later attempt to explore and master their world. Securely attached infants will engage in more active exploration than will those who are less securely attached. Similarly, the degree of attachment also influences the emergence of the child's sense of self (self-concept). More securely attached infants appear to be more effective help seekers, more cooperative and more able to relate to others emotionally than their less securely attached counterparts. As Sroufe notes, they become more socially skilled pre-schoolers.

Temperament

Attempts to identify people by personality date back to ancient Greek times. In his writings, the physician Hippocrates (460–337 BC) identified four bodily fluids (humours) – black bile, yellow bile, phlegm and blood. A melancholic (sad) temperament was associated with black bile, a choleric (angry) temperament with yellow bile, a phlegmatic (cool) temperament with an excess of phlegm and a sanguine (cheerful, happy) temperament with too much blood. More recently, Sanson and Rothbart (1995, p. 2) define temperament as '. . . individual differences in reactivity to internal and external stimulation, and in patterns of motor and attentional self-regulation'.

Trends and issues

Attachment and later victimisation behaviour

Troy and Sroufe (1987) have reported a very interesting study concerning the relationship between a child's attachment history and a tendency to 'victimise' others at 4 to 5 years of age. In this study, the investigators used the Ainsworth and Bell (1970) strange situation test to identify secure attachment, anxious–avoidant attachment and anxious–resistant attachment.

1 Secure attachment
Securely attached infants felt confident that a care-giver was available and accessible. This allowed them to explore their environment in a confident and competent manner.

2 Anxious–avoidant attachment
This was characterised by a pattern of care-giver rebuff. When these children expressed emotional needs under stress they would ignore or move away from their care-giver.

3 Anxious–resistant attachment
The care-giver was insensitive and inconsistently available to the child, which resulted in ambivalent contact-seeking by the child. Under stress, such children would mix angry behaviour with comfort-seeking behaviour, continue to fuss or pout and not settle down.

Troy and Sroufe found that at 5 to 6 years of age children with an avoidant attachment history were more likely to be victimisers than securely attached infants. They were 'hostile, anti-social and socially and emotionally isolated from others'. Children with a resistant attachment history were more likely to be victims than others. That is, such children were stressed by social situations and seen by teachers as more dependent, helpless and socially inept (Sroufe 1973).

The concept of **temperament** has received an increasing amount of research interest in the last 20 years or so. In their New York Longitudinal Study (NYLS), Thomas et al. (1963) gathered information on 141 children from middle and upper socioeconomic groups families using an interview procedure. The series of interviews with parents began when the children were 3 months old, and were supplemented with direct assessments of the children during their school years. In the interviews factual information was sought about what the children could do and how they did it. Analyses of the parent interviews revealed nine categories of temperament that were empirically scorable.

temperament behaviours that comprise relatively stable characteristics of a person's personality.

1 Activity level: the motor component of a child's behaviour.
2 Rhythmicity: the predictability or otherwise in a child's behaviour, e.g. the sleeping–waking cycle.
3 Approach–withdrawal: the nature of the child's initial response to new stimuli.
4 Adaptability: the child's response to new or altered situations.
5 Threshold of responsiveness: the level of stimulation needed to evoke a response.
6 Intensity of reactions: the energy level of a child.
7 Quality of mood: the balance of pleasant, joyful versus unpleasant, crying behaviour.
8 Distractability: the readiness of the child to be distracted from a task.
9 Persistence: the length of time a child remains on task.

Children differ in temperamental characteristics, such as willingness to 'approach' new experiences.

Thomas and Chess (1977, p. 9) defined temperament in terms of 'behavioural style'. This refers to the 'how rather than the what (abilities or content) or the why (motivation) of behaviour. That is, temperament is concerned with the way in which an individual behaves'. For example, two infants may be equally skillful at playing and yet differ markedly in how they play. Thus, one may be quick and decisive in play while the other is slow and reflective.

Thomas et al. (1969) were firmly committed to an interactionist view of development in which an individual's innate predisposition exists in relationship to the environment. They argued for the notion of 'goodness of fit', whereby optimal individual development was possible when there was a balance between the individual's properties and the demands of the environment.

From their nine temperament variables, the NYLS team derived three subtypes of temperament style. 'Easy' children, who made up 40 per cent of their sample, are adaptable, approachable, regular in bodily function, positive in mood and mild in intensity. As such, infants with an 'easy' temperament coped with changes in routine, smiled at strangers, had regular feeding and sleeping patterns and could tolerate frustration.

'Difficult' temperament children had the opposite characteristics. They made up some 10 per cent of the sample and were inclined to withdraw in the face of new experience, did not cope well with new routine, were irregular in bodily function, negative in mood and high in intensity. Such infants were characterised by adjustment problems to new routines, had irregular sleeping and eating patterns, were negative in mood and had frequent bouts of crying and temper.

'Slow to warm up' children, comprising 15 per cent of the sample, were characterised by negative withdrawal responses to new stimuli, coupled with slow adaptability to new situations. They showed mild reactions, whether positive or negative, and tended to have more regular biological functions than 'difficult' children.

The Australian Temperament Project

The Australian Temperament Project (ATP) conducted by Prior, Sanson, Smart and Oberklaid (2000) represents the first '. . . large-scale longitudinal study of temperament and its relationships with the emotional and behavioural development of Australian children from infancy to adolescence' (Prior et al. 2000, p. 1). The study followed 2443 families and was '. . . planned to investigate whether children with particular kinds of temperaments were at higher risk for developmental and behavioural problems' (Prior et al. 2000, p. 3).

The authors presented a well-accepted definition of temperament as 'individual differences in attentional, emotional, and behavioural self-regulation, along with the relative level of emotional reactivity, which together give a unique flavour to the individual' (Prior et al. 2000, p. 3). The authors concluded that temperament does matter and influences a child's predisposition to adjustment problems in the home and school. They also concluded that '[t]emperament has a significant long-term influence on positive adjustment and socially adaptive behaviour, as shown particularly in the studies of resilience in the face of adversity' (Prior et al. 2000, p. 64). Different aspects of the findings of the AT project are reported in other chapters of this textbook.

Temperament and behaviour problems

Thomas and Chess (1977) have reported on the relationship between temperament and behaviour disorders in children. The researchers used a longitudinal study to follow the children in the NYLS through to adolescence. From their research, Thomas and Chess (1977, p. 46) concluded that: 'temperamental characteristics play significant roles in the genesis and evolution of behaviour disorders in children'. In general, reviews of the literature indicate that the associations between early temperamental characteristics and later adjustment are modest (e.g. Rothbart and Bates 1998). A difficult temperament, defined in terms of intense negative affect and constant demands for attention, is associated with later internalising and externalising behaviour (e.g. Bates et al. 1991). Caspi et al. (1995) have reported that early resistance to control, impulsivity, irritability, and distractability are associated with later externalising behaviour and social alienation.

Temperament and parenting

Usefulness of the concept of temperament

There are a number of ways in which the concept of temperament contributes to our understanding of children's development. In the first instance, it helps us to understand individuality in children. It is now better understood that from birth infants vary strikingly in behavioural characteristics (Buss & Plomin 1975), such as fussiness, soothability, alertness, and sleeping and waking patterns. Second, the concept of temperament has alerted developmental psychologists to the role of genetic factors in individual development (Matheny 1980; Goldsmith & Gottesman 1981). In a special edition of the *Journal of Pediatric Nursing* (1995, vol. 10) the issue of temperament, its measurement and implications for parenting was presented in a series of articles.

A contemporary view of infancy

In reviewing infancy research a number of writers have commented on the changes that have occurred in the field in the last quarter of a century (Belsky et al. 1989; Parke 1989; Horowitz & Columbo 1990; McCall 1990, Schaffer 2000). In their review, Horowitz and Columbo (1990, p. 173) note that research into infancy has established a sound foundation of knowledge such that it has 'made impressive and important advances in knowledge of infant behaviour and development'. More specifically, Parke (1989) has identified three important shifts in emphasis in the study of social development in infancy.

1   A greater emphasis on social interactions and relationships. While the study of infant cognitive and perceptual development is well established, researchers are now giving greater emphasis to the study of infant social behaviour (for example, in terms of parent–infant, and infant–sibling research). Moreover, efforts are now being made to integrate social interaction with infant cognitive and motor development.
2   A renewed interest in the study of infant emotional development is a major thrust in contemporary infancy research. Particular emphasis is being given to understanding how emotional expression helps to regulate the interaction.
3   A study of the biological basis of infant social behaviour and personality attributes such as temperament.

The nature of infant development

In reviewing the literature, Parke (1989) believes that developmental psychologists are now less interested in the strong form of discontinuity theory (for example, the stage theories of Freud and Piaget). Instead, emphasis is now on more subtle questions regarding the nature of discontinuity/continuity when they occur and the behaviour showing one or the other, the identification of the mechanisms involved and the role of innate factors such as temperament in developmental theory.

Infancy as an identifiable period

Parke (1989) takes the view that rather than attempting to designate arbitrarily when infancy begins and ends, a broader life-span perspective should be taken.

For example, the nature of infancy will vary as a function of, among other things, adults' own experiences at the time. Thus, Tinsley and Parke (1988) found that grandfathers' involvement with their infants varied as a function of the grandfather's age. Grandfathers aged 50–55 were more involved with their infant grandsons than younger grandfathers (still pursuing a career) or older grandfathers (distracted by illness or the cares of old age).

Critical periods of development

Early emphasis was given to the idea that deficiencies at sensitive periods of the infant's life would lead to impaired development in later years. Parke (1989, p. 23) argues that evidence is accumulating to challenge 'the assumption of non-reversibility'. For infants who are classified as insecurely attached, the potentially harmful affects of such experiences can be reversed if family circumstances change: 'behaviour is modifiable at a variety of developmental points, and that later behaviour is not necessarily determined in a fixed fashion by early experiences' (Parke 1989, p. 23).

The direction of influence during infancy

In evaluating contemporary research, Parke (1989) believes that research interest has moved away from the effect of the parent on the child's development to the study of how parent and infant influence each other.

The unit of analysis

At various times, the study of infancy research has focused attention on the individual, the dyad, triads and families. At present, the emphasis is on the family system and the infant in the context of the family (Parke 1989). See quiz at the end of this chapter.

The family life-cycle: 8

Preparing for motherhood

Pregnancy is a very significant time in the life-cycle of the family and those involved. In a major study of women's experience of pregnancy, Sherefsky and Yarrow (1973, p. 239) concluded that:

a first pregnancy is a time of intensified psychological activity directed toward preparing for the culmination in labor and delivery and for the new tasks and commitment thereafter. It is an intra psychic experience in which the woman tends to be primarily engrossed in immediate physiological changes and emotional developments in response to all aspects of pregnancy.

Similarly, Priel and Besser (2000, p. 437) have summarised the general literature noting that

. . . the transition to motherhood supports the view of pregnancy and the postpartum period as a time when issues of both interperson relations and identity and self esteem come to the fore, imposing a reassessment of the individual's autonomy and close interpersonal relationships.

The authors found that women who coped well with their first pregnancy were high in nurturance and ego strength and could visualise themselves as mothers. In another study, Osofsky and Osofsky (1980) found that during pregnancy women undergo considerable stresses and upheavals. Fears entertained by women included:

- whether or not the child will be normal;
- the nature of physical changes in the body;

- the birth process and how the experience will affect them;
- changes to home and work patterns;
- changes in relationship to their partner.

In their summary of the literature, Osofsky and Osofsky (1984, p. 375) concluded that:

the woman's adjustment to pregnancy depends to a considerable extent on her circumstances and her earlier relationships with her own mother, the effects of the pregnancy on her life and work patterns and her ability to adjust to them and the support that is available to her from her husband, family and the community.

Goals of pregnancy

Campbell (1989) has suggested that during pregnancy a woman is seeking to accomplish several psychological tasks.

Acceptance of pregnancy. The mother-to-be must deal with any feelings of ambivalence about her pregnancy and come to accept the child as part of herself. Complicating factors may involve whether or not the pregnancy was planned, the financial status of the family, the marital status of the mother, and the support of significant others in the nuclear and extended family. The mother must also resolve issues concerning career planning, fears regarding the pregnancy, conflicts with her own mother and the realisation of the dramatic changes occurring in her own life.

Resolution of fears and anxieties about childbirth. Some mothers will attempt to ignore their fears by denying them, while others will attempt to deal with them through childbirth classes, and discussion with significant others about the birth process (Campbell 1989).

Acceptance of the mother's role. In accepting the role of mother, the woman is confronted with the responsibility of motherhood. Possible factors influencing this adjustment include the mother's previous experience with pregnancy (if any) and the woman's relationship with her own mother.

Acceptance of the completion of pregnancy. According to Campbell (1989), during this stage the mother is mentally preparing herself for the birth and the emergence of the new baby that has been such a significant part of her for nine months.

In summary, Delmore-Ko et al. (2000, p. 634) concluded their study of parents' adaptation to parenthood noting that '...the transition to parenthood is a time of substantial change as individuals' identities evolve from being solely husband and wife to becoming father and mother as well as their relationship shifts from couple to family unit'.

A psychoanalytic perspective

In the psychoanalytic tradition, consideration of the nature of expectant motherhood focuses on the mother's relationship with her own mother. Bydlowski (1984) has argued that by giving birth a woman meets and comes close to her own mother. She becomes a continuation of her own mother while at the same time becoming different from her: 'Through birth and above all through her first child the woman pays her debt to her own mother' (Bydlowski 1983, p. 134).

Chapter summary

Our understanding of the nature of infant development has changed considerably since the publication of the first edition of this text in 1993. Advances in the nature of our understanding of genetics (See chapter 4) and developments in theoretical understanding (See chapter 4) have contributed significantly to this understanding. In particular, appreciation of the way the infant contributes in a very active sense to their own development is shaping our thinking.

Discussion questions

1 What are the major differences between Freud's and Erikson's views of infancy?
2 What did behavioural, or learning, theory contribute to our understanding of infants' emotional development?
3 How do the nativist and cognitive/constructivist views of emotional development differ?
4 Discuss the concept of attachment as reflected in various psychological theories.
5 How did Thomas and Chess (1977) define temperament?
6 Summarise the main changes that have occurred in our understanding of infant development in the last 25 years.

Quiz

1 **The nature of infant development**

| Development is a continuous Process with new events or change, occurring in a steady, orderly, continuous fashion. | 1 2 3 4 5 | Development occurs in discrete steps or stages with the organisation of behaviour at each stage being different from the preceding one |

2 **Infancy as an identifiable period in the life-cycle**

| Infancy is a focal period in its own right with its own identifiable features | 1 2 3 4 5 | Infancy should not be considered as a special period and should be Placed in an overall Life-span perspective |

3 **Critical periods of development in infancy**

| There exists in infancy certain critical periods when the individual is sensitive to experience and the experiences during these times are irreversible in their effect | 1 2 3 4 5 | Behaviour shaped during the critical or sensitive periods can later be modified or changed and the outcomes are not irreversible |

4 **Direction of influence during infancy**

| During infancy it is the parent who influences, directs or shapes the infant | 1 2 3 4 5 | Influence shaping development during infancy is bi-directional, with both parent and infant Influencing each other |

5 **The unit of analysis or study during infancy**

1	2	3	4
The individual (infant or parent)	the dyad e.g. mother–child father–child	the triad e.g. mother–father –infant	the full family group e.g. including grand-parents

Activities

1 Score the dimensions in the quiz on p. 179 relating to developmental issues in infancy according to your own understanding and compare your answers to the views of Parke (1989). Circle the number closest to the statement that best represents your belief.

2 In small groups discuss the meaning of motherhood for women. Discuss this topic in relation to variables such as (a) culture (b) the age of the mother and (c) the mother's relationship with her own parents. One place to start the discussion could be the various reasons for having children.

3 Complete the 'Self Review Quiz' in the CD-ROM to assess your understanding of the content presented in this section. Use your quiz results as a basis for reviewing any chapter content about which you are uncertain.

See your CD

Selected websites

Child Adolescent Psychological and Educational Resources <www.caper.com.au>

Kidslife – Making Parenting Easier <www.kidslife.com.au>

Parenting – Science and Practice <www.parentingscienceandpractice.com>

4

Toddlerhood

Matthew (on left) aged 4 months

Matthew aged 5 years

Matthew aged 8 years

9 Physical Development of Toddlers

'You Must Run at Least Twice as Fast as That'

Well, in our country,' said Alice, still panting a little, 'you'd generally get to somewhere else – if you ran very fast for a long time, as we've been doing'. 'A slow sort of country', said the Queen. 'Now, here, you see, it takes all the running you can do, to keep in the same place. If you want to get somewhere else, you must run at least twice as fast as that!'.

Lewis Carroll, Through the Looking Glass

KEY TERMS AND CONCEPTS

- Instinct practice play
- Surplus energy
- Sensori-motor
- Development theory
- Sensori-motor play

- Symbolic play
- Logico-mathematical
- Physical knowledge
- Father's role

Introduction

As toddlers emerge from infancy, dramatic changes are taking place in their physical development. As far as their mobility is concerned, they are relatively independent of their parents. A glance around any supermarket will usually identify some harried parent trying to control a toddler while attempting frantically to fill their basket or trolley with groceries.

Toddlers have discovered the advantages of standing and walking. Much to their parents' concern they are now able to reach the top of kitchen benches, tables and door knobs, opening up whole new worlds for exploration. Standing on tip-toe they can reach for knives or saucepans. Although a little unsteady on their feet at first, toddlers revel in their new found mobility, charging from room to room in the house, squealing with delight. Stairs are a fatal attraction and the despair of parents. In parks, the raised cement edges of flower beds are another challenge for the child's developing physical skills. Bruises on the shins and lower legs are the red badge of courage for the toddler striving to refine walking and running skills.

This chapter discusses the toddler's physical growth, change in appearance and motor development. The nature, functions and types of children's play are examined, together with some theoretical explanations of play and the phenomenon of superhero play. Other topics include the role of doing in the learning process, and the prevalence, nature and prevention of childhood accidents. The Family Life-cycle: 9 is devoted to the father's role in the family system.

Toddlers developing physical skills prepare them for even greater achievements.

Physical growth

During toddlerhood children's developing physical skills shift dramatically from a position of high dependency on the caregiver to a growing independence. Their emerging curiosity and mastery of locomotor skills facilitate their exploration of the wider world. Meanwhile their parents provide a secure base to whom they can return from time to time.

In contrast to the rapid growth during infancy, physical growth slows during the toddler period. The charts in Figure 9.1 give the relative height and weight rates during infancy and toddlerhood for girls and boys. It can be seen that physical growth slows after infancy and is characterised during toddlerhood by a slow but steady gain or rate of change.

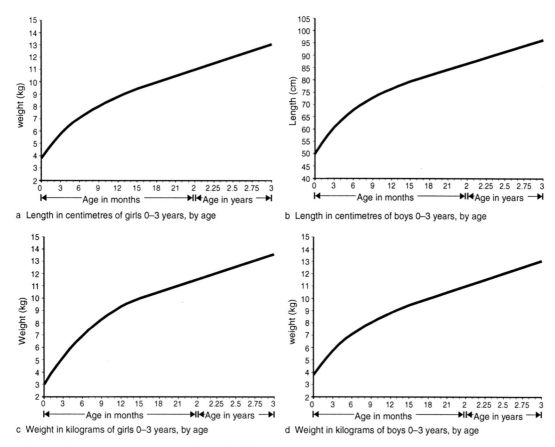

a Length in centimetres of girls 0–3 years, by age

b Length in centimetres of boys 0–3 years, by age

c Weight in kilograms of girls 0–3 years, by age

d Weight in kilograms of boys 0–3 years, by age

Figure 9.1 Average heights and weights for infants and toddlers
Source: Adapted from the Child Adolescent Health Service (SA) booklet for parents (1988)

Appearance

Body fat

One conspicuous change in body appearance from infancy to toddlerhood is a decrease in body fat. At the end of the first year of life the amount of body fat peaks at 22 per cent of total body weight. This accounts for the characteristic profile of a protruding stomach. Then in the course of the next few years the percentage of body fat decreases to 12.5–15 per cent at 5 years of age (Illingworth 1987). During these early years, the toddler gradually assumes a more upright stance. Muscle tone improves while the protruding stomach disappears and the child becomes leaner and more muscular.

Facial changes

During the toddler period the child's skull length increases and there is a forward movement of the jaw. The upper jaw is developing rapidly to allow for the emergence of the teeth (Breckenbridge & Murphy 1969).

Motor development

Parents usually take great pride in the toddler's physical feats. The child's fast-developing skills of walking, running and exploring, accompanied by an insatiable curiosity, are a source of constant amazement for parents. Toddlers' ability to walk and the resulting independence they gain from their parents expand their horizons considerably. A variety of things capture their attention, from the fluff on the carpet to the coverings on the stereo speakers (which can be picked at when the parents' attention wanders!).

Fine motor skills

During the toddler years, there is a rapid development in the acquisition of fine motor skills, such as drinking through a straw, eating with a fork and spoon, and eating an ice-cream cone. As parents know only too well, the 2-year-old is typically able to reach for distant objects with one hand without requiring support from the other. Toddlers are also generally able to imitate vertical and circular strokes with a crayon, turn the pages of a book, build a tower of blocks (three to four in height), pull off socks and help find armholes when dressing.

The 3-year-old builds on previous skills and can balance taller towers of blocks (9 to 10), trace a square and copy a circle. At this age little food is spilt while feeding and the child can pick up small objects, button or unbutton clothes, and so forth.

Gross motor skills

Gross motor skills develop as the child masters standing, walking and running. At the same time, reaching and throwing are developed. Typically a 2-year-old is able to stand upright, pick up objects from the floor without falling over, run,

---

Trends and issues

A parent's view of a toddler's physical skills

A toddler's emerging physical skills cause parents to hold their breath at the dinner table as the toddler exclaims 'Me do it!', while grabbing the half-full mug of juice and drinking from it. Then, as the toddler is distracted by something else, the mug of juice is held precariously while the child reaches for a spoon on the table.

Breakfast-time finds a father making an omelette for his 2-year-old son. Matthew has been up since 6.30 am and is kicking a balloon around in the lounge, stopping for a visit to the potty, because potty training is under way and he is proud of his efforts (even if his aim is a little astray at times!). Finally the omelette is ready and loud shouts of 'No – me!' indicate that Matthew wants to carry the plate to the table. Dad gives him the plate and he totters carefully to the table, leaving the plate balanced precariously on the edge. Refusing Dad's help, he climbs onto the chair (bolstered with a cushion for extra height). Using a fork with some dexterity now, he is able to pick up pieces of omelette and feed himself. Then a cry of 'Dink peese' alerts Dad (who is furiously gulping down some toast and boiling-hot coffee) to his son's immediate needs. Asked what he would like to drink, Matthew is down from the chair in a flash, pulling open the fridge door and pointing to the apple juice. Dad has the temerity to suggest a drink of milk but is greeted with a loud protestation of 'No'! The apple juice is poured into a cup and with Matthew once more sitting at the table, some is drunk and some is spilled.

kick, walk up and down steps unaided, walk backwards and sit in a chair.

At 3 years of age the toddler can rise from a squatting position, balance on the toes, and walk in a straight line by placing one foot in front of the other. A 3-year-old can catch a ball with both arms extended, run smoothly and easily, walk without support up a flight of stairs and ride a tricycle.

The 3-year-old's gross motor abilities include riding a tricycle.

Children and play

It is ironic that play is such a pervasive feature of our lives and yet we understand so little about it. The lack of serious study of play is perhaps understandable in view of cultural and professional attitudes that view play as frivolous, juvenile and time-wasting. Observations about play date back to ancient times, however. The Greek philosopher Plato is often cited as the first person to recognise the practical value of play – for example, he advocated letting children play with apples to help them to learn to count. At a later date, Aristotle believed that children's play helped to prepare them for adult life. In more recent times, during the history of early childhood care in Australia, attention has frequently been called to the role of play in children's lives. The *Annual Report of the Kindergarten Union of South Australia* (1936–37) contains the following poem, attributed to Charlotte Gilman:

> To the people of place and power
> Who govern and guide the hour;
> To the people who write and teach,
> Ruling our thought and speech;
> And all the captains and kings
> Who command the making of things –
> Give me the good ye know –
> That I, the child, may grow!
> Light, for the whole day long
> Food that is pure and strong,
> Housing and clothing fair,
> Clean water and clean air,
> Teaching from day to day
> And room – for a child to play.
> Cited in Creaser 1990, p. 4.

To date, there is no comprehensive understanding or theory of play. Pellegrini and Smith (1998, p. 577) have noted that

> [b]oth child developmentalists and animal ethologists agree that play behavior is enjoyable, and that players, typically children or juveniles, are concerned with means over ends, and that the

Play provides many opportunities for social interaction.

activity appears to be 'purposeless', or to occur for its own sake.

Many of the current views and theories contradict one another. The problem with most theories is that they tend to single out a predominant aspect, such as surplus energy, and treat it as a fundamental fact about play.

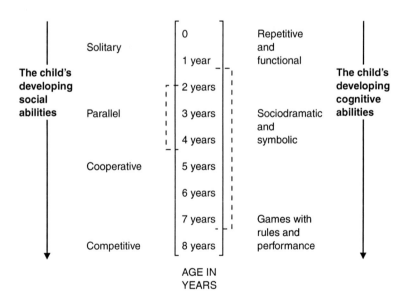

Figure 9.2 Development sequence of play
Source: Adapted from Creuser 1990

Theories of play

Instinct practice theory

Theories of play were first formulated in the nineteenth century. Groos (1861–1946) devoted himself to the study of play in animals and young children (Groos 1989). He theorised that animals and human beings have instincts (an innate tendency to be active in ways that ensure survival). Play is the means by which instinctive activities are practised and perfected. First, it involves the practice of physical skills and their coordination – that is, the mastery of the physical self. Second, it provides practice, in miniature, of the roles the animal or child will fulfil when grown up: for example, a kitten playing with wool is perfecting the skills that will be needed later for hunting.

Groos also studied children's imaginative symbolic play. In such play children 'convert' everyday objects into whatever takes their fancy: a chair can become a hospital bed, for example. Groos believed that although children can and do distinguish between the 'real' and the 'pretend' in such play, they still maintain the illusion that what is pretended is real. They do so because such illusion provides them with greater freedom.

Groos's writings have had a strong influence on educationalists such as Maria Montessori, whose teaching methods reflect the preparatory aspects of play (Montessori 1975). In Montessori education, children are provided with miniature versions of adult equipment, such as chairs, and encouraged to imitate adult activities.

> **Instinct practice theory**
> a theory formulated by Groos, that play helps to refine and develop instinctive activities.

The psychoanalytic explanation of play

When Sigmund Freud developed his theory of psychoanalysis at the beginning of the twentieth century, he formulated no distinct theory of play, but was indirectly interested in it as an expression of children's emotional life and as a possible clue to their emotional problems. Freud attached particular importance to the repetitious and symbolic nature of play. He thought, for instance, that children's tendencies to repeat words when they first hear them is the way they practise their capacities. Repetition of games or hearing the same story over and over again also help children understand that the world in which they live has some stability and predictability. Freud also believed that children's imaginative play and fantasies reveal something about their inner life. Psychologists today frequently use imaginative play with dolls and other toys for clinical diagnosis and therapy (Axline 1974; Gardner 1975).

Surplus energy theory

This theory is based on the idea that the energies of the body are designed for, and appropriately directed towards, meeting safety and physiological needs, such as the need for shelter, food or warmth. In our society, however, children are in a privileged position because adults basically provide for these needs. So, having surplus energy at their disposal, children play.

Developmental theory of play

Piaget (1962) proposed a developmental theory of play indicating a progression in play behaviours from imitative to symbolic to rule-governed play. The focus is on identifying particular types of play associated with certain ages.

Summary

Pellegrini and Smith (1998) have argued that overall, the dominant theoretical view in child development has related to the 'deferred benefits' theory (e.g. Groos 1898, 1901). '[D]uring the period of extended childhood, children engage in play to learn and practice those skills necessary to be functioning adult members of society'(p. 581). An alternative view that has some support (e.g. Bateson 1976) is that play should not be considered as an imperfect version of some later adult activity. Rather, it serves some discrete developmental purpose at that particular time and place in the child's development.

Definition of play

It is perhaps a little easier to define play than to theorise about it. Catherine Garvey (1977) has argued that there are certain descriptive characteristics of play that are critical to its definition. These are:

sensori-motor play
play involving the senses and motor skills.

1 Play is pleasurable – it is valued by the player.
2 Play has no extrinsic goals – play is for play's sake.
3 Play is spontaneous and voluntary.
4 Play involves active engagement on the part of the player (just doing nothing – being bored – is not pleasurable and is therefore not play).

Types of play

Taking the above characteristics of play, it is possible to identify four types of play relevant to young children:

1 Sensori-motor play
2 Symbolic play (sociodramatic)
3 Construction
4 Play with rules.

1 Sensori-motor play

Sensori-motor play really begins when the infant starts manipulating fingers and toes. As the child gets older, sensori-motor play is identified with developing some body mastery, such as balancing games. Much of the very young child's play is solitary in nature and has little of the interaction with other children that characterises play at a later age. It is also repetitive, a simple act being repeated a number of times, such as fitting blocks together.

Play engages many of the senses.

In a Special Review Section edited by Pellegrini and Smith in *Child Development* (1998) the issue of 'physical activity play' was considered from a number of different theoretical and research perspectives. Pellegrini and Smith commented on the relative paucity of research into children's physical activity play. As they noted, such play:

> . . . may involve symbolic activity or games with rules; the activity may be social or solitary, but the distinguishing behavioral features are a playful context, combined with what Simons-Morton et al. (1990) describe as moderate to vigorous physical activity, such that metabolic activity is well above resting metabolic rate.

VIEWPOINT

What is play?

'It's where you can do what you want without getting yelled at'
Marilyn, 7 years

'Like playing cricket – it's like having fun and its doing things and it's – I still can't think of the right word'
Jake, 7 years

'Going outside and playing with your friends'
Belinda, 11 years

Activities such as running, jumping and climbing would fit physical activity play.

Pellegrini and Smith (1998) have identified a number of different types of play, namely (i) rhythmic stereotypes; (ii) exercise play; and (iii) rough and tumble play. They have identified a number of broad features associated with each type of play.

Age trends. Rhythmic sterotypic (described as gross motor movements e.g. body rocking with little apparent purpose) play peaks in infancy. Exercise play dominates in early childhood declining in late primary school, while rough and tumble play peaks in late primary.

Gender differences. Pellegrini and Smith report no sex differences in relation to rhythmic stereotypes. However, males tend to exceed females in relation to both exercise and rough and tumble play.

2 Symbolic play

With the ability to retain images of objects during the second year of life (Piagetian notion of object permanence, see chapter 7), the young child is able to think representationally and express these ideas in **symbolic play**. Thus, children take objects that they find and by their actions create symbols: for example, a pencil is used as a rocket or a box becomes a bed. This is the make-believe fantasy play that dominates much of the activity of the pre-schooler. The symbols created by the young child are diverse, fluid and dynamic. Such symbolisation matures and becomes more elaborate, reaching its highest form of expression in **sociodramatic play**. Thus, when Maria pretends to be a doctor and Sue a nurse they may play out an elaborate theme. They are not wasting their time, for each child is integrating the knowledge she has acquired from her real experiences.

symbolic play
imaginative play in which one object is used to represent another.

sociodramatic play
the most elaborate form of symbolic play in which a theme is enacted.

The criteria for sociodramatic play are as follows.

a The child undertakes a make-believe role and imitates behaviour.
b Make-believe objects are substituted for real objects: a block becomes a truck.
c Verbal descriptions are substituted for actions: for instance the child says 'I will help fix your truck, save you and then come back and pick you up'.

d   The child persists in the role-play for a length of time.

e   At least two players are involved.

Creaser notes that sociodramatic play can be found in children as young as 1 year, although it is usually more in evidence at 2 years. 'Until that time infants and toddlers use familiar objects in a functional and often very repetitive way' (Creaser 1990, p. 7). Sociodramatic play reaches a peak between 4 and 6 years of age, before giving way to the final play stage, that of games with rules (see Figure 9.2). In late infancy and toddlerhood, children's play is of a parallel nature. Each player is caught up in her or his own world and cooperative play emerges only slowly. Competitive play follows on from cooperative play as children strive to 'win' or 'be first'.

3 Construction

Construction is generally defined as forms of art work, such as painting, clay modelling or block building. Central to a construction is an expression of a symbol which, once completed, represents a static product. Construction, although symbolic, is goal-oriented. For example, in symbolic play the symbols change: a wooden block can become a truck, boat or electric shaver in a matter of minutes. In construction activity, the child intellectually decides to make or paint, say, a house and holds that image until the task is completed.

4 Games with rules

Play helps children understand their world.

These are the social games of competition that begin during the pre-school years but are more characteristic of middle childhood – games such as marbles, monopoly, football, netball, that are organised by rules. Children must confine their actions within the context of rules and are not free, as in symbolic play, to change quickly into a new role or even to change themes or outcomes. Games with rules require a highly socialised child.

Functions of play

Socialisation

Play helps children to rehearse social skills and gain a better idea of the nature of the give and take in relationships.

Mental health

Erikson (1950) suggested that a child gains a sense of mastery or control over events through play. Play teaches children to think ahead, to anticipate the consequences of their own actions.

Accumulation of information

Children accumulate facts, improve their use of language and modify their understanding of the world through play.

Cognitive development

According to Piaget (1953), symbolic play leads to an increasing differentiation of the objective and the subjective, with a consequent decrease in egocentrism. That is, the child learns to see the world from another's perspective. The acting out of different roles during play might also facilitate the development of social behaviours such as sharing, cooperation and altruism. A similar outlook has been expressed by the Russian psychologist Vygotsky (1978, p. 129):

> In their play children project themselves into adult activities of their culture and rehearse their future roles and values. This play is in advance of development . . . In play a child is always above his average age, above his daily behaviour. In play it is as though he were a head taller than himself.

Superheroes like to dress up or down!

The development of attitudes and personality traits

It has been argued that thematic play is especially crucial in the development of creativity, intrinsic motivation, perseverance and self-confidence (Feitelson and Ross 1973).

An interesting discussion of the nature and function of play has been presented by Panksepp (1998). Panksepp has considered the idea of children's play in relation to attention deficit hyperactivity disorders, concluding that 'We may be taking a major step toward promoting childhood mental and physical health when we, as a society, begin to recognise and affirm the right of children to really frolic for a few hours each day' (p. 97).

Summary

In concluding their paper on play, Pellegrini and Smith (1998) identified a number of future research areas that would more fully inform us regarding the nature and function of play. They called for further naturalistic studies into play to provide insight into age trends and gender differences. In a related fashion, they identified the need for further study relating to the benefits of play, e.g. in relation to strength, endurance and skill development. They also called for more research into the function of exercise play and children's cognitive development. They made a particular call for more research into 'rough and tumble' play. Their call is particularly important, given that Lieberman (1997) has identified 'play' as one of the first–order elements in human functioning.

The role of doing in learning

> I hear and I forget.
> I do and I understand.
> Anon.

logico-mathematical Piaget's term for knowledge gained about the relationships between objects as a result of our interaction with them.

physical knowledge Piaget's term for knowledge of the physical properties of objects gained from direct physical experience of them.

Observation of young children will quickly establish their intense preoccupation with manipulating and handling objects. As discussed in chapter 3, Piaget identified two different types of knowledge: **logico-mathematical** and **physical knowledge** (Piaget 1965, 1972). Logico-mathematical knowledge involves learning about the properties and relations that belong not to things themselves but rather to our interactions with things (Elkind 1974). Williams and Kamii (1986) give the example of comparing red and white balls. The notion of their difference is created by the individual and is not a property of either the red or the white ball. Thus, when children search for square blocks among a pile of blocks, they are using logico-mathematical knowledge because they are making a relationship between blocks that are square and those that are not. In contrast, physical knowledge comes about when the child builds a house from the square blocks.

Piaget (1970) believed that logico-mathematical and physical knowledge develop together. Piaget's theories help educators appreciate that young children acquire knowledge not only through their senses but by manipulating, handling and acting on objects. For example, children discover the properties of water by pouring, drinking and mixing. This is why it is essential for children to manipulate objects in the learning process (Williams & Kamii 1986). Such action is not mindless; rather, a 'mental action' usually accompanies a 'physical action'. For example, when we squeeze a fruit to see how ripe it is, the important part of the action is the mental part, without which the external act would be mindless manipulation (Williams & Kamii 1986, p. 25). For the precept quoted at the beginning of this section to be valid then, 'doing', or manipulation, must be accompanied by mental process or reflection.

Trends and issues

Superhero play

Leslie (3 years of age) is visiting his 4-year-old friend and is fully outfitted with a Star Wars mask, shield and sword. As he and his friend are playing, Leslie suddenly draws his sword and assumes a fighting stance accompanied by a challenging shout. His friend turns from his own play and the two are now prepared to do battle against the 'forces of evil'. Superhero play has struck.

In *Socialising the Superheroes*, Cupit (1989) draws attention to the role of superhero play in Australian children's lives. Contemporary superheroes include Batman and Superman. Earlier counterparts included figures such as Buck Rogers, Wonderwoman and Captain America. Kostelnik et al. (1986) have identified features of superheroes including:

- amazing powers such as speed, strength and endurance;
- wisdom such that others look to them for guidance;
- a knowledge of right and wrong;
- a high standing in society.

Superhero themes

According to Cupit (1989) and Kostelnik et al. (1986), a number of dominant superhero themes are played out in the course of any film or television episode. These are:

1 an opening situation identifying the characters;
2 a sudden threat;
3 a capture and chase;
4 a vanquishing of the threat;
5 resolution of the problem and accolades for the superhero, including explicit or implicit moral stance or approbation of the superhero.

Cupit (1989) identifies a number of concerns that adults have about such play. These include:

- the promotion of an aggressive atmosphere in play;
- an increased risk of accidents and injury;
- exclusivity such that others cannot join in;
- excessive imitation, which limits creative play;
- noisiness;
- the limitations of the play themes;
- the avoidance of positive emotional interactions;
- emphasis on male dominance;

- excessive use of threatening language;
- the imposition of certain values;
- the use of violence to resolve interpersonal problems.

In superhero play, boys are usually either 'leaders' or 'followers', while girls who participate usually take, or are assigned, the role of 'followers' (Cupit 1989). Cupit encourages the reader to consider what such sociodramatic play is teaching children about sex roles. Cupit observes that such play usually occurs out of doors during free-play periods. Children usually wear appropriate superhero clothing and equipment, participate in a non-specific activity such as shouting names and engage in aggressive acts.

Why do superheroes appeal to children?

Both Cupit (1989) and Kostelnik et al. (1986) have found that superhero play appeals to children because:

- it involves physical activity or fun;
- the sociodramatic play releases tension;
- simple repetitive scripts make participation easy;
- identifying with other children in play scripts facilitates social acceptance.

Dealing with superhero play

Three common adult responses to superhero play include banning the play (e.g. see articles in *Young Children, Childhood Education*), replacing the play with other types of play or extending the play (Cupit 1989). Boyd (1997) and Cupit (1989) have argued that while banning the play is the most common response, it is probably the least useful reaction. Boyd (1997, p. 27) concludes by noting that 'I believe that banning superhero play is not the most productive manner for dealing with our concerns about increased violence in our classrooms'. Cupit (1989) suggests that the most valuable strategy is to replace the play script by:

1 having the children question what their superheroes do;
2 using superhero stories to provide extension activities: for example, Star Wars battles Turtle might lead to a discussion of conflict resolution;
3 counteracting values portrayed in stories by using alternative themes: for example, by making the female role a more active one.

The risk of injury is highest for younger children.

Accidents in early years

Parents are only too aware of the risk of accidental injury to children, particularly to toddlers. Carefully compiled hospital statistics have helped to increase community awareness of the toll of accidental injury to children (O'Connor 1982; Pearn 1985). All evidence now suggests that accidents are the biggest killer in childhood after the first year of life (Major 1980; Clyde 1983; Leditschke 1989).

Some statistics

Australian statistics on accidental injury to children (Clyde 1983) reveal a similar pattern of causes to those reported in European countries and in the United States. As reported by Laflamme and Eilert-Peterson (1998, p. 206); 'Injuries constitute one of the greatest threats to the health of children in the industrialised world'. Some insight into these causes is provided by Leditschke (1989), who has found that in Australia accidents are responsible for a quarter of the deaths of children from 1 month old to the late primary and early secondary school years.

The nature of accidents: Their psychological antecedents

Accidents that children have vary according to their sex and age. In a report on the literature pertaining to psychological characteristics of childhood accidents, Matheny (1987) has noted that boys are injured more than girls, that poisonings are more common among toddlers and street accidents more common among primary school children. According to Leditschke (1989), authorities aiming to prevent childhood injury should consider three aspects of childhood injury:

1 Who is injured.
2 The agent causing the injury.
3 The environment in which the injury occurs.

Trends and issues

Thomas and the cat

Thomas was a 15-month-old toddler. He and his parents had been visiting a friend who lived in a first-floor apartment. Thomas had spent most of the visit playing with the friend's cat. While Thomas's parents were getting ready to leave, the cat pushed the apartment door ajar and Thomas followed it out onto the second-storey landing. His parents, who were distracted with tidying up and saying goodbye, did not notice Thomas leaving the apartment. Suddenly they heard a soft thump, followed by a cry from Thomas.

Rushing out onto the landing and fearing the worst, they peered over the ledge of the guard-rail but could not see their child. Next they rushed down the stairs and halfway down they saw Thomas lying on the ground crying. He had followed the cat, squeezed under the guard-rail and fallen three-quarters of a metre onto a grassed area under the steps. Thomas was crying and gasping for breath. A doctor was called and fortunately found nothing broken, although Thomas had a rather nasty cut above his eye.

Table 9.1 Causes of death of Australian children, by age

Age	Cause of Death
0–1 month	Prematurity and congenital abnormalities
1–12 months	Sudden Infant Death Syndrome (SIDS)
1–2 years	Drowning, scalds, poisons
5–7 years	Road accidents
12–14 years	Cycle accidents

Sources: Based on Clyde 1983, Major 1980 and Leditschke 1989

Adults have a role to play in reducing injury.

Wortel et al. (1994) identified three types of strategies to prevent injury, namely:

- adoption of safety measures (e.g. use of seat belts);
- supervision of the child;
- education of the child regarding safety measures.

Let us apply Leditschke's formula to the Trends and Issues case study 'Thomas and the cat'. The person injured was a 15-month-old toddler. The agent causing the injury related to inadequate safety rails on the stairs, some lack of parental supervision, and a child's natural curiosity. The environment was a first-floor apartment. To prevent further accidents of this kind, these three factors, relating to physical antecedents, should be taken into consideration. However, accidents also have psychological precursors.

The most difficult problem to be faced in preventing childhood accidents involves modifying the child's behaviour (Leditschke 1989). To do this, the behaviour might be conceptualised in terms of 'how–why–what'. The 'how' of behaviour relates to behavioural style or temperament. In a review of

Accident proneness in children has been linked to temperament.

over 700 children, Manheimer and Mellinger (1967) found that the children who suffered more accidents were more aggressive, impulsive and inattentive. We have seen in chapter 8 that 'temperament', as defined by Thomas et al. (1977), incorporates nine dimensions of behaviour – activity level, quality of mood, intensity of reactions, adaptability, approach – withdrawal, persistence, rhythmicity, distractability and threshold of responsiveness. The argument put forward by Leditschke is that children prone to accidents are most likely to be high in activity, impulsive and easily distracted. Similar findings have been reported in the Australian research of Russell and Russell (1989).

The 'why' of behaviour in Leditschke's terms refers to motivation. Children's injuries often occur when they are attempting to imitate the behaviour of another child or adult. There is also a risk-taking component to injury: children low in self-esteem are more prone to risk-taking and less able to evaluate the risks involved.

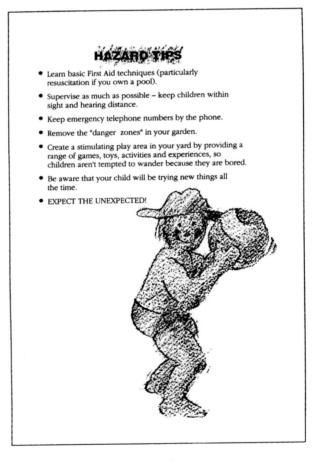

Figure 9.3 Advice to parents on backyard safety
Source: *Playing it Safe*, reprinted with the permission of Child Accident Foundation of Australia.

Programs to prevent childhood accidents

In 1979 in Australia, the Royal Australasian College of Surgeons sponsored the Child Accident Prevention Foundation. The philosophy of the foundation is based on the idea that younger children must be protected from injury and older children must be taught how to protect themselves. Programs to prevent accidents should take into account not only the physical aspects of the child's environment (such as access to swimming pools, busy roads, poisons etc.), but also the psychological characteristics of individual children that might increase their proneness to accidents.

In examining the literature, it is evident that strategies to teach pre-schoolers about health and safety have primarily utilised behavioural strategies. Research conducted by Laflamme and Eilert-Peterson (1998) argued for 'passive' protection strategies for attending to the safety of young children. They suggest that the focus should be on attention to home design, building structures that take into consideration the needs of young children.

The family life-cycle: 9

Birth of the first child: The father

With the advent of the first child, the couple system becomes a family system. New roles must be developed as the parent couple form a unit to care for the child.

The emphasis on the role of the mother in psychological literature has a long history. As Earls (1976, p. 209) points out:

> The physical needs of infants for nourishment and affection appear to be so obviously fulfilled by mothers that Western psychology has been able to comfortably ignore the relationship of men to infants. If fathers are considered at all, it is usually in relation to the extent that they provide a supportive environment generally, and contribute to a good marriage specifically. Direct interaction between fathers and young children is usually regarded as accessory to maternal behaviour and responsibility.

Sigmund Freud's opinion of parenting roles was that children view their parents differently at different stages in their lives. Since the child's first intimate contact is normally with the mother or with someone who fulfils the mother's role, Freud believed that she will always be the child's first love. The choice of the mother as the first love object is closely connected with all Freud's ideas, that are generally subsumed under the heading of 'the Oedipus complex'. Freud used the myth of Oedipus (see chapter 3) to explain how a boy becomes afraid that he will be castrated by his father for his incestuous feelings towards his mother. This castration anxiety leads to repression of his desire for his mother and hostility towards his father, which later gives way to identification with his father. In 'Analysis of a phobia in a five year old boy' (Freud 1909), Freud identified a form of sexual rivalry between a father and his son for the mother's affection. Thus, according to Freud, it is not until the child is five years of age that the father becomes a psychologically significant figure.

During the 1950s, John Bowlby also emphasised the importance of the mother–infant relationship (basing his ideas on Freud's theory). Mothers are biologically prepared for child-care: 'If mothers don't look after babies, then babies are not going to prosper' (Bowlby 1976, p. 41).

It was not until the late 1960s to early 1970s that research began to examine the father's role in the first years of the child's life. Diverse issues have been studied, such as father–infant interaction (Pederson & Robson 1969; Lamb 1977) and the effect of the father on the child's intellectual development (Jordan, Radin & Epstein 1975). Fathers have now become the focus of broader research interest, given the changing nature of family composition in Western countries such as Australia (Lamb 1981; Parke 1981; Russell & Wright 1982; Renouf 1991; Conrade & Ho 2001; see also The Family Life-Cycle: 2). Research reported by Hudson et al. (2000), indicates interesting differences in first-time mothers' and fathers' self-efficacy and parenting satisfaction. Fathers consistently had lower self-efficacy scores and fathers of male infants reported greater parenting satisfaction scores than fathers of female infants. The authors of the research suggested that the findings highlighted the need for alternative models of parent education for mothers and fathers.

A growing number of families, for instance, have elected on role reversal, with the man staying at home to raise the children, while the woman goes out to work, as in the case of one Victorian family in which the 'house husband':

> has been caring for the house, his two sons – Andrew, six, and Simon, 20 months – and his step-daughter, Jacqueline, 17, while his wife goes off each day to Kyneton where she is employed as a social worker.

> 'He gets the two older children off to school in the morning, does the housework, takes Simon to a local play group, and brings the baby along when he works as a parent-helper in Andrew's grade at . . . school'.

The Age, 26 December 1984.

Russell and Wright (1982) have noted a number of significant points regarding the role of fathers in Australian families.

1 *Child-care competence.* Fathers are just as competent as mothers at child care. Fathers are equally able to perform tasks such as feeding, changing and bathing the child.

2 *Attachment.* As we have seen, until relatively recent times the mother–infant relationship was regarded as both unique and necessary for the child's emotional and social development. However, there is now an emerging body of evidence to suggest that under both laboratory and home conditions infants 'from around six months of age display attachment behaviours to their fathers in much the same way as they display them to their mothers' (Russell & Wright 1982, p. 4).

3 *Play.* Russell and Wright (1982) report figures for the United States and Australia that indicate that fathers spend between 1.7 and 2.8 hours per week on child-care tasks such as feeding and nappy changing. This contrasts sharply with the 18 hours per week that unemployed mothers spend on child-care tasks in Australia (Russell 1983). Fathers consistently spend more time playing with their children than performing child-care tasks (Russell & Wright 1982).

Russell and Wright conclude that fathers in Australia are becoming more involved in child-care, although men are not taking over child-care responsibility as rapidly as women are moving away from it and into the workforce.

Chapter summary

There is little doubt that one of the most noticeable developments in young children concerns their mastery of their body and the improvement in their coordination. Parents watch with a mixture of fear and admiration as children 'test' their skills in terms of running, climbing, skipping and jumping. Their mastery is a source of considerable pride to both the child and the parent.

Discussion questions

1 What constitutes work and what constitutes play in early childhood?
2 Discuss the various definitions of play given in this chapter and formulate your own definition.
3 Which superheroes are found in contemporary children's play? Identify features of these superheroes that might appeal to children.
4 Discuss the link between temperament and accident proneness.
5 How do Australians view the role of the father in the family?

Activities

1 What are the toddler's major achievements in terms of gross and fine motor skills?
2 List the contrasting characteristics of work and play in two columns as shown in the example. Imagine your 'play' column is really labelled 'work'. Could you justify encouraging these qualities in your classroom? Discuss.
3 Individuals or groups are each allocated a theory of play to research and then outline its major features to the class.

Selected websites

Child Adolescent Psychological and Educational Resources <www.caper.com.au>

Kidsafe – Child Accident Prevention Foundation of Australia <www.kidsafe.com.au>

Fathers play a significant role in child raising.

10 Cognitive Development of Toddlers

'What's One and One and One and One?'

'Can you do addition?' the White Queen asked. 'What's one and one and one and one and one and one?'

'I don't know', said Alice. 'I lost count.'

'She can't do Addition, the Red Queen interrupted. 'Can you do Subtraction? Take nine from eight'.

'Nine from eight I can't, you know,' Alice replied very readily: 'But –'

'She can't do Subtraction', said the White Queen. 'Can you do Division? Divide a loaf by a knife – what's the answer to that?'

Lewis Carroll, Through the Looking Glass

KEY TERMS AND CONCEPTS

- Schema
- Constructive argument
- Sensori-motor period
- Tertiary circular motion
- Equilibration
- Crystallised intelligence
- Fluid intelligence

- Mental age
- Chronological age
- Intelligence quotient
- Intelligence tests
- Zone of proximal development
- Postnatal depression

Introduction

Accompanying the toddler's considerable advances in physical development are changes in the way the child thinks (advances that would go some way towards eventually helping Alice answer the questions put to her by the White Queen and the Red Queen!). In this chapter consideration is given to the toddler's increasingly sophisticated ways of thinking about the world. The concept of intelligence is discussed and various theoretical approaches to the study of cognition are outlined. As I have noted in chapters 3 and 7, a significant contributor to our knowledge in this field is Jean Piaget, but even though his first research was published between 1924 and 1932, his work was not recognised in Australia until the 1960s. Similarly, the Russian psychologist Lev Vygotsky was researching and writing about children's thinking over approximately the same period of time, but his ideas are only now finding acceptance in countries such as Australia. The Family Life-cycle: 10 considers the role of the mother after the birth of the first child.

Cognitive development and intelligence

Cognitive development and more particularly, the idea of intelligence, has always fascinated psychologists. Why do some people, such as Einstein or Beethoven, have exceptional abilities? Are such gifts present at birth or do they develop over time? Is intelligence a stable factor or does it change as the individual ages? Cognitive development and the influences shaping it are complex issues, as illustrated by the Gryphon's dialogue with Alice in *Alice in Wonderland*:

> 'I couldn't afford to learn it', said the Mock Turtle with a sigh. 'I only took the regular course.'
>
> 'What was that?' inquired Alice.
>
> 'Reeling and writhing, of course, to begin with,' the Mock Turtle replied: 'and then the different branches of Arithmetic – Ambition, Distraction, Uglification, and Derision.'
>
> 'I never heard of 'Uglification', Alice ventured to say. 'What is it?'
>
> The Gryphon lifted up both its paws in surprise. 'What! Never heard of uglifying!' it exclaimed. 'You know what to beautify is, I suppose?'
>
> 'Yes', said Alice doubtfully: 'it means – to – make – anything – prettier.'
>
> 'Well, then', the Gryphon went on, 'if you don't know what to uglify is, you *are* a simpleton.'

Carroll 1982, pp. 126–7.

Early attempts to understand the activities of the mind can be traced back to the Greek philosophers. Plato distinguished between the intellectual, emotional and moral facets of the mind. Aristotle collapsed Plato's three-fold distinction into the duality of the cognitive or intellectual capacities and the emotional or moral facets.

In the nineteenth century, the concept of intelligence achieved a new focus and prominence through the writings of the British scientist Francis Galton (1869). Following a line of thinking developed by Charles Darwin (1859), which emphasised the hereditary as opposed to environmental facets of development, Galton maintained that individual differences in our capacities were also innate. Drawing on his studies of hereditary genius, Galton explained the range of mental power he observed among people in terms of 'general abilities' and 'special aptitudes'.

As a basis for further consideration of the concept of intelligence, Piaget's views of cognitive development during the toddler stage will be considered, followed by a description of Lev Vygotsky's theory.

Theoretical foundations: Piaget

schema
an Piagetian terms, a pattern of action or a mental structure; plural, schemata.

Piaget's painstaking observational research of children's behaviour has provided those who work with children with important insight into the way children understand the world around them at different ages. In progressing from sensori-motor through pre-operational and concrete operations to formal operations and thought, the individual moves through differently organised theories of the world and self. The core structural element is the **schema**, which, correct or not by adult standards, permits the child to take in, organise and make sense of information, and use it to make assumptions about the future. In Piagetian terms, development is the increase in scope of the child's schemata. It is important to understand that according to Piagetian theory, a child's view of the world differs from that of an adult. The child's view, however, is not an incomplete adult view, but rather represents a different theoretical organisation of presented evidence.

constructive development
occurs when a child actively participates by finding personal meaning in a situation, making decisions and sharing viewpoints with peers.

In Piaget's theory, development is **constructive** in as much as the child actively participates in the process. Development is a product of the interaction between maturation and learning. Thinking, knowing, imagining and remembering are all processes that are included in the meaning of the term 'cognition'.

Piaget consistently revised and reworked his ideas on the nature of development. In a contribution to a text by Mussen (1960), Piaget explained that his theory had not been completed and that he considered himself to be his own chief revisionist. His theory of children's cognitive development moved from a rather fixed conception of stages and substages to a greater awareness of the impact of the complex interactions between the child and the environment.

A miniature Copernican revolution

Piaget's careful observations of his own children's growth initially provided him with important insight into the way a toddler's thinking develops. Reading Piaget transforms the way we view children. Through Piaget's writings, we see the toddler as a fascinating individual who is actively processing information about the world in an attempt to make sense of a very complex environment.

By the end of the first year, infants have already passed through the first four stages of the **sensori-motor period**, moving from a few reflex behaviours and vague perceptions of the world to a growing recognition of relatively permanent objects. They have become skilled at manipulating objects such as toys and have made significant leaps in language development. As skilled imitators, they revel in repeating sounds they hear around them.

The sensori-motor period is so-called because the infant's earliest signs of intelligence appear in terms of sensory perceptions and motor activities: during this period of development the young child will begin to follow a moving object, notice noises and reach for objects and toys. Although these may appear to be small achievements in themselves, Piaget believed that in the first two years the child effects 'a miniature Copernican revolution' (Piaget 1967).

By two years of age the child is walking and is free, independent and able to seek out new experiences. According to Piaget, the toddler is in the last two phases of the sensori-motor period – substages 5 and 6 (see Table 10.1). Abilities attained in earlier substages are consolidated and extended in the last two substages.

> **sensori-motor period**
> Piaget's first cognitive development stage in which infants use their senses and motor skills to explore their environment.

Substage 5: tertiary circular reactions (12–18 months)

During the fifth stage of the sensori-motor period, the child does not simply repeat movements, as in substage 4 (see chapter 7), but experiments to see what will happen. This active experimentation helps extend the child's notion of space and size relationships, time sequences and causation. For example, Piaget (1952) describes an experiment conducted with his daughter Jacqueline. A cardboard rooster was placed outside her playpen with its head and tail at different openings between the bars. To get this new toy into her playpen Jacqueline had to push it back, stand it up and bring it (head or tail first) through the bars. Piaget recorded that it took four days and 39 attempts for his daughter to solve this particular problem, but once she had solved it she was able to repeat the exercise without fail.

At the dinner table, the toddler may drop peas or pieces of potato onto the floor, watching with interest to see where they fall. Then, the child may drop the peas from various positions and heights. By experimenting in this way, the child is trying to see what will happen to the peas when position and height are varied. This illustrates two aspects of tertiary circular reactions.

1   The child is trying to assimilate new objects into the usual schema of dropping. When peas are dropped from different positions, the toddler discovers that they drop in different ways and behave differently when they hit the floor.
2   The child is interested in these inconsistencies and so may have to accommodate the old schema of 'dropping' to allow for new information.

Toddlers' behaviour is therefore tertiary and circular, in as much as they want to repeat a pleasurable action.

Another feature of the fifth substage is the child's discovery and use of a means to achieve an end. For example, my son Matthew (2½ years) used a

Trends and issues

Circular reactions and Pooh Bear

An example of tertiary circular reactions can be found in the A. A. Milne story, *The House at Pooh Corner*. Pooh is walking in the forest holding a fir cone when he trips, drops the cone into the river and watches it emerge on the other side of a bridge:

'That's funny', said Pooh. 'I dropped it on the other side, and it came out on this side! I wonder

if it would do it again?' And he went back for some more fir cones. It did. It kept on doing it. Then he dropped two in at once and leant over the bridge to see which of them would come out first; and one of them did; but as they were both the same size, he didn't know if it was the one he wanted to win or the other one. So the next time he dropped one big one and one little one.

Milne 1984 edn, p. 94.

miniature hockey stick to retrieve a ball that was out of arm's reach under a settee. Matthew discovered that he could pull the ball to him by hooking it in the curved end of the stick.

In substage 5, the toddler can also correctly follow a visible sequence of movements involving an object. Piaget described his observations of his daughter:

> Jacqueline watches me hide my watch under cushion A on her left, then under cushion B on her right; in the latter case she immediately searches in the right place. If I bury the object deep she searches for a long time, then gives up, but does not return to A (Piaget 1954, p. 67).

Even if the object successively disappears in a number of places the toddler will look for it in the last place it was seen. This is different from the reaction of substage 4, in which the infant would look for the object in the place it was previously discovered. That is, in substage 5 the object has acquired a permanence of its own.

Table 10.1 Substages 5 and 6: the last substages of Piaget's sensori-motor period

Stage	Age	Abilities
Sensori-motor period	0–2 years	Use of five senses to relate to the world
Substage 1	0–1 month	Modification of reflexes
Substage 2	1–4 months	Primary circular reactions
Substage 3	4–8 months	Secondary circular functions
Substage 4	8–12 months	Coordination of secondary reactions: attainment of object permanence
Substage 5	12–18 months	Tertiary circular reactions
Substage 6	18–24 months	Representational thought
Pre-operational period	2–7 years	Language and symbolism
Concrete operations period	7–11 years	Can apply simple logic to solve problems
Formal operations period	11+ years	Abstract reasoning

Substage 6: representational thought (18–24 months)

Although the infant appears to have made great advances in the first five sub-stages of the sensori-motor period, they are insignificant compared to the development in substage 6, when toddlers begin to do their 'grouping' mentally rather than physically. The child becomes capable of representing invisible displacements. Before this, children essentially are not capable of thought and language (Ginsberg & Opper 1979) and are therefore limited to the world of sensory experience.

In substage 6 they enter the phase of symbolic thought: they can represent to themselves in images or symbols how they might actually do something without actually doing it. Piaget calls this the 'invention of new means'. When toddlers fail to solve a problem using a familiar schema, they will consider the situation mentally and then use a schema never before applied.

For example, Piaget (1952) described how he played with his child Lucienne (16 months of age) by hiding his watch in a matchbox. First, he left the matchbox open wide enough for Lucienne to get her fingers inside and pull out the chain. Then the opening was closed to a narrow slit so that she could not get her fingers in. As Piaget noted, Lucienne paused over this problem for a moment, opening and closing her mouth as she mimicked what to do. Then she put her finger into the slit, and opened it wide enough to pull out the chain. Piaget understood Lucienne's behaviour to mean she was mentally solving the problem by her motor imitation of the desired act. By opening her mouth she represented to herself how to open the matchbox. Lucienne was on the verge of thought.

In Piaget's sub-stage 6, the child is exploring the world and performing experiments upon it.

Vygotsky and intellect

Apart from Piaget, as indicated earlier there is another theorist who has made, and continues to make a significant contribution to our understanding of children's cognitive development is Lev Vygotsky. His writing also informs our understanding of the concept of intelligence.

Lev Semenovich Vygotsky (1896–1934) was a Russian psychologist whose contribution to our understanding of children's cognitive development is now beginning to be understood and appreciated in Australia. Although Vygotsky was a very deep thinker, he was also a very practical man who founded and directed a number of research institutes, including the first Russian institute for the study of handicapped children (Kozulin 1988). Vygotsky was committed to Marxist doctrine but his interpretation of it led to a suppression of his writings until Krushchev denounced Stalinism in 1956. The first English translation of his work *Thought and Language* appeared in 1962.

Vygotsky emphasised that human capacities, such as attention, memory and consciousness, have their beginnings in human social life. He was critical of mainstream Western views of education and psychology where the emphasis was on individual development and where collective functioning was generally ignored. As noted by Holaday, LaMontagne and Marciel (1994) Vygotsky's theory was (i) instrumental; (ii) cultural; and (iii) genetic.

1   *Instrumental*. His theory was instrumental in as much as '[p]eople actively modify the stimuli they encounter and use them as instruments to control conditions and regulate their own behavior' (Holaday et al. 1994, p. 16). As such, a feature of Vygotsky's theory was that individuals are active agents in creating their own development and learning.

2   *Cultural*. There is no doubt that language was seen by Vygotsky to play a crucial role in the development of thinking (Vygotsky 1962). 'Language is a cultural tool created to organise thinking' (Holaday et al. 1994, p.16).

3   *Genetic*. A third component of his theory emphasised genetics in a developmental sense. Interactions with others were understood to facilitate the development of higher order mental functions from lower order mental functions. According to Vygotsky, child development is made up of periods of relatively stable growth, crises and transformation. The development of an individual can come to a standstill or even regress. 'Child development, then, could be described as a series of qualitatively different stages' (Van Der Veer 1986, p. 528).

Table 10.2 Vygotsky's stages of development

Stage	Age
Infancy	0.2–1 year
Early childhood	1–3 years
Pre-school period	3–7 years
School period	7–13 years
Adolescence	13–17 years

Vygotsky (1984) identified five stages in child development (see Table 10.2). Each of these stages is a so-called stable period preceded and concluded by a period of crisis (Van Der Veer 1986). At around 12 months of age the toddler faces a new period of crisis or transformation which is associated with three new developments – namely walking, speech and emotional reactions. For Vygotsky, the child's language development was paramount, and he made the distinction between thought and speech development in the first two years of life. However, at about 2 years of age the two curves of development of I thought and speech come together to initiate a new form of behaviour. In Vygotsky's (1988) view this is a momentous time in the toddler's cognitive development: speech begins to serve intellect and thoughts begin to be spoken. The onset of this stage is indicated by two unmistakable objective symptoms:

1   a sudden active curiosity about words and questions about every new thing;
2   the resulting rapid increases in the child's vocabulary.

The zone of proximal development

It is through Vygotsky's **zone of proximal development** that the full implications of the notion of the social nature of the young child are now being recognised. In Vygotsky's words: 'Human learning presupposes a specific social nature and a process by which children grow into the intellectual life of those around them' (Vygotsky 1978, p. 88). Human learning is viewed as interactive and it is the competent nature of the child that is emphasised. Vygotsky believed that a child's progress in concept attainment achieved through interaction with an adult would provide a more sensitive gauge of the child's intellectual abilities than an intelligence test where the child was principally working alone. He described the 'zone of proximal development' as '. . . the distance between the actual developmental level as determined by through problem-solving under adult guidance or in collaboration with more capable peers' (Vygotsky 1978, p. 86).

zone of proximal development (ZPD)
the 'gap' between what individuals can achieve alone and what they can achieve with the help of a more knowledgable person.

   A number of researchers have drawn upon Vygotsky's notion of the zone of proximal development (ZPD) in their own studies of how children learn (Wood et al. 1978; Bruner & Haste 1987; Wood, D. 1988). In a block assembly task in which mothers were asked to teach their 4 to 5-year-old children, Wood identified five instructional options available to mothers: (i) general verbal encouragement; (ii) specific verbal instruction; (iii) assistance in choosing materials for a task; (iv) preparing materials for assembly in a task; and (v) demonstration.

   He reports that 'the children who learned most about the task were exposed to a style of instruction that combined showing and telling in a specific pattern' (Wood, D. 1988, p. 79). Mothers using such a pattern would suggest to the child a block to choose and offer more help if the child still did not understand. When the child followed a suggestion, however, these mothers would immediately step back and allow the child to assume responsibility for what happened next. Wood calls such an instructional style 'contingent teaching':

These mothers ensured that the child was not left alone when he was over-whelmed by the task, and also guaranteed him greater scope for initiative when he showed signs of success (Wood, D. 1988, p. 79).

In summary, Wertsch and Rogoff (1984, p. 1) define the ZPD as '. . . the phase in development in which the child has only partially mastered a task but can participate in its execution with assistance and supervision of an adult or more capable peer'.

Holaday et al. (1999) describe two important dimensions of the ZPD, namely (i) 'joint collaboration'; and (ii) 'transfer of responsibility'.

1   As the authors describe it, 'joint collaboration' is best viewed as active, shared participation for the purpose of solving a problem. The adult or peer, by virtue of their greater understanding of the problem, actively facilitates or encourages the child in their own definition and redefinition of the problem to promote the achievement of a solution.

2   '[T]ransfer of responsibility' refers to the ' adult's decreasing role in regulating and managing behaviour or task performance. The child is given more opportunities to perform the task independently' (Rogoff 1986; Holaday 1994, p. 19).

An important element in promoting cognitive development is 'scaffolding'. Rogoff and Gardner (1984, p. 109) describe it as occurring when a more competent or able adult or peer adjusts the learning situation or task conditions '. . . to produce appropriate understanding of a particular problem for a learner at a particular level of ability'. In general terms, it refers to the process whereby a more knowledgeable adult or peer provides the appropriate support and input to facilitate the problem-solving of another and then gradually withdraws the degree of support and control as a function of the other's increasing mastery of the problem.

In summary, Van Der Veer (1986) argues that Vygotsky made three original contributions to our understanding of human development:

1   his description of the crisis-like character of development;
2   the importance of the role of speech;
3   his emphasis on the social nature of the young child.

Intelligence

The definition of intelligence

The word 'intelligence' has many meanings to the lay person, although such meanings usually relate to 'knowing about things' and the 'capacity for knowledge'. Would you consider a person intelligent if they had:

• completed a university degree but abused narcotics?
• worked so hard they had experienced three heart attacks by 35 years of age?

- completed frontier-breaking scientific research but could not manage their financial affairs and were intensely jealous people?

Piaget (1962) opted for a broad definition of intelligence. He linked it with the concept of **equilibration**. That is, intelligence is not a trait but rather a process involving the three central concepts of schema, assimilation and accommodation. A schema refers to a recurring action pattern that guides behaviour. An infant's schemata are overt, involving sensori-motor behaviour, while an older child carries out schemata mentally. Assimilation is the incorporation of new knowledge into existing schemata. Accommodation is the modification of schemata to incorporate new knowledge that does not fit existing schemata. Equilibration refers to the individual's search for a balance between the two processes of assimilation and accommodation.

> **equilibration**
> the search for a balance between what the child already knows (assimilation) and the child's new experiences (accommodation).

Vygotsky placed instruction at the heart of human development, and defined intelligence as the capacity to learn through instruction. In fact, he was one of the first psychologists to study the links between cognitive development and education (Vygotsky 1978). His concept of the zone of proximal development described earlier in this chapter is a critical aspect of the instructional process.

Why conceptions of intelligence matter

Sternberg (2000) identified four reasons why people's conceptions of intelligence matter:

1 Ideas about intelligence influence how individuals evaluate their own and other's intelligence.
2 People's implicit theories of intelligence inform the development of theories of intelligence.
3 Implicit theories can be helpful when a researcher suspects problems with more explicitly stated theories.
4 Understanding and appreciating implicit theories can help understand developmental and cross-cultural differences.

Raymond Cattell (1963) distinguished two types of intelligence: **crystallised** and **fluid**. Crystallised intelligence is measured by tests of vocabulary, general knowledge and reading comprehension, and is therefore subject to educational and cultural influences. Fluid intelligence requires the individual to understand complex relationships, think abstractly, reason inductively and be able to form concepts. Such intelligence is considered to have a hereditary base and to be less influenced by intensive education and acculturation.

> **crystallised intelligence**
> according to Cattell, a type of intelligence that comprises knowledge based on education and culture.

To David Wechsler, who developed the widely used Wechsler Intelligence Scale for Children, 'Intelligence is the overall capacity of an individual to understand and cope with the world around him' (Wechsler 1974, p. 5). Wechsler argues that intelligence is a global entity that is multifaceted and avoids singling out specific abilities, such as abstract reasoning, as important.

> **fluid intelligence**
> according to Cattell, a type of intelligence that is hereditary and involves the ability to think and reason abstractly.

In defining intelligence, Miles (1957) refers to the standardised tests that have been developed for the purpose of determining whether a person is intelligent.

It is the items on these tests (or more strictly, the person's behaviour in producing correct responses to these items) that are regarded as constituting the exemplaries of the word 'intelligent'. Intelligence, in other words, is *what intelligence tests measure* [italics added]. (Miles 1957, p. 29).

The concept of multiple intelligences has been developed by Gardner (1972, 1984) and Sternberg (1985). Gardner (1972, 1984, 1999) believes that seven forms of intelligence can be identified, including: (i) linguistic; (ii) logical-mathematical; (iii) spatial; (iv) musical; (v) interpersonal – dealing with others; (vi) intrapersonal knowledge of self; and (vii) bodily-kinaesthetic. Gardner suggested that the first two types were valued and emphasised in the mainstream Western school system. Intelligence tests typically assess only the linguistic and logical–mathematical types of intelligence. Gardner observes that the relative importance of these seven types of intelligence varies over time and across cultures. In some cultures, for example, it might be more important to have well-developed personal skills than the ability to add or subtract quickly. Gardner makes the point that while on the whole, linguistic and logical–mathematical skills are important, we should be sensitive to the possibility that in the future other types of intelligence might be equally important.

From the sample of definitions of intelligence given here, it is obvious that there is no simple definition of the term. Contemporary definitions would probably include that intelligence refers to:

- a process;
- a wide range of skills, such as vocabulary or mathematical reasoning;
- ability to profit from experience;
- the ability to use new information;
- the ability to adjust to new situations.

Metaphors for intelligence

Sternberg (2000) has identified seven metaphors representing experts' ideas about intelligence.

1 *Geographic*: Using this metaphor, intelligence is viewed as 'a map of the mind'(p. 10).
2 *Computational*: In this metaphor, the 'basic unit of analysis is the elementary information process (or component) (p. 10). Computer simulation is used to explore the nature of intelligence.
3 *Biological*: Here experts examine structures in the brain linking parts of the brain to certain intellectual functions.
4 *Genetic–epistemological*: Piaget is the main exponent of this metaphor. The notion of 'schema' .
5 *Anthropological*: As noted by Sternberg (2000, p. 11), 'The question here is that of what forms intelligence takes as a cultural invention'.
6 *Sociological*: Researchers such as Vygotsky have elaborated on this view, emphasising the importance of soialisation in the development of intelligence.

7 *Systems*: 'The systems metaphor is based on the notion that intelligence is a complex system that integrates many levels of analysis, including geographic, computational, anthropological, sociological and others' (Sternberg 2000, p. 12).

Metaphors, as noted by Sternberg (2000), are neither right or wrong, but provide different ways of understanding and discussing a concept like intelligence.

Intelligence tests

In 1905 the French scientist Alfred Binet was asked by the French Ministry of Education to develop a test that could be used to identify mentally defective children in French schools so that they could be taught separately. In his original test, Binet used 30 items that were of varying degrees of difficulty.

> [L]et us recall to mind precisely the limits of the problem for which we are seeking a solution. Our aim is, when a child is put before us, to take the measurement of his intellectual powers, in order to establish whether he is normal or if he is retarded (Binet & Simon 1905, p. 191).

Binet and Simon's tests were soon being used by French school authorities to identify children in need of special instruction and to predict school performance. A number of terms and concepts have been developed as a result of Binet's research. A 6-year-old child who performs as well on an intelligence test as an average 7-year-old is said to have a **mental age** (MA) of seven. **Chronological age** (CA) refers to the actual age of the child. In 1914 a German psychologist by the name of Stern proposed the formula:

$$\frac{\text{Mental age (MA)}}{\text{chronological age (CA)}} \times 100 = \textbf{intelligence quotient (IQ)}$$

Since the early works of Binet and Simon (1905), Galton (1883), Cattell (1890) and others, various intelligence tests have been introduced. Two of the most commonly used scales for measuring intelligence are those developed by Alfred Binet and David Wechsler, both of which have been adapted for use in Australia. Recent editions of each of these tests are described here.

The Stanford–Binet scale

This individually administered intelligence scale may be used with individuals of all ages from 2 years to adult. A recent version of the Stanford-Binet scale is the fourth edition (Thorndike et al. 1986) and comprises 15 tests grouped into four major categories: verbal reasoning, quantitative reasoning, abstract visual reasoning and short-term memory. Test-takers complete only those subtests appropriate to their age group. A vocabulary subtest is first administered to determine the person's most appropriate 'entry level' for the remaining tests. Next the examiner determines a basal level (least difficult) and a ceiling level (most difficult) on each of the tests appropriate to the person's age group. These

mental age
a measure of intellectual ability in terms of the average ability at a particular age, which may not be the same as an individual's actual age (chronological age).

chronological age
the actual age of an individual; compare mental age.

intelligence quotient (IQ)
the ratio of an individual's mental age (MA) to chronological age (CA) multiplied by 100.

raw data are converted to standard age scores (SAS) and are used to determine how the person has performed relative to the normative age groups.

The Stanford–Binet must be administered by a properly qualified professional who is capable of simultaneously presenting the instructions in a standard format, scoring the test-taker's responses and determining the appropriate items at which to begin and discontinue testing.

The Wechsler intelligence scale for children (WISC III)

The WISC III is a recent version of the Wechsler intelligence scale for children (Wechsler 1991). It is the most widely used individually administered measure of intellectual ability in children of school age in Australia, and is one of a family of Wechsler scales (the others being for pre-schoolers or adults). Wechsler tests are based on an alternative model of intellectual assessment to the Binet scale and yield three scores: verbal intelligence quotient, performance intelligence quotient and full-scale intelligence quotient. In this way, the measurement of the child's intelligence does not rely solely on verbal ability.

The WISC III consists of 13 subtests, including a new performance scale, known as symbol search. With a view to holding the child's interest and attention, many of the stimulus materials are presented in colour. An important aspect of the WISC-III is that it aims to assess the child's upper and lower ability levels as accurately as possible. During picture completion, if a child gives incorrect answers to the first two age-appropriate items, the preceding questions are administered in reverse order until the child answers two consecutive questions correctly. As with the Stanford-Binet, this test should be administered only by highly trained academics or professionals.

Intelligence testing is used to complement the information that teachers gather about school children through classroom assessment. Generally, intelligence tests are administered and interpreted by guidance officers or school counsellors only when requested by parents or principals.

As already noted, tests of intelligence were originally conceived to predict educational performance. To this end, they could be considered as relatively successful with correlations between school grades and IQ averaging around .40 to .50. The correlations tend to increase with age (McGew & Knopik 1993).

Children's views of intelligence

Various writers have examined how children view the concept of intelligence. Yussen and Kane (1985) interviewed year 1 to year 6 primary school children using questions relating to their definition of intelligence, the signs of intelligence and changes in intelligence over time. Developmental trends were noted, with older children having a more differentiated and internalised view of intelligence than younger children. Approaching the issue of intelligence from a motivational perspective, Dweck (1999) classified children as 'entity' or 'incremental' theorists. Entity theorists believed that intelligence was something you were born with. Consequently there was not much one could do to change one's intelligence, and these children were often afraid to make mistakes in front of others. Incremental theorists believed that one's intelligence was not constant across the life span and that learning was a method for increasing one's intelligence.

A critique of intelligence tests

School performance. As noted earlier, intelligence tests were initially developed to predict school performance and this continues to be the main use of such tests (Sternberg 1992). Correlations between measures of IQ and school grades are moderate (McCall 1977). Past and present school performance is as good, if not better, than intelligence tests in predicting future school performance.

Stability of intelligence. There is very little evidence for stability of general intelligence from infancy to childhood. However, after 10 years of age, IQ stability is reasonably high – of the order of +.70 to +.90, particularly where the measurements are taken at short time intervals (Cronbach 1984; Gustafsson & Undheim 1992). Nonetheless, individuals can still undergo quite substantial changes in intelligence test scores of the order of 30–40 points (Francois 1990).

Cultural bias. A significant criticism of intelligence tests is that they are biased in terms of their language, pictures and content in favour of white middle-class children, thereby disadvantaging children from low socioeconomic and different ethnic backgrounds. In an effort to offset such criticism non-verbal tests of intelligence have been developed (Brown et al. 1992; Raven 1986).

Careful consideration is now being given to the future of standardised intelligence tests, both overseas (Lawson 1992; Sternberg 1992) and in Australia (Jenkinson 1991). To avoid problems with the use and abuse of such tests, it is advised that:

> intelligence testing devices be restricted to persons who can demonstrate competence both in administering and interpreting. A knowledge of the techniques of test construction, a background in psychology, a supervised internship in administering and interpreting, and an adequate knowledge of the clinical aspects of child study are recommended (Lawson 1992, p. 133).

Language development

The study of children's acquisition of language is one of the most exciting features of developmental psychology. Our understanding of how language develops has undergone radical change in the last two decades.

> During the course of the child's first two years, notable developments occur in lexical, semantic, and grammatical aspects of language (Tamis-Lemonda et al. 1998, p. 676).

> What one tends to overlook is the sheer magnitude of the child's achievement. Simply learning the vocabulary is an enormous undertaking. The fact is that for many years after starting to talk a child learns new words at a rate of more than 10 per day. Yet little is known about how children do it . . .

By the age of three years children will have mastered the basic structure of their native language and will be well on the way to communicative structure . . .

Acquiring their first language is the most impressive intellectual feat many people will ever perform (Miller and Gildea 1987, p. 86).

In the bus queue, a three year old was talking animatedly to her mother. The mother stared straight ahead, silent – until suddenly she exploded, her voice furious, detonating, 'That's all I ever hear from you! – chatter, chatter, chatter!' The little girl's lively, intelligent face changed, and she looked wary, self-conscious, off-balance and silly. I wondered what else a mother expected to get from a three-year-old. What else has a small child to give? And what gift could one have that is more tender, more joyous, more remarkable? (Berg 1972, p. 11).

Down the street an old man shuffles past a pram. The baby babbles away. 'Shut up you little bleeder!' says the old man with hate. 'Shut up!' (Berg 1972, p. 11).

'The acquisition of language is a peculiarly human characteristic' (Baldwin 1980, p. 429). In the space of two to three years children will progress from their first word (at 12 to 18 months) to speaking fluent grammatical sentences at three to four years of age. Observing my own son's language development, I became acutely aware of just how fast a child acquires language. When he was 18 months old, Matthew was using one- and two-word utterances, such as Mum, Dad, drink, Mum – drink, no. But by 24 months it was possible to identify sentences, such as 'Daddy – drink please' or 'Daddy – I want cake'.

By any gauge, then, a child's learning of language is an impressive feat. The speed and size of the accomplishment is best grasped in table form (see Table 10.3).

Table 10.3 The development of language

Child's Age (months)	Type of Vocalisation	Achievement
0–11	Babbling	Contextual understanding: objects are recognised in context
12–15	1–2 word utterances	Object recognition
16–18	Short sentences	Transition period: object recognition in various contexts
19–24 25–	} Language	Symbols and labels used with greater dexterity: language becomes more complex

What is language?

A newborn infant will cry from hunger or coo with happiness. Your pet cat will 'meow' when it is time to be fed. An autistic child may take an adult's hand and put it on a toy that he or she wants to play with. These are all instances of communication that do not actually involve language. However, when a child says 'I want a cup of milk' or a deaf child gives the appropriate sign language for 'drink', or older children are involved in some verbal dispute over a game in the playground, language is used as the means of communication. That is, in the second set of examples symbols are used and the use of symbols is basic to true language. A symbol is something that can stand for or represent something else, such as a picture of a cup. Thus, the child asking for a 'cup' of milk is using a symbol (word) which stands for or represents the object, cup. Children arguing in the playground are using a sophisticated form of language in which a pattern of words (symbols) is used to present their arguments.

It is true that animals emit sounds and gestures that other animals understand. For example, seagulls exhibit a complex set of sounds and gestures when they cluster around food, and other seagulls understand such communication. But the birds' sounds and posturings are largely the result of instinct and are responded to instinctively. This is not necessarily so when humans use language to communicate. For example, the word 'tea' means a meal to some people, but for others it refers to a drinking beverage. Animal 'language' is used in a fixed format, but humans have the unique ability to arrange symbols into new and meaningful combinations.

To step back a little though, we should define some basic terms including 'speech', 'language' and 'communication'. As noted by Owens (1996, p. 7), 'Speech is a verbal means of communicating or conveying meaning'. The important thing is that speech requires precise neuromuscular coordination including voice regulation. Owens (1996, p. 8) defines language as '. . . a socially shared code or conventional system for representing concepts through the use of arbitrary symbols and rule-governed combinations of those symbols'. English, French, Chinese and any other 'language' has its own unique set of symbols. Speech and language form part of the larger process of 'communication'. 'Communication is the process participants use to exchange information and ideas, needs and desires' (Owens 1996, p. 11).

The emergence of language

Babbling

Babies are born able to make sounds – crying, **babbling**, and cooing. Within a few months of their baby's birth, parents listening to their infant cooing and babbling in the crib will invest many of their baby's utterances with meaning and intention. For instance, a baby's cry may be met with the mother's response of 'Oh! So you want to play, eh?'. Moreover, analysis of mother–infant vocal utterances (Stern 1977) shows that when addressing a baby in the first month of the baby's life, a mother typically alters the pitch of her voice (raising or lowering it), stresses words or syllables (that is, gives a sing-song quality to her voice), and uses a pattern of vocal burst followed by a pause (imagining that the infant is talking back). This type of speech has been referred to as **motherese**. By the second month of life, the infant is engaging in vocal play in which many different sounds are produced (Jones and Guidon 1972). These articulated sounds involve vowel sounds (a, e, i, o, u) and then various consonants. Even deaf infants go through the babbling stage.

babbling
the alternating vowel and consonant sounds made by a young infant in the first months of life.

motherese
a type of speech used by the mother to address the young infant.

Sound imitation

lattation
repetitive sounds
made by the young
infant at about
6 months of age.

Jones and Guidon (1972) have identified a stage in language development called
the 'sound imitation' period. During this period they have identified two phases:
1 **Lattation**. After 6 months of age infants are aware of the sound they
   produce and because of the pleasure they derive from these sounds, they
   repeat them: for example, 'ga, ga, ga'.

echolalia
imitation by the
infant of the speech
of others, appearing
at around 9 months
of age.

2 **Echolalia**. Around the ninth month of life, infants begin to imitate sounds in
   their environment selectively, such as the sounds care-givers make.

One-word utterances

At approximately 1 year of age, one-word utterances (such as ta-ta, ma-ma)
appear. The meaning of the word can vary considerably. Thus, the word
'ma-ma' may be a greeting when the mother returns from the shop, or it may
be used to attract the mother's attention, or it may mean 'get me a drink'.

**holophrastic
speech**
one-word
utterances that
express a complete
thought, appearing
at about 1 year of
age.

Holophrastic speech occurs when one word stands for a whole sentence.
Regardless of the language to which the child is exposed, the earliest meaningful sounds are consonants produced with the tongue in front of the mouth.
Holophrastic speech refers to single-word utterances that may express complex
intentions and meanings. These words are generally labels for persons, objects
or acts.

Two-word utterances

At around 18 to 24 months, two-word utterances become identifiable in the
child's language: 'See doggie'; 'Where Daddy?'. Thus, the words 'Dink peese'
at 18 months meant 'Can I have a drink of juice please?' Even though children
of this age do not reproduce all the words spoken to them, they imitate the most
important words. They also seem to have acquired the grammatical rule of
word order – subject, verb, object: 'I getting ball'.

telegraphic speech
early utterances
(18–24 months)
that leave out most
of the articles,
prepositions and
conjunctions.

Telegraphic speech is the term used to describe short sentences of this kind.
Basically, the meaning intended by the child is still derived from the context

1 the child invents new sentences;
2 the sentences follow rules:

noun phrase (NP)	=	modifier (M)	+	noun (N)
(big ball)		(big)		(ball)

morpheme
the smallest unit of
meaning in spoken
or written language.

At a later stage (2½ years), noun–verb combinations emerge: 'Daddy
gone'. There is a striking uniformity across languages in the meaning
expressed by simple two-word utterances. Grammatical **morphemes** appear:
prepositions such as 'in' and 'on', articles such as 'an', forms of the copula
(linking words) such as 'is' or 'are', verb tenses, and inflections such as '-ing'
or '-ed'. Starting from the age of 18–24 months, the use of morphemes
gradually increases over the next two or three years, although they are not
necessarily correctly used all the time for months or even years later.

Sentences

The next step involves whole sentences. By the time children are 2 years of age they usually have an effective vocabulary of 300 words. This extends to 1000 words at 3 years, and between 3 and 5 years of age about 50 words per month are added. As the child's language develops there is a gradual reduction in situational cues and an emergence of symbols. From 2 years of age children learn to follow instructions, such as, 'Get your socks from the bedroom please'. Word usage extends beyond nouns and verbs to the inclusion of prepositions and adjectives.

Theories of language development

We have seen that, while there is evidence that animals have some capacity to learn and utilise language, in humans this capacity far exceeds that of any other mammal. Language serves an enormous functional purpose for children. It allows them to discriminate between objects and situations and to generalise from one situation to another. For example, to call another a 'friend' conveys a great deal of information. When children understand a word like 'hot' their behaviour in the presence of an object such as a fire is shaped. Language also serves to help children evaluate the appropriateness of certain behaviour. For example, reward or punishment is implied by the words 'good' or 'bad', as in 'That's a good boy'.

How children acquire language is subject to considerable debate. Bloom (1983) described the process as akin to 'magic', while Gleitman and Wanner (1982) described the process as 'mysterious'. As such, Bohannon and Bonvillian (1997) have bemoaned the fact that theory construction has generally lagged behind research.

A stimulus–response theory of language development

As noted in chapter 3, behaviourists share a common focus on describing overt, observable behaviour. Behaviourists eschew mentalistic concepts which are not subject to observation. In relation to language theory the focus is upon observable environmental conditions (stimuli) that co-occur and predict overt verbal behaviours (responses).

Using the concepts described in chapter 3, a child would learn the word 'juice' in the following manner using principles of classical conditioning. The juice (unconditioned stimulus – UCS) fed to a thirsty infant (Matthew) causes a physiological response (unconditioned response – UCR). Matthew's father in saying the word 'juice' just prior to giving the child the juice is providing a conditioned stimulus (CS). Gradually the word 'juice' becomes a conditioned response (CR). Then, once a CS (word) comes to elicit a CR it can be used as an UCS to modify the response to another CS. For example, if a new word such as 'cake' is frequently used in association with the word 'juice' the new word may come to elicit a CR to the word 'juice'.

Apart from classical conditioning as described in chapter 3, operant conditioning fills in the gap to explain other means by which speech is acquired. According to Skinner (1957, p. 31), 'A child acquires verbal behaviour when relatively unpatterned vocalisations, selectively reinforced, gradually assume forms which produce appropriate consequences in a given verbal community'. Skinner's behaviourist view specified that each word and word combination was learned. Reinforcement, imitation and association are significant in the acquisition of language. Seen from such an empirical viewpoint, language becomes a set of habits that the child learns in response to outside circumstances.

'DOG' —'doggy'—'yes', a doggy' (Reinforcer)======S–R strengthened

'kitty'—'no', that not a doggy' (punisher) ======S–R weakened

However, as Campbell and Wales (1970, p. 242) point out, 'It is a matter of controversy whether the acquisition of language can be accounted for within current versions of psychological theories of learning'. The stimulus–response theory has been strongly criticised in terms of its ability to explain language development (Howlin 1980; Maratsos 1983). Basic criticisms are that human language development is far too complex a phenomenon to be explained by reinforcement theory. Children could not possibly master the grammatical structures of their language as quickly as empirical evidence suggests if they had to depend upon stimulus–response reinforcement mechanisms.

Social learning theory (see chapter 3) has also been called upon to explain language development in children. Using this theory, it is argued that children acquire language by observing and imitating adults. That is, parents serve as models for the child's language development. One criticism of the social learning theory approach is that the speed with which language is acquired by the young child makes it unlikely that imitation alone is responsible.

Linguistic theories of language development

A number of writers emphasise that behavioural explanations of language development have reduced in importance (Cochrane 1972). Linguistic approaches assume that language has a structure or grammar that is relatively independent of language use. Noam Chomsky's research and writings (1965, 1976) have had a significant impact on current views of language development. Chomsky proposed that an innate language acquisition device accounted for a child's rapid acquisition of language and that every child has a basic sense of grammar. He was arguing for some commonality to the rules followed in the range of languages used by humans. As noted by Owens (1996, p. 36), 'He was interested in a theory of the universal grammatical rules of language, rules with biological bases'.

Chomsky proposed two levels of linguistic processing: the 'phrase-structure' elements refer to the essential underpinnings of all sentence organisation and are universal regardless of the language being used. Transformational rules refer to the rearrangement of the phrase-structure elements based on a specific language and are not universal.

Chomsky's psychological model was two-tiered in nature. The actual sentences we use are called 'surface structures' while 'deep structures' are found inside the brain and contain the inherent phrase–structure rules. Transformational rules mediate between surface and deep structures.

Following early linguists' observations regarding commonalities in children's acquisition of language, Chomsky proposed some in-born language acquisition mechanism which he called the 'language acquisition device' (LAD). 'Thus, the infant is "prewired" for linguistic analysis' (Owens 1996, p. 42).

Limitations in the theory proposed by Chomsky relate to the fact that adult speech is very different from child speech. The mechanisms proposed by Chomsky to account for language acquisition could not explain why children use one- and two-word utterances.

Socio-linguistic theory

To date, the various attempts to explain language acquisition have focused on the structure and form of language – on the 'bits' and 'pieces' of language. In contrast, socio-linguistic theory focuses more on the communicative context. Language is then viewed as a means for achieving some end within the communicative context. Emphasis is given to the role of the care-giver in children's language development. Thus, socio-linguistic theory, while drawing upon the belief that there is some underlying structure to language, argues that children express their intention in speech. Initially, it is argued the care-givers play a role in imputing intention. For example, just prior to feeding, the baby may be fussing and the mother will interpret this fussing, saying 'Oh, you are so hungry aren't you?' These conversational bouts (Golinkoff 1983) are taught by the parents and imitated by the infants. Language acquisition proceeds as the infant matures and complex interactions continue between the child and adults.

Contemporary views of language acquisition

Nelson (1985, 1986) puts forward a constructivist view of language acquisition. Her neo-Piagetian theory also draws on the work of Bruner (1983) and Vygotsky (1978). She proposes that, within a constructivist framework, it is the child's experience with the world that is the foundation for developing understanding. This constructivist view presents the child as an active participant in the development of language – a view that contrasts strongly with the stimulus–response theory of language acquisition. Nelson's theory of language development suggests that at first, the young child's understanding of the world is made up of separate actions (Genishi 1988). Repeated experiences gradually provide a mental representation of an event or experience. At the core of all this is 'action'. For example, a child develops a mental representation of a ball and through interaction or play with a ball learns not only to recognise the ball but what it can be used for. 'Thus, the child's language learning proceeds from action and experience to concept to words and not from word to concept to experience' (Genishi 1988, p. 18). Language development is expanded upon in later chapters.

Birth of the first child: The mother: Postnatal depression

Women have always played a central role in families: 'The expectation for women has been that they would take care of the needs of others, first men, then children then the elderly (McGoldrick 1989, p. 29). Furthermore, marriage is seen as a more hazardous state for women than men (Avis 1985; McGoldrick 1989). It is ironic that, while men in Western cultures (such as the Australian mainstream culture) are often ambivalent about marriage, fearing that they will be 'trapped' or 'lose their freedom', it is the women who suffer most in terms of depression, marital dissatisfaction, poor physical health, low self-esteem and lack of autonomy (Avis 1985).

In the life-cycle approach to families, pregnancy and childbirth represent a very significant point in a woman's life and in the life of the family of which she is or becomes part. As far as childbirth is concerned, studies of women's actual experience have produced inconclusive findings. Research by Waldenstrom et al. (1996) report that childbirth was assessed as positive by 77 per cent of women, with no difference being reported by multiparas and primaparas. Factors contributing to the positive experience were (i) support from the mid-wife; (ii) duration of labour; (iii) pain; (iv) expectations of the birth; (v) involvement in the birth process; and (vi) surgical procedures.

Therese Benedik (1950) believes that as a developmental event, motherhood plays a significant role in the formation of a woman's personality, in as much as it physiologically completes maturation and psychologically channels motherliness. Bibring et al. (1961) have argued that first pregnancies include an element of crisis, in so far as crisis refers to a decisive stage or turning point in the life of the mother-to-be.

Following the birth of her first child, adjustment or crisis are likely to occur for the mother in a number of areas:

1 From a psychoanalytic perspective, the birth of the first child is significant in terms of the mother's relationship with her own mother: their relationship becomes that of equals. At the same time, the relationship with the father of the child is reassessed as the family unit shifts from being dyadic to triadic.
2 Secondly, the birth of the first child involves acceptance by the woman of her biological role. Rheingold (1964) also discusses the birth of the first child as representing a 'degree in femininity'.
3 Childbirth involves a change in status. That is, motherhood is accompanied by the learning of new and unfamiliar tasks. For example, the mother may leave her job for a period of time and concentrate on child care and domestic duties.

The complexity of change that greets the new mother is sometimes better captured in fiction writing than in the research accounts in journals and textbooks. Ann Roiphe writes in *Up the Sandbox*:

And with each feeding, each soothing, each moment we live together, I grow into him. My spirit oozes out, I feel myself contracting and him expanding and the ties between us solidify. And I am almost his possession. My selfish purposes are also served. Instead of being as I was before I conceived a child, a bit of dark matter orbiting aimlessly, brooding on my own molecular disintegration, I am now a proper part of society (Roiphe 1970, p. 12).

Postnatal depression

Despite its prevalence and known history since the fourth century BC, mental disturbance following childbirth is still a little understood phenomenon. The Greek physician Hippocrates believed the disturbance was caused by the stoppage of the normal secretion of milk, which was then directed to the brain instead of to the breast. In the seventeenth century, a common medical opinion held that postnatal depression was caused by vapours arising from the uterus to the brain.

In the last decade, research strongly suggests that the months following childbirth pose a substantial risk for 10 to 15 per cent of mothers, who may suffer marked depressive illness during this time (Stamp 1994; Astbury et al. 1994). As noted by Stamp, Williams and Crowther (1996, p. 218), '[t]his represents a major public health issue for childbearing women in Australia'.

Doughty (1988) has identified three separate conditions that may be associated with a woman's reaction to the birth experience.

1 Three-day or maternity blues are experienced by up to 50 per cent of women three to five days after delivery. A feature of this condition is uncontrollable crying that can be triggered by the smallest of events.
2 Postnatal psychosis affecting one woman in 1000 occurs within a few weeks of delivery.

A feature of this condition is a distortion of the mother's reality and delusional thinking. Suicide and infanticide may occur.

3 Postnatal depression is a condition that, according to Doughty, is more severe than maternity blues but less severe than postnatal psychosis.

Postnatal depression may occur one month after the birth of the baby and is usually of four to six weeks' duration but can last up to two years. Symptoms include sadness, futility, inability to cope, feelings of being overwhelmed, mood swings, insomnia and panic attacks. Stamp, Williams and Crowther (1996) provide a summary of the factors associated with developing postnatal depression, including interpersonal factors such as (i) a past history of mood disorder; (ii) interpersonal factors (e.g. problematic marital relationships); and (iii) environmental facts (e.g. adverse life events and stress).

The condition is viewed as a combination of biological and psychosocial factors. For example, there is evidence of a link between postnatal depression and a drop in the levels of the hormones progesterone and oestrogen 24 to 36 days after delivery (Doughty 1988). Psychosocial stressors include feelings of entrapment and loss of identity, the mother's relationship with her partner, poor marital and family relationships and financial concerns. Various screening devices have been developed to identify postnatal depression including The Edinburgh Postnatal Depression Scale and the Postpartum Depression Screening Scale (Beck & Gable 2001). Treatment (drugs and counselling) facilitates full recovery.

One woman's experience
Mary (aged 33 years) is married with four children. Her husband, John, is a teacher and before the birth of their first child Mary was a junior primary teacher. They had been married for 15 years. Their fourth child was born in October 1988 by emergency caesarean section. Talking about the birth, Mary said that having a caesarean section 'changed it all, because I felt no control over the birth happenings. John was told that he could not be at the birth (because of its emergency nature) as we were on the way to the theatre'.

Some two weeks after returning home from hospital with her healthy baby, Mary reported the gradual onset of the following symptoms:

- concerns over the financial situation of the family;
- insomnia;
- intense, unexplainable bouts of anxiety;

- somatic sensations (tingling in her hands);
- depression;
- bouts of crying.

'At first I thought it was just having the new baby at home and coping with the other three children', said Mary.

In the months that followed, the symptoms became worse. 'I started to think that it could not be just tiredness – it must be something mental because the other kids were behaving so well', Mary explained. 'Looking back on it, I can see that the problems that distressed me so much (such as financial concerns) were more imaginary than real, but at the time they were frighteningly real to me.' The feelings were mainly in evidence at night: 'I would lie awake at night with the feelings and the more I thought, the worse they got. My husband was wonderfully supportive but the feelings got worse', Mary recalled. 'It got so bad I thought I was having a breakdown and then I knew I needed outside help', she continued.

Mary sought help from a psychologist and her local doctor. Psychological assessment showed a significant level of postnatal depression (measured on the Edinburgh postnatal scale: see Cox et al. 1987), but no evidence of any personality disorder. Mary was prescribed anti-depressants and received counselling. After five and a half months, the symptoms began to abate.

'Looking back on the experience I would advise women to seek outside help', Mary recommended. Early warning signs are when 'things get out of perspective and you can't think through everyday situations, such as whether the dinner will be ready on time'.

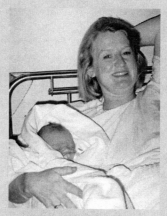

Motherhood plays a significant role in the development of a woman's personality.

Chapter summary

In this chapter consideration has been given to the significant growth and development in young children's cognitive development. In particular, the contributions made by Piaget and Vygotsky have been described in some detail. There is no doubt that these two theorists have contributed significantly to our understanding in a multi-disciplinary sense. In a related way, the issue of the concept of 'intelligence' has been presented in some detail. The child's own world is enriched by a developing competence with language. The reader is strongly encouraged to visit the websites listed at the end of this chapter to obtain further information.

Discussion questions

1   Piaget believed development to be a 'constructive' process. Explain and discuss.
2   What are the primary features of substages 5 and 6 of Piaget's sensori-motor period?
3   What do you understand by the terms mental age, chronological age and intelligence quotient and what are their distinguishing features?
4   How do Australians view the role of the mother in the family?
5   Critically, examine the various explanations for how children acquire language and present the underlying features of the various theories in class.

Activities

1   Compile statements about the nature of intelligence and write each on a 7–5 cm card (30 to 40 cards are needed). The statements may be true or false, for example: 'As they become older people become less intelligent'.

Procedure
   a   Form small groups of four or five. Each person is dealt six or seven cards, and the rest of the cards are placed in the centre of the group.
   b   Each person discards the statements they disagree with into the centre and picks up cards with statements they agree with.
   c   Finally, each person should have a 'hand' of cards (one card or more) that epresents their beliefs regarding the nature of intelligence.
   d   Each person in turn then justifies their choice of cards, making reference to information in the textbook.
   e   The group then decides on a description of 'intelligence' to present to the larger group.
2   View the film *Multiple Intelligence*, by Howard Gardner and discuss the concept, contrasting it with other views of intelligence.

Selected websites

American Psychological Association <www.apa.org/releases/ intell.html>

Theories of Intelligence <www.igs.net/~cmorris/spectrum/html>

History of Intelligence Tests <www.indiana.edu/~intell/index.html>

The Jean Piaget Archives <www.unige.ch/piaget/presentg.htm>

Lev Semenovich Vygotsky <www.massey.ac.nz/~Alock/virtual/ project2.htr>

11 Social and Emotional Development of Toddlers

'And He Knelt Before the Little Child'
'Who hath dared to wound thee?' cried the Giant, 'Tell me, that I may take my big sword and slay him'.
'Nay', answered the child: 'but these are the wounds of love'.
'Who art thou?' said the Giant, and a strange awe fell on him, and he knelt before the little child.

Oscar Wilde, The Selfish Giant

CHAPTER OUTLINE

KEY TERMS AND CONCEPTS

- Anal stage
- Autonomy versus shame and doubt
- Psychosocial aspect
- Transactional view of development
- Authoritarian
- Authoritative
- Permissive
- Nuclear family
- Extended family
- Blended family
- Sole-parent family

Introduction

From previous chapters we have seen that rapid advancements in gross and fine motor skills allow toddlers to enjoy a sense of physical independence from their care-givers. Similarly, the development of thinking skills allows toddlers to experiment with their environment and learn to interact with it. All this takes place within the larger domain of family life as the care-givers learn to adjust to having a child in their midst. In the still larger domain of the culture within which the family lives, the young child is learning to interact with the broader community.

In addition to these physical and cognitive changes, toddlers develop significantly in their social and emotional relationships. An emerging sense of self or 'me' is reflected in a growing awareness of separateness from others. During toddlerhood, children learn to recognise when significant others are pleased or displeased with their behaviour. As children become more aware of the larger world and their place in it, their emotional responsiveness to the world increases in subtlety and sophistication.

This chapter takes as its central theme the idea of 'relationships', perhaps as reflected in the little child's 'wounds of love'. Russell (2000, p. 109) has noted that '[c]hildren's lives, like those of adults, are played out primarily through relationships with others, especially close relationships'.

This chapter further describes the views of Freud and Erikson, who have both contributed to our understanding of the social and emotional development of children. The development of the toddler's social relationships with family and peers will then be discussed. Other issues examined in this chapter are day-care, behavioural problems, and the effect of hospitalisation on young children. The Family Life-cycle: 11 presents the concept of the 'blended' family.

Children's relationships within the family context

In a broad-based series of studies, Alan Russell and colleagues have explored how children's relationships are developed and enacted within the family context (Russell 2000; Russell & Saebel 1997; Russell et al. 1998; Russell & Russell 1994). A central theme identifiable in Russell and colleagues' research is that '. . . the behaviours, attitudes, roles and strategies experienced in parent–child relationships tend to be replicated in subsequent close relationships (Sroufe & Fleeson 1986)' (Russell 2000, p. 110). Russell develops the notion of 'replication' to include the idea that if the parent–child relationship embodies reasoning and collaboration, children can be expected to learn and enact such behaviours in later relationships.

Theoretical foundations

Consideration will be given here to the views of Freud and Erikson before considering more contemporary theorising.

Freudian theory

According to Freud, at about the age of 18 months toddlers enter the **anal stage** of development (the second of Freud's psychosexual stages – see Table 11.1 and chapter 3). Physically at this time children are maturing in the lower trunk region, and this maturation includes the development of the sphincter muscles, which control urination and defecation. About this time also, parents are placing an emphasis on toilet training. Together, these forces shift the focus of attention of sexual energy from the oral to the anal erogenous zone. As Freud expresses it:

> Faeces are the child's first gift, the first sacrifice on behalf of his affection, a portion of his own body which he is ready to part with, but only for the sake of somebody he loves (Freud 1955, p. 81).

By understanding faeces 'as a gift', the child is then in a position to 'express active compliance with his environment and by withholding them [faeces], his disobedience' (Freud 1955, p. 186).

The risk for the child and parents at this stage is that toilet training may become a major source of conflict. Children need sufficient time to experience the pleasures offered by the anal zone. If they become fixated at this stage, the fixation may be expressed in later life as 'withholding' the gift. Thus, as adults these individuals may become excessively obstinate: either obsessively neat and organised or very untidy.

anal stage
the second of Freud's psychosexual stages, during which the anal area is the primary 'erotic' zone and the child gains special pleasure from the elimination or retention of faeces.

Table 11.1 The anal stage: the second of Freud's psychosexual stages of development

Ages	Stages
Infancy	Oral
1½–3½ years (approx.)	Anal
3½–5½ years (approx.)	Phallic
5½–12 years (approx.)	Latency
Adolescence	Genital

Parents reading this text may be able to relate these comments to their experience of toilet training their own child or children. For example, they may recall the subtle pressure that results from comparisons with the advances made by other children in toilet training. They may also remember the pride they experienced when their toddler finally urinated in the potty for the first time. Usually young children are very pleased with their 'accomplishment' and often want to share it by showing their 'good deed' to the care-giver.

During the anal stage of development, according to Freudian theory, the child's developing relationship with the mother is of primary importance. It is the mother who is the focus of the child's attention.

Erik Erikson: Autonomy versus shame and doubt

According to Erikson, by their second year, children have developed a clear perception of self – a sense of separateness and personal identity. At this time their basic task is to learn when to hold on and when to let go. Erikson labelled the conflict that must be resolved at this stage as '**autonomy versus shame and doubt**'.

autonomy versus shame and doubt the second of Erikson's psychosocial stages of development, during which toddlers experience a sense of autonomy when successful in their striving for independence but shame or doubt as a result of parental prohibitions.

In Erikson's words, 'As his [the toddler's] environment encourages him to "stand on his own feet" it must protect him against meaningless and arbitrary experiences of shame and doubt' (Erikson 1963, p. 244). At this stage, young children begin to experience their 'autonomous will'. The task of parents is to recognise children's needs for autonomy and not be too rigid in terms of outer control. Children in turn will increasingly assert this autonomy – for example, by saying 'No'! Erikson argues that parental outer control must be firmly reassuring while allowing children to experience choice.

If children are denied free choice, they may experience doubt and risk developing a 'precocious conscience'. Shame, in Erikson's terms, is 'rage turned against the self': 'He who is ashamed would like to force the world not to look at him, not to notice his exposure. He would like to destroy the eyes of the world' (Erikson 1963, p. 227). Shame during toddlerhood may often be associated with toileting functions, so that children may come to believe that their bodies and wishes are evil and dirty.

Table 11.2 'Autonomy versus shame and doubt': the second of Erikson's psychosocial stages

Ages	Stages
Infancy	Basic trust versus mistrust
1½–3½ years (approx.)	Autonomy versus shame and doubt
3½–5½ years (approx.)	Initiative versus guilt
5½–12 years (approx.)	Industry versus inferiority
Adolescence	Identity versus role confusion
Young adulthood	Intimacy versus isolation
Adulthood	Generativity versus stagnation
Maturity	Ego integrity versus despair

A comparison of Freud's and Erikson's theories

In his theory of social and emotional development, Freud (1940) described the child's relationship to his or her mother as 'unique without parallel, established unalterably for a whole life-time as the first and strongest love object and as the prototype for all later love relations' (p. 188).

Freud's theory has been most influential in the broad impact it has had on:

1   our understanding of developmental phases in children;
2   our understanding of the effects of separation and institutional care on children;

According to Erikson parents should be firmly reassuring but allow their children to experience choice.

3   legal and social policy concerning children and the family (it is now almost a given principle that a primary factor in child development is the continuity of sensitive care-giving);

4   the introduction into lay language of the concepts of ego and superego (conscience);

5   the importance attached to the early years in terms of personality formation, highlighting the impact of parenting methods on children's development.

Erikson's theory overlaps Freud's but differs in several very important aspects. Erikson emphasised the ego, or the study of the more conscious adaptive and coping functions of the personality, in its interactions with the broader social and cultural forces that have an impact on children. Erikson has added to personality development what he has called the **psychosocial aspect.** That is, children have certain psychosocial tasks to complete in terms of their relationship with parents, family and society. Erikson's theory, in contrast to Freud's, emphasises the life span and the tasks to be accomplished at different points in one's life. The individual, in conjunction with parents and later, significant others (such as a partner), must resolve the conflicts that occur at each stage (such as in the 'autonomy versus shame or doubt' stage of toddlerhood) and in doing so, undergoes a developmental crisis before proceeding to the next stage.

Erikson's theory of personality development is unusual in two ways. First, the child can work on the current developmental task while preparing for the next stage and, second, the child is born with a 'growth' plan. Thus, a task not completed at one stage of development may be completed during a later stage. Erikson optimistically recognised that, while the child's earliest relationships are formative, these influences do not always determine personality development.

psychosocial aspect
the development of the child in the larger social setting of family and culture.

Toddlers gradually move from symbiotic union with their mothers to establishing a sense of separateness and personal identity.

rapprochement
according to Mahler, describes the phase in which a toddler discovers that personal identity can be achieved while maintaining or re-establishing a harmonious relationship with the mother.

transactional view of development
the view that development is a two-way interaction between child and environment.

Reflected in Erikson's theory is the respect he holds for the resiliency and resourcefulness of children, who can learn to compensate for early adverse circumstances.

Contemporary theories of development

Modern applications of psychoanalytic ideas to our understanding of toddlerhood are manifold. In a review of the psychoanalytic contribution to our understanding of the infant's life, Horner (1985) suggests that three ideas are paramount. In the earliest months:

1   the infant does not differentiate self from others;
2   the infant regards herself or himself as all-powerful;
3   failure to distinguish (differentiate) self can impede the infant's future development.

Mahler (1961) and Mahler et al. (1975) suggest that during toddlerhood individuals are primarily concerned with moving from a symbiotic union with their mothers to an established sense of separateness and personal identity. In reviewing Mahler's ideas, Horner (1988) notes that toddlers experience various emotions during the **rapprochement** phase, ranging from anxiety and depression at separateness, to a fear of being dominated by the mother again, to pleasure and elation at discovering new things. Rapprochement refers to the toddler's discovery that attaining identity does not mean losing the love and security provided by the mother. Mahler et al. (1975) believe that two behavioural patterns characterise the toddler phase: shadowing and darting away. These behavioural patterns 'indicate both [the child's] wish for reunion with the love object and his fear of re-engulfment by it' (Mahler et al. 1975, p. 79).

A transactional view of development

Horner (1988) has argued for a **transactional view of development** in toddlerhood. A transactional model of development emphasises 'the plastic character of the environment and of the organism as an active participant in its own growth' (Sameroff & Chandler 1975, p. 235). That is, children's behaviour is more than simply a response to their environment. To this end, Horner (1988) considers children's own developmental progress during infancy (such as walking, attainment of language, ability to sustain interaction with others) in relation to the adults in the children's lives. Thus, as children gain mastery in terms of locomotion, parents' expectations of their children change. Parents delight in a toddler's newfound skills of walking, running and climbing, but in turn, their expectations of the toddler change and their vigilance increases because there is a greater risk of physical injury (see chapter 9, 'Accidents in the early years'). Similarly, as toddlers walk more, adults carry them less, but this in turn makes toddlers cling more to their parents (watch any toddler and parent in the supermarket). Clinging is one form of contact between toddler and parent. As children are able to move around and discover previously hidden things (they can open the refrigerator, for instance), parents must put things out of reach: 'Toddlers whine and coerce, then, largely as a function of parents' refusals and prohibitions' (Horner 1988, p. 11).

Horner also sets language development in a transactional perspective. As children begin to understand and use language, so parents expect toddlers to understand verbal instructions. It is much easier for a parent to say 'Stop that' than to intervene physically, and so what is happening here relates to parental expectations of compliance, which in turn can enhance toddlers' language development (Horner 1988).

For Horner, the child's behaviour during toddlerhood should be viewed as a process:

> Viewed from this standpoint rapprochement is not a process of dealing with lost symbiotic bliss but a process of restoring positive equilibrium following perturbations in the relationship – a process of re-attaining basic love and security when frustrations and resistance with their correlated affects have been effectively dealt with (Horner 1988, p. 13).

Social development and parenting

An increasing amount of research in the last decade has examined the nature of toddler socialisation. As toddlers grow and develop in the second and third year of life, reaching out to others in the family, the social world becomes an important part of children's overall development.

The toddler and family life

For the toddler, becoming part of a family involves developing relationships with different members of the family (Dunn & Munn 1985). It also involves developing an understanding of the routines, rules, jokes, games and sanctions involved in family life. Dunn and Munn (1985, p. 480) note that 'Very little is known at present about children's entry into family life'. One line of research inquiry, however, indicates that toddlers are aware of and sensitive to the emotional life of the family. Dunn and Munn (1985) have found that toddlers do have some understanding of how or what will upset or annoy a brother or sister and some understanding of their mother's feelings or reactions when they do something that has been forbidden. The fact that toddlers will comfort a family member suggests a 'practical understanding of the emotional state of the other family member and how to alleviate it' (Dunn & Munn 1985, p. 49). Similarly, the research of Cummings et al. (1981) indicates that toddlers are responsive to the distress and anger of family members. By and large, however, the means by which the toddler is socialised into the world of the family is barely understood.

Parenting young children

In recent years a number of significant reviews of the parenting literature have appeared (Collins et al. 2000; Gray & Steinberg 1999; Bradley & Corwyn 1999; Vandell 2000; Maccoby 2000; Geary & Flinn, 2001; Bornstein, in press). The Australian writers, Bowes and Watson (1999) have considered the issue of parenting in the broad context of family life emphasising that parenting behaviour needs to be seen in an historical context (see Chapter 8).

What is parenting?

One might well ask, what is parenting? The *Concise Oxford Dictionary* defines a parent as 'One who has begotten or borne offspring, father or mother', or as Bradley and Corwyn (1999, p. 339) note: 'Parenting is what parents do to take care of their children, rather like the classic response to what is intelligence (i.e., it's what intelligence tests measure)'.

What do parents do to parent?

Bradley and Corwyn (1999) have used systems theory to identify a number of tasks involved in parenting namely: (i) sustenance; (ii) stimulation; (iii) support; (iv) structure; and (v) surveillance. The first three tasks are linked to Maslow's hierarchy of needs providing for the basic food, water and safety needs of the child (see chapter 3). In structuring the home environment, parents are sensitive to the ways in which the needs of the child are met, e.g. the individual needs of children should be accommodated. Finally, the task of monitoring – 'keeping track of the child' – and being aware of their where-abouts is important.

The authors argue that there is some 'suggestive' evidence that these five parenting tasks are linked to optimal outcomes in terms of the positive adaptation of children.

Parenting practices

Developmentalists have been interested in the nature of parental child-rearing beliefs and attitudes, and this interest has spawned a number of different lines of research. For example, researchers have examined :

1 gender differences in parenting (Russell & Russell 1994; Russell & Saebel 1997; Conrade & Ho 2001);
2 cross-cultural differences in parenting practice (Chen et al. 2000);
3 the relative influence of parenting on socialisation vs other forces such as peers (Harris 1998; Vandell 2000).

A concept central to these various lines of research is that of 'parenting style'. Parker and colleagues (1979) identified four parenting styles, while Baumrind (1967, 1971) operationalised three different styles described in more detail here.

Trends and issues

Effects of physical punishment

Martin (1975) reviewed the literature of 27 studies of harsh punishment. By 'harsh' was meant harsher than the rest of the community. In 25 of the studies, harsh punishment at home correlated with aggression against other children, teachers and society. It was found that harshly punished children were more likely to become antisocial delinquents in adolescence. The study also found that critical and derogatory parents are more likely to produce withdrawn and anxious children than violent children, especially if the child is a boy and the hostile parent is the father.

Intergenerational effects of physical punishment

Quite apart from the direct effects of physical punishment on children, there is convincing evidence that harsh punishment is transmitted across generations (Berkowitz 1993). Simons et al. (1991) found that grandparents who engaged in aggressive parenting had children who became, in turn, aggressive parents. That is, there was intergenerational influence at work in the adoption of a parenting style.

A useful summary of the effects of corporal punishment has been reported in a position paper written on the topic by Paintal, as referred to in chapter 1 (1999).

Parenting styles

Baumrind (1966; 1971) has identified three different types of parenting style, namely **authoritarian**, **authoritative** and **permissive**. According to Baumrind, both authoritarian and authoritative parents are directive and have clear expectations about how their children should behave, but authoritarian parents are dictatorial and unbending. Such parents have rules that they expect their children to follow. Permissive parents, on the other hand, exercise little control over their children.

The characteristics of the three types of parenting style are as follows:

Authoritarian parents. The parents' word is law. Misconduct is punished.
1   They are disinclined to reason with the child on points of disagreement.
2   They rely heavily upon punishment rather than positive reinforcement to influence the child.
3   They discourage the child from expressing herself or himself or developing independence.
4   They are cold and distant in their relationship with the child.
5   They are highly status-conscious.

Permissive parents. They make few demands on their children.
1   Anarchy frequently reigns and discipline is lax.
2   They are typically non-controlling and non-demanding.
3   They have few (if any) rules that the child must follow.
4   They themselves tend to be poorly organised and/or ineffective in running their household.
5   Relationships with their child are warm, but they offer little positive guidance to help the child develop.

Authoritative parents. They favour a democratic style of child-rearing.
1   They set limits and enforce rules but are ready to bend them if, after listening to their child's requests and questions, they think the situation merits change. Rule-making is democratic rather than dictatorial.

authoritarian
a dictatorial style of childrearing in which unquestioning obedience is expected from children.

authoritative
a democratic style of childrearing, in which parents give firm guidance while listening to their children's ideas.

permissive
a lax style of childrearing in which parents make few demands of their children, imposing few rules and offering little positive guidance.

2   They are prepared to justify their points of view by reasoning with their child.

3   They are rewarding rather than punitive, and encourage self-expression and growth towards independence.

4   They are, in general, warm and nurturant towards their child.

According to Baumrind (1966; 1971), the three parenting styles appear to produce the following results:

1   The sons of authoritarian families tend to be distrustful, unhappy and hostile, and neither the sons nor the daughters are high achievers.

2   The children of permissive parents are the least self-reliant and self-controlled and the most unhappy. The boys tend to be low achievers, but the girls do quite well at school.

3   The children of authoritative parents are the most self-reliant, self-controlled, content, friendly and cooperative, and are high achievers.

Sex-based differences in parenting style

Australian researchers (Russell 2000; Russell et al. 1998; Russell & Saebel 1997) have examined sex-based differences in parenting style. Confirmation of the research by Russell and colleagues has been presented by Conrade and Ho (2001), indicating that mothers are more likely than fathers to be perceived as authoritative, being more responsive to children's feelings and being more likely to offer explanations for rules and disciplinary practices.

Cultural differences

A reasonably robust finding of a great deal of research concerns cross-cultural differences in parenting style (Arrindell et al. 1994). Marked differences in parenting style are apparent between individualistic cultures, e.g. Australian and collectivist cultures, e.g. Chinese.

The relative influence of parents and other socialising influences

VIEWPOINT

What is a friend?

'Someone who shared their toys with you'.

Tim, 6 years

'It's where somebody is really kind and you can trust them and who will be nice to you and you to them and you can depend on them'.
Briony, 8 years

'Someone who likes you – someone you can depend on'.
Belinda, 11 years

Harris (1998, p.15) published a book in which she was highly critical of the nurture assumption which Harris defines as the belief that '. . . parents are the most important part of the child's environment and can determine, to a large extent, how the child turns out'. The thesis proposed by Harris generated a good deal of controversy. Arguments presented by Vandell (2000) and Maccoby (2000) have pointed to the role of multiple causation agents associated with socialisation.

Relationship with peers

An increasing amount of research has been devoted to toddlers' development of friendships and their peer relationships.

Trends and issues

In the supermarket

In a study of mothers' and toddlers' interactions in supermarkets, Holden (1983) observed that controlling toddlers' behaviour is a difficult task for parents. Toddlerhood, with the child rapidly developing cognitive and social skills, is a very interesting stage of development for both parent and child. At about this time, parents' expectations of children's abilities increase concurrently with toddlers' greater grasp of language. Parents' self-esteem is often related to their ability to control toddlers (Holden 1983): bad behaviour on the part of the toddler may reflect badly on the parent, who wishes to be seen as a good and competent parent.

Holden (1983) discovered two major categories of control that are frequently used by mothers in supermarkets: reactive and proactive. In using a reactive control method, mothers responded to their toddlers' demands by using one or more of the following strategies: reasoning, power assertion, silence, acknowledgment of their child's desire or diversion. A proactive approach involved trying to avoid potential conflict by distracting the child with conversation or some other activity. Holden argues that the proactive approach is more beneficial than a reactive one because it helps to avoid frequent conflicts, which can be unpleasant and tiring and which can ultimately influence the care-giver's self-esteem. In turn, toddlers can benefit from a proactive approach because:

1   they learn what behaviour is acceptable in supermarkets;
2   they can learn from the experience of the interaction;
3   mothers are socialising their children using techniques other than power assertion.

For example, Vandell and Mueller (1980, p. 189) have described a friendship between 8-month-old boys:

> The boys actively chose one another as the preferred playmates, and in their play, the two boys showed the most sophisticated play of the play group's game. Years later when Robert moved away, he continually asked for Loren and Loren repeatedly asked for Robert.

Gottman (1983) suggests that the interest in the nature of children's friendships is more than academic. In his analysis of the literature, he argues that 'having a close friend is of critical importance for the physical and psychological health of adults who undergo a variety of life crises' (Gottman 1983, p. 1). Gottman links this to research involving children who go through childhood friendless.

It has been observed that pre-school friendship groups 'engage in more positive exchanges, mutuality and sharing than do non friend dyads' (Furman & Masters 1980, p. 1041). However, the less developed verbal and cognitive skills of toddlers could be considered to influence the developmental course of friendship relations. Howes (1988) notes that the early toddler period is in fact marked by stable friendships. That is, toddlers can differentiate among playmates and will direct more attention to one child than another. Toddler friendships involve the child not only physically but also emotionally (Howes 1983). Howes has identified stages in the development of peer relations during the toddler period.

Early toddler period (13–24 months)

During this early stage, friendships are stable and involve complementary or reciprocal play (Howes 1988). That is, toddlers have the ability to exchange turns and roles. The complementary nature of friendship relations involves the toddlers' ability to offer (toys or food), receive (take something from another) or play hide-and-seek. To achieve such ends, a child must have the cognitive ability to assume the role of the other child (Mueller and Lucas 1975).

Late toddler period (25–36 months)

During this period, toddlers are more flexible in their friendships in that they have a greater number of friends than previously (Howes 1988). They are more able to communicate meaning: that is, any two toddlers are able to share an understanding of the central idea or theme of an interaction between them (Howes 1985). As toddlers develop cognitively they are able to distinguish between different types of friends and they are able to use symbols in interacting with friends: a stick becomes a doll, for example.

Family relationships

In their study of the social nature of early conflict, Hay and Ross (1982, p. 112) concluded that 'children's social skills are acquired and refined, not only through their pleasant harmonious encounters, but also through conflict'. As any parent or child-care worker will testify, conflict does appear to increase during the toddler years. Such conflict can involve family as well as peers.

Having a friend is important for a child's development.

Toddlers and day-care

Modern society and the family within society is undergoing rapid change. A study of the constituent nature of the Australian family today would indicate that a range of family forms is now identifiable, such as **nuclear family**, **extended family**, **blended family** and **sole-parent family** (see also chapter 2).

For many years, the commonly expressed view was that the traditional nuclear family was the most desirable form of family within which to raise children – desirable, that is, in terms of the children's psychological health. This view is under attack because cross-cultural research indicates that a striking diversity of family forms all appear to function adequately in their own context. For example, in traditional Aboriginal societies, polygamy was practised and teenaged girls were married to older men. In contemporary urban Aboriginal groups, Collman (1979, p. 392) has distinguished three types of marriage, namely: 'firestick or tribal marriage', 'kangaroo' (de facto) relationships, and ceremonial marriage in accordance with Australian law.

As indicated in chapter 2, increasing numbers of Australians are opting for alternative family forms including never-married one-parent households, homosexual or lesbian unions, de facto relationships and communal living. In Australia, as in other Western countries, the number of sole-parent families has been increasing in the last decade. Sole-parent families are most often headed by women, whose standard of living is frequently below the poverty line. The widespread poverty of mother-custody families can be attributed to a number of factors, namely:

1 The supporting parent's benefit, upon which many custodial mothers rely, often fails to meet their financial needs.
2 Fathers frequently fail to comply with maintenance agreements.
3 Women caring for children at home cannot earn an income.

In the last two decades, we have witnessed a major shift in the way we rear children in Australia, and this is particularly characterised by the extensive use of day-care for infants and toddlers. As more women enter the workforce the question that arises concerns the effect of day-care on infant and toddler development.

Child-care research has occurred in two phases (McCartney & Galanopoulos 1988). The first of these began in the 1960s when the relationship between women's greater participation in the workforce and the increasing use of substitute child-care became apparent. Researchers were interested in whether day-care was in some way harmful to children's development (emotional, social and intellectual). According to McCartney and Galanopoulos (1988), this first wave of research led to the conclusions that:

- attachment to parents is not affected by day-care;
- day-care children tend to be more aggressive than children cared for at home by parents;

nuclear family
a couple and their children living in the same dwelling.

extended family
a nuclear family plus grandparents and/or other relatives.

blended family
a family resulting from the remarriage of one or both adults, who bring with them children from the previous marriage.

sole-parent family
a family in which the children are raised by the mother or father alone.

- day-care may help the intellectual development of children from disadvantaged backgrounds.

The second wave of day-care research during the 1980s focused on the quality of care offered, which varies in just the same way as it does in children's home environments. Factors researched included child–staff ratios, quality of staff training, amount of staff supervision, quality of day-care programming and back-up resources for staff.

In a review of the field, Jay Belsky (1990) has sounded a very timely warning concerning just how little we know about the effects of day-care on infant and toddler development. Belsky stresses the limitations of the first phase of research, which was largely based on studies conducted in high-quality centres, such as those run by universities, which were not representative of day-care centres in general. In 1978, Belsky and Steinberg wrote that, if children receive excellent day-care, their attachment to their parents remains unaltered and their sociability may even be enhanced. In 1987, however, Belsky concluded that entry into day-care in the first year of life is a 'risk factor' which can impair child attachment and heighten aggressiveness, non-compliance and withdrawal in later school years. One year later Belsky (1988, p. 402) wrote that:

> more than 20 hours per week of non-parental care, at least as experienced on a routine basis in the United States, is a risk factor in the development of insecure infant–parent relationships and subsequent aggression and non-compliance.

It may not be so much the amount of non-parental care (that is, greater than 20 hours per week) in the first year that influences subsequent child development in this way but 'rather the nature of some of the families that rely upon such care. In other words, risk may be a function of growing up in a family using non-parental care extensively in the first year' (Belsky 1988, p. 403).

At a policy level, Belsky (1990) has called for a setting aside of old North American political ideas that day-care represents a 'collectivisation' of child-rearing. With recent United States statistics indicating that 53 per cent of all mothers with infants under 1 year of age are in the workforce, Belsky (1990) recommends large infrastructure investment in day-care which, in particular, would facilitate:

1 parental leave policies allowing one parent to be at home during the child's first year without fear of job loss;
2 the opportunity for parents to work part-time in the child's first year;
3 good quality day-care facilities.

To this end, a third phase of research into the effect of non-parental care on early infant and toddler development is now becoming evident (Belsky & Rovine 1988; Schanchere 1990). Researchers are now more aware of the influence of complex variables such as the presence of family conflict, which are best viewed in the context of the family system. Melhuish (2001) in a review of the literature argued that research has now established the significance of the 'quality' of day care for young children's development. Data from longitudinal research (e.g. Sylvaet al. 1999) has identified the complex links between home environment, socio-economic status, the quality of day-care and child developmental outcomes.

Behavioural problems

At present, the nature of behavioural problems in 2- and 3-year-old children is not well understood. Part of the reason for this is the assumption made by many parents and the professionals who work with children that behavioural problems will be outgrown.

Definition

In a review of the literature, Cross and Slee (1988) note that many terms have been used to describe behaviourally disordered children, including 'having a severe behavioural disorder'; 'non-compliant', 'antisocial', 'hyperactive' and 'having a conduct disorder'. The label 'conduct disorder' has been adopted by psychiatrists as part of their formal classification system. The Diagnostic and Statistical Manual III-R of the American Psychiatric Association (1987, p. 55) states that the 'essential feature' of a conduct disorder:

> is a persistent pattern of conduct in which either the basic rights of others or major age-appropriate societal norms or rules are violated. The behaviour pattern typically is present in the home, at school, with peers, and in the community.

Prevalence

The reported prevalence of behavioural disorders in the normal population varies from 4 per cent to 20 per cent, depending upon the specific criteria used for diagnosis (Webster-Stratton 1983). Australian research suggests figures ranging from 6 per cent (Mitchell 1985) to 10–15 per cent (Glow & Glow 1984; Slee 1986). According to Cross and Slee (1988, p. 29), 'children with severe behavioural disorders are relatively common with about one child in 10 having a major problem'.

Current trends

In the United States the number of children with severe behavioural disorders 'is increasing and far exceeds resources for dealing with them' (Webster-Stratton 1983, p. 33). Edgar (1985) points to a similar pattern of increasing disturbance among Australian youth.

Developmental trends

Webster-Stratton (1983) notes that normal aggressive behaviours do peak in the toddler age range (Hartup 1974). Importantly though, evidence suggests that behavioural problems are persistent and that toddlers who are severely aggressive in the early years continue aggressive behaviour in later life (Richman et al. 1982; Campbell et al. 1986). Barron and Earls (1985) found that 54 per cent of the children identified with behavioural problems at the age of 3 years continued to manifest high levels of behavioural problems in their first year at school. As Cross and Slee (1988, p. 30) note:

> The literature is clear in showing that it is likely that disruptive behaviour will persist over time. In adolescent years it may well manifest as various forms of delinquency, and later in adulthood as antisocial and perhaps criminal behaviour . . . In short, children do not 'outgrow' their 'bad behaviours.

What causes behavioural problems?

Findings from various fields of research have identified child-related, parent-related and background factors that influence behavioural problems in young children.

Child-related characteristics

The behaviour of children is intricately interwoven with characteristics such as decreased cognitive functioning (Richman et al. 1982). The issue of temperament has also been related to behavioural problems in children (Thomas et al. 1968; Bates et al. 1985).

Parent-related characteristics

Maternal perceptions of young children's behavioural problems have been linked with personal adjustment difficulties – particularly maternal depression (Webster-Stratton 1989; Slee 1990). Mothers' reports of low marital satisfaction and negative life stressors were also positively correlated with critical or physically negative maternal behaviours.

Background factors

A number of background factors have been linked to young children's behavioural problems, including their higher prevalence among first-borns (Campbell et al. 1982); large family size (Richman et al. 1988); and sole-parent households (Cohen & Minde 1983).

Hospitalisation

As reported by Whelan and Kirkby (1995), significant changes have occurred regarding family access to child patients over the years and they cite the 1947 policy document of the Royal Children's Medical Hospital as evidence:

Patients are not allowed visitors unless they have been in hospital for a period of 4 weeks, after which time only the parents or guardians (no friends or relatives are allowed) are permitted to visit on each alternate Sunday in each month, between the hours of 2.00 pm and 3.30 pm. Parents or guardians of patients dangerously ill are allowed to visit as often as the doctors consider necessary.

It is now better understood that admission to hospital can be stressful for young children and a number of factors have been linked to the child's reaction. In a study of Australian children, Kapelis (1983) reports that slight psychological upsets can occur in as many as 92 per cent of children. Similarly in research conducted by Whelean and Kirkby (1995) the authors argued that '[c]hildren have been reported to show a variety of negative behavioral and emotional reactions to illness and hospitalization' (p. 131).

Despite this growing appreciation of the impact of hospitalisation on children, the Canadian researchers Woodgate and Kristjanson (1996, p. 233) noted that '[r]elatively little is known about hospitalized young children and how they respond to pain'. These same authors have utilised a combination of a gate control theory of pain and family systems theory to understand children's pain response as a '. . . dynamic process influenced by the interacting individual, family and environmental factors' (p. 235).

Children's fears and anxieties about hospital are important not just in themselves but because they can affect the illness and the course the illness takes. An important part of the problem with hospitalisation is that it brings a radical change in the routine and rhythm of the children's lives. Children are separated from the familiar world of parents, siblings and peers. At the same time, they must submit their freedom, privacy and sense of control to strangers. In hospital, children see and hear others in pain. Sleeping and waking times are different; the bed is different and strange; there are different sights, sounds and smells. If their concept of time is not well developed, children may have little or no idea of when the stay in hospital will end.

Coping with hospitalisation

A number of characteristics have been linked to a child's ability to deal with the hospital experience and these may be grouped under the main headings of child-related characteristics and organisational factors.

Child-related characteristics

Age. As Klinzing and Klinzing (1977) conclude in their review of the literature, most researchers agree that children less than 5 years of age are more vulnerable to emotional upset from hospitalisation than older children. One explanation for this has been put forward by Bowlby (1960), who believes it is due to the separation of young children from their parents. At about 6 months of age, babies will demonstrate clear distress at separation when they are hospitalised; that is, they cry when separated from their parents. Bowlby describes three phases of behaviour in children separated from their parents upon admission to hospital:

1   protest: the child cries and is upset;
2   despair: the child is obviously unhappy and withdraws;
3   detachment: the child shows a loss of interest in care-givers.

Cognitive level. There is a body of research evidence linking children's understanding of hospitalisation with their cognitive development (Bibace & Walsh 1980; Perrin & Gerrity 1981). Perrin and Gerrity (1981) discovered a systematic progression, with age, in children's understanding of illness-related concepts. Thus, they found that kindergarten children typically related illness to punishment for their own misbehaviour. Children in middle childhood had begun to develop and associate a concept of 'germs' with illness. During early adolescence an increasing sophistication of thinking allows children to relate illness to multiple causes.

Personality of the child. There is evidence that children's personalities may influence their adjustment to hospitalisation. Stacey et al. (1970) discovered that the following categories of children were most vulnerable to the impact of admission to hospital:

1   Only children, youngest children and children from extended family households;
2   Children who respond unfavourably to tests of interpersonal communications, responsiveness and aggression;
3   Children whose mothers are themselves either very anxious or very unconcerned at the child's hospitalisation;
4   Children whose mothers report that they react poorly to strange adults or children;
5   Children who rarely visit the houses of other children;
6   Children who have recently experienced a traumatic separation, such as a divorce in the family.

Organisational factors

The hospital environment. Klinzing and Klinzing (1977) report that the sensory and motor restrictions that are frequently associated with hospitalisation can stress the child. Providing opportunities for play, recreation and education may help offset the listlessness, depression and unhappiness that can result from the enforced inactivity.

Contact with Parents. Giving parents plenty of opportunities to be with their children helps to offset the impact of hospitalisation.

Helping the hospitalised child

Various strategies have been used to alleviate children's stressful reactions to hospitalisation. Azarnoff (1983) describes the use of hospital tours and booklets to familiarise young children with hospitals, while films and video-tapes showing hospitals and hospital procedures have also been used (Kapelis 1983). In a study conducted in Adelaide, Kapelis (1983) found that viewing a videotape entitled *Doctors and Nurses* increased children's knowledge about hospitals and helped to reduce the children's level of anxiety regarding hospitals.

In a review of New Zealand hospitals and their care of children, Miltich-Conway and Gibbs (1989) put forward the following suggestions to make hospitalisation a less stressful experience for children.

1 *Preparation.* Parents can help alleviate children's anxiety by talking with hospital personnel themselves so that they can explain procedures to their child.
2 *Talking.* Parents and hospital staff should be sensitive to young children's feelings and reasoning (for instance, their idea that illness is a punishment) and allow the child to express such fears.
3 *A special toy.* Creating a 'home away from home' with a special toy or object may help the child.
4 *Play.* The therapeutic effect of play before and after hospitalisation may help children cope with anxiety.
5 *Pre-admission visits.* Visiting the hospital/ward beforehand can help to familiarise children with the hospital environment.
6 *Living-in.* One parent rooms in with the child during hospitalisation.
7 *Visiting.* Regular and frequent visits by parents can help a child cope with hospitalisation.

The family life-cycle: 11

The blended family

> *Australian society has been passing through a transition from being dominated by one family type, parents and their offspring, to being one of diversity, where a wide range of different family and non-family types are common.*

National Population Council 1987, p. 1.

A growing percentage of all marriages consists of remarriages (ABS 2000). Many men and women who remarry have children. One family type resulting from remarriage is the step or blended family. In a study of people who remarry, McDonald (1989) found that the most common reason for remarrying was that marriage exemplified the couple's love and commitment to one another and provided security for self and children.

Johnstone (1984) describes a blended family as a family grouping in which one or both adult partners have previously been married or in a de facto relationship, and have children from that relationship. An increasing amount of research attention is now being given to the particular psychological problems associated with blended families (McGoldrick & Carter 1980; Johnstone 1984).

McGoldrick and Carter (1980, p. 268) note that from a family systems perspective we all carry into our new relationships 'the emotional baggage of unresolved issues from important relationships'. More particularly, these authors identify particular problems:

1 problems associated with each individual's family of origin which arise anew in a blended family;
2 problems brought into the new relationship from the first marriage;
3 problems relating to issues surrounding separation or divorce.

According to McGoldrick and Carter (1980), a number of rather predictable emotional problems occur in blended families:

1   *New roles.* The formation of a blended family plunges family members suddenly into multiple and often ambiguous roles: for example, overnight a bachelor becomes a spouse and stepfather. One direct result of this is the problem of what the children should call their stepfather.
2   *Ambiguous boundaries.* Other significant problems include: who should discipline the children; who are the 'real' members of the family, and so forth. It is very difficult to draw one simple boundary around the blended household as one can do with new families.
3   *Affective problems.* There are a range of emotions unique to the blended family. For instance, if the mother has left the children of her first marriage, she may experience a great deal of guilt. Loyalty conflicts occur: children will usually feel a natural loyalty to their real parents and this can generate conflict.
4   *Solutions to conflict.* Given that blended families are usually formed against a backdrop of hurt and confusion, there is a tendency to smooth over conflicts rather than 'rock the boat' (McGoldrick & Carter 1980).

The complex tasks facing blended families in our society are deserving of more research. Only the barest outlines of problems facing the blended family have been alluded to here.

Chapter summary

In this chapter 'relationships' have been highlighted as a significant feature of the toddlers developing social world. Developments in theorising have pointed to the complexity of multiple causes shaping children's development. The issue of how best to parent achieves a sharper focus in the light of the toddler's mobility, and striving for greater autonomy and independence. In turn, the developing family faces significant issues such as child-care as mothers re-enter the paid workforce.

Discussion questions

1   Identify the main similarities and differences between Freud and Erikson's theories of toddlers' psychological development.
2   From a 'transactional' perspective, explain how parents' expectations of their children change as the children develop.
3   Consider how you were raised in terms of the three parenting styles – authoritarian, authoritative, permissive.
4   Summarise and discuss research regarding the nature of behavioural problems.
5   What particular issues or problems do blended families face?

Activities

1   From your own experience of separation from parents upon hospitalisation, make a list of the your feelings and relate this to your developmental age at the time. Identify the 'buffer' factors or the things that helped you deal with the situation or

that you believe could help children deal with such separations. Compile a list of all the factors identified by group members.

2   Visit or phone your local day-care centre and obtain a list of attributes that the centre believes enhance the quality of the day-care service it offers. Compare the list with the current understanding of the effects of day-care on children.

3   Complete the 'Self Review Quiz' on the CD-ROM to assess your understanding of the content presented in this section. Use your quiz results as a basis for reviewing any chapter content about which you are uncertain.

Selected websites

Child Adolescent Psychological and Educational Resources <www.caper.com.au>

Kidslife – Making Parenting Easier <www.kidslife.com.au>

The Pre-school Years

5

Nicholas at 4 years

Nicholas at 6 years

Nicholas at 10 years

12 Physical Development of Pre-schoolers

'. . . And If It Makes Me Larger . . .'

Soon her eyes fell on a little ebony box lying under the table: she opened it, and found in it a very small cake, on which was lying a card with the words EAT ME printed beautifully on it in large letters. 'I'll eat', said Alice, 'and if it makes me larger, I can reach the key, and if it makes me smaller, I can creep under the door, so either way I'll get into the garden, and I don't care which happens!

Lewis Carroll, Alice's Adventures in Wonderland

CHAPTER OUTLINE

KEY TERMS AND CONCEPTS

- Enuresis
- Primary enuresis
- Secondary enuresis
- ADHD
- clumsiness

Introduction

The 4-year-old pre-schooler is barely recognisable from the 2-year-old toddler who gleefully exercised new-found physical abilities on hapless parents or who could not easily be reasoned with when denied a brightly coloured toy that had caught his or her eye.

Four-year-olds are past the naming stage of asking 'What's that?' ('Wazzat?') and are now curious to know 'Why?'. When pre-schooler Matthew sits in the kitchen watching his father prepare dinner the 'whys' are apt to fly thick and fast: 'Why do you put salt in the soup, Dad?'; 'Why is pepper hot?'; 'Why do you chop the leaves off celery?'; and on and on it goes.

At 4 years of age, children can answer their parents' questions clearly. Their attention span is increasing and cooperative play with other children becomes a little easier.

The pre-schooler's body shape has changed dramatically. The little protruding tummy so characteristic of the toddler has disappeared and the child now walks in a more erect fashion. Jumping and climbing have long since been mastered. Pre-schoolers have acquired new eye–hand coordination that makes riding their first bicycle a pleasure, while fine motor coordination enables them to dress themselves. In the Family Life-cycle 12, the traumatic effects of the loss of a child for a family are presented.

Physical growth

Arnold Gesell (1974) gives a full description of young children's physical development. At a glance, the developmental markers passed between 2 and 6 years of age are quite impressive. It is important to appreciate that there are wide individual differences in the age at which various markers are passed. By 6 years of age, the young child has grown to two-thirds of adult height and has acquired many sophisticated physical skills, such as those of dressing, toileting and feeding. The following details are taken from Gesell (1974) and Illingworth (1987).

- *Speed of physical growth*. The speed of physical growth is steady but unspectacular.
- *Sex differences in growth*. Males and females grow at approximately the same rate.
- *Weight gain*. Weight gain during this time averages 2 kilograms per year. By 5 years of age, the young child's weight at 12 months (10 kilograms) has doubled.
- *Height*. Height increases by an average of 7.6 centimetres per year during the pre-school period.
- *Activity level*. There is a developmental peak in activity level between 18 and 23 months (Routh et al. 1978). It would appear that the period between 2 and 3 years of age is naturally a physically active time (Routh et al. 1974).

Motor development

Gross motor skills

During the pre-school and early childhood years, young children continue to make advances in mastering gross motor skills. They have gained control of the erect standing posture, walking has become second nature, and reaching and throwing skills have been further refined. Three-year-olds can jump off the bottom step and ascend stairs with alternating feet; balance on one foot for seconds at a time; ride a tricycle and catch a ball with both arms extended forward.

The 4-year-old has a very steady walking gait and uses long, confident steps. In terms of physical abilities, 4-year-olds can engage in such complex motor acts as whirling around in a circle without falling down and turning somersaults. Along with having an improved sense of balance, they can also stand on their toes, hop on one foot and catch a ball while flexing their arms at the elbow.

Pre-schoolers are quickly developing complex physical skills.

Fine motor skills

During the pre-school period, the child is developing and refining reaching for, grasping and manipulating small objects. The 3-year-old is able to scribble with a crayon, build a tower of about 10 blocks, use a fork and pour from a jug. The pre-schooler is also mastering dressing, if helped with buttons and shoelaces.

Motor learning theory

To understand more about the development of motor skills, one group of theorists has stressed the significance of the link between the intake of sensory information and the representations and storage of this information in memory. Schmidt (1988) proposed a motor schema theory for explaining the performance of new skills and the change of well-learnt movements. Schmidt proposes that when a movement is performed four aspects are stored in memory:

- the position of the body and relevant information regarding the environment in performing the movement;
- storage of parameters relevant to carrying out the movement;
- the results of performing the movement; and
- the sensory feel of performing the movement.

Information is then stored in the memory in terms of 'schemas' regarding the performance of the movement. 'We learn skills by learning rules about the functioning of our bodies, forming relationships between how our muscles are activated, what they actively do and how these actions feel' (Schmidt 1988, p. 488).

Toilet training

Basically parents are concerned to know when and how to toilet train their young child and what to do about problems they might encounter. Parents often worry about being too lax or too strict in their approach to toilet training their child. Questions parents commonly ask themselves are: 'How will I know when my child is ready to toilet train?' and 'How can I best help my child to learn to use the toilet?'(Bainer & Hale 2000).

Attitudes towards toilet training

Beliefs about toilet training have changed over the years. In the 1950s and 1960s, early and strict toilet training was emphasised. Parents often confused early toilet training with precociousness in children and would take pride in the toileting achievements of their children. However, in recent years parents have been encouraged to take a more relaxed attitude towards toilet training (Walker 1978; Bainer & Hale 2000).

When to toilet train

It is now more widely understood that bowel and bladder control is a developmental skill that is acquired largely when the child is ready (Bollard & Nettlebeck 1987). In the newborn, bowel and bladder movements are reflexive. As the young child develops, some conscious awareness occurs. Some of the complexity of development associated with toilet training is captured by Knobloch and Pasamanick (1974, p. 204), who note:

In order to be completely 'toilet trained' the child must: consciously associate the excretory act with certain internal sensations, with a particular and appropriate place, and with certain words; voluntarily inhibit relaxation of the sphincters and terminate that inhibition (release) voluntarily; verbalise or otherwise indicate the need; differentiate between stimuli from the bladder and bowel and inhibit or release the appropriate sphincter; and foresee sufficiently the urge to urinate or defecate – a formidable series of tasks, the complexities of which are not always appreciated.

Sex differences

Sex differences are apparent in terms of readiness for toilet training, with girls generally establishing control earlier than boys.

Individual differences

There are wide individual differences in the age at which children attain bowel and bladder control. Many books on child-rearing practices suggest that systematic toilet training is generally ineffective and may lead to later emotional maladjustment unless it is started when the toddler is 18 months or older (Largo & Stutzle 1977). In a large-scale New Zealand study (1265 children), Fergusson et al. (1986) found that by 8 years of age all but 3.3 per cent of children had attained bladder control. Factors predictive of the age of attainment of nocturnal bladder control were:

- a family history of **enuresis**, or the inability to control the bladder;
- the child's developmental level at 1 and 3 years;
- the child's early sleep patterns.

From the New Zealand study, it was suggested that:

- there may be a hereditary or genetic contribution;
- children slower to develop at 1 and 3 years of age had problems, indicating a maturational factor in bladder control;
- infants who slept for long periods were later in attaining bladder control than those who slept for short periods.

enuresis
the inability to control the discharge of urine; see also primary enuresis, secondary enuresis.

Methods of toilet training

Foxx and Azrin (1973) and Azrin et al. (1974) have developed tests in three areas to determine a child's readiness to toilet train, namely:

1   What bladder control does the child have? Does the child stay dry for several hours? Does the child know the bodily signs indicating a readiness to urinate?
2   Is the child's physical development sufficiently well advanced; for example, can the child walk from room to room?

3   Has the child sufficient understanding of language to be able, when asked, to walk with the parent to the bathroom or identify various parts of the body.

Toilet training and operant conditioning

Azrin and Foxx (1976) have developed a procedure based on operant conditioning techniques (see chapter 3) for training in bladder control and they claim the same procedures can be applied to bowel training. They describe this procedure as follows (Foxx & Azrin 1973, p. 436):

> The general method was to provide an intensive learning experience that maximised the factors known to be important for learning. The learning factors maximised were a distraction free environment, a large number of trials, consideration of important responses, operant reinforcement for correct responses, a variety of reinforcers, quality of the reinforcers, frequency of reinforcement, manual guidance, verbal instruction, immediacy of reinforcement, immediacy of detection of incorrect responses and negative reinforcement for incorrect responses.

Azrin and Foxx (1976) believe that it is essential for the parent to have several uninterrupted hours alone with the young child when setting up the toilet training program. A supply of drinks and snacks should be readily available. A doll (the type that wets itself) is used as a role model: the parent praises the doll if wetting occurs on the toilet and scolds it if wetting occurs in the pants. When the procedure is started with the child, a dry pants check is carried out every five minutes, with potty trials every 15 minutes (the child takes off his or her pants and sits on the potty). A type of potty chair that plays a brief tune when urine strikes two metal electrodes on the base of the potty is recommended. When the child urinates in the potty a reward is given. According to Azrin and Foxx (1976), the average child can be toilet trained in four hours using this technique.

Trends and issues

Nocturnal enuresis in children

'Enuresis' is the involuntary passage of urine beyond the age at which voluntary control is usually acquired' (Neal 1989, p. 978). According to this Australian researcher, this age may be around 5 years, as about 70 per cent of children have achieved dryness by this stage. By 10 years of age, 90 per cent of children have achieved voluntary control. As described by Neal, primary enuresis occurs when the child is never consistently dry and secondary enuresis is when there has been a period of dryness of at least one year after the age of 3 years. The enuresis may be diurnal, nocturnal or both. Nocturnal bed wetting is by far the most common variety.

Sex differences
There are no sex differences in the number of dry days at 4 years. In the 4 to 10 age group, more boys than girls show enuretic behaviour, while after the age of 11 years no sex differences are apparent.

Family background
Research indicates that most children with enuresis have at least one parent who was similarly affected as a child (Bollard & Nettelbeck 1989).

Causes

A number of possible causes can be identified including the following:

- *Delayed maturation.* There are individual differences in maturation of attaining urinary control.
- *Emotional factors.* Almost all the evidence suggests that emotional factors play little part in primary enuresis but are almost always present in secondary enuresis.

Treatment

Behavioural therapy using learning/conditioning theory has been increasingly popular over the past 30 years as the method of choice. The child lies on a sensor pad that triggers an alarm (bell or light) upon contact with urine. The apparatus is battery operated. The Australian clinical psychologists Bollard and Nettlebeck (1989) have developed a technique for treating enuresis based on this approach.

Attention deficit hyperactivity disorder (ADHD)

According to Gimpel and Kuhn (2000), the onset of **attention deficit hyperactivity disorder (ADHD)** symptoms is usually noted during the pre-school years, although the diagnosis typically occurs somewhat later. ADHD generally describes a pattern of childhood behaviour comprising impulsiveness, difficulties in sustaining attention, and over-activity. In the Australian population, a prevalence rate of 3–5 per cent exists. A number of elements of ADHD will be discussed here, but the reader is referred to important reviews of the literature for a better understanding of the issue (e.g. Vance & Luk 2000; Saunders & Chambers 1996).

Attention deficit hyperactivity disorder (ADHD) a complex set of behaviours involving impulsiveness, inattention and over-activity.

Diagnosis

Males, children in lower socioeconomic scale families, children living in urban areas and children with mothers who have a high school level of education or less are more likely to exhibit ADHD symptoms (Barkley 1990). Hancock (1996) has called attention to the concern that the disorder is being over-diagnosed. The ICD-9 (International Classification of Diseases) and the DSM-III (Diagnostic and Statistical Manual of Mental Disorders) had different approaches to diagnosis. Now, however, the development of 'hyperkinetic disorder' in ICD-10 and 'attention-deficit/hyperactivity disorder' in the DSM-IV have brought the classification criteria closer. One of the key criteria now generally agreed upon relates to 'pervasiveness', which generally means the disorder must occur across two settings.

Developmental course

ADHD is frequently viewed as a developmental disorder involving delayed development in neurological maturation. As Gimpel and Kuhn (2000) point out, in this circumstance one might expect pre-school children to be at greater risk for over-diagnosis because of its developmental nature, and because they are not yet at school it is difficult to establish the diagnosis across two settings.

In fact, research reported by Gimpel and Kuhn (2000) concluded that reliance on parental reports was associated with over-diagnosis and they recommended using the full DSM-IV criteria across settings with multiple informants.

Co-morbidity

Another element of ADHD is its co-morbidity with other disorders such as conduct disorder, learning disorders, anxiety and bi-polar disorders. In a significant review of the literature, the Australian researchers (Vance & Luk 2000) concluded that ADHD is associated with several co-morbid psychiatric conditions.

The Australian Early Intervention Network (AusEinet) has identified the need to publish guidelines for early intervention programs for young children with ADHD. Hazel et al. (2000), in a critical examination of best practice and treatment for the disorder, identified future research needs to include (i) the identification of age-appropriate outcome measures; (ii) greater use of multi-modal treatment studies; (iii) greater study of pharmaco-therapies and longitudinal studies of adjustment of the children to interventions.

Clumsy children

clumsiness
an impairment of the child's ability to perform skilled motor acts usual for the child's age.

In a playground, schoolyard or during a physical education lesson, a parent or teacher can readily identify a wide range of gracefulness in children. Developmentally the **clumsiness** of a toddler is usually looked upon with some amusement by an adult. Few parents or teachers would be made anxious by such 'clumsy' behaviour at this early age. Even in primary school or in early secondary school, adults will make allowances for some inaptitude in physical prowess. What, then, is meant by clumsiness in a child?

Description and definition of clumsy children

The Australian researchers Knuckey and Gubbay (1983, p. 9), have noted:

> Parents and professionals who manage children take for granted the processes of maturation, including the acquisition of motor skills, which transform the unco-ordinated infant into a graceful young adult.

However, there do exist a number of children who lag significantly behind their peers in the development of these important skills and who, according to Knuckey and Gubbay, have been aptly described as 'clumsy children'.

In a major study of Australian children, Gubbay (1975) found an incidence of 6.7 per cent of school children with motor inaptitude. Illingworth (1987, p. 332) comments that, developmentally:

> [c]lumsy children are usually regarded as normal for several years, and then they begin to get into trouble at school or worry their parents because of their awkwardness. Mothers commonly say their children 'fall a lot', 'always has bruises

on his legs', 'is 'awkward with his hands', 'cannot pedal a cycle', and say that the teacher complains that 'his writing is bad' or that the child 'doesn't seem to hold a pen properly'.

Such a child may be accused of being lazy, careless or poorly behaved. Perhaps the child is poor at sport and in some cultures that can mean rejection by peers. As Illingworth (1987) notes, clumsiness in a child is often associated with poor concentration, lack of coordination and inability to discriminate left from right, as well as with learning disabilities. Knuckey and Gubbay (1983, p. 19) define a clumsy child as one who is:

> mentally normal without bodily deformity and whose physical strength, sensation and coordination are virtually normal by the standards of routine, conventional neurological assessment, but whose ability to perform skilled purposive movement is impaired.

Causes

In searching for causes of clumsiness in children, two major possible contributing factors have been noted.

1 *Organic causes.* Neurological causes have been posited as a contributing factors to clumsiness (Illingworth 1987).
2 *Environmental causes.* Researchers have identified environmental factors, such as malnutrition either in utero or in the early months of life, as being associated with clumsiness (Illingworth 1987).

Prevalence

Problems in attempting to estimate prevalence have arisen because of the difficulties in defining clumsiness. Poor coordination is often a result of clumsiness. Other terms such as motor impairment, developmental dyspraxia and visuo-motor disability are used interchangeably with clumsiness. Research from Australia indicates that some 6 to 10 per cent of young children are poorly coordinated (Johnston et al. 1987).

Prognosis

Johnston et al. (1987) have developed a test (the South Australian Motor Coordination Screening (SAM) test) for screening poor coordination in 5-year-olds. This simple-to-administer test can be used by teachers, nurses and doctors. The test has explicit pass/fail criteria and has been proved to correctly identify 90 per cent of children with poor coordination (Smyth et al. 1991).

In Knuckey and Gubbay's (1983) study, 24 children were re-examined eight years after an original diagnosis of clumsiness. Those who originally had mild or moderate clumsiness were normal on follow-up, but those children who were initially severely affected were still clumsy eight years later. Evidence such as this suggests that help given early can improve motor and social skills and reduce the prevalence of related behaviour disorders (Johnston et al. 1987). It may also be possible to prevent the poor self-concept so often found in clumsy children if early counselling of parents and teachers is provided. As Johnston et al. (1987) note, the early identification of these children at school entry is desirable.

Children and drawing

Australian psychologist Jacqueline Goodnow (1977) argues that children's drawings often indicate general aspects of development and skill. That is, drawings can reflect how children think, what they attach importance to and thenature of relationships they consider to exist between objects. Similarly, the Australian academic Shelley Phillips (1986, p. 53) notes that '[t]he originality of young children can be seen in their use of things, interpretations and drawings, all of which are affected by cognitive development'.

The study of children's drawings has a long history. Burt (1921) identified a number of major stages related to the child's development. For Burt, drawing was a method of self-revelation that needed language and that provided valuable access to the child's imagination. The stages identified by Burt (1921, pp. 319–27) are summarised here.

Stage 1: scribble (2–3 years)

a   Purposeless pencil drawing enjoyed for motor expression.
b   More purposive drawing, with the child paying attention to the drawings.
c   Imaginative drawings modelled on an adult drawing.
d   Localised scribbling in which the toddler seeks to copy parts of an object.

Stage 2: line drawings (4 years)

During this stage, single movements of the pencil replace the massive and rather random scribbling of the previous stage.

Stage 3: descriptive symbolism (5–6 years)

At this stage, drawing concentrates on the human figure, with the focus on head, body, arms, eyes and facial features, but with little attention to shape or detail.

Stage 4: realism (7–9 years)

At this time in the child's life, drawing still symbolises rather than represents reality, but now more detail is apparent. The child may ornament human figures with clothing and jewellery.

Figure 12.1 The development of children's drawing

Stage 5: visual realism (10–12 years)

With the development of physical skills, the child's techniques improve. The child is now able to copy or trace the work of others and may begin to produce two- and three-dimensional drawings.

Stage 6: regression (12–14 years)

According to Burt, at this time, children's drawings exhibit a regression, which he ascribes to emotional conflicts.

Stage 7: artistic revival (14+ years)

At this stage of development, drawings are used to tell a story.

Gender differences in human figure drawing

Brown (1990), in a study of the drawings of 526 children aged between 5–11 years, argued on the basis of the presence or absence of specific characteristics that girls were more developmentally mature than boys.

Cognitive development in human figure drawing

An argument has been made that children's drawings can be used to assess their intellectual and cognitive development. Aikman, Belter and Finch (1992) found that human figure drawings were not good predictors of IQ scores or achievement test scores. However, Chappell and Steitz (1993) concluded there was an identifiable relationship between human figure drawings and Piaget's stages of cognitive development, with drawing levels increasing with cognitive ability.

Emotional development and human figure drawing

Koppitz (1968) has examined in some detail the way in which human figure drawings can be used to indirectly assess children's feelings and emotions. The approach used is to ask children to 'draw a whole person, not just a head'. 'The person a child knows best is himself; his picture of a person becomes therefore a portrait of his inner self, of his attitudes' (Koppitz 1968, p. 5). The attitudes, anxieties and concerns of children as reflected in their drawings have been identified in terms of 38 signs to be found on children's human figure drawings (Koppitz 1968). The signs are listed under the three headings of (i) quality signs; (ii) special features; and (iii) omissions.

Using Koppitz's (1968) indicators, Yama (1990), in a study of Vietnamese refugees, concluded that human figure drawings could provide a useful index of client adjustment. Hibbard and Hartmann (1990) also used Koppitz's indicators in a study of sexually abused children aged 5–8 years, concluding that the drawings of such children reflected more anxiety and emotional indicators than the drawings of a control group of non-abused children.

In summary, 'the evolution of spontaneous drawing is related to the child's psycho-affective maturation' (Wallon & Baudoin 1990, p. 338). Assessment of a child's drawings can provide important clinical information regarding the child's development.

The family life-cycle: 12

The loss of a child

One aspect of the family life-cycle, the impact of which is often overlooked, occurs when parents lose a baby – either through miscarriage, spontaneous abortion, stillbirth, or the death of the baby shortly after birth. In fact, while these events are surprisingly common, their impact on the parents and the course of the family life-cycle is only just beginning to be understood. It is estimated that 10 to 14 per cent of pregnancies terminate through miscarriage when the foetus is expelled by natural means before the twenty-fifth week of pregnancy (Wetzel 1982).

As we have seen in previous family life-cycle items, very little research attention has been given until recently to the psychological effects of becoming a parent. Even less attention has been paid to the psychological impact on parents of losing a baby through miscarriage or stillbirth.

Miscarriage

There are many reasons why miscarriages occur (Hager 1987). In the case of a healthy woman experiencing her first miscarriage, substance abuse and environmental causes should be seriously considered as contributing factors. Statistically, however, the most likely cause of miscarriage is some genetic abnormality in the foetus.

In considering the literature, Day and Hooks (1987) note that depression is a common mental state following a miscarriage. This mental state results from intense feelings of loss and grief, although frustration and anger can also contribute to it, as can fear of personal vulnerability and concerns about the possibility of future miscarriages. Day and Hooks (1987) also observe that relatives and friends are often at a loss to know how to help because miscarriage is such an enigma. However, these same authors have found that recovery from miscarriage can be linked to family strength or 'resilience' (see chapter 21). The degree of cohesion in families – that is, how interdependent and supportive family members are – is linked to the successful resolution of depression following miscarriage.

Stillbirth

An intra-uterine foetal death is a traumatic experience for parents (Woods and Esposito 1987; Page-Lieberman & Hughes 1990). Mothers and fathers must come to terms with the intense grief associated

with such loss. The hospital staff are also faced with crucial questions, such as: 'Who will tell the parents? Which of various delivery options will be chosen? Should the parents see the baby after delivery?'

Once foetal death has been diagnosed, two courses of action are available to hospital personnel (Woods & Esposito 1987). The labour can be induced or the pregnancy can continue under observation while awaiting spontaneous onset of labour. If the latter course is adopted, hospital staff are faced with having to deal with the often confused and/or angry feelings of the mother and her family. The mother may be confused as to the reasons for such a course of action. At the same time, she is attempting to come to grips with the fact of the death of her baby. Woods and Esposito (1987) note that once the onset of labour has occurred, the parents experience other feelings of which the hospital staff should be aware.

- *Fear.* Given that there is little to look forward to after delivery the mother may worry about the child's appearance, especially if the baby has been carried in utero for several days.
- *Guilt.* The parents must deal with their sense of responsibility for the baby's death. For example, they may blame their behaviour during pregnancy, such as eating or drinking habits.
- *Anger.* The parents may be angry at the death of their baby and this anger may be directed at the hospital staff.
- *Loneliness.* The baby's death may cause the parents to ask themselves such questions as 'Why us?' or 'Why our baby?'. They may experience intense feelings of isolation and abandonment as a result of their shattered dreams.

Fathers and perinatal death

Given fathers' increasing participation in the pregnancy and birth process (see chapter 9), researchers are now considering how fathers deal with perinatal death. Many fathers are caught between their own grief and the needs of their partner, while fearing that expression of their own grief will worsen the situation (Page-Lieberman & Hughes 1990).

Coping with a perinatal death

Page-Lieberman and Hughes (1990) give the following guidelines for helping parents to cope with a perinatal death.

- Respect individual coping styles during labour and delivery. The father is performing many tasks and does not want to be deserted.
- Give parents the choice of a room on the postpartum unit or a general floor. Choose carefully which general floor, by communicating with staff to make sure that they are prepared to work with grieving parents.
- Ensure that parents have ample time and privacy to hold their baby.
- Suggest that if possible, extended family members see the baby.
- If parents refuse or are reluctant to see or hold the baby, ask them if they would like to hear about the baby. Having the nurse describe the infant often lessens parents' fears or fantasies about the baby's looks.
- Call the child by name, or if the child is not named, use 'your daughter' or 'your son'.
- Point out positive characteristics of the infant (colour of hair, etc.). Foetuses, as well, have noteworthy traits, such as a strong heartbeat during a difficult labour, or a well-shaped head.
- Speak with the grandparents and acknowledge their loss of a grandchild. Stress the importance of their full support in grieving, especially a willingness to discuss the baby.
- Review the labour process and praise parents for the decisions they made.
- Recognise guilt as a normal reaction but ignore the reason. Help parents to recognise the process.

- Ask parents what plans they have to remember or say goodbye to their baby. If seemly, offer suggestions of what others have found comforting.
- Encourage couples to tell each other how they feel, and prepare them for individual styles of mourning.
- After a healthy baby is born, discuss grief for a previous loss.
- Avoid stiff professional behaviour. Showing sorrow demonstrates that staff recognise the extent of the parents' loss.
- Sit down when talking with bereaved parents. It is the best body language.
- Ask parents if they want their names to be given to bereavement groups. Encourage the participation of parents in such support activities.

The impact of a baby's death on the family
Pregnancy loss is a significant and potentially powerful stressor in the lives of many families. At present, our understanding of how families cope with such a loss is limited by our understanding of the complex nature of the grieving process and of the factors that facilitate adjustment to such a loss. It is only now that researchers are beginning to appreciate that such a loss, unless dealt with at the time, can have a significant impact on the life-cycle of the family.

Chapter summary

As noted by O'Brien (1994, p. 164), 'Changes in the movement pattern for locomotion and manipulation are due to children's increased body awareness and cognitive control over their bodies. This in turn allows them greater control to meet environmental demands'. The pre-school period is a time of exciting development and change in terms of children's acquisition of gross and fine motor skills.

Discussion questions

1   What are the major developmental tasks facing children at 2, 3, 4 and 5 years of age?
2   What physical features help determine the best time to toilet train?

3   What psychological theory have Azrin and Foxx (1976) used as a basis for develop-
     ing toilet training skills in children? Explain its application.
4   What is meant by 'enuresis'?
5   What psychological effects could 'clumsiness' have on children?

Activity

Collect a range of drawings from children aged 2, 4, 6, 8, 10 and 13 years. Present them
to the class and discuss them in terms of the developmental features displayed by the
drawings.

Selected websites

Child Adolescent Psychological and Educational Resources <www.caper.com.au>

AusEinet <www.AusEinet.flinders.edu.au>

13 Cognitive Development of Pre-schoolers

'I Wonder if I was Changed in the Night?'

'Dear, dear! How queer everything is today! And yesterday everything happened just as usual: I wonder if I was changed in the night? Let me think: was I the same when I got up this morning? I think I remember feeling rather different. But if I'm not the same, who in the world am I? Ah, that's the great puzzle!'

Lewis Carroll, Alice's Adventure in Wonderland

KEY TERMS AND CONCEPTS

- Egocentrism
- Conservation
- Animism, artificialism and realism
- Imaginary companion
- Telegraphic speech
- Stimulus–response theory
- Social learning theory

Introduction

Children's understanding of the world and their place in it undergoes rapid development during the pre-school years. This understanding is accompanied by significant changes in their use of language. The pre-schooler's behaviour is dramatically different from that of a child during the 'terrible twos' (just ask any parent!). The temper tantrums, refusals to comply and use of the word 'No!', so characteristic of the 2-year-old, contrast sharply with the 4- to 5-year-old's ability to comprehend instructions, comply with requests and generally reason about the world.

This chapter focuses on the nature of children's cognitive development in the pre-school period. More particularly, consideration is given to a number of theorists, namely Piaget, Bruner and Vygotsky, and their views of the way children's thinking develops during this period. An examination is also made of children's language development in the pre-school years.

Various topics related to pre-schoolers' cognitive development are discussed, namely: the intriguing nature of pre-schoolers' 'magical' ways of thinking; the importance of fairytales; the role of computers; and preparing for school. The Family Life-cycle: 13 is devoted to the effects on children of media violence viewed on television.

Theoretical foundations

The impact of Piaget's theory on views of child development was first felt in Australia during the late 1950s and early 1960s. Piaget presented to professionals (teachers, nurses and psychologists) and to parents a rich and persuasive vision of the child that was based on the idea that development was primarily cognitive; human change was a matter of the child's **epistemological development**, the child's increasingly rational theory of the way the world worked (Levine et al. 1983, p. 34).

Piaget's views on cognitive development were drawn from sensitive and painstaking observations of the everyday behaviour of his own three children. In working with older children, Piaget used a method of conversational inquiry in which he gently and sympathetically explored the child's explanation of the world and events in it. His research was largely responsible for presenting to parents and educators the image of the thinking child – an image that has continued to influence our views of children. Piaget's stages of cognitive - development are outlined in Table 13.1.

One of the major accomplishments of the pre-operational child is the development of **symbolic functions**. 'Symbolic functioning is the ability to make one thing represent a different thing which is not present' (Ault 1983, p. 42). The young child pushing a small cube along the floor and saying 'meow' knows the plastic cube is not a cat. Rather, the plastic cube signifies something for the child. Piaget argued that signifiers may (i) be symbolic, that is, the cube may resemble a cat; or (ii) be signs (c-a-t) or words that are arbitrary. In

epistemological development
development of the child's knowledge base.

symbolic functions
cognition that enables one object or action to represent another.

relation to (ii) it would be natural to assume that the rapid development of children's thought is merely a reflection of their language development – that words provide them with concepts and that therefore, once they learn the appropriate word they have also achieved the concept embodied in it. But Piaget argued that words are first learned and then come to represent concepts as a result of the child's own experiences with them. As Piaget presented it, the symbols are therefore private before they develop into conventional symbols.

Piaget believed that the young child's capacity to use symbols to represent some aspect of reality begins early in the sensori-motor period. By the end of the sensori-motor period, imitation is possible in the absence of a model. Children pass very quickly from what looks like imitation to symbolic play.

Table 13.1 The pre-operational period: the second of Piaget's stages of cognitive development

Stage	Age	Abilities
Sensori-motor period	0–2 years	Use of five senses to relate to the world
Pre-operational period	2–7 years	Language and symbolism
Concrete operations period	7–11 years	Can apply simple logic to solve problems
Formal operations period	11+ years	Abstract reasoning

The development of symbolic functions

The development of symbolic functions may be inferred from four types of activities (Ault 1983):

1   *The search for hidden objects.* To be able to search for a hidden object children must have some mental representation of the object and of unseen movements. As we saw in chapter 7, a child in the early sensori-motor period will not look for an object even though he or she watches it being hidden under a cloth.

2   *Delayed imitation.* This is imitation some time after the event has been observed. For example, my son Matthew (at 2 years and 5 months of age) suddenly began crying 'I want my Mummy' one evening after his mother had walked out of the room. When his mother returned I described his behaviour. She commented that he was probably imitating his 5-year-old friend in the apartment below. The previous day Matthew had seen his friend Tyson cry 'I want my Mummy' when Tyson's mother went out shopping.

3   *Symbolic play.* In using symbolic play the child may treat one object as though it were another: for example, an object such as a long-handled brush may be treated as if it were a guitar. One object represents another in the child's imagination.

4 *Use of language.* Certainly, during the pre-operational period, language comes to be used symbolically. Piaget holds that the development of symbolic functions precedes language: that is, children must have a mental image of 'mother' before they can say 'Mama'. Language, then, serves to help young children:

- to control their own behaviour;
- to classify and organise their environment.

Characteristics of pre-operational thinking

Piaget (1967) identified three characteristics of the pre-operational child's view of the world:

- centration;
- a focus on states versus transformation;
- irreversibility versus reversibility.

Centration

According to Piagetian theory, the pre-operational child is centred (egocentric). That is, the pre-schooler is likely to concentrate on a single feature or limited portion of a task that is interesting to him or her but to ignore other meaningful aspects of the work. This indicates that the pre-operational child is easily distracted by the appearance or the spatial properties of an object. Flavell (1963, p. 60) defines the concept as follows:

> Egocentrism denotes a cognitive state in which the cogniser sees the world from a single point of view only, his own but without knowledge of the existence of viewpoints or perspectives and without awareness that he is a prisoner of his own viewpoint.

egocentrism (centration) the inability to distinguish between one's own point of view and that of another person.

Interestingly, in his later writings Piaget switched from the term **egocentrism** to **centration** because egocentric has the additional connotation of 'being overly concerned with self' (Vyuk 1981). Piaget's belief in centration was based on a series of experiments such as the following.

Piaget and Inhelder (1956) presented a model of three mountains to children of different ages (see Figure 13.1). A doll was placed at various locations (positions 1, 2, 3 and 4) around the mountains and children were asked to say how the mountains looked to the doll from each location. Children under 6 years of age tended to choose a picture or replica that depicted their own view and not the doll's view. In Piaget and Inhelder's explanation, the pre-operational child is 'rooted to his own viewpoint in the narrowest and most restricted fashion so that he cannot imagine any other perspective but his own' (Piaget and Inhelder 1956, p. 242).

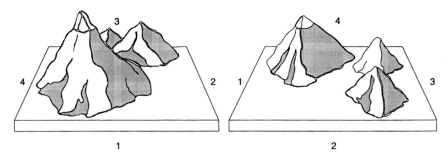

Figure 13.1 The three mountain task

Criticism has been levelled at the idea that young children cannot imagine any other perspective but their own. Research by Borke (1975) has demonstrated that when presented with tasks that are age-appropriate, children as young as 3 or 4 years have a high likelihood of correctly representing another's perspective. Similarly, non-centrated results have been obtained on other perspective tasks. Shatz and Gelman (1973) report that in their research 4-year-olds used shorter sentences and simpler utterances when talking to 2-year-olds than when talking to their peers. Maratsos (1973) observes that when asked to indicate the position of a toy to a sighted adult, 3- and 4-year-old children pointed with their fingers. However, when the same adult covered her eyes the children tried as best they could to describe the toy's position.

In a more recent criticism of Piaget's concept of egocentrism, Bruner (1987) argues that:

> The problem is not with competence but with performance. It is not that the child does not have the capacity to take another's perspective but rather that he cannot do so without understanding the situation in which he is operating (Bruner 1987, pp. 92–3).

That is, we may be underestimating the child's capacity to take the perspective of another.

States versus transformations

Another facet of pre-schoolers' thinking, as described by Flavell (1963), involves their focus on states rather than on transformations. That is, in pre-schoolers' thinking the focus is static: they are unable to represent the transformation that something may undergo from one state to another. For example, in pouring water from a short, wide glass to a tall, thin glass the child does not understand that the state can be transformed: that the same volume of water only partially fills the wide glass but fills the thin glass completely (see Figure 13.2). Pre-operational children focus on the beginning and end of the task but have difficulty with the transformation that occurs in between.

Irreversibility versus reversibility

Older 'concrete operational' children's thinking is characterised by reversibility. Thus, they may recognise that the change of shape caused by pouring the water into a long, thin glass can be undone by pouring the water back into its original container. However, pre-operational children, according to Piagetian theory, cannot conceive of such a possibility.

Experiments in pre-operational children's thinking

The features of centration, states versus transformations and irreversibility versus reversibility are characteristic of the pre-operational child's understanding of the world. These characteristics are frequently cited to help explain a number of compelling experiments demonstrating pre-operational children's thinking. That is, the experiments provide pre-operational children with real challenges as they attempt to solve certain problems.

As pre-schoolers begin to take a wider interest in the world around them, to ask 'why, to imitate events, to engage in pretend play and solve quite complex practical problems, one might think that their cognitive development is complete. Piagetian research suggests that this is not so. The evidence is that pre-school children do not feel as confident with their newly gained symbolic or conceptual skills as they do with perception and action. This has been revealed through a series of ingenious experiments, initially conducted by Piaget, involving:

- conservation;
- seriation;
- class inclusion.

Conservation

Constancy or **conservation** is a property of objects and events that assists the individual to live an orderly life. Basically, conservation means that an object retains certain properties no matter how its form changes. In Piagetian theory it refers to the idea that fundamental properties of objects – such as weight, number or volume – remain the same despite external changes in their shape or arrangement.

> **conservation**
> in Piagetian theory, the retention by an object or substance of certain properties, regardless of changes in shape and arrangement.

The conservation experiments

Experiments have been conducted in relation to conservation with liquids, solids, number and length. Three of the classic experiments are shown in Figure 13.2. In the various conservation tasks, the children see the experimenter alter some feature of a display and must decide whether or not something has changed. For example, in the number task, the child is asked if the two rows have the same number of coins or if either the top or the bottom row

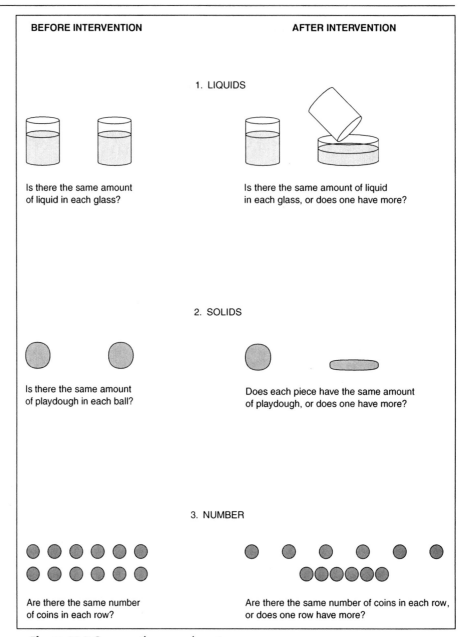

BEFORE INTERVENTION

AFTER INTERVENTION

1. LIQUIDS

Is there the same amount
of liquid in each glass?

Is there the same amount of liquid
in each glass, or does one have more?

2. SOLIDS

Is there the same amount
of playdough in each ball?

Does each piece have the same amount
of playdough, or does one have more?

3. NUMBER

Are there the same number
of coins in each row?

Are there the same number of coins in each row,
or does one row have more?

Figure 13.2 Conservation experiments

has more. Children above the age of 3 years will usually say the rows have the
same number of coins. Then, the child watches while the top row is spread out.
Again the child is asked whether the two rows have the same number of coins
or whether one row has more than the other. Pre-operational children typically
reply that the bottom row has more 'because they are all bunched up', or the top
row has more because 'they are all spread out'. In contrast, children at the next
stage (concrete operations) will say that both rows still have the same number.

Explanations of non-conservation

One explanation for the pre-schooler's failure to conserve is the confusion of outward appearance with substance, in as much as the child centres on one dimension of the problem (such as length of the line or height of the water) and ignores the other dimensions (such as density of the line). It is also possible that the young child focuses on state rather than on the transformations between states, and this could lead to some misunderstanding of the issue. Both these explanations follow the Piagetian view.

Some compelling research evidence has also been gathered against centration and state explanations of non-conservation. Anderson and Cuneo (1978) showed 5-year-old children rectangular biscuits that varied in width and height. They were asked to say how happy they would be to get such biscuits to eat. The children used a rating scale with a sad face at one end and a happy face at the other. The researchers discovered that even pre-schoolers used width and height to rate the biscuits and that they did not centre on only one aspect of the problem.

In addition, the British psychologists McGarrigle and Donaldson (1974) offer some alternative explanations for children's inability to conserve when given the previously described Piagetian tasks. They conclude from their research that there are 'clear indications that traditional procedures for assessing conservation seriously underestimate the child's knowledge' (McGarrigle and Donaldson 1974, p. 347). They suggest that in changing an attribute of the experiment, such as the length of the line, the experimenters influence the children's interpretations of the experimenter's utterances.

Seriation

Another characteristic of the pre-operational child's thinking is **seriation**, or the ability to arrange objects according to some quantified dimension such as length, size or weight. For example, children may be given a number of sticks of various lengths and be asked to arrange them from shortest to longest. A pre-operational child might pick up two sticks from one pile, compare them and put the shorter on the left. Then the child might take up another stick from the pile, compare it with only one of the two previous sticks, and if it were shorter, place it on the left, with no regard for its length relative to the original stick.

seriation
the ability to put objects or quantities into a logical sequence.

A Piagetian explanation is that the pre-operational child can focus on only one aspect of the problem at a time. An older child might complete the task by looking at the whole pile, removing the shortest stick, looking at those remaining, removing the next shortest, and so on. Each time the older child would consider the entire problem as well as the developing arrangement. To educators it is quickly apparent that the achievement of seriation is a critical development in terms of understanding numbers and learning arithmetic.

Class inclusion

class inclusion
the ability to
associate a subset
of objects (such as
red apples) with
the larger grouping
to which it belongs
(fruit).

A third distinguishing feature of the pre-operational child in Piagetian theory is **class inclusion**. In one version of the Piagetian experiment to demonstrate this, young children are asked a number of questions about seven blue beads and three white beads, all of which are wooden:

Adult: Do you see these beads? Some are white and some are blue. What are the white ones made of?

Child: Wood.

Adult: What are the blue beads made of?

Child: Wood.

Adult: Are there more blue beads or more wooden beads?

Child: Blue beads.

The pre-operational child will typically say there are more blue beads. The same problem arises where a young child has difficulty understanding the relationship between a city, the state in which it is located and the country which contains them both. The Piagetian explanation again focuses on the characteristic of centring. Because pre-schoolers have trouble focusing their attention both on the parts (white/blue) and the whole (wood), they make errors when answering the questions.

Trends and issues

Preparing for school: Parental influence

The general quality of family life has been consistently shown to have a major bearing on the way a child copes with the demands of school (G. H. Childs pers. comm.). This is reflected most obviously in the child's attainment scores in key subject areas such as mathematics and reading. Stott et al. (1988) have established that how well children benefit from school is not determined by intellectual ability alone, but by:

- how well children pay attention, concentrate on learning and avoid distraction;
- how motivated the child is in terms of an active, positive approach to school and response to the teacher.

Such behaviours have been found to predict the child's academic achievement as well as, if not better than, scores on standard intelligence tests, and to combine with intelligence quotient scores in giving a much stronger total prediction of school achievement. More particularly, these kinds of 'on task' and motivational factors appear to be particularly important during the first years of school in terms of establishing later behaviour.

Recent Australian research conducted by Childs (unpub.) with children beginning school in Adelaide and Whyalla (South Australia) has highlighted the critical role played by the family in shaping the development of 'on task' and motivational behaviours. Childs has found major differences in attention/concentration and motivation as a consequence of the way parents prepare their children for school. The most severely disadvantaged children were those from low-skilled/low-income families, with boys showing these effects more strikingly than girls.

Childs (unpub.) believes that a great deal depends on the general expectations for competent behaviour that parents apply to their children on a day-to-day basis. These expectations may be reflected in a whole range of pre-school activities, household chores, family rules and patterns of communication. They might emerge in the emphasis parents give to telling and sharing stories, playing games requiring focused attention or insisting that the child listen to parental instructions. In more general terms, parent expectations might be reflected in the amount of focused parent–child interaction, or the amount of unrestricted television viewing allowed. Clearly, though, parents play a crucial role in preparing children for the demands of school.

The 'magic' world of the pre-schooler

In his earliest writings, Piaget (1929) described a number of intriguing features of a pre-operational child's thinking: magic and omnipotence, animism, artificialism and realism.

Magic and omnipotence

As Piaget (1929) understood it, pre-schoolers believe that everyone thinks as they do and shares their wants and feelings. Not only is the world created for the child but the child can control the world. Thus, the sun comes out when the child goes for a walk and the night comes when the child goes to bed. Vestiges of this magical thinking are found in rhymes of childhood: 'Rain, rain go away' and 'Never step on the cracks in the pavement'.

Animism

By **animism** Piaget meant that for the pre-operational child the world of nature is alive, conscious and has a purpose. Thus, young children may believe that the sun will follow them to light the way. Piaget has identified four stages of animism:

1   Up to the age of 4 or 5 years, the child believes that almost everything is alive and has a purpose – for example, 'a naughty chair bumped the child'.
2   During this second stage (5–7 years) only objects that move have a purpose: for example, floating clouds provide shade.
3   In the next stage (7–9 years), only objects that move spontaneously are thought to be alive: for example, cars move but they are not alive.
4   In the last stage (9–12 years), the child understands that only plants and animals are alive.

animism
according to Piaget, the belief of the pre-operational child that inanimate objects are alive.

Artificialism

Artificialism in the pre-operational child is closely related to animism and reflects the child's belief that human beings create natural phenomena. For example, when asked how the moon came to be, the pre-operational child might say 'because we came alive'. Piaget (1929) recounts how his little daughter, seeing the clouds of smoke rising from her father's pipe, assumed he was responsible for the clouds in the sky in Switzerland where they lived.

As they grow older, children proceed from purely artificial explorations to ones that are half artificial and half natural (such as, the sun comes from clouds, but the clouds come from people's homes). Finally, by 9 to 10 years of age, the child has a natural explanation for phenomena such as how the sun and stars came to be.

artificialism
according to Piaget, the belief of the pre-operational child that certain aspects of the natural environment are manufactured by people.

Realism

realism
according to Piaget, the confusion by the pre-operational child of external reality with the child's own thought processes and subjective understanding; the child's belief that wishes, thoughts and feelings are 'alive'.

Realism for the pre-operational child is the idea that words, pictures, dreams and feelings are equally real. Thus, a name is real and is part of the thing named. In the story of *Rumpelstiltskin* the magic and power of names is emphasised: for example, the queen must guess Rumpelstiltskin's name in order to win her child back. In *Alice in Wonderland*, a conversation between Alice and Humpty Dumpty illustrates the idea of realism, showing that as children grow older they realise that names are not an intrinsic part of the object named but come from elsewhere.

'And only one for birthday presents, you know. There's glory for you!'

'I don't know what you mean by "glory",' Alice said.

Humpty Dumpty smiled contemptuously. 'Of course you don't till I tell you. I meant "there's a nice knock-down argument for you!"'

'But "glory" doesn't mean "a nice knock-down argument"', Alice objected.

'When I use a word', Humpty Dumpty said in rather a scornful tone, 'it means just what I choose it to mean – neither more nor less'.

'The question is', said Alice, 'whether you can make words mean so many different things'.

'The question is', said Humpty Dumpty, 'which is to be master – that's all'.

(Carroll 1982)

Imaginary companions of pre-schoolers

The cartoon series 'Calvin & Hobbes' provides a very good example of a young child with an imaginary companion – a 'tiger called 'Hobbes'. As defined by Svendson (1934, p. 988) an imaginary companion is '. . . an invisible character, named and referred to in conversation with other persons or played with directly for a period of time, at least several months, having an air of reality for the child but no apparent objective basis'.

Research by Pearson et al. (2000) discovered that over 46 per cent of 5- to 12-year-olds reported experiences of imaginary companions. As the authors noted: 'These findings were unexpected as previous studies had suggested that imaginary companions were experienced by fewer, much younger children'(p. 13). The same authors noted that more girls than boys reported having imaginary companions.

Gleason, Sebanc and Hartup (2000) note that the developmental significance of imaginary companions has been difficult to determine in the light of the limited research into the topic. In contrast to some of the better known imaginary companions such as 'Hobbes' in 'Calvin & Hobbes' and *Winnie the Pooh*, research indicates that imaginary companions are usually human, they may occur singly or in groups, they are most frequently children, and usually male (Taylor 1999).

Many children enjoy having an imaginary companion.

Children and fairytales

In the introduction to his book *The Uses of Enchantment*, which deals with the role of fairytales in children's lives, Bruno Bettelheim (1982) is critical of much of contemporary literature available to children because it fails to stimulate and nurture the resources a child needs.

> For a story truly to hold the child's attention, it must entertain him [sic] and arouse his curiosity. But to enrich his life, it must stimulate his imagination; help him develop his intellect and clarify his emotions; be attuned to his anxieties and aspirations; give full recognition to his difficulties, while at the same time suggesting solutions to the problems which perturb him. In short, it must at one and the same time relate to all aspects of his personality (Bettelheim 1982, p. 5).

Bettelheim believes that it is the folk fairytale that best fulfils these needs.

The popularity of fairytales among countless generations of children strongly suggests that such stories appeal in some way to some basic needs in us all. It is possible from the countless fairytales that exist to identify a few basic themes as well as similar plots, characters and storylines.

Themes A frequently occurring theme is the discovery of another world, such as a past or future society, including an initiation and the experience of trials and tribulations in the course of a journey: for example, *Hansel and Gretel* or *The Tin Soldier*. Another theme is that of some initial misfortune being overturned, leading to a happy ending, of which *Cinderella* is a classic illustration.

Story line In fairytales, a story line frequently concerns something that is forbidden, such as a forbidden room or door. The story line deals with the breaking of the taboo and the evil powers that are then released – in early fairy-tales, evil is as omnipresent as virtue (Bettelheim 1982). The hero or heroine must experience the trials and tribulations of breaking the taboo before finally succeeding. The story line often involves a journey or flight of some kind. The fairytale *The Wild Swans* is an example of this kind of story line. According to Howarth (1989, p. 59), 'the reason fairytales are so engrossing is that they speak to the basic questions children ask themselves. As one child put it, "they think about what I think about"'.

Characters Alongside the main characters there is frequently a helpful, gentle and kindly animal or bird that possesses magical powers: for example the birds that nourish Cinderella. Another popular character is frequently an ugly creature who, more often than not, is under some spell. One example of a tale with an ugly creature is *Beauty and the Beast.*

Trends and issues

Reading to your child

As noted in chapter 10, various theories have been proposed to account for children's language acquisition. One challenge faced by the various theories is their ability to explain the very rapid growth in word learning such that by 6 years of age an English speaking child will have a vocabulary of approximately 6000 words (Anglin 1993). It appears that direct teaching cannot easily account for such a rapid rate of word acquisition, so attention has been given to the means by which children learn words incidentally from their environment. Storybook reading has been researched to understand whether children learn from listening to storybook reading. Reviews of research (e.g. Bus, van Ijsdoorn & Pellegrini 1995)

suggest there is a positive correlation between story-book reading and vocabulary development. It has also been established that the style of storybook reading is associated with a child's word acquisition such that a more interactive adult storybook reading style using open-ended questions, praise can positively influence language development. Research by Senechal (1997) indicates that pre-school children make more gains in vocabulary after repeated readings of a storybook than after a single reading. Repeated exposure to the story line and pictures appeared to facilitate their memory search for novel labels. Senechal (1997) also found that asking labelling questions during repeated readings of a book was a very powerful means for encouraging the acquisition of expressive language (see Chapter 7).

Developmental perspectives and fairytales

In the broadest sense, Bettelheim (1982) comments that 'Myths and fairy stories both answer the eternal questions: What is the world really like? How am I to live my life in it? How can I truly be myself?' Bettelheim goes on to observe that the fairytale develops and unfolds in a way that conforms to the way a child thinks. In fairytales, young children can identify fears and anxieties that symbolise their own fears and anxieties as they make their way in life. Fairytales therefore help young children to deal with their own anxieties and fears (Lubetsky 1989).

> Children often do not respond to direct questions about their feelings. Fairy-tales not only provide entertainment for a child but a creative way to provide anxiety reduction, fantasy fulfilment, reflections back on earlier times, and a window to the future. The stories are represented as fantasy, yet many confront real conflicts in development with hopeful, satisfying results (Lubetsky 1989, p. 253).

Bruner and child development

In chapter 7, we have seen that Jerome Bruner posits three stages in the cognitive development of the child: the representational, iconic and symbolic. Although Bruner's theory acknowledges a deep intellectual debt to the thinking of Piaget and Vygotsky, his theorising about the nature of child development differs from theirs in a number of important ways.

Reality is constructed

Bruner places a great deal more emphasis than Piaget on the notion that humans actively construct meaning from the world. In *Actual Minds, Possible Worlds* (1986), Bruner cites Goodman's notion of a 'constructivist' philosophy.

> Contrary to common sense there is no unique 'real world' that pre-exists and is independent of human mental activity and human symbolic language; that which we call the world is a product of some mind whose symbolic procedures construct the world (Bruner 1986, p. 95).

According to Bruner children learn through social interaction.

As such, the world we live in is 'created' by the mind. Bruner argues that the idea that we 'construct' the world should be quite congenial to developmental or clinical psychologists who observe that humans can attach quite different meanings to the same event. The constructivist notion has also been explicated by Gregory Bateson (see chapter 3).

Development is culturally and historically embedded

Bruner (1986) and Bruner and Haste (1987) emphasise that human development must be understood in its cultural and historical context. In Bruner's words (1986, p. 67), 'It can never be the case that there is a 'self' independent of one's cultural–historical context'. To this end, Bruner's outlook is closely connected with Vygotsky's view (see chapters 3 and 10). Culture is the means by which 'instructions' about how humans should grow are carried from one generation to the next (Bruner 1987). That is, culture helps transmit knowledge and understanding (see Chapter 1).

The child as a social being

Bruner and Haste (1987, p. 11) observe that 'we are now able to focus on the child as a social being whose competencies are interwoven with the competencies of others'. Bruner and Haste are critical of the legacy bequeathed by Piaget, suggesting that while the child is active in the construction of the world, the picture that emerges is one of a rather isolated child working alone at problem-solving tasks. Bruner and Haste emphasise that the child is in fact a social operator, who through a social life 'acquires a framework for interpreting experience, and learns how to negotiate meaning in a manner congruent with the requirements of a culture' (Bruner & Haste 1987, p. 1).

Bruner's research and writing is having an important impact on developmental psychologists' understanding of the developing child. By emphasising the constructive nature of cognitive development and the influence of cultural factors, Bruner has added a richer dimension to our understanding of the nature of children's thinking.

Children and computers

Since the first edition of this textbook, computers have come to play a significant role in the futures of today's children. Computers are now widely used in industry and commerce, and most Australian schools use computers in one form or another. Computers are now used in a wide range of activities to promote children's learning, including drawing, writing and story experiences, as well as to provide enjoyment and entertainment (Elliott 1985; Hancock 1988). However, as Selwyn and Bullon (2000) have noted, while virtually every British child had used a computer at school at least once during the school year '. . . the nature of pupils' engagement with ICT [information and communication technology] varied considerably' (p. 321).

Computers/cognitive skills and 'screenagers'

Hancock (1988) has drawn attention to the database facilities that computers offer young children. Teaching children to retrieve information electronically is simply an extension of teaching them to gather information from books, film

Computers and children

Today, many children in economically developed countries spend so many hours alone in front of the computer screen that, in fact, we have a new non-nuclear family system: a father–mother and child/children–computer(s)' (Fomichova & Fomichova 2000, p. 1). In many ways, the computer has replaced the television as a significant part in children's lives.

It is very easy to understand why children (and adults) find computers so attractive. Computers provide children with extrinsic rewards in terms of almost immediate feedback from the games and activities, plus a range of entertaining sound effects and graphics. The reinforcement they receive helps establish the behaviour of playing the games. Computers provide individualised instruction delivered at the student's own pace, allowing for a variety of learning styles.

Of course, the increasing presence and use of computers, particularly in Western industrialised countries raise lots of concerns for parents. Children's competencies in their use of computers are linked to their image and picture of themselves. However, even in countries where computers are widely available not all people have access to such technology, which raises concerns about social equality. There are also concerns that computers emphasise visual and sensori-motor skills at the expense of the development of linguistic skills. For children, the challenge with the use of computers is how to teach them to establish themselves as individual, creative thinkers able to use their own brain for problem-solving and creative thinking.

and audiovisual facilities. Database skills can help children develop cognitive skills in classification and analysis of information. Older children can be taught to develop their own databases on specific subjects, such as a database of the pets owned by the children in a class or of the occupations of their parents. Over and above this rather early, rather simplistic outlook regarding the use of computers in schools, Fomichova and Fomichova (2000, p. 1) have noted that one of the fundamental questions regarding the use of computers in schools concerns '. . . how to formulate and create optimal cognitive preconditions for successful children–computer interaction'. As the same authors go on to note,

> Fifteen years ago a typical nuclear family consisted of a father, mother, and children. Now many children in economically developed countries spend so many hours alone in front of the computer screen that, in fact, we have a new non-nuclear family system: a father–mother and child/children–computer(s) (p. 1)

Fomichova and Fomichova (2000) have argued that one of the pre-conditions to introducing children to ICT is that we need to teach children to establish themselves as '. . . autonomous, creative thinkers, i.e. how to use effectively one's own brain in terms of language, number, information processing, problem-solving and creative thinking' (p. 2).

Psychological theories and computer use

As (ICT) makes an ever greater impact on our everyday lives and the lives of children and adolescents, efforts are being made to help explain and understand its impact. Consideration is given to the psychological basis for ICT (e.g. Morgan, Morgan & Hall 2000).

Behavioural theories can be used to help explain children's attraction to, and use of computers. Computers provide children with extrinsic rewards in terms of almost immediate feedback from the games and activities, supplemented by a range of entertaining sound effects and graphics. The variable ration schedule of reinforcement (see chapter 3) helps establish the behaviour.

More cognitively-oriented theories (e.g. Wishart 1990) have identified the fact that computers provide individualised instruction delivered at the student's own pace, and allowing for a variety of learning styles.

Most recently, researchers such as Muir, Nazarian and Gilmer (1999) have utilised a constructivist perspective (see chapter 3) to help understand and explain how students best learn in an ICT context.

Computers and literacy skills

In the information age, the ability to access, process, manipulate and evaluate information from a variety of sources quickly and effectively is a very important set of skills for a child to acquire (Elliott 1985). Computers are especially useful for encouraging the development of literacy skills such as reading and writing. Children can also use specific computer programs for drawing or painting, which enable them to experiment with line, colour and shape. In relation to writing, children can move from computer drawing or painting to the incorporation of letter shapes into their work. The next step is the acquisition of keyboard skills to encourage writing, in conjunction with learning handwriting skills. In later school years, the word processing capacities of computers facilitate text creation, editing and story production. With extra facilities attached to the classroom computer, children can communicate their stories to other classrooms, schools or states within a country. Computer-based reading programs can be used to supplement textbooks and library materials.

Computer games

In chapter 9, consideration was given to the idea of children's play and the idea of games. Along with the advent of computers another dimension has been added to the games children play. Typical responses to a general question regarding what they like about their favorite computer games elicited the following comments from my children:

> 'It has lots of fun games in it.' (Christopher, 7 years)
> 'You have to go on a journey and find things.' (Nicholas (10 years)
> 'You can make a character and it is unpredictable.' (Matthew, 13 years)

A worldwide billion dollar software industry has developed around the production of computer games. There is no doubt that the games are very appealing to most children with their stunning visual and sound effects with the latest offering enticing interactive opportunities. The effect of computer games on children's social, emotional and cognitive development has become a hotly debated topic. Typically, the debate polarises around the argument that computer games are 'bad' for children impacting on their general health (e.g. reducing their participation in physical activity, increasing the level of obesity), social development (violent video games are linked to anti-social acts) and cognitive development (e.g. reinforcing convergent thinking).

Alternatively, researchers suggest that computer games promote learning through visualisation, experimentation, creativity and the development of manipulation skills (Betz 1995; Leutner 1990; Amory et al. 1999). In particular, researchers such as Quinn (1994) have examined the pedagogical features of computer games concluding that many computer games do in fact lack adequate pedagogical features that would stimulate learning. In an effort to redress this problem the South African researchers (Amory et al. 1999) have proposed a game development model which attempts to create a link between pedagogical features and game elements.

As yet, our understanding of the impact of our increasingly computerised world on children has been given little research attention. Debate still rages over the role computers should play in children's lives.

Trends and issues

How long should children play video games?

Many parents feel uneasy about the length of time children spend playing video games. What is the appropriate number of hours in terms of the video gaming per day for kids? How long is the acceptable duration for the video game?

My 10-year-old son, Nicholas, said his favourite game is where you have a special laser gun and you have a certain time to finish a certain level. He said that sometimes the games can teach you to be aggressive and use bad or poor language.

Nicholas believes a child should be able to play a video game for half an hour.

Mathew, our 13-year-old, said his favourite game is one where you can pick a certain character and you can upgrade your skills to become better, for example, at casting spells. Matthew believes an older child should be able to play for an hour at a time. Matthew thinks that computer games can sometimes be helpful for getting rid of stress.

To date, there appears to be little information available regarding how long a child should watch/play video games, but generally young children should play for less time than older children and all children should be taught some skills for regulating and monitoring their own time spent playing. For example, children could set up a clock with an alarm set for a certain time period.

My children and I discussed some ideas for parents and children for video watching and they suggested the following guidelines might be helpful. What do you think?

What can parents do?

Matthew & Nicholas's Parent Video Quiz

	Score = 1	0
1 Do you talk to your children about right and wrong before renting/buying video games?	yes	no
2 Do you accompany your child when renting a game or see the game they have rented?	yes	no
3 Do you talk about the most suitable game for your child with your child e.g. discuss the amount of violence in the game?	yes	no
4 Do you watch the game or play the game with your child?	yes	no
5 Do ask what games your child's friends play?	yes	no

Total
5/5 = perfect video parent
3/5 = average video parent
1/5 = poor video parent.

Point One is based around the idea that violent or aggressive video games could provide an opportunity for some discussion between the parent and child about what values or behaviour the video game is teaching. It increases the option for the child to manage or regulate their own game-playing behaviour.

Point Two suggests that the ideal is for the parent to supervise the child in selecting a game and also provides opportunity for discussion about the type of game being selected and the reason why (e.g. fun, to relieve boredom, popular game) the game is selected.

Point Three suggests that different types of games will appeal to boys and girls and to children with different personalities.

Point Four provides opportunity for the parent and child to interact and share ideas about how long the game should be played for, as well as about the type of game being played.

Point Five highlights that children's friends are very influential in the popularity of some types of games. Often a child will want to play a certain game to 'fit in' with his/her friends and if the parent knows about this they can talk over issues such as peer pressure with their child.

Language and the pre-schooler

In chapter 10, consideration was given to the nature of language and the various theories that have been proposed to account for language development in children.

Language development

There is a real growth in the language use of the pre-school child. As noted by Owens (1996), a significant growth occurs in the 4-year-old child's ability to develop and convey a simple story and use ever more complex sentences. This accompanies an expansion in vocabulary to between 1500–1600 words (Lipsitt 1966). As noted by Owens (1996, p. 100), '[L]anguage becomes a real tool for exploration, and the four-year-old is full of questions. He [sic] may ask several hundred in a single day, causing parents to wonder why they ever longed to hear their child speak'. The 'why' question (Why is the sky blue? How deep is the ocean? How do fish breathe under water?) is ubiquitous at this time.

During the late pre-school/early junior primary school level, the child is capable of using very adult-like language with a vocabulary in excess of 2000 words. Stories can be told in detail and a sense of humour is quite apparent. It has been estimated that by 6 years of age, English-speaking children will have a vocabulary of approximately 10 000 words (Anglin 1993).

Developing communication in pre-schoolers

There is a body of research indicating that mothers speak to their pre-school child in a manner different from their speech to other adults. Snow (1977) identified that mothers speech to young children ('motherese') is pitched at a higher tone, often accompanied by exaggerated intonational patterns identified by many questions and directives and syntactically simple. Research had previously identified different styles in maternal communication with children. For example, Nelson (1977) identified an (i) object-oriented referential style; and (ii) a self-oriented expressive style of language acquisition.

- **object-oriented referential style:** parents using this style asked frequent questions, spoke concisely and were responsive in their communication;
- **self-oriented expressive style:** here the parents used longer sentences with many directives and actively intruded on the child's actions.

Research interest focused on whether there was any relationship between maternal communication style and children's language development. As noted by Kloth et al. (1998), while research suggests that speech style differences exist among mothers, outcomes in terms of children's language acquisition are mixed. Their own research has identified three maternal communication styles, namely:

Trends and issues

Optimal development

Developmental psychology has helped us better understand that across the life-span there are certain developmental tasks that are best achieved at certain ages in order to promote optimal development. The nature of these tasks have certain similarities across communities and cultures. For example, for the very young child developing a sense of safety and security is important (e.g. see Erikson, ch. 3). For the toddler acquiring language skills and physical skills and learning to control impulses are important. Around 2–3 years of age it is appropriate that the young child is able to be more independent of their parents. Depending on how well they have achieved earlier tasks they are possibly better equipped to achieve greater independence and spend more time apart from the parents. Of course, individual children will vary greatly in terms of when they achieve independence.

Research also suggests that apart from individual differences there are cultural differences in the way young children's behaviour is viewed. For example research (Hughs & More 1997) indicates that Australian Aboriginal parents tend to emphasise cooperation, harmony and spiritual connectedness through family and kin relationships. Aboriginal children learn through observation and imitation of adults rather than through being verbally taught. Traditional Aboriginal society is very different to western society where there is a stronger focus on the individual and competition to achieve, often at the expense of others. It could be expected then that parents from different cultural groups will hold different views regarding issues such as when it is appropriate for children to achieve some independence from adults.

Perhaps there is a need to be mindful and respectful of how our views regarding childrearing are shaped by our cultural background.

Trends and issues

Chimpanzee talk

Gardner and Gardner (1969) set out to teach a chimpanzee (Washoe) American Sign Language, which is based on a system of gestures. Training the chimpanzee began when she was 1 year old. A system of rewards for correct responses was used. Following four years of training, Washoe had learnt some 160 signs. Washoe was able to generalise signs: she could sign 'more' and use it to request 'more' tickling or 'more' hair brushing. Once she had learnt a number of signs, she began using them in combination: for example, 'Hurry open'.

Was Washoe using language? According to the fundamental definition of language presented in this text, it appears that she was displaying basic language skills. That is, she was using symbols and combining them meaningfully. However, unlike the child's rich inventive use of language, the chimpanzee's skills were limited. Washoe learned sign language only after intensive training. In contrast, children apparently use language spontaneously .

- 'Non-intervening': here mothers do not pressure their child to respond verbally and their communication is characterised by pauses in conversation, few requests for information and long monologues.
- 'Explaining': mothers using this style are relatively talkative, giving the child few opportunities to take over, providing a lot of information and using labelling and yes/no questions, long monologues and short speaker pause times.
- 'Directing': this communication style uses language to direct and control the child, with warnings and negations being frequent.

Kloth et al. (1998) identified associations between maternal language style and mother and child characteristics. Their findings demonstrated an association between low education level and 'directive' style. They point to other research linking a 'directive' style with a slower rate of language acquisition (e.g. Nelson 1973; Akhtar et al. 1991). In contrast, they note a positive correlation between the 'explaining' style' and the child's language level, suggesting that the overall amount of speech is correlated with the rate of a child's language acquisition. Kloth et al. (1998) also identified developments in the mother's style as the child grows older, with a move toward a more 'non-intervening style'. It was also found that mothers used a more 'explaining style' with boys than girls.

Comparing young children's conversational style with peers and adults

As noted earlier, young children of 3 years of age or so are quite linguistically competent, equipped with a comprehensive vocabulary and some knowledge of syntax and a grasp of the idea of conversational turn-taking. None-the-less, any adult will confirm how difficult it sometimes is to carry on a conversation with a 3- to 4-year-old. At any time the child may ignore questions, change the topic or abruptly walk away to commence another activity. Explanations for the observation of apparent difficulties in communicating with a young child have raised questions regarding how well children can carry on a conversation with a peer compared to with an adult.

Dyslexia

Research into dyslexia has a long history in relation to the fields of medicine, psychology and education. It is estimated that 3–10 per cent of the population suffer from dyslexia with rates varying according to age and the diagnostic criteria used. Generally, children who experience particular difficulty in learning to read and/or write are of concern to teachers and parents. As a group, such children are generally of average or above average intelligence, have few if any significant social or emotional problems and have received appropriate educational support. Failure to achieve age-appropriate reading and writing skills generally characterises dyslexic children. Initially, the disorder was associated with some impairment in visual–perceptual processing skills, e.g. as

Children, the family and television

If parents could buy package psychological influences to administer in regular doses to their children, I doubt that many would deliberately select Western gunslingers, hopped-up psychopaths, deranged sadists, slap-stick buffoons and the like, unless they entertained rather peculiar ambitions for their offspring. Yet such examples of behaviour are delivered in quantity, with no direct charge, to millions of households daily. Harried parents can easily turn off demanding children by turning on a television set; as a result today's youth is being raised on a heavy dosage of televised aggression and violence (Bandura 1963, p. 46).

The figures are almost common knowledge these days – 99 per cent of Australian homes have a television. Surveys indicate that television viewing is a major occupation of children before and after school during the week, with 52 per cent of children watching more than three hours of television per day (McCann & Sheehan 1985). As early as 1978, the Senate Standing Committee on Education and the Arts in Australia noted that 20 per cent of Australian children were avid viewers of television. Moreover, many of these children had very little rapport with family or friends – their constant companion was the television set.

As reported by Kennedy (2000), in the United States, while children spend 1.3 hrs per week reading and 1.7 hrs per week studying, they watch at least 12 hrs per week of television.

Hearn (1990) examined people's motivations for media use. Reasons given for watching television included:

1   as a means of managing arousal (to change mood) – television as entertainment and relaxation;
2   for social needs – companionship gained from watching television together;
3   to obtain information – educational use.

Interestingly, Meadows (1986) observes that it is somewhat of a misnomer to identify television watching as a leisure activity, because even when family members watch a program together their viewing tends to be passive, non-critical and a non-social event.

As reported by Holman et al. (1984), greater parental control of programming was associated with less television viewing by children. In a survey of Australian television, McCann and Sheehan (1985) found that 51.3 per cent of programs and 53 per cent of program hours contained violence. Some 96.7 per cent of crime shows were violent, with cartoons (85.7 per cent) followed closely by action adventure shows (73.7 per cent). They also found that 32.9 per cent of violence was gratuitous and unnecessary to the development of the plot or theme.

Effects of media violence on viewers

Robinson et al. (2001, p. 17) have argued that 'Violence is pervasive in television, movies and video games. Children's television programming contains even more violence than prime-time programming: it has been estimated that by the age of 18 years, US children witness 200 000 acts of violence on television alone, (Huston, Donnerstein & Fairchild 1992).

The effects of viewing media violence fall under three categories:

1   *Learnt aggression.* According to the social learning theory approach (see chapter 3), children imitate or copy acts of aggression. The research of Sheehan (1983) linked media violence and aggressive behaviour, although there was no evidence that there was a causal relationship over time.
2   *Arousal effect.* Hearn (1990, p. 177) argues that 'most media is ultimately consumed for its arousal value'. This is supported by studies that point to the arousal effect of media violence (for example, Kelley 1985).
3   *Desensitisation.* With repeated exposure to violence, the arousal of individuals declines as they desensitise to the events (Linz et al. 1984). This suggests that some emotional blunting to violence is occurring.

Robinson et al. (2001, p. 17) have concluded that '[t]he relationship between exposure to aggression in the media and children's aggressive behavior is well documented'.

While these three effects of media violence can be identified, to understand the impact of television on children it is necessary to consider the context in which the child watches television. More particularly, the family plays a significant role in the child's reaction to what is seen.

In an intervention based on Bandura's social cognitive theory (see chapter 3), Robinson et al. (2001) described an intervention to reduce television, videotape and video game violence in primary school children. They concluded that their findings '... support the causal influences of these media on aggression and the potential benefits of reducing children's media use'.

characterised by letter reversal where a child would treat a 'b' as a 'd' or vice versa. In a major review of the field, Simpson (2000) argued that current consensus viewed dyslexia as a pervasive deficit in the language system as opposed to problems with visual or temporal processing or with automatising skills.

Chapter summary

The research of Piaget provides a significant base from which to further understand the cognitive development of the young child. Developing language skills allow the child to give 'voice' to their observations and understanding of the world around them. Technological change in mainstream Western industrialised countries is providing young children with new challenges relating to computer literacy.

Discussion questions

1   What is meant by the term 'symbolic functions'? Cite examples from your own experiences with children.
2   Explain the three features of pre-operational thinking described in this chapter.
3   What is meant by the term 'conservation'? What are the explanations for non-conservation in young children?
4   What key features distinguished Bruner's views of child development from those of Piaget?
5   Identify the roles you think computers play in children's lives today.
6   What are the various stages associated with the development of language?

Activity

Select a fairytale, such as *Cinderella*, or a movie involving a fairytale. Consider the nature of the theme, story line and characters, and discuss your findings with others. Consider the link between the nature of the fairytale and child development issues, such as fears of abandonment or the struggle for identity.

Selected websites

IT Forum <http://it.coe.uga.edu/itforum/paper18/paper18.html>

The Jean Piaget Archives <www.unige.ch/piaget/presentg.htm>

Australian Children's Television Foundation <www.actf.com.au>

National Institute on Media and the Family <www.mediaandthefamily.org>

14 Social and Emotional Development of Pre-schoolers

'How Happy We are Here!'

Every afternoon as they were coming from school, the children used to go and play in the giant's garden. It was a large lovely garden, with soft green grass. Here and there over the grass stood beautiful flowers like stars, and there were twelve peach trees that in the spring-time broke out into delicate blossoms of pink and pearl, and in the Autumn bore rich fruit. The birds sat in the trees and sang so sweetly that the children used to stop their games in order to listen to them. 'How happy we are here!' they cried to each other.

Oscar Wilde, The Selfish Giant

CHAPTER OUTLINE

KEY TERMS AND CONCEPTS

- Phallic
- Initiative versus guilt
- Children's fears
- Conflict
- 'Easy', 'intermediate' and 'difficult' temperaments

- Adjusting to school
- Child abuse
- Bullying
- Sibling conflict

Introduction

In terms of children's social and emotional development, the pre-school period is a time of rapid change. The typical pre-schooler is acquiring social skills at a rapid pace and these skills are developed and refined in terms of play and friendships established with other children. At the same time, the child is beginning to identify more strongly with parents and friends of the same sex.

The nature of family life is also changing dramatically. At this time in the family life-cycle a second child may be making his or her presence felt. Parents may find that the first child is experiencing some difficulties understanding how to share his or her parents' love and they may witness regressive behaviour, such as thumb-sucking, bed-wetting or other behavioural manifestations of the child's conflict.

In this chapter, consideration is given to various theoretical approaches to understanding the pre-schooler's social and emotional development. The theory provides a basis for exploring issues relevant to this period of the child's life and this stage of the family life-cycle – children's fears, the child's developing sense of self, conflict, school adjustment, child abuse, and bullying. Sibling relationships are discussed in The Family Life-cycle: 14.

Theoretical foundations

During the pre-school years the young child's emerging personality takes more definite shape. Both Freud and Erikson considered in some detail the tasks facing the child at this time.

Freudian theory

> Have you ever noticed that men feel called on to prove that they are men, while women do not have to assert their femininity, in order to be counted as women?

> . . . To be a woman is to be as human beings were meant to be, full of love and serenity . . . while to be a man is to attempt something unnatural (Sontag 1966, p. 72).

In chapter 11 we saw that during the anal stage (Freud's second psychosexual stage of development) the child's **libidinal** energy is centred on the **erogenous zone** of the anus, and out of this arises the prime source of conflict with parents; that is, toilet training. At the same time, in the context of the toddler's emerging physical development, a struggle with parents often ensues around the issue of 'freedom versus dependency'. Thus, the child's frequently expressed wish of 'Me do it!' reflects part of his or her struggle to be free of parental restraint and to exercise newly developing physical capabilities. The next stage of psychosocial development identified by Freud is the phallic stage (see Table 14.1).

libidinal
associated with instinctive energies and desires.

erogenous zone
parts of the body that at different ages are susceptible to pleasurable feelings.

Table 14.1 Freud's third psychosexual stage of development: the phallic phase

Ages	Stages
Infancy	Oral
1½–3½ years (approx.)	Anal
3½–5½ years (approx.)	Phallic
5½–12 years (approx.)	Latency
Adolescence	Genital

phallic stage
the third of Freud's psychosexual stages, during which the young child's libidinal energy shifts to the genitals.

As outlined in chapter 3, Freud used the myth of Oedipus to explain his theory that, during the **phallic stage**, a boy becomes afraid he will be castrated by his father because of his incestuous feelings towards his mother. This castration anxiety leads to a repression of his desires for his mother and an expression of hostility for his father. Hostility later gives way to identification with his father.

In a later development of his theory, Freud used the Greek myth of Electra, who was instrumental in the murder of her own mother, to explain the sex-role development in females. The girl develops penis envy (counterpart to castration anxiety). Her anxiety is resolved by identifying with her mother and assuming similar sex-role characteristics.

Erikson's theory

initiative versus guilt
the conflict faced by children in the third of Erikson's psychosocial stages of development, in which they discover behavioural limits.

The stage of Erikson's psychosocial theory corresponding to the pre-school years is known as **initiative versus guilt** (see Table 14.2). Given that pre-school children have learnt to control their own physical movements, the scene is now set for the next stage, that of using his or her new-found abilities. Children now try to be more independent of their parents and according to Erikson this involves:

- freer movement and establishment of wider goals – for example, the development of friendships;
- a grasp of language and its potential, hence the 'why' questions;

Table 14.2 'Initiative versus guilt': Erikson's third psychosocial stage

Ages	Stages
Infancy	Basic trust versus mistrust
1½–3½ years (approx.)	Autonomy versus shame and doubt
3½–5½ years (approx.)	Initiative versus guilt
5½–12 years (approx.)	Industry versus inferiority
Adolescence	Identity versus role confusion
Young adulthood	Intimacy versus isolation
Adulthood	Generativity versus stagnation
Maturity	Ego integrity versus despair

- development of imagination through physical coordination and language use.

In Erikson's view, at this stage children's physical and emotional development provides greater opportunity for them to be more fully themselves. It is a time of heightened interest in the individual's own sexuality. On the other hand, according to Erikson, if children are not able adequately to complete the separation from the parents and remain tied to them for direction, they run the risk of developing a sense of guilt.

Who am I? The developing sense of self

The question 'Who am I?' assumes a special significance during the early years of childhood when, according to a number of researchers, a sense of self emerges (Kagan 1981; Kaye 1982; Bullock & Lutkenhaus 1990). In fact, Bullock and Lutkenhaus (1990, p. 217) believe that the emergence of a sense of self 'profoundly affects how children react to their own and others' behaviours'.

To backtrack a little, though, the writings of the psychologist William James (1910), at the beginning of the twentieth century, provide us with important insight into the question of just how it is that a child develops a sense of self. James suggested that the 'self' is composed of two parts, the 'me' and the 'I'. The 'me' component is 'the sum total of all a person can call his' (James 1910, p. 44). For the young child, the 'me' aspect consists of the actual qualities that define the self. For example, 'me' is composed of my body, my clothes, my toys and so on. James believed that each individual orders these components of 'me' into a hierarchy, assigning different values to material, social and spiritual components. Thus, young children may attach a great deal of significance to their toys (material) and less importance to social aspects of themselves, such as their ability to make friends. The second component of James's analysis of self, the 'I', reflects that part of the self through which individuals understand the world around them and are aware of themselves in the world.

'Who am I?'

Self-awareness in toddlerhood

Research conducted with children shows that awareness of self, self-concept and a sense of identity develop from birth. It is during the toddler period that a sense of separateness and distinctiveness from others emerges. In a groundbreaking study of five infants, Dixon (1957) found that by 12 months of age the infant demonstrates a recognition of self and others. Another significant study by Amsterdam (1972, p. 304) found, using the 'mirror and rouge' technique (whereby rouge was dabbed on a child's nose), that 'the child's ability to locate a red spot on the face shows that he associates his own face with the face in the mirror'. This ability represents the emergence of a sense of self. If the toddler reached for the red spot of rouge on his or her face, and not for the reflection in the mirror, it was believed that the child was aware that he or she was the person in the mirror. Subsequent researchers (such as Lewis & Brookes-Gunn 1979) have replicated Amsterdam's findings. Lewis and Brookes-Gunn reported that infants as young as 15 months touch their reddened noses.

Children's developing sense of self is reflected in their use of language. Parents of toddlers will be familiar with the emergence of the 'Me do it!' statement from their young children; a statement that may relate to any task from feeding themselves to putting on shoes, to pouring juice into a cup. Their language and accompanying actions (such as crying if not allowed their way) point strongly to their awareness of themselves as separate individuals who can assert their will and demonstrate their competence. Leaving the security of their care-givers and wanting to make their own way in the world is part of this developing sense of self.

Children's understanding of selfhood

As Damon and Hart (1982) have noted, the advantage of studying the sense of self of pre-schoolers as opposed to that of toddlers is their language ability. Broughton (1978) conducted an important study into children's sense of self by asking them various open-ended questions such as, 'What is the self?' 'What is the mind?' (reported in Damon & Hart 1982).

Early childhood

According to Broughton, during early childhood the self is understood in physical terms: children distinguish themselves from others in terms of physical appearance, such as different height, weight or skin colour. The young child will also confuse self, mind and body.

Middle childhood

Around 8 years of age Broughton's second level of self-knowledge emerges, such that children distinguish between mind and body. That is, children realise that they are different from other children, not only because of their different physical appearance but also because of different thoughts and feelings that they have.

Conflict

According to the *Macquarie Dictionary*, conflict denotes a 'battle or struggle, esp. a prolonged struggle; strife . . . controversy; a quarrel . . . discord of action, feeling, or effect; antagonism, as of interests or principles . . . a striking together; collision'. Hay (1984, p. 2) describes conflict as an opposition between two individuals 'when one person does something to which a second person objects'.

While conflict may be an important aspect of human relations, conflict as evidenced in children's relations has received scant attention. In the research that has been conducted into conflict among children, some sex differences and developmental trends have been identified.

Sex differences

There is a body of evidence to suggest that boys engage in direct conflict more often than girls (Miller et al. 1986; Shantz 1986; Slee 1990). A study of 1100 Australian school children ranging in age from 5 to 13 years, revealed that males were significantly more likely than females to report that they responded to conflict with conflict (Slee 1990). Using a similar strategy to that employed by Kagan et al. (1982), children were told: 'Imagine you are playing with a toy of yours and another child of the same age comes up and takes it away from you. What would you do?' As indicated in Table 14.3, 52.9 per cent of the males said that they would 'hit or fight or grab the toy back'(direct conflict), compared to 33.3 per cent of the females. However, females were more likely to make an 'assertive response' indicating they did not like such behaviour and asking for the toy back (Table 14.3).

Table 14.3 A comparison of conflict resolution styles and feelings regarding conflict in males and females aged 5–13 years (per cent of sample)

| | Conflict Style | | | | |
	Do Nothing	Mediate	Direct Conflict	Don't Know	Be Assertive
Males	7.8	31.7	52.9	0.4	7.3
Females	13.4	36.8	33.3	1.1	15.4

| | Feelings | | | |
	Angry	Neutral	Happy	Sad
Males	61.1	9.9	6.0	23.0
Females	47.6	7.9	2.8	41.7

Developmental trends

Aboud (1982) observes that in the 5 to 9 year age range there is an increasing use of a reconciliation to resolve conflict. In contrast, Kagan et al. (1982) report an increasing tendency for children to respond to conflict with conflict as they grow older. This developmental trend in children's response to conflict has also been clearly demonstrated by the study mentioned above (Slee 1990), in which 29.7 per cent of 5- to 6-year-olds indicated a conflict response to conflict compared to 71.8 per cent of 11- to 13-year-olds (see Table 14.4).

Table 14.4 Children's conflict resolution styles and feelings regarding conflict: a comparison of four age groups

	Conflict Style				
Age	Do Nothing	Mediate	Direct Conflict	Don't Know	Be Assertive
5–6 years	14.9	46.5	29.7	0.7	8.2
7–8 years	14.8	34.9	36.7	1.8	12.5
9–10 years	3.7	25.9	55.8	0.0	14.6
11–13 years	4.6	13.0	71.8	0.0	10.7

	Feelings			
Age	Angry	Neutral	Happy	Sad
5–6 years	42.1	5.2	5.2	47.5
7–8 years	47.0	11.4	3.2	38.4
9–10 years	70.7	8.2	5.8	15.3
11–13 years	72.5	16.8	1.5	9.2

Affective reactions

In a review of the field, Shantz (1987, p. 300) notes that 'children's moods and emotions during and after disputes are uncharted areas'. Some interesting preliminary findings emerge from the previously mentioned study of Australian school children's affective reactions to conflict (Slee 1990). The children were asked to indicate how they would feel if another child took a toy away from them. They were to choose from a facial expression representing one of the four emotions of 'angry', 'neutral', 'happy' or 'sad'. From Table 14.4 it can be seen that boys reported they were significantly more likely (61 per cent) than girls (48 per cent) to express angry feelings during conflict, and girls were more likely than boys to express sad feelings (41.7 per cent versus 23 per cent). These findings are consistent with the results of an observational study conducted by Miller et al. (1986), who discovered that girls are significantly more likely than boys to express anger indirectly during conflict. It therefore seems possible that girls are experiencing anger in response to conflict but are reporting it or expressing it differently from boys.

Interestingly, there were also developmental trends in affective reaction to conflict. From Table 14.5 it can be seen that older children reported more anger in response to conflict than did younger children.

These findings and a review of the literature indicate that parents and educators should be aware of a number of points when faced with conflict in children (Slee 1990).

- It is important that adults and children appreciate that conflict is part of everyday life and that it can be used creatively.
- Children need to be alerted to alternative strategies for resolving conflict apart from the win–lose option.
- There may be age differences in children's approach to conflict resolution that reflect their intellectual and social development.
- Males and females may respond differently to conflict, and sex and age differences may be apparent in the feelings engendered by conflict.

Adjusting to school

It is all too easy for adults to forget what it was like to start school. For the young child, starting school means moving from one system (the family) where the routine, rules and organisation are well known, to a new system (the school) where new routines, rules and a different level of organisation are required. A longitudinal study in South Australia has followed 260 children during their first year at 22 kindergartens in metropolitan Adelaide (Slee 1986b). At the beginning of the year, 13.3 per cent of the children were rated by their teachers as 'poorly/very poorly adjusted'. By the end of their first year in kindergarten some 5.7 per cent of the children received the same rating. A significant number of this 5.7 per cent (33 per cent) were the same children who were rated as 'poorly/very poorly' adjusted at the beginning of the year. These figures indicate that a percentage of children continue to be poorly adjusted to school in the course of the first year.

The research of Nelson et al. (1999) has further confirmed the link between parental assessment of pre-school temperament (particularly negative

Adjusting to school is an issue for a small number of children.

emotionality) and teacher-rated adjustment in year three. Research evidence also indicates that the effects are more long-lasting than the first year and can extend well into primary school (Chazan & Jackson 1974, Nelson et al. 1999).

Teachers' perceptions of school adjustment

Teachers consider children to be well adjusted if they:

- settle into the routine of kindergarten;
- cooperate with other children;
- relate well to the teacher;
- are proficient at language;
- are sociable and mix easily (Slee 1986a).

Children's temperaments

temperament
behaviours that comprise relatively stable characteristics of a person's personality.

One factor that has received some attention in relation to early school adjustment is **temperament.** This factor refers to the way an individual interacts with people and objects in the environment: the 'how' rather than the 'what' or 'why' of behaviour (see chapter 4). From the nine temperament categories of activity, rhythmicity, distractability, approach, adaptability, persistence, sensory threshold, intensity and mood, the diagnostic clusters of 'easy', 'intermediate' and 'difficult' can be derived. 'Easy' children are rhythmic, approaching, adaptive, mild and positive, but 'difficult' children have the opposite profile. Carey et al. (1977) found a significant positive correlation between the temperament category of adaptability and teachers' rating of school adjustment in 5- to 7-year-old children.

Australian kindergarten children rated by their teachers as well adjusted in term 1 were adaptable to new situations, positive in mood, willing to approach new situations, and low in intensity (Slee 1986b). That is, four out of five of the temperament categories comprising the diagnostic temperament categories of 'easy', 'intermediate' and 'difficult' correlated significantly with teachers' ratings of kindergarten adjustment in term 1. Overall, 'easy' children were perceived by their teachers to be significantly better adjusted than 'difficult' children. In the course of the year, however, the strength of the relationship between kindergarten adjustment and temperament profiles weakened. The most likely explanation for this finding is that most children do adjust in the course of time. Further research is required to facilitate identification of the small groups of children who experience long-term adjustment difficulties (Slee 1986b).

The Australian Temperament Project (ATP) described in chapter 8 examined a number of aspects of temperament and school adjustment.

From a review of the literature it is possible to devise a number of guidelines for parents and teachers to help young children to adjust to school in the early years.

- Respect children's feelings about starting school by observing their behaviour and developing a plan to help them in a warm, nurturant fashion.

- Consider the effect of your own temperament and personality on children's behaviour.
- Set effective limits on children's behaviour and enforce these limits consistently.
- Use role-plays to help children understand how their behaviour affects others.
- Provide children with the opportunity to learn from each other with minimal adult supervision, for example, through sand and thematic play.
- Provide the opportunity for socially competent children to teach other children.
- Allow the children to talk about their fears and anxieties.
- Parents should establish contact with school staff before their child starts school.
- If problems arise, acknowledge them and deal with them openly.
- Allow for children's individual differences in starting school.

Child abuse

It is now better understood that child abuse is a significant problem in Australian society and it is increasingly coming to be recognised as such by professionals working with children (Briggs 1987; Clare & Roe 1990; Strang, 2000), and by parents and community leaders. The fact that the problem has been acknowledged only relatively recently is in all probability a product of the slow rate of change in relation to attitudes towards children in Australian society and a reflection of the status children have in our society. Although customs such as female infanticide, swaddling and the deliberate maiming of children are now outlawed in our society, it is only relatively recently that legislation has been passed abolishing corporal punishment in schools in some states, such as South Australia (see chapter 1, Trends and Issues: Children and punishment). Mandatory reporting of child abuse is now in place in South Australia, New South Wales, Queensland, Tasmania and the Northern Territory. Victoria and Western Australia have a voluntary reporting system. As Strang (2000) has noted: 'The sanctioning of the abuse of children has been based on a number of social conditions and beliefs, some of which have been challenged only in recent years' (p. 2). Strang goes on to note that such beliefs include the notion of inherent evilness of children requiring harsh disciplinary measures, and the belief that children are the property of adults (see chapter 1).

Defining child abuse

In 1981, the Australian Welfare Administrators' Conference defined child abuse as:

> a situation wherein a parent(s) or other person(s) having the care, custody, control or charge of a child inflicts or allows to be inflicted on the child physical

injury or gross deprivation which causes or creates substantial risk of death or disfigurement, or creates or allows to be created a substantial risk or injury other than by accidental means. The definition includes sexual abuse or sexual exploitation of the child (Department for Community Welfare 1986, p. 2).

Types of abuse

A number of different types of abuse have been identified (South Australian Child Protection Council 1989; Strang 2000), including:

- **Physical abuse**. This refers to any non-accidental injury inflicted on a child – beatings, burns, scalds or poisonings.
- **Sexual abuse**. Any sexual behaviour imposed on a child under the age of 18 years – incest, unlawful sexual intercourse, molestation, exhibitionism.
- **Emotional abuse**. This refers to a consistent attitude or behaviour towards a child which is detrimental to, or impairs, the child's emotional and/or physical development – verbal aggression, isolation, emotional rejection.
- **Neglect**. Any serious omission or commission by a person that jeopardises or impairs the child's physical, intellectual or emotional development. For example, a neglected child may be consistently dirty.

Young children and the issue of abuse

Australian research has emphasised that the young child is most at risk of abuse (Goldman & Goldman 1989). On an Australia-wide basis, Richardson (1990) reports that, for children under 18 years of age during 1989–90, 42 695 cases of child maltreatment were reported, 18 333 of which were substantiated, while a further 2572 cases were assessed as 'child at risk'. Strang (2000, p. 4) notes that overall '[w]hat we do know is that since statistics have been kept by welfare departments, the numbers of children reported and confirmed as having been abused have increased'.

Preventing child abuse

As Clare and Roe (1990, p. 3) point out:

> The effects of child abuse on children are often long lasting. Some children suffer permanent physical injury and many others suffer emotional and psychological trauma which lasts throughout adult life.

In Australia a range of government and non-government initiatives have been directed towards the problem of child abuse. In many states of Australia legal reforms have been implemented and assistance and training provided to community and self-help groups. NAPCAN (National Association for the Prevention of Child Abuse and Neglect) provides an important focus for research and the dissemination of information regarding child abuse. Protective behaviours programs have been introduced into schools.

The protective behaviours program

Clare and Roe (1990) note that this program was brought to Australia in 1984 and following trials in Victoria and South Australia it is now used Australia-wide. It has two main themes:

- We all have the right to feel safe all the time.
- Nothing is so awful that you cannot talk about it with someone you trust.

In broad outline, two sessions are required to address these two themes. In the course of the sessions, children are taught to identify their body's early warning signs to let them know when they are not feeling safe. They are encouraged to establish a network of people to whom they can go if they are not feeling safe. The program also targets other areas where children may not feel safe, such as bullying at school.

In an interview study of 250 Australian families caring for 565 children aged between 3 and 12 years, Briggs (1987) found that it was difficult for parents to discuss the issue of sexual abuse with their children:

> Their excuses for not talking about the subject were various, concealing a wide-spread and deeply rooted embarrassment relating to adult sexual behaviour (Briggs 1987, p. 24).

In summary, there is now a greater awareness of the issue of child abuse and the need to address the problem at a number of different levels. Strang (2000, p. 9) has noted that

> [t]he greatest chance we have to prevent violence in society is to raise children who reject violence as a method of problem-solving, who believe in the right of the individual to grow in a safe environment and who strive to value the unique contribution all our citizens and especially our children can make to our future.

Trends and issues

Children's fears: Living in an uncertain age

It is tempting for adults to dismiss children's fears of such things as animals, the supernatural and physical events such as lightning as simply being vivid aspects of an overactive imagination. To this extent, adults fail to realise that children's fears reflect something of their understanding of the world and their place in it (Ollendick & King 1991; Gullone & King 1997). Jersild et al. (1975, p. 319) have defined fears as a 'variety of apprehensions, ranging from acute fears to a more complicated kind of uneasiness'. Research conducted in Australia, the United States and Europe has identified a number of features of children's fears, including some concerning sex differences and age trends.

Sex differences

There is evidence that females have more fears than males (Ollendick et al. 1985; Slee & Cross 1988; King et al. 1989b; Burnham & Gullone 1997; Gullone & King 1997). In a study of 1243 Australian children and adolescents, Slee and Cross (1988) found females had on average 11.0 fears and males 7.6. Possible explanations for this finding include the effects of socialisation: for example, in Western societies it is 'permissible' for girls to have more fears than boys. Another possible, and perhaps related, explanation is that some girls are reporting fears without actually having them (continued overleaf).

Developmental trends

There is conflicting evidence concerning the number of fears that children have at different ages. Lapouse and Monk (1953) found no relationship between the number of fears and age. However, other studies have reported a significant decline in the number of fears between the ages of 4 and 19 years (Slee & Cross 1988; Gullone & King 1997): younger children appear to have more fears than their older counterparts. Slee and Cross also report that across the age range, animal and supernatural fears in younger groups give way to fears of war and social fears among older children. As noted by Nicastro & Whetsell (1999, p. 393), in their review of the literature, '...fears appear to surface and change as a result of the varying abilities of children across age groups.' Data from the Slee and Cross study (1988) are presented in Table 14.5 to highlight developmental trends.

Fears: individual differences

Research reported by Gullone and King (1997) highlight that while most normative fears are transient there appears to be a trait or temperamental component in relation to fearfulness. Gullone and King (1997) have found that there is some stability over time in an individual's level of fearfulness. As the authors of the study note, the clinical implications of this finding relate to identifying individuals at risk for developing fears or phobias.

Implications for parents and educators

As noted by Nicastro and Whetsell (1999, p. 392), 'Today's children face increased stressors'. The stressors arise from a variety of sources, e.g. environmental (media portrayal of earthquakes and hurricanes), interpersonal (increased family disruption, e.g. divorce) and intra-personal (e.g. mental health problems). In considering how best to respond to children's fears it is important to consider developmental trends and gender differences as discussed here. Individual children respond in different ways to fearful situations, affecting how they cope with the fear.

Table 14.5 The most frequently occurring fears of children aged 4–19 years (N = 1243)

4–7 years (N = 379)		8–12 years (N = 540)		13–19 years (N = 324)	
Fear	%	Fear	%	Fear	%
1. Snakes	74.6	War	77.4	War	76.5
2. Burglars	66.8	Burglars	76.9	Snakes	68.0
3. Falling from heights	66.8	Snakes	76.3	Burglars	65.4
4. Left alone at night	55.4	Falling from heights	63.7	Falling from heights	63.0
5. Wild animals	53.0	Getting lost	56.0	Not being liked	53.1

Note Percentages do not add up to 100 per cent because each child reported more than one fear.

School bullying

A related aspect of the broad issue of the victimisation of children relates to bullying. Being bullied or victimised is a very old phenomenon. The fact that some children are frequently and systematically harassed and attacked by other children has been described in many novels and plays (such as Thomas Hughes's *Tom Brown's School Days*, published in 1857). Many of us have had first-hand experience of being bullied from our school days.

To help orient us to the issue, the following case-notes involving a parent and her year six child, with whom I worked in the course of a year, outline some of the instances of bullying suffered by the child. The family was referred to me by their local doctor. As described to me by the boy in the first session:

> One thing that happened to me was that in year five I was bashed up at school by one of the kids. One day this kid just started bashing me up and he knocked me to the ground and kicked me in my legs and body. The worst thing though was that while I was being bashed up the other kids just stood around and did nothing to help. But it did not stop there and from term one week one the bullying went on. From the hitting it went to name calling and excluding me from groups. Rotten food was put in my locker, my sports equipment was stolen or broken. If I tried to play basketball the kids would tell me to 'get lost'. I hated it so much I hid in the computer room or library. It just went on and on through the year.

Presently there is also a great deal of discussion regarding the level of violence in Australian society as attested to by media reports and major federal (Sticks & Stones 1994) and state enquiries (ACT 1995; WA (1996). To appreciate why school bullying is fast emerging as an educational issue it is necessary to see it in the context of contemporary dominant themes of social change in Australian culture, including those of patriarchy, authoritarianism, masculinity, femininity and violence (Smith et al. 1999; Smith 2002).

The present situation

> The best fun was to make Lenora cry. She was so pale and thin, she had none of the fat of her carnivorous class-mates. She swept across the yard like a little straw broom, trying to keep herself stiff and ready for attack. Playtime or classtime made no difference to Lenora. She had no friends and there was nothing she could do that was better or different from anything anyone else could do. The opportunities for taunting her were endless. She was a small grey magnet for bullies. In an instant she might be surrounded by jeering, laughing faces that did not leave until she cried. The moment her tiny eyes filled up with tears the crowd would begin to disperse. By the time her face was awash with salty water she was alone. It was not the crying anyone wanted to watch, it was just the fact they could make her do it that was funny. Danny McGee was in training to be a bully. He watched the bigger kids closely. He saw how they pinched and shoved in line until some kid got into trouble for turning around and shouting at them. How they lied like sweet-faced little angels to the teachers. How they teased and tormented small defenceless kids, like Lenora Luffhead (Blacklock 1995, p. 54).

While bullying at school has long been recognised as existing in Australian literature, the empirical study of the phenomenon really did not begin until 1989–90. In the last six years the term 'bullying' has become much more widely used, although it is still a much misunderstood term. The work of Dan Olweus from Norway and Peter Smith from England have provided a powerful impetus for Australian research into bullying. A commonly accepted definition of the term which draws on their thinking is that bullying is: 'Repeated intimidation, over time, of a physical, verbal or psychological nature of a less powerful person by a more powerful person or group of persons'. Bullying is now accepted to be a subset of aggressive behaviour which has its own defining characteristics.

The following information regarding the extent of bullying in Australia is based on research involving approximately 25 500 primary and secondary students from over 60 Catholic, independent and public schools around Australia. The data have been collected using the Peer Relations Questionnaire (PRQ) developed by Rigby and Slee (1995) in response to teachers' requests for a standardised method for assessing the nature and extent of school bullying. The psychometric properties of the PRQ have been assessed (Rigby & Slee 1991) and evidence presented to the effect that it is a valid and reliable self report measure of school bullying.

School bullying is an international issue.

Frequency of bullying

Data from over 25 500 Australian students across more than 60 schools (Rigby & Slee 1999) provides the basis for the following broad conclusions regarding bullying (Table 14.6).

Overall, between one in five and one in seven students reported being bullied several times a week or more. Bullying is more frequently reported by younger students and girls generally report less bullying than boys. In secondary school the amount of bullying is highest in year levels eight and nine.

Duration of bullying

A feature of the definition of bullying referred to earlier is that it involves repetition. While most bullying lasts a 'day or two', for a disturbingly high

Table 14.6 The frequency of bullying

- Between one in five and one in seven students report being bullied 'once a week or more'
- More bullying occurs in primary than secondary schools
- In primary schools bullying is highest in the lower years
- In secondary schools bullying is highest in years 8 and 9
- Males typically report being bullied more than females
- Females and males typically report being bullied in different ways (e.g. physical or verbal)

Based on Australian surveys of over 25,000 students from more than 60 schools

percentage of students it lasts months or more. Research now leaves us in little doubt regarding the cumulative effects of being subject to repetitive acts of violence.

Safety from bullying

As already mentioned, an important element of bullying is a power imbalance between the bully(s) and victim and so safety at school is a pertinent question.

We asked students if school is a safe place for young people who find it hard to defend themselves from attack from other students? Among both males and females bullied at 'least once a week', approximately one-third of students saw their school as 'never/hardly ever' a safe place (Table 14.7).

Table 14.7 School children's judgments of the safety of their school for young people who find it hard to defend themselves, according to gender, age group and frequency of being bullied (percentages)

Age in years		Never bullied		Bullied less than once a week		Bullied once a week or more	
		8–12	13–18	8–12	13–18	8–12	13–18
Yes it is safe	Boys	28.2	24.0	18.8	12.2	11.0	8.5
	Girls	31.3	20.0	18.4	9.1	16.7	7.3
Usually safe	Boys	63.8	64.1	71.3	69.7	63.6	58.1
	Girls	61.8	68.9	73.0	73.9	63.5	64.3
Hardly ever safe	Boys	6.4	8.7	8.9	14.7	19.2	22.6
	Girls	5.5	9.4	7.1	15.7	16.5	22.9
Never safe	Boys	1.5	3.2	1.1	3.5	6.3	10.9
	Girls	1.4	1.7	1.5	1.4	3.3	5.5
Total N	Boys	1445	6294	1214	3011	911	2221
	Girls	1316	4654	792	1851	636	972

Source: Adapted from Rigby & Slee 1999

Table 14.8 Percentages of school children reporting being bullied by peers in different ways, according to gender and age group

		8–12 Years			13–18 Years		
		Never	Sometimes	Often	Never	Sometimes	Often
Being teased	Boys	50.1	38.0	11.9	52.6	38.8	8.6
	Girls	52.6	38.8	8.6	58.1	33.5	8.4
Hurtful names	Boys	49.7	36.4	13.9	56.0	33.1	10.8
	Girls	49.6	38.4	12.0	56.7	33.2	10.1
Left out	Boys	65.9	26.9	7.3	75.7	18.8	5.5
	Girls	58.7	32.3	9.0	69.0	24.4	6.6
Threatened	Boys	71.5	22.7	5.8	74.4	19.8	5.9
	Girls	84.9	12.6	2.5	87.8	9.7	2.5
Hit/kicked	Boys	63.5	28.5	8.0	72.4	21.3	6.3
	Girls	77.2	18.9	3.9	88.5	9.3	2.2
Total	Boys		3320			10,657	
N	Girls		2587			6973	

Source: Adapted from Rigby & Slee 1999

Types of bullying

As part of the definition referred to earlier, bullying manifests itself in different ways. The data presented in Table 14.8 indicates types of bullying experienced 'often' by the 25,500 students in the Australian sample.

From Table 14.8 it can be seen that bullying may be physical, verbal or psychological. Physical bullying occurs more with boys and emotional and verbal threats occur more often for girls.

The effects of bullying

The following profiles of bullies and victims are based on Australian research conducted principally by Associate Professor Ken Rigby and myself (Table 14.9).

Generally, our findings confirm that bullying is a physically harmful, psychologically damaging and socially isolating aspect of an unnecessarily large number of Australian children's school experience. The damaging physical effects have been highlighted in Australian studies linking poor health, depression and suicidal ideation with bullying. Psychological well-being (e.g. self-esteem and happiness) has been shown to suffer with bullying, while loneliness and alienation from peers are also linked with victimisation. See Smith et al. (1999) and Slee and Rigby (1998) for a comprehensive international discussion of bullying.

Table 14.9 Profiles of bullies and victims

Outcomes	Bullies	Victims
Physical	• girls typically suffer poor health	• generally suffer poor physical health
Social	• are about average in socio-metric status	• are often rejected by other students
	• have some friends at school	• typically feel lonely and isolated at school
	• usually dislike school	• generally dislike school
Psychological	• are generally depressed	• are generally depressed
	• are not anxious	• typically suffer from anxiety
	• are average in self esteem	• are usually low in self esteem
	• do not have strong tendency towards internal or external locus of control	• usually have an external locus of control
	• generally have poor conflict resolution skills	• are about average in conflict resolution skills
Academic ability	• typically over-estimate their academic ability	• typically underestimate their academic ability
Home environment	• often come from homes lacking in cohesion and support	• often come from homes typified by too much closeness and overprotectiveness

Source: Phillip Slee, *The PEACE Pack* (2000)

Interventions to reduce school bullying

In 1994 a federal government inquiry into violence in Australian schools concluded that while violence was not a major problem in Australian schools,
bullying was. A recommendation of the inquiry was for the development of
intervention programs to reduce school bullying. At a state level, some govern-
ments (e.g. Western Australia 1995 and ACT 1996) have funded investigations
into school bullying and similarly reported that it is a major concern.

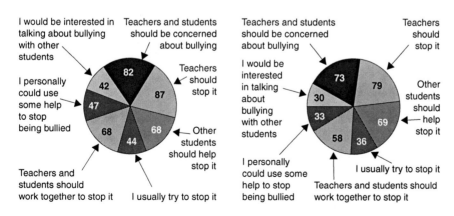

Figure 14.1 Students' opinions about action to stop bullying (n = 25 210 students
expressed as a percentage)

Source: Slee and Rigby, (1998)

Figure 14.2 Bullying through the eyes of children

Student's beliefs regarding interventions

To help understand what Australian students think should be done, students were asked their opinion about what school interventions could be used to reduce bullying. These findings are presented in Figure 14.1.

From the results in Figure 14.1 it can be seen that students are strongly of the opinion that the school community should act to stop bullying, although responsibility for stopping it is largely attributed to teachers. A good third of students would personally be interested in talking about the problem, although further treatment of this data shows that younger primary school students are more interested in talking about it than are older secondary students.

Attitudes towards victims

Research into the attitudes of children towards victims of bullying (Rigby & Slee 1991) indicates that the majority of children studied (approximately 80 per cent from year 4 to year 10) were supportive of victims. However, for both males and females support for victims diminished from year 4 to year 10. Support for victims showed a slight increase around year 12. It is possible that schools may act so as to inculcate stereotypical male values, which run counter to the development of empathic responses towards others (Askew 1989), with the result that 'bullying is the only way in which boys are able to demonstrate their manliness' (Askew 1989, p. 63).

One factor identified in children's attitudes to bullying is a 'rejection of weak children' (for instance, 'I wouldn't be friends with kids who let themselves be pushed around') (Rigby & Slee 1991). In relation to a second factor, 'approval of bullying', a proportion of children studied by Rigby and Slee said that 'It's OK to call some kids nasty names'. Overall, the study concluded that while the majority of children believe it is right to intervene to stop bullying, a small proportion think it should be ignored or sanction it (Rigby & Slee 1991).

The nature of bullies and victims

Bullies usually have strong aggressive tendencies and a positive attitude towards violence (Olweus 1989; Slee & Rigby 1993). They lack empathy towards and feelings of guilt about the victim. Bullies may target children who complain, seek attention and who are emotionally and physically weak.

Olweus (1989) has indicated that victims are usually anxious, sensitive and quiet, with low self-esteem and negative attitudes towards themselves: '[T]he behaviour and attitude of the victims seem to signal to others that they are

Programs like the PEACE Pack are being used to reduce school bullying.

insecure and worthless individuals who will not retaliate if they are attacked or insulted' (Olweus 1989, p. 16). While Olweus (1989) suggests that the majority of victims may be described as above, there is an identifiable group of victims whom he has labelled as 'provocative', who combine both anxious and aggressive patterns. Research suggests (Slee & Rigby 1993) that victims are not necessarily anxious but rather are introverted in nature.

The family life-cycle: 14

Sibling relationships

In the literature on child development surprisingly little attention has been given in the past to the study of sibling relationships and the importance of such relationships for individual and family development. In part, this oversight reflects the legacy of the psychoanalytic view that it is the parents who are the primary influence in the child's life.

There is now an emerging body of research concerned with the nature of sibling relationships (Lamb & Sutton-Smith 1982; Dunn 1984, 1988; Honig 1986). As Honig (1986, p. 37) notes, 'Becoming a big brother or a big sister, although an exciting and tumultuous time for preschool-aged children, requires complex growth oriented adaption'. Early research on sibling relationships has focused on issues such as birth order, age gap and gender.

Birth order

A great deal of attention has been given to differences between first-born and later-born children. Being the first-born child has been associated with greater 'success' in life, higher intelligence and so forth. In a critical review of the voluminous research in this field, Lamb and Sutton-Smith (1982, p. 153) concluded that birth order has little explanatory power in terms of psychological outcomes: '[I]t remains a puzzle that so many thousands of studies have been devoted to such minimal end'.

Sex differences

Sutton-Smith (1982) and Dunn (1984) have also addressed the issue of the effect of the sex of siblings on each other. For instance, 'It is often said that a boy growing up with several sisters will be rather 'feminine' in his interests and that a girl with brothers will be a 'tomboy' (Dunn 1984, p. 65). Such a picture, as Dunn goes on to note, is a gross oversimplification of a very complex situation.

Dunn and Kendrick (1982) observed siblings at home when the younger sibling was 8 and then 14 months of age. The researchers noted that older siblings were more friendly towards their new brothers or sisters if they were the same sex. One possible explanation for this is that with siblings of different sex, jealousy may prevent such close friendliness, because mothers may tend to interact more with the younger sibling if he or she is of the opposite sex to the older child.

Reactions to the birth of a sibling

Typical reactions of the first child in a family to the birth of a brother or sister include an increase in behavioural problems or regressive behaviour (Dunn & Kendrick 1982). Certainly 'jealousy' of the new arrival is commonly observed by parents. Behavioural disturbance is greatest in children under 5 years of age:

> The birth of a brother or sister must in itself involve a major shift of a symbolic kind – a change in the child's conception of himself within the family, and indeed of himself as a person. The presence of a sibling provides a focus for frequent discussion by mother and child of another person. The baby as a person with wants, intentions, likes and dislikes, with rights, possessions and gender; as a rival for the attention, love, approval and disapproval of the parents (Dunn & Kendrick 1982, p. 56).

Sibling conflict

Dunn makes various observations about the factors influencing the quality of sibling relationships, including:

- conflict between siblings is very much a part of normal family life;
- family structure variables such as the sex of the children and age gaps have no influence on the quality of the relationships;
- the temperament of the siblings is linked to conflict;
- the emotional climate of the family is related to sibling conflict;
- the behaviour of parents towards siblings in conflict is related to the frequency of the conflict.

This last point will be addressed a little more fully.

The role the parent plays in relation to sibling conflict is important (Dunn 1988). For example, one point of view is that parental interventions increase sibling conflict, given that children are quarrelling to gain attention or to cause parental intervention. Such intervention deprives children of the opportunity to learn how to resolve conflict. In the psychological literature, it is widely believed that parental involvement in sibling quarrels escalates the frequency of conflict, although research suggests that the picture is somewhat more complex than this (Dunn & Munn 1986). Mature adult interventions involving discussion of rules and feelings would contribute to the development of relatively mature forms of sibling behaviour during conflict.

Bank and Kahn (1982) have identified two groups of ineffective parenting styles associated with sibling conflict: conflict-avoiding parents and conflict-amplifying parents.

Conflict-avoiding parents. With this parental style, the adults intervene constantly to mediate the children's conflict. Fearing direct conflict themselves, such parents negotiate for their children, even though the youngsters could solve the conflict themselves. Such parents are oversensitive to sibling conflict. Over-protectiveness may not allow children sufficient opportunity to vent aggressive or angry feelings and does not allow them to learn the skills of negotiating and compromise.

Conflict-amplifying parents. This parental style subtly encourages sibling conflict. The suggestion here is that through their aggressive interactions the children are meeting the parents' deeply seated needs relating to their own aggressive impulses or feelings.

In summary, recent research has drawn attention to the importance of the quality of sibling relationships in the family. Growing up with brothers and sisters has an important effect on a child's relationships with his or her parents. Moreover, the nature of the relationships between siblings also has an impact on children's growth and development and ultimately affects other relationships within the family system.

School programs to reduce bullying

It is important that intervention programs be implemented as early as possible to counter the effects of children's aggressive behaviour (Slee 2001). To this end, Slee (2001) has developed a program to counter the effects of school bullying, known as the Peace Pack (see website <www.caper.com.au>).

Chapter summary

The pre-school period represents a time of transition – transition from family to school life – from siblings to peers – from parents to teachers. The break is often a sharp one for parents, who feel the 'loss' of their child as they move into other worlds. New challenges confront the young child in relation to adapting and coping with the changing circumstances with which they are confronted.

Discussion questions

1   How do Freud and Erikson differ in their views of the nature of the social and emotional development of pre-schoolers?
2   What is the 'mirror and rouge' technique and how is it used to understand selfhood in toddlers?

3   What different types of child abuse have been identified?
4   Discuss possible sources of stress that could create adjustment problems for children beginning school.
5   Discuss the definition of bullying and the features that distinguish it from other forms of child–child conflict.

Activities

1   Interview a number of children regarding 'what frightens them most.' Share your answers in class.
2   Devise a list of questions to ask a sibling (your own brother or sister, if you have one) about conflict, conflict resolution and parents' reaction to conflict.
3   View the various websites addressing the issue of bullying identified in the CAPER website http://www.caper.com.au and summarise major findings in relation to the (i) definition of bullying; (ii) its incidence; and (iii) its effects.

4   Complete the 'Self Review Quiz' on the CD-ROM to assess your understanding of the content presented in this section. Use your quiz results as a basis for reviewing any chapter content about which you are uncertain.

Selected website

Child Adolescent Psychological Educational resources <www.caper.com.au>

6

Middle Childhood

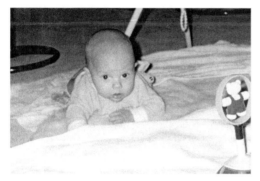

Ben aged 15 weeks

Ben aged 1 year

Ben aged 7 years

15 Physical Development in Middle Childhood

'If One Only Knew the Right Way to Change Them –'
So she set the little creature down, and felt quite relieved to see it trot away
quietly into the wood. 'If it had grown up,' she said to herself, 'it would have
made a dreadfully ugly child: but it makes rather a handsome pig, I think.'
And she began thinking over other children she knew who might do well as
pigs, and was just saying to herself, 'If one only knew the right way to
change them – 'when she was a little startled by seeing the Cheshire Cat
sitting on a bough of a tree a few yards off.

Lewis Carroll, Alice's Adventures in Wonderland

CHAPTER OUTLINE

KEY TERMS AND CONCEPTS

- Locomotive activities
- Manipulative activities
- Norms
- Somatotype
- Endomorph

- Mesomorph
- Ectomorph
- Obesity
- Socialisation

Introduction

Considerable advances have been made in our understanding of the nature of children's physical growth and development thanks to the work of such psychologists as Arnold Gesell (see chapter 6). For all that, developmental psychologists can sympathise with Alice's ruminations about the pig. More particularly, a great deal remains to be understood about the relationship between aspects of children's physical growth and their psychological development in middle childhood. This chapter explores some of these links. Other topics discussed include girls' participation in sport and the relationship between food and physical activity. The Family Life-cycle: 15 focuses on the effect of parental conflict on children.

Gross motor development

The Australian Sports Commission (1997) reports that greater than 30 per cent of Australians do not exercise. They also report that if only 10 per cent of this group began regular exercise approximately $600 million would be saved on Australia's health bill, given the major health benefits associated with exercise. The 'Active Australian' vision (Australian Sports Commission 1991), similar to the United States 'Healthy People' campaign, has set a focus on physical activity with one priority being increased participation in vigorous physical activity. As noted by Rice and Howell (2000), it is estimated that nearly half of American children aged between 12–21 are not vigorously active on a daily basis.

Activities such as hopping, jumping, skipping and climbing are gross motor movements. They are **locomotor** activities using the whole body. When the child is bending, pushing or swinging we have examples of non-locomotor activities. A **manipulative** activity involves throwing, catching and striking. A fundamental movement pattern can combine these. For example, running and picking up a ball may include locomotor, non-locomotor and manipulative activities. All too often, adults' attention focuses on the very young child's developing physical activity and less attention is paid to physical capabilities during the middle years of primary school.

locomotor
descibes movement from one place to another.

manipulative
describes activities involving the use of the hand.

Developmental norms

Gesell (1974) and his associates developed norms (standards or measurements of behaviour) that chart children's growth and development (see chapter 6). The **norms** refer to what happens when in a child's development. In chapter 6 the norms that chart girls' and boys' growth in height are listed. Norms are not absolutes. They simply provide statistics for basic comparisons: what is normal for one individual is not necessarily normal for another.

During middle childhood, a child's growth in height is steady at about 6.5 to 7 centimetres per year. Weight gain during middle childhood is steady at about 10 to 15 kilograms per year.

norms
accepted standards against which individual performance can be compared.

Trends in health-related physical fitness

Pangfazi (2000) and Biddle and Gondas (1996) have noted that the explanations for adverse changes in health-related physical fitness of children are likely to be found in a complex relationship involving physical fitness, changes in leisure activities, and changes in societal concerns regarding the safety of children left unsupervised as they walk or ride to school or play outside of the home. In many Western industrialised countries such as Australia (e.g. Brown & Brown 1996; Dollman et al. 1998), concerns are being expressed that the decline in health-related fitness in school children will follow into adulthood and have significant health impacts. Apart from the long-term

concerns, Drummond (2001) has argued on the basis of his research of young adolescent South Australian boys that societal changes have resulted in '... increasing pressure for boys to focus upon their bodies as a vehicle for social and cultural acceptance'(p. 40). In particular, the desirability of attaining a muscular, athletic body with no extraneous fat may place undue pressure on young males. Drummond argues that problems arise where there is a mismatch between the stereotypic model of what a body should look like in terms of sport and boys' perceptions of their own bodies. Where the discrepancy is great the risk is that boys will reduce their participation in physical activity.

During middle childhood changes are occurring in the child's musculoskeletal development.

Musculoskeletal changes

During middle childhood, changes are also occurring in the child's musculoskeletal proportions. There is an increase in musculoskeletal growth as well as an increase in heart strength and lung capacity. Such changes influence the child's endurance in sporting activities. Changes in body proportion mean that the child loses the squat, chubby appearance of the pre-schooler and becomes taller, more slender and more graceful in appearance and movement (Maresh 1966).

Sex differences

Appearance. Any classroom teacher will tell you about the differences in physical appearance of boys and girls in the middle childhood. Boys are usually taller and heavier than girls, except for the years immediately preceding puberty. The growth spurt for girls is between 10 and 14 years (see chapter 18 for more details), while for boys it occurs from 12 to 16 years of age (Maresh 1966). Girls therefore reach physical maturity earlier than boys.

Performance. Because physical growth during middle childhood proceeds at a slow, even pace, children have the opportunity to consolidate and develop their interests and skills. Adults who spend time with children will testify that there are wide individual differences in children's motor skills. Up to middle childhood there are minimal differences between boys and girls in their ability to acquire and execute motor skills. However, as is also true during the pre-school years that girls tend to have better balance and coordination than boys, while boys have greater physical strength. In a study of children between 5 and 12 years of age, Keogh (1965) found that boys could run faster and had greater endurance than girls, were better at throwing and had greater grip strength. Girls, on the other hand, demonstrated greater skills in gymnastics. However, despite equivalent performance abilities, girls tend to drop out of sport as middle childhood progresses, particularly in the later years.

Growth in height and weight during middle childhood is steady.

Somatotype

From the time of Hippocrates, attempts have been made to categorise people by their physique. Sheldon (1940) has identified three dimensions of physique.

Endomorph. This physique is characterised by a round body, with small bones, smooth skin and little hair on the body. Endomorphs are not well-muscled and are at a disadvantage in activities that require them to move quickly or overcome their body weight. One advantage is that the endomorphic individual's large surface area facilitates participation in water sports, making it easier to float.

endomorph
a body type characterised by roundness and smoothness.

Mesomorph. The mesomorphic individual has large bones and well-developed muscles. In stature such an individual is square and rugged, and marked by a predominance of muscle. The shoulders are broad and the waist relatively thin.

mesomorph
a well-developed, well muscled body type.

Ectomorph. This individual is straight and linear in physique. Bones are thin and muscles are small. The ectomorph's shoulders are narrow and lack muscle support. Such individuals are often physically agile, with good body control, but may lack resilience in body contact sports.

ectomorph
a long, thin body type.

Sheldon related his research of physical characteristics to personality. He found that endomorphic individuals were associated with the temperamental trait of viscerotonia, characterised by sociability and a love of relaxation, comfort and food. Mesomorphic individuals were typified by a love of physical adventure and exercise, accompanied by a marked preference for aggressiveness, assertiveness and action (somatotonia). The temperamental trait associated with ectomorphy involved restraint, inhibition and concealment. Such individuals were found to be typically reactive and uncertain of themselves in social situations (cerebrotonia).

Support for Sheldon's theory of the association between body type and personality comes from research such as that conducted by Wells and Siegal (1961), who asked subjects to rate the psychological characteristics of silhouettes resembling Sheldon's body types. The subjects rated endomorphs as warm-hearted, good-natured and lazier than others, mesomorphs as masculine and adventuresome, and ectomorphs as ambitious and more tense than others. However, the correlation between body type and personality may well be a function of social expectation. For example, a strong, active individual may be encouraged by parents to be adventuresome, dominant and self-reliant. In a New Zealand study, Williams et al. (1989) failed to find any statistically significant relationship between physique and the personality characteristics of assertiveness, aggressiveness, dominance and aggression. However, they noted that while the results were not statistically significant, there was some positive association, suggesting that further research is needed.

Somatotype and motor performance

As Sheldon found, human beings come in different sizes and shapes. A glance around any classroom of children in middle childhood will reveal an assortment of body shapes. The three body types identified by Sheldon can be found in boys and girls, but boys tend to be associated more often with the mesomorphic body type than girls. Very few individuals are 'pure' types. Research conducted by Sills and Everett (1953) and Lindegard (1956) has revealed the following relationships between physique and motor performance.

- Individuals with a tendency towards endomorphy have a lot of weight to carry, which can limit their participation in certain sporting activities.
- The ectomorph is relatively poorly protected by muscle and is therefore prone to sports injury.
- The mesomorph's ruggedness and strength predisposes such an individual to physical activity.

Trends and issues

Getting girls to play sport

As noted by the Australian researcher James (1999), it is often erroneously assumed that young girls prefer to sit and talk with each other than participate in physical activity during lunch and recess time.

In her study of young teenage girls, James reported on complaints by the girls that they were often refused access to a school gymnasium by the boys at lunch time to play basketball. Girls reported that they were restricted to the role of spectators unless invited to play by the boys, at which point they were often the butt of jokes and ridicule. In her study, James utilised the concept of 'public spaces', building on a body of emerging research which indicates that the '[t]he meanings associated with public spaces are not the same for males and females' (James 1999, p. 11). James cited the writings of Franck and Paxon (1989), who noted that in Western

societies the more private domestic spaces are typically the domain of females while men control the more public, open spaces. There is a social aspect to this behaviour with boys using 'teasing' to exclude girls from certain public spaces (James 1999).

The findings from the study by James indicated that a range of factors shaped girls' participation in an activity such as basketball. 'Extrinsic' factors included the boys' physical domination of public spaces, their use of verbal taunts to intimidate the girls and their more competitive attitude. 'Intrinsic' factors related to girls' concern regarding their physical appearance and athletic abilities. James recommended that schools use observational studies, action research and surveys (See CD on methodology) to '. . . empower both boys and girls to redress the imbalance in schoolground spaces' (James 1999, p. 15).

 See your C

Girls and sport

As already established in this chapter, at the primary school level there are few appreciable physiological explanations to help understand sex-related differences in physical performance.

Eston et al. (1989) found that the fitness levels of British year 11 and year 12 girls are lower than those of their male counterparts. According to Williams (1989), girls and boys bring very different expectations to their physical education lessons. The same author notes that in British schools more male than female teachers take physical education lessons and more male than female teachers run after-school sport programs. This means that boys have positive role models, while girls do not. Furthermore, the domination of playground activity by boys has been well documented. Such domination allows the boys to practise important physical skills, such as throwing, catching and kicking a ball; skills that girls, therefore, do not have the opportunity to practise.

Williams (1989, p. 178) comments: 'The unwitting reinforcement of differential treatment in terms of approved play activity is something which all primary schools need to consider'.

A number of myths are associated with women's sporting involvement, but each of these can be countered by the true facts. To show how ridiculous such myths really are, Menzies (1985, p. 23) has applied similar arguments to males. For example:

> Boys should be banned from all contact sports. Unlike girls their reproductive organs are not protected, and they could be hurt in such a way as to damage their potential as fathers.

> . . . Males should be banned from climbing mountains, since they aren't as able as females to adjust to high altitudes.

In her book *The Second Sex*, Simone de Beauvoir (1952, p. 331) emphasises that:

> in sports the end in view is not success independent of physical equipment; it is rather the attainment of perfection within the limitation of each physical type; the featherweight boxing champion is as much a champion as is the heavy weight; the woman skiing champion is not inferior to the faster male champion; they belong to two different classes. It is precisely the female athletes, who being positively interested in their own game, feel themselves least handicapped in comparison with the male.

Although myths such as those identified by Menzies may not be as prevalent in Western society today, many people are still ignorant of the value of exercise, believing that girls are in some way unsuited for extended and vigorous activity (Howarth 1987).

Girls' attitudes toward sport are heavily influenced by a number of factors including socialisation, family, school, media and culture.

Girls' participation is sport is influenced by society's views of femininity.

Socialisation

Socialisation is the ongoing process by which humans are transformed from biological organisms at birth to human beings fully able to participate in society (D'Alton & Bittman 1976; McGurk 1978). It takes place over the course of the individual's lifetime. The process of socialisation can take place in a number of ways:

1   reinforcement – the provision of reward and punishment in the acquisition and performance of social roles;
2   teaching – a direct and deliberate process by one or more individuals;
3   observational learning – the learning and performance of a role or task by observing it being performed by significant others.

socialisation
the process by which individuals acquire the values, attitudes and knowledge of the society (or subgroups of society) to which they belong.

The outcomes of socialisation are two-fold:

- the transmission of society's cultural values, attitudes and norms to the individual;
- the development of personality in the individual.

Research by Garcia et al. (1995), indicates that overall girls and women participate in less physical activity than boys and men. As reported by Park and Wright (2000), the New South Wales Schools Fitness and Physical Activity Study noted that the participation rate in physical activity was 20 per cent less for young women than for young men of the same age. Park and Wright (2000) argued for a social constructivist view of gender, observing that the image girls have of themselves is not simply shaped but rather girls are '. . . active in selecting, rejecting and adapting social meanings and practices which they incorporate into their own sense of what it is to be male and female' (Wright 1997, p. 16). Given the significance of sport in the 'Australian way of life', Park and Wright further argue that while sport significantly shapes the way boys view their masculinity, for girls playing sport presents a significant risk to their femininity. That is, for girls sport challenges 'ideal' notions of what it is to be feminine. For example, in the document *Girls Gain Ground*, published by the South Australian Education Department (n.d.), a number of myths were identified that characterise girls and physical activity, e.g. 'If girls play sport they will develop bulging muscles' or 'girls are more likely to be injured than boys'. Simultaneously girls who play sport seriously challenge the notion of sport as a dominant male province, hence the common putdown, 'You're playing like a girl'.

The family

Psychological research shows that parents treat newborns differently according to gender (Goldberg & Lewis 1972; Chafetz 1974). Parents often inculcate gender-appropriate behaviour in their children from birth. For example, this may occur through their choice of clothes colour (pink for girls and blue for boys) or through verbalisation ('big boys don't cry').

Schools

In a British study conducted by Clarricoates (1980) of teachers' perceptions of differences between boys and girls, the following features emerged:

- Teachers saw boys as lively, adventuresome, aggressive, boisterous, self-confident, independent, energetic and loyal.
- Girls were considered by teachers to be obedient, tidy, neat, conscientious, orderly, fussy, catty, bitchy and gossiping.
- In commenting on the results of this research, Howarth (1987) observes that girls are often seen as lacking attributes for success and even in activities that favour girls, such as gymnastics, their poise, elegance and control is viewed less favourably than the confidence and energy of boys.

The media

An examination by Browne (1990) of physical education textbooks recommended for senior high school students in Australian schools revealed considerable gender bias. In relation to both written content and illustrations, Browne reports a 70 to 90 per cent bias in favour of males. She cites an earlier study by Kahle (1987), which indicated that between 59 and 90 per cent of the illustrations in such textbooks were male dominated. Referring to the UK, Spender (1989, p. 65) observes that:

> teachers find there is no shortage of material which is designed for boys. Most textbooks assume that the average human being is male, that male experience is the sum total of human experience and that the activities of males are inherently more interesting and significant.

There is no doubt that girls' bodies undergo significant physical changes during puberty and that better nutrition is resulting in these changes occurring at an earlier age in Western societies. The suggestion is that these changes are more frequently associated with the development of negative perceptions of the body among girls than boys (Rhea 1998). Park and Wright (2000), citing Wright and Dewar (1997), have noted that from a social perspective the critical 'gaze' that girls are subject to as part of their socialisation is a more important factor than the physical changes themselves.

> The obsession that Western culture has with the youthful, slim and sensual body that adorns magazine covers and media commercials throughout the world is likely to be just as powerful an influence on young women's choices as the physical changes themselves (p. 16).

Culture

The evidence is that physical activity is significantly associated with positive psychological (e.g. self-esteem) and physical benefits (greater skeletal health) (Health Education Authority 1998). In Australia, a survey of 3092 New South Wales' girls indicated that the level of sports participation of girls from non-English speaking backgrounds was significantly lower than those from Anglo-Australian culture (Vescio, Taylor & Toohey 1999). Their finding supported earlier research by Taylor and Toohey (1998), which identified various barriers to sports participation among adult females from various cultural background including Chinese, Croatian, Greek, Italian, Lebanese, Serbian and Vietnamese. These barriers included time constraints, lack of company, family responsibilities, lack of information about sports, and lack of sports skills and poor facilities. Findings from the Vescio et al. (1999) study indicated that barriers to participating in sports included 'time constraints', lack of company and lack of sports skills.

By encouraging physical activity, adults can help children develop positive attitudes toward sport.

Food and physical activity

To improve the quality of our lifestyle and function at our mental and physical peak we need to eat well. Throughout the many stages in an individual's life from infancy to adulthood, the amount of food needed by the body varies, but generally the types of foods that are best for us do not change.

The most common nutrition problem in Australia is overeating. Being over-weight is defined as being more than 10 per cent above acceptable weight, while the definition of obese is being more than 20 per cent above acceptable weight (Fanning 1980). If we eat more food than the body uses, the excess is stored as fat. For every extra 30 000 kilojoules (7000 calories) we eat, we store 1 kilogram of body fat (1 calorie = approximately 4 kilojoules).

For the overweight, and in particular the obese, there are important reasons for controlling weight. There is a strong relationship between obesity and the likelihood of illness and greater risk of such diseases as hypertension, heart disease, gall bladder disease and maturity onset diabetes. Being overweight contributes to high blood pressure and an increased cholesterol level (Boulton & Magarey 1988). When linked to smoking and drinking, being overweight can place a real strain on the heart and lungs and lower a person's stamina (Clyde 1983).

In Australia, eating habits have undergone great changes in the last decade, particularly in relation to 'fast food'. Occasionally eating take-away food, such as pizza, chicken, chips and hamburgers, causes no apparent harm to an individual's health (Fanning 1980). However, if such fast food becomes a regular part of our diet, we lose control over our salt and fat intake. Too much salty, fatty food, without an accompanying increase in the consumption of fruit, vegetables and whole grain foods, is associated with the development of life-threatening degenerative diseases such as cardiovascular disease and diabetes.

Obesity

Fanning (1980) suggests that 20 per cent of Australian school children are overweight and similar figures have been provided by Boulton and Magarey (1988). This figure accords with United States (Erickson, Robinson; Haydel, Killen 2000). However, Boulton and Magarey (1988) point out the problems associated with labelling a child '**obese**', because cultural attitudes towards the ideal body shape vary considerably. In Western countries thinness is idealised, but in South Pacific countries such as Samoa and Tonga being overweight correlates with social status. Nevertheless, Boulton and Magarey (1988) emphasise that being overweight is disadvantageous for a person's physical and psychological health.

obese
being excessively overweight; more than 20 per cent heavier than the acceptable weight.

Obesity in Australian children has been attributed to overindulgence in junk and fast foods, as well as sweets, combined with lack of exercise. The blame may lie with 'persuasive TV advertisements promoting energy-dense foods that [are] all too available at home and in the school canteen' (*The Advertiser*, 11 September 1987, p. 25). To help prevent obesity, parents should encourage children 'to help plan and cook meals, grow vegetables and read the labels on processed food', as well as motivate and encourage their children to control their weight. In a South Australian study, Morton (1990) found that television advertising for food runs contrary to healthy eating guidelines.

Developmental course of obesity

There is no evidence that obesity in infancy correlates with obesity in later childhood (Boulton and Magarey 1986). However, in summarising the research evidence, Boulton & Magarey (1986) note that it is clear that the longer children remain obese the higher the probability that they will become obese adolescents and adults. All the evidence suggests that around 90 per cent of obese adolescents will become obese adults. In healthy Australian children, the proportion of fat babies (in the top 20 per cent for fatness at 3 to 6 months) who remain fat at age 8 is 23 per cent for boys and 11 per cent for girls (Boulton & Magarey 1988).

The hazards of obesity

In a review of the health hazards of obesity, Boulton and Magarey (1988) noted that they should be considered in terms of immediate and delayed physical and psychological problems. The evidence indicates that obese children are at an increased risk of elevated plasma triglyceride levels, hyperinsulinemia, hyper-cholesterolemia, hypertension and decreased release of growth hormone.

Obese children are also at risk of being stigmatised, given Australian society's emphasis on thinness as being physically attractive. This would increase psychological problems, should the child remain obese into adolescence and adulthood.

It is commonly believed that overweight children are unhappy with their weight. Braet, Mervielde and Vandereycken (1997) report that a clinical group of obese children scored higher on parental reports of both emotional and behavioural problems compared with a non-clinical sample. Myers, Raynor and Epstein (1998) found that decreases in percentage overweight during obesity treatment predict improvements in children's psychological functioning.

Trends and issues

Children's rough and tumble play

The issue of children's play was considered in broad detail in chapter 9. Piaget proposed a developmental theory of play documenting a progression in play behaviours from imitation of others to symbolic play to rule-governed play. Vygotsky (1933) (see chapter 9), in accordance with his emphasis on social experience and language, highlighted the importance of representational play.

> Play creates a zone of proximal development in the child. In play, the child always behaves beyond his average age, above his daily behaviour; in play it is though he were a head taller than himself (Vygotsky 1933, p. 102).

As noted, play has never been universally defined but various types of play have been identified. For example, rough and tumble (R & T) play was first identified by Harry Harlow in his observations of rhesus monkeys. He described their R & T play to include chasing, running, fleeing, wrestling, falling and play fighting. Accompanying R & T play is the 'play face', described by Harlow as an open mouthed, teeth-bared expression which while looking fierce conveys a non-aggressive intent.

Children have been observed to engage in R & T play including the 'play face' accompanied by laughter, smiles and shouting to convey a non-aggressive intent. Considerable research has examined R & T play in children (Blurton-Jones 1976; Reed & Brown 2000). Activities encapsulating R & T play include games such as 'chasey' and 'king of the mountain'. Boys typically engage in more R & T play than girls. The benefits of R & T play have been documented to include an association with enhanced problem-solving ability and academic achievement among boys.

Promoting physical activity

As noted by Rice and Howell (2000), there has been a downward trend in the amount of physical activity among children in the United States of America. In an examination of methodology used in relation to physical activity, Rice and Howell (2000) have clarified issues relating to terminology. They cite research by Caspersen, Powell and Christenson (1985, p. 126) which defines physical activity as '. . . any bodily movement produced by skeletal muscles that results in energy expenditure'. These authors differentiate this from 'exercise', which is defined as '. . . physical activity that is planned, structured, repetitive and purposive in the sense that improvement or maintenance of one or more components of physical fitness is an objective'. In turn, the authors delineate 'physical fitness as '. . . related to the movements that people perform: physical fitness is a set of attributes that people have or achieve'. As they note, physical fitness can be thought of as an outcome.

The evidence supporting the positive benefits of exercise continues to mount (Hughs 1984; Paffenbarger & Hyde 1984). A great deal of attention has been given to the benefits of physical activity for promoting health in adults. It has been suggested that exercising for 15 to 60 minutes at 50 to 85 per cent of maximal functional capacity three to five times per week has the most benefit. Activities such as swimming, jogging, bicycling, skipping and hiking use large muscle groups in an aerobic fashion.

In Australia, there is some concern among the community at large that children are increasingly adopting a sedentary lifestyle. Twenty per cent of children in a Victorian survey reported that exercise was a 'non-event' and said they had been 'turned-off' by unpleasant school experiences with physical activity (Wicks 1987).

Exercise and prime time television

Overweight and obesity have been strongly associated with the amount of timethat individuals watch television, such that the more time youth watch television the more likely they will be overweight (King et al. 1999). In a study reported by King et al. (1999), exercise scenes on television generally depicted males, whites and adults; sports and games were the most frequent types of exercise, and gyms and clubs were the most frequent locations. It is often assumed that children have an innate interest in physical activity, but this is not necessarily so. It remains, then, for educators to consider the means by which they may motivate children's interest in physical activity.

Factors influencing participation

Age

The research of Godin and Shephard (1986) indicates that from primary school to early adolescence children's attitudes shift from the notion that physical activity is fun to the more adult idea of indulging in physical activity to improve health. As students move through high school there is also an increasing tendency for them to drop out of physical education (Butcher 1983).

Sex differences

All the evidence suggests that in the 10 to 17 year age group more boys than girls are physically active (Anderson et al. 1986; Godin & Shephard 1986). Moreover, Godin and Shephard (1986) discovered that girls' participation in physical education decreases in school years 7, 8 and 9 as they become involved in less strenuous activity. The consequence is a decline in girls' level of physical fitness (Butcher 1983). There are a number of possible reasons for this decline in interest.

Firstly, there is a set of factors associated with cultural values that emphasise boys' participation in hard physical activity, while girls are socialised with different expectations regarding participation in physical activity (Hasbrook 1986). Secondly, the earlier maturation of girls can lead them to adopt what they perceive to be appropriate adult behaviour, which may include a more sedentary lifestyle (Godin & Shephard 1986).

Improving children's attitudes towards sport

In reviewing the literature it is apparent that there are a number of different ways in which children's attitudes towards sport could be encouraged in a more positive fashion.

The family

There is a need for education programs that alert parents to the fitness level of children. One of the aims of such programs should be to change parental attitudes in favour of encouraging their sons and daughters to exercise.

School

Schools might be encouraged to adopt a more positive attitude to sport by making physical activity an integral part of the curriculum. It is still possible to find teachers who will use exercise as a punishment for misbehaviour (for example, making a child do laps of the oval), and this attitude should be discouraged.

The media need to adopt a more proactive stance towards coverage of women's sport. Similarly, television programs could be used more to promote healthy images of the value of correct eating and exercise habits.

> **VIEWPOINT**
> **Why do parents fight?**
> 'Sometimes because one wants to go one place and one wants to go somewhere else'
> Jonathan, 8 years
>
> 'Because they don't like what the other has done'
> Jarrad, 12 years

The family life-cycle: 15

'Mum and Dad are fighting again!'

Efforts to understand what aspects of marital conflict create adjustment problems in children have led to the recognition that there are both direct effects on adjustment and indirect effects mediated through quality of parenting and parent–child relationships (Kelly 2000, p. 964).

In the context of the family life-cycle, the advent of a child or children adds a new dimension to a couple's life. In a longitudinal study of 58 South Australian couples who became parents for the first time, a number of important findings emerged in terms of the impact of children on the couple's lives (Baum 1989). Along with the advent of a child, parents typically reported:

- changes in the nature of the marital relationship with particular reference being made to less sex, less time together, tiredness and financial strain;
- changes in their friendship network – for example, the women had more contact with friends in the local neighbourhood than before the birth of the child;
- more time spent with relatives since the birth (especially the women).

These changes in the nature of the primary relationship provide a basis for increased marital conflict. In turn, this confronts children with the task of dealing with such conflict. As Dunn and Munn (1985, p. 480) note:

Becoming a member of family involves for a child not only the development of relationships but a growing understanding of the affective relationships among these individuals and of the particular routines, rules, expectations, jokes, games, prohibitions, and sanctions of family life.

Developmental changes in children's understanding of emotions

It is now clear that from the earliest months of life babies are responsive to maternal emotional states (Stern 1977; Slee 1983; 1984). Research by Cummings et al. (1981) found that in the family context there are developmental changes in children's response to anger expression by family members. At 1 to 1½ years of age toddlers often react emotionally to anger in others (that is, they showed overt distress or anger). Developmentally, children are less likely to express emotion in response to emotional display as they get older (Buss & Plomin 1975) and as they improve their social skills (Zahn-Waxler & Radke-Yarrow 1982). In a study of 5- to 9-year-old children, Corell and Abramovitch (1987) found that the youngest children in the family cite themselves as the cause of marital anger, but the older children are likely to attribute cause to siblings, fathers and ongoing family events.

The impact of parental disharmony on children

'Exposure to anger between others is likely to be aversive for children' (Cummings 1987, p. 978). In a study of 5-year-old children, Cummings (1987) found that background anger is a stressor for children and increases aggressive behaviour. An emerging body of evidence is now linking parental disharmony with behavioural and emotional problems in children (Richman et al. 1982; Slee & Cross 1990; Cummings & Cummings 1988). A review of research by Kelly (2000) concluded that 'direct' effects of marital conflict on children impacted on children's modelling of parental behaviours, failure to acquire various social skills and various physiological effects. In relation to 'indirect' effects, Kelly (2000, p. 966) noted '[p]ersistent, intense marital discord, and marital dissatisfaction, pervasively undermines the quality of parenting, including discipline, parent–child aggression and affective responses'.

Children's strategies for coping with parental disharmony

Research by Jenkins et al. (1989) indicates that 18 per cent of 7-year-old children in the London area were living in disharmonious homes. The children's reactions to parental disharmony principally involved intervention (telling parents to stop) or comforting the parent(s) after the quarrel (see Table 15.1).

Table 15.1 Children's use of coping strategies in response to parental quarrels

Strategy	Children using %
Intervention in parental quarrels (modes of intervention)	71
Going to sit beside the parent	24
Telling the parents to stop	40
Distracting them	15
Taking sides	15
Making other comments about quarrels	10
Crying	32
Actively encouraging parents to make up afterwards	40
Seeking contact with a sibling	59
Confiding in siblings	40
Confiding in friends	18
Offering comfort to parents after a quarrel	62
Frequently blaming themselves for parental quarrelling	24
Obtaining information about quarrel from parents	41
Perceiving beneficial aspects of parental quarrels	41

Source Jenkins 1989

Reviewing the literature, Cummings and Cummings (1988) have identified a number of categories of children's response to background anger:

1   escape or avoidance, such as leaving the room;
2   support-seeking, as in clinging to the parent(s) during the quarrel;
3   positive reappraisal, such as smiling to avoid showing feelings;
4   distancing, such as failing to respond to the quarrel at all.

Figure 15.1 reproduces a model devised by Cummings and Cummings (1988) setting out the key elements involved when children are faced with adults' angry behaviour. It can be seen that there are four major domains influencing children's response to adult anger.

1   *Child characteristics/background.* Here emphasis is given to variables such as the child's developmental level, sex, family history and temperament.
2   *Context.* The context refers to the setting for the anger expression.
3   *Stress and coping.* This domain refers to factors such as cognition, feeling and physiological

arousal which influence children's responses and their coping strategies.

4   *Outcomes.* Exposure to background anger can result in an adaptive outcome, such as expressing or talking over the reaction, or a maladaptive outcome, such as an angry outburst.

The four major domains identified are not part of a theoretical formulation but do help us to organise the factors that may affect a child's reaction to parental quarrels (Cummings & Cummings 1988).

Kelly (2000, p. 966) summarised a review of research into the topic, noting that '[t]he manner in which parents resolve their conflict has been determined to affect the impact of high conflict on children's adjustment. Chronic, unresolved conflict is associated with greater emotional insecurity in children'. Kelly goes on to note that

[f]ear, distress and other symptoms in children are diminished when parents resolve their significant conflicts, as opposed to no resolution, and when parents use more compromise and negotiation methods rather than verbal attacks.

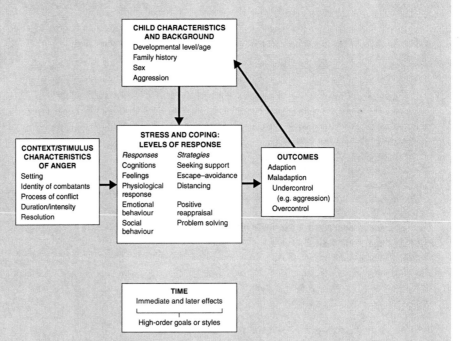

Figure 15.1 Key elements in children's coping with adult anger

Chapter summary

Middle childhood is at one and the same time a period of consolidation – consolidation of physical skills – and a time of change. Parents and teachers are only too well aware of the differences in physical development which characterise any two boys or girls setting them apart from their peers. Salient issues emerging here relate to engagement in, and enjoyment of, physical activity and issues related to eating behaviour. A significant question to consider concerns the messages children are learning from their schooling, the media and their leisure activities regarding how to value and respect their own health and well-being.

Discussion questions

1 Outline the characteristics of different somatotypes, highlighting the links with personality and motor performance.
2 Discuss Simone de Beauvoir's comment on women and sport (see p. 000).
3 Discuss your memories of the school playground and how it was used by girls and boys.
4 What images of women's participation in sport are promulgated by the media?
5 What role do you think the media play in promoting healthy eating?
6 What understanding do we have of young children's ability to interpret emotion?
7 Referring to Figure 15.1, identify how children might cope with conflict at home.

Activities

1 Conduct a 'media survey' of your local newspaper by examining the sports section over a period of time (e.g. one week) and counting the frequency of reports on male and female sports activity, the prominence given to such activities, the photographs taken and so forth.
2 View any 'soapie' over a regular time period (e.g. one week), identifying how sport is portrayed, the type of physical activity engaged in by the main characters. One might also examine the 'eating patterns' of the main characters.

Selected websites

Website for Health Promoting Schools <www.sahps.net>

Child Adolescent Psychological and Educational Resources <www.caper.com.au>

16 Cognitive Development in Middle Childhood

'Grown-ups Love Figures'

Grown-ups love figures. When you tell them that you have made a new friend, they never ask you any questions about essential matters. They never say to you, 'What does his voice sound like? What games does he love best? Does he collect butterflies?' Instead they demand: How old is he? How many brothers has he? How much does he weigh? How much money does his father make?' Only from these figures do they think they have learned anything about him.

Antoine de Saint-Exupery, The Little Prince

KEY TERMS AND CONCEPTS

- Concrete operations
- Conservation
- Classification
- Seriation
- Theory of mind
- Pre-riddle
- Cognitive congruency principle
- Learning style
- Auditory learning style
- Visual learning style
- Kinaesthetic learning style
- Moral development
- Concrete-experience learning style
- Abstract–conceptual learning style
- Reflective–observation learning style
- Active-experience learning style
- Deep learning
- Surface learning
- Heteronomous morality
- Autonomous morality
- Immanent justice
- Egocentrism
- Realism
- Justice concept
- Autonomous reality

Introduction

In *The Little Prince*, Antoine de Saint-Exupery reminds us that there are other ways of looking at and understanding the world apart from through adult eyes. During the primary school years, children make significant strides in terms of their cognitive development. This chapter describes the nature of some of the changes that occur in the way children think about and understand their world in middle childhood. The Family Life-cycle: 16 looks at counselling children in families.

Theoretical foundations

Jean Piaget has made a significant contribution to our understanding of children's cognitive development during middle childhood. From Table 16.1 it can be seen that Piaget places the primary school child largely within the concrete operations period. In the sensori-motor period, the child accomplishes a number of significant cognitive skills, including the achievement of object permanence and the imitation of actions. The second stage of cognitive development – the pre-operational period – sees the remarkable achievement of the development of symbolic thought, accompanied by the associated language development. According to Piaget, the third stage of cognitive development – concrete operations – is no less remarkable for its achievements than the previous stages.

Concrete operations stage

During the **concrete operations** stage, children's thinking exhibits a number of identifiable features. The notion of 'concrete' thought, as presented by Piaget (1963), incorporates the idea of what can be seen, touched or manipulated. The child is caught up in thought processes that focus on 'concrete' realities. The idea of 'operations' in Piagetian terms refers to the increasingly internalised nature of thought. The operations that can be performed during this stage include:

- reversibility;
- conservation;
- ordering of objects by number, size or class (classification);
- an ability to relate to time and space.

concrete operations
according to Piaget, the stage between 7 and 11 years of age during which children begin to understand the relationship between things in the world but still cannot think in abstract terms.

Reversibility

Children achieve reversibility when they understand that opposite numbers can cancel each other out: for example, that the addition $3 + 2 = 5$ can be reversed by the equivalent subtraction $5 - 2 = 3$. Similarly, they can understand that when an identical volume of water is poured from one container to another of

Table 16.1 The period of concrete operations: the third of Piaget's stages of cognitive development

Stage	Age	Abilities
Sensori-motor period	0–2 years	Use of five senses to relate to the world
Pre-operational period	2–7 years	Language and symbolism
Concrete operations period	7–11 years	Can apply simple logic to solve problems
Formal operations period	11+ years	Abstract reasoning

different dimensions, the volume of water remains the same, even though the shape of the container is different (see chapter 13).

Conservation

conservation
in Piagetian theory, the retention by an object or substance of certain properties, regardless of changes in shape and arrangement.

Concrete-operational children realise that whether a mathematics problem is presented as $2 + 3 + 1 = 6$ or $3 + 2 + 1 = 6$, it still adds up to 6. Reversibility occurs or must be present to solve the problem $2 \times 3 = 6$ or $6 \div 2 = 3$. **Conservation** is described more fully in chapter 13. According to Piaget, the development of conservation occurs sequentially.

Classification

class inclusion
the ability to associate a subset of objects (such as red apples) with the larger grouping to which it belongs (fruit).

In mastering classification, or **class inclusion**, children learn how to deal with the whole and parts of the whole at the same time. For example, if there are six oranges and three bananas and a child is asked whether there are more apples, more bananas or more fruit, a child who is not at the stage of conservation may answer that there are more oranges. That is, the child's answer can be somewhat unpredictable because she or he cannot understand the concept of class (fruit) and subclasses (bananas); that is, the child cannot conceive of the whole and the parts at the same time.

Annett (1959) studied the way 300 children aged 5 to 11 years classified four sorts of cards depicting plants, animals, furniture and vehicles. The task of the children was to sort the cards by group and then indicate why the cards belonged together. The results of the study revealed that young children (5 to 6 years) were very confused about the classification process. Between the ages of 8 and 11 years, children were much more able to sort the cards into the four groups. The formation of valid concepts depends on accurate sorting of similar and dissimilar properties.

seriation
the ability to put objects or quantities into a logical sequence.

A concept called **seriation** is related to classification. Seriation involves the ability to order objects according to, say, size or position: for example, sorting a number of sticks according to length. The pre-operational child can complete such a task but will typically go about it in a random fashion. According to Piaget, pre-operational children do this because they cannot appreciate that one element, B, can simultaneously be smaller than A, and bigger than C. That is, pre-operational children cannot deal with the notion that A > B > C and then infer that A > C, but they can infer what a series looks like and solve the task visually. In contrast, in the concrete operations stage, 7- to 8-year-olds approach the task systematically, first finding the largest stick and then the remaining ones. That is, the concrete-operational child has no difficulty with the concepts of 'bigger than' and 'smaller than'. The understanding of children's cognitive development has implications for appreciating a range of other developments including humour.

Theory of mind

Premack and Woodruff (1978) introduced the idea of '**theory of mind**' as part of their efforts to understand the cognitive and language abilities of chimpanzees – 'An individual has a theory of mind if he imputes mental states to himself and others'(1978, p. 515).

> **theory of mind**
> the ability to impute mental states to self and others.

As we spend time with others we take into account their feelings, thoughts and behaviour in order to try and understand why individuals behave as they do. Indications of the existence of theory of mind awareness is found in everyday language usage such as 'I think she was upset' or 'I'm sure you will like this'. To understand that children have a developing sense of one another, researchers must first rule out the possibility that the child is: (i) behaving egocentrically (e.g. indicating that another child wants something based not on their knowledge of the other's desire but on their own desire); or (ii) simply using past experience to infer something about another child.

Children's humour

Q: What do you call Postman Pat after he has retired from his job?

A: Pat!

Humour is a universal phenomenon and there have been many studies of humour in children and adults (for example: Freud 1938; Wolfenstein 1954; Grotjahn 1957; McGhee 1979). Various theoretical explanations have been offered to explain humour.

Psychoanalytic theory

Sigmund Freud (1938) argued that humour relates to sexual or aggressive impulses and that it allows a person to release tension in an acceptable fashion so that it is discharged without danger of punishment or loss of love. More particularly, Freud emphasised the role of humour as a defensive

> **VIEWPOINT**
> Why did the chicken cross the road?
> Because he wanted to get run over!
> 5-year-old
>
> What does a tiger do when it climbs up a tree?
> It falls down!
> 5-year-old
>
> What is black and white and pink and bounces on a trampoline?
> A sunburnt penguin on a trampoline!
> 6-year-old
>
> How many ears does Davey Crockett have?
> Three. A left ear, a right ear and a wild frontier!
> 9-year-old
>
> What do you get if you put five ducks into a peanut butter jar?
> Peanut butter and quackers!
> 9-year-old

process protecting the individual from anxiety. As Freud (1960, p. 233) notes, 'Humour can be regarded as the highest of these defensive processes'.

Social theory

Another interpretation is that humor helps enhance interpersonal relations, and group unity (Chapman 1983; Fine 1983).

Physiological theory

Physiologists emphasise the role of humour in the reduction or relaxation of the cardiovascular system, modulation of the neuroendocrine system and enhancement of the immune system (Berk 1994; Berk et al. 1989).

Cognitive developmental theory

Cognitive explanations emphasise the importance of the child's thinking processes and the cognitive challenge of humour. McGhee (1979) proposes that humour lies in being able to predict and see the incongruity of an event: that is, that humour is a product of a discrepancy between an expectation and some incongruent outcome or punch line. For example:

Parent (on phone): Doctor, doctor, come at once! Our baby swallowed a pen.

Doctor: I'll be right over – what are you doing in the meantime? *(The obvious expectation is that the parents are trying to save the baby's life.)*

Parent: Using a pencil. *(Incongruous punch-line of the joke.)*

OR

Q: How many psychologists does it take to change a light bulb?

A: Only one, but the light bulb has to want to change!

According to McGhee (1979), humour develops in four stages that are closely related to children's developing cognitive abilities.

Stage 1. Toddlers or young children become capable of imagining that some objects represent other objects (for example, a spoon becomes a telephone). Young children often find such representations humorous.

Stage 2. Children's increasing verbal fluency plays an important role, so that they think that misnaming an object either deliberately or accidentally is funny: for example, when an adult pretends that a hand is an animal. In the latter part of this stage, humour becomes more social, as the child uses it to initiate contact with adults or other children.

Stage 3. According to McGhee, at about 3 years of age the nature of children's humour changes, extending to conceptual incongruity: for example, hearing animals talk through the use of puppets. At this stage, children are increasingly using context to make judgments about what is and what is not funny.

Stage 4. As young children's language skills improve, they realise that things may not always be as they seem. That is, words and actions may have more than one meaning. At this stage, children are capable of understanding the multiple meanings of words and we witness the first enjoyment of riddles and 'knock-knock' jokes. Initially, though, children engage in **pre-riddles** – 'knock-knock' jokes without punch lines. They then create their own joke endings. The child has an appreciation of what a joke or riddle is, but does not truly have the language or cognitive ability to 'get' the joke and consequently will laugh at any response that follows the riddle. For example:

pre-riddles
a riddle without a punch-line.

> Why is an elephant so fat?
> Because she has too many babies.

That is, the answer makes no real sense.

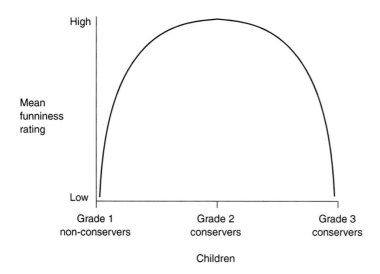

Figure 16.1 The inverted U function

Humour and cognition

The development of humour has been linked with Piaget's four developmental periods (see Table 16.1). McGhee (1976, p. 420) notes that 'more pleasure should be derived from achieving insight into a joke which is understood only after some optimal moderate amount of effort than one which is either very easily understood or extremely difficult'. Zigler et al. (1967) proposed a **cognitive congruency principle**, which incorporates the idea that cartoons that make fewer cognitive demands on children will elicit a lower humour rating than those that are in keeping with a child's cognitive level. Drawing on the work of Zigler et al., McGhee (1976) proposes an inverted U function linking humour and cognitive development (see Figure 16.1). In McGhee's research, children in the groups were read stories including jokes such as:

cognitive congruency principle
states that a child finds funniest those jokes that relate to the child's cognitive developmental level.

Mr Jones went into a restaurant and ordered a whole pizza for dinner. When the waiter asked if he wanted it cut into six or eight pieces Mr Jones said, 'Oh, you'd better make it six! I could never eat eight'.

The results of McGhee's research suggest that humour appreciation is greatest soon after subjects have acquired the concepts incorporated in a joke and smallest when subjects have not acquired the concepts or have mastered them several years previously.

Research by Varga (2000) challenges the idea of there being too close a link between Piagetian stages and humor development. Varga examined young children's use of 'hyperbole', described as 'expressions of exaggerated incongruity intended to achieve a special effect'(p. 142). The prediction is that the expression of hyperbole is associated with a cognitive level associated with the Piagetian stage of concrete operational thought. Varga's research indicated the even 4- to 5-year-old children have the cognitive skills for appreciating and expressing the double meaning in hyperbolic statements.

Trends and issues

Students' approaches to learning and study

In an Australian study of secondary and tertiary students, Biggs (1987) developed two measures, which he called the Learning Process Questionnaire (LPQ) and the Study Process Questionnaire (SPQ). The SPQ is suitable for use with tertiary students, while the LPQ is its secondary school equivalent. Biggs identified two distinct approaches to learning: surface and deep. Biggs also takes into account a student's motives: for example, whether the purpose of learning is to gain academic qualifications or to gain the highest mark. Students who adopt a **deep learning** approach are interested in the academic task, search for meaning, relate the task to themselves, integrate parts of the task into the whole and try to theorise about the task. Students who adopt a **surface learning** approach see the task as a means of achieving an end, such as gaining a good mark to be accepted for tertiary studies. Such students do not relate aspects of the task to a whole, worry about the time pressure involved, avoid personal meaning and rely on rote learning.

In considering the question of application, Biggs argues that the SPQ profiles indicate an individual's general orientation to learning. Identification of a student's orientation can help a teacher to decide how to approach individual students. For instance, a teaching strategy for 'deep' students is to play a facilitating role, allowing students to pursue their own interests (thereby generating their own connections).

---

deep learning
an approach to learning involving a search for meaning and relationship.

surface learning
a means-to-an-end approach to learning.

learning style
a person's preferred mode of taking in and storing information.

Approaches to learning/learning style

It is now better understood that individuals differ in the way they absorb, retain and process new information. The study of student **learning style** is now a well-established field of research in Australia, Great Britain, Sweden and the USA (Murray-Harvey 1994). Dunn et al. (1995) presented research findings indicating that individuals can identify their own learning style and benefit when taught through their preferred style.

Definition of learning style

There is considerable debate concerning the concept of learning style in the research literature. Keefe and Monk (1986, p. 16) define learning style as:

the composite characteristics of cognitive, affective, and physiological traits that serve as relatively stable indicators of how learners perceive, interact with and respond to, the environment. It is demonstrated in that pattern of behaviour and performance by which an individual approaches educational experiences. Its basis lies in the structure of neural organisation and personality which both molds and is molded by human development and the learning of experiences of home, school and society.

A definition with a somewhat different emphasis is presented by Lemlech (1984, p. 42):

[L]earning styles emanate from natural, inborn inclinations. The individual's learning style manifests itself through preferred senses and personality characteristics.

Different learning styles in children are well recognised by teachers.

These two definitions capture nicely the major source of disagreement in the study of learning styles; namely argument about the relative influence of personality and situational factors in approaches to learning (Biggs 1987). Broadly speaking though, learning style indicates that students learn through various means, with preferences for learning reflected in terms of **auditory**, **visual** and **kinaesthetic** modalities. As Shaughnessy (1998, p. 141) notes:

A person's learning style is the way he or she concentrates on, processes, internalises, and remembers new and difficult academic information or skills. Styles often vary with age, achievement level, culture, global versus analytic processing preference, and gender.

auditory learning style
learning through hearing.

visual learning style
learning through seeing.

kinaesthetic learning style
learning involving the whole body.

Children have different learning styles.

Measurement of learning style

A number of different measures of learning style have been developed to assess primary, secondary and tertiary students' learning style.

1 *The Learning Style Inventory.* Dunn et al. (1979) have developed a 104-item instrument that measures learning style in 22 areas and identifies students' learning styles in terms of (i) emotional, e.g. motivation to please parents and teachers; (ii) physical, e.g. food and drink intake; and (iii) sociological, e.g. learning alone or with peers; and (iv) environmental, e.g. noise and light level preferences for learning.

2 *The Kolb Learning Style Inventory* (Kolb 1976). This 12-item self-report measure is founded on Jung's concept of types or styles. Learning is viewed as a four stage cycle beginning with concrete experiences which provide the basis for observation and reflection upon experiences. The two essential dimensions are (i) **concrete experience** and **abstract conceptualisation**; and (ii) **active experimentation** and **reflective observation**. Loo (1999) reports problems with the factor analytic structure of the inventory but supports its use as a pedagogical tool.

3 *The Study Process Questionnaire (SPQ)* (Biggs 1987). As described by Murray-Harvey (1994, p. 376), the SPQ conceives student learning '. . . as a composite of motives and strategy dimensions termed surface, deep, achieving and deep achieving approaches, which categorise important differences in the way in which students approach their learning'. Each approach to learning is defined by a question related to the student's motivation for learning and the strategy that the student employs to achieve it (Biggs 1992; 1995). As such, the SPQ measures six dimensions of student learning: surface motive (SM), surface strategy (ST), deep

concrete experiencing learning style
as defined by Kolb, learning through actual experience.

reflective observational learning style
as defined by Kolb, learning that involves thinking about something that has been experienced.

motive (DM), deep strategy (DS), achieving motive (AM) and achieving strategy (AS). Research supports the factorial structure of the SPQ (Sachs & Gao 2000).

Apart from learning style, researchers have also given consideration to the different approaches that students adopt to learning and study (see Trends and issues: Students' approaches to learning and study, p. 336).

Application of learning style

An emerging body of research links the appropriate assessment and use of learning style to improvement in students' academic performance. According to Hodges (1983, p. 17), 'learning styles research has revealed that students learn faster and with less effort when they are taught through their individual learning styles'. For example, in a meta-analysis of the Dunn and Dunn model it was found that students whose characteristics were accommodated by teaching responsive to their learning styles could be expected to archive 75 per cent of a standard deviation higher than those whose styles were not accommodated (Dunn et al. 1995). Dunn et al. (1989, p. 56) note:

> When permitted to learn difficult academic information or skills through their identified preferences, children tend to achieve statistically higher test and attitude scores than when instruction is dissonant with their preferences.

Trends and issues

Homework and developmentally appropriate practice

Anyone who has stood outside a school at dismissal time would be aware of the school students leaving for home with school bags crammed full of books and materials, much of which is to be used to complete homework activities. Generally, the idea is that homework helps consolidate school learning, and there is some evidence to support this idea. Nonetheless, as Corno (1996) indicates, homework can be a source of frustration for both students and parents.

From an early age children are aware that they have certain tasks to complete at home relating to school work. Warton (2000) has identified a developmental progression in children's understanding of their homework responsibility ranging from year 2

children remembering that they should do their homework without being reminded.

Hoover-Dempsey and Sandler (1995) identified common themes regarding parental ideas and practices about school homework; including, (i) the unique characteristics of children; (ii) the nature and extent of parental involvement; (iii) expectations about independent work.

Hoover-Dempsey and Sandler (1995) and Balli (1998) all report that the benefits of parental involvement are 'tempered by the extent to which parental involvement strategies are developmentally appropriate and by the match between parental involvement strategies and teacher expectations' (Balli 1998, p. 145). For example, Balli (1998) found that students sometimes reported that children found problems and inconsistencies between parent ideas about homework assignments and teacher understanding.

Learning strategies of Aboriginal children

It is a well-documented fact that Australian Aboriginal children in the mainstream school system are seriously disadvantaged. Many Aborigines leave school barely literate and numerate (Bourke & Parkin 1977; Coker 1981; Boulton-Lewis et al. 1988; Hughs & More 1997).

Aborigines as a group consistently score much lower in English, reading, writing and arithmetic tests than any other identifiable group in Australia. They also leave school at an earlier age and at a lower achievement level than the national average (Coker 1981, p. 3).

A range of cultural, socioeconomic and geographic factors could account for this finding, including poverty, poor housing, lack of opportunity for self-determination and Aboriginal identity, and low self-esteem. Geographic factors are also implicated including the isolation of many Aboriginal settlements, which is in turn related to poor resourcing and high teacher turnover.

Research has contributed important insight into possible differences between Aboriginal and non-Aboriginal people that may have implications for the application of learning style theory to Aboriginal education. Aborigines have superior visual memory to non-Aboriginal people (Kearins 1976). Davidson (1979) discovered that Aborigines prefer to work with the 'whole' concept, whereby all relevant parts can be considered at one time. Dasen's (1974) research suggests that Aborigines employ a concrete, reality-based mode of reasoning. On the other hand, in mainstream Australian schools, the emphasis of teaching strategies is on verbal memory, a sequential mode of processing information from parts to the whole and rational hypothetical reasoning (Knapp 1981). Buckley (1996) and Harris (1992) have described the major learning processes of Aboriginal people as:

- observation and imitation;
- personal trial and error;
- real life participation;
- learning context-specific skills rather than general principles;
- person oriented rather than information oriented learning.

However, a cautionary note has been sounded by Knapp (1981) and Eckermann (1988), who have warned against the temptation to infer from such research results too much too easily regarding Aboriginal learning style. Observations regarding Aboriginal learning style are frequently based on a 'fairly simplistic analysis of traditional Aboriginal values' (Eckermann 1988, p. 8). For example, it has been argued that a traditional hunting-gathering lifestyle has led to an emphasis on acute visual-perceptual abilities in locating events in space, a focus on the present and events in real-life context. At the same time, according to this argument, the nomadic lifestyle with few real possessions and no need of a cash economy has not necessitated the development of literacy and numeracy skills. Hughs and More (1997) note, 'We conclude that while there is not evidence for a single Aboriginal learning style, there are some recurrent learning styles which are more likely among Aboriginal students'(p. 18). They further note that these recurrent styles warrant attention by teachers in attending to individual differences between students.

A question raised by research findings concerns the extent to which such features are inherent in regarding Aboriginal learning style . Taking account of the rather simplistic analysis of Aboriginal lifestyle, Boulton-Lewis et al. (1988, p. 32) concluded from their research:

that the differences in Aboriginal cognitive strategies that have been identified in other research could be learned differences dependent on different learning contexts rather than on inherent cognitive differences.

McInerney et al. (1998), in a comparative study of Aboriginal, Anglo and immigrant Australian year 7 to 11 year students' motivational beliefs, discovered a remarkable similarity in learning goal orientations. They distinguished between mastery goal orientations reflected in students' metacognitive knowledge, strategy usage and internal control beliefs. Where small differences did exist, Aboriginal students were more influenced by social goals.

Trends and issues

Effective teaching

The question of what constitutes effective teaching is one that has interested teachers, parents and school administrators for many years. In Australia the issue is both political and educational, given current economic constraints and the related debate over school staffing.

One of the most comprehensive overseas investigations into the nature of effective teaching was conducted by Walberg (1984). In an analysis of 3000 studies relating to the topic, Walberg identified a number of key techniques an effective teacher might employ.

1 *Positive reinforcement.* The most important indicator of effective teaching was the careful and judicious use of Skinnerian reinforcement techniques.
2 *Feedback.* By providing students with feedback about their performance, the teacher can help shape their learning in significant ways. Feedback, either written or verbal, is an important part of the process of effective teaching.
3 *Cooperative learning.* The use of small group techniques in the classroom along with a positive attitude to cooperative learning facilitates the learning process.
4 *Classroom atmosphere.* Classroom cohesiveness, student satisfaction and student goal directiveness facilitate learning.
5 *Questioning.* The teacher's skillful use of questioning, particularly higher order questioning that requires something more from the student than simple recall, is associated with effective teaching.

The Australian researcher Yates (1988, p. 4) describes five conditions that 'contribute directly to successful classroom teaching'.

1 *An opportunity to learn.* Sufficient time should be given to the curriculum. Opportunity to learn also refers to the teacher's ability to cover or complete the set curriculum.
2 *An academic focus.* Learning should be task-oriented and teacher- (not student-) directed. Teachers should communicate their high expectations regarding students' learning capabilities.
3 *Classroom management practices.* Teachers should have a 'proactive' managerial style and be able to anticipate possible classroom problems before they arise. A 'well-managed' classroom where students are on task, rather than waiting for the teacher's attention or misbehaving, promotes learning.
4 *Active teaching principles.* Specific instructional skills that include an active task orientation, good questioning techniques, clear modelling of required behaviour, clear instruction and sound feedback, promote academic learning.
5 *'Success' experience* for the students with regard to their academic work. 'Successful practice thus consolidates the learning process' (Yates 1988, p. 6).

In framing their argument, Yates and Yates (1990, p. 226) comment that 'knowledge transmission is essentially a social process'. As part of this social process, children learn through observation and imitation, and so an important role of the teacher is to establish optimal conditions in the classroom promoting such learning.

According to Yates (1988), effective teachers possess two qualitatively different sets of skills: (i) management skills, which help to maintain an orderly classroom environment; and (ii) instructional skills, which help to orient and motivate students. The impact of these two components on student achievement is mediated by students' response to to instruction, which includes factors such as paying attention, concentrating on the task and contributing time to the learning process. Figure 16.2 shows the elements of successful teaching as conceptualised by Yates and Yates (1990).

Westwood (1996), in a review of the concept of effective teaching, emphasised that effective teaching also embraces effective relationship skills with students.

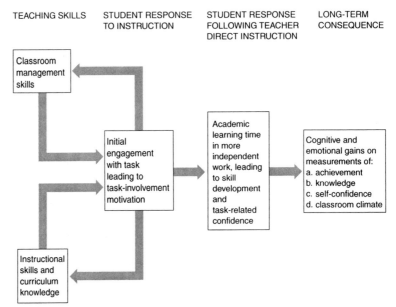

Figure 16.2 The sequence of effects in successful teaching

Source: Yates and Yates 1990

Effective teaching establishes optimal conditions in the classroom to promote learning.

Moral development

A party for young children provides a rich field for the astute child observer to consider the issue of **moral development**. Typical scenes include fights between or among children over a toy or drink, the sharing of enjoyment as the party candles are blown out, children playing together cooperatively in the sandpit and adults admonishing children 'not to fight' or to 'play together nicely'. Adults are sometimes confused as to why it apparently takes children so long to understand the ideas of right and wrong.

The *Macquarie Dictionary* defines morality as 'conformity to the rules of right conduct; moral or virtuous conduct . . . a doctrine or system of morals; ethics; duties . . .'. In William Shakespeare's play *Measure for Measure*, a character observes, 'Some rise by sin and some by virtue fall.' The point being made by Shakespeare is that it is not enough to have a sense of right and wrong; we must also know how to act according to this understanding (Schumacher 1977, p. 151).

The story of Louis Slotin, as told by the scientist-philosopher Jacob Bronowski (1960), drives home the point made so many centuries ago by Shakespeare. Slotin was a nuclear physicist working on the atomic bomb project at the Los Alamos National Laboratory in New Mexico, USA, in 1946. At one crucial point in an experiment involving the radioactive substance, plutonium, Slotin badly misjudged something and a chain reaction involving plutonium was initiated. To stop the reaction, Slotin parted the plutonium pieces with his bare hands. This was virtually an act of suicide for it exposed him to a very large dose of radiation. He then had his seven co-workers mark their exact positions in the room so that measurements could be made of their degree of exposure to radioactivity. Slotin subsequently died from the radiation exposure but his companions recovered. Slotin's courageous act highlights the features of morality as defined earlier, namely quality of action in regard to what is right and wrong and consideration of others' welfare.

The question facing developmental psychologists is how a child comes to develop a sense of right and wrong and learns to act on this understanding. In the following section, consideration is given to various theoretical explanations for moral development along with a critique of contemporary developmental theory.

Psychoanalytic theory of morality

According to Freud (1955), that part of the personality most directly concerned with morality is the superego. Freud argues that we inherit a rudimentary form of conscience as part of the **superego** present in outline at birth. Freud proposes that as part of our evolutionary history, humankind was left with a predisposition for the development of conscience, which was then fleshed out in terms of the development of the superego.

> **moral development**
> the development of the values, attitudes and beliefs that help people distinguish right from wrong.

> **superego**
> in Freudian theory, that part of the personality incorporating the internalised values held by the individual and corresponding to the internalised injunctions of the parent.

The superego is fully developed through the resolution of the Oedipus complex (see chapter 3). The young child of 5 to 6 years of age internalises or 'introjects' a father image (representative of both parents) that forms a division with the ego. In identifying with the external authority of the parents the child accepts parental rules and prohibitions. The superego takes on the power to exact unquestioning obedience and to punish the self, and this punishment is experienced as guilt:

> A great change takes place only when the authority is internalised through the establishment of a super-ego. The phenomenon of conscience then reaches a higher stage. Actually, it is not until now that we should speak of conscience or a sense of guilt (Freud 1961, p. 72).

In his book *Civilisation and its Discontents*, first published in 1930, Freud asks what means a civilisation employs to inhibit aggressiveness and how a person comes to have a sense of guilt. He proposes that there are two stages in developing a 'bad conscience'. In the first stage the individual's sense of guilt arises from the fear of losing love.

> Such people habitually allow themselves to do any bad thing which promises them enjoyment, so long as they are sure that the authority will not know anything about it or cannot blame them for it. They are afraid only of being found out (Freud 1961, p. 72).

In the second stage the ego, another major aspect of an individual's personality, will often struggle on behalf of the third component of personality (id) against the exacting demands of the superego. If the ego should succeed in disobeying the superego, it will experience the condemnation of the superego in the form of guilt. According to Freud (1961), two origins of a sense of guilt are (i) fear of authority; and (ii) fear of the superego. The guilt that arises out of a fear of authority demands the renunciation of instinctual satisfactions, while the second source of guilt demands both renunciation and punishment for the forbidden wishes.

Over time, Freud's views regarding the nature of children's moral development have been heavily criticised. Such criticisms include the idea that introjection cannot completely account for mature moral judgments such as those made by the nuclear scientist, Louis Slotin.

Social learning model of moral development

According to this theory, all behaviour, including moral behaviour, is learned (Bandura & Walters 1963; Bandura 1977). Humans, especially children, are constantly observing the behaviour of others and such observation generates possibilities for later organised behaviour. Reinforcement is a key element in the development of moral behaviour and is mediated in three ways:

1   in terms of an individual's expectancy that reinforcement for a particular behaviour will occur;
2   by the personal values an individual holds;

3   by inner control, which guides a person's behaviour, often in the absence of reinforcement.

According to social learning theory, moral development in children occurs mainly through the parents' physical intervention. For example, to stop one child hitting another the parents may physically intervene. As the child develops, social sanctions in the form of rewards or punishments replace physical intervention. Finally, external sanctions such as rewards and punishment are replaced by greater symbolic inner control whereby individuals monitor their own behaviour.

'Character education'

An influential line of thinking related to understanding moral development is that of 'character education'. Kilpatrick (1992, p. 15) described this as 'the idea that there are traits of character children ought to know, that they learn these by example, and that once they know them, they need to practice them until they become second nature'. A key element in character education is the use of traditional stories, myths, poems and other narratives to provide powerful models in moral development. Research by Narvaez et al. (1999) in research with children from grades 3 and 5 identified developmental differences in moral theme understanding. They note that for adults who educate for character they '. . . should be aware of children's differential interpretations of stories that seem perfectly clear to adults' (p. 483). They go on to note that their findings have serious implications for curriculum development because '[a] curriculum that works with one age may not work for another' (p. 483).

Cognitive–developmental theory and moral development

Piaget's pioneering work on moral development is described in his book *The Moral Judgement of the Child* (1965). Piaget developed a procedure in which he would tell children a story involving some moral dilemma and then ask them what the characters in the story should do. Two of the stories he told were as follows (Piaget 1965, p. 122):

> A little boy who is called John is in his room. He is called to dinner. He goes into the dining room. But behind the door there was a chair and on the chair there was a tray with fifteen cups on it. John couldn't have known that there was all this behind the door. He goes in the door, knocks against the tray, bang go the fifteen cups and they all get broken.

> Once there was a little boy whose name was Henry. One day when his mother was out he tried to get some jam from the cupboard. He climbed up onto a chair and stretched out his arm. But the jam was too high up and he couldn't reach it and have any. But while he was trying to get it he knocked over a cup. The cup fell down and broke.

Questions that could then be put to children regarding these two stories include:

- Which of the two children is the naughtiest and why?
- Are the two children equally guilty?

The answers a child gives to questions such as these provide the basis for further questioning about their moral reasoning. Analysis of children's responses to such stories led Piaget to conclude that there are three stages in the development of respect for rules and a sense of justice.

Stage 1: Heteronomous morality, moral realism or morality of constraint

According to Piaget (1932), moral growth is part of the total development of the child and as such is related to mental growth. Stage 1 of moral reasoning is characteristic of young children up to 7 or 8 years of age. Rules, obligations and commands are external and sacred because they are laid down by adults.

A key concept in the child's moral reasoning during stage 1 is that of immanent justice. According to this concept, the proper punishment for any wrongdoing is inherent in the act of wrongdoing and punishment must follow as surely as night follows the day. Punishment for any wrongdoing is inevitable and retributive. Frequently a child's judgment of the degree of punishment required for an act of wrongdoing exceeds that of an adult. According to immanent justice, any behaviour that shows obedience to adults and their rules is good, and any act not conforming to the rules is bad. The letter of the law applies. Piaget defines moral realism as:

> the tendency to regard duty and the value attaching to it as self subsistent and independent of the mind, as imposing itself regardless of the circumstances in which the individual finds himself (Piaget 1932, p. 111).

immanent justice
the notion that punishment for wrongdoing is inevitable, an inherent part of the wrongdoing.

The concept of **immanent justice** and being punished for disobeying is illustrated in A. A. Milnes's *Winnie the Pooh*, when Pooh Bear falls into a gorse bush while trying to steal honey and he muses on his fate:

> 'It all comes, I suppose,' he decided as he said goodbye to the last branch, spun round through time and flew gracefully into a gorse bush, 'it all comes of liking honey so much. Oh, help!'

Piaget proposed two basic explanations of children's moral reasoning during stage 1.

**egocentrism
(central)**
the inability to distinguish between one's own point of view and that of another person.

1   *Cognitive structure.* The significant element here is the **egocentrism** of the child's thinking, such that the child assumes that everyone's view of events is the same as his or hers. Since the child has difficulty comprehending another's viewpoint it is also difficult for the child to appreciate the needs and circumstances of other people upon which moral judgments must be made.

A second feature associated with cognitive structure is the **realism** of the child's thinking. That is, the child may reify (or make real) wishes, thoughts and feelings and perceive them as 'thing-like' entities. Thus, a young child may wish to hurt his friend by pushing him over and when subsequently he sees his friend fall over he may believe he was responsible for the action. That is, he cannot distinguish between an impulse and his actually committing the deed.

2 *Experience*. Adult control and constraint impinge heavily on the young child's moral reasoning. This inequity in power will heavily influence a child who has, as yet, an incomplete view of herself or himself as a person and what she or he wants. The child will therefore tend to yield to adults' suggestions and wishes without really knowing why.

realism
according to Piaget, the confusion by the pre-operational child of external reality with the child's own thought processes and subjective understanding; the child's belief that wishes, thoughts and feelings are 'alive'.

Stage 2: The development of the justice concept

At about 7 to 8 years of age the child's concept of morality changes, according to Piaget. Now the child gains pleasure from engaging in rule-governed play where rules are recognised as essential for regulating the game as a social activity. This contrasts with the first years of life where children play with little regard for rules. In Lewis Carroll's *Alice in Wonderland*, Alice reflects on this aspect of play while watching the Queen's game of croquet:

> 'I don't think they play at all fairly,' Alice began in a rather complaining tone, 'and they all quarrel so dreadfully and one can't hear oneself speak and they don't seem to have any rules in particular: at least if there are nobody attends to them and you've no idea how confusing it is all the things being alive' (Carroll 1982, p. 112).

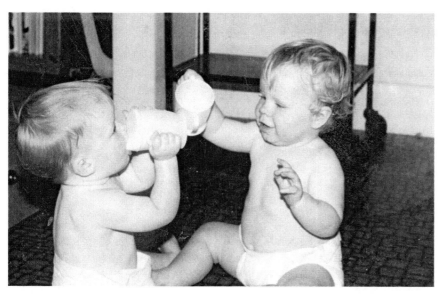

Learning to share and cooperate is part of moral development.

In fact, it is through children's interaction with peers that they learn something about the give and take of relationships and of the nature of equality. Beliefs in immanent justice and evaluating an act in terms of objective consequences give way to ideas of reciprocal punishment. Punishment must be equivalent to the misdeed: if a child hits another then the victim has the right to hit the other back just as hard.

Stage 3: The stage of autonomous morality or moral relativism

Groundwork for this stage has been laid in the preceding stages and evidence that the child has adopted an autonomous conception of morality emerges at about 12 to 13 years of age. The child now gives heavy consideration to motives, intentions and individual circumstances when making moral judgments. As Piaget (1932, p. 316) expresses it, 'One does not apply the same law to all, but takes into account the personal circumstances of each'.

Evaluating Piaget's theory of moral development

Support for Piaget's views of children's moral development is at best mixed. There is some support for Piaget's concept of developmental changes in moral reasoning and for the links between moral judgments and cognition.

Developmental changes. There is a body of evidence supporting the developmental trend for heteronomous to autonomous conceptions of justice, at least in Western cultures (Stuart 1967; Cowan et al. 1969).

Moral judgments and cognition. There is some research evidence to support the view that a child's development of the concept of justice reflects progress in cognitive capacities (Cudrin unpub.; Caring unpub.). Piaget has provided us with a stage-based approach to moral development that accounts for the hierarchical and directional nature of moral development.

Kohlberg's theory of moral development

One theorist who has extended Piaget's developmental stage sequence is Lawrence Kohlberg. Kohlberg (1966) believed that moral judgment develops through a series of three levels and six stages (see Table 16.2). The development of his theory was based on interviews with boys aged 10 to 16 years. He followed the Piagetian tradition of asking children to judge the morality of conduct in stories such as the following:

> Radium was needed to treat an ill wife. The husband had not the money to purchase this nor could he borrow the money. As his wife was dying he asked the druggist to sell him the radium cheap or let him pay later. The druggist refused. So the man broke into the shop and stole the radium. Should he have done this?

Responses to stories such as these were used by Kohlberg to differentiate three levels of moral development. He asked children questions that tapped into their feelings regarding whether or not the central figure (hero) in the story should act according to the law or according to his own or others' needs. Following a child's response, a series of probes or questions were asked to reveal the thinking underlying the child's first replies.

In considering responses, Kohlberg was not interested in statements about whether an action was right or wrong but the reasons why a child thought an action was right or wrong. For example, one person might say stealing is wrong because the thief could get caught, while another might say it is wrong because it undermines the moral fabric of society. These two different reasons for the same answer indicate very different moral reasoning.

The three-level scheme developed by Kohlberg is more complex than that of Piaget. It deals with changes in moral reasoning across the life-span. As presented by Kohlberg, only a small proportion of mature adults will attain the highest levels of moral reasoning.

As described by Gilligan (1982, p. 27), Kohlberg's six stages:

> trace a three-level progression from an egocentric understanding of fairness based on an individual's need (stages one and two), to a conception of fairness anchored in the shared conventions of societal agreements (stages three and four), and finally to a principled understanding of fairness that rests on the free-standing logic of equity and reciprocity (stages five and six).

Level 1: Preconventional level – Egocentric orientation

In the first two stages, there is an egocentric orientation to morality: the child responds to right and wrong in terms of the physical consequences of an act or in terms of the brute physical power of those who determine the rules.

Stage 1: Punishment and obedience orientation. At this stage justice is determined by power, status and possessions, and the physical consequences of an action determine its rightness or wrongness. Thus, the child will work to avoid punishment and defer to power.

Stage 2: Instrumental relativist orientation. The orientation of the child to justice may be captured by the attitude 'You scratch my back and I'll scratch yours'. Justice is determined in a very pragmatic way and right action consists largely of having one's needs met.

Level 2: Conventional level – social orientation

At this level the child's orientation to justice is in terms of loyalty to the family or peer group. Loyalty also encompasses conformity to expectations.

Stage 3: Interpersonal concordance. During this 'good boy–nice girl' stage, good behaviour conforms to the idea of the golden rule or that which pleases others or is approved by them.

Interaction amongst peers is crucial for moral development.

Stage 4: Law-and-order orientation. The individual orients strongly to authority, the laws of the land and the maintenance of social order. The more personal concerns of stage 3 are replaced by a concern for the maintenance of society.

Level 3: Post-conventional level – principles orientation

Essential to moral reasoning at this stage is an understanding not only of the law but of its philosophical basis. There is a clear effort to define moral values and principles that can be applied regardless of the authority of individuals or the needs of society.

Stage 5: The social contract orientation. Right action is generally determined in terms of general individual rights that have been critically examined and agreed upon by the whole of society. There is an emphasis upon the legal obligations but with the flexibility to change the law should the situation demand it.

Stage 6: Universal ethical principled orientation. The issue of right and wrong is determined by a decision of conscience reliant on self-chosen ethical principles that relate to some universal consistent trait.

Qualities of stage development in Kohlberg's theory

As described by Duska and Whelan (1975), there are four qualities of stage development inherent in Kohlberg's theory. These qualities have important implications for the development of moral reasoning in individuals.

Invariance in stage development. Duska and Whelan (1975) note that the stages in Kohlberg's theory occur in terms of a predetermined sequence. Moral

Table 16.2 The key features of Kohlberg's theory of moral development

Stage	Focus of Attention	Source of Motivation
LEVEL 1		
Stage 1	The physical consequences of the act	Justice is determined by power and the physical consequences of an act determine its rightness or wrongness.
Stage 2	Meeting one's own needs	Justice is determined by what 'you can do for me'– 'You scratch my back and I'll scratch yours'.
LEVEL 2		
Stage 3	Peer group evaluation	The idea of justice relates to what the individual's family or peer group will think and conforming to their expectations.
Stage 4	Social group norms	A law-and-order orientation guides a person's sense of justice. The emphasis is on maintaining social order.
LEVEL 3		
Stage 5	What society has sanctioned	Justice is determined by 'right' action with regard to the rights of the individual as agreed upon by society.
Stage 6	Higher ethical order/ conscience	Higher ethical principles guide a person's ideas regarding justice.

development, then, moves in an orderly and predetermined fashion, shaped by the interacting forces of maturation and experience.

Level of comprehension. According to Duska and Whelan, a person at stage 2 of moral reasoning who identifies good and bad in terms of having his or her own needs met cannot comprehend reasoning at stage 4 with its commitment to duties to society. That is, people cannot comprehend moral reasoning at a point more than one stage beyond their own.

Movement to higher stages of moral reasoning. Reasoning at one stage beyond their own level is appealing to people because they can appreciate that such reasoning solves the sort of problems and moral questions they face.

The role of disequilibrium in the movement through the stages. Movement through to higher stages of moral reasoning is effected when 'a person's cognitive outlook is not adequate to cope with a given moral dilemma' (Duska & Whelan 1975, p. 49). That is, a person is motivated to look for more and more adequate ways of resolving moral issues.

Criticism of Kohlberg's theory

Two of the more prevalent criticisms of Kohlberg's theory of moral development concern the notion of stages and the universality of the stages.

Foremost among the criticisms of his theory is the concept of stages that underpins his theory. One of the dangers inherent in stage theories (to which Kohlberg's theory is no exception) is that of creating artificial separations while overlooking variations within stages and similarities between stages

(Meadows 1986). Meadows has also argued that it is not clear just what they are stages of, given that moral judgments require a complex response that includes feeling as well as cognition.

Kohlberg argues that his stages are universal, claiming that data gathered in Mexico, Taiwan, Great Britain, Turkey and the USA support his views. In a review of research, Simpson (1974) has challenged this claim, citing limitations in Kohlberg's research, such as culturally biased data-gathering procedures. More recent research has supported Simpson's earlier assessments (Harkees et al. 1981).

Carol Gilligan's model of moral development

The writings of Carol Gilligan have drawn our attention to further possible limitations in Kohlberg's theory.

In testing Kohlberg's theory, one recurring feature is the apparent inability of the majority of females to move beyond level 2 (conventional level: stage 3 – interpersonal concordance). That is, females appear to be largely oriented to judging moral standards in terms of living up to what is expected of them, showing concern for others and respect. According to Kohlberg (1971), women's moral development is limited by their inability to see beyond 'relationships', which generally 'bound' their moral experience.

Carol Gilligan (1982) argues that instead of being arrested at a certain stage, female moral development is simply but importantly different from male moral development. In the broadest sense, she notes that much contemporary psychology has adopted the male life as a norm.

According to Gilligan, the moral development of females differs from that of males.

The penchant of developmental theorists to project a masculine image and one that appears frightening to women, goes back at least to Freud . . . who built his theory of psychosexual development around the experiences of the male child that culminate in the Oedipus complex (Gilligan 1982, p. 6).

Gilligan agrees with Kohlberg that the moral development of men and women occurs in conjunction with their social interaction. However, according to Gilligan, the nature of the interaction between men and women differs and, as such, different moral stages evolve for each sex. She considers moral development in relation to women's lack of power in Western patriarchal society. Gilligan (1982, pp. 62–3) argues that because of the imbalance of power in a male-dominated society, females develop a sense of responsibility based on the universal principle of caring.

The experiences of inequality and interconnection inherent in the relation of parent and child, then give rise to the 'ethics of justice and care, the ideals of human relationship'.

According to Gilligan (1982), in moral development the individual's basis for decision-making moves from the needs of the individual to the needs of society and finally to universal principles (see Table 16.3).

Gilligan (1977) has noted that contemporary research on the moral judgment of women differs from the research of Freud, Piaget and Kohlberg and provides a different insight into the nature of moral development. In this conception, the moral problem is seen to arise from conflicting responsibilities rather than from competing rights. For its resolution it requires a mode of thinking that is contextual and inductive rather than formal and abstract.

Gilligan's work (Gilligan 1977, 1982; Gilligan et al. 1988) has challenged psychologists to reconsider the very nature of moral development as proposed by early theorists. Her writings and thought represent a significant contribution to the field.

Table 16.3 Gilligan's model of moral development

Perspective	Orientation
1. The initial concern of the individual is with survival where being moral is being submissive to society. The transition to the next stage is made by a reinterpretation of selfishness/responsibility such that the individual takes on a more responsible perspective	EGOCENTRIC
2. The focus is on goodness, where being moral is first and foremost not hurting others. The transition to the next stage occurs when the individual takes into account themselves as well as others	SOCIETAL
3. The injunction against hurting others is the key component. The conception of *caring* for others is the most adequate guide to solving moral dilemmas	UNIVERSAL PRINCIPLE

Children's understanding of death

In helping children understand death, the Australian author William Nelson (1985, p. 3) writes: 'Parents are well advised to view the loss of a loved one as a family crisis: an event that disrupts the family's emotional life and thereby has significance for all members of the family'. Today's children increasingly are exposed to the experience of death in the media, their homes and even in schools. Corr (1998, p. 443) argued that, 'All too often the needs of children and adolescents who encounter issues related to death are not properly acknowledged or appreciated by adults'. Understanding how children and adolescents view death is increasingly being applied to postvention or critical incident de-briefing in schools relating to incidents such as suicide, homicide or accidental death/injury (Leenaars & Wenckstern 1998).

VIEWPOINT
Do you know what it means to say that something is 'alive' or 'living'?
'When it is moving (but some things are alive and don't move) – Oh! When it grows'
Jac, 7 years

'To breathe'
Katie, 8 years

'Being alive, breathing, sharing with others'
Sarah, 11 years

Theoretical approaches

As Ellis and Stump (2000, p. 65) note, 'It is the consensus of many researchers who have studied children's concepts of death that beliefs about death proceed through stages as the child develops cognitively'. The work of Piaget (1967) regarding children's conceptions of life is central to this view.

The research of Nagy (1948), Melear (1973), Lonetto (1980), Florian (1985), and Hoffman and Strauss (1985) has also helped us to understand children's conceptions of death from a cognitive–developmental perspective. The concepts central to an understanding of death are: of (i) irreversibility (once a living thing dies, its physical body cannot regenerate); (ii) non-functionality (once a living thing dies its biological functioning ceases); and (iii) universality (the understanding that all living things die) (Speece & Brent (1987).

Stages in children's understanding of death

Young children (5 years and less). Such children have a limited under-standing of death often believing that death is reversible using inactivity and immobility as criteria for death. In an Australian study, Wainwright (unpub.) found that young Sydney children believed that a doctor or a hospital could bring a person back to life after the person had died.

Primary-school-aged children. According to Nagy (1948), during middle to late childhood, children develop a more realistic concept of death and gradually come to terms with their own mortality. During this period children come to see death in terms of an ending of bodily functions: that there is no pulse or respiration (Anthony 1971). However, children in this age group are still egocentric enough in their thinking to believe that while death may happen to older people it will not happen to them (Phillips 1986). So concepts of irreversibility and permanence are present.

Adolescents. An increasing ability to think in more abstract terms enables pre-adolescents and adolescents to think of death in more adult terms including universality – all living things die. There is also a search for a religious and philosophical understanding of death.

An alternative framework

Kastenbaum (1981), Rochlin (1967) and McIntyre et al. (1972) proposed a second approach to understanding children's conceptions of death. This approach has certainly not received as much attention as the cognitive–devel-opmental view. It emphasises the study of children's conceptions of death within an ecological context. That is, children's views of death should be understood in the particular social and cultural context in which the child is raised. For example, in Australian Aboriginal cultures there is an important spiritual component to death (Williams 1982). Aboriginal people understand physical reasons for ill-health but also believe spiritual agents play an important role in sickness and death, as shown in the following extract from the book *The Kaurna People* (Education Department of South Australia 1989, p. 104):

> The sun, 'teendo', is said to be a female having several sisters, all of whom shed a malevolent influence over mankind. One of the evils inflicted by this malignancy begins as a very painful cough, which is most likely the result of pulmonary disease, and consequently often fatal.

> When very ill, the sick person expectorates into the palm of his hand and offers the sputa to the sun. If she is induced to be propitiated, the patient is soon relieved, if the reverse, she says, 'Noornte oornte, wirrilla pallone ningko', 'Go away, quickly dead you'.

Understanding an Aboriginal child's conception of death according to this ecological model would necessitate an appreciation of the cultural norms shaping Aboriginal people's understanding of death.

Limitations to research

While our understanding of children's conception of death has been enhanced by research, there is now an increased awareness of the limitations of contemporary methodologies. Berzonsky (1987) comments:

> [L]inguistic ability may account for at least some of the difficulty preschool subjects have when asked to judge whether or not an object is 'alive'. The word 'alive' may not be mapped on to the child's concept of life.

Wenestam (1984) also observes that children's verbal responses to interview questions may not accurately reflect their understanding of death. The task therefore remains to further develop our understanding of the way children view death.

The family life-cycle: 16

Counselling children in families

Verna brought her son Todd (5 years old) for counselling, citing Todd's preoccupation with death as the primary concern. Todd had recently taken to constantly asking his mother questions about what it was like to die and whether everyone went to heaven. He would often ask these questions after watching TV programs such as 'McGuyver'. In the course of counselling it also emerged that Todd's mother was seriously worried about the possibility of losing of her son. Her concern had been activated by a friend's recent loss of her 5-year-old daughter in a car accident. As a single mother, Verna felt particularly vulnerable and had many questions regarding her own life without Todd. As the mother's own concerns were addressed, her child's fear of death declined.

What constitutes problem behaviour?
As is indicated by the preceding case study, just because a child is referred for counselling it does not mean that there is anything wrong with the child (Slee 1987). In addition, it may be that factors other than problem behaviour may bring a child to the attention of professionals, such as marital distress or lack of parental knowledge about child-rearing. In considering the question of what is a problem child, a number of different factors must be considered.

Burbank, cited in Morrison, Macdonald & LeBlanc (2000), once said, '[I]f we paid no more attention to plants than we have to our children we would now be living in a jungle of weeds'. This statement highlights the need for research to better understand the nature of behaviour problems experienced by some children. One thing that will be encountered by clinical psychologists treating a child referred for counselling is a diversity of opinion regarding the cause of the child's problem and the preferred mode of treatment. For instance, some psychologists might believe that the child's misbehaviour arises out of patterns of learning that bring the child into conflict with peers and adults. Other psychologists would look to the child's developmental history for answers regarding maladaptive behaviour. Still others would consider the child's broader family and social background in seeking answers. However, among this diversity of opinion which draws on various behavioural and developmental theories, there is some consensus regarding a number of features of the referred child's behaviour (Herbert 1975):

1 *Duration*. How long has the behaviour problem persisted?
2 *Frequency, intensity or number*. There is cause for concern when the behavioural problem occurs often, is severe or when there are a number of problems.
3 *Focus of concern*. Herbert suggests that when the nature of the child's behaviour problem is such that it monopolises the energy and resources of the family, then it is a source of concern.

Another perspective on the task of defining behaviour problems has been suggested by Werner (1982). He advocates defining behaviour problems in terms of deviation from normal development. He has identified two criteria. Fixation refers to behaviour that persists beyond the age when such behaviour would be considered developmentally appropriate. For example, a 7-year-old who wets the bed would be considered to have a behaviour problem, given that most children have control over night-time urination by 4 to 5 years of age. Regression refers to cases where a child who has achieved mastery of a level of development (such as toileting) reverts to behaviour characteristic of an earlier age.

Treating the child – treating the family!
The child's behaviour, such as bed-wetting, tantrums, or refusal to go to school, is presented by the parents as a problem. One approach is to treat the child. Another approach, using a more systems-oriented perspective, is to view the child as one part, and only one, of a larger system – the family. This orientation in itself shifts the focus of treatment from the child to the whole family.

One developing method of treatment falls within the ambit of family systems theory. Coppersmith (1982) observes that when a family seeks treatment for a child or adolescent they usually ascribe 'blame' to the individual child or adolescent and want the individual 'fixed' as soon as possible.

Within a family counselling perspective most counsellors firmly believe that children's difficulties are not necessarily caused by their families (Combrinck-Graham 1990). Most, however, regard the family as the primary healing environment and they respect the special energy of children's contributions to change in the whole family. As such, counsellors emphasise working with the whole family and not just the identified or referred child. They adopt the view that children's problems are a functional part of the family system. Wachtel (1990) has noted that counsellors will orient to the family through questions such as: 'What is the function of the child's symptoms in this family? Whose concern or voice in the family is the child expressing?'

The family systems approach to child counselling is a major force in current thinking regarding the counselling of children and is currently providing new means for working with children and families (White 1986; Parry & Doan 1994).

Chapter summary

A 'not so quiet' revolution is taking place in our understanding of the way children in middle childhood are thinking and learning. The research of Piaget has demonstrated for us the advances in young people's thinking skills. Research has now offered a significant challenge to reconsider our estimation of the nature and extent of children's cognitive development. Accompanying these changes, important developments are occurring in our understanding of the way they reason about moral issues and other events such as loss or grief which impact on their lives.

Discussion questions

1   What are the identifiable features of children's thinking during the concrete operations stage according to Piagetian theory? How do these features influence children's understanding of the world?
2   How does the psychoanalytic view of humour differ from the cognitive–developmental perspective?
3   What is meant by the term 'learning style'?
4   Clarify and discuss Yates's five conditions for successful classroom teaching.
5   What are the main features of the theoretical approaches to the study of moral development – psychoanalytic, social learning (behaviourist) and cognitive–developmental?
6   Compare and contrast Carol Gilligan's views of moral development with those of Kohlberg.
7   What are the main features of children's conceptions of death seen from a cognitive–developmental perspective?

Activities

1   Individually or in groups, think of primary or secondary school teachers whom you remember most vividly and who influenced you in a positive fashion. Make a list of the qualities that made them effective teachers. Discuss your ideas with the whole group.
2   View an episode of a selected current 'popular' sitcom and identify the features of the main characters in terms of Kohlberg's six substages.
3   Collect a series of jokes told by children from pre-school to adolescence. Attempt to classify the jokes in terms of cognitive development.

Selected websites

Fernside Online <www.fernside.org> This organisation is a non-profit organisation serving grieving children and their families.

Katharine School of the Air, Aboriginal Education Program: <www.assoa.nt.edu.au> This web site provides a distance education program providing an educational service to rural Aboriginal students who have little access to conventional schools.

The Jean Piaget Archives <www.unige.ch/piaget/presentg.htm>

Child Adolescent Psychological and Educational Resources <www.caper.com.au>

17 Social and Emotional Development in Middle Childhood

'– Things That Make Children Sweet-tempered'

'When I'm a Duchess' she said to herself (not in a very hopeful tone though), 'I won't have any pepper in my kitchen at all. Soup does very well without – Maybe it's always pepper that makes people hot-tempered', she went on, very pleased at having found out a new kind of rule 'and vinegar that makes them sour – and barley-sugar and such things that make children sweet-tempered. I only wish people knew that: then they wouldn't be so stingy about it, you know'.

Lewis Carroll, Alice Through the Looking Glass

KEY TERMS AND CONCEPTS

- Latency
- Industry versus inferiority
- Self-concept
- Self-esteem
- Self-dynamism
- Social skills

Introduction

The world of the primary school child is to a large extent a world closed to adults in so much as it is a society of its own. There is a timeless quality associated with this period of children's lives. Primary school children move into their own world of magic, fairytale and ritual, which by its very secrecy excludes adults. In her book *To Kill a Mockingbird* (1960), Harper Lee allows us an all too rare glimpse into the secret world of children, a world characterised by secrets, rituals and rules. The success of the *Harry Potter* series of books captures significant themes which entrance primary school children. 'Harry Potter is a wizard! Along with Ron and Hermione, his best friends, Harry is in his third year at Hogwarts School of Witchcraft and Wizardry' (Rowling 1999). A further contemporary glimpse into the world of middle childhood is provided by *Bart Simpson's Guide to Life* (Groening 1993). This book offers all sorts of 'advice' about parents, school and peers for primary school children.

In this chapter consideration is given to a number of theoretical and research findings relating to primary school children's social and emotional development. Topics discussed include the development of self-concept and self-esteem, the nature of children's friendships and cooperation, the causes of stress and coping with it, and the consequences of divorce for children. In addition, behaviour management and school discipline are examined in terms of William Glasser's theory. The Family Life-cycle: 17 looks at families, children and chronic illness.

Theoretical foundations

As for younger children, the writings of Sigmund Freud and Erik Erikson have made an important contribution to our understanding of the social and emotional world of middle childhood.

Sigmund Freud

According to Freud (Grinker 1968), during the middle childhood period – the **latency period** – the child's sexual urges are relatively dormant awaiting their turbulent awakening during adolescence (see Table 17.1). The child spends time mastering a variety of tasks and acquiring different interests, and energy is devoted to the broad task of learning. The interests of the child are extended beyond the immediate family to school and peers, as illustrated in the following excerpt from Harper Lee's *To Kill a Mockingbird*.

latency period
in Freud's theory, a period of development (6–12 years) in the child's life when sexual impulses are relatively dormant.

> The second grade was grim, but Jem assured me that the older I got the better school would be, that he started off the same way, and it was not until one reached the sixth grade that one learned anything of value. The sixth grade seemed to please him from the beginning: he went through a brief Egyptian

Period that baffled me – he tried to walk flat a great deal, sticking one arm in front of him and one in back of him, putting one foot behind the other. He declared Egyptians walked that way; I said if they did I didn't see how they got anything done . . . (Lee 1960, p. 65).

Harry Potter was a highly unusual boy in many ways. For one thing, he hated the summer holidays more than any other time of the year. For another, he really wanted to do his homework, but was forced to do it in secret, in the dead of night. And he also happened to be a wizard (Rowling 1999, p. 7).

Trends and issues

Eriskson and self-esteem

Erik Erikson believed that an adult's self-esteem is largely dependent upon childhood experiences (Erikson 1977). More particularly, it is dependent upon the resolution of three basic tensions in the early years of life, namely trust versus mistrust, autonomy versus shame and doubt, and initiative versus guilt (see Table 17.2). Erikson believed that these tensions are sequential: that is, resolution of one tension prepares the child for the next one. Additionally, the earlier these three tensions are addressed and resolved the better equipped the child will be for coping with later life situations.

Table 17.1 The 'latency' stage: the fourth of Freud's psychosexual stages

Ages	Stages
Infancy	Oral
1½–3½ years (approx.)	Anal
3½–5½ years (approx.)	Phallic
5½–12 years (approx.)	Latency
Adolescence	Genital

Erik Erikson

industry versus inferiority
the fourth of Erikson's psychosocial stages, in which the child aims at productivity and mastery, but feels inferior if these are not achieved.

Erikson's fourth stage of life-cycle development, that of **industry versus inferiority** (5½ to 12 years; see Table 17.2), parallels the latency period in Freudian theory. According to Erikson, during this time the 'inner stage seems all set for "entrance into life", except that life must be school life, whether school is field or jungle or classroom', and the child is set 'to win recognition by producing things'. Thus, the child is prepared to develop a sense of industry, developing perseverance and adjusting to the 'inorganic focus of the tool world' and becoming 'an eager and absorbed unit of a productive situation' (Erikson 1963, p. 124).

The importance of this stage in Erikson's scheme of things is emphasised by Cole (1970, p. 132), who observes that 'The industrious child who at eight or ten feels like a reasonably capable person and acts like a reasonably resourceful one is on his way to something more than a job'. The risk that the child runs during this stage is that he or she will develop a sense of inferiority – a sense of inadequacy resulting in feelings of worthlessness. Significant others in the child's life can contribute to this by denigrating the child's efforts.

Table 17.2 'Industry versus inferiority': the fourth of Erikson's psychosocial stages

Ages	Stages
Infancy	Basic trust versus mistrust
1½–3½ years (approx.)	Autonomy versus shame and doubt
3½–5½ years (approx.)	Initiative versus guilt
5½–12 years (approx.)	Industry versus inferiority
Adolescence	Identity versus role confusion
Young adulthood	Intimacy versus isolation
Adulthood	Generativity versus stagnation
Maturity	Ego integrity versus despair

Self-concept and self-esteem

Self-concept

Self-concept refers to a relatively stable set of perceptions or beliefs that a person uses to describe herself or himself. One way to understand the idea of self-concept is to imagine viewing yourself in a 'special' mirror that reflects not only your physical attributes but also other aspects, such as likes, dislikes, sporting and academic prowess, and so forth. The reflection in this 'special' mirror would be your self-concept. Reflected appraisal and social comparison influence the development of self concept. As proposed by Fitts (1971) in a review of the literature, self-concept is powerfully influenced by the way others (such as parents, teachers, peers) respond to us.

self-concept
the picture one has of oneself.

In middle childhood, self-concept is influenced by the appraisal of significant others and by comparison with peers.

Self-esteem

Pope et al. (1988, p. 2) argue that the terms **self-concept** and **self-esteem** are often used interchangeably, albeit incorrectly.

> Self esteem is an evaluation of the information contained in the self concept, and is derived from a child's feelings about all the things he is. If a child places a high value on being a superior student but is himself only an average or poor student, his self esteem will suffer.

Developmental changes in self-concept

In chapter 14, consideration was given to the development of a sense of self from birth. Researchers such as Oppenheimer (1991) point out that the self-concept does not exist at birth, but that around 6 to 7 months of age the infant comes to recognise 'self' from surroundings. Self-concept at this early stage is almost entirely physical, entailing as it does in a 7-month-old the dawning recognition that the hand moving past the face 'belongs' to him or her.

In the early pre-school years young children typically describe themselves in terms of physical characteristics, e.g., 'I am a boy with red hair'. In part, this tendency reflects the early concrete operational thinking of children of this age.

The implications of healthy self-concept/self-esteem development

As children are developing the perceptions they have of themselves contribute to healthy growth and development. Research indicates that children with realistic self-concepts and higher levels of self-esteem engage in fewer negative health behaviours (Dielman et al. 1984; Petersen-Martin & Cottrell 1987). More particularly, research indicates that healthy self-concept and self-esteem development is inversely linked to psychological adjustment (Dusek 2000).

Harter's model of self-esteem development

Harter's (1983) writings are referred to here because they provide a developmental perspective. Key terms in the model include:

i   *Global self-esteem.* the overall value a child places on her/himself and the generated feelings of worthiness held (Harter 1989). The terms 'global self-esteem' and 'self-esteem' can be used interchangeably.
ii *Self Concept.* This is the basic description a child attaches to her or himself and represents the ideas, attitudes/beliefs that a child possesses.

The model developed by Harter uses a hierarchical structure. Global self-esteem comprises four second-order dimensions identified as competence, power, moral worth and acceptance. Under each of the four second-order dimensions are the more specific domains that indicate how the second-order dimensions are manifested. In Harter's model, global self-esteem is more than the sum of its parts and it is not sufficient to sum up the parts to arrive at a measure of global self-esteem. Self-concept refers to the second-order dimensions as measured by the domains of scholastic competence, athletic competence, physical appearance, behavioural conduct and peer social acceptance. Figure 17.1 presents a representation of Harter's model.

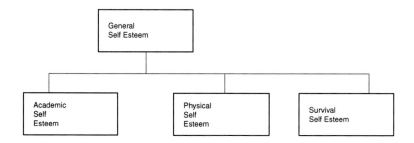

Figure 17.1 A representation of Harter's view of self-esteem.

In her work, Harter (1983) raised a number of questions concerning the development of self-esteem. In the first instance, she believed that the dimensions of competence, power, moral worth and acceptance were likely to be expressed differently according to children's developmental level. In a related way she questioned whether certain dimensions may be more important than others at certain developmental stages. Another question concerned whether her model was appropriate for children at all developmental stages.

Friendship in middle childhood

Other than love, no other facet of human relationships has occupied more attention in the arts, literature and the social sciences than friendship. The ancient Greeks set great store by the notion of friendship. This is reflected in Homer's epic poem *The Iliad*, in which the friendship of Achilles and Patroclus is a key element. It was grief and anger at Patroclus's death that made Achilles return to the battle to take vengeance on Hector. In ancient Greece good friends shared each others' fortunes and misfortunes and supported each other with complete truth and faithfulness. In the fourth century BC, the Greek philosopher Aristotle devoted a considerable portion of the *Nicomachean Ethics* to an analysis of friendship. According to Aristotle, perfect friendship was only possible between the good and one could not be friends with too many people.

Contarello and Volpato (1991) have studied friendship as portrayed in historical literary texts through the ages. They suggest that the meaning of the term 'friendship' has changed over time. They contrast the meaning of the term in classical times, where it denoted a voluntary and chosen bond available only to free men, with medieval France where it referred to kin showing basic family solidarity and also to lovers. From their research of literary texts they believe the '. . . central core of friendship would appear to be intimacy, respect, mutual help, shared activity, confrontation' (Contarello & Volpato 1991, p. 70).

Turning to children, and from a more contemporary perspective, psychologists' attention to the topic of children's friendships has waxed and waned during the twentieth century (Rubin 1980). In the 1920s and 1930s researchers showed considerable interest in the topic and this was followed by a long period of relative neglect before a resurgence of interest in the 1970s. Rubin (1980) credits the lack of interest in the topic during the middle period to assumptions inherent in the prevailing psychoanalytic viewpoint concerning the primacy of the mother–child relationship. 'Compared to this "first" relationship children's relationships with one another were seen as being of little real importance' (Rubin 1980, p. 13). Presently there is a considerable renewal of interest in the topic of children's friendships and their peer relationships more generally (Slee & Rigby 1998).

Harry Stack Sullivan and 'chums'

The psychology of H. S. Sullivan is not well known. Along with Adler (1927), Horney (1937) and Fromm (1947), Sullivan (1953) was one of the first to rebel against orthodox psychoanalytic thought. These four theorists are often grouped together because of their mutual concern for the role of self and the importance of interpersonal processes in the development of personality and psychopathology. Perhaps the identifying feature of Sullivan's theory is the emphasis he gives to interpersonal relationships. Sullivan views the individuality of each person as a function of such relationships.

Sullivan identifies two broad classes of needs:

1   *The need to satisfy our biological wants*, for food, sex or sleep. He also identifies the need for physical contact as crucial. In this regard observations of children's responses to cuddling and the behaviour of individuals deprived of contact comfort lend some weight to his argument.

2   *The need for a sense of security*, involving a feeling of wellbeing and comfort. In Sullivan's view, not only is this need for a sense of security satisfied through meeting the child's observable needs but it could also be positively or negatively affected by unverbalised attitudes of the caregiver towards the child.

self-dynamism
Sullivan's term for the active, achieving, protective part of the self.

Sullivan believes that the growing child's sense of self is a function of the history of the child's personal relationships with significant others. The sum of these percepts influences what Sullivan called **self-dynamism**. This concept refers to the self as perceived by the individual, the self as a doer and protector of the sense of security.

Sullivan emphasises that children can be best understood through the relationships they have with their parents and friends. He suggested that establishing a close friendship is a significant developmental task for pre-adolescents. Parents are the first to help children realise they are not isolated, self-sufficient individuals, but Sullivan believes that parents can carry children only so far in their development. Friendships and the friends children have provide a whole new basis for helping children in their development. Friendship helps children develop and engenders mutual respect: it is a relationship in which each person has a chance to grow and contribute to the development of another. Sullivan identifies three broad stages in children's friendships:

1 Between 2 and 5 years of age children's most important relationships are with adults, on whom they rely to meet their physical, social and emotional needs.
2 Between 4 and 8 years children turn increasingly to their playmates as friends.
3 From 8 to 11 years 'chumship' dominates.

Sullivan attached a great deal of importance to the development of chumship. He believed that during the chumship phase children are learning how to help another person grow and develop.

The nature of children's friendships undergoes developmental change.

> All of you who have children are sure that your children love you; when you say that you are expressing a pleasant illusion. If you will look closely at one of your children when he finally finds a chum – somewhere between eight and a half and ten years – you will discover something very different in the relationship, namely that your child begins to develop real sensitivity to what matters to another person (Sullivan 1953, p. 245).

Middle childhood is a significant time, when children find their place among their peers. Peers become as important, if not more so, than parents. The issue of the importance of peers in an individual's life is taken up again in chapter 20 in the discussion of adolescent development.

What is a friend? A developmental perspective

At 2 years of age my son Matthew would ask 'My friend Jac play with me?', by which he meant could we invite the next-door neighbour's child over to play with him. In Matthew's eyes, Jac was his friend because he could play with him. Certainly, children form friendships for many different reasons. Some generally agreed upon conditions marking the friendships of children and adolescents include:

- a degree of 'reciprocity' or mutual regard;
- a general desire to spend more time in each other's company than with others;
- enjoyment of each other and fun.

As summarised by Bagwell et al. (1998, p. 140), '. . . friendship is a mutual relationship between two children in which reciprocal liking is quintessential'.

Over time, children's concept of friendship undergoes some developmental change (Selman 1976; Bigelow 1977; Hartup 1978; Rubin 1980; Berndt 1986). The researcher Berndt (1986) found that sixth-graders were more likely than third-graders or kindergarten children to identify intimacy and trust as features of friendship. The younger children emphasised play or association as a feature of friendship. The young child (3 to 5 years) tends to view friends as 'momentary physical playmates' – a friend is the person the child is playing with at any particular time (Rubin 1980, p. 38).

Social skills and friendship

social skills
acceptable learned behaviours that gain positive responses from others.

A great deal of attention has been given to the study of **social skills** in adults (Trower et al. 1978) but it is only comparatively recently that the focus has turned to children. In relation to children, the topic is important because:

1 socially isolated or unpopular children have been found to be deficient in skills such as cooperation and a positive response to peers (Gottman et al. 1976; Oden & Asher 1977);
2 inadequate social skills in children have been associated with poor academic performance (Cartledge & Milburn 1986);
3 children deficient in social skills have a high incidence of school maladjustment (Hill 1989; Mathur & Rutherford 1991; Ladd et al. 1996).

Bagwell et al. (1998) have identified that mutual friendship in year five of primary school is associated with positive life status adjustment as adults.

Cartledge and Milburn (1986, p. 7) define social skills as 'socially acceptable learned behaviours that enable the person to interact with others in ways that elicit positive responses and assist in avoiding negative responses from them'. Trower et al. (1978) highlight some of the complexity of defining social skills and explain how social skills are acquired. They believe that social skills are developed by a combination of factors, such as:

- the imitation of others;
- reinforcement;
- the opportunity to observe and practise behaviour;
- the development of cognitive abilities;
- some innate potential.

According to Rubin (1980), friendship requires the following skills:

1 the ability to gain entry to a group;
2 the ability to be a supportive, caring and approving playmate;
3 the ability to manage conflict successfully, which means being able to express one's own rights and feelings while remaining sensitive to the rights and feelings of others.

From this brief overview it is apparent that the development of friendships is a complex and important task for children. Greater understanding of the

Making friends at school requires complex social skills.

relationship between social skills and friendship would provide insight into the difficulties some children have in making friends. What seems imperative is that serious consideration is given by those who work with children to the significant role that friends play in children's lives.

Stress

Like adults, children experience stress in their lives. There is a tendency for adults to view childhood through rose-tinted glasses and consider it to be a carefree and idyllic time. In his book *My Brother Jack*, George Johnston describes the early childhood of two children (himself and his brother) growing up in Australia after the Second World War. In powerful images he describes the impact of his parents' quarrels on him and his brother as children.

> One must allow for time's foreshortening, but I can hardly recall a night when I was not awakened in panic by the stormy violence of my parents' quarrels. Often Mother would run from the house in the dead of the night, swearing never to return, and there was one specially terrible occasion when Jack and I were awakened in the sleep-out by the sound of Mother, who was outside in the rain and darkness, whimpering like an animal as she tried to crawl into hiding beneath the Dollicus (Johnston 1964, p. 39).

Psychological research indicates that stresses are with us from birth. According to Lipsett (1983, p. 162), 'there is much that occurs in the normal life of the newborn, and in the child developing throughout the first year that is patently stressful'. Other researchers confirm this view (Honig 1986; Compas 1987).

The nature of stress

The term 'stress' was introduced into medicine in the 1930s by Hans Seyle, who studied stress as a physiological response to demanding conditions, which he called 'stressors' (Seyle 1956). He emphasised that stress was a stimulus event of sufficient severity to produce disequilibrium in the homeostatic physiological system.

Today, various definitions of stress are to be found in the literature. In general, the definitions emphasise that stress is likely to arise when demands exceed a person's ability to cope, or where an individual's personal resources are overtaxed. The Australian researcher Rosemary Otto (1989, p. 345) notes that: 'there is now wide agreement that stress constitutes an internal response at both the emotional, experiential and physiological levels to a "lack of fit" between a person and environment'.

Not all stress is harmful. According to Erikson (1970), healthy physiological development involves confronting various crises throughout the life-span. Sigmund Freud (1949) emphasises that individuals experience conflicts between self and instinctual urges on the way to achieving successful adulthood. Piaget and Inhelder (1969) also believed that conflict experienced in the course of social interaction facilitates children's cognitive development. There is a level of stress that enables us to perform at peak efficiency and which then dissipates once the task is completed.

The more harmful form of stress produces physiological changes such as increased blood pressure and heart rate. Such stress does not disappear. At the experiential level the individual may identify feelings of tension, nervousness, sleeplessness, along with a sense of 'losing control'.

Dealing with stress

Seyle (1974) indicates that there are four basic ways people cope or deal with stress:

1 by removing the stressor – if a child is being bullied he or she might avoid contact with the person or gang of children;
2 by refusing to allow neutral situations to become stressors – a child may refuse to allow anger towards another to become a source of stress;
3 by dealing with the stressors – the child victim of a bully might confront the individual concerned;
4 by finding ways of calming themselves in the face of stressors.

Causes of stress in children

Ecological variables

A number of ecological factors have been identified as affecting the mental health of children including:

1 parental circumstance;
2 parental discipline;
3 birth of a brother or sister;
4 divorce;
5 hospitalisation;
6 children's fears;
7 child abuse.

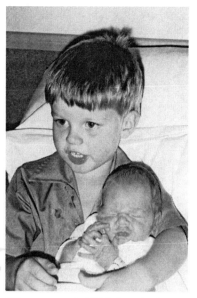

When a second child is born in the family, the older sibling may experience some stress.

1 Parental circumstance. The research of Michael Rutter (1979) has established that there are six family variables strongly associated with mental illness in children:

i severe marital discord;
ii low social status;
iii overcrowding or large family size;
iv father's criminality;
v psychiatric disorder of the mother;
vi committing a child to care of welfare agencies, for example, foster care.

From Rutter's research it has emerged that the rate of psychiatric disorder in children is a function of the number of family risk factors present in the child's life. A single stress factor by itself does not place the child at risk but the presence of two or three factors in combination produces a four-fold increase in the rate of psychiatric disorder, while four or more such factors produced a ten-fold increase. One factor broadly implicated as a significant stressor in children's lives is domestic violence. Australian research indicates that children exposed to domestic violence compared to those who are not exhibit (a) significantly higher emotional and behavioural problems; (b) lower levels of social competence; (c) a greater tendency to choose aggressive responses in conflict situations (Mathias et al. 1995).

2 Parental discipline. As outlined in chapter 11, Baumrind (1967; 1982) has identified three key types of parental discipline including (i) authoritarian; (ii) permissive; and (iii) authoritative. Baumrind argues that the first two methods are stressful for children because adult coercion or overindulgence denies the child the opportunity to make choices and to be responsible for themselves or their actions. Authoritative parents are not being overbearing or intrusive but are willing to impose restrictions in areas in which they believe they have greater insight than the child. Baumrind believes that energetic, friendly children have caring parents who have high expectations which are clearly communicated and consistently but not inflexibly enforced.

3 Birth of a brother or sister. Not a great deal is known about children's reactions to the birth of a brother or sister. It can be a stressful event, particularly if the baby is seen by the older sibling as competition or as a replacement for himself or herself (Marecki et al. 1985). Dunn (1981) found that more than half of 40 children aged between 2 and 3 years became tearful and had sleeping difficulties and toileting problems following the birth of a sibling. It is important, therefore, not to overlook the possibility that a child may experience some stress when a new member is added to the family.

4 Divorce of parents. The divorce of parents is one of the most traumatic events a child can experience. Often the stress associated with divorce is prolonged as there is usually a period of disharmony leading up to the separation or divorce. Research suggests that for many children, emotional disturbance following a divorce tends to get worse before it gets better (Hetherington 1989; Wallerstein & Kelly 1980). Younger children are more likely than older children to regress behaviourally because they worry about being abandoned and/or feel they have caused the divorce. As such, they can become immature in their behaviour and may be tearful, irritable or aggressive. Primary-school-aged children are prone to bouts of depression and/or a deterioration in their schoolwork. Overall, girls seem to adjust better to divorce than boys, particularly where they are in the custody of their mother.

As reviewed by Callan and Noller (1987), Australian and overseas research is serving to highlight the variable response of children to divorce. Rodgers (1996, p. 174), in an examination of the Australian literature pertaining to the social and psychological wellbeing of children from divorced families, concluded that 'There is no scientific justification for disregarding the social and psychological significance of parental divorce, and the importance of support services for children and parents should not be underestimated'.

5 Hospitalisation. The Australian Bureau of Statistics (1992) reported survey findings that 323 000 children under the sage of 14 were admitted to hospital at least once over a 12-month period. Australian parents report that hospitalisation is a significant stressor for families (Slee & Murray-Harvey 1998). Going into hospital can be a stressful experience for children. The stress reactions may be transient or of a long-term nature. Kapelis (1983) reports that a slight psychological upset resulting from hospitalisation can occur in as many as 92 per cent of children. Separation from parents, unfamiliar surroundings, disruption of routine and painful medical procedures are factors contributing to stress in hospital. Younger children, in particular, are likely to equate hospitalisation with punishment for some real or imaginary misdeed. Various strategies such as films, hospital tours, books and play kits have been used to offset the stressful impact of hospitalisation (see chapter 11). The general agreement is that these methods do help to reduce the level of stress and anxiety a child feels and assist post-operative recovery. Surprisingly then, Whelan and Kirby (1995), in a survey of hospitals in Victoria, found that less than 10 per cent of the hospitals had formal programs for preparation.

6 Children's fears. Australian children aged between 4 and 19 years are subject to a range of fears (Slee & Cross 1989). For example, a fear of wild animals is a concern of 53 per cent of 4- to 7-year-olds, although one must allow for wide individual differences.

The research showed that females report more fears than males. Age trends were also apparent, with younger children exhibiting more fears than older children. It is quite possible that if the fears are not addressed and dealt with that they may constitute a source of stress for children.

A fear of wild animals is a major concern of young children.

A fear of wild animals, often expressed by younger children is not found to the same extent in older children.

Personal variables

1 Sex of the child. The sex of the child is consistently identified in the research as a factor associated with stress. As Honig (1986, p. 54) notes, 'Male children are more vulnerable than female children'. Boys have been found to be at greater risk of disruptive behaviour problems following major stressors such as divorce (Emery 1982). Masten et al. (1988, p. 747) observe that 'being a girl appears to be "protective" in some manner with respect to a number of problems of adaption, at least in early and middle childhood'.

2 Intellect of the child. Masten et al. (1988) have noted that general intellectual ability is associated with adjustment. In a study of children from third to sixth grade, Garmezy et al. (1984) assessed three groups of children: (i) normal; (ii) with a heart defect; and (iii) mainstream physically handicapped. From their study it appeared that IQ functioned as a protective factor in terms of the effects of life stressors.

Resistance to stress

Research is now focusing on factors that mediate a child's ability to resist stress (Campos 1987; Masten et al. 1988). Moderating variables that have been investigated include locus of control (Johnson & Sarason 1978) and social support (Nichols et al. 1972). In relation to locus of control, it appears that children with an internal rather than an external locus of control, who consequently believe they have some influence and control over their lives, are more resistant to the effects of stress. Children who have a wide network of social support – family and friends – are more able to cope with stressful life events. In sum:

> The literature on environmental stressors in childhood, in addition to documenting the importance of situational differences, also points to the importance of individual differences, both personal and familial, in the nature of adaption (Masten et al. 1988, p. 746).

Stressful life events and adjustment

The relationship between stressful life events and adjustment is one that has gained increasing research attention in the psychological literature. As stressful life events are recognised as part of the fabric of life for children as well as adults, it is understood that such events create adaptive problems that must be surmounted. An evolving outlook now assumes that all individuals are susceptible to stressful life events, which, in turn, can be associated with negative physical and psychological outcomes (Dohrenwend & Dohrenwend 1974; Compas 1987; Honig 1986). There is an accumulating body of evidence that chronic stressful life events may have multiplicative adverse effects on children's adjustment (Rutter 1984). One study by Gersten et al. 1974) showed that the number of stressful life events experienced by children correlated with parental ratings of increased conflict with parents and a higher level of anxiety in children. In a timely warning, though, Berden and Althaus (1990) point out that 'the interaction between life events and changes in the behavioural–emotional functioning of children is a very complex one'. More research is needed to tease out the relationship.

The measurement of stressful life events in children

Using the approach developed by Holmes and Rahe (1967), Coddington (1972) devised a life-event questionnaire for use with children and adolescents. Adult judges were used to assess the stress values of events for children. Since this pioneering work, other similar life events schedules for children have been developed (Monaghan et al. 1979; Swearingen & Cohen 1985; Murray-Harvey & Slee 1998).

Critics of the procedure that uses adults to assess children's stressful life events support their arguments with demonstrated differences between children and adults in the judgment of event stressfulness. Yeaworth et al. (1980, p. 95) question whether 'adults can validly impute the psychological adjustment required by adolescents and children when they experience specific changes'. Sensitivity to such criticisms has led to the development of various stressful life event inventories that use children's and adolescents' views of event stressfulness rather than those of adults (Yeaworth et al. 1980; Brown unpub.).

The two variables described in a previous section (ecological and personal) have been shown by research to be linked to stressful reactions in children. As adults, we risk overlooking the possibility that children may experience stress because they do not necessarily react verbally or non-verbally to stressors in the same way as adults. Moreover, in our increasingly complex society children are subject to stress as they are 'hurried' through childhood by adults preoccupied with early school enrichment programs and school activities, leaving little time for children to experience childhood (Elkind 1987). As such, there is a growing concern among individuals who work with children about the role of stress in children's lives and their ability to cope. More research is needed to identify those life events that are stressful through a child's eyes.

Resilience or invulnerability to stress

In psychological research there has been a growing interest in studies of children's resilience or invulnerability to stress. South Australian research by Howard, Dryden and Johnson (1999) was prompted by a concern that a rising proportion of young children were starting school with significant needs (economic, social and psychological) which placed the children 'at risk'. They defined 'risk' as '. . . environmental factors that either singly or in combination have been shown to render children's failure to thrive more likely'(p. 308). In particular, they refer to robust research findings conducted by West and Farrington (1973) which still has currency today and that identified risk factors to include (i) low family income; (ii) large family size; (iii) parental criminality; (iv) low intelligence; and (v) poor child-rearing techniques. As Howard et al. (1999) have noted, the focus on 'risk' has led to a number of innovations and interventions at school level, particularly in relation to curriculum reform, the development/extension of school counselling services, the implementation of behaviour management policies, mandatory notification of child abuse and various social justice policy initiatives.

Rutter (1987) has noted that although many children exposed to stress develop social, emotional and behavioural problems, some children will prove resilient in the face of adversity and develop healthy psychosocial functioning. For example, in a 30-year longitudinal study of infants on the Hawaiian island of Kauai, Werner (1989, p. 76) took a special interest in:

certain 'high risk' children who, in spite of exposure to reproductive stress, discordant and impoverished home lives and uneducated, alcoholic or mentally disturbed parents, went on to develop healthy personalities, stable careers and strong interpersonal relations. We decided to try to identify the protective factors that contribute to the resilience of children.

Garmezy (1983, p. 73) defines the so-called protective factors as 'those attributes of persons, environments, situations and events that appear to temper predictions of psychopathology based upon an individual's risk status'. According to Garmezy (cited in Bernard 1991, p. 3), the resilient child is one who 'works well, plays well, loves well, and expects well'.

Rutter (1984) has also been interested in how a surprisingly large number of children become normal, successful adults despite disadvantaged and stressful childhoods. Compas (1987) has identified three broad factors associated with invulnerable or resilient children:

1   constitutional characteristics of the child, such as temperament, high self-esteem, internal locus of control and autonomy;

2   a supportive family environment characterised by warmth, cohesiveness and closeness;

3   a supportive system provided by some organisational agency, such as social welfare.

VIEWPOINT

Why do parents get divorced?

'Because they don't like each other any more'
Aimee, 7 years

'Sometimes they have fights and decide they don't like each other'
Caitlin, 11 years

Effects of divorce

During the 1990s, divorce rates in Australia were such that almost one in two marriages ended in divorce. Early marriage (particularly teenage marriage) is strongly associated with high divorce rates (Roden 1989). The Australian Bureau of Statistics (ABS 1996) reported a continuing upward trend in the divorce rate for currently married men and women. As noted by Clarke-Stewart et al. (2000), in the United States 20 million children are living in one-parent families, with more than one million children experiencing the effects of the divorce of their parents each year.

According to Hetherington (1989, p. 2), who reviewed research on children's adjustment to divorce and remarriage:

During the first two years following divorce, most children and many parents experienced emotional distress; psychological health and behaviour problems; disruptions in family functioning; and problems in adjusting to new roles, relationships and life changes associated with the altered family situation.

Clarke-Stewart et al. (2000), in evaluating the literature, concluded that divorce can have a detrimental effect on school-age children in relation to '. . . school achievement, self-esteem, and psychological adjustment'. The same authors go on to note that while differences in outcomes for children from divorced and non-divorced parents are:

. . . consistent across studies, long-lasting across time, and statistically significant, little agreement exists about the extent, severity, and duration of these problems, because children's responses to parental marital transitions vary widely (Amato 1994).

Highlighting this point, a study by Clarke-Stewart et al. (2000, p. 304) of the effects of divorce on very young children concluded that:

. . . children's psychological development was not affected by parental separation per se: it was related to mothers' income, education, ethnicity, child-rearing beliefs, depressive symptoms and behaviour.

This conclusion is consistent with the findings of Australian research into the impact of divorce conducted by Dixon, Charles and Craddock (1998). However, as O'Connor et al. (2000) have noted, the simple question of whether there is an association between parental divorce and children's adjustment difficulties has been replaced by the search for multiple mechanisms by which 'divorce-related factors confer risk'. For example, these authors have researched the question of whether some aspects of children's adjustment to parental divorce is genetically mediated.

Children's feelings about separation

Paul Amato (1987) explored Australian children's feelings regarding their parents' separation and divorce: 'Overall, the pattern of responses is consistent with previous studies indicating that many children react to parental separation with feelings of distress and sadness' (Amato 1987, p. 615). Children showed a range of reactions, with a minority of children being pleased at the separation. He categorised children's reactions as:

1 *negative* – 'I wasn't happy. I used to cry' (girl aged 9 years);
2 *neutral* – 'It didn't really bother me because I was only 6 at the time. Everyone says they're sorry if they know Mum and Dad are divorced, but it doesn't really worry me' (boy aged 16);
3 *positive* – 'When Dad was happy he was nice, but sometimes he got mad and then he got pretty mean. It was pretty quiet when he was gone, and after that he wouldn't belt any of us and smack us or do anything bad to us' (girl aged 9 years).

The impact of divorce

There may be a long period of disharmony between the parents leading up to the divorce and after the separation conflict between parents may escalate rather than decline (Hetherington et al. 1979). This view is supported by research done by Rutter (1971), who notes that much of the disturbance in children stems from such discord rather than from the separation itself. Kelly (2000) has concluded in her review of the literature that marital conflict is a more important predictor of child adjustment than is divorce or post-divorce adjustment.

The research findings of Hetherington (1989) indicate that boys are more vulnerable to the impact of divorce than girls. A psychoanalytic explanation for this finding is that the absence of the father could lead to the non-resolution of the Oedipus complex (see chapter 3). Other explanations for the poorer adjustment of boys point to the greater aggressiveness of boys, their greater level of non-compliance than girls and the tendency of boys to receive less care from female care-givers because they are perceived to be tougher and less needy than their sisters (Hetherington 1989).

Australian research is generally consistent with overseas research. Approximately one-third of Australian parents reported that their children had been badly affected at the time of separation (Burns 1980). However, the majority felt their children had subsequently adapted successfully.

Jones (2000) has identified a number of factors buffering children in high conflict marriages including:

- a good relationship with at least one parent;
- parental warmth;
- support of brothers and sisters;
- good self-esteem and peer support, particularly for adolescents.

Mediating factors

In reviewing the literature, Kurdek (1981) has identified four categories of factors that mediate children's response to divorce:

1   cultural beliefs, values and attitudes surrounding modern life – for example, that it is 'wrong' or against religious beliefs to divorce;
2   the stability of the post-divorce environment and the social supports available to the restructured sole-parent family;
3   the child's individual psychological competencies for dealing with stress;
4   the nature of the family interaction in period before and after the separation.

Behaviour management in school

In any school there is a small group of children alienated by the existing school system. Their alienation is reflected in their dropping out of school, their inability to form close relationships with teachers and a tendency to find the curriculum irrelevant to their basic needs. Slee (1992) has strongly argued that the increasing alienation of students in our school system inevitably results in resistance and alienation. The important question then becomes what can be done to make school a more attractive place to be, a place where the curriculum better meets the child's needs.

The seriousness and nature of behaviour management in schools

In a study of teacher's views of discipline, Adey et al. found in their metropolitan school survey of 1335 primary and secondary South Australian teachers that over one in five teachers reported 'serious' or 'very serious' discipline problems in schools. As reported by Adey et al. (1991), the most common discipline problems faced by primary teachers, which occur on a daily basis, include: hindering other students, work avoidance, talking out of turn, infringing class rules, not being punctual, unnecessary noise, rowdiness, out-of-seat behaviour, and verbal and physical abuse of other students. A disturbing feature of their findings was that in primary schools, pupil verbal and physical aggression occurred in about one in six classes almost daily.

Burke et al. (1994, p. 2) have noted in their paper dealing with behaviour management in Australian primary schools: 'The research indicates that disruptive and anti-social student behaviour is a product of intrapersonal, interpersonal and contextual factors'. In this regard, Slee and Knight (1992) have convincingly argued that school organisational structure, policy development and administrative procedures are related to the nature and incidence of disruptive and anti-social behaviour within schools (Slee et al. 1997).

William Glasser and reality therapy

Glasser is perhaps best known as the founder of the Institute for Reality Therapy in Los Angeles. He was born in 1925 and began practice as a psychiatrist in 1957 in Los Angeles. His early writings reflect the influence of Freud but by 1960 he had rejected Freudian ideas because of their focus on early childhood experiences. Instead, Glasser strongly emphasised the need to focus individuals' attention on the present. As his thinking developed, he accepted the ideas inherent in humanistic psychology with its emphasis on self-actualisation, identity, significant others and so on. In a succession of books, the most recent of which is *Control Therapy* (1984), he identified strongly with the psychological theories of Abraham Maslow, Carl Rogers and other humanistic thinkers.

Glasser's first and pivotal idea is that human development is based upon the actualisation of five basic internal psychological and physiological needs (Glasser 1984).

1 *The need to survive and reproduce.* Glasser believes that this need is located in what he calls part of the 'old brain'. The task of this need is to keep the body functioning.
2 *The need to belong.* This need includes the need for friends, family and love. Glasser comments that 'While most educators try to make their schools friendly places they don't pay enough attention to the fact that needs do not turn off in the classroom' (cited in Brandt 1988, p. 39). He further claims that alienation at school comes about in part because students do not have the opportunity to associate with other children in a friendly, rewarding fashion.
3 *The need for power.* Glasser (cited in Brandt 1988, p. 39) describes this need in the following terms: 'Another need, perhaps harder to satisfy than friendship, is to gain the continuing sense that "I have some power, I'm somebody; people pay attention to me"'. In the school setting, children often do not have a sense of feeling important and having some control, especially in the classroom itself.
4 *The need for freedom.* Glasser believes that one important need is that for self-expression.
5 *The need for fun.* Laughter, humour and fun are also seen to be essential by Glasser.

In Glasser's view, our behaviour is always an attempt to fulfil one or more of these five basic needs and students will function more adequately when their needs have been met.

> We all have needs built into our genetic structures, and everything we do is our attempt to satisfy them. For example, we all need to struggle to survive (most children do understand this), but we also have a need for love and belonging (Glasser, cited in Brandt 1988, p. 39).

A second fundamental idea of Glasser's is that people are essentially decision-making beings. People create their own personalities by the decisions they make in seeking to actualise and reconcile their psychological and physical needs. Individuals (even young children) should be taught to take responsibility for their own lives and the effect of their actions on others. Glasser links decision-making with identity: strong decision-makers develop a strong sense of identity.

A third idea underpinning Glasser's theory draws on the humanistic ideal that there is no such thing as a 'bad' person. He believes that there is only bad or irresponsible behaviour. As such, he advocates an unconditional positive regard for others. Given this outlook, one can appreciate that Glasser argues against negative reinforcement (such as threats to behave) and physical punishment (such as caning). Similarly, criticism, sarcasm and other forms of verbal abuse lead people to give up rather than take control of their lives.

A fourth element of Glasser's theory concerns the emphasis he gives to the quality of interpersonal relations. Glasser believes that relationships between people are the means by which people realise their physical and psychological needs.

School discipline

Glasser's theory has found increasing acceptance as a method of discipline in Australian schools. For example, the South Australian Education Department's Discipline Management Policy draws on some of Glasser's ideas.

Glasser has stated that 'discipline problems do not occur in classrooms in which students' needs are satisfied' (cited in Gough 1987, p. 658). Glasser has been highly critical of behavioural or stimulus–response approaches to discipline, which rely on scare tactics (punishment) and on doing something 'to' the student. Glasser formulated a 10-step school-wide approach for dealing with discipline problems. Conceptually, the 10 steps involve three graded stages.

According to Glasser, when student's needs are satisfied disruptive problems are less likely.

Stage 1

At this first stage the teacher is asked to evaluate critically the appropriateness of the discipline methods currently used. Thus the teacher sets aside some quiet time for reflection, to list the strategies used with a particular student (or students) with whom discipline problems are being experienced. The basic question the teacher asks is, 'What am I doing to discipline this student?'

Stage 2

During this stage the intention is to have the students face up to their own behaviour. If the first three steps have been completed with no resulting change in the student's behaviour, the student is told in a positive, caring manner, 'Please stop your disruptive behaviour'. The point made here is to indicate clearly to the student that the behaviour is unacceptable.

Stage 3

The last steps involve isolation of increasing severity. The idea of 'time out' is invoked to give staff and student time to reflect and demonstrates that the behaviour cannot be continued, while allowing the student to continue to be part of the school community.

For example, at this step 'time out' is introduced at the classroom level: that is, the student is removed to a quiet corner of the classroom. This conveys the message to the student that he or she is being isolated from the classroom community.

In terms of the program, Glasser emphasises that the student is given the choice of changing his or her behaviour: that is, the student has the opportunity to actualise his or her needs in a way that does not inhibit the learning of others in the school community. It is emphasised that the Glasser 10-step method is most effective when the whole school uses it and there is liaison between home and school.

In summary, while the focus in this section has highlighted one particular approach to behaviour management, the Australian writer Louise Porter (1995) has provided a very comprehensive review of various approaches to the issue and you are strongly referred to her text. Slee et al. (1998) have utilised a case study approach to examine the application of behaviour management to a school situation.

The family life-cycle: 17

Families, children and chronic illness

Newacheck and Taylor (1992) report that for the United States 31 per cent of children are affected by chronic illness, 9 per cent are moderately affected and 2 per cent are severely affected. More broadly considered, Shute (1998, p. 135) notes that, '[d]espite the difficulty of establishing incidence precisely, it is quite clear that there are substantial numbers of children with chronic illnesses living in industrialised nations today'.

As Shute (1998) has noted, chronic illnesses cannot be cured, but need to be managed on a long-term, often life-long basis. Shute documents that in the 1970s the most common childhood chronic conditions were asthma, epilepsy, cerebral palsy and orthopaedic conditions. In the 1980s, with improving medical technology, conditions like cancer, and end-stage renal failure were added to the list. With medical support, the majority of children will survive to at least young adulthood and the family obviously plays a significant role in supporting and helping the child cope with illness.

Davis (1963), in a study of families in which there was a child with polio, reported two major family response styles to the health of a child, namely normalisation and dissociation. Darling and Darling (1982), in a study of families with a child with a birth defect, identified four response styles including, normalisation, altruism, crusadership and resignation.

Knafl and Deatrick (1990) have utilised the 'family management style' (FMS) to describe how families define and manage the chronic illness of their child, considered in relation to their socio-cultural context. As Knafl et al. (1996, p. 324) note, families must make multiple adaptations in coping with a child's chronic illness, including, 'Making sense of the illness, mastering treatment regimens, adapting the family routine and budget to the demands of the illness, creating a normal life for the child in spite of the illness, and negotiating with health care and school professionals ...'.

In their research, Knafl et al. (1996) identified five FMSs, including (i) thriving; (ii) accommodating; (iii) enduring; (iv) struggling; and (v) floundering. Their study involved extensive interviews with 63 families with a school-age child with a chronic illness. Shute (1998) has noted the difficulties of defining just what a chronic illness is. In the Knafl et al. (1996) study, the authors characterised chronic illness as having (i) a greater than three-month duration; (ii) a stable or progressive illness course; (iii) relatively normal life-span despite impairment; and (iv) a necessary active management plan to minimise serious illness consequences.

1   *Thriving*: in these types of families the overriding theme was normalcy, with the parents continuing to view the child as normal despite the illness.
2   *Accommodating*: while these families also emphasised normalcy in dealing with their child, there was greater negatively regarding their situation.

3   *Enduring*: as described by Knafl et al. (1996), 'difficulty' was the overriding theme in this FMS, where negativity was accompanied by a great deal of effort in illness management.
4   *Struggling*: Here the parents were in a great deal of conflict with regard to managing the child's illness, with different parental views conflicting about how best to cope.
5   *Floundering*: 'Confusion' was the identifying element in this FMS and the 'parents typically viewed the child as a tragic figure or as a problem child whose illness combined with other academic or behavioural problems to create a difficult parenting situation' (Knafl et al. 1996, p. 321).

In summary, while there is an emerging body of research providing important insight into how a family adapts and manages the various tasks associated with having a child with a chronic illness, further research is warranted, in the light of advancing medical technology.

Chapter summary

The social/emotional world of the primary school child is an increasingly complex one. In particular, the pull of the peer group is particularly strong, influencing the behaviour and feelings of the child. One unfortunate outcome of the changes concerns the impact of stress on the individual. In this chapter consideration has been given to a range of individual, social and societal factors impacting on primary-school-age children. The time has come to listen attentively to children's voices as partners in any research endeavour and policy development. Viewing children as 'experts' is a prerequisite for taking into account how children understand and react to their experiences. It would represent a significant shift in outlook to give credence to the view that children are the 'experts' when it comes to their own, joys, worries, concerns or viewpoints. In turn, this would translate into engaging children as partners in any endeavour related to research and policy development. Perhaps a pertinent question to ask at this point concerns what our research and policy-making procedures would look like if we respected children as collaborators rather than viewing them as 'subjects' to be studied.

Discussion questions

1   What is the difference between self-esteem and self-concept?
2   What is the difference between perceived and ideal self?
3   Explain Sullivan's idea of 'chums' in relation to friendship.

4   How do children develop social skills?

5   Based on the discussion in this chapter, define 'stress' in your own words.

6   What ecological and personal factors affect stress in children?

7   What link is there between stressful life events and school adjustment?

8   What effect does divorce have on children?

9   What are the four fundamental ideas underpinning Glasser's approach to school discipline? How do these ideas relate to other theoretical approaches to child behaviour, e.g. learning theory?

Activities

1   Using the references in this text, research the concept of 'resilience' or 'invulnerability' to stress. In particular, identify those factors that contribute to children's resilience to stress. How might these factors be further enhanced in terms of their effectiveness in the home or at school?

2   Select a topic from this chapter (such as stress or the effect of divorce on children) and conduct a literature survey. Discuss the results of your survey in class.

3   Complete the 'Self Review Quiz' on the CD-ROM to assess your understanding of the content presented in this section. Use your quiz results as a basis for reviewing any chapter content about which you are uncertain.

Selected websites

An on-line journal of peace and conflict resolution <www.trinstitute.irg/ojpcr>

Child Adolescent Psychological and Educational Resources <www.caper.com.au>

A list of useful conflict resolution links to other sites <www.io.com/~ellie/conflict.html>

Adolescence

7

Aimee aged 8 years

Aimee aged 14 years

Aimee aged 16 years

18 Adolescent Physical Development and Health Issues

'So Typical'

The spot on my chin is getting bigger. It's my mother's fault for not having known about vitamins. I pointed out to my mother that I hadn't had my vitamin C today. She said 'Go buy an orange'. So typical! Nigel came around today. He hasn't got a single spot yet. My grandma came by today. She squeezed my pimple. It has made it worse. I will go to the doctors on Saturday if the spot is still there. I can't live like this with everybody staring.

Sue Townsend, The Secret Diary of Adrian Mole age 13¼

KEY TERMS AND CONCEPTS

- Puberty
- Growth spurt
- Hypothalamus
- Pituitary gland
- Gonads
- Menarche
- Secular trends
- Sex-role
- Gender identity
- Androgyny
- Anorexia nervosa
- AIDS

Introduction

The sentiments expressed by the teenager, Adrian Mole capture some of the complexity surrounding the physical changes that occur during this period of life. The term 'adolescence' is derived from the Latin *adolescere*, which means 'to grow up' or 'to grow to maturity'. Adults' feelings about adolescents are often pessimistic or somewhat ambivalent. The eighth century BC Greek poet Hesiod's opinion of the youth of his time would not be out of place today:

> I can see no hope for the future of our people if they are dependent on the frivolous youth of today for certainly all youth are reckless beyond words . . . When I was a boy, we were taught to be discreet and respectful of elders, but the present youth are exceedingly wise and impatient of restraint.

In this chapter consideration is given to significant aspects of adolescent physical development and the health-related issues of suicide, anorexia nervosa, AIDS and drug use. The Family Life-cycle: 18 is devoted to the 'empty nest' syndrome.

The study of adolescence

G. Stanley Hall (1904) is usually acknowledged as the first psychologist to identify adolescence as an important stage of human development. A notable feature of Hall's view was his idea of storm and stress as characterised by:

> lack of emotional steadiness, violent impulses, unreasonable conduct, lack of enthusiasm and sympathys . . . previous selfhood is broken ups . . . and a new individual is in the process of being born. All is solvent, plastic, peculiarly susceptible to external influences (Hall 1904, p. 26).

A key element of Hall's thinking involved the concept of recapitulation. That is, all individuals live through each of the major evolutionary steps of the human race as a whole. In Hall's view, adolescence recapitulates the stage of emerging civilisation (Hall 1904).

Following Hall, the study of adolescence was given further impetus with the research of Erik Erikson (1963, 1968) and Piaget and Inhelder (1969). In Erikson's psychosocial theory of development across the life-span, the formation of an identity is the key task of the adolescent period. Erikson believed that there was more to adolescence than simply 'storm and stress', and his work considerably enriched contemporary thinking regarding this important period of life.

Piaget and Inhelder provided new insight into the nature of adolescent cognitive development. In their stage approach to cognitive development, they highlighted adolescence as a period during which the individual attains the ability to reason in an abstract manner.

Currently, a burgeoning interest in the adolescent period is reflected in increasing research in the field, the results of which are challenging much contemporary thinking regarding the nature of adolescence (Irwin 1987; Heaven & Callan 1990; Collins 1991).

Trends and issues

Economic conditions and theorist's views

In a timely article, Enright et al. (1987) drew our attention to the need to consider the socio-historical context when evaluating child development issues. In a major review of the theoretical literature regarding the nature of adolescence, they observed a number of important trends. They discovered that psychological theories of adolescent development are strongly associated with the economic conditions of the time. Thus, during periods of depression or economic retraction, 'theories of adolescence emerge that portray teenagers as immature, psycho-logically unstable and in need of prolonged participation in the educational system' (Enright et al. 1987, p. 553). Quite the reverse applies during periods of economic boom, when theories of adolescence reflect adolescents' competencies and downplay the need for further education.

Enright et al. (1987) make the point that developmental psychology may play an important ideological role in society. This role may be directed at maintaining the status quo in society, even when there is some cost to optimal personal development.

Images of adolescence

In their paper, Violato and Wiley (1990) review the images of adolescence in English literature through the ages from Geoffrey Chaucer (1340–1400) to Charles Dickens (1812–1870). Violato and Wiley conclude that, in the main, literary works portray adolescence as 'a time of turbulence, excess and passion, which is in consonance with Hall's (1904) depictions' (Violato & Wiley 1990, p. 263). For example, in William Shakespeare's *The Merchant of Venice* and *Romeo and Juliet* youth is depicted as a time of 'excess', 'passion', and 'sensuality'. In *Romeo and Juliet*, the exuberant Romeo kills Mercurio and Tybalt during some irresponsible sword play. The impetuous, passionate nature of youth is shown in the betrothal of Romeo and Juliet in one night, and their respective suicides upon believing each other dead.

While one popular conception of adolescence is that it is a period of 'storm and stress', other points of view are also found among psychological researchers. The Australian writers Connell et al. (1975) argue on the basis of their research that adolescence is not an especially stormy period, and that for many individuals it is a fairly undramatic and uneventful time.

At this point it is worthwhile revisiting the usefulness and validity of the concept of developmental stages such as 'adolescence' or 'youth', touched upon in chapter 1. As discussed in chapter 1, mainstream developmental psychology has emphasised the 'qualities' that help us identify and appreciate the nature of the challenges facing us as we grow and develop.

It serves as a useful heuristic to help organise our thinking around child and adolescent development. Serious debate is now being engaged in to consider alternatives to simple linear classification of the developmental process identified by normative transitions. Present discussion emphasises that:

> . . . the focus on youth is not on the inherent characteristics of young people themselves, but on the construction of youth through social processes (such as schooling, families or the labour market). Young people engage with these

institutions in specific ways, in relation to historical circumstances (Wyn & White 1997, p. 9).

Historians such as Kett (1977) have specifically argued that adolescence is a life stage created to meet the demands of industrial labour for a skilled labour force.

Galambos and Leadbeater (2000), in a review of trends in adolescent research, have noted that current views of adolescence continue to think of it in terms if 'risks and opportunities'. They identify 'challenges' in terms of adolescent's engagement in risky behaviours, and issues with poverty, homelessness and unemployment. They identify opportunities in relation to better nourishment and access to financial resources. The optimistic conclusion to their review is that in the new millennium we stand to benefit from on-going research into adolescence.

Physical development

puberty
the attainment of sexual maturity; in girls, the beginning of menstruation; in boys, the first production of live sperm.

At about 10 to 12 years of age the individual enters **puberty**. This event signifies sexual maturity and the word is derived from the Latin *pubertas*, meaning age of manhood. It is usually considered to date from the onset of menstruation in girls and the first production of live sperm in boys. However, these two observable changes represent only a small part of the complex process known as puberty.

Puberty is associated with the growth spurt and is a universal characteristic of adolescence that comprises the most extensive and rapid change in postnatal life (Grumbach et al. 1974). The onset of hormonal activity also occurs at puberty. This activity falls under the influence of the central nervous system, and involves the hypothalamus, the pituitary gland (both of which are located at the base of the brain) and the gonads (ovaries and testes).

hypothalamus
a structure in the forebrain that controls a range of autonomic functions, such as body temperature.

The **hypothalamus** is located in the central core of what is sometimes known as the 'old brain', because of its similarity to the brain in more primitive creatures. The hypothalamus is about the size of the tip of a person's index finger. This organ serves a significant function in regulating the body's internal environment, such as body temperature. When it is cold, signals from the hypothalamus cause the blood vessels in the skin to contract, thereby reducing heat loss from the body. The hypothalamus also appears to be involved in regulating the sex drive, hence its importance during adolescence (Tortora & Anagnostakos 1987).

pituitary gland
an organ located beneath the hypothalamus that controls many hormonal secretions.

At the lower end of the hypothalamus is the **pituitary gland**, which controls many hormonal secretions. Hormones travel throughout the body and influence many aspects of behaviour (Tortora & Anagnostakos 1987).

gonads
the sex glands, which regulate sex drive; in females, the ovaries; in males, the testes.

The ovaries in women and testes in men (known collectively as the **gonads**) are part of the endocrine system. During adolescence there is some physical growth of the gonads and their secretions regulate the secondary sex characteristics such as growth of the breasts in women and growth of facial hair in men (Tortora & Anagnostakos 1987).

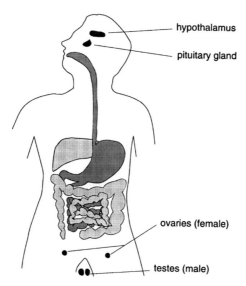

Figure 18.1 Glands involved in the hormonal activity that begins at puberty

The onset of puberty

There are a number of factors influencing the age of onset of puberty including genetic determinants, culture and the environment in which the adolescent is raised. For girls, the onset of puberty is signalled by the **menarche** (the first menstrual period) at around 12 to 14 years (Mackay et al. 1992). In boys, various bodily changes indicate the attainment of puberty.

menarche
a female's first
menstrual period.

Primary sex characteristics

At birth, male testes are present but are only about 10 per cent of their final size. During puberty they grow rapidly. Enlargement of the penis and the onset of ejaculation also occur during puberty (Tanner 1973). The penis is capable of erection from birth but during adolescence erection occurs in relation to sexually provocative stimuli.

In girls, breast budding and menstruation are associated with the growth in size of the ovaries. It is the ovaries that produce and secrete the hormones needed for menstruation, pregnancy and the development of secondary sex characteristics.

Secondary sex characteristics

The development of secondary sex characteristics involves features that are not directly related to sexual reproduction, such as the growth of body hair and voice changes. The first secondary sex characteristic to develop in males is the growth of pubic hair, followed by underarm and facial hair. Skin becomes coarser and thicker during puberty and the sebaceous or fatty glands are activated during this time, often resulting in troublesome acne. Boys' voices change around 13 years of age, gradually deepening in pitch (Tanner 1970).

For girls, the onset of puberty is signalled by secondary sex characteristics such as changes in the size and shape of the hips, which grow wider and rounder with the enlargement of the pelvic bone. Rapidly following these changes are breast development and the appearance of pubic hair (Tanner 1970).

Secular trends in physical development

secular trends
the trend for people to develop earlier and to be larger than in former eras.

Using historical sources, scientists have charted what have been called **secular trends** in development. For example, Tanner (1970) has argued for a secular trend in relation to the mean age of menarche (see Figure 18.2). On average, menarche arrives four months earlier per decade. In noting this trend, the researchers Marder et al. (1975, p. 47) comment:

> At the same time the average age of leaving school or tertiary education is increasing. The implications of an earlier average physical maturity, on the one hand and an increasing period of some form of economic dependence, are profound.

Similar secular trends have been reported by Harper and Collins (1975, p. 29) for Australian adolescent boys:

> The average height of fifteen year old boys in 1914 was 158.7 centimetres, in 1937 it was 166.4 centimetres, in 1954 it was 168.7 centimetres and in 1970 it was 169.1 centimetres. Weight showed a similar increase in fifteen year olds and rose from an average of 46.9 kilograms in 1914 to 58.1 kilograms in 1970. The average boy at maturity is expected to be 3 centimetres taller and 4.5 kilograms heavier than his father, and probably will reach puberty at about nine months earlier.

Evidence for the increase in height and weight of individuals can be seen in the clothing and furnishing of past generations. A more dramatic illustration of the physical changes is evident in an examination of the armour worn by medieval knights, which would by any standards cramp a present-day 13-year-old adolescent (Muus 1970). Other historical comparisons reveal a similar trend:

> The seats in the famous La Scala opera house in Milan, Italy, which was constructed in 1776–1778, were thirteen inches wide. Thirty years ago most states outlawed seats that were less than eighteen inches wide. In 1975 comfortable seats will need to be 24 inches wide. The feet of the American male at the present time grow one third of an inch every generation, which means an upward change of one shoe size per generation. Today the shoes worn by the average male are 9–10B, while his grandfather in all probability wore a size 7 shoe (Muus 1970, p. 170).

A number of factors have been proposed to account for the physical changes in modern adolescents, including better nutrition, improved living standards and medical breakthroughs in the treatment of childhood diseases. However, '[v]ariability is the rule, rather than the exception, for all pubertal processes' (Brookes-Gunn 1988, p. 365). An adolescent's reaction to puberty is dependent upon many social and psychological factors.

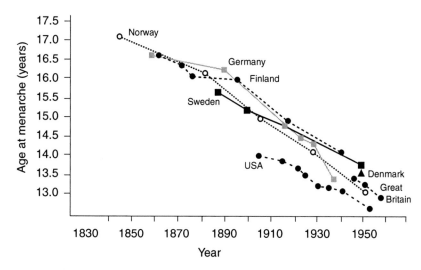

Figure 18.2 The secular trend in the mean age of menarche for various countries
Source: Adapted from Tanner 1970

Early and late maturation: Psychological effects

According to Brookes-Gunn (1988), three points are valid in relation to individual variation in pubertal development. Although she has described these points in relation to girls' maturational timing, similar comments could be made of boys' development.

1   There is individual variation of the mean age of the onset of puberty. While the average age of onset of breast buds in American girls is 11 years, the range is from 8 to 13 years.
2   The 'sequence' of timing of pubertal events is not standard. Thus, although the sequence in American girls is usually breast buds followed by the appearance of pubic hair, in about half of girls pubic hair appears first.
3   Thirdly, the speed of passage through puberty varies. The 'average' girl takes four years to develop mature breasts, but some girls can proceed through the development in one and a half years.

Consequences of early and late maturation

Two contrasting views have been presented to account for the consequences of early and late maturational development.

1   *The Deviance Hypothesis.* This view as represented by the writings of Alsaker (1995) proposes that being off time causes difficulties for the adolescent because it places him/her in a socially deviant category.

2   *The Developmental Stage Termination Hypothesis.* The view (e.g. Petersen
     & Taylor, 1980) presented here proposes that early maturation puts adoles-
     cents at risk because it leads to their involvement in roles and activities
     (e.g. dating) for which they lack appropriate skills.

Research (Williams & Currie 2000) has highlighted the complex interplay
between pubertal status and self-concept with their research suggesting that the
onset of puberty may impact differently on the self-esteem of male and female
students.

Sex differences

Boys' and girls' progression through puberty differs in a number of important
respects (Tanner 1973; Brookes-Gunn 1988). For girls, the growth spurt and
the onset of the development of secondary sex characteristics typically occurs
earlier than for boys. In detailed longitudinal research, Eveleth and Tanner
(1977) demonstrated that the growth spurt is earlier in girls, while Lipsitz
(1979, p. 4) draws out the implications of this difference:

> The fact is that there is no more variable group that we can deal with than adol-
> escents, especially young adolescents . . . Because of this extreme variability,
> there can be a six year span in biological development between a quickly devel-
> oping girl and a slowly developing boy, and here I am only talking about
> biological age (Lipsitz 1979, p. 4).

The impact of pubertal timing on boys

Boys who mature earlier than their peers are taller, heavier and more muscular.
Early social maturation carries with it advantages for boys while late maturation can generate problems (Coleman & Hendry 1990). Early maturing boys
have been found to be more relaxed, more popular, less dependent and more
attractive to both adults and peers than their later maturing counterparts
(Coleman & Hendry 1990). They have a better self-image than girls of the
same age (Petersen et al. 1983; 1988). However, the research of Williams and
Dunlop (1999) indicates that off-time maturers (early or late maturers) are at
greater risk for delinquency and are more likely to engage in antisocial behaviour such as alcohol/drug use, delinquency and early sexual activity, lending
support for the 'deviance' hypothesis. One explanation for the increased likelihood of early maturers engaging in risk-taking behaviour is due to their
friendship with older peers (Silbereisen et al. 1989).

The impact of pubertal timing in girls

Until recently, little was known about the psychological consequences for girls
of being early or late maturers (Brookes-Gunn 1988):

> It has been hypothesised that being on time is more advantageous than being off
> time, and that early maturing girls are at more of a disadvantage than late

maturers because the former are more deviant compared to their male and female counterparts (Brookes-Gunn 1988, p. 368).

Similar observations have been made by Jones and Mussen (1958) and Peskin and Livson (1972), who have noted that early maturing girls will frequently try to hide their changing physical appearance from their peers under baggy jumpers.

However, this seemingly clear picture of the psychological consequences of early maturation for girls is clouded somewhat by a number of variables. Faust (1960) reported that early menstruation was regarded as a liability for girls in school year 6 but as a social advantage for those in years 7 and 8. That is, it would appear that while early maturation is a disadvantage to young girls when they are developmentally ahead of the majority of their peers, it can be an advantage at an older age when it provides a desirable link with older adolescents. As such, peer evaluations can be a powerful influence in determining the impact of the event upon an individual child. Similar to early maturing boys, early maturing girls, while more popular with peers, are at greater risk for engaging in delinquent activities, using drugs and alcohol and experiencing early sexual intercourse.

Sex-role development

As already noted in this chapter, adolescence brings with it considerable physical changes – a point that highlights the quantitative and qualitative differences between the sexes. Two terms commonly used in the literature to describe sex-role development are **sex-role** and **gender identity**.

Cunningham (1990, p. 133) defines sex-role as consisting of 'those activities, interests and tasks that are socially prescribed for men and women'. That is, sex-role is the role that society perceives to be appropriate to a person's biological sex. Douvan (1979, p. 79) defines gender identity as 'an early body-related sense of the self as male or female'. That is, it is the ability of the individual to identify himself or herself as male or female. Gender is social, not biological, and gender identification is expressed behaviour that is learned rather than inherited.

sex-role
learned behaviour that society deems appropriate for a person's sex; compare gender identity.

gender identity
a person's sense of self as male or female; compare sex role.

It is important to make the distinction between sex-role and gender identity because the two do not always go together. In rare instances where genital abnormalities at birth make the identification of the biological sex of the individual difficult, it has been shown that a member of one sex can be raised 'rather' successfully as a member of the opposite sex (Cunningham 1990). Money (1968) identified 19 cases in which there was a discrepancy between the child's chromosomal sex and the gender label applied to the child. In all 19 cases the children came to define themselves in terms of the sex-role assigned to them rather than in accordance with their chromosomal sex. Such evidence highlights the important role of psychological and social forces in determining sex-role.

It also appears that neither gender identity nor sex-role necessarily determines sexual preference, such that males and females can be heterosexual or homosexual with little apparent detriment to their psychological functioning. Cunningham (1990) observes that sex-role activities and sex traits do not always go together. Thus, a football player (pursuing a masculine interest) can be compassionate and caring (feminine traits).

Theories of sex-role development

An important question associated with gender identity and **sex-role** concerns how adolescents acquire these attributes. A number of theories have been proposed in answer to this question.

Sex-role development is a much debated topic.

Psychoanalytic theory

Freudian theory has made a significant initial contribution to our understanding of sex-role development and elements of this theory were briefly discussed in chapter 3. Freud (1955) proposed that an important feature in the development of sex-role is the resolution of the Oedipus complex at about 4 or 5 years of age. The nature of the child's love for her or his mother is initially based on the meeting of the child's needs. At about 4 or 5 years of age the child begins to develop incestuous feelings for the parent of the opposite sex (phallic stage). Competition with the same-sex parent for the love of the opposite-sex parent is eventually resolved and the child comes to identify with the same-sex parent, taking on the characteristics and attributes of this parent. That is, in resolving the Oedipus complex, boys assume the sex-role of the father and girls, in resolving the Electra complex, take on the sex-role of the mother.

In terms of Freudian theory, sex-role development is largely completed during early childhood. Freud's theory therefore has little relevance for adolescence, apart from the implication that the success or otherwise of the resolution of the Oedipus and Electra complexes may have long-term consequences for later sexual adjustment.

Contemporary views of sex-role development give little credence to psychoanalytic theory:

> There is little support for Freud's key notion of defensive identification with the aggressive parent. Instead children are much more likely to mimic warm or socially powerful adults than they are to imitate threatening individuals who are competing with them (Cunningham 1990, p. 135).

More specifically, the theory has been criticised on grounds that awareness of genital differences in young children is a minor element in identity development, that there is no good reason to think of male genitals as superior to female genitals and for the assumption that Freud made that the father was the disciplinarian in the home, thus overlooking the mother's role in this regard.

Behavioural theory

An alternative view of sex-role development has been proposed by behavioural (or social learning) theory (Mischel 1970). The concepts of classical and operant conditioning explained in chapter 3 are pivotal in the behavioural theory of sex-role development. According to this theory, sex-roles are learnt by the same processes as those by which other behaviours are learnt. Thus, boys and girls learn their sex-roles through the contingent application of rewards and punishments.

According to behavioural theory, children learn their sex-roles through imitation or observational learning. The principles underlying this theory were expounded by Albert Bandura (1971; see chapter 3). Children's concepts of sex stereotypes are based on their own observations of how adults behave, whether in real life, on television or in books. According to Cunningham (1990, p. 136), 'Social learning theories probably provide the most successful explanation of sex role development to date'.

Cognitive–developmental theory

In cognitive–developmental theory, children are thought to develop sex-roles in specific stages (Kohlberg 1966). As their cognitive development proceeds, so they acquire sex-roles. Kohlberg proposed the following stages in children's sex-role development (Brookes-Gunn & Matthews 1979).

In the first stage children divide the world up into male and female, recognising over time that they belong to one of these groups. We can hear this process at work when a 3-year-old says to her friend 'You pretend to be the Mummy and I'll be the Daddy'.

The second step involves attaching a 'value' to people, attitudes and behaviours of the same sex. During this time, children will seek out same-sex individuals to emulate. However, Kohlberg (1966) does not believe that such imitation should be confused with behavioural theory. Rather, it arises through valuing behaviour in the individual of the same sex and desiring to imitate that person. According to Kohlberg, behavioural theorists explain that:

> sex-typed behaviour and attitudes are acquired through social rewards that follow sex-appropriate responses made by the child or by a relevant model. The social learning theory syllogism is: I want rewards, I am rewarded by doing boy things, therefore I want to be a boy. In contrast, cognitive theory assumes this sequence: I am a boy, therefore I want to do boy things, therefore the opportunity to do boy things is rewarding (Kohlberg 1966, p. 89).

Finally, according to Kohlberg, in the last stage the child identifies with the same-sex parent, while valuing the same-sex people and their activities. As Brookes-Gunn and Matthews (1979, p. 118) observe, 'To a cognitive developmentalist, identification represents a positive, internal process motivated by the child's active search for understanding and striving toward mastery of the world.'

In an Australian study using a cognitive–developmental framework, Bussey (1983) argues that children must accomplish four cognitive tasks before their sex-role behaviour is significantly influenced by others:

1 realising the existence of two groups of people: males and females;
2 identifying that they belong to one of these groups;
3 being able to encode behaviour as male and female appropriate;
4 realising that they are subject to a similar set of expectations to that applied to other children of their sex.

Ethological theory

Geary and Bjorklund (2000) have reviewed the contribution of evolutionary theory to our understanding of developmental psychology. As noted in chapter 3, ethology originally concerned the study of animal behaviour. A core explanatory principle was natural selection which explains species-wide adaptive behaviour designed to ensure the survival of an animal species in a particular ecological niche.

In relation to gender differentiation in childhood, Geary and Bjorklund (2000, p. 60) argue that '[f]rom an evolutionary perspective, these sex differences are predicted to be a reflection of and a preparation for sex differences in adult reproductive activities'. In this way, boys' competitive behaviour and striving for dominance is preparation for adult male competition over mates. In contrast, girls' greater sociability, social responsiveness and cooperativeness prepares them for involvement in social groups in which to raise their young.

Feminist theories

Feminist theory has made an important contribution to our understanding of the development of gender identity. While a number of different forms of feminism exist, all offering slightly different perspectives, they share common ground in emphasising the critical role of the social environment in shaping gender development.

Various schools of feminist thinking exist, each emphasising different aspects of gender.

Liberal feminism. This line of thinking emphasises the role of socialisation in shaping the development of children's gender. As noted by Burr (1998, p. 16), 'Liberal feminists assume that girls and boys are born with equal potential to develop a variety of skills and abilities and that it is only through our child-rearing practices that they learn to become typically feminine or masculine.'

Radical feminism. This viewpoint identifies 'patriarchy' as the central issue, such that women have been oppressed not only as a class by men but also oppressed in their private and personal relations with men. As Burr (1998) has noted, the movement has been instrumental in encouraging 'feminist' research and in challenging the mainstream methods and practices of research and for encouraging research about and for women.

Socialist feminism. As described by Burr (1998), this outlook represents a dual systems theory in as much as gender issues are shaped by the economic system and gender relations, and the interaction between the two. As described by Burr, to understand women's oppression, an examination of the gender division of labour in the household, as well as in the workforce, is necessary.

Integrating perspectives

Maccoby (2000), in an overview of gender development, has called for a more integrated approach for explaining gender development. As she notes, 'In the last century, there have been substantial changes in gender roles and the relationships between the sexes, changes that have occurred much too rapidly to be explained in genetic terms' (p. 405). Maccoby goes on to note that this amount of rapid change underscores the significant role of social factors in explaining gender development.

Femininity and masculinity

Developmental psychologists have long been interested in femininity and masculinity and particularly its measurement.

The Australian writer Ann Oakley (1972, p. 189) notes: 'On the whole, Western society is organised around the assumption that the differences between the sexes are more important than any qualities they have in common'. This attitude has led psychologists to the predominant view that good mental health in adolescence and early adulthood is dependent upon the acquisition of sex-appropriate personality traits (Cunningham 1990). Traits typically associated with the sexes comprise:

Males
- aggressiveness
- competitiveness
- dominance
- adventuresomeness

Females
- nurturance
- caring
- understanding
- passivity

Three models of healthy sex-role development have been proposed in the psychological literature (Whitely 1983).

Congruence model

This model proposes that for the most positive outcome, men should adopt a strong masculine sex-role identity and women should adopt a strong feminine sex-role identity.

Androgyny model

The *Macquarie Dictionary* defines androgynous as follows:

> 1. *Bot.* having staminate and pistillate flowers in the same inflorescence. 2. being both male and female; hermaphroditic. 3. having both masculine and feminine characteristics.

androgyny possession of both male and female personality characteristics.

The **androgyny** model emphasises the value of a person having both male and female characteristics. Early measures of masculinity and femininity assumed they were bi-polar constructs of a single dimension. Constantinople (1973) was critical of such an outlook, suggesting that instead of thinking of masculinity and femininity as a fixed entity it might be better thought of as a social construction arising out of ways that humans organise their social experience. Such an outlook is counter to the view that links psychological health with appropriate sex type.

Psycho-dynamic theory would suggest that pathology with a lack of appropriate femininity in women and masculinity in men. Contrary to such a view, Bem (1974) argued that in fact women and men who showed extreme sex-typing were less well adjusted than others. She further argued that femininity and masculinity can unduly prescribe our behaviour to narrow roles. That is, under certain circumstances it is a strength to have recourse to either 'typically' masculine or 'typically' feminine traits. While intuitively appealing, the androgynous model is not without its critics and Burr (1997) provides a succinct summary of such criticisms, e.g. explaining why society would focus so much attention on repressing certain characteristics in one half of the population while encouraging them in the other half.

Masculinity model

The proposition put forward in this model is that masculine traits are an advantage to both sexes.

Support for this third view is found in the research of Antill and Cunningham (1980). In a study using a variety of masculinity–femininity traits, they concluded that Australian male and female students who described themselves primarily with masculine characteristics displayed higher self-esteem than those with more feminine self-concepts. Their results run counter to the ideas expressed in the androgyny model. Researchers have explored some personality characteristics of androgynous persons, and have generally found such people to be mentally healthy (Bem & Lenney 1976; Bem, Martyna & Watson 1976), to have positive self-concepts (O'Connor, Mann & Bardwick 1978), and to be adaptable and behaviourally flexible (Bem & Lenney 1976).

Explanations offered by Cunningham (1990) for the contradiction in findings include the need to specify which aspects of the self and personality adjustments are measured. Thus, Cunningham (1990) describes research by Marsh (1987) where masculinity predicted self-concept in those areas where Australian boys had higher self-concepts, such as mathematics, and femininity predicted self-concepts in areas where girls had higher self-concepts, such as relationships with same-sex peers. Obviously more research is needed to untangle the relationship between sex-role and aspects of development such as self-concept.

The task of developing a sexual identity

The task facing adolescents in terms of sex-role development is a difficult one. In Australian society, where higher value is generally placed on masculine than on feminine traits and behaviour, the task is certainly a challenging one (Antill & Cunningham 1980). The task facing Australian adolescent girls in developing a sex-role is different from that facing boys. The double bind for girls is that if they embrace behaviour expected of a healthy adult they risk being described as unfeminine, but if they adopt feminine behaviours they risk being labelled as immature. For boys, Australian society makes it very difficult to transcend a masculine model of sex-role in order to adopt a more androgynous outlook. This is because Australian society encourages the masculine attributes of dominance, strength and competitiveness and downgrades the feminine attributes of tenderness, caring and sensitivity to others.

Adolescent health issues

Boss, Edwards and Pitman (1995), in a comprehensive analysis of the status of young Australians, argued that '. . . on average, the physical health status of all Australians has improved over the last 10 years', while also noting that '[u]nfortunately, good health is not always a reality for certain groups of the

VIEWPOINT

What would lead a young person to take his or her own life?

'Family problems that they see no solution to'
Belinda, 18 years

'Depression, lack of love, don't feel needed'
Rosie, 18 years

'Parental pressure – a world that doesn't understand – loneliness'
Julie, 17 years

'Stressed out with school – family problems – drugs – sexual abuse'
Shannon, 17 years

Australian child population' (p. 102). The same authors identify at-risk groups to include Aboriginal and Torres Strait Islanders, and rural and homeless children. It is generally accepted by researchers and social policy advocates that adolescence is a critical period for the development and adoption of healthy life-style behaviours (e.g. eating habits, exercise). In reviewing the literature concerning the nature and type of problems facing children and adolescents it can be argued that the problems experienced by children and young people are significant, and there is no sign they are diminishing. In the remainder of this chapter, a number of health issues pertinent to youth will be addressed.

Trends and issues

Adolescents and suicide

As Zubrick et al. (2000) have noted as many as one in five Australian children aged from 4 to 17 have significant mental health problems. In Australia, more people die from suicide than motor vehicle accidents and young Australians experience particularly high rates of suicide (Baume & McTaggart 1998). A similar pattern exists among New Zealand youth (Beautrais 2000). In reviewing suicide trends in Australian metropolitan and non-metropolitan areas, Baume and McTaggart (1998) noted that over the last 30 years suicide rates in the 15–34 age range have increased

almost four-fold (see Figure 18.4). A broad overview of suicide rates is presented in the Australian Bureau of Statistics breakdown by gender and age (See Figure 18.3).

Typically, males employ more violent means of suicide, although in both sexes hanging is the preferred method. In females the impact of this on the overall rate has been offset by a decline in suicide by drug overdose, which was previously the preferred method (Baume & McTaggart 1998). A similar pattern exists among New Zealand youth (Beautrais 2000).

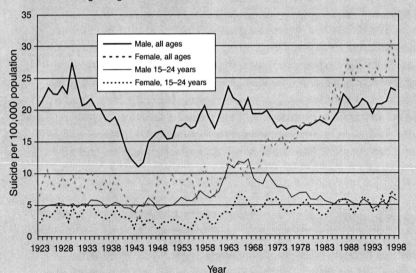

Figure 18.3 Suicide rates (standardised) per 100 000 population 1923–98

Source: ABS 2000 'Australian Social Trends' (2000), cat. no. 4102.0

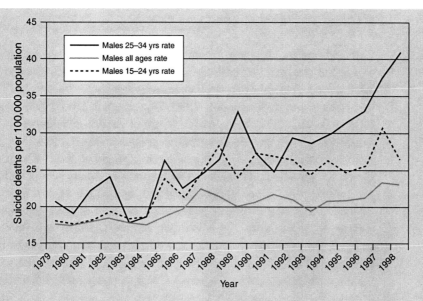

Figure 18.4 Male suicide rates (standardised) per 100 000 males, by age 1979–98

Source: ABS 2000 'Australian Social Trends' (2000), cat. no. 4102.0

While at least some of the increase in suicide rate is a statistical artefact – that is, it has come about as a result of changes in coronial classification practices – Hassan (unpub.) largely agrees with the conclusions of Kosky (1987) regarding the real rise in youth suicide, which can be explained by a number of factors. One such factor is the increase in youth unemployment and associated fear of economic deprivation, which have had a significant impact on the mental health of Australia's youth. Youth unemployment is on the increase in Australia and is now as high as 18.1 per cent for males and 19.5 per cent for females in the 15 to 19 age group. Changes in the organisation, composition and structure of the Australian family (see chapter 2) may also be a contributing factor to the increasing youth suicide rate (Hassan unpub.).

The extent of suicidal behaviour among Australian youth should be a source of considerable concern to health professionals and the wider community alike (Kosky 1987; Hassan unpub. According to Balson, an Australian psychologist, 90 per cent of suicide victims give repeated warnings of their intentions and talk of their suicide as close as a week

before their death (*The Sunday Age*, 26 July 1992). However, in seeking to understand more fully why young people commit suicide, some insight might be gained by looking behind the statistics at the human face of Australia's youth, as revealed in the following examples:

> *A lot of love and care, that's all I want. That's hardly asking anything at all.*

A 17-year-old homeless girl found dead with a needle in her arm (cited in *The Age*, 2 January 1988).

> *A few nights back, a 14-year-old girl injected battery acid into her veins. She died horribly ... alone ... in sheer agony ... without hope ... a body racked by terrible pain on the verge of death ... for what? Battery acid straight into her veins ... at 14.*

(Social worker, cited in *The Bulletin*, 12 January 1988).

Eating disorders in adolescence

Eating disorders are certainly not confined to adolescence and it is well to appreciate that their manifestation in adolescence has its precursors in pre-adolescence. A body of Australian research conducted by Marika Tiggemann (e.g. Tiggemann & Pennington, 1990; Tiggemann & Dyer 1995; Tiggemann & Wilson-Barrett 1998) has clearly identified gender differences in body dissatisfaction, with women manifesting greater dissatisfaction than men. This difference is confirmed in young children. Rolland et al. (1997), in a study of the eating attitudes and behaviours of Australian primary school children (aged 8–12years), reports that 50 per cent of girls and 33 per cent of boys wanted to be thinner and 40 per cent of girls and 24 per cent of boys had dieted to lose weight. As reported by the Australian writers Griffiths and Furmill (1995, p. 2), 'Dieting has been associated with an eight-fold rise in the risk of the development of dieting disorders, such as anorexia and bulimia nervosa ...' Bulimia nervosa and anorexia nervosa are apparently related disorders.

Prevalence of eating disorders

Bulimia nervosa

As reported by Blinder and Chao (1994), bulimia was first described in 1797. The syndrome describes a behaviour pattern characterised by ravenous eating followed by self-induced vomiting. Weiss et al. (1994) report that bulimia typically begins between 16 and 19 years of age and at least 90 per cent of suffers are female (DSM-IV 1994).

As reported by Fisher et al. (1995) in a review of eating disorders, approximately 1–5 per cent of adolescent girls meet the criteria for bulimia nervosa, while 10–50 per cent report engaging in occasional self-induced vomiting. Ben-Tovim (1988) reports that for the Australian population, bulimia was found in 1–2 per cent of all women. The essential features of bulimia nervosa include recurrent episodes of binge eating, a feeling of lack of control over eating behaviour during binges, self-induced vomiting, use of laxatives or diuretics, strict dieting and a persistent concern with body weight.

Oliver (1998) has noted a recent cultural shift pertinent to eating disorders, namely the valorisation of female thinness. Indicative of such a shift is that Marilyn Monroe as a film star of the 1950s had a body size 16 contrasting with Jamie Lee Curtis as a film star of the 1980s with a body size of 8 to 10. As Markula (1995, p. 425) notes:

> Popular women's magazines are saturated with images of beautiful, thin and tight models.

Anorexia nervosa

Anorexia nervosa is an eating disorder associated with food and weight control. It has been recognised as a clinical entity for centuries. In this disorder, weight loss is typically achieved by restricting food intake, but laxatives, diuretics and self-induced vomiting may also be used.

The disorder is most frequently diagnosed in adolescents, with approximately 0.5 per cent of the female population exhibiting some features of the syndrome (Paige 1983). The number of diagnosed anorexics is increasing (Harding 1985).

Approximately one-third of anorexics are overweight before the initiation of self-imposed weight control (Root & Powers 1983). Second-born children appear to be at greater risk of developing the disorder (Humphries et al. 1982). As Harding (1985, p. 276) notes:

> The dieting anorexic is frequently a member of a family under extreme stress from family disagreements, divorce and separation. The anorexic is often a perfectionistic, self critical, obsessed individual with little psychological insight.

The Diagnostic and Statistical Manual of Mental Disorders (1987) lists the following criteria for diagnosis:

- intense fear of becoming obese which does not diminish with weight loss;
- disturbance of body image – for example, claiming to be fat when emaciated;
- refusal to maintain a body weight greater than normal weight for height and age;
- in females, absence of at least three consecutive menstrual cycles.

anorexia nervosa
an eating disorder characterised by extreme reduction of food intake and loss of at least 25 per cent of original body weight.

Theories of anorexia nervosa

Biological theories

The biological view is that some dysfunction of the hypothalamus (see Physical Development) brings about anorexia. The evidence to support this view is scarce. Although anorexics do suffer from abnormal hormone secretions (which is why their menstrual cycles cease), these abnormalities seem to be more an effect than a cause. Thus, if an anorexic can be induced to gain weight, hormonal and menstrual functioning will return to normal (Crisp 1980).

Psychoanalytic theory

This theory proposes that anorexia nervosa involves a regression to the oral or anal stage and represents an attempt to avoid the conflicts arising from adolescent sexuality (Richardson 1980). In this view, the anorexic will therefore often show the personality characteristics associated with these stages, including stubbornness, obstinacy and a fixation with eating and bowel control.

Psychodynamic theory

Given psychodynamic theory's greater emphasis on the role of the ego in personality development (see chapter 3), anorexia nervosa is seen to arise from various ego deficits (Irwin 1984; Akridge 1988). According to Akridge (1988, p. 26), 'The pursuit of thinness by the young, female adolescent is a struggle for control and a sense of personal identity'. A contributing factor is that many anorexics suffer from disturbed body image, viewing themselves as too fat even though they are too thin (Anderson 1983).

Behavioural theory

In accordance with the principles of behavioural or learning theory outlined in chapter 3, anorexia nervosa would be regarded as a learned condition. The individual would receive some reinforcement for their eating behaviour, perhaps through the attention they receive.

More recent formulations include cognitive behavioural theories which build on the advances that have been made in relation to understanding psychiatric disorders such as depression (Beck et al. 1979), panic disorder (Barlow et al. 1998), and bulimia nervosa (Wilson & Fairburn 1998). As explained by Fairburn, Shafran and Cooper (1999), in their cognitive behavioural treatment of anorexia nervosa, the extreme need to control eating overlies the Western societies' preoccupation with judging self-worth in terms of body shape and weight.

Family systems theory

Based on the principles of Bateson (see chapter 3), family systems theory is increasingly being viewed as a means of treatment. According to Minuchin et al. (1978), the family becomes organised around the symptom of anorexia nervosa in order to avoid interpersonal conflicts. That is, the symptoms of the anorexic person serve the function of distracting the family's attention from other conflicts. The features of 'anorexic families' include (Minuchin et al. 1978):

1   enmeshment, whereby there is a lack of real role boundaries and a confusion of roles, with the tasks of each family member not clearly defined;
2   over-protectiveness – in as much as members seek to protect one another or a particular member of the family;
3   rigidity – the family holds quite rigid beliefs, such as loyalty to other family members;
4   conflict avoidance – members evade rather than deal with conflict.

In sum, the family systems approach appears to hold some hope for the treatment of anorexia. Anderson (1983, p. 18) observes that:

> The highest probability of developing anorexia nervosa is in a perfectionistic and self critical individual, who goes on a diet during the early teenage years to lose 5–20 pounds, and who comes from a family of upper middle class socio-economic status which is stressed in various ways.

Treatment using family systems theory involves reducing conflict and tension within the family system (Carino & Chmelko 1983). More appropriate role relations and clearer role boundaries are encouraged. The Australian family therapist Michael White (1983) has developed an approach to treatment based on the view that there is a link between anorexia nervosa and certain rigid, implicit family beliefs, which entail:

1 'loyalty' to one another, to the extent that if family loyalty is betrayed feelings of guilt are induced;

2 rigid role prescriptions for women, for example, women are expected to be sensitive, devoted and self-sacrificing.

3 White also argues that anorexic families are characterised by a view of reality dominated by the notion of 'insightfulness'. That is, family members believe they know one another's minds. In actual fact, White believes such 'insightfulness' frequently 'blinds' members to the destructive character of such beliefs. White's approach to treatment is to challenge the family members' strongly held beliefs regarding the effects of 'loyalty', rigid role prescriptions and insightfulness.

The 'objectification of women'

> [Men] *act* and *women appear*. Men look at women. Women watch themselves being looked at . . . Thus she turns herself into an object – and most particularly an object of vision: a sight (Berger 1972, p. 47).

There is no question that adolescence, particularly for girls, is a time when many changes – some quite striking – occur in terms of body shape and size. Paradoxically, as their bodily shape becomes less angular and rounder and softer, their culture (mainstream Western) is telling them in very powerful terms that 'thin is beautiful'. As the New Zealand researcher Markula (1995, p. 424) has noted, '. . . women's bodies come in a variety of shapes and weights . . . the media portray only thin and tight models'. As the author goes on to note, many feminist scholars argue strongly that this fashion ideal is oppressive to women.

Markula raised the question of why women continue to read such magazines, diet or engage in strenuous exercise regimes with a view to obtaining some fashion ideal. As she notes, 'Can one simply assume that most women are unaware of how they contribute to their own suppression through their everyday behavior'(p. 425). Her research indicated that women's everyday life was far more complex than such a simple conclusion would have us believe and that behaviour is not simply a function of ignorance or lack of education.

While Markula gathered her data from university-aged women, research by Oliver (2000), involving young adolescent girls, emphasised the 'objectification' of young women's bodies, as referred to by Berger. Oliver's research highlighted the role of 'fashion'.

> It is partially through fashion that they begin to judge themselves and each other, a requisite factor if this oppression is to continue, to determine whether they are or are not the ideal image (p. 242).

Oliver argued strongly that health promotion among young girls should actively educate them regarding the oppressive and disempowering nature of such cultural images. It is interesting to speculate regarding the possible link between adolescent reading habits involving women's health and fitness magazines and the use of eating-disordered diet methods, e.g. laxatives or intentional vomiting.

Acquired Immune Deficiency Syndrome (AIDS)

AIDS
acquired immune deficiency syndrome, the end of a spectrum of disease caused by a virus that attacks and exhausts key parts of the body's natural defence system.

First identified in 1981, **AIDS** has become a worldwide health crisis. As reported by McMurray (1997), the HIV epidemic now has an incidence rate of 16 000 new cases per day. Neither a vaccine to prevent infection, nor a cure is expected for several years. The first case of AIDS in Australia was identified in January 1982. By February 1995, 2341 cases had been diagnosed. Of these, 96 per cent were males, of whom 72 per cent were in the age group 25–44 years (Li et al. 1996). In New Zealand, 128 cases had been reported by 21 April 1989.

What is AIDS?

In 1981, doctors in California and New York began to notice that a number of previously healthy homosexual young men were being diagnosed with opportunistic diseases usually found in people with suppressed immune systems (Fauci 1986). AIDS is the end of a spectrum of disease caused by the human immunodeficiency virus (HIV). This particular virus attacks and exhausts key parts of the body's natural defence system. HIV is carried in the blood, semen and bodily secretions of infected individuals. It can be transmitted through intercourse and the transfer of blood, such as a blood transfusion from a mother to her baby. More specifically, it is transmitted through unprotected sexual intercourse and the transfer of infected blood, particularly through sharing infected needles and other drug-injecting equipment.

Incidence in adolescents

Lawrance et al. (1990) note that in the United States 21 per cent of known AIDS cases were in the 21 to 29 age group. Given that the average latency period for the virus is five to seven years, this means that most of these people were exposed to HIV as adolescents, either through sexual contact, intravenous drug use or both behaviours. In Australia, Greig and Raphael (1988) report that 61 per cent of deaths have occurred in the under-40 age group and 23 per cent in the under-30 age group. The general conclusion from the literature is that AIDS is a young person's disease.

Understanding AIDS

Various researchers have explored the issue of the knowledge that children and adolescents have of AIDS (USA – Schvaneveldt et al. 1990; Canada – King et al. 1989a; Australia – Greig & Raphael 1988; Greig & Raphael 1989; Turtle et al. 1989). The general conclusion to be drawn from these studies is that children and adolescents do not 'appear to have got the message about AIDS prevention. They are aware of the concept of AIDS but may have responded by denying their risk' (Greig & Raphael 1988, p. 26).

Children's perceptions of health and illness vary considerably, depending upon such factors as the stage of cognitive development. From a cognitive–developmental perspective, young children of pre-school age with an egocentric perspective are likely to believe that illness is caused by forces such as the 'sun' or 'wind' and that magical procedures (a word or gesture) can make one feel better. During middle childhood a more sophisticated outlook emerges: children's thinking is less influenced by notions of magic and is more logical in nature, so that they are able to understand illness in terms of 'germs'. In adolescence, the acquisition of abstract reasoning allows children to understand that illness is a complex process. Thus, in the case of AIDS, 'accurate knowledge of AIDS is directly related to children's age' (Shelley et al. 1990).

Attitudes towards AIDS

As reported by Peterson and Peterson (1987), older Australian adolescents rank AIDS as more of a threat than any other problem including unemployment, crime, drugs and nuclear war. New Zealand writers have also found that adolescents are a particularly vulnerable group, given that '[a]dolescence is a time of experimentation with a range of behaviours, both sexual and social, and intense conformity to peer group norms' (*The HIV/AIDS Epidemic: Toward a New Zealand Strategy* 1989, p. 11). Similar results have been reported for Australian teenagers (Gallois & Callan 1990).

In sum, the presence of AIDS underlines the urgent need for more research into adolescent sexuality. Educational efforts directed at adolescents should be sufficiently broad-based to take into account the broader social context of the adolescent world, such as the pressures that arise from the need to conform to peer group norms. Researchers such as Connors and Heavan (1990) are exploring the relationship between personal beliefs and attitudes towards AIDS sufferers, while Greig and Raphael (1989) are addressing the important question of how to educate Australian adolescents about AIDS prevention.

Adolescent risk-taking and AIDS

Various explanations have been offered for adolescents' apparent resistance to the need for safe practice to avoid exposure to HIV, including '[a] predilection by adolescents for risk-taking which distinguishes them from adults' (Greig & Raphael 1989, p. 11). New Zealand research (1997) has established that among adolescents,

> . . . many young people are engaging in high levels of risk-taking behaviour, such as not wearing helmets when riding bicycles and motor cycles, consuming alcohol on a weekly basis, not using contraceptives, carrying weapons and contemplating self-harm (p. 459).

Adolescence and the use of public space

Recent attention has been given to the manner in which boys and girls use public space. Research conducted by Kandy (1999) was prompted by adolescent girls' claims that they were only allowed access to the public space of the school basketball courts as spectators to the boys unless the boys were 'bored', in which case they were invited to play and subsequently 'ridiculed'. They cite research by James (1998) that girls desire a more equitable access to recreational space. This finding is consistent with earlier research that adolescent boys use and dominate public spaces in a manner which limits girls' access to such space (Girls in Space consortia 1997). The picture emerging confirms earlier research that girls and boys are socialised in different ways such that public space has a different meaning for each. Historically, men have controlled and dominated the more public spaces and women control the more domestic private spaces.

The development of such behaviour has been noted by Voss (1997) who identified three forms of social interaction between 5- and 7-year-olds, including (i) teasing; (ii) disputing; and (iii) playing. The teasing arose when space was limited while disputes occurred when space was invaded, with boys being more likely to 'initiate invasions' with associated attempts to impose rules and assert control. The Girls in Space (1997) consortia indicated the adolescent boys' use of and domination of public space threatened teenage girls and restricted their access to and use of space.

Drug use

> Drugs make you happy for a while and then you get hooked on it. A lot of people do it just to impress their friends, then some of them can't get out of it. (*The Advertiser*, 28 September 1990).

Increasing drug use is a common facet of adolescence in many Western countries. For example, in England, Wright and Pearl (1995) report that over the last 25 years there has been a four-fold increase in high school students' use of, or knowledge of those using illicit drugs. In Australia, surveys suggest that depending on the nature of the drug and the time of the survey, drug use is either increasing or decreasing (Donnelly & Hall 1994).

Factors associated with drug use indicate that there is a higher rate of abuse amongst certain at-risk populations. For example, drug abuse has been associated with school non-attendance (Lennings 1996) and family disruption (Miller, Maguin & Downs 1997).

From Table 18.1 it can be seen that for young Australians in 1998, marijuana topped adolescent drug use. A number of psychological explanations for drug use by adolescents have been identified (Wilks & Callan 1990).

Social learning theory

Social learning theory has made an important contribution to our understanding of the psychology of human development (see chapter 3). Key elements of the theory include the imitation and the modelling of the behaviour of significant others in the individual's life, such as peers, parents or teachers. According to this model, drug-taking is influenced by significant others in the adolescents' lives.

Table 18.1 Summary of illicit drug use in Australia, 1998

Substance/behaviour	Drugs ever used	Drugs recently used[a]	Mean age of initiation
	(per cent)	(per cent)	(years)
Marijuana	39.1	17.9	18.8
Pain-killers/analgesics[b]	11.5	5.2	19.6
Tranquillisers/sleeping pills[b]	6.2	3.0	23.3
Steroids[b]	0.8	0.2	21.4
Barbiturates[b]	1.6	0.3	19.8
Inhalants	3.9	0.9	17.5
Heroin	2.2	0.8	21.7
Methadone[c]	0.5	0.2	22.1
Amphetamines[b]	8.8	3.7	20.0
Cocaine	4.3	1.4	22.2
Hallucinogens	9.9	3.0	18.4
Ecstasy/designer drugs	4.8	2.4	22.5
Injected illegal drugs	2.1	0.8	20.7
Any illicit drug	46.4	22.8	18.8
None of the above	53.6	77.2	..

(a) Used in the last 12 months.
(b) For non-medical purposes.
(c) Non-maintenance.
Source: National Drug Strategy Household Survey 1998.

Sociocultural model

The social context is significant for understanding adolescent drinking: 'Adolescents learn to drink or not according to whether drinking is approved and sanctioned by others' (Wilks & Callan 1990, p. 199). It is the values, attitudes and beliefs that society holds towards activities such as alcohol drinking that helps to shape behaviour.

Social–psychological model

This approach emphasises the importance of adolescent self-esteem, depression and alienation in influencing drug-taking. For example, in relation to alienation, the implication is that cultural forces and the pressures arising from an industrial society underpin adolescents' temptation to use drugs as a form of escapism.

Drug education programs

Booth and Samdal (1997) have argued that schools provide significant opportunities for health promotion, although in Australia little research has been conducted to understand the current status of health promotion in schools.

In an analysis of a New Zealand alcohol/drug education program, Newport (1989) suggests that programs are ineffective when:

- they provide only information and facts;
- they use scare tactics;

- they use 'one-off' guest speakers or a single lecture on the danger of alcohol or other drugs.

Newport emphasises that any drug education program needs to be related to the social and historical context. It should take into account elements such as peer pressure and should be part of an ongoing health education program.

Protective factors in adolescent health behaviour

Research has identified various protective factors pertinent to health. For example, links have been established between the value attached to healthy behaviours and positive health practices. Peer and parental models for healthy behaviour correlate significantly with adolescents' participation in health behaviours. Research by Jessor, Turbin and Costa (1998) with American adolescents, has identified proximal (health-related) and distal (conventionally-related) protective factors.

Proximal factors: include the value adolescents attach to health-related behaviour, the perceived effects of health-compromising behaviour and parents who model healthy behaviour.

Distal factors: include a positive orientation to school, friends who model conventional behaviour, involvement in prosocial activities and church attendance.

Health promoting schools

The World Health Organisation Health Promoting Schools framework (see website p. 412) presents a comprehensive holistic approach to fostering health within a school and community context, utilising health and education personnel in a common effort to promote healthy behaviour. As described by Booth and Samdal (1997, p. 365), 'A health promoting school concept is based on a holistic view which recognises the different physical, social and mental dimensions of health . . .' A health-promoting schools framework has been used to address health-related problems such as eating disturbance, body image problems and smoking (Neumark-Sztainer 1996; O'Dea & Abraham 2000).

The family life-cycle: 18

The empty nest syndrome

An important stage in the family life-cycle identified by various theorists has been called the 'empty nest syndrome'. This occurs when the children have grown to adulthood and leave the family home to establish a life and home for themselves (Hill 1986).

Raup and Myers (1989) distinguish between the empty nest 'experience' and the empty nest 'syndrome'. The latter is a maladaptive response to the family life-cycle transition when the children have left home. As noted by Raup and Myers (1989), parents – especially mothers – are prone to experiencing overwhelming grief, sadness, dysphasia and depression, although 'relatively few women experience the plethora of negative emotions and adjustment difficulties that are diagnosed as the "empty nest" syndrome.' However, clinicians have observed that this syndrome certainly does affect some individuals and families.

Case study

When the Fox family began counselling, they consisted of the father Glen (45 years), mother Janette (41 years) and daughter Vanessa (16 years). An older son had died two years previously in a car accident. The reason that they had requested help was that Vanessa was 'uncontrollable' and had 'run away from home'. At the first session Glen was quite emotional (crying frequently), Janette was calm and Vanessa was angry, frequently shouting when an argument developed. During the next six sessions, Glen and Janette expressed considerable grief over their son's death and emphasised that they feared for their daughter, given that she wanted to leave home permanently. However, it emerged in the course of counselling that the primary concern of the parents was the fear of their own loneliness once their daughter left home. A number of significant marital issues were addressed in the course of counselling. The 'empty nest' syndrome had caught them unprepared to face their 'new' life as a couple.

Responses

The response of parents to their last child leaving home varies in relation to personal, social and cultural factors.

Personal. When the last child leaves home, parents will often engage in a process of reviewing the 'success' or otherwise of their parenting years. The question that arises is whether the parents are able to view the child-rearing years as personally successful or whether they can see only missed opportunities. The outcome of this evaluation will influence parents' adjustment to the last child's departure.

Another personal issue facing the parents, particularly women who have devoted much of their life to child-rearing, is whether they as individuals or as a couple can successfully fill the void in their lives left by their last child's departure (Raup & Myers 1989).

Social. The reasons for the departure of the last child can influence parental adjustment to this life-cycle phase. For example, it may be more socially acceptable to the parents if the child leaves home to marry than to set up home alone. Parents may also view the departure of sons differently from that of daughters. For example, it may be more acceptable for the son to leave home than for the daughter because the parents may believe that a woman's role is to care for ageing parents.

Cultural. Different cultures may hold widely differing views about how and when a child can leave home.

Adjustment to the 'empty nest'

Various factors affect parents' adjustment to the empty nest. Raup and Myers (1989) have found that:

- women fulfilling traditional family roles often have the greatest difficulty in adjusting;
- adjustment is influenced by the degree of investment or involvement in the maternal role at the time a child plans to leave;
- adjustment is frequently difficult if there is a lack of alternative roles;
- parental adjustment can be more difficult if children leave home earlier than expected.

More research is needed to clarify the nature of the factors that might facilitate adjustment.

Chapter summary

In the context of rising concerns regarding the health and well-being of young people in many countries a strong call is being made by many to seriously address the significant issues currently facing them. The issues are complex and multi-faceted and are intimately linked to political, structural and social changes currently taking place in most countries around the world as they attempt to deal with issues such as the globalisation of economies.

Discussion questions

1   Is adolescence a time of 'storm and stress' or is it a relatively uneventful period? Use your own experience to illustrate the discussion.
2   What evidence is there that economic conditions influence views of adolescents, as Enright et al. (1987) suggest?
3   How do various psychological theories explain sex-role development?
4   Relate the concepts of early and late maturation to your own development and discuss their implications in terms of your own experience.
5   What relationship is there between the various social pressures brought to bear on today's adolescent and the eating disorder, anorexia nervosa?
6   Why is AIDS such an important issue in terms of adolescent development?
7   How do various psychological theories explain adolescent drug use?

Activities

1   Select a novel dealing with adolescence (for example, George Johnston's *My Brother Jack*). What image of adolescence is portrayed in the novel?
2   How are adolescents portrayed in the media (newspapers, TV 'soapies', magazines)? Discuss your findings.
3   Devise an effective media program to alert adolescents to the dangers of AIDS.

Selected websites

Youth Studies Australia <www.acys.utas.edu.au>

South Australian Health Promoting Schools Communication Network <www.sahps.net>

Child Adolescent Psychological and Educational Resources <www.caper.com.au>

19 Cognitive Development in Adolescence

'Alone'
From childhood's hour I have not been
As others were – I have not seen
As others saw – I could not bring
My passions from a common spring –
From the same source I have not taken
My sorrow I could not waken
My heart to joy at the same tone –
And all I loved – I loved alone . . .

Edgar Allen Poe (1829) from Childhood's Hour

KEY TERMS AND CONCEPTS

- Formal operations
- 'La méthode clinique'
- Information processing
- Developmental tasks
- Cycle of learning
- Imaginary audience
- Personal fable

Introduction

The nature of adolescent thinking has been the subject of a good deal of research. During adolescence individuals acquire a greater flexibility in the way they think and their cognitive abilities come to more closely resemble those of an adult. Adolescents are able to think in abstract terms and consider at length the nature of complex concepts such as beauty, truth and justice. This skill is promoted by their ability to entertain different ideas at the same time and to hypothesise about possibilities. In adolescence, individuals develop further their ability to put themselves in the place of another and then to consider such questions as 'What would it be like to be a person from a different cultural background?'

In this chapter we examine the way adolescents' thinking develops, particularly the transition from the concrete operational way of thinking that prevails in middle childhood to the formal operational thought of adolescence. The new skills acquired with formal operational thought are identified and discussed.

Other topics covered in this chapter include the information-processing view of adolescent cognitive development, Havighurst's developmental tasks, the SOLO taxonomy for understanding adolescent learning, adolescent decision-making and social cognition. Adolescent–parent conflict is examined in the Family Life-cycle: 19.

The nature of adolescent thinking

As Keating (1980, p. 211) observes:

> To ask the question 'What is the nature of adolescent thinking?' is to imply that there may be something unique or special about it, something that distinguishes it from the thinking of a child, which it succeeds, or from the thinking of a adult, which it precedes, or both.

Using a neo-Piagetian framework and drawing heavily on the work of Barbara Inhelder and Jean Piaget, Keating identifies five ways in which the thinking of adolescents differs from that of younger children.

1 Thinking about possibilities

Compared to the thinking processes of a child, adolescent thinking is usually considered to be more closely tied to possibilities rather than to concrete realities (Keating 1980). The adolescent is more capable than the child of thinking in abstract terms and this opens up the way to thinking about possibilities.

The 'pendulum' problem described by Inhelder and Piaget (1958) illustrates this point. Given a scientific problem to solve, such as what determines the time it takes for a pendulum to complete its swing, adolescents will usually construct hypotheses and carry out 'experiments' to find the answer. Piaget asked children of different ages to solve this problem. Possibilities for testing included:

- varying the length of the string;
- varying the weight of the object swung by the string;
- varying the height at which the pendulum is released.

Concrete operational children typically could not solve this problem because they did not know how to test possibilities systematically. Formal operational children would systematically vary one factor at a time while holding the others constant. After trying two different lengths of string with a 100 gram weight and then with a 200 gram weight, one 15-year-old girl correctly concluded: 'It is the length of string that makes it go faster or slower. The weight doesn't play any role' (Inhelder & Piaget 1958, p. 75).

2 Thinking through hypotheses

A second feature of adolescent thinking identified by Keating (1980) relates to hypothesis development. For example, a primary-school child presented with the hypothetical question 'If all cats were pink and you had a cat, would your cat be pink too?' would laughingly dismiss the suggestion that cats are pink because he or she would know that it is not possible for cats to be pink. The adolescent can make logical connections between the two statements – if all cats are pink and then it would follow that his or her cat would be pink too.

3 Thinking ahead

Planning is an identifiable feature of formal operational thought (Keating 1980). Inhelder and Piaget (1958) demonstrated the existence of the planning component in adolescent thinking with a chemistry experiment. Four out of five test tubes were labelled 1, 2, 3, 4 and the fifth was labelled g. Adding g to some combination of 1, 2, 3 or 4 would give a yellow mixture. The task of the child or adolescent was to find the correct combination. Typically, the primary-school child attempted to solve the problem by trial and error – by adding a few drops of g to each of the test tubes. The adolescent in the formal operations stage typically devised a plan of action. For example, one often-used plan was to add g to the four test tubes, then pick up test tube 1 combined with g and add it to test tube 2 and so on, keeping a note of what had already been tried.

4 Thinking about thoughts

The formal operations child, unlike the concrete operations child, has the ability to think about thinking. One facet of this ability is the 'great fascination among adolescents for probing their own internal states, whether cognitive or emotional' (Keating 1980, p. 215): that is, the ability of adolescents to talk for hours, usually with peers, regarding their ideas and feelings.

5 Thinking beyond old limits

Adolescents in the formal operations stage have the advantage of being able to apply their new thinking skills not only to experimental situations but to a consideration of many topics that they may have never considered before.

Theoretical foundations

Piaget and formal operations

formal operations
Piaget's name for the fourth stage of cognitive development from about 11 years of age onwards, during which individuals acquire the ability to think in abstract terms.

Piaget has made an enormous contribution to our understanding of adolescent cognitive development: his theory of **formal operations** 'remains the pre-eminent account of adolescent cognition' (Moshman & Neimark 1982, p. 351).

From about 11 years of age, adolescents enter what Piaget called the formal operations period. They are now able to think beyond the present and can appreciate possible relations among sets of elements. Hypotheses can be set, which can then be confirmed or refuted.

Experiments with children conducted by Inhelder and Piaget (1958) allowed them to identify differences in the nature of thinking across the age groups. One of these experiments is known as the bending rods task. A number of flexible rods were attached to the side of a frame. The rods varied in length, width and material (wood or metal), and various weights could be attached to the end of the rods so that they bent. The primary-school aged child was asked to explain whether the amount the rods bent related to the length, width or material of the rods, or to the weight attached, or to any combination of these factors. An excerpt from Inhelder and Piaget (1944, p. 50) helps to explain one young child's reasoning:

> 'Some of them bend more than others because they are lighter [he points out the thinnest rods] and the others are heavier.' The interviewer hands him a short thick rod, a long thin one, and a short thin one and asks him to show how a thin rod can bend more than a thick one. The child places a 200-gram weight on the long thin rod and a 200-gram weight on the short thick one without seeming to notice that the thin rod he has chosen is also the [longer] of the two. 'You see', he says. The interviewer then asks whether it is better to make the comparison that the child just made or to compare instead a short thick rod with a short thin one. 'These two', the child answers, pointing to the long thin rod and the short thick one. The interviewer asks why. 'They are more different', the child says, over-looking the critical idea of holding all other factors equal while the effects of thickness are explored.

The young child's attention focuses primarily on one aspect of the problem at a time – for example, the 'heaviness' of the rods. The child may vary one set of factors while forgetting about the influence of other factors.

Table 19.1 Formal operations: the fourth of Piaget's stages of cognitive development

Stage	Age	Abilities
Sensori-motor period	0–2 years	Use of five senses to relate to the world
Pre-operational period	2–7 years	Language and symbolism
Concrete operations period	7–11 years	Can apply simple logic to solve problems
Formal operations period	11+ years	Abstract reasoning

In contrast, adolescents are much more capable of experimenting, and isolating variables to determine their effect. The adolescent approaches the problem much more systematically by:

- making good guesses (hypotheses) about the possible answer;
- being able to manipulate in an abstract way several factors that might in combination provide the answer, such as the length, thickness and weight of the rods;
- conducting a systematic experiment to test possible hypotheses.

An adolescent approached the bending rods experiment as follows (Inhelder & Piaget 1958, p. 60):

> The interviewer first asks her what factors are involved here. 'Weight, material, length of the rod, perhaps form,' she answers. The interviewer then asks if she can prove her hypotheses. The subject compares the 200- and 300-gram weights on the same steel rods. 'You see, the role of weight is demonstrated,' she explains. She then proceeds to isolate each of the other variables and to discover the relationships among them. Throughout she shows a clear understanding that the effects of any variable can only be demonstrated when all of the other factors are held constant.

A critique of Piaget's theory of cognitive development

Gardner (1979, pp. 73–4) acknowledges the tremendous contribution that Piaget has made to our understanding of the child's cognitive development as follows:

> Whatever its ultimate scientific fate, Piaget's contribution has over the past few decades provided a major impetus for research in developmental psychology. Before Piaget began research into the child's special cognitive and conceptual powers most work consisted of either sheer descriptions of objective features of the child's existence (physical milestones, preferred activities, motoric activities), anecdotal accounts of individual children, including ones displaying unusual abilities or difficulties, or broadly speculative interpretations of the course of growth.

The rise to prominence of Piagetian psychology coincided with the declining influence of behaviourism (Halford 1989). At the same time, the writings of cognitivists such as Bruner and Vygotsky were gaining ascendance. Halford (1989) observes that if the 1960s represented a period of optimism regarding the application of Piagetian psychology to understanding children's cognitive development, then the 1970s produced a reassessment resulting in some disillusionment with the theory. According to Halford, the disillusionment can be attributed to research that challenged many of Piaget's assumptions regarding the nature of cognitive development and to the failure of Piaget's research to reap the anticipated rewards in some applied areas. The following represents an overview of some of the major criticisms of Piagetian theory.

Methodology

A feature of Piaget's experimental method, ***la méthode clinique***, was his careful interviewing of the child. His child-centred approach in his earliest work consisted of an open-ended discussion with the child. From an empirical perspective, as outlined in chapter 1, Piaget's interview technique has been criticised as too subjective and value-laden. Criticism has also been directed at the reliance on verbal introspection of immature minds.

Ages and stages

One of the most trenchant criticisms of Piagetian theory is directed at the sequence of stages and the nature of children's behaviour within the stages (Gardner 1979), particularly the four criteria for stage development as described by Inhelder 1975:

1 a period of formation and progressive organisation of mental operations;
2 the progressive hierarchical development of one stage upon another;
3 relative similarity on the attainment of each stage;
4 a directional and hierarchical nature.

Major concerns have been expressed that an age/stage approach overlooks the part played by differences in mental and environmental factors in shaping a child's behaviour.

Language and Piaget's tasks

'So here's a question for you. How old did you say you were?'
Alice made a short calculation, and said 'Seven years and six months.'
'Wrong!' Humpty Dumpty exclaimed triumphantly. 'You never said a word like it!'
'I thought you meant "How old are you?"' Alice explained.
'If I'd meant that I'd have said it', said Humpty Dumpty.

(Carroll 1982)

As part of Piaget's interview technique, language is a very significant element that he uses to try to discover the course of children's cognitive functioning. Phillips (1969, p. 4) comments:

He observes the child's surroundings and his behaviour, formulates a hypothesis concerning the structure that underlies and includes them both, and then tests that hypothesis by altering the surroundings slightly – by rearranging the materials, by posing the problem in a different way, or even by overtly suggesting to the subject a response different from the one predicted by the theory.

For example, in a simple conservation task the format might be as follows:
Arrange two rows of objects (such as one cent pieces or buttons), about 10 in each row so that there is a one to one correspondence and the two rows are of equal length. Ask the child 'Are there the same number of buttons in each row?'

If he or she agrees, say 'Watch me now' as you lengthen one of the rows, and then repeat the question 'Are there the same number of buttons in each row?' Depending upon the child's answer, you might ask the child about the reason for the answer, rephrase the question or reset the experiment to repeat it.

McGarrigle and Donaldson (1974) and Donaldson (1978) are critical of the language used in such experiments. A child may take the repetition of the question as a cue to alter his or her first judgment, reasoning along the lines that if the researcher has altered the experimental set-up then perhaps a different answer is warranted. Donaldson also argues that sometimes the language used will carry so much weight that it will override the meaning of the situation, leading the young child to make errors in judgment. In sum, while Piaget's theory of cognitive development and the conclusions drawn from it have come under increasing scrutiny, the fact remains that few viable alternative frameworks have been developed (Halford 1989).

In an overview of current theorising about cognitive development, Thelen and Smith noted that 'viewed from above' Piaget's theory has captured the grand sweep of development' and that '. . . Piaget's cognitive theory fits the orderliness of development on a large scale (Thelen & Smith 1994, p. 21). They argue that on a more detailed scale the theory fails to capture the '. . . complexity and messiness of cognitive development in detail' (pp. 21–2). They cite Donaldson's (1978) work among others as indicating that when variations are made to Piagetian tasks there are confusing and contradictory findings. In particular, Thelen and Smith (1994) challenge central tenants of Piagetian theory, namely that:

1 children develop from an impoverished beginning state. They note that infancy research suggests that in fact the young infant is 'highly competent' (see chapter 9);
2 there are global discontinuities in cognition across stages. They cite evidence that in fact there are early precursors to abilities;
3 *monolithic cognitive growth*. In fact there is wide individual variation in development and competencies.

Thelen & Smith (1994, p. 22) note that 'Cognitive development does not look like a marching band; it looks more like a teeming mob'.

Adolescent language development

As noted by Nippold (2000), while it was once believed that language development is largely completed by late childhood (and still is according to some textbooks in developmental psychology!), it is now better understood that there is significant growth in language during the adolescent years. Whitmire (2000) notes that adolescence is a time of considerable physiological and psychological change (see chapters 18, 19 and 20). Language development becomes increasingly sophisticated and refined during the adolescent years. Nippold (2000) provides a useful framework for considering adolescent language development under the headings of 'pragmatics', 'syntax' and 'semantics'.

Pragmatics

Rinaldi (2000) observes that the attempt to distinguish the semantics of language from that aspect of language open to interpretation has a long history. McTear and Conti-Ramsden (1992) identified the field of 'pragmatics' as concerning the individual's abilities to interpret meaning, taking into account the linguistic and non-linguistic content. There is a significant body of evidence to suggest that during adolescence significant changes occur in the nature and manner in which language is used. As cited in Nippold (2000), during adolescence when peers become more significant, conversations with peers increase in number, particularly among girls, but not at the expense of conversations with parents. Generally, the topics of conversation differ with peers and parents, with adolescents increasingly likely to discuss personal issues with friends. Finally, Nippold (2000) reports that significantly higher levels of animation and affect are used with peers than with parents during adolescence.

Syntax

As already noted in this chapter, cognitive development undergoes significant change during adolescence. In this regard, as reported by Nippold (2000), an examination of adolescent written language indicates an increasingly sophisticated use of syntax, especially under conditions of 'persuasive' writing where the intention is to convince an audience of a particular argument. The use of longer sentences, appropriate linkages between ideas by words such as 'therefore', 'and', 'but', and the emergence of a coherent line of argument, come to exemplify adolescent language use.

Semantics

A body of research has considered the increasingly sophisticated use and understanding of aspects of language such as proverbs (e.g. 'A stitch in time saves nine'). Researchers including Rinaldi (2000) and Nippold (1998) have examined the development of semantics in language use. Nippold (1998) also considered other types of figurative language such as metaphors, similes and idiom. Owens (1995) has identified the use of slang as an important aspect of adolescent language development.

In summary, there is no doubt that language development continues to undergo change during the adolescent period, although in many ways it is an under-researched topic.

Indigenous language development

In considering the issue of language development, there are significant issues for Indigenous students, particularly in countries such as Australia.

- approximately 90 out of 250 Indigenous languages are still spoken in Australia today (Walsh 1993);
- many Indigenous students are expected to learn about everyday life in English while their mother tongue is considered a second language;
- Some words such as 'Granny' have different meanings in Aboriginal language where it refers to a combination of grandmother and grandchild;
- there are no equivalents to 'hello' or 'please' or 'thank you' in Indigenous language;
- when speaking, traditionally oriented Indigenous children will not readily look an adult in the eye as such behaviour is considered 'rude' or 'cheeky'.

Australian Aboriginal students and the school experience

In considering the issue of Australian Aboriginal students and schooling, a number of prominent issues arise. Harslett (1998) has reported research indicating that while Aboriginal students in both rural and urban schools seek an education and want to complete their final year of secondary education a high number of these students feel alienated from school. This is reflected in 'absenteeism, dropping out, misconduct, and non engagement in learning' (Harslett 1998, p. 1). Research conducted by Harslett and colleagues indicated that Aboriginal students ranked classroom boredom and negative relationships with teachers as significant reasons for school absenteeism. Their findings were consistent with a range of other research, indicating that a common factor of poor relationships with teachers contribute to school dropout (Partington, Godfrey & Harris 1997).

Poor school attendance by Aboriginal students has been the focus of recent research (e.g. Rothman 2001; DETYA 2000).

> Despite initiatives which have been introduced by the Commonwealth and State/Territory governments in the last 20 years to improve participation in, and outcomes from, education among Indigenous students, they continue to be the most educationally disadvantaged student group in Australia, with consistently lower levels of academic achievement and higher rates of absenteeism than among non-Indigenous students (DETYA 2000, p. 1).

Allowing for difficulties in collecting reliable data, Rothman (2001) reports in a study of South Australian students that Indigenous students' school absence rates are approximately 60 per cent higher than non-Indigenous students absence rates. The implications of low attendance have been highlighted in the DETYA report, where it was noted that regular attendance is generally agreed to strongly correlate with school success.

Information processing theory: understanding development

This approach to human development draws on the analogy of the human mind with a computer. Based on the thinking of E. C. Tolman (1932), **information processing** examines how animals and humans use information from their

information processing
the taking in, storing and using of information by humans and animals.

environment to direct their behaviour. Like the computer, the human mind takes in information, acts on the information, stores it and is capable of retrieving the information and generating responses. Thus, the processes involved include:

1   gathering and representing the information – encoding;
2   storing or retaining the information;
3   accessing or retrieving the information.

A simplified model of information processing is shown in Figure 19.1.

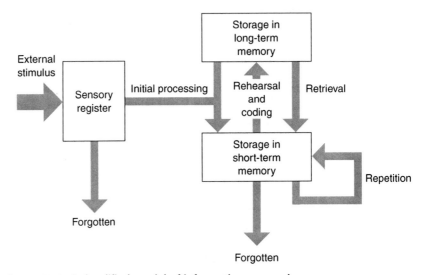

Figure 19.1 A simplified model of information processing

The information processing approach in psychology has been used to address such issues as how thinking is organised, cognitive strategies in problem solving and the role of short-term memory in learning. The general view of information processing theorists is that over time a person develops an increasingly more complex and sophisticated 'computer' (mind) for solving problems, a 'computer' that stores more and more knowledge and develops ever better strategies for solving problems.

A number of critical claims by Piaget regarding conservation and transivity problems have to do with the interaction of the amount of information a child receives with the kind of information (Halford 1982; Bryant & Trabasco 1971). For example, the likelihood of a child providing a correct response to a conservation problem is partly a function of how much information there is and how varied it is. The research of Keating and Bobbitt (1978) with children aged 9, 13 and 17, found 'evidence that late childhood and very early adolescence are a prime time for maturation of the information processing system' (Keating 1980, p. 242).

In sum, while theories such as information processing have added another perspective to our understanding of children's cognitive development, the fact is that such a contribution is still relatively small. As such, researchers such as Keating (1982) are sceptical of the extent of the contribution.

Trends and issues

Adolescent decision-making

The nature of adolescent decision-making, particularly in the context of the family, has been the subject of psychological research both overseas and in Australia (Poole & Gelder 1984; Cashmore & Goodnow 1985; Dornbusch et al. 1985; Brown & Mann 1988; Moore et al. 1990).

Developmental and cultural aspects
Australian researchers have made an important contribution to the understanding of age-related changes in children's decision-making capabilities (Mann 1985). Among children of 8 to 14 years of age, Mann et al. (1984) found a gradual increase in the discriminating use of decision-making rules; that is, the use of majority rule and turn-taking to resolve decisional problems. Older children are more likely to use turn-taking than majority rule. Children from more collective cultures, such as Japan, use the turn-taking decision rule more than children from more individualistic cultures, such as Australia, implicating culture as a variable influencing decision-making style (Mann et al. 1985).

Decision-making in families
Dornbusch et al. (1985) have examined decision-making in adolescents in relation to Baumrind's style of parenting (chapter 11). Their results show that authoritarian parents are likely to be the sole source of decision-making in the family. With a permissive style of parenting, adolescents made decisions by themselves while authoritative parents were more likely to engage in joint decision-making with their adolescent children. The same authors also found

that the decision-making process was different in mother-only households from that in two-parent households. In mother-only households, youths are perceived as more likely to make decisions without direct parental input.

The Australian researchers Poole and Gelder (1984, p. 66) characterise adolescence as 'a time when the relative influence of the family diminishes, that of the peer group increases, and there is an emergence of increasing self autonomy in decision making'. In a sample of 520 Australian students, they found that the adolescents generally saw themselves as making most of the decisions influencing their lives. Family members still played a role with adolescents valuing the opinion of the mother and the father. Females considered the opinion of their mothers to be important while males were more influenced by their fathers.

The study by Brown and Mann (1988) of 304 adolescents in the 12 to 16 age group in South Australia, has thrown more light on the effects of family structure and parental involvement on adolescent decision-making. Brown and Mann found that female adolescents were involved in more family decisions than males. They also reported that when both parents model high involvement in decision-making the adolescents in the family tend to be more involved than when only one parent provides such a model. They have used social learning theory to explain their findings. Interestingly, Brown and Mann found that 'adaptable' families – where '[a]daptability refers to a family's ability to change and adapt to new roles and rules' (p. 84) – had adolescents who participated in more decision-making than less adaptable families.

R. J. Havighurst and developmental tasks

One theorist who has made an important, if underrated, contribution to our understanding of child and adolescent development is Robert Havighurst. In Havighurst's (1953) view, development is not one long, slow uphill climb, but consists of both steep gradients where learning is difficult and plateaus where the individual can coast in terms of development. One example of this is a child who must work hard to master the art of catching a cricket ball, but who, having mastered the skill, can then 'coast' for years. Havighurst's theory addresses the issue of children's cognitive development as well as other aspects of development. His views provide some contrast to cognitive–developmental and information processing theories.

The nature of developmental tasks

A question often asked by parents is 'How well is my child doing?' Masten and Coatsworth (1998, p. 206) have noted that '[e]valuations of how a child is doing in life generally reflect expectations based on pooled knowledge about child development that are culturally transmitted from one generation to the next'. As the same authors go on to note, the expectations and concerns are often reflected in popular culture, e.g. the milestones noted in child-rearing books. For example, a list of developmental tasks has been presented in *The National Mental Health Strategy Monograph* (2000)

developmental tasks
in Havighurst's theory, tasks that must be completed during certain periods of a person's life.

Havighurst describes **developmental tasks** as 'those things that constitute healthy and satisfactory growth in our society' (1953, p. 2). He elaborates further that:

> [a] developmental task is a task which arises at or about a certain period in the life of the individual, successful achievement of which leads to happiness and to success with later tasks, while failure leads to unhappiness in the individual, disapproval by society, and difficulty with later tasks (Havighurst 1953, p. 2).

He believes that inner and outer forces set up certain developmental tasks for the individual, and he identifies three such forces:

1 The biology of the individual, involving physical maturation, such as learning to walk or learning to relate to the opposite sex during adolescence.
2 Cultural forces, such as learning to read and write.
3 The personal values and aspirations of the individual, such as aspiring to become a doctor or engineer.

Developmental tasks in childhood and adolescence

Early childhood

Havighurst has identified nine key tasks to be accomplished during this period of development.

1 Learning to walk.
2 Learning to take solid food.
3 Learning to talk.
4 Learning to control the elimination of bodily waste.
5 Learning about sex differences and sexual modesty.
6 Achieving physiological stability.
7 Forming simple concepts regarding social and physical reality.
8 Learning to relate oneself emotionally to parents, siblings and other people.
9 Learning to distinguish right and wrong and developing a conscience.

Middle childhood

During this period nine developmental tasks are faced by the individual.

1   Learning physical skills necessary for ordinary games.
2   Building wholesome attitudes towards oneself as a growing organism.
3   Learning to get along with age-mates.
4   Learning an appropriate masculine or feminine role.
5   Developing fundamental skills in reading, writing and calculating.
6   Developing concepts necessary for everyday living.
7   Developing a conscience, morality and a scale of values.
8   Achieving personal independence.
9   Developing attitudes towards social groups and institutions.

Adolescence

Havighurst identifies 10 developmental tasks during this period.

 1 Achieving newer and more mature relations with members of both sexes.
 2 Achieving a masculine or feminine role.
 3 Accepting one's physique and using the body effectively.
 4 Achieving emotional independence of parents and other adults.
 5 Achieving some assurance of economic independence.
 6 Selecting and preparing for an occupation.
 7 Preparing for marriage and family life.
 8 Developing intellectual skills and concepts necessary for civic competence.
 9 Desiring and achieving socially responsible behaviour.
10 Acquiring a set of values and an ethical system as a guide to behaviour.

A developmental task during adolescence includes establishing relationships with peers.

Selverstone (1989) believes that the 10 developmental tasks during adolescence may be clustered into four main categories:

1   Identity, which involves the determination of the question 'who am I?'.
2   Connectedness, which includes establishing relationships with peers.
3   Power – the development of a sense of control and power.
4   Hope/joy, which is achieved via the accomplishment of the previous three tasks.

According to Havighurst (1953), there is a right moment for teaching or developing a task. That is, there is a moment or time in the individual's life path when it is most opportune to be exposed to the learning involved in a task. Havighurst also adopts a broad outlook about the nature of tasks, believing that they extend beyond the individual to the cultural–historical context in which the individual is growing or developing.

The SOLO taxonomy: understanding human learning

The Australian researchers Biggs and Collis (1982) have developed a system of learning called the Structure of the Observed Learning Outcome (SOLO) taxonomy. SOLO is based on neo-Piagetian ideas and has been influenced by information processing concepts. According to Biggs and Collis (1982), there are four basic stages of intellectual functioning between birth and the end of adolescence.

1   *Sensori-motor*. During this stage children are concerned with their immediate environment and with the development of sensori-motor abilities.
2   *Iconic*. In this period of the child's life the major concern is the development of symbolism, so that words and images come to stand for events.
3   *Concrete symbolic*. During this stage the child's symbolic capacity develops further to facilitate the manipulation of classes and groups.
4   *Formal*. This stage involves the development of abstract concepts and events.

cycle of learning
the sequence of understanding through which a learner proceeds in mastering a task or absorbing a body of knowledge.

The SOLO taxonomy is aimed at detecting the quality of students' learning by finding out where the student is in terms of a **cycle of learning**. The cycle of learning has five general levels (Biggs & Telfer 1987).

1   *Prestructural*. At this level in the cycle, the child can attempt a set task, such as answering a question, but is capable of very little else. For example, if a child at the prestructural level is asked a question such as 'What causes lightning?', the child will be distracted easily and a likely response will be 'I don't know'. Similarly, if teaching a skill such as playing soccer is attempted, the child will not be able to kick the ball.
2   *Unistructural*. At this level in the learning cycle, the child will focus on the question posed or the activity to be learned, but typically centre on just one aspect, such as learning to kick the ball in a straight line.

3 *Multistructural.* Here the child can attend to more than one aspect of the task – can run at the ball, kick it and follow on – but will stop running on after kicking.

4 *Relational.* According to Biggs and Telfer (1987), the relational level in the cycle is a higher level of functioning that enables the child to attend to parts of the whole in an integrated fashion. At this level the child can play a game of soccer in an organised fashion, attending simultaneously to the various physical facets of the game.

5 *Extended abstract.* At this highest level, the individual is using abstract reasoning to think about strategies and tactics involved in the task and to appreciate the aesthetics or underlying philosophy, for example, to appreciate the historical significance of soccer.

Biggs and Telfer (1987) place a great deal of emphasis on the concept of the learning cycle, arguing that it is a process through which an individual moves in learning a task. They believe that overall the SOLO taxonomy has wide application in the learning setting.

Trends and issues

Optimistic students

As Yates (1995, p. 23) notes, 'Optimism, the simple belief that positive events outweigh the negative, is widely respected as a normal, natural and healthy personality attribute'. A number of writers and researchers have examined the concept of optimism (Seligman 1990; Fischer & Leitenberg 1986; Peterson & Bossio 1991). In particular, Peterson and Barrett (1987) have used the term 'explanatory style' to describe the way in which individuals explain the causes of events in their lives. Optimistic individuals are considered to attribute good outcomes in their lives to stable, global and internal causes. Pessimistic individuals explain good outcomes as due to factors that are transitory, specific and due to unstable elements such as luck, the stars or fate. Yates and colleagues have examined the concept of explanatory style in relation to Australian students. In their longitudinal study of primary and lower secondary school students, Yates et al. (1998) report that explanatory style is stable over a number of years, that it develops in primary-school-age children, is related to gender, with males being more pessimistic than females, and is associated with measures of depression. Yates et al. (1995, p. 33) also report a link between optimistic thinking and '. . . the child's desire to learn and to understand mathematics, and to holding positive attitudes towards certain teaching behaviours'.

Social cognition and ego development

One feature of adolescent development that has been observed by parents, teachers and psychologists relates to adolescents' self-consciousness and related egocentrism or concern for how they appear in the eyes of others. This outlook is often reflected in particular concern with negative social evaluation from peers. David Elkind (1967, 1968, 1970) has extensively researched the issue of adolescent egocentrism, arguing that 'formal operational structures allow for abstract and hypothetical centred thought, but that initially the transition from concrete to formal thought engenders a novel form of egocentrism in which the individual imagines her- or himself to be a target of everyone else's thoughts' (Pesce & Harding 1986, p. 83).

The imaginary audience

Elkind (1967, 1970) has stressed the importance of the **imaginary audience** (IA) as one form of adolescent egocentrism. This concept accounts for adolescents' concern that they are the focus of other people's attention. With this preoccupation, adolescents are then continually constructing or reacting to an audience:

> It is an audience because the adolescent believes that he will be the focus of attention, and it is imaginary because in actual social situations, this is usually not the case unless he contrives it to be so (Elkind 1967, p. 1030).

For example, as is understandable, adolescents going through the physical changes of puberty (see chapter 18) might feel self-conscious about their appearance (awkwardness, budding breasts, voice changes etc.). Adolescents' wish for privacy could be associated with their perception that they are being scrutinised or evaluated by others (Pesce & Harding 1986).

Elkind and Bowen (1979) have developed an 'imaginary audience scale' designed to assess the willingness of adolescents to reveal themselves to an audience. In their study, Elkind and Bowen (1979) found that year 8 students were more unwilling to reveal themselves to an audience than students in years 4, 6 or 12. This finding was thought to be the result of year 8 students' recent entry into the formal operations period: these students were exhibiting a by-product of early formal stage development egocentrism. Currently, however, findings regarding the relationship between the imaginary audience and cognitive development are equivocal, with researchers such as Pesce and Harding (1986) reporting a higher sensitivity to an imaginary audience around years 8 and 9 regardless of cognitive level.

Personal fable

Another adolescent delusion according to Elkind (1967) is that of the **personal fable** (PF). This involves adolescents' conviction that their own feelings are unique and that they are not subject to the risks and limitations of others. Elkind (1967) gives the example of the adolescent girl who says to her mother 'You just don't know how it feels to be in love'. That is, the girl believes her experience is unique and beyond the capacity of others to appreciate. Researchers have postulated that this attitude may account for some of the seemingly reckless behaviour of adolescents such as drug use or failure to use safe and proper contraception (see chapter 18; Elster et al. 1980; Irwin & Millstein 1986).

Taken together, the constructs of 'imaginary audience' and 'personal fable . . . have provided distinctive explanations of adolescent angst, self consciousness, and susceptibility to peer pressure' (Vartanian 1997, p. 246). Researchers (Lapsley 1993; Vartanian 1997) have identified interpersonal relations as a significant manifestation of IA and PF. The suggestion is that IA and PF emerge in response to the adolescents' struggle to balance '. . . interpersonal needs of connection with, and individuation from, parents' (Vartanian 1997, pp.

246–7). IA and PF emerge as the adolescent struggles with the development of identity and maintaining closeness and connectedness with others while managing psychological separation from parents. In particular, the PF plays a significant role in establishing a separate sense of self.

The family life-cycle: 19

Family conflict

The family plays an important role in facilitating the adolescent's smooth transition to young adulthood (Noller & Patton 1990). Sound family relations are important in the development of important aspects of the adolescent's personality, such as a healthy self-concept.

Disagreements between adolescents and their parents

Adolescence is commonly regarded as a period when young people come into a good deal of conflict with their parents. Although the popular notion of a general revolt against parents during adolescence has not been supported by research, relationships do generally deteriorate somewhat (Rigby & Rump 1981). The issues upon which adolescents and their parents often disagree have been examined in a number of studies (for example,

by Coleman et al. (1977) in England; Papini & Sebby (1988) in the United States, and most recently by Rigby & Dietz (unpub.) in Australia).

In the Australian study, conducted in Adelaide, South Australia, adolescent children (aged 14–16 years) from 56 families and their mothers and fathers were asked independently to indicate whether there had ever been disagreements between parents and the adolescent with respect to each of 19 selected issues. In general, family members concurred in their judgments regarding the matters on which there had been disagreement. Table 19.2 gives the percentages of adolescents who reported having had disagreements with their parents on each of the issues.

Do these disagreements have any further significance? Evidently yes. No matter how the range of disagreements was assessed in this study by mothers, fathers or adolescents, in families where

Table 19.2 Female and male adolescents reporting disagreement with parents on selected issues

Female respondents (N = 32)		Male respondents (N = 24)	
1. Untidiness	81%	1. Money	92%
2. Helping at home	75%	2. Helping at home	79%
3. Use of telephone	66%	3. Use of telephone	71%
4. Noise level	63%	4. Time to be home at night	67%
5. Money	63%	5. Homework	63%
6. Appearance	63%	6. School attitude	63%
7. Homework	63%	7. Family outings	63%
8. Manners	53%	8. Appearance	63%
9. Time to be home at night	53%	9. Untidiness	58%
10. School attitude	50%	10. Noise level	54%
11. Use of leisure time	50%	11. Manners	50%
12. Meal times	44%	12. Smoking or drinking	50%
13. Family outings	44%	13. Use of leisure time	46%
14. Social, political or religious beliefs	38%	14. Future career	42%
15. Choice of friends	38%	15. Choice of friends	42%
16. Privacy	34%	16. Privacy	38%
17. Opposite sex friend	34%	17. Meal times	33%
18. Future career	31%	18. Opposite sex friend	29%
19. Smoking or drinking	25%	19. Social, political or religious beliefs	25%

adolescents tended to be significantly more negative, not only in their attitudes towards parental authority but also in their attitudes towards non-parental authorities such as the police or teachers. In short, the disagreements had ramifications beyond the home, extending into the wider community.

Conflict resolution styles

In a study of 354 Australian adolescents drawn from mainstream and migrant families, four conflict resolution styles were identified (Peterson unpub.). Some 37 per cent of families reported heated discussion to resolve conflict, while the equivalent figure for arguing angrily was 29 per cent, for fighting physically 8 per cent, and for avoidance 26 per cent. There appear to be sex differences in parent–adolescent conflict, with female family members taking 'a more active role than males in the positive as well as the negative aspects of domestic negotiation' (Peterson 1990, p. 73).

Chapter summary

In this chapter consideration has been given to the significant changes which occur in the nature of adolescent thinking and to the particular developmental tasks facing adolescents. Ongoing developments in language and a greater facility to think in more abstract terms presents the adolescent with greater opportunity to reflect on the nature of things including that of self.

Discussion questions

1. In what ways does adolescent thinking differ from the thinking of children in middle childhood?
2. What are some of the major criticisms of Piagetian theory? Discuss.
3. What are the key elements of the information processing model?
4. Identify the main features of Havighurst's developmental theory.
5. What is the 'cycle of learning' in the SOLO taxonomy?
6. Explain the term 'imaginary audience'.

Activities

1. Outline how decision-making was achieved in the family in which you grew up.
2. Interview a number of adolescents with regard to the 19 issues causing disagreement listed in this chapter. Compare your results with those obtained by Rigby and Dietz (unpub.) and discuss your findings.

Selected websites

Youth Studies Australia <www.acys.utas.edu.au>

The Jean Piaget Archives< www.unige.ch/piaget/presentg.htm>

International Education Journals <www.iej.cjb.net>

Child Adolescent Psychological and Educational Resources <www.caper.com.au>

International Education Journal <http://iej.cjb.net>

20 Social and Emotional Development in Adolescence

'Two of the Fairest Stars'
Two of the fairest stars in all the heaven,
Having some business, do entreat her eyes
To twinkle in their spheres till they return.
The brightness of her cheek would shame those stars,
As daylight doth a lamp, her eyes in heaven
Would through the airy region stream so bright,
That birds would sing, and think it were not night.
See how she leans her cheek upon her hand.
O that I were a glove upon that hand,
That I might touch that cheek.

William Shakespeare, Romeo and Juliet, *Act 2, Scene 2 Lines 15–23*

CHAPTER OUTLINE

KEY TERMS AND CONCEPTS

- Genital stage
- Identity versus role confusion
- Peer groups, cliques and crowds
- Eros
- Ludas
- Storge

Introduction

A burgeoning body of research into adolescence, as reflected in a number of reviews of the field (Lerner & Galambos 1998; Galambos & Leadbeater 2000), has provided some insight into the world of the adolescence. In the Australian context the sentiment expressed by Collins (1991) that very little research has been conducted into adolescence largely still holds true and his call for more research into adolescence remains valid.

As we have seen in chapter 18, the physical changes occurring in this single phase of the life-cycle are quite dramatic, characterised by a sudden growth spurt, pimples, appearance of body hair and development of the reproductive organs. At the same time, adolescents acquire a greater capacity for rational and abstract thought associated with risk-taking, limit testing and experimentation. For some individuals, youth – particularly early youth – represents a time of increased self-consciousness and egocentrism.

Adolescents face major developmental landmarks, including achieving independence from parents, acquiring the right to leave home and school, vote, have sex, drink alcohol and drive a car. At this time, many young people make significant decisions about their future careers. In contemporary Australia, adolescents must also come to grips with other important issues that have implications for their future life. These include the lack of employment opportunities and the extended time that must often be spent at school as a result; health issues such as AIDS and drug abuse; and broader questions regarding the future, such as conservation of the environment.

This chapter describes the theories of adolescent social and emotional development expounded by Freud and Erikson, and focuses on the special topics of peer groups, loneliness, friendship, unemployment, delinquency and attitudes towards institutional authority. In this second edition, consideration is given to the Australian research of Connell (1987, 1990, 1995) into over 15 years of research into the development of 'masculinity'. The Family Life-cycle: 20 touches on the future prospects of today's young people.

Theoretical foundations

As in other aspects of development, both Sigmund Freud and Erik Erikson have made significant contributions to our understanding of adolescent social and emotional development.

Sigmund Freud

genital stage in Freudian theory, the period beginning in adolescence characterised by the reawakening of sexual feelings.

We saw in chapter 17 that according to psychoanalytic theory the primary school child is in the latency period with regard to emotional development. This period is then followed in adolescence by the **genital stage** (Table 20.1).

According to Freud, after the latency period the hormonal changes of puberty herald the re-emergence of sexual feelings. Freud believed that the genital stage was associated with a re-awakening of previously suppressed Oedipus and Electra complexes (Stafford-Clark 1971). As a consequence, boys become rebellious and challenge parental authority, particularly that of their fathers, while girls increasingly defy their mothers.

Another feature of the adolescent period is a degree of narcissism, or preoccupation with self as a love object (Stafford-Clark (1971). More attention is paid by both sexes to their physical appearance. As part of the Oedipus and Electra complexes, Freud believed that homosexual feelings would be an element of adolescents' sexual interest. Alternatively, the adolescent could show a tendency to fall in love with a 'thinly disguised parent figure of the opposite sex' (Stafford-Clark 1971, p. 107).

Anna Freud (1964, p. 98) wrote:

> Puberty is rightly regarded as a time when numerous neurotic disturbances may be expected to appear. It is less well known that puberty also removes certain neurotic symptoms which are typical for the years preceding it.

Table 20.1 The genital stage: the last of Freud's psychosexual stages

Ages	Stages
Infancy	Oral
1½–3½ years (approx.)	Anal
3½–5½ years (approx.)	Phallic
5½–12 years (approx.)	Latency
Adolescence	Genital

In the light of this comment, the upheavals and disturbances normally associated with adolescence may be an indication that adolescent development is occurring.

While Sigmund Freud's theory prompted a great deal of controversy regarding the nature of adolescent emotional development, it has now largely given way to more contemporary theories.

Erik Erikson

In Erikson's theory of psychosocial development, adolescence is associated with the fifth stage, that of **identity versus role confusion** (see Table 20.2). In his book *Childhood and Society* (1963, p. 254) Erikson wrote:

> The adolescent mind is essentially a mind of the moratorium, a psychosocial stage between childhood and adulthood, and between the morality learned by the child, and the ethics to be developed by the adult.

In the fifth of Erikson's psychosocial stages, the developing youth is faced with physical and emotional changes. Adolescents realise that they are leaving

identity versus role confusion
the fifth of Erikson's psychosocial stages, in which there is a search for identity involving an intense exploration of personal values, beliefs and goals.

Table 20.2 'Identity versus role confusion': the fifth of Erikson's psychosocial stages

Ages	Stages
Infancy	Basic trust versus mistrust
1½–3½ years (approx.)	Autonomy versus shame and doubt
3½–5½ years (approx.)	Initiative versus guilt
5½–12 years (approx.)	Industry versus inferiority
Adolescence	Identity versus role confusion
Young adulthood	Intimacy versus isolation
Adulthood	Generativity versus stagnation
Maturity	Ego integrity versus despair

childhood behind and preparing to take their place in the world. As Erikson (1963, p. 253) puts it:

> The growing and developing youths, faced with this physiological revolution within them, and with tangible adult tasks ahead of them are now primarily concerned with what they feel they are.

The task facing the adolescent is to integrate the results of the previous four stages into a complete ego:

> The integration now taking place in the form of ego identity is, as pointed out, more than the sum of the childhood identifications. It is the accrued experience of the ego's ability to integrate all identifications with the vicissitudes of the libido, with the aptitudes developed out of endowment and with the opportunities offered in social roles (Erikson 1963, p. 253).

Role confusion is based on doubt regarding one's sexual identity but, as Erikson (1950) notes, in most instances it is the inability to settle on an occupational identity (see Unemployment, this chapter) that disturbs the adolescent. Role confusion is reflected in teenagers' questions such as 'Who am I?'. It can also be seen in strong identification with cliques and 'in-groups' and in clannish behaviour that excludes outsiders who differ in terms of their culture, race or in such petty aspects as incorrect dress. According to Erikson, the developing sense of identity is evident in a sense of psycho-social well-being and of being 'at home' in one's body, family and social world (Erikson 1959). Personal identity develops within the context of community relationships where the relationships become increasingly salient to the individual.

Contemporary views on adolescent development

In the context of contemporary society, factors such as the lengthening of time between physical maturity and the attainment of adult status can invoke difficulties in identity development. In the context of social and economic marginality for youth in many Western societies there are significant implications for identity formation. Cote and Allahar (1996, p. 74) view adolescence in late modernity as characterised by an 'identity moratorium', where the risk is that they will be side-tracked or 'lost' where adolescence can be the 'most destructive or wasted period of their lives'. As described in chapter 3, the ecological theory of Bronfenbrenner (1979) provides an integrated way of looking at adolescent development.

By middle childhood children have achieved a sense of self and a gender identity, as well as some knowledge of their intellectual and physical skills. In adolescence, however, the individual is faced with a reawakening of sexual urges, which is now reflected in a need to establish intimacy with others. New responsibilities must be addressed in terms of society's demands for the individual to establish a work role and prepare to take her or his place in the adult world. In contemporary Western society there are particular pressures arising from structural changes which have significant implications for identity formation.

Trends and issues

Adolescent communication with parents

A number of prominent Australian researchers have examined the nature of communication between adolescents and parents (Ochiltree 1984; Noller & Callan 1990; Noller & Patton 1990). Ochiltree (1984) has argued that many of today's parents, who themselves were raised in more affluent and opportunistic times, are ill-prepared for the task of raising adolescents in contemporary Australia. Parents today are increasingly finding that they have to provide care for young adults confronting the reality of a shrinking employment market and the need to remain longer at school. In a study of 296 adolescents aged 13–17 years, Noller and Callan (1990) found that they perceived their fathers in a different way from their mothers. Fathers were seen as less able to recognise adolescents' point of view and were perceived as initiating fewer conversational contacts. Adolescents also saw their fathers as more judgmental and less willing to negotiate. They reported that they were more guarded and defensive in their communication with their fathers (Noller & Callan 1990, p. 360).

Boys and masculinity

Since the publication of the first edition of this text, the issue of the general health and well-being of boys has come to the attention of researchers, educators and welfare workers. Issues (e.g. youth suicide) touched upon in - chapter 19 have heightened awareness of the problems facing today's youth.

Healey (1997) has summarised some of the 'risks' associated with growing up in Australian society. In the case of boys, the development of a sense of identity and the determination of the nature of their relationships with others has been written about in terms of the development of masculinity. As Connell (1996) has noted, debate regarding 'boys' issues' is alive in a diverse range of countries including Australia, Germany, Japan and the United States. For example, a South Australian school has begun a special program for year 9 and 10 boys who are at risk of leaving school early (*The Advertiser* 2001, p. 33).

Connell (1996) has challenged a number of preconceptions regarding the notion of masculinity.

1 the idea that there is such a thing as a unitary 'male sex role' has been replaced by the idea of 'multiple masculinities'. 'Different cultures, and different periods of history, construct masculinity differently' (Connell 1996, p. 209).

2 Connell challenges the notion of a single 'hegemonic' masculinity, noting that different forms of masculinity can co-exist although some masculinities may be privileged over others, e.g. sporting heroes (Phoenix & Frosh 2001).

3 According to Connell, organisations such as schools play a significant role in defining and sustaining how masculinity is defined.

4 Masculinity is constantly being refined, changed such that 'From body-builders in the gym, to managers in the boardroom, to boys in the elementary school playground, a whole lot of people are working very hard to produce what they believe to be appropriate masculinities' (Connell 1996, p. 210).

5 As Connell notes, masculinities are 'layered' in the sense that one expression of masculinity may 'mask' or act as a thinly disguised veneer for a contradictory expression, e.g. overt heterosexual behaviour masks some homosexual desire.

6 Finally, Connell, notes that masculinities are 'amenable to change', as evidenced by historical changes in the way masculine behaviour is constructed.

Presently, in countries such as Australia there is a lively debate developing regarding boys' issues and the associated notion of masculinity (Gilbert & Gilbert 1998; Biddulph 1997; Browne & Fletcher 1995).

Peer groups

The peer group and adolescent social relations have provided the basis for a considerable body of research in developmental psychology. Broadly speaking, the concept of peer groups is used to refer to social relationships (other than kinship ones) that exist between young people, including group or dyadic relationships (Salmon 1979). There is a general consensus among psychologists that the peer group has considerable developmental significance.

Peer group structure

peer group
a group of children
approximately the
same age.

The nature of the **peer group** has been described in some detail by the Australian researcher Dexter Dunphy (1963), who observes:

In the socialisation of the individual his transition from the nuclear family to wider adult society can take place in many ways. In western urban society, the peer group is one important avenue through which this can occur.

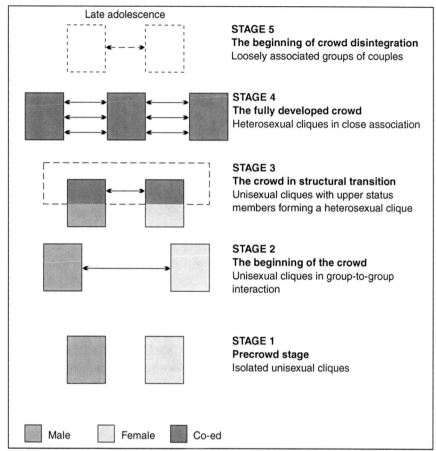

Figure 20.1 A schematic representation of age-changes in peer group structure
Source: Adapted from Dunphy 1963

Dunphy based his research on naturalistic observations of peer group interaction and interviews with adolescents in Sydney. In what is regarded as a classic study in psychology, he observed peer group interaction on street corners, in milkbars, in homes, at parties and on Sydney beaches. He describes two types of groups, namely **cliques**, which are small with an average of six members, and **crowds**, which are large and are usually composed of two to four cliques.

Cliques and crowds perform different functions. Cliques are for talking and crowds for mixing, as at parties and other large social gatherings. The formation of a crowd shows developmental trends, as indicated in Figure 20.1.

Stage 1. In the early adolescent period, peer group development usually involves single-sex cliques that are fairly isolated from cliques of the opposite sex.

Stage 2. In stage 2 there is a move towards heterosexuality in the composition of the group. Interaction at this point is usually considered 'daring' and undertaken in the security of the group. The upper status members of the group are usually responsible for initiating interaction.

cliques
in adolescence, a small group of about six individuals, as described by Dunphy (1963).

crowd
in adolescence, a large group consisting of two or more cliques, as described by Dunphy (1963).

Stage 3. The third stage witnesses the formation of heterosexual cliques for the first time, although members maintain contact with unisex cliques.

Stage 4. In stage 4, the fully developed crowd can be identified, with heterosexual cliques in close association.

Stage 5. In late adolescence, the crowd begins to disintegrate and is replaced by a loosely associated group of couples.

In a study of Sydney adolescent peer groups, James and Wearing (1985, p. 149) found support for Dunphy's observations regarding the influence of the peer group. More particularly, James and Wearing's research highlights the role the peer group plays in helping the adolescents' developing 'sense of individuality and personal competence'. They emphasised that the influence of the peer group was 'alive and well' in the lives of Australian adolescents in the 1980s, although 'the shared house and the informal friendship network may have replaced the more traditional "gang" and sport and work groups as a means of establishing identity and self-clarification' (James & Wearing 1985, p. 149). Such a change might reflect changing social structure in Australian society as seen, for example, in the greater mobility of families today.

Attention has now turned to understanding the broader social world of the adolescent peer group (Serafica & Blyth 1985). Questions asked concern how the peer group and family of the adolescent differ in nature and what purpose each serves. From one point of view, the peer group has the important function of helping the young person in his or her transition from a family-dependent child to a relatively independent adult (Sebald 1989). A contrasting point of view is that the peer group is of questionable value in aiding the growing-up process because of its advocacy of immature values and norms. However, both viewpoints acknowledge that today's adolescents live in a peer subculture where in-group standards heavily influence values, attitudes, beliefs and behaviour (Sebald 1989). Adolescents use two reference groups – family and peers – for different purposes. The family is the primary source of reference for issues relating to finance, education and career plans, while the peer group is sought out for information relating to the type of clothes to wear, dating and social events.

Loneliness

Brennan (1982) has reported that 'adolescence seems to be the time of life when loneliness first emerges as an intense recognizable phenomenon' (p. 269). In a review of research, Wildermuth (1990) found that 22 per cent of Australian adolescents are 'so very lonely'. Loneliness in adolescence has been explored from a number of different theoretical points of view. Sullivan (1953) suggests that loneliness arises out of a lack of or a need for intimacy. Erikson (1963) believes that loneliness occurs as a result of the 'identity crisis' experienced by the adolescent if the individual fails to resolve the conflict of intimacy. Behavioural theory would account for loneliness in terms of failure to have the need for companionship reinforced.

The longing of humans for contact has been dramatically illustrated in the research of Spitz (1954) and Bowlby (1951; 1953), who demonstrated that infants in hospital need more than just physical care and will deteriorate psychologically and physiologically when deprived of human love and affection. For example, in one study Spitz found that over half of the deaths of infants hospitalised during the First World War were due to such deprivation.

A number of factors contribute to adolescent loneliness (Mijuskovic 1986; Hansell, Mechanic & Brandolo 1986), including:

- a sense of separation from parents as the primary reference group, which can be disruptive of significant interpersonal relationships, such as happens when adolescents leave home;
- cognitive developments that allow adolescents to think in terms of possibilities and choices, which may in turn increase their awareness of themselves as separate individuals;
- an increasing sense of freedom during adolescence, which in itself can be a lonely and confusing element in the young person's life;
- adolescents' struggle with their new identity in relation to physiological and psychological changes, which can enhance the sense of inadequacy;
- the adolescents' struggle to find meaning in terms of their lives, which if not resolved can increase the sense of loneliness.

Apart from these psychological factors, Mijuskovic (1986) and Kroger (1982) also identify social or sociological factors that can induce loneliness in an individual, including the 'in limbo' experience of adolescents in Western society, who in terms of status, are neither adults nor children. In Western society, the ethic of competition in schools in relation to academic and sporting pursuits can create a feeling of isolation as a result of failure to live up to the expectations and standards of others. The changing family structure has contributed to the adolescent's feeling of loneliness:

> [A]ccelerating levels of marital discord, tensions, divorce, separation, working mothers, parental role confusion, family mobility have all contributed to a progressive sense of loneliness in today's adolescent (Mijuskovic 1986, p. 944).

Some personality characteristics also tend to promote loneliness, including low self-esteem, apathy and aimlessness, shyness and self-consciousness. Highly introspective adolescents spend more time alone (Mijuskovic 1986 Buchholz & Catton 1999). Research with 13–19 year old Chinese adolescents concluded that lonely youth possessed smaller social networks, had fewer close friends of both sexes and received less support from their classmates. Generally, they reported less satisfaction with relationships outside the family. Lonely adolescents were less trusting of others (Hamid & Lok 2000).

In sum, while loneliness can arise at any time in an individual's life, the many developmental changes occurring during the adolescent years appear to make adolescents particularly prone to loneliness (Wildermuth 1990).

Friendships

The concept of friendship was touched upon in chapter 17. Reference was made to the developmental component in the nature of friendships from childhood to adolescence. Newman (1982, p. 531) has observed that as adolescents become less conforming and more independent in their judgments, 'They are less likely to seek peer friendships in order to be accepted by a clique or crowd and are more interested in honesty and commitment in a relationship'.

Serafica and Blyth (1985) have reviewed research relating to the study of adolescent friendships during this century. Research since the 1930s has focused on factors determining choice of friends, stability of friendships, personality development and developmental changes in the conceptualisation of friendship. Current research is concerned with the issue of how friends select and influence one another. Intimacy and its relationship to friendships has also received research attention in the 1980s and 1990s.

Friendship and intimacy

One theorist who has influenced our views of the nature of friendship during childhood and adolescence is H. S. Sullivan (see also chapter 17):

> The special significance of intimacy in adolescent friendship stems from the work of Sullivan (1953) who argued that interpersonal relations proceed through three developmental stages, each dominated by a particular psychosocial task (Townsend et al. 1988, p. 421).

Early adolescence is characterised by the need to find a 'chum' (Townsend et al. 1988). A 'chum' meets the special need of interpersonal intimacy (see

'I just need a friend.'

chapter 17). The outcome of finding a 'chum' leads to enhanced self-esteem and personal adjustment.

The results of the study by Townsend et al. of New Zealand adolescents has lent broad support to Sullivan's original thoughts regarding 'chums'. They concluded from their study that psychological adjustment in early adolescence was more dependent 'on having a close relationship with a peer than on being relatively popular with a number of peers' (p. 431). They also found evidence of enhanced self-esteem in those adolescents who had an intimate friendship. This finding is consistent with Sullivan's (1953) view that it is the nature and not the extent of interpersonal relations that is associated with personal adjustment.

Unemployment

The Australian researchers Patton and Noller (1984, p. 399) observe that:

> An examination of labour statistics since the early 1970s shows that the youth group 15 to 19 years has the highest percentage of unemployment as well as a greater rate of annual increase in unemployment than any other age group.

An ABS publication *Labor, Special Article – The Youth Labor Market* (1998) noted that 'As young people move out of full-time education, there are marked changes in the characteristics of their labor force participation' (1998, p. 1). In this article it is noted that the teenage unemployment rate was 18.9 per cent compared to 11.9 per cent for 20–24 year olds and 5.6 per cent for persons aged more than 25 years.

Trends. In Figure 20.2, reproduced from the ABS (1998) special article, the teenage full-time unemployment rate peaked in June 1992 at 34.1 per cent, followed by a downward trend to 1994, then remaining relatively steady up to June 1998 at between 27 per cent and 29 per cent.

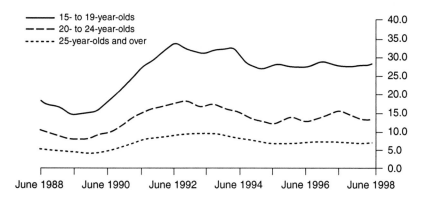

Figure 20.2 Full-time unemployed rate, trend
Source: ABS 1998

The psychological significance of unemployment

One psychological framework that helps explain the significance of employment is based on Erik Erikson's psychosocial stages. Gaining employment is an important element in the resolution of the crisis during the fifth stage (identity versus role confusion). Employment indicates the end of adolescence (Patton & Noller 1984). A first job is 'the capitalist equivalent of initiation rites in primitive society' (Windschuttle 1979, p. 55).

Feather (1987) has reviewed the psychological impact of unemployment on Australian youth. Research generally identifies a high level of reported depression among individuals, particularly when they have high initial confidence of obtaining employment and express a strong desire for work. Long-term unemployment is more strongly associated with depression than short-term unemployment. Unemployment has also been linked with lower self-esteem scores. Long-term unemployment is accompanied by behaviour such as increased smoking, reduced participation in sport, greater alcohol consumption, more visits to the doctor and a general loss of social contact.

In view of the importance attached to employment in Western society, it is not unreasonable to expect that unemployment has a distressing effect upon young people. There is no simple answer to this problem, although the most obvious solution is the provision of work that matches young people's education and ability (O'Brien 1990). O'Brien advocates a multifaceted approach to dealing with unemployed youth. Options include education and counselling, job-training courses and a change in society's attitude regarding the legitimacy of unemployment.

Juvenile delinquency

Writing on the dimension of the juvenile delinquency problem in Australia, Mukherjee (1985, p. 19) emphasises that 'Juvenile delinquency is considered to be a matter of grave concern in nearly all countries'. Further to this, Rutter, Giller and Nicholson (1998) have argued that in an international context there has been an increase in juvenile crime.

The extent of the problem

Rutter, Giller and Hagell (1998) have summarised international trends in juvenile crime, indicating that:

- one-third of all reported crime is linked to juveniles;
- the most common crime involves theft;
- violent crime is on the increase;
- males commit more crimes than females (there may be an under-estimation of female juvenile crime);
- one-third of offenders report committing at least one violent crime.

In Australia, a major report compiled by the Criminal Justice Commission (1992) found key findings to include:

- juvenile involvement in crime has increased in the last 20 years;
- juvenile crime is at the least extreme end of property crime;
- re-offenders are responsible for the majority of juvenile crime;
- most children appearing before the courts do not re-offend.

It is difficult to determine the extent of the problem because it is difficult to define what is meant by juvenile delinquency (Collins 1975; Mukherjee 1985). As Mukherjee (1985, p. 37) observes, 'The fact of the matter is that we simply do not know how much and what types of unlawful behaviour are perpetrated by individuals from different segments of the population'.

Similarly, compiling statistics on crime presents problems (Mukherjee 1985). Should we examine arrest rates or should we take into account the probability that more crime is committed than is reported? From his analysis of Australian statistics, Mukherjee argues that far fewer juveniles are arrested for violent crimes such as homicide and serious assault than members of the general population. However, juveniles are significantly overrepresented in arrests for crimes such as burglary and car theft.

Theories of juvenile delinquency

Coventry and Polk (1985) have identified three theoretical perspectives accounting for delinquency.

The individual perspective

From this perspective, features of an individual's make-up are seen to influence personality so that delinquency results. This perspective has played a dominant role in shaping research and policy regarding delinquency in Australia, because it not only explains why delinquency occurs (a personality predisposition towards violence), but also indicates what can be done to prevent it (such as punishment to correct such deviance).

Group-centred perspective

One source of theories regarding delinquency is that it often occurs in groups as a direct result of peer group activities (Coventry & Polk 1985). Research interest here focuses on the dynamics of peer group interaction, which encourages or discourages delinquent acts.

In Australia there has been some concern of late with the issue of 'youth gangs'. As Perrone and White (2000, p. 1) have noted, such '. . . fears have been fuelled, in no small part, by the surge in media reports promoting negative images of youth street activities: random violence, drug taking and distribution, and a range of other socially disruptive, illegal and/or predatory criminal activities.' The authors go on to note that such 'moral panics' are not a new

Trends and issues

Attitudes towards institutional authority

In recent years a number of studies conducted mainly in Britain and Australia have strongly supported the generality of the concept of attitude towards institutional authority as it applies to adolescents (Rigby & Rump 1981; Murray & Thompson 1985; Emler & Reicher 1987; Rigby et al. 1987). These studies confirm that among adolescents (as among older people) individuals who are favourably disposed towards one kind of institutional authority, such as the police, tend to feel more positive about other institutional authorities, such as teachers.

Measurement

Measurement of attitude to authority among adolescents has included the use of projective tests (Coleman 1980), but more frequently multi-item Likert scales have been employed. The most recently developed measure is the Children's Attitude towards Institutional Authority Scale (Rigby et al. 1987). This scale consists of 30 items, half positively and half negatively keyed, with subscales tapping attitudes towards the police, the law, teachers and parents: for example 'You can respect the police'. The subscales yield results that are positively and significantly intercorrelated. The total scale is highly reliable and suitable for use with adolescents.

Studies

Published studies employing reliable measures with adolescent subjects have indicated the following:

1 Contrary to popular opinion, adolescents are predominantly positive in their attitudes towards authorities such as parents, the police and teachers. Only a small minority among large samples of adolescents assessed in Britain and Australia have expressed negative attitudes towards such authorities (Murray & Thompson 1985; Rigby et al. 1987).

2 During early adolescence (up to the age of 15 years), adolescents tend to become less favourable in their attitudes towards both parental and non-parental authorities (Rigby & Rump 1981; Rigby et al. 1987). In later adolescence, there are some indications that they become more positively disposed (Coleman 1980).

3 In general, male and female adolescents have similar attitudes towards institutional authorities (Rigby 1989). Nevertheless, in several studies significant gender differences have been reported. Female adolescents had higher mean pro-authority scores in a study of Roman Catholic students in South Australian secondary schools (Rigby & Densley 1985), and also in a study conducted among school children in Scotland (Reicher & Emler 1985). The cultural milieu in which such attitudes develop can have implications for gender differences.

4 Religious beliefs and practices are related to attitudes towards institutional authority. Among Roman Catholic students in Australia, those expressing belief in God and attending church more frequently scored significantly higher on an attitude-towards-institutional-authority scale (Rigby & Densley 1985).

5 Parental influence on attitudes towards authority is particularly strong. Students attending the University of Nottingham in England were found to have attitudes to institutional authority that were highly positively correlated with those of their parents (Rigby 1988a).

6 Some personality correlates of attitude to authority have been explored. Adolescents differing in their attitudes to institutional authority have not been found to differ significantly in degree of extroversion or in neuroticism; nor have they been found to differ reliably in the desire to dominate others (Rigby 1988b). However, adolescents who are relatively anti-authority have been shown to have higher degrees of psychoticism on the Eysenck Personality Questionnaire (Rigby & Slee 1987; Heaven 1989). Somewhat unexpectedly, pro-authority adolescents have been found to have a more internal locus of control (Heaven 1989).

7 Finally, links have been established between attitudes towards institutional authority and self-reported delinquent behaviour. Adolescents with relatively unfavourable attitudes to authority are more likely than others to engage in a range of delinquent activities (Reicher & Emler 1985; Rigby et al. 1989).

In this developing area of enquiry, further studies are still needed to determine what factors, particularly in the school and home environments, contribute to producing such wide variations between individual adolescents in their attitudes towards institutional authority (see Rigby 1990 for an overview of this topic).

phenomenon. Unfortunately, the media reports have an unfounded 'racialised' character wrongly attributing such behaviour to Lebanese or Asian youth gangs (Perrone and White 2000).

Structural perspective

A third perspective on delinquency, identified by Coventry and Polk (1985), is based on the structure of Australian society. That is, poverty, inequality and so forth are thought to account for delinquent acts. From this perspective, research and policy development is directed towards understanding the relationship between societal structure and delinquency.

Intervention strategies

In considering intervention strategies, key findings from international research highlights the predictable developmental trajectories beginning in early childhood, such that delinquency in adolescence is strongly associated with behaviour problems in early childhood (Bor et al. 2001). Coventry and Polk (1985) note that each of these three perspectives exerts some influence on policy and program intervention strategies. In a study of personality and attitudinal components of delinquency, Rigby et al. (1989, p. 689) make a plea for an 'interactionist perspective on delinquent behaviour according to which individual as well as environmental factors are acknowledged'. Bor et al. (2001, p. 1) conclude that on the basis of evidence that the best predictor of aggression at 14 years of age is aggression at age 5, '. . . effective early intervention programs can be among the most productive crime prevention strategies'.

Adolescent love

Love has held an endless fascination for writers, poets and philosophers down the ages and there is no shortage of definitions or descriptions of love. Definitions of love in the literature range from an emphasis on its unselfish, altruistic nature to its passionate, ecstatic nature and to the beneficial, productive nature of love (Lee 1974). In the psychological literature love has been variously defined as an 'emotion', a 'need', a 'set of behaviours', and as 'an attitude' (Rubin 1970).

According to Lee (1974), there are three different 'types' of love, namely **eros**, **ludas** and **storge**.

Eros. This type of love generates powerful attraction, usually involving the physical appearance of the beloved.

Ludas. Love is a game and something to be enjoyed while at the same time it involves a playful, hedonistic lack of commitment to the relationship.

Storge. This style of loving is the slow, steady, deeply affected kind.

eros
Lee's (1974) name for love involving an immediate and powerful physical attraction.

ludas
Lee's (1974) name for a playful type of love characterised by lack of commitment.

storge
Lee's (1974) name for deep love that develops slowly and steadily.

Dating

Adolescent love and romantic relationships are now being more widely researched (Connolly & Johnson 1996; Connolly et al. 2000; Connolly et al. 1999). Whatever the style or combination of styles of love enjoyed by a couple there is usually a period of dating involved. The Australian researcher Marta McCabe (1984) has identified a number of functions of adolescent dating:

- the possibilities it provides for recreation and fun;
- the signals it provides regarding the status of the individuals (high status individuals date more frequently);
- the opportunity for socialisation and personal growth;
- the opportunity for companionship;
- the means it provides for determining mate or partner selection.

Dating behaviour during adolescence can be influenced by various factors (McCabe 1984).

Maturation

A key element in adolescent dating is that of biological and psychosocial maturation. The biological changes involve the attainment of full reproductive maturity for males and females. McCabe uses the Eriksonian theory of psychosocial maturity to explain the necessity for the development of a sexual identity in adolescence. Dating provides adolescents with the opportunity to explore relationships where there is a certain level of commitment, and provides 'opportunity for both partners to explore sexual roles which may be included later in identity formation' (McCabe 1984, p. 164).

Social maturation

In Western society a number of forces that influence dating behaviour serve to discourage sexual activity among youth. One such force is religion, particularly the Judaeo-Christian religions, which discourage premarital sexual relations. Schools are another such force, especially private schools, which tend to be more restrictive than state schools concerning students' sexual attitudes and behaviour.

Personal meaning

McCabe believes that the personal meaning adolescents attach to physiological and social influences also affects adolescent dating behaviour. For example, a belief that there should be no sex before marriage will influence an adolescent's dating behaviour accordingly.

Trends and issues

The quality of family life

The family provides children with their first significant experience of relationships. From this foundation, children are able to move into the world beyond the family and establish relationships outside the family. Research by Erikson (1963) underlines that the developmental tasks facing adolescents involve separating from the family and establishing an identity for themselves. Nevertheless, the quality of parental care and home life remains a significant facet of adolescent development. In a study of Australian adolescents, Finlayson et al. (1987) found that the quality of family relationships influenced adolescents' school performance, emotional well-being and their indulgence in problem behaviour.

According to Chubb and Fertman (1992), adolescents who feel they belong in a family differ significantly from those who feel that they do not belong in several ways. Belonging was defined as the degree to which adolescents felt they were members of the family on an equal basis with other members of the family unit. Adolescents who felt they belonged:

1 had higher self-esteem;
2 had a more internal locus of control;
3 had a greater sense of belonging to groups other than the family, such as school;
4 spent more time with their families;
5 were more actively involved with their families.

Adolescence: a synthesis

In chapters 18, 19 and 20 consideration has been given to the considerable physical, cognitive and social/emotional changes taking place during the period known as adolescence. The extent of these changes is best understood in relation to the adjustments taking place in terms of biological changes, changes to self and family and peer relationships. A systems perspective (See chapter 3) draws our attention to the multiple, interrelated levels of organisation in which the various changes take place. A systems perspective also highlights that for example, while significant hormonal changes (e.g. those associated with menarche) are occurring, in and of themselves they are not sufficient to explain or account for the complexity of the changes. Rather, in a dynamic manner they interact with other factors such as the timing of their onset and the social, cultural and historical significance attached to their occurrence.

The family life-cycle: 20

Youth, change and the future

The anthropologist Margaret Mead (1970) proposed that we are living in a post-figurative world and that young people are united in their concern about the dangers this planet faces (see chapter 1). In Mead's view, the task facing youth in this post-figurative world is to act on their knowledge of the crises facing the world to help lead their elders towards redeeming the future.

Many studies, both overseas and in Australia, indicate that today's youth face the future with considerable fear and trepidation (Boughton et al. 1987;

Slee & Cross 1988). The fear of nuclear annihilation is an important element in adolescents' view of the future (Slee & Cross 1988). They are also becoming increasingly concerned about the destruction of the environment (Knoblauch 1992).

From a somewhat broader perspective, the basic concerns of Australian adolescents were found by Poole and Evans 1988 to be as follows:

1 personal and family relationships;
2 life-course concerns, including career and employment;
3 communication;

4   personal development;
5   leisure;
6   concern with social and ethical issues.

The most frequently mentioned concerns were personal relationships (23 per cent), education (21 per cent), jobs (20 per cent), personal development (10 per cent), money (6 per cent), leisure (5 per cent), relationships with the opposite sex (5 per cent) and the future (3 per cent). The academic courses students were taking, gender and level of aspiration influenced the nature of the concerns expressed. In a New Zealand study (McGee & Stanton 1992), four types of stressful life events were identified: problems relating to self-image and independence; academic and physical competence; parental conflict; and moving residence and school.

Adolescents in Singapore and Australia differ in their orientation to the future (Poole & Cooney 1987). Young people in Singapore were more concerned with the nature of their own country, education and politics, while their Australian counterparts were more focused on environment, lifestyle and personal relationships.

If young people in this post-figurative world are to act on their knowledge and understanding of the threat our planet faces, it is important to encourage them to feel that they have the power to be able to change events. Moreover, if we are to understand adolescent behaviour within a family context, we must first have some appreciation of adolescents' concerns.

Chapter summary

Significant issues face the adolescent including the development of intimate relationships, and determination of an occupational role. Consolidation of physical and cognitive development allows the individual to give voice to more abstract concepts dealing with 'love' and loneliness'. As noted in this chapter, other significant issues pertain to the development of gender identity. A range of social, cultural and psychological forces means that the problems being faced by young people today are significant ones.

Discussion questions

1   How did Freud and Erikson differ in their theoretical views regarding the nature of adolescent development?
2   Discuss Dexter Dunphy's five stages of peer group development in relation to your own observations.
3   Discuss Sullivan's (1953) contention that it is the nature and not the extent of interpersonal relations that is associated with personal adjustment.
4   What are the factors contributing to adolescent loneliness? Discuss in the light of your own experience.
5   How does friendship in adolescence differ from that in childhood?
6   Summarise and discuss the principal findings relevant to attitudes to authority in adolescence.
7   Discuss McCabe's (1984) finctions of dating.
8   Summarise the research fundings of Connolly and colleagues referred to in this chapter and discuss the implications of the findings for understanding adolescent intimate relationships.
9   What major concerns facing adolescents today have been identified by research?

Activities

1   Referring to the literature discussed in this chapter, identify what you believe to be the major significance of entry into the workforce for adolescents (independence, identity etc.). Interview a number of adolescents with a view to understanding more about their attitudes towards employment and their beliefs about the impact of unemployment on youth.
2   Critically evaluate a social commentary on the nature of culture and society such as that written by Eckersley (1998) or Glover et al. (1998) and present your understandings in class.
3   Complete the Self Review Quiz on the CD-ROM to assess your understanding of the content presented in this section. Use your quiz results as a basis for reviewing any chapter content about which you are uncertain.

Selected websites

International Education Journal <www.iej.cjb.net>

Child Adolescent Psychological and Educational Resources <www.caper.com.au>

Australian Institute of Criminology <www.aic.gov.au>

An on-line journal of peace and conflict resolution <wwwtrinstitute.irg/ojpcr>

Youth Studies Australia <www.acys.utas.edu.au>

Studying Human Development

8

Studying human development

21 Towards a Life-span Perspective

'I Love a Broad Margin to My Life . . .'

I love a broad margin to my life. Sometimes, in a summer morning, having
taken my accustomed bath, I sat in my sunny doorway from sunrise till noon,
rapt in a revery, amidst the pines and hickories and sumachs, in undisturbed
solitude and stillness, while the birds sang around, or flitted noiseless
through the house, until by the sun falling in at my west window, or the noise
of some traveller's wagon on the distant highway, I was reminded of the
lapse of time. I grew in these seasons like corn in the night, and they were far
better than any work of the hands would have been. They were not times
subtracted from my life, but so much over and above my usual allowance.

Henry David Thoreau, Walden

KEY TERMS AND CONCEPTS

- Positivism
- Paradigm
- Intimacy versus isolation
- Generativity versus stagnation
- Ego integrity versus despair
- Authentic identity

Introduction

Methods of child study are evolving and being adapted to better capture the broader influences that shape the developing individual. This chapter highlights recent developments in the study of children and adolescents, including changes in methodology and related changes in the way in which we see the growing child in the broader contexts of family life and the culture to which the family belongs.

Furthermore, although this text focuses on the development of children and adolescents, it is important to appreciate that the individual continues to grow beyond adolescence. To this end, the methods used to study child and adolescent development may have to be further refined to identify the nature of changes occurring during adulthood and old age. The Family Life-cycle: 21 focuses on the concept of resilient families and the key features that help them negotiate times of crisis.

'I love a broad margin to my life.'

Recent developments

Methods of child study

The scientific study of child development is a relatively recent phenomenon. Our understanding of the nature of child development has been considerably advanced by research in the field and the fruits of these endeavours have been highlighted in this text. The body of this research evidence is grounded in a 'positivist empiricist' framework (see chapter 2), and the basic beliefs and methodology have been outlined in previous chapters.

Although it has various meanings, the term **positivism** is generally applied to the belief that empirical, scientific methodology is the most effective means of gaining knowledge about the world (Slee 1987). This belief is currently under scrutiny. As Bullivant (1978, p. 240) observes: 'In all the social sciences, traditional methodologies are seemingly being challenged'. Instead of these traditional methodologies, various alternative methodologies for understanding human behaviour have been proposed (Harr & Secord 1972; Reason & Rowan 1981; Manicas & Secord 1983; Reason 1987).

In relation to developmental psychology, one consequence of this shift in methodology is that less emphasis is now placed on stages of development and greater importance is given to understanding the 'role of discourse and dialogical process' in development (Bruner & Haste 1987, p. 11). That is, increasing attention is now being given to the 'competent' child, who interacts in a very active way with the environment and who is busy constructing meaning out of such interactions. The contributions of writers such as Vygotsky (1984) encourage contemporary researchers to consider how the abilities of the child interact with and build upon 'the intercession and scaffolding of adults and peers' (Bruner & Haste 1987, p. 9) – how the child's development results from interaction with those around the child, particularly sensitive adults and peers who are able to provide a foundation for the child to learn and discover for her- or himself. As Galambos and Leadbeater (2000) have noted in their review of trends in adolescent research:

> We also point to changes in our research tools that allow for more comprehensive statistical pictures of the patterns and processes of developmental changes as well as a more in-depth qualitative picture of the diversity of adolescent experiences both within and across different cultures and ethnic or racial groups (p. 289).

positivism
a branch of philosophy advocating the use of the methods and principles of the natural sciences in the study of human behaviour.

Trends and issues

Constructing childhood

As noted in chapter 1, Ariès (1962) called to our attention the socially constructed nature of childhood through his assertion that 'in medieval society childhood did not exist' (p. 125). That is, once weaned, children participated in daily life according to their abilities just as adults do. From the fifteenth century on Ariès argued there was a growing awareness that children were somehow 'different'. This 'difference' came to be slowly reflected in social, political and economic ways and the institutionalisation of the idea is today reflected in our school system and the development of specialist hospitals and health-care facilities. James and James (2000 p. 35) noted:

There is now widespread if not universal acceptance of the premise that childhood is indeed socially constructed; that children are worthy of study in their own right, and that children are competent social actors who may have a particular perspective on the social world that we, as adults, might find worth listening to.

Seeing children anew

The methodological advances in the child development field challenge us to consider anew the way we see children. Various views of children are outlined

We are being challenged to consider how we see children.

in chapter 1 and linked to psychological theories, with emphasis on how our views of children are embedded in a historical–cultural and philosophical context. Edgar (1995, p. 15) has argued for a '"cultural" view of child development' . . . wherein '. . . we are bound to see the family as the key mediating structure of that culture, the crucible in which is forged the child's developing competence'. See CD-ROM for details of methods of child study.

Contemporary thinking regarding the nature of children has built upon, and in many ways moved beyond, the views of theorists outlined in chapter 1. Theories such as those of Jerome Bruner (1987) have helped to free us from the constraints of rather simplistic views of the child as a *tabula rasa*, or blank slate. Furthermore, researchers such as Margaret Donaldson (1974) and Carol Gilligan (1988) have built upon the considerable contributions of Piaget and are presently challenging us to think beyond the rather naive view that the young child is bound up in egocentrism.

Present-day thinking gives greater emphasis to children's interpersonal capabilities (from the earliest age), their social nature and their caring responsiveness to others. We are now in a better position to understand how children, in an endeavour to make sense of their experience, construct their own understanding of the world and develop their own theories about it. More specifically, the writings of Carol Gilligan (1982; 1988) present a real challenge to the theoretical and experimental foundations of developmental psychology to free itself from a patriarchal, male-oriented view of human development.

The individual is part of the system.

The individual as part of a system

In the first edition of this text a strong call was made to heed the call of systems thinking as a means for better appreciating the nature of human development. Developmental psychology has its roots in the study of the individual, as Kaye (1985, p. 40) points out: 'Traditional developmental psychology takes the individual as its unit of analysis; the child's parents and other family members are conceptualised as potential influences upon the child's development'.

This fundamental idea is now being challenged from a variety of quarters. Thus, the developmental psychologists such as Bronfenbrenner (1977), Sameroff (1982) and Bruner and Haste (1987) highlight the need to appreciate the broader context – social and cultural – in which the individual grows. Changes in methodology point to the need for researchers to 'focus on the child as a social being whose competencies are interwoven with the competencies of others' (Bruner & Haste 1987, p. 11).

In this regard, contemporary systems thinking offers some exciting new possibilities in the child development field. Systemically oriented psychologists such as Kaye (1985) and Minuchin (1985), drawing on the work of Bateson (see chapter 3), emphasise the need to view the individual as an interdependent contributing part of a system that influences that individual's behaviour. This view entails a very different outlook on the individual – one in which the emphasis is on how the child or adolescent grows as part of a system rather than on internal psychological processes.

Minuchin (1985) acknowledges that a systems orientation is not the prevailing mode in developmental psychology. However, she expresses some optimism that a move in this direction is evident and she cites as supporting evidence research in developmental psychology that:

- increasingly advocates a constructivist view, whereby the child is considered to be an active, construing individual rather than a passive, reactive organism (Piaget 1952; Vygotsky 1984; Bruner 1987);
- emphasises the bi-directionality of interactive behaviour, involving not only dyads but triads (Bell 1978; Kreppner et al. 1982);
- recognises the role of the father and siblings in influencing individual development (Russell 1983; Lamb 1981);
- entails a consideration of the contextual factors that have an effect on human growth (Piaget 1952; Samaroff 1982; Bronfenbrenner 1977).

In sum, methodological developments in a diverse range of fields in the social sciences including counselling, nursing and public health, to name but a few, are challenging researchers to consider alternative ways to understand various aspects of development. One further example of the alternative ways being proposed is presented in the narrative writing approaches exemplified in the writings of Jerome Bruner (1986; 1990).

Irwin (1996) has proposed a number of metaphors to help understand how researchers have approached the study of human development. Two such examples include the metaphor of 'mind as a machine' or the mind as a 'conditioned reflex'. Irwin has proposed that narrative psychology presents an alternative metaphor derived from the arts and literary criticism and hermeneutics '. . . and is a metaphor that holds that people are essentially writers of the stories of their lives' (p. 109). Certainly a number of researchers (e.g. Polkinghorne 1988; Georgesen et al. 1999) have taken up the challenge of researching human development in a narrative mode. For example, Georgesen et al. (1999, p. 1255) have used a narrative approach which they describe as consisting '. . . of the stories that the individual has constructed to give a sense of overall meaning to his or her life' to explore the relationship between childhood teasing and personality.

Trends and issues

'Emerging adulthood'

Arnett (2000, p. 3) has argued that 'In effect, a new period of life has opened up between adolescence and adulthood as a normative experience for young people in industrialised societies'. In support of his view, Arnett (1997; 2000a; 2000b) has cited the changing demographics in many Western industrialised countries including Australia. These include a rise in the median age of marriage for women and men, an increase in age at first childbirth for women, and the proportion of young people completing tertiary education. Arnett (2000b) has proposed a new theory of development from the late teens through the early 20s labelled 'emerging adulthood'. As Arnett (2000a, p. 3) has argued, '. . . it is a period of life characterised for many young people by a high degree of change, experimentation, and instability (Rindfuss 1991) as they explore a variety of possibilities in love, work, and worldviews (Arnett 1998, in press; Arnett, Ramos, & Jensen, in press)'. Certainly, the views proposed by Arnett warrant further research as part of a broader understanding of life-cycle theory.

Competent family functioning

The study of the impact of family interaction patterns and family development on behaviour and personality development has until recently fallen within the domain of sociology, and '[t]here has been little effort to merge sociologically oriented studies of family systems with psychologically based interest in developmental changes in the individual family members' (Krepper et al. 1982, p. 375). Increasingly though, attempts are being made to connect consideration of 'family dynamics' and 'family structure' with the development of the individual.

A particular feature of this research has been a greater focus on 'competence' or 'healthy' family functioning.

An underlying theme of this text is that a great deal of our understanding of individuals and families is based on a set of assumptions about human nature. To this end, much psychological research has focused on what is wrong or dysfunctional with people and families. In Kohn's words (1991, p. 498):

> The belief persists in this culture that our darker side is more persuasive, more persistent, and somehow more real than our capacity for what psychologists call pro-social behaviour. However, in the last decade there have been strong moves by psychologists to better understand how some individuals and some families cope better than others.

From an individual perspective, Cowen (1991) has argued for the need to research more carefully the concept of 'wellness', which he defines as related to good physical health and psychological well-being, and which is denoted by a sense of belonging, control and basic satisfaction with one's lot in life. Significant contributions to wellness include:

- doing a job well or communicating skilfully with others;
- resilience, or resistance to stress;
- systems support in terms of the family or school;
- empowerment.

Certainly the family makes an important contribution to the achievement of wellness in individuals (Haley 1980; Bagarozzi & Anderson 1989; Sabatelli & Anderson 1991). Various therapists and researchers have contributed to our understanding of the identifying features of healthy family functioning.

According to Virginia Satir (1964), the cornerstone to healthy family functioning is 'communication'. She believes that communication is harmonious when family members are able to express themselves openly without fear of rejection or retaliation. She also maintains that in healthy families clearly identified family rules used in a flexible manner help guide family members' behaviour.

The research and writing of Olson et al. (1983) regarding the circumplex model of the family have also contributed to our understanding of healthy family functioning. According to Olson and associates, there are two key dimensions crucial to good family functioning. The first is cohesion – the extent of closeness among family members. Families can be too close and enmeshed, or too distant and disengaged. The second dimension involves adaptability: families can be low on adaptability and too rigid in their functioning. They may be unable to alter or modify roles, or the atmosphere may be too chaotic, with parents unable to discipline children effectively, for example. According to the circumplex model, balanced and well-functioning families score moderately on the two dimensions of cohesion and adaptability.

Minuchin (1974) and Haley (1980) emphasise the role of the family's organisational structure in helping the family to function effectively. Adopting a systems approach, both Minuchin and Haley highlight the need for clear boundaries between the various sub-systems in a family. Parents should have a clear idea of their roles in the family and delineate these in terms of their expectations of the roles children play. For example, there should be open, clearly defined rules to identify status differences between family members, one such rule being that parents have the role of disciplining children.

Inherent in the structural/strategic view of effective family functioning presented by Minuchin and Haly is the idea of hierarchical organisation, with members of the family clearly understanding their role(s) in the hierarchy. Another feature of the structural/strategic view is that during moments of crisis in the family (such as the birth of a child), the family is capable of adapting to changed circumstances. Healthy families are capable of applying appropriate strategies to solve the crises and problems that arise as part of the life-cycle.

In summary, it is of considerable value for researchers to develop a greater understanding of the manner in which individuals and families can function in a healthy, adaptive fashion. The Australian writers Callan and Noller (1987) and Bowes and Hayes (1999) provide excellent overviews of marriage and the family in which they consider this issue.

Researchers such as Kaye (1985) and Minuchin (1985) argue for a greater recognition of the commonality of systemic theory and developmental psychology. Such a task is a deceptively simple one. It requires a dramatic shift from viewing and understanding the intrapsychic processes of the individual to appreciating human development as part of a larger system. To paraphrase Kaye (1985), a systems approach means that a system such as a family becomes the object of study in its own right. Moreover, a family is not simply the 'algebraic' sum of its parts because this would not entail special analysis. To explain processes at a systems level instead of at an individual level amounts to advocating a new **paradigm**. Moves towards better understanding the nature of dynamic systems are reflected in the writings of such theorists as Thelen and Smith (1998), Svyantek and Brown (2000); and von Geert (2000), as described in chapters 1 and 3 of this text.

paradigm
a pattern, model or example; a world view.

Development across the life-cycle

The debate over whether human development is a life-long process or whether it stops with adolescence is an ongoing one. As noted in chapter 3, Freud emphasised the significance of the first years as the formative ones in human development. The argument following from this view is that the study of adults is of little relevance to developmental psychology. That is, while it may be acknowledged that individuals continue to change past adolescence, such changes are for the most part considered to be cultural and not the result of 'gene expression', nor are they age-linked or universal.

Alternatively, other theorists such as Erik Erikson (chapter 3) and Arlin (1975) maintain that human development continues across the life-cycle. Shanahan et al. (2000) have called attention to a number of features characterising a systems view of development. Firstly they have emphasised that along with the shift to a dynamic-systems representation of human development,

> . . . the prominent place of plasticity in many theories acknowledges that change can occur at any level of organisation in the ecology of human development and that intra-individual variability is possible across the entire life-span (p. 421).

Secondly, in adopting a more contextual 'life-history' view of development, consideration is given to secular trends, e.g. changes in the onset of puberty and health status of children. Thirdly, a greater appreciation of individual differences has restricted the degree to which developmental psychology is looking for generalisability. Finally, the understanding of the impact of multiple contexts and multi-directional influences on development has contributed significantly to an appreciation of life-cycle development.

Development does not begin and end with childhood.

Age-related development

During childhood major developmental achievements (such as walking or talking), which exert a major influence on the individual child's relationship with those in her or his environment, occur within a specific age range. In contrast, the developmental landmarks in adulthood (establishing a relationship, bearing children or becoming a grandparent), which also trigger significant changes in the individual, are neither age-linked nor universally experienced. As such, attaching specific time periods to adult life-events is less important at one level. At another level, the 'timing' of such events is often quite critical. Neugarten (1968) uses the term 'social clock' to describe each culture's sense of timing for events such as marriage and child-bearing. Neugarten believes that individuals are sensitive to being 'off-time'– for example, bearing children later in life than expected in that culture.

Contributors to life-cycle theory

Levinson (1978) believes that Carl Jung (1875–1961), a student of Freud's, should be considered the founder of the modern study of adult development. Jung disagreed with Freud's emphasis on the early childhood years and intrapsychic conflicts. Jung placed more emphasis on the second half of life as an important period of development and on the roles of religion, mythology and culture in shaping our lives.

Erik Erikson

Erik Erikson made a significant contribution to life-cycle theory with his eight stages of development, the first five of which have already been discussed in this text. Stages 6–8 are the final stages covering the adult years.

Stage 6: Intimacy versus isolation. With adulthood comes the task of establishing a true intimacy with other adults. Establishing oneself in a relationship is an important step. The risk is that some individuals will fail at this task and in the face of the difficulty of the task opt to withdraw and isolate themselves.

Table 21.1 Erikson's psychosocial stages: adulthood

Ages	Stages
Infancy	Basic trust versus mistrust
1½–3½ years (approx.)	Autonomy versus shame and doubt
3½–5½ years (approx.)	Initiative versus guilt
5½–12 years (approx.)	Industry versus inferiority
Adolescence	Identity versus role confusion
Young adulthood	Intimacy versus isolation
Adulthood	Generativity versus stagnation
Maturity	Ego integrity versus despair

The final stage of the life-cycle (stage 8), according to Erikson, involves achieving a sense of completeness.

Stage 7: Generativity versus stagnation. The task facing the mature adult relates to the felt need for productivity and creativity in work and establishing a base for guiding the next generation. Dangers emanating from this stage include a sense of 'going nowhere' and doing nothing important, resulting in a sense of stagnation.

Stage 8: Ego Integrity versus despair. In this final stage, a sense of wholeness and completeness of a life well lived should be achieved. Problems arise if the focus of the individual is regret and despair over wasted chances and unfortunate choices.

Levinson

Writing in 1978, Levinson researched the life-cycle concept and proposed that it evolves through a series of 'eras', each lasting approximately 25 years. During each era certain tasks present themselves and the extent to which the tasks are accomplished determines how much satisfaction or turmoil the individual experiences. An era is a time of life in the broadest possible sense. Each era has its own distinctive and unifying quality or 'character of living', which is shaped by biological, psychological and social aspects. In moving from one era to the next, basic changes occur in the 'fabric of life' and the transition can take as long as six years. The major eras consist of (1) early childhood; (2) early adulthood; (3) middle adulthood; and (4) late adulthood.

1 Early childhood transition. This includes the period up to adulthood and is normally lived out within the family or equivalent social unit. Tasks associated with this time include developing a sense of separateness (a 'me'), widening the social world to include school and peers and developing an identity during adolescence.

2 Early adulthood. This era represents the peak time for biological functioning and the development of an adult identity. As noted by Levinson (1978) six crucial tasks are to be accomplished in the time period between leaving high school and the late twenties, namely:

i   achieve some autonomy from the family of origin;
ii achieve some balance between exploring and experimenting with lifestyles and achieving a stable lifestyle;
iii forming a 'dream' or guiding vision to help realise one's place in the adult world;
iv developing a 'mentor' relationship, where the older individual has a part to play in helping the younger person realise their 'dream';
v   developing an occupation;
vi realising a love relationship.

3 Middle adulthood. According to Levinson, after the age of 40 an old era has come to an end and a new season has begun. Changes occur in biological and physiological functioning; there is a generational shift so that the individual becomes more a part of the establishment. Finally in terms of career there is an opportunity to realise the fruit of one's labours.

4 Late adulthood. In late adulthood the person moves from 'centre-stage' and gives up some of the recognition, power and authority enjoyed in the past.

There is a limited amount of emerging research to support the validity of Levinson's schema of developmental periods that were largely based on his impressionistic interpretations of his considerable interview material.

Sheehy

A life-span development view is proposed by Sheehy (1976), based on detailed interviews with 115 men and women. Sheehy believes that we all go through developmental stages bound approximately by chronological age, and that within each of us there is an underlying impulse towards change. Externally, our life is shaped by events such as culture and family, while internally it is shaped by how we evaluate our participation in the outer world. According to

Sheehy, the periods between stages are 'passages'. She identifies four stages, labelled rather fancifully as:

1 breast to breakaway;
2 the trying twenties;
3 passage to the thirties;
4 deadline decade: the mid-life passage.

authentic identity
Sheehy's (1976) concept of a personal identity that evolves from an individual's struggle with life events.

According to Sheehy, in striving to face the various conflicts at each stage we earn an **authentic identity**, which is not based on our parents or what our culture says we should be. It is an identity carved out of our own struggles with life events at each stage.

The family life-cycle: 21

Resilient families

The concept of the resilient child is one that has been highlighted by the research of Rutter (1971) and Garmezy (1983). A great deal of psychological research has focused, as a legacy of its Freudian past, on the negative aspects of child behaviour such as emotional problems (e.g. aggression, anxiety and depression). Recently there has been a shift in approach and greater emphasis is now given to the resilience and capable competent components of children's behaviour. This outlook is consistent with an emerging view of children as active, construing individuals whose development is shaped by their own volition. In a similar vein, an emerging body of research is now devoted to the study of resilient families (Garmezy 1985; Kaye 1985; Amato 1987; Rae-Grant et al. 1989).

In this series on the family life-cycle, we have seen that the family experiences various nodal points in its development at which a crisis may develop. In the life-cycle of the family system, a crisis comes about in two ways. It may occur around the period of stress as the family is in transition from one stage to the next. For example, the birth of the second child requires certain adaptations on the part of the parents and existing child to accommodate the new member. A crisis can also develop because the family becomes 'stuck' at a certain point in its development and fails to move from one stage to the next. The recognition of such crisis points in the development of the family points to the need to study 'well functioning (effective, adaptive) families' (Kaye 1985, p. 50).

In an examination of Australian families, Amato (1987) argues that it is the quality of the interpersonal strengths and resources possessed by a family that helps it manage crises most resiliently. A group of researchers have studied nearly 1400 families over the life-cycle to identify those strengths that contribute to family resilience in times of stress (Olson et al. 1983; McCubbin et al. 1988; McCubbin & McCubbin 1988). The strengths required by the family vary from one stage of the life-cycle to the next. Overall, however, resilient families have in common:

1 various celebrations that help to stabilise the family in crisis, (for example, birthdays are acknowledged);
2 an element of hardiness encompassing individual family members' beliefs in a sense of control or influence over their life;
3 a routine (for example, specific times for meals or to accomplish set tasks);
4 traditions of honouring certain key events in the life of the family.

Social capital of families.
There has been a significant growth in interest in the concept of 'social capital'. While our society has generally recognised other forms of 'capital', such as financial and human (education), social capital has also now been recognised. In Coleman's (1988) seminal study, consideration was given to the benefits that accrue from social connectedness in communities and within families. Coleman defined 'social capital' as those aspects of the social structure, personal relations and network of relations that best facilitate actions within the structure. As noted by Desmond et al. (1998, p. 12), 'social capital refers to features in the social organization, such as social networks, expectations, and trust, that facilitate coordination and cooperation for mutual benefit'. Research is now emerging which indicates that social capital has significant relations with children's well-being (Drielsma 2000).

In summary, the further study of resilient, healthy, well-functioning families would provide us with important insight into how to optimise such conditions in families under stress.

A cautionary note

In presenting human development within a life-cycle framework it is important to note the reservations of a number of theorists including Germain (1994) regarding such an outlook. Germain has argued against the view that the life-cycle should be considered as some fixed, linear progression through a sequence of stages characterised by normative assumptions regarding family forms or child-bearing. As noted in chapter 1 of this text the demographics of many Western industrialised nations including Australia are changing dramatically. Germain (1994, p. 259) has noted that various life-cycle models '. . . do not take into account cultural and historical contexts, differences in male and female socialisation, variations in sexual orientations, and the influences of poverty and oppression'.

Chapter summary

In this chapter human development has been presented within a life-cycle context. Attention has been drawn to sweeping demographic and broad societal changes impacting on the nature of development across the teenage and early adulthood years. At the same time it is now better understood that development does not begin and end with childhood but that within a broad systemic framework development occurs across the life-cycle.

Human development is best viewed within a broad life cycle perspective.

Discussion questions

1   Re-examine the various views of child development described in chapter 1 and discuss the influence of such views on contemporary thinking about children.
2   How do the theories of Piaget, Vygotsky and Bruner challenge us to think differently about children's development?
3   What differences are there between the systems perspective on child and adolescent development and the view of traditional psychology?
4   Based on your reading of this chapter, should human development be considered a life-cycle process?
5   Compare and contrast the life-span development views of Erikson, Levinson and Sheehy.

Activities

1   Identify those factors in your family that contributed to healthy development, that is, the interpersonal resources possessed by your family. Discuss how such qualities enhanced your own development.
2   Complete the 'Self Review Quiz' on the CD-ROM to assess your understanding of the content presented in this section. Use your quiz results as a basis for reviewing any chapter content about which you are uncertain.

The tradition of family celebrations is one of the strengths of resilient families.

Selected websites

Child Adolescent Psychological Educational Resources
<www. caper.com.au>

Youth Studies Australia <www.acys.utas.edu.au>

Glossary

accommodation in Piaget's theory, the modification of mental structures to incorporate new knowledge.

active–experiencing learning style as defined by Kolb, learning through active participation.

adolescence a term for teenagers derived from Latin *adolescere*, meaning 'to grow to maturity'.

agent an individual who has the ability to initiate, direct, manage or control his or her own behaviour.

AIDS acquired immune deficiency syndrome, the end of a spectrum of disease caused by a virus that attacks and exhausts key parts of the body's natural defence system.

alleles gene factors that determine specific characteristics.

amniocentesis medical procedure for detecting foetal abnormalities by withdrawing a sample of the amniotic fluid and performing chromosomal analyses.

anal stage the second of Freud's psychosexual stages, during which the anal area is the primary 'erotic' zone and the child gains special pleasure from the elimination or retention of faeces.

androgyny possession of both male and female personality characteristics.

animism according to Piaget, the belief of the pre-operational child that inanimate objects are alive.

anorexia nervosa an eating disorder characterised by extreme reduction of food intake and loss of at least 25 per cent of original body weight.

Apgar test a test routinely used to assess the physical condition of newborn babies.

artificialism according to Piaget, the belief of the pre-operational child that certain aspects of the natural environment are manufactured by people.

assimilation in Piaget's theory, the incorporation of new information into the child's existing patterns of thought and behaviour.

associational knowledge a type of knowledge identified by Tripodi (1981) that indicates the extent of the relationship between two variables.

attachment the primary social bond between one individual and another.

attachment behaviour behaviour that promotes contact and/or proximity of an infant to the care-giver.

attention deficit hyperactivity disorder (ADHD) a complex set of behaviours involving impulsiveness, inattention and over-activity.

auditory learning style learning through hearing.

authentic identity Sheehy's (1976) concept of a personal identity that evolves from an individual's struggle with life events.

authoritarian a dictatorial style of child-rearing in which unquestioning obedience is expected from children.

authoritative a democratic style of child-rearing, in which parents give firm guidance while listening to their children's ideas.

autonomous morality a sense of right and wrong determined by the individual, not by others.

autonomy versus shame and doubt the second of Erikson's psychosocial stages of development, during which toddlers experience a sense of autonomy when successful in their striving for independence but shame or doubt as a result of parental prohibitions.

babbling the alternating vowel and consonant sounds made by a young infant in the first months of life.

basic trust versus mistrust refers to the first of Erikson's psychosocial stages in which the infant develops the ability to rely on others and believe in his or her own capacity to deal with his or her own needs and those of the world.

behaviourist focusing on observable behaviour and its causes.

birth emergence of young from body of mother.

blastocyst a hollow ball of approximately 100 cells that forms in the very early stages of development following conception.

blended family a family resulting from the remarriage of one or both adults, who bring with them children from the previous marriage.

canalisation genetic predisposition towards the development of certain characteristics in the species, such as walking.

cathexis the focusing of mental energy on a particular action or memory.

cause–effect knowledge as defined by Tripodi (1981), a type of knowledge that identifies the cause of an event.

central tendency in statistics, the typical or central value of a set of scores.

chromosome one of 46 small thread-like structures in the nucleus of human cells containing the genetic code in the form of DNA.

chronological age the actual age of an individual; compare mental age.

circular reaction any behaviour that the infant repeats.

class inclusion the ability to associate a subset of objects (such as red apples) with the larger grouping to which it belongs (fruit).

classical conditioning learning in which a neutral stimulus elicits a certain response by repeated association with another stimulus that already elicits the response.

clique in adolescence, a small group of about six individuals, as described by Dunphy (1963).

clumsiness an impairment of the child's ability to perform skilled motor acts usual for the child's age.

cofigurative Margaret Mead's description of a culture in which children learn from their peers.

cognition the way we know about the world through the use of thinking, reasoning, learning and remembering.

cognitive congruency principle states that a child finds funniest those jokes that relate to that child's cognitive developmental level.

cognitive–constructivist emphasising the interrelatedness of cognition and emotion in the developing scheme of emotions.

concrete operations period according to Piaget, the stage between 7 and 11 years of age during which children begin to understand the relationship between things in the world but still cannot think in abstract terms.

concrete-experiencing learning style as defined by Kolb, learning through actual experience.

conditioned reflex occurs when a previously neutral stimulus acquires the ability to produce a response through association with an unconditioned stimulus (a stimulus that evokes a response that has not been learned).

conservation in Piagetian theory, the retention by an object or substance of certain properties, regardless of changes in shape and arrangement.

constructive development occurs when a child actively participates by finding personal meaning in a situation, making decisions and sharing viewpoints with peers.

constructivism a school of thought in psychology that emphasises the subjectivity of experience and the role of individuals in actively construing their world.

constructivist emphasising the subjectivity of our experience and the role of individuals in actively construing meaning in their world.

correlation in statistics, the relationship between two sets of scores.

critical awareness a process of enquiry in which the researcher's own values and attitudes make a contribution.

crowd in adolescence, a large group, consisting of two or more cliques, as described by Dunphy (1963).

crystallised intelligence according to Cattell, a type of intelligence that comprises knowledge based on education and culture.

cycle of learning the sequence of understanding through which a learner proceeds in mastering a task or absorbing a body of knowledge.

deep learning an approach to learning involving a search for meaning and relationship.

deoxyribonucleic acid (DNA) a complex chemical containing the genetic code that guides development.

development takes into account the effect of experience on an individual.

developmental psychology the study of the individual from conception.

developmental tasks in Havighurst's theory, tasks that must be completed during certain periods of a person's life.

Down syndrome an inherited disorder, first described by John Langdon Haydon Down in 1866, resulting from an extra copy of chromosome 21.

drives in Freudian theory, powerful instinctive desires, such as hunger or thirst.

dynamic systems theory the spontaneous emergence of higher order forms of functioning as a result of recursive, circular interactions among simpler components.

dyzygotic twins individuals with different genetic blueprints who have developed from two different eggs fertilised at the same time; compare monozygotic twins.

echolalia imitation by the infant of the speech of others, appearing at around 9 months of age.

ectomorph one of Sheldon's three body types, a long, thin body type.

ego in Freudian theory, the conscious self, the realistic rational part of the personality that mediates between the instinctual demands of the id and the superego.

egocentrism (centration) the inability to distinguish between one's own point of view and that of another person.

ego integrity versus despair the last of Erikson's psychosocial stages, in which the crucial task is to achieve the sense of a life well lived.

embryo the developing human being during the first eight weeks following the implantation of the ovum in the uterine wall.

empiricism the view that knowledge is derived solely from experience.

enactive representation the ability to experience the world through actions, or doing.

endomorph one of Sheldon's three body types, best characterised by roundness with fairly weak muscle and bone development.

engrossment a term describing a father's preoccupation with his newborn child.

enuresis the inability to control the discharge of urine; see also primary enuresis, secondary enuresis.

epistemological development development of the child's knowledge base.

epistemology the study of the theory of how we acquire knowledge.

equilibration the search for a balance between what the child already knows (assimilation) and the child's new experiences (accommodation).

erogenous zones parts of the body that at different ages are susceptible to pleasurable feelings.

eros Lee's (1974) name for love involving an immediate and powerful physical attraction.

event sampling a method of observation in which the focus is on a specific event, such as a conflict episode between children.

existentialism a philosophy emphasising the importance and value of the individual and the role of freedom, responsibility and choice in determining behaviour.

experiential child refers to the concept that children develop solely as a product of their experience.

extended family a nuclear family plus grandparents and/or other relatives.

field experiment an experiment in which independent variables are deliberately manipulated in a naturalistic setting.

field study the investigation of naturally occurring events at the time and place that they occur.

fine motor refers to movements requiring precision and dexterity, as in manipulative tasks; compare gross motor.

fluid intelligence according to Cattell, a type of intelligence that is hereditary and involves the ability to think and reason abstractly.

foetal alcohol syndrome a serious condition involving various physical defects and mental retardation in children born to alcoholic mothers.

foetoscopy screening technique in which the foetus is viewed through an endoscope.

formal operations period Piaget's name for the fourth stage of cognitive development from about 11 years of age onwards, during which individuals acquire the ability to think in abstract terms.

gender identity a person's sense of self as male or female; compare sex role.

generativity versus stagnation the seventh of Erikson's psychosocial stages, in which the crucial task is to be productive and creative.

genes biological units of heredity involving a self-reproducing DNA particle located in a particular chromosome.

genetics the scientific study of heredity.

genital stage in Freudian theory, the period beginning in adolescence characterised by the reawakening of sexual feelings.

genotype the actual genetic composition of the organism.

Gestalt a school of thought in psychology suggesting that the perceived organised whole is more than the sum of its parts.

gonads the sex glands, which regulate sex drive; in females, the ovaries; in males, the testes.

gross motor refers to movements of the entire body or of major parts of the body; compare fine motor.

growth progressive anatomical and physical changes of a living being; compare development.

habituation the eventual disappearance of a response following repeated presentation of a stimulus.

heteronomous morality a sense of right and wrong established by rules imposed by outside authorities, such as parents.

holophrastic speech one-word utterances that express a complete thought, appearing at about 1 year of age.

humanism a school of thought in psychology that emphasises individuals, their personal experience and potential for development.

humanistic emphasising individuals, their personal experience and potential for development.

hypothalamus a structure in the forebrain that controls a range of autonomic functions, such as body temperature.

hypothesis a testable proposition.

hypothetical–developmental knowledge as identified by Tripodi (1981), the description of events using general concepts.

iconic representation the ability to use mental images or pictures to represent experience.

id in Freudian theory, that part of the personality containing all of the basic impulses or drives.

ideal self an idealised image of oneself and what one might become.

identity versus role confusion the fifth of Erikson's psychosocial stages, in which there is a search for identity involving an intense exploration of personal values, beliefs and goals.

imaginary audience refers to attention that adolescents tend to imagine is focused on them.

imitation copying or reproducing behaviour.

immanent justice the notion that punishment for wrongdoing is inevitable, an inherent part of the wrongdoing.

industry versus inferiority the fourth of Erikson's psychosocial stages, in which the child aims at productivity and mastery, but feels inferior if these are not achieved.

infertility the inability to conceive.

information processing the taking in, storing and using of information by humans and animals.

iniquitous child refers to the idea that children are inherently evil.

initiative versus guilt the conflict faced by children in the third of Erikson's psychosocial stages of development, in which they discover behavioural limits.

instinct practice theory a theory formulated by Groos, that play helps to refine and develop instinctive activities.

instincts in Freudian theory, forces that exist behind the tensions caused by the needs of the id.

intelligence quotient (IQ) the ratio of an individual's mental age (MA) to chronological age (CA) multiplied by 100.

intimacy versus isolation the sixth of Erikson's psychosocial stages, in which the crucial task is to establish true intimacy.

justice concept according to Piaget, the child's concept of morality at about 7–8 years of age, involving rules and reciprocity.

kinaesthetic learning style learning involving the whole body.

knowledge in action research that emphasises practice rather than theory.

laboratory study research conducted in a carefully controlled, artificial environment.

la methode clinique see **methode clinique**.

latency period in Freud's theory, a period of development (6–12 years) in the child's life when sexual impulses are relatively dormant.

lattation repetitive sounds made by the young infant at about 6 months of age.

learning style a person's preferred mode of taking in and storing information.

libidinal associated with instinctive energies and desires.

libido a relatively fixed quantity of energy in each individual that primarily relates to the sexual drive.

locomotor describes movement from one place to another.

logico-mathematical knowledge Piaget's term for knowledge gained about the relationships between objects as a result of our interaction with them.

ludas Lee's (1974) name for a playful type of love characterised by lack of commitment.

manipulative describes activities involving the use of the hand.

maturation the changes that occur in an organism as it fulfils its genetic potential; compare development.

mean in statistics, the average of a set of scores obtained by summing all scores and dividing the total by the number of scores.

mechanistic emphasising the role of experience and the cause–effect nature of behaviour.

median in statistics, the value in a series of scores which has as many scores above it as below it.

meiosis the process of cell division of sex cells, resulting in four new cells.

menarche a female's first menstrual period.

mental age a measure of intellectual ability in terms of the average ability at a particular age, which may not be the same as an individual's actual age (chronological age).

mesomorph one of Sheldon's three body types, best characterised by a predominance of muscle and bone.

méthode clinique (clinical method) the method of interviewing adopted by Piaget to help him understand the child's thought processes.

mitosis the process of cell division for body cells by which chromosomes in each cell replicate to form a second set of chromosomes, which then separate from the original cell to form a new, identical cell.

mode in statistics, the most frequently occurring value in a set of scores.

monozygotic twins individuals with identical genes who have developed from the same fertilised egg.

moral development the development of the values, attitudes and beliefs that help people distinguish right from wrong.

morpheme the smallest unit of meaning in spoken or written language.

motherese a type of speech used by the mother to address the young infant.

nativist refers to the idea that emotions are innate, or inborn.

naturalistic experiment the study of one event in relation to another as they occur in their natural environments.

new paradigm research new methods for conducting research that are outside the main scientific tradition.

niche-picking the selection, as people age, of aspects of their environment to which they will respond in terms of personality, intellect and motivation.

non-standardised interview an interview in which the questions are largely determined by the respondent's answers.

normal distribution in statistics, a symmetrical distribution (bell-shaped) of a set of scores, where most values fall around the central area of the curve (the mean) and the frequency of the scores fall off to either side of the mean.

norms accepted standards against which individual performance can be compared.

nuclear family a couple and their children living in the same dwelling.

obese being excessively overweight; more than 20 per cent heavier than the acceptable weight.

object permanence the understanding that objects can exist independently of one's interaction with them.

oocyte name given to the egg cell when it is released from the ovary.

operant conditioning behaviour that results from the rewarding or punishment of voluntary behaviour by stimulus consequences.

organismic emphasising the contribution individuals make to their own development.

paradigm a pattern, model or example; a world view.

participatory and wholistic knowing a mode of enquiry that is more systemic than the Newtonian scientific view.

peer group a group of children of approximately the same age.

perceived self one's view of oneself: self-concept.

permissive a lax style of child-rearing in which parents make few demands of their children, imposing few rules and offering little positive guidance.

personal fable the delusion of adolescents that their own experiences and feelings are unique and cannot be understood by others.

phallic stage the third of Freud's psychosexual stages, during which the young child's libidinal energy shifts to the genitals.

phenomenology a philosophy that focuses on the world as it appears to the individual.

phenotype the physical or behavioural traits in an individual that reflect both genetic and environmental factors.

physical knowledge Piaget's term for knowledge of the physical properties of objects gained from direct physical experience of them.

pituitary gland an organ located beneath the hypothalamus that controls many hormonal secretions.

placenta a mass of tissue in the uterus through which nutrients are transmitted from mother to foetus and waste products filtered from foetus to mother.

population in statistics, a group of individuals sharing at least one common characteristic.

positivism a branch of philosophy advocating the use of the methods and principles of the natural sciences in the study of human behaviour.

postfigurative Margaret Mead's description of a culture in which children learn from their forebears.

pre-operational period Piaget's name for the stage between 2 and 7 years of age, during which children acquire the ability to represent the world using symbols, such as language.

pre-riddle a riddle without a punch-line.

prefigurative Margaret Mead's description of a culture in which adults learn from their children as well as vice versa.

preformist refers to the view that a miniature adult exists in the egg or sperm.

primary enuresis is said to occur when the child is never consistently dry.

primipara a woman giving birth for the first time.

psychoanalysis the method for treating mental disorders, developed by Sigmund Freud, in which the underlying defect, the motive behind behaviour, is rendered conscious.

psychoanalytic theory of play views play as an outlet for emotion.

psychodynamic focusing upon the dynamic interaction between the conscious and unconscious in affecting behaviour.

psychosocial in Erikson's theory, describes the interactions between child and family and between child and culture.

psychosocial aspect the development of the child in the larger social setting of family and culture.

puberty the attainment of sexual maturity; in girls, the beginning of menstruation; in boys, the first production of live sperm.

punishment any stimulus that results in the suppression or reduction of a behaviour.

quantitative-descriptive knowledge according to Tripodi (1981), a type of knowledge that describes the links between two variables.

rapprochement according to Mahler, describes the phase in which a toddler discovers that personal identity can be achieved while maintaining or re-establishing a harmonious relationship with the mother.

reaction range the broadest possible expression of a genotype.

realism according to Piaget, the confusion by the pre-operational child of external reality with the child's own thought processes and subjective understanding; the child's belief that wishes, thoughts and feelings are 'alive'.

reflective observational learning style as defined by Kolb, learning that involves thinking about something that has been experienced.

reflexes involuntary actions of muscles.

reinforcement any stimulus that increases the likelihood of a behaviour recurring.

research design a general plan for the research to be undertaken.

sample in statistics, a subset of a population.

scaffolding Vygotsky's term for the way in which a mature person skilfully encourages a learner to acquire a new skill or understand a concept.

schema in Piagetian terms, a pattern of action or a mental structure; plural, schemata.

scientism the idea that all true knowledge arises from the use of empirical scientific method.

secondary enuresis involuntary passing of urine when there has been a period of dryness of at least one year after the age of 3 years.

secular trend the trend for people to develop earlier and to be larger than in former eras.

selectionist refers to the view that neuronal networks are modified by environmental influence.

self-actualisation the individual's full use of talent, capacity or potential.

self-concept the picture one has of oneself.

self-dynamism Sullivan's term for the active, achieving, protective part of the self.

self-esteem one's evaluation of information one holds about oneself.

sensori-motor period Piaget's first cognitive development stage in which infants use their senses and motor skills to explore their environment.

sensori-motor play play involving the senses and motor skills.

seriation the ability to put objects or quantities into a logical sequence.

sex role learned behaviour that society deems appropriate for a person's sex; compare gender identity.

skewed distribution in statistics, occurs when a set of scores is asymmetrical.

social capital refers to networks which provide a basis for trust, cooperation and perceptions of safety.

social skills acceptable learned behaviours that gain positive responses from others.

socialisation the process by which individuals acquire the values, attitudes and knowledge of the society (or subgroups of society) to which they belong.

sociodramatic play the most elaborate form of symbolic play in which a theme is enacted.

sole-parent family a family in which the children are raised by the mother or father alone.

somatotype physique expressed in terms of extreme types.

standardised interview interview in which set questions are asked of all respondents in the same age group.

storge Lee's (1974) name for deep love that develops slowly and steadily.

structure in Piagetian theory, the way a child organises his or her experience of the world.

superego in Freudian theory, that part of the personality incorporating the internalised values held by the individual and corresponding to the internalised injunctions of the parent.

surface learning a means-to-an-end approach to learning.

surplus energy theory of play proposes that play occurs only after basic needs have been met.

symbolic functions cognition that enables one object or action to represent another.

symbolic play imaginative play in which one object is used to represent another.

symbolic representation ability to represent experience by using symbols.

telegraphic speech early utterances (18–24 months) that leave out most of the articles, prepositions and conjunctions.

temperament behaviours that comprise relatively stable characteristics of a person's personality.

tertiary circular reaction occurs when a child actively uses trial and error to learn more about the world.

theory of mind the ability to impute mental states to self and others.

time sampling arbitrary division of the stream of behaviour under observation into equal time intervals, which are scored for the presence or absence of specified behaviours.

transactional view of development the view that development is a two-way interaction between child and environment.

virtuous child refers to Rousseau's notion that the child is inherently good.

visual learning style learning through seeing.

zone of proximal development (ZPD) the 'gap' between what individuals can achieve alone and what they can achieve with the help of a more knowledgable person.

References

Acker, S. (1988), 'Teachers, gender and resistance', *British Journal of Sociology of Education* 9, pp. 307–22.

Adler, A. (1927), *The Practice and Theory of Individual Psychology*, Harcourt Brace Jovanovich, New York.

Ainsworth, M. (1973), 'The development of infant–mother attachment', in B. Caldwell and H. Ricciuti (eds), *Review of Child Development Research* vol. 3, University of Chicago Press, Chicago.

Ainsworth, M. D. S. and Bell, S. M. (1970), 'Attachment, exploration and separation: illustrated by the behaviour of 1 year olds in a strange situation', *Child Development* 41, pp. 49–67.

Ainsworth, M. D. S. and Bell, S. M. (1974), 'Mother–infant interaction and the development of competence', in K. Connolly and J. Bruner (eds), *The Growth of Competence*, Academic Press, London.

Ainsworth, M. D. S. and Wittig, B. (1969), 'Attachment exploratory behaviour of one-year-olds in a strange situation', in B. M. Foss (ed.), *Determinants of Infant Behaviour*, vol. 4, Methuen, London.

Ainsworth, M. D. S., Bell, S. M. and Stayton, D. J. (1974), 'Infant–mother attachment and social development: socialisation as a product of reciprocal responsiveness to signals', in M. P. M. Richards (ed.), *The Integration of a Child into a Social World*, Cambridge University Press, London.

Ainsworth, M., Blehar, M., Waters, E. and Wall, S. (1978a), *Strange Situation Behaviour of 1 Year Olds*, Lawrence Erlbaum, Hillsdale, New Jersey.

Ainsworth, M. D. S., Blehar, M. C., Waters, E. and Wall, S. (1978b), *Patterns of Attachment*, Lawrence Erlbaum, Hillsdale, New Jersey.

Akhtar, N., Dunham, F. and Dunham, P. J. (1991), 'Directive interactional early vocabulary development: the role of joint attentional focus', *Journal of Child Language* 18, pp. 41–9.

Akridge, K. (1988), 'Anorexia nervosa', *Journal of Obstetric, Gynaecologic and Neonatal Nursing* January/February, pp. 25–30.

Alasker, F. D. (1995), 'Pubertal timing overweight and psychological adjustment', *Journal of Early Adolescence*, 12, pp. 396–419.

Alsaker, F. D. and Flammer, A. (1999), *The Adolescent Experience: European and American Adolescents in the 1990s*, Erlbaum, Mahwah N.J.

Allen, F. C. L., Scannell, E. D. and Turner, H. R. (1998), 'Guilt and hostility as coexisting characteristics of bulimia nervosa', *Australian Psychologist* 33, pp. 143–7.

Amato, P. (1987), *Children in Australian Families: the Growth of Competence*, Prentice-Hall, Sydney.

American Psychiatric Association (1987), *Diagnostic and Statistical Manual of Mental Disorders (DSM-III-R)*, American Psychiatric Association, 3rd edn.

Ames, A. (1951), 'Visual perception and the rotating trapezoidal window', *Psychological Monographs* 65 (7), p. 234.

Amsterdam, B. (1972), 'Mirror self-image reactions before age two', *Developmental Psychobiology* 5, pp. 297–305.

Anastasiou, N. J. and Stengel, A. H. (1980), 'Education physicians in child development: why, what and how', in M. J. Guralnick and H. B. Richardson (eds), *Paediatric Education and the Needs of Exceptional Children*, University Park Press, Baltimore.

Anderson, J., Lorenz, B. and Pease, S. (1986), 'Prediction of sport participation from children's gender, past participation and attitudes: a longitudinal analysis', *Social Sports Journal* 3, pp. 101–11.

Anderson, N. H. and Cuneo, D. O. (1978), 'The height plus width rule in children's understanding of quantity', *Journal of Experimental Psychology* 107, pp. 335–78.

Anderson, S. (1983), 'Anorexia nervosa and bulimia: a spectrum of eating disorders', *Journal of Adolescent Health Care* 4, pp. 15–21.

Andrew, L. B. (1984), *New Conception: a Consumer's Guide to the Newest Fertility Treatment*, St Martin's Press, New York.

Andrews, B. and Brewin, C. R. (2000), 'What Freud did get right', *The Psychologist* 13, pp. 605–7.

Anglin, J. M. (1993), 'Vocabulary development: a morphological analysis', *Monograph of the Society for Research in Child Development* 58, (10).

Annett, M. (1959), 'The classification of instances of four common class concepts by children and adults', *British Journal of Educational Psychology* 29, pp. 223–36.

Anthony, S. (1971), *The Discovery of Death in Childhood and After*, Penguin, London.

Antill, J. K. and Cunningham, J. D. (1980), 'The relationship of masculinity, femininity and androgyny to self esteem', *Australian Journal of Psychology*, 32, pp. 195–207.

Apgar, V. (1953), 'A proposal for a new method of evaluation of the newborn infant', *Current Researches in Anesthesia and Analgesia* 32, pp. 260–7.

Apgar, V., Holaday, D. A., James, L. S., Weisbrot, I. M. and Berrien, C. (1958), 'Evaluation of the newborn infant – second report', *Journal of the American Medical Association* 168, pp. 1985–8.

Appleton, T., Clifton, R., and Goldberg, S. (1975), 'The development of behavioural competence in infancy', in F. D. Horowitz (ed.), *Review of Child Development Research*, University of Chicago Press, pp. 101–86.

Ariès, P. (1962), *Centuries of Childhood*, Vintage Books, New York.

Arnett, J. J. (1997), 'Young people's conceptions of the transition to adulthood', *Youth and Society* 29, pp. 3–23.

Arnett, J. J. (2000), 'Emerging adulthood. A theory of development from the late teens through the twenties', *American Psychologist*, May, pp. 469–80.

Askew, S. (1989), 'Aggressive behaviour in boys: to what extent is it institutionalised?', in D. P. Tatum and D. A. Lane (eds), *Bullying in Schools*, Stoke-on-Trent, Trentham Books, pp. 59–71.

Aspin, L. J. (1987), *The Family: an Australian Focus*, Longman Cheshire, Melbourne.

Astbury, J., Brown, S., Lumley, J. and Small, R. (1994), 'Predicting postnatal depression among pregnant women', *Birth* 23 pp. 218–23.

Ault, R. (1983), *Children's Cognitive Development*, Holt, Rinehart and Winston, New York.

Australian Bureau of Statistics (1990), *Causes of Death, Australia*, catalogue no. 3303.0, Australian Bureau of Statistics, Canberra, table 8.

Australian Bureau of Statistics (1992), *The Labour Force, Australia,* February 1992, Australian Bureau of Statistics, Canberra, catalogue no. 6203.0.

Australian Bureau of Statistics (2000), *Australian Social Trends, 2000*, Australian Bureau of Statistics, Canberra, catalogue no. 4102.0.

Australian Bureau of Statistics (2002), *Australian Social Trends, 2002,* Australian Bureau of Statistics, Canberra, catalogue no. 4102.0.

Australian Sports Commission (1997), *Active Australia: A National Participation Framework*, Australian Sports Commission, Canberra.

Avis, J. (1985), 'The politics of functional family therapy: a feminist critique', *Journal of Marital and Family Therapy* 11, pp. 127–38.

Axline, V. M. (1974), *Play Therapy*, Ballantine Books, New York.

Azarnoff, P. (1983), *Preparation of Young Healthy Children for Possible Hospitalisation: the Issues*, Paediatric Projects, Monograph 1.

Azrin, N. H. and Foxx, R. M. (1976), *Toilet Training in Less Than a Day*, Pocket Books, New York.

Azrin, N. H., Sneed, T. J. and Foxx, R. M. (1974), 'Dry bed training: rapid elimination of childhood enuresis', *Behaviour Research and Therapy* 12, pp. 147–56.

Bagarozzi, D. A. and Anderson, S. A. (1989), *Personal, Marital and Family Myths: Theoretical Formulations and Clinical Strategies*, W. W Norton, New York.

Bahn, D. (2001), 'Social learning theory: its application in the context of nurse education', *Nurse Education Today*, 21, pp. 110–17.

Baldwin, A. (1980), *Theories of Child Development*, 2nd edn, Wiley, New York.

Ball, S. J., Demo, D. H., and Wedman, J. F. (1998), 'Family involvement with children's homework: strategies and practices', *Elementary School Journal* 95, pp. 435–50.

Bandura, A. (1963), 'What TV violence can do to your child', *Look*, 22 October, pp. 46–52.

Bandura, A. (1971), *Psychological Modelling: Conflicting Theories*, Aldine, Chicago.

Bandura, A. (1977), *Social Learning Theory*, Prentice-Hall, Englewood Cliffs, New Jersey.

Bandura, A., Ross, D. and Ross, S. A. (1963), 'Vicarious reinforcement and imitative learning', *Journal of Abnormal and Social Psychology* 67, pp. 601–7.

Bandura, A. and Walters, R. (1963), *Social Learning and Personality Development*, Holt, Rinehart and Winston, New York.

Bank, S. and Kahn, M. D. (1982), *The Sibling Bond*, Basic Books, New York.

Barker, R. G. (1963), *The Stream of Behaviour*, Appleton-Century-Crofts, New York.

Barker, R. G. and Wright, H. R. (1955), *Midwest and its Children: the Psychological Ecology of an American Town*, Row and Peterson, New York.

Baron-Cohen, S., O'Riordan, M., Stone, V., Jones, R. and Plaisted, K. (1999), 'Recognition of faux pas by normally developing children and children with Asperger Syndrome or high-functioning autism', *Journal of Autism and Developmental Disorders* 29, pp. 407–18.

Bates, J. E., Maslin C. A. and Frankel, K. A. (1985), 'Attachment security, mother–infant interaction and temperament as predictors of behaviour problem ratings at age three years', in I. Bretherton and E. Waters (eds), *Growing Points of Attachment Theory and Research, Monographs of the Society for Research in Child Development* 209, pp. 167–93.

Bateson, G. (1972), *Steps to an Ecology of Mind*, Ballantine, New York.

Bateson, G. (1979), *Mind and Nature*, Flamingo, UK.

Battye, P. and Slee, P. T. (1985), 'The demise of the person in social work', *Australian Social Work* 38, pp. 23–31.

Baum, F. (1988), *Nothing or No-one Could Have Told Me What It Was Going to Be Like*, part 1, a report prepared for the South Australian Health Commission, Adelaide.

Baum, F. (1990), *Nothing or No-one Could Have Told Me What It Would Be Like*, part 2, a report prepared for the South Australian Health Commission, Adelaide.

Baumrind, D. (1966), 'Effects of authoritarian parental control on child behaviour', *Child Development* 37, pp. 887–907.

Baumrind, D. (1967), *Child Care Practices Anteceding Three Patterns of Preschool Behaviour*, Genetic Psychology Monographs 75, pp. 43–88.

Baumrind, D. (1971), *Current Patterns of Parental Authority*, Child Development Psychology Monographs 4, pp. 1–107.

Baumrind, D. (1982), 'Are androgynous individuals more effective persons and parents?' *Child Development* 53, pp. 44–75.

Beautrais, A., Joyce, P. R. and Mulder, R. T. (1998), 'Youth suicide attempts: a social and demographic profile', *Australian and New Zealand Journal of Psychiatry* 32, pp. 349–57.

Beauvoir, S. de (1952), *The Second Sex*, Penguin, Harmondsworth, UK.

Beck, C. T. and Gable, R. K. (2001), 'Further validation of the post partum depression screening scale', *Nursing Research* 50, pp. 155–8.

Begley, D. J., Firth, J. and Hoult, J. (1980), *Human Reproduction and Developmental Biology*, Macmillan, New York.

Bell, R. Q. (1978), 'A reinterpretation of the direction of effects in studies of socialisation', *Psychological Review* 75, pp. 81–95.

Belsky, J. (1988), 'Infant day care and socioemotional development: the United States', *Journal of Child Psychology and Psychiatry* 29, pp. 397–406.

Belsky, J. (1990), 'Infant day care, child development and family policy', *Society*, July/August, pp. 10–12.

Belsky, J. and Rovine, M. (1988), 'Nonmaternal care in the first year of life and security of infant–parent attachment', *Child Development* 59, pp. 157–67.

Belsky, J., Rovine, M. and Fish, M. (1989), 'The developing family system', in M. R. Gunnar and E. Thelen (eds), *Systems and Development. The Minnesota Symposia on Child Psychology*, vol. 22, Lawrence Erlbaum, Hillsdale, New Jersey.

Belsky, J. and Steinberg, L. D. (1978), 'The effects of day care: a critical review', *Child Development* 49, pp. 929–49.

Bem, S. L. and Lenney, E. (1976), 'Sex-typing and the avoidance of cross-sex behaviour', *Journal of Personality and Social Psychology* 33, pp. 48–58.

Bem, S. L., Martyna, W. and Watson, C. (1976), 'Sex typing and explorations of the expressive domain', *Journal of Personality and Social Psychology* 34, pp. 1016–23.

Ben-Torion, D. I. (1988), 'DSM – 111, draft DSM –111 and the diagnosis and prevalence of bulimia in Australia', *American Journal of Psychiatry* 145, pp. 1000–2.

Berden, G. F. M. G., Althaus, M. and Verhulst, F. C. (1990), 'Major life events and changes in the behavioural functioning of children', *Journal of Child Psychology and Psychiatry* 31, pp. 949–57.

Berg, L. (1972), *Look at Kids*, Penguin, Harmondsworth, UK.

Berndt, T. J. (1986), 'Children's comments about their friendships', in M. Perlmutter (ed.), *The Minnesota Symposia on Child Psychology*, vol. 18, Lawrence Erlbaum, Hillsdale, New Jersey.

Bernstein, J., Potts, N., Mattox, J. H. (1985), 'Assessment of psychological dysfunction associated with infertility', *Journal of Obstetric, Gynecological and Neonatal Nursing*, Nov./Dec., pp. 63–6.

Bertalanffy, L. von (1968), *General Systems Theory*, Braziller, New York.

Bertenthal, B. I. (ed.) (1991), 'Canalization of behavioural development', *Developmental Psychology* 27, pp. 3–35.

Berzonsky, M. D. (1987), 'A preliminary investigation of children's conceptions of life and death', *Merrill-Palmer Quarterly* 33, pp. 505–13.

Bettelheim, B. (1982), *The Uses of Enchantment*, Penguin, Harmondsworth, UK.

Bibace, R. and Walsh, M. E. (1980), 'Development of children's concepts of illness', *Paediatrics* 66, pp. 912–17.

Bibring, G. L., Dwyer, T. G., Huntingdon, T. S. and Valenstein, F. (1961), 'A study of the psychological processes in pregnancy and the earliest mother–child relationship', *Psychoanalytic Study of the Child* 16, pp. 9–72.

Biddle, S. and Goudas, M., (1996) 'Analysis of children's physical activity and its association with adult encouragement and social cognitive variables' *Journal of School Health* 2, pp. 75–8.

Biddulph, S. (1997), *Raising Boys: Why Boys are Different – and How to Help Them Become Happy and Well-Balanced Men*, Finch Publishing, Sydney.

Bigelow, B. J. (1977), 'Children's friendship expectations: a cognitive–developmental study', *Child Development* 48, pp. 246–53.

Biggs, J. B. (1987), *Student Approaches to Learning and Studying*, ACER, Melbourne.

Biggs, J. and Collis, K. F. (1982), *Evaluating the Quality of Learning: The SOLO Taxonomy*, Academic Press, New York.

Biggs, J. B. and Telfer, R. (1987), *The Process of Learning*, Prentice-Hall, Australia.

Binet, A. and Simon, T. H. (1905), 'Méthode nouvelle pour le diagnostic du niveau intellectuel des anormaux', *Anée Psychologique* 11, pp. 191–244.

Birnholz, J. C. (1981), 'The development of human fetal eye movement patterns', *Science* 213, pp. 679–81.

Bjorklund, D. A. and Pellegrini, D. (2000), 'Child development and evolutionary psychology', *Child Development* 71, pp. 1687–708.

Blake, W. (1971), *Songs of Innocence*, Dover Publications, New York.

Blinder, B. and Chao, K. (1994), 'Eating disorders: an historical perspective', in L. Alexander-Mott and D. Lumsden (eds) *Understanding Eating Disorders: Anorexia Nervosa, Bulimia Nervosa and Obesity*, Taylor and Francis, Washington D.C.

Bloom, B. S. (1964), *Stability and Change in Human Characteristics*, Wiley, New York.

Bollard, J. and Nettelbeck, T. (1989), *Bedwetting*, Chapman and Hall, London.

Booth, M. L. and Samdal, O. (1997), 'Health-promoting schools in Australia: models and measurement', *Australian and New Zealand Journal of Public Health* 21, pp. 365–9.

Bor, W., Najman, J. M., O'Callaghan, M., Williams, G. M., and Anstey, K. (2001), *Aggression and the Development of Delinquent Behaviour in Children*, Australian Institute of Criminology, pp. 1–6.

Borduin, C. M., Mann, B. J., Cone, L. and Borduin, B. J. (1990), 'Children's concept of family', *The Journal of Genetic Psychology* 151, pp. 33–43.

Borke, H. (1975), 'Piaget's Mountains Re-visited: Changes in the Ego-centric Landscape', *Developmental Psychology* 11, pp. 240–3.

Boss, P., Edwards, S., and Pittman, S. (1995), *Profile of young Australians: Facts, Figures and Issues*, Churchill Livingstone, Melbourne.

Boughton, R., Kenyon, Y., Laycock, L., Lewin, T. and Thomas, S. (1987), 'Australian children and the threat of nuclear war', *The Medical Journal of Australia* 147, p. 3.

Boulton, T. J. C. and Magarey, A. (1986), 'The growth of fat: continuity from infancy to age 8 and family influence', *Australian Paediatric Journal* 22, p. 329.

Boulton, T. J. C. and Magarey, A. (1988), 'Cholesterol and obesity in childhood – implications for future health', *Australian Journal of Early Childhood* 13, pp. 10–15.

Boulton-Lewis, G. M., Neill, H. and Halford, G. S. (1988), 'Information processing and scholastic achievement in Aboriginal Australian children in south-eastern Queensland', *The Aboriginal Child at School* 14, pp. 42–57.

Bourke, C. J., Rigby, K. and Burden, J. (2000), *Improving the School Attendance of Indigenous Students*, DETYA report, DETYA, July.

Bourke, S. F. and Parkin, B. (1977), 'The performance of Aboriginal students', in S. F. Bourke and J. P. Keeves (eds), *The Mastery of Literacy and Numeracy*, ACER, Melbourne.

Bower, T. G. R. (1971), 'The object in the world of the infant', *Scientific American* 225, pp. 30–8.

Bower, T. (1977), *The Perceptual World of the Child*, Fontana Books, London.

Bowlby, J. (1951), *Maternal Care and Mental Health*, World Health Monograph no. 2, WHO, Geneva.

Bowlby, J. (1953), 'Some pathological processes set in train by early mother–child separation', *Journal of Mental Science* 99, pp. 265–73.

Bowlby, J. (1960), 'Separation anxiety', *International Journal of Psychoanalysis* 41, pp. 89–113.

Bowlby, J. (1969), *Attachment and Loss, vol. 1: Attachment*, Basic Books, New York.

Bowlby, J. (1973), *Attachment and Loss, vol. 2: Separation: Anxiety and Anger*, Basic Books, New York.

Bowlby, J. (1976), 'Bowlby on latch-key kids: an interview with Nicholas Tucker', *Psychology Today* 2, pp. 37–41.

Bradley, R. H. and Corwyn, R. F. (1999), 'Parenting', in L. Baltes and C. S. Tamis-Le Mond (eds), *Child Psychology: A Handbook of Contemporary Issues*, Psychology Press, Philadelphia.

Braet, C., Merielde, I. and Vandereychen, W. (1997), 'Psychological aspects of childhood obesity', *Journal of Paediatric Psychology* 22, pp. 59–71.

Brandt, R. (1988), 'On students' needs and team learning: a conversation with William Glasser', *Educational Leadership*, March, pp. 38–45.

Brazelton, T. B. (1962), 'A child oriented approach to toilet training', *Paediatrics* 29, pp. 121–8.

Breckenbridge, M. and Murphy, M. N. (1969), *Growth and Development of the Young Child*, W. B. Saunders and Co., New York.

Breen, D. (1975), *The Birth of a First Child*, Tavistock Publications, London.

Bridges, K. (1932), 'Emotional development in early infancy', *Child Development* 3, pp. 324–31.

Briggs, F. (1987), 'South Australian parents want child protection programs to be offered in schools and preschools', *Australian Journal of Early Childhood* 12, pp. 20–5.

Brodie, B. (1974), 'Views of healthy children toward illness', *American Journal of Public Health* 64, pp. 1156–9.

Bronfenbrenner, U. (1972), *Influences on Human Development*, Dryden Press, Hillsdale, Illinois.

Bronfenbrenner, U. (1977), 'Toward an experimental ecology of human development', *American Psychologist* 32, pp. 513–31.

Bronowski, J. (1960), 'A moral for an age of plenty', *Saturday Evening Post* 233 (20), 12 November.

Brookes-Gunn, J. (1988), 'Antecedents and consequences of variations in girls' maturational timing', *Journal of Adolescent Health Care* 9, pp. 365–73.

Brookes-Gunn, J. and Matthews, W. S. (1979), *He or She: How Children Develop Their Sex-Role Identity*, Prentice-Hall, Englewood Cliffs, New Jersey.

Broughton, J. (1978), 'Development of concepts of self, mind, reality and knowledge', *New Directions for Child Development* 1, pp. 75–100.

Brown, J. E. and Mann, L. (1988), 'Effects of family structure and parental involvement on adolescent participation in family decisions', *Australian Journal of Sex, Marriage and Family* 9, pp. 74–85.

Brown, L. P. (unpub.), 'Stressful life events as perceived by children', unpublished doctoral thesis, University of Rochester, 1985.

Brown, L., Sherbenou, R. J. and Johnson, S. K. (1990), *Test of Non-verbal Intelligence*, Pro-Ed, Brisbane.

Brown, W. J. and Brown, P. R. (1998), 'Children's physical activity and better health', *ACHPER Healthy Lifestyles Journal* 43, pp. 19–23.

Browne, J. (1990), 'Gender bias in physical education textbooks', *The Australian Council for Health, Physical Education and Recreation Journal* 127, pp. 4–6.

Browne, R. and Fletcher, R. (eds), (1995), *Boys in Schools: Addressing the Real Issues – Behaviour, Values and Relationships*, Sydney, Finch Publishing.

Bruner, J. S. (1956), 'Freud and the image of man', *Partisan Review* 23, p. 323.

Bruner, J. (1962), *The Process of Education*, Cambridge, Massachusetts, Harvard University Press.

Bruner, J. (1966), *Studies in Cognitive Growth*, Wiley, New York.

Bruner, J. (1982), 'The transactional self', in J. Bruner and H. Haste (eds), *Making Sense: the Child's Construction of the World*, Methuen, London.

Bruner, J. (1986), *Actual Minds, Possible Worlds*, Harvard University Press, Cambridge, Massachusetts.

Bruner, J. (1987), *Child's Talk*, Norton, New York.

Bruner, J. and Haste. H. (1987), *Making Sense. The Child's Construction of the World*, Methuen, London.

Bryant, P. E. and Trabasso, T. (1971), 'Transitive inferences and memory in young children', *Nature* 232, pp. 456–8.

Bullivant, B. M. (1978), 'Towards a neo-ethnographic method for small group research', *Australian and New Zealand Journal of Sociology* 14, pp. 239–49.

Bullock, M. and Lutkenhaus, P. (1990), 'Who am I? Self understanding in toddlers', *Merrill-Palmer Quarterly* 36, pp. 217–38.

Burnham, J. J. and Gullone, E. (1997), 'The fear survey schedule for children II: a psychometric investigation with American data', *Behaviour Research and Therapy* 35, pp. 165–73.

Burns, A. (1980), *Breaking Up: Separation and Divorce in Australia*, Nelson, Melbourne.

Burns, A. and Goodnow, J. (1979), *Children and Families in Australia: Contemporary Issues and Problems*, Allen & Unwin, Sydney.

Burt, C. (1921), *Mental and Scholastic Tests*, P. S. King and Son, London.

Bus, A. G., Van Ijsdoorn, M. H. and Pellegrini, A. D. (1995), 'Joint book reading makes for success in learning to read: a meta-analysis on intergenerational transmission of literacy', *Review of Educational Research* 65, pp. 1–21.

Buss, A. H. and Plomin, R. (1975), *A Temperament Theory of Personality Development*, Wiley, New York.

Bussey, K. (1983), 'A social cognitive appraisal of sex-role development', *Australian Journal of Psychology* 35, pp. 135–43.

Butcher, J. (1983), 'Socialisation of adolescent girls in physical activity', *Adolescence* 18, pp. 753–66.

Butterfield, J. and Covey, M. J. (1962), 'Practical epigram of the APGAR score', *Journal of the American Medical Association* 181, p. 353.

Butterworth, G. and Hopkins, B. (1988), 'Hand–mouth coordination in the new-born baby', *British Journal of Developmental Psychology* 6, pp. 303–14.

Bydlowski, M. (1984), 'Mothers' desire to have a child', in P. O. Hubinot, *Ontogeny of Attachment*, Karger, Basel.

Callan, V. J. and Noller, P. (1987), *Marriage and the Family*, Methuen, Sydney.

Campbell, I. E. (1989), 'Common psychological concerns experienced by parents during pregnancy', *Canadian Mental Health*, March, pp. 2–5.

Campbell, R. and Wales, R. (1970), 'The study of language acquisition', in J. Lyons (ed.), *New Horizons in Linguistics*, Pelican, New York.

Campbell, S., Breaux, A., Ewing, L., Ezumowski, E. and Pierce, E. (1986), 'Parent identified problem pre-schoolers: mother–child interaction during play at intake and one-year follow-up', *Journal of Abnormal Child Psychology* 14, pp. 125–440.

Camras, L. A. (1988), 'Darwin re-visited: an infant's first emotional facial expressions', in I. H. Oster (ed.), *Emotional Expression in Infants: New Perspectives on an Old Controversy*, Symposium, International Conference on Infant Studies, Washington, DC.

Capra, F. (1988), *Uncommon Wisdom: Conversations with Remarkable People*, Flamingo, UK.

Carey, W. B. (1970), 'A simplified method for measuring infant temperament', *Journal of Paediatrics* 77, pp. 188–94.

Carey, W. B. (1985), 'Clinical use of temperament data in pediatrics', *Journal Development and Behavioural Paediatrics* 6, pp. 137–42.

Carey, W. B., Fox, M. and McDevitt, S. C. (1977), 'Temperament as a factor in early school adjustment', *Paediatrics* 60, pp. 621–4.

Caring, L. C. (unpub.), The relation of cognitive styles, sex and intelligence to moral judgement in children, unpublished doctoral dissertation, New York University, New York, 1970.

Carino, C. and Chmelko, P. (1983), 'Disorders of eating in adolescence: anorexia nervosa and bulimia', *Nursing Clinics of North America* 18, pp. 343–52.

Carpenter, G. (1974), 'Mother's face and the newborn', *New Scientist* 61, p. 742.

Carraher, T., Carraher, D. and Schliemann, A. (1985), 'Mathematics in street and schools', *The British Journal of Developmental Psychology* 3, pp. 21–31.

Carroll, L. (1982), *Alice's Adventures in Wonderland. Through the Looking Glass*, Penguin, New York.

Carter, E. A. and McGoldrick, M. (1980), *The Family Life-Cycle: a Framework for Family Therapy*, Gardner Press, New York.

Cartledge, G. and Milburn, J. F. (eds) (1986), *Teaching Social Skills to Children*, Pergamon, New York.

Cashmore, J. A. and Goodnow, J. J. (1985), 'Agreement between generations: a two-process approach', *Child Development* 56, pp. 493–501.

Casperson, C., Powell, K. and Christenson, G. (1985), 'Physical activity exercise and physical fitness: definitions and distinctions for health-related research', *Public Health Reports* 100, pp. 126–31.

Cath, S. H., Gurwitt, A. R. and Ross, J. (1982), *Father and Child Development Perspectives*, Little Brown and Co., Boston.

Catherine, J., Brack, M. S., Donald, P., Orr, M. D. and Ingersoll, G. (1988), 'Pubertal maturation and adolescent self esteem', *Journal of Adolescent Health Care* 9, pp. 280–5.

Cattell, J. McK. (1890), 'Mental tests and measurements', *Mind* 15, pp. 373–80.

Cattell, R. B. (1983), 'Theory of fluid and crystallised intelligence: a critical experiment', *Journal of Educational Psychology* 54, pp. 1–22.

Chafetz, J. (1974), *Masculine, Feminine or Human*, Peacock Publications, Itasca, Illinois.

Charlesworth, W. and Kreutzer, M., 'Facial expressions of infants and children', in P. Ekman (ed.), *Darwin and Facial Expression*, Academic Press, New York.

Chazan, M. and Jackson, S. (1974), 'Behaviour problems in the infant school: changes over two years', *Journal of Child Psychology and Psychiatry* 18, pp. 201–9.

Childs, G. H. (unpub.), A survey of learning style difficulties among school beginners from Adelaide and Whyalla, unpublished report.

Chomsky, N. (1965), *Aspects of Theory of Syntax*, MIT Press, Cambridge, Massachusetts.

Chomsky, N. (1976), *Reflections on Language*, Pantheon, New York.

Clapp, D. (1985), 'Emotional responses to infertility: nursing interventions', *Journal of Obstetric, Gynecologic and Neonatal Nursing*, November/December, pp. 32–8.

Clare, C. and Roe, D. (1990), *Keeping Our Children Safe. Protective Behaviour Programs in Early Childhood Settings*, Australian Early Childhood Resource Booklets, Australian Early Childhood Association, Canberra.

Clarke-Stewart, A. K. (1998), 'Historical shifts and underlying themes in ideas about rearing young children in the United States: Where have we been? Where are we going?', *Early Development and Parenting* 7, pp. 101–17.

Clarke-Stewart, K., Vandell, D., McCartney, K. and Owen, M. T. (2000), 'Effects of parental separation and divorce on very young children', *Journal of Family Psychology* 14, 2, pp. 304–26.

Clarricoates, K. (1980), 'The importance of being Earnest … Emma … Tom … Jane: the perception and categorisation of gender deviation in primary schools', in R. Deem (ed.), *Schooling for Woman's Work*, Routledge and Kegan Paul, pp. 39–51.

Cleverley, J. and Phillips, D. C. (1976), *From Locke to Spock*, Melbourne University Press, Melbourne.

Clifton, R., Perris, E. and Bullinger, A. (1991a), 'Infants' perception of auditory space', *Developmental Psychology* 27, pp. 187–98.

Clifton, R. A., Williams, T. and Clancy, J. (1991b), 'The academic attainment of ethnic groups in Australia: a social psychological perspective', *Sociology of Education* 64, pp. 111–26.

Cloe, C. and Roe, D. (1990), *Keeping our Children Safe. Protective Behaviours Programmes in Early Childhood Settings*, Australian Journal of Early Childhood Resource Booklets, Australian Early Childhood Association, Canberra.

Clyde, M. (1983), *Children Can Grow – If We Let Them*, Australian Journal of Early Childhood Resource Booklets 3, Australian Early Childhood Association, Canberra.

Cochrane, K. J. (1972), 'Current developments in the assessment of language and its uses in educational and clinical situations', *The Slow Learning Child* 19, pp. 153–64.

Coddington, R. D. (1972), 'The significance of life events as etiologic factors in the disease of children: a survey of professional workers', *Journal of Psychosomatic Research* 16, pp. 7–18.

Cohen, D. G., Stern, V. and Balaban, N. (1983), *Observing and Recording the Behaviour of Young Children*, Teachers College, New York.

Coker, J. G. (1981), 'Aboriginal schooling', *The Aboriginal Child at School* 9, pp. 3–5.

Cole, G. F., Hungerford, J. and Jones, R. B. (1984), 'Delayed visual maturation', *Archives of the Disabled Child* 59, p. 107.

Cole, R. (1970), *Erik H. Erikson: the Growth of His Work*, Souvenir Press, London.

Coleman, J. C. (1980), *The Nature of Adolescence*, Methuen, London.

Coleman, J. C. (1988), 'Social capital and the creation of human capital', *American Journal of Sociology* 94, pp. 95–120.

Coleman, J. C. and Hendry, L. (1990), *The Nature of Adolescence*, Routledge, London.

Coleman, J. S., George, R. and Holt, G. (1977), 'Adolescents and their parents: a study of attitudes', *Journal of Genetic Psychology* 130, pp. 239–45.

Collins, J. K. (1969), 'Adolescence', *The Forum of Education* 28, pp. 106–13.

Collins, J. (1975), 'Adolescent delinquency–orientation', in J.Y. Collins (ed.), *Studies of the Australian Adolescent*, Cassell, Sydney.

Collins, J. K. (1991), 'Research into adolescence: a forgotten era', *Australian Psychologist* 26, pp. 1–9.

Collins, W. A. and Laursen, B. (1999), *Relationships and Developmental Contexts. The Minnesota Symposium Child Psychology*, vol. 30, Lawrence Erlbaum, New Jersey.

Collman, J. (1979), 'Western children and the significance of the domestic group to urban Aboriginals in Central Australia', *Ethology* 18, pp. 379–97.

Combrinck-Graham, L. (1990), 'Developments in family systems theory and research', *Journal of the American Academy of Child and Adolescent Psychology* 29, pp. 500–12.

Compas, B. E. (1987), 'Coping with stress during childhood and adolescence', *Psychological Bulletin* 101, pp. 393–403.

Compayre, G. (1896), *The Intellectual and Moral Development of the Child*, trans. Mary Wilson, Appleton, New York.

Connel, R. (1996), 'Teaching the boys: new research on masculinity and gender strategies for schools', *Teachers College Record* 98, pp. 206–35.

Connel, R. (1998), 'Masculinities and globalisation', *Men and Masculinities* 1, 3–23.

Connell, R. W. (1975), *How to do Small Surveys – a Guide for Students in Sociology*, Kindred Industries and Allied Trades, 2nd edn, School of Social Sciences, Flinders University, Adelaide.

Connell, W. F., Stroobant, R. E., Sinclair, K. E., Connell, R. W. and Rogers, K. W. (1975), *12 to 20: Studies of City Youth*, Hicks Smith and Sons, Sydney.

Connellan, J., Baron-Cohen, S., Wheelwright, S., Batki, A. and Ahluwalia, J. (2000), 'Sex differences in human neonatal perception', *Infant Behaviour and Development* 23, pp. 113–18.

Connolly, J., Craig, W., Goldberg, A., and Pepler, D. (1999), 'Conceptions of cross-sex friendships and romantic relationships in early adolescence', *Journal of Youth and Adolescence*, 4, pp. 481–94.

Connolly, J. A., Furman, W. and Konarski, R. (2000), 'The role of peers in the emergence of heterosexual romantic relationships in adolescence', *Child Development* 71, pp. 1395–408.

Connolly, J. A. and Johnson, A. M. (1996), 'Adolescent romantic relationships and the structure and quality of close interpersonal ties', *Personal Relationships*, 3, pp. 185–95.

Connors, J. and Heaven, P. C. L. (1990), 'Belief in a just world and attitudes towards AIDS sufferers', *The Journal of Social Psychology* 130, pp. 559–60.

Conrade, G. and Ho, R. (2001), 'Differential parenting styles for fathers and mothers: differential treatment for sons and daughters', *Australian Journal of Psychology* 53, pp. 29–35.

Coppersmith, E. I. (unpub.), Development reframing: 'He's not bad, he's not mad, he's just young', unpublished paper, University of Massachusetts, 1984.

Coppersmith, I. (1982), 'From hyperactive to normal but naughty: a multi-system partnership in de-labelling', *International Journal of Family Psychology* 3, pp. 131–44.

Corno,L. (1996), 'Homework is a complicated thing', *Educational Research in Education* 59, pp. 27–30.

Cote, J. E. and Ailatiar, A. L. (1996), *Generation on Hold: Coming of Age in the Late Twentieth Century*, New York University Press, New York.

Covell, K. and Abramovitch, R. (1987), 'Understanding emotion in the family: children's and parents' attributions of happiness, sadness and anger', *Child Development* 58, pp. 985–91.

Coventry, G. and Polk, K. (1985), 'Theoretical perspectives and juvenile delinquency', in A. Borowski and J. M. Murray, *Juvenile Delinquency in Australia*, Methuen, Sydney.

Cowen, E. (1991), 'In pursuit of wellness', *American Psychologist* 46, pp. 404–8.

Cowan, P. A., Langer, J., Heavenrich, J. and Nathanson, M. (1969), 'Social learning and Piaget's cognitive theory of moral development', *Journal of Personality and Social Psychology* 11, pp. 261–74.

Cox, J. L., Holden, J. M. and Sagavsky, R. (1987), 'Detection of post natal depression', *Journal of Psychiatry* 150, pp. 782–6.

Crane, P. and Dee, M. (2001), *Young People, Public Space and New Urbanism*, Youth Studies Australia, 20, pp. 11–18.

Creaser, B. (1990), *Rediscovering Pretend Play*, Australian Early Childhood Resource Booklets 4, Australian Early Childhood Association, Canberra.

Crews, F. (1997), *Freud Scientifically Reappraised. Testing the Theories and the Therapy*, Wiley, New York.

Crisp, A.H. (1980), *Anorexia Nervosa*, Academic Press, London.

Crnic, L. S. and Pennington, B. F. (1987) (eds), 'Developmental psychology and the neurosciences', *Child Development* 58, pp. 533–713.

Cronbach, L. J. (1984), *Essentials of Psychological Testing*, 4th edn, Harper Row, New York.

Cronly-Dillon, J. R. and Perry, G. W. (1976), 'Tubulin synthesis in developing rat visual cortex', *Nature* 261, pp. 581–3.

Cross, D. G. and Slee, P. T. (1988), 'Behaviourally disordered children: current issues and future direction', *Australasian Journal of Special Education* 12, pp. 28–33.

Cudrin, J. M. (unpub.), The relationship of chronological age, mental age, social behaviour and number of siblings to the Piagetian concept of moral judgement development, unpublished doctoral dissertation, University of North Carolina, 1965.

Cummings, E. M. (1987), 'Coping with background anger in early childhood', *Child Development* 58, pp. 976–84.

Cummings, E. M. and Cummings, J. L. (1988), 'A process-oriented approach to children's coping with adults' angry behaviour', *Developmental Review* 8, pp. 296–321.

Cummings, E. M., Zahn-Waxler, C. and Radke-Yarrow, M. (1981), 'Young children's responses to expression of anger and affection by others in the family', *Child Development* 52, pp. 1274–82.

Cunningham, J. (1990), 'Becoming men and women', in P. C. L. Heaven and V. J. Callan (eds), *Adolescence: an Australian Perspective*, Harcourt Brace Jovanovich, Sydney, pp. 133–51.

Cupit, C. G. (1989), *Socialising the Superheroes*, Australian Early Childhood Resource Booklets, Australian Early Childhood Association, Canberra.

Cureton, T. K. (1947), *Physical Appraisal and Guidance*, Mosby, St. Louis.

D'Alton, S. and Bittman, M. (1976), *The Social Experience: an Introduction to Sociology*, Nelson, Melbourne.

D'Souza, N. (1990), 'Aboriginal children: the challenge for the end of the millenium', *Children Australia* 15, pp. 14–15.

Damon, W. and Hart, D. (1982), 'The development of self understanding from infancy through adolescence', *Child Development* 53, pp. 841–64.

Damon, W. and Lerner, R. M. (1998), *Handbook of Child Psychology*, 5th edn, John Wiley and Sons Inc., New York.

Darwin, C. (1959), *On the Origin of Species by Means of Natural Selection*, Harvard University Press, Cambridge, Massachusetts (first published 1859).

Darwin, C. (1965), *The Expression of the Emotions in Man and Animals*, University of Chicago Press, Chicago (first published 1872).

Darwin, F. (1958), *The Autobiography of Charles Darwin*, Dover Publications, New York.

Dasen, P. R. (1974), 'The influence of ecology, culture and European contact in cognitive development in Australian Aborigines', in J. W. Berry and P. R. Dasen (eds), *Culture and Cognition: Readings in Cross-Cultural Psychology*, Methuen, London.

Davidson, G.R. (1979), 'An ethnographic psychology of Aboriginal cognitive ability', *Oceania* 10–11, pp. 270–93.

Davis, F. (1963), *Passage Through Crisis: Police Victimised Their families*, Bobbs-Merril, Minneapolis.

Day, R. D. and Hooks, D. (1987), 'Miscarriage: a special type of family crisis', *Family Relations* 36, pp. 305–10.

Day, R. H. and McKenzie, B. E. (1985), 'Perception and perceptual development', in N. T. Feather, *Australian Psychology: Review of Research*, Allen & Unwin, Sydney.

De Casper, A. J. and Fifer, W. P. (1980), 'Of human bonding: newborns prefer their mothers' voices', *Science* 208, pp. 1174–6.

De Loach, J. and De Mendoza, O. (1987), 'Joint picturebook interactions of mothers and one year old children', *British Journal of Developmental Psychology* 5, pp. 111–23.

De Marco, R. and Sydney, K. (1989), 'Enhancing children's participation in physical activity', *Journal of School Health* 59, pp. 337–40.

DeMaria, W. (1981), 'Empiricism: an impoverished philosophy for social science research', *Australian Social Work* 34, pp. 3–8.

Denholm, C., Horniblow, T. and Smalley, R. (1992), 'The times they are still a'changing', *Youth Studies* 11, pp. 18–26.

Department for Community Welfare (SA) (1986), *Child Abuse: Guidelines for Professionals*, Department for Community Welfare, Adelaide.

Dixon, C., Charles, M. A. and Craddock, A. A. (1998), 'The impact of experiences of parental divorce and parental conflict on young Australian adult men and women', *Journal of Family Studies* 4, pp. 21–34.

Dixon, J. (1957), 'Development of self recognition', *Journal of General Psychology* 91, pp. 241–50.

Dobson, J. C. (1970), *Dare to Discipline*, Tyndale, Wheaton, Illinois.

Dohrenwend, B. W. and Dohrenwend, B. P. (1974), *Stressful Life Events: Their Nature and Effects*, Wiley, New York.

Dollard, J. and Miller, N. E. (1950), *Personality and Psychotherapy*, McGraw-Hill, New York.

Doman, G. (1983), *How to Teach Your Baby to Read*, Doubleday, New York.

Donaldson, M. (1978), *Children's Minds*, Fontana/Collins, London.

Donnelly, N. and Hall, W. (1994), *Patterns of Cannabis Use in Australia*, National Drug Strategy Monograph Series, no. 27, Australian Government Publishing Service, Canberra.

Dornbusch, S. A., Carlsmith, J. M., Bushwall, P., Ritter, D., Leiderman, H., Hastorff, A. H. and Gross, R. T. (1985), 'Single parents, extended households and the control of adolescents', *Child Development* 56, pp. 326–41.

Doughty, J. (1988), 'Postnatal depression', *Mind*, winter, pp. 12–15.

Douvan, E. (1979), 'Sex role learning', in J. C. Coleman, *The School Years*, Methuen, London.

Drielsma, P. (2000), *Hardwiring Young Brains for Intimacy*, National Child Protection Clearing House, 2, pp. 6–11.

Drummond, M. (2001), 'Boys' bodies in the context of sport and physical activity: implications for health', *Journal of Physical Education New Zealand*, 34, pp. 36–42.

Ducan, A. T. (1969), 'Motivation achievement in an industrialised society', in S. S. Dunn and C. M. Tatz, *Aborigines and Education*, Sun Books, Melbourne.

Dunn, J. (1984), *Sisters and Brothers*, Fontana, London.

Dunn, J. (1988), 'Sibling influences on childhood development', *Journal of Child Psychology and Psychiatry* 29, pp. 119–27.

Dunn, J. and Kendrick, C. (1982), 'The arrival of a sibling', *Health Visitor* 55, p. 156.

Dunn, J.F., Kendrick, C. and MacNamaee, R. (1980), 'The arrival of a sibling: changes in patterns of interaction between mother and first born child', *Journal of Child Psychology and Psychiatry* 22, pp. 1–18.

Dunn, J. and Munn, P. (1986), 'Becoming a family member: family conflict and the development of social understanding in the second year', *Child Development* 56, pp. 480–92.

Dunn, K. (1981), 'Madison prep.: alternative to teenage disaster', *Education Leadership* 38, pp. 386–7.

Dunn, R., Beaudry, J. and Klavas, A. (1989), 'Survey of research on learning styles', *Educational Leadership* 3, pp. 50–8.

Dunn, R., Dunn, K. and Price, G. E. (1979), *Learning Style Inventory*, Price Systems, Lawrence, Kansas.

Dunn, R., Griggs, J., Olson, J., Gorman, B. and Beasley, M. (1995), 'A meta-analytic validation of the Dunn and Dunn learning styles model', *Journal of Educational Research* 88, pp. 353–61.

Dunphy, D. C. (1963), 'The social structure of urban adolescent peer groups', *Sociometry* 26, pp. 230–46.

Dusek, J. B. (2000), 'The maturing of self-esteem research with early adolescents', *Journal of Early Adolescence* 20, pp. 231–40.

Duska, R. and Whelan, M. (1975), *Moral Development: a Guide to Piaget and Kohlberg*, Paulist Press, New York.

Duvall, E. M. (1971), *Family Development*, Lippincott, New York.

Earls, F. (1976), 'The fathers (not the mothers): their importance and influence with infants and young children', *Psychiatry* 39, pp. 209–26.

Eckermann, A. K. (1988), 'Learning styles, classroom management, teacher characteristics and rural–urban Aboriginal people: some thoughts', *The Aboriginal Child in School*, pp. 3–19.

Eckersly, R. (1988), *Casualties of Change: the Predicament of Youth in Australia*, Commission for the Future, CSIRO, Australia.

Eckersley, R. (1998), 'Refining progress: Shaping the future to human needs'. Sixth Australian Institute of Family Studies Conference, Melbourne 25–27 November.

Edgar, D. (1985), 'Possible directions for an Australian family policy', *Australian Journal of Sex, Marriage and Family* 1, pp. 146–56.

Edgar, D. (1995), 'Family impacts on the development of the child', *Australian and New Zealand Journal of Psychiatry* 29, pp. 14–22.

Education Department of South Australia (1989), *The Kaurna People: Aboriginal People of the Adelaide Plains*, Education Department of South Australia, Adelaide.

Eichorn, D. H. (1979), 'Physical development: current foci of research', in J. Osofsky (ed.), *Handbook of Infant Development*, Wiley, New York, pp. 253–343.

Elkind, D. (1967), 'Egocentrism in adolescence', *Child Development* 38, pp. 1925–34.

Elkind, D. (1968), 'Adolescent cognitive development', in J. F. Adams (ed.), *Understanding Adolescence*, Allyn & Bacon, Boston.

Elkind, D. (1974), *Children and Adolescents*, Oxford University Press, New York.

Elkind, D. (1987), 'The child yesterday, today and tomorrow', *Young Children*, May, pp. 6–11.

Elkind, D. and Bowen, R. (1979), 'Imaginary audience behaviour in children and adolescents', *Developmental Psychology* 15, pp. 38–44.

Elliott, A. (1985), 'Developing technological literacy: a new challenge for early childhood education', *Australian Journal of Early Childhood* 10, pp. 3–9.

Elster, A. B., Panzarine, S. and McAnarney, E. R. (1980), 'Causes of adolescent pregnancy', *Medical Aspects of Human Sexuality* 14, pp. 69–87.

Emery, R. E. (1982), 'Interparental conflict and the child of discord and divorce', *Psychological Bulletin* 92, pp. 310–30.

Emler, N. and Reicher, S. (1987), 'Orientations to institutional authority in adolescence', *Journal of Moral Education* 16, pp. 108–16.

Enright, R. D., Levy, V. M., Harris, D. and Lapsley, D. K. (1987), 'Do economic conditions influence how theorists view adolescents?', *Journal of Youth and Adolescence* 16, pp. 541–59.

Erikson, E. H. (1963), *Childhood and Society*, Penguin Books, Harmondsworth, UK.

Erikson, E. H. (1968), *Identity, Youth and Crisis*, Faber, London.

Erikson, E. (1977), *I Need to Be Me: the Emergence of Self*, W. H. Freeman, Madison, Wisconsin.

Erickson, S. J., Robinson, T., Farish, H. and Killen, J. (2000), 'Are overweight children unhappy? Body mass index depressive symptoms and overweight concerns in elementary school children', *Archives of Pediatrics and Adolescent Medicine* 154, pp. 931–5.

Eshkevari, H. S. (1988), *Development in the First Three Years of Life: a Cultural Perspective*, Kitchener Press, Beverly SA.

Eston, R., Threfall, T. and Brodie, D. (1989), 'The effects of gender on health related fitness measures in preadolescent children', *Physical Education*, Associated Research Supplement no. 5.

Evans, C. S. (1979), *Preserving the Person: a Look at the Human Sciences*, IVP, Illinois.

Eveleth, P. and Tanner, J. M. (1977), *Worldwide Variation in Human Growth*, Cambridge University Press, Cambridge.

Eysenck, J. H. (1979), *The Structure and Measurement of Intelligence*, Springer-Verlag, New York.

Fairbairn, C. G., Shafran, R. and Cooper, Z. (1999), 'A cognitive behavioural theory of anorexia nervosa', *Behaviour Research Therapy* 37, pp. 1–13.

Fanning, E. A. (1980), 'Our changing life-style: its effects on child nutrition and dental health', *Australian Journal of Early Childhood* 5, pp. 17–21.

Fantz, R. L. (1963), 'Pattern vision in newborn infants', *Science* 140, p. 296.

Fauci, A. S. (1986), 'The acquired immune deficiency syndrome: an update', *Annals of Internal Medicine* 104, pp. 800–13.

Faust, M.S. (1960), 'Developmental maturity as a detriment in prestige of adolescent girls', *Child Development* 31, pp. 173–84.

Feather, N. T. (1987), 'The psychological impact of unemployment: empirical findings and theoretical approaches', in N. T. Feather (ed.), *Australian Psychology: Review of Research*, Allen & Unwin, Sydney.

Feitelson, D. and Ross, G. (1973), 'The neglected factor in play', *Human Development* 16, p. 222.

Fergusson, D. M., Horwood, L. J. and Shannon, F. T. (1986), 'Factors related to the age of attainment of noctural bladder control: an 8 year longitudinal study', Paediatrics 78, pp. 884–90.

Fischer, K. W. (1987), 'Relations between brain and cognitive development', *Child Development* 58, pp. 623–32.

Fisher, M., Golden, N., Debra, M. D., Katzman, K, Kreipe, R., Rees, J., Schebendach, J., Sigman, G., Ammermann, S. and Hodderman, H. (1995), 'Eating disorders in adolescents: a background paper', *Journal of Adolescent Health* 16, pp. 420–37.

Fischer, M. and Leitenberg, H. (1986), 'Optimism and pessimism in elementary school-aged children', *Child Development* 57, pp. 241–8.

Fisher, S. and Greenberg, C.R. (1996), *Freud Scientifically Reappraised Testing the Theories and the Therapy*, Wiley, New York.

Fitch, S. and Labrosse, D. (1997), *If You Could Wear My Sneakers!* Doubleday, Toronto.

Fitts, W. H. (1971), *The Self Concept and Self Actualisation*, W. H. Freeman, Nashville, Tennessee.

Flavell, J. H. (1963), *The Developmental Psychology of Jean Piaget*, Van Nostrand, London.

Florian, V. (1985), 'Children's concept of death: an empirical study of a cognitive and environmental approach', *Death Studies* 9, pp. 133–41.

Foerster, H. von (1973), 'Cybernetics of cybernetics (physiology of revolution)', *The Cybernetician* 3, pp. 30–2.

Formichova, O. and Formichova, V. (2000), 'Computers and the thought-producing self of the young child' *British Journal of Educational Technology* 31, pp. 213–31.

Fox, G. L., Bruce, C. and Combes-Orme, T. (2000), 'Parenting expectations and concerns of fathers and mothers of newborn infants', *Family Relations* 49, pp. 123–31.

Foxx, R. M. and Azrin, N. H. (1973), 'Dry pants: a rapid method of toilet training children', *Behaviour Research and Therapy* 11, pp. 435–42.

Franck, K. A. and Paxson, L. (1998), .Women and urban public space: research design and policy issues', in I. Altman and E. Zube (eds) *Human Behaviour and Environment: advances in Theory and Research*: *Public Places and Spaces*, vol. 10, Plenum Press, New York.

Francois, G. R. (1990), *The Lifespan*, 3rd edn, Wadsworth, Belmont, California.

Frankenburg, W. K., Dodds, J., Fandal, A., Kazuk, E. and Cohrs, M. (1975), *The Denver Developmental Screening Test*. Reference Manual, University of Colorado Medical Center, Denver.

Fraser, B. G. (1976), 'The child and his parents: a delicate balance of rights', in R. Helfer and C. H. Kempe (eds), *Child Abuse and Neglect*, Ballinger, Cambridge, Massachusetts.

Freud, A. (1946), 'The psychoanalytic study of infantile feeding disturbances', *Psychoanalytic Study of the Child* 2, pp. 119–32.

Freud, A. (1964), *The Psychoanalytic Treatment of Children*, Schocken Books, New York.

Freud, S. (1905), 'Wit and its relation to the unconscious', in *The Basic Writings of Sigmund Freud*, Modern Library, New York.

Freud, S. (1909), 'Analysis of a phobia in a five year old boy', *The Standard Edition of the Complete Psychological Works of Freud,* Hogarth Press, London.

Freud, S. (1935), *A General Introduction to Psychoanalysis*, Simon and Schuster, New York.

Freud, S. (1938), 'Wit and its relation to the unconscious', in *The Basic Writings of Sigmund Freud*, Modern Library, New York.

Freud, S. (1940), 'An outline of psycho-analysis', *The Complete Works*, vol. 23, Hogarth Press, London.

Freud, S. (1955), 'An infantile neurosis and other works', *The Standard Edition of Complete Psychological Works*, tr. J. Strachley, vol. 17, Hogarth Press, London.

Freud, S. (1960), *Jokes and Their Relation to the Unconscious*, Norton Library, New York.

Freud, S. (1961), *Civilisation and its Discontents*, W. W. Norton, New York.

Freud, S. (1963), *A General Introduction to Psycho-analysis*, trans. R. Riviere, Touchstone Books, New York.

Freud, S. (1964), *The Psychoanalytical Treatment of Children*, Schocken Books, New York.

Freud, S. (1974), *Two Short Accounts of Psycho-analysis*, Penguin, Harmondsworth.

Fromm, E. (1947), *Man for Himself*, Rinehart, New York.

Funder, K. (1989), 'Images of Australian families', *Family Matters* 25, pp. 26–8.

Furman, W. and Masters, J. (1980), 'Peer interaction, socio-metric status and resistance to deviation in young children', *Developmental Psychology* 16, pp. 229–36.

Galambos, N. L. and Leadbetter, B. J. (2000), 'Trends in adolescent research for the new millenium', *International Journal of Behavioural Development*, 24, pp. 289–94.

Galton, F. (1869), *Hereditary Genius: an Imaginary Inquiry into its Laws and Consequences*, Macmillan, London.

Galton, F. (1883), *Inquiries into the Human Faculty and its Development*, Macmillan, London.

Garcia, A. W., Broda, M. A., Frenn,M., Coviak, C., Pender, N. and Ronis, D. (1995), 'Gender and developmental differences in exercise beliefs among youth and prediction of their exercise behaviour,' *Journal of School Health*, 65 pp. 213–19.

Gardner, H. (1972), *The Quest for Mind*, Coventure, London.

Gardner, H. (1979), 'Developmental psychology after Piaget: an approach in terms of symbolisation', *Human Development* 73, p. 88.

Gardner, H. (1984), 'Human intelligence isn't what we think it is', *US News and World Report*, March 19, pp. 75–8.

Gardner, R. A. (1975), *Psychotherapeutic Approaches to the Resistant Child*, Jason Aronson, New York.

Gardner, R. A. and Gardner, B. (1969), 'Teaching sign language to a chimpanzee', *Science* 165, pp. 664–72.

Garmezy, N. (1983), 'Stressors of childhood', in N. Garmezy and M. Rutter (eds), *Stress, Coping and Development in Children*, McGraw-Hill, New York, pp. 43–84.

Garmezy, N. (1985), 'Stress-resistant children: the search for protective factors', in J. E. Stevenson (ed.), *Aspects of Current Child Psychology Research, Journal of Child Psychology and Psychology Book Supplement no. 4*, Pergamon, Oxford.

Garmezy, N., Masten, A. S. and Tellegren, A. (1984), 'The study of stress and competence in children: a building block for developmental psychopathology', *Child Development* 55, pp. 97–111.

Garvey, C. (1977), *Play*, Harvard University Press, Cambridge, Massachusetts.

Gauld, A. and Shotter, J. (1977), *Human Action and its Psychological Investigation*, Routledge and Kegan Paul, London.

Gelcer, E. and Schwartzbein, D. (1989), 'A Piagetian view of family therapy: Selvini-Palazzoli and the invariant approach', *Family Process* 28, pp. 439–56.

Genishi, C. (1988), 'Children's language: learning words from experience', *Young Children*, November, pp. 16–23.

Gergen, K. (1971), *The Concept of Self*, Holt, Rinehart and Winston, New York.

Germain, C. (1994), 'Emerging conceptions of family development over the life course', *Families in Society* 12, p. 3.

Gersten, J., Langner, T., Eisenbert, J. and Orzeck, L. (1974), 'Child behaviour and life events: undesirable change or change per se?' in B. S. Dohrenwend and B. P. Dohrenwend (eds), *Stressful Life Events*, Wiley, New York, pp. 159–70.

Gesell, A. (1974), *The First Years of Life: a Guide to the Study of the Pre-School Child*, Methuen, London.

Gibson, F., Ungerer, J. A., McMahon, C. A., Leslie, G. I. and Saunders, D. M. (2000), 'The mother–child relationship following In Vitro Fertilisation (IVF): infant attachment, responsivity and maternal sensitivity', *Journal of Child Psychology and Psychiatry* 41, vol. 8, pp. 1015–23.

Gilbert, R. and Gilbert, P. (1998), *Masculinity Goes to School*, Allen & Unwin, Sydney.

Gilby, R. L. and Pederson, D. R. (1982), 'The development of the child's concept of the family', *Canadian Journal of Behavioural Sciences* 14, pp. 110–21.

Gilligan, C. (1977), 'In a different voice: women's conceptions of self and morality', *Harvard Educational Review* 47, pp. 481–517.

Gilligan, C. (1982), *In a Different Voice: Psychological Theory and Women's Development*, Harvard University Press, Cambridge, Massachusetts.

Gilligan, C., Ward, J. V. C. and Taylor, J. (eds) (1988), *Mapping the Moral Domain: a Contribution of Women's Thinking to Psychological Theory and Education*, Harvard University Press, Cambridge, Massachusetts.

Ginsburg, H. and Opper, S. (1979), *Piaget's Theory of Intellectual Development: an Introduction*, Prentice-Hall, Englewood Cliffs, New Jersey.

Given, J. E., Jones, G. E. and McMillen, D. (1985), 'A comparison of personality characteristics between invitro fertilisation patients and other infertile patients', *Journal of Invitro Fertilisation and Embryo Transfer* 2, p. 1.

Glasser, W. (1984), *Control Theory*, Harper and Row, New York.

Gleason, T. R., Sebanc, A. M. and Hastup, W. (2000), 'Imaginary companions of preschool children', *Developmental Psychology*, 36, pp. 419–28.

Glover, S., Burns, J., Butler, H. and Patton, G. (1998), 'Social environment and the emotional wellbeing of young people', *Family Matters* 49, pp. 11–16.

Glow, R. A. and Glow, P. H. (1984), 'From trait to category of child behaviour disorders: advances in the use of the Adelaide Parent Rating Scale', in R. A. Glow (ed.), *Advances in the Behavioural Measurement of Children*, vol. 1, Greenwhich, Connecticut, New Jersey.

Goble, F. G. (1974), *The Third Force: the Psychology of Abraham Maslow*, Pocket Books, New York.

Godin, G. and Shephard, R. J. (1986), 'Psychosocial factors influencing intentions to exercise of young students from grades 7 to 9', *Research Quarterly of Exercise Sport* 57, pp. 41–52.

Goldberg, S. and Lewis, M. (1972), *Play Behaviour in the Year Old Infant*, Bordwick Publishers, USA.

Goldman, R. J. and Goldman, J. D. G. (1989), 'The prevalence and nature of child sexual abuse in Australia', *Australian Journal of Sex, Marriage and Family* 9, pp. 94–106.

Goldsmith, H. H. and Gottesman, I. I. (1981), 'Origins of variation in behavioural style: a longitudinal study of temperament in young twins', *Child Development* 51, pp. 91–103.

Goodnow, J. (1977), *Children's Drawing*, Fontana Open Books, Glasgow.

Goodnow, J. J., Cashmore, J., Cotton, S. and Knight, R. (1984), 'Mothers' developmental timetables in two cultural groups', *International Journal of Psychology* 19, pp. 193–205.

Goodnow, J. J., Knight, R. and Cashmore, J. (1985), 'Adult social cognition: implications of parents' ideas for approaches to development', in M. Perlmutter (ed.), *Social Cognition: Minnesota Symposia on Child Development*, vol. 18, Lawrence Erlbaum, Hillsdale, New Jersey.

Goolishian, H. A. and Anderson, H. (1987), 'Language systems and therapy: an evolving idea', *Journal of Psychotherapy* 24, pp. 529–38.

Gottesman, I. I. (1963), 'Genetic aspects of intelligent behaviour', in N. R. Ellis (ed.), *Handbook of Mental Deficiency*, McGraw-Hill, New York, pp. 253–96.

Gottlieb, G. (1991), 'Experiential canalization of behavioural development: theory', *Developmental Psychology* 27, pp. 4–13.

Gottman, J. M. (1983), 'How children become friends', *Monographs of the Society for Research in Child Development* 48, p. 3.

Gottman, J., Gonso, J. and Schuler, P. (1976), 'Teaching social skills to isolated children', *Journal of Abnormal Child Psychology* 4, pp. 179–97.

Gough, P.B. (1987), 'The key to improving schools: an interview with William Glasser', *Phi Delta Kappan*, May, pp. 656–62.

Granger, C. R. (unpub.), Young adolescents' knowledge of infant abilities, unpublished PhD dissertation, University Micro Films International, 1982.

Greig, R. and Raphael, B. (1988), 'AIDS and adolescents: getting the message across', *Mind* 3, pp. 24–7.

Greig, R. and Raphael, B. (1989), 'AIDS prevention and adolescents', *Community Health Studies* 8, pp. 211–19.

Griffin, H. and Prior, M. (unpub.), Young people and the nuclear threat, unpublished manuscript, La Trobe University, 1987.

Griffiths, R. and Farnill, D. (1995), 'Primary prevention of dieting disorders: an update', *Primary Prevention* 1, pp. 1–7.

Grinker, R. R. (1968), 'Conceptual progress in psychoanalysis', in J. Marmor (ed.), *Modern Psychoanalysis*, Basic Books, New York.

Groos, K. (1989), *(a) The Play of Animals, (b) The Play of Man*, Appleton, New York.

Grossman, K. E. and Grossman, K. (1990), 'The wider concept of attachment in cross-cultural research', *Human Development* 33, pp. 31–47.

Grotjahn, M. (1957), *Beyond Laughter*, McGraw-Hill, New York.

Gruber, H. E., Girgus, J. S., Banuazizi, A. (1971), 'The development of object permanence in cats', *Developmental Psychology* 1, pp. 9–15.

Grumbach, M. M., Grave, G. D. and Mayer, F. E. (1974)(eds), *Control of the Onset of Puberty*, Wiley, New York.

Gubbay, S. A. (1975), *The Clumsy Child: a Study of Developmental Apraxic and Agnostic Ataxia*, W. B. Saunders, London.

Guilder, J. (1991), 'Why are so many Aboriginal children not achieving at school?' *The Aboriginal Child at School* 19, pp. 42–53.

Gullone, E. and King, N. S. (1997), 'The fears of youth in the 1990s: on temporary normative data', *The Journal of Genetic Psychology* 154, pp. 137–53.

Gustafsson, J. E. and Undheim, J. O. (1992), 'Stability and change in broad and narrow factors of intelligence from ages 12 to 15 years', *Journal of Educational Psychology* 84, pp. 141–50.

Hadeed, A. J. and Siegal, S. R. (1989), 'Maternal cocaine use during pregnancy', *Pediatrics* 5, pp. 205–10.

Hager, A. (1987), 'Early pregnancy loss: miscarriage and ectopic pregnancy', in J. R. Woods and J. L. Esposito (eds), *Pregnancy and Loss: Medical Therapeutics and Practical Considerations*, Williams and Wilkins, New York.

Haith, M. M. (1990), 'Progress in understanding of sensory and perceptual procession early in infancy', *Merrill-Palmer Quarterly* 36, pp. 1–25.

Haley, J. (1980), *Learning Home: the Therapy of Disturbed Young People*, McGraw-Hill, New York.

Halford, G. S. (1982), *The Development of Thought*, Lawrence Erlbaum, Hillsdale, New Jersey.

Halford, G. S. (1989), 'Reflections on 25 years of Piagetian cognitive developmental psychology, 1963–1988', *Human Development* 32, pp. 325–57.

Hall, G. S. (1904), *Adolescence: its Psychology and its Relations to Physiology, Anthropology, Sociology, Sex, Crime, Religion and Education*, vols 1 and 2, Appleton-Century-Crofts, New York.

Hall, J. A. (1985), *Nonverbal Sex Differences*, Johns Hopkins Open University Press, Baltimore.

Hamerton, J. L., Briggs, S. M., Gianelli, F. and Carter, C. V. (1961), 'Chromosomal studies in detection of parents with high risk of second child with Down's Syndrome', *Lancet* 281, pp. 788–91.

Hamilton, A. (1981), *Nature and Nurture: Aboriginal Child-Rearing in North-Central Arnhem Land*, Australian Institute of Aboriginal Studies, Canberra.

Hancock, J. (1988), 'Learning with data bases', *Journal of Reading* 32, pp. 582–90.

Harding, S. E. (1985), 'Anorexia nervosa', *Paediatric Nursing*, July/August, pp. 275–7.

Harkees, S., Edwards, C. P. and Super, L. M. (1981), 'Social roles and moral reasoning: a study in a rural African community', *Developmental Psychology* 17, pp. 595–601.

Harper, J. and Collins, J. K. (1975), 'The effects of early or late maturation on the prestige of the adolescent girl', in J. K. Collins (ed.), *Studies of the Australian Adolescent*, Cassell, Stanmore, New Jersey.

Harper, P. A. (1962), 'Development of bowel and bladder control', in P. A. Harper (ed.), *Preventative Paediatrics, Child Health and Development*, Appleton-Century-Crofts, New York, pp. 27–35.

Harr, R. and Secord, P. F. (1972), *The Explanation of Social Behaviour*, Basil Blackwell, Oxford.

Harris, J. R. (1998), *The Nurture Assumption: Why Children Turn Out the Way They Do*, Free Press, New York.

Harris, R., Nilsson, J. and Bond, M. (unpub.), Psychosocial changes on couples undergoing IVF Treatment, Flinders University of South Australia.

Harris, S. G. (unpub.), Milingimbi Aboriginal learning contexts, PhD thesis, Univ. of New Mexico, 1977.

Harslett, M. (1998), *Good relationships and good school experiences: that's what is important to Aboriginal students*, Aboriginal Pedagogy Conference, 10–11 November.

Harter, S. (1983), 'Developmental perspectives on the self', in P. H. Mussen, *Handbook of Child Psychology*, Wiley, New York.

Harter, (1989), 'Causes, correlates and the functional role of global self worth: a life span perspective', in J. Kolligan and R. Sternberg (eds), *Perceptions of Competence and Incompetence Across the Lifespan*, Yale University Press, New Haven.

Hartup, W. (1974), 'Aggression in childhood: developmental perspectives', *American Psychologist* 29, pp. 336–41.

Hartup, W. W. (1978), 'Children and their friends', in H. McGurk, *Issues in Childhood Social Development*, Methuen, London.

Hasbrook, C. A. (1986), 'The sport participation social class relationship: some recent youth sport participation data', *Social Sports Journal* 3, pp. 154–9.

Hassan, R. (unpub.), Unlived lives: trends in youth suicide, paper presented at Conference on Preventing Youth Suicide, Adelaide, 1990.

Hassan, R. and Carr, J. (1989), 'Changing patterns of suicide in Australia', *Australian and New Zealand Journal of Psychiatry* 23, pp. 226–34.

Havighurst, R. J. (1953), *Human Development and Education*, Longman, New York.

Hay, D. (1984), 'Social conflict in early childhood', in G. Whitehurst (ed.), *Annals of Child Development*, vol. 1, 1–44, Greenwich, CT:JAI.

Hay, D. F. and Ross, H. S. (1982), 'The social nature of early conflict', *Child Development* 53, pp. 105–13.

Hayes, A. (1990), 'Developmental psychology, education and the need to move beyond typological thinking', *Australian Journal of Education* 34, pp. 235–41.

Hazell, P., Ongan, T., Hutchins, P., Foreman, D., Keating, D. A., Dunne, A., Bannerman, N. C. and Sly, K. (2000), 'Best practice in diagnosis and treatment for attention deficit hyperactivity disorder: reserch and guidelines', *Australian Journal of Early Childhood*, 25, pp. 34–46.

Healey, J., Hassan, R. and Mckenna, R. B. (1985), 'Aboriginal families', in D. Storer (ed.), *Ethnic Family Values in Australia*, Prentice-Hall, Sydney.

Healey, Y. (1997), *Issues for the Nineties*, The Spinney Press, Melbourne.

Health Education Authority (1998), *Young and Active? Policy Framework for Young People and Health Enhancing Physical Activity*, Health Education Authority, London.

Hearn, G (1990), 'Adolescents and mass media: interrelationships', in P. C. L. Heaven and V. J. Callan (eds), *Adolescence: an Australian Perspective*, Harcourt Brace Jovanovich, Sydney.

Heaven, P. C. L. (1989), 'Locus of control and attitudes to authority among adolescents', *Personality and Individual Differences* 9, pp. 181–3.

Heaven, P. C. L. and Rigby, K. (1987), 'Attitudes toward authority and the EPQ', *Journal of Social Psychology* 127, pp. 359–60.

Hepper, P. G. (1988), 'Foetal soap addiction', *Lancet* 1, pp. 1347–8.

Herbert, M. (1975), *Problems of Childhood*, Pan, London.

Hesse, H. (1970), *Poems*, trans. J. Wright, Farrar, Straus and Giroux, New York.

Hetherington, E. M. (1989), 'Divorce: a child's perspective', *American Psychologist* 31, pp. 851–8.

Hetherington, E. M. (1999), 'Social capital and the development of youth from nondivorced, divorced and remarried families', in W. A. Collins and B. Laursen *Relationships as Developmental Contexts. The Minnesota Symposia on Child Psychology*, vol. 30, Lawrence Erlbaum, New Jersey.

Hetherington, E. M., Cox, M. and Cox, R. (1979), 'Family intervention and the social, emotional and cognitive development of children following divorce', in L. Vaugh and T. B. Bruzelton (eds), *The Family Setting Priorities*, Science and Medical Publishers, New York.

Hill, R. (1986), 'Life cycle stages for types of single parent families: of family development theory', *Family Relations* 1, pp. 19–29.

Hill, T. (1989), 'Neglected and rejected children: promoting social competence in early childhood settings', *Australian Journal of Early Childhood* 14, pp. 11–16.

Hobbes, T. (1931), *Leviathan*, Basil Blackwell, Oxford.

Hodges, H. L. B. (1983), 'Learning styles', *Arithmetic Teacher* 30, pp. 17–20.

Hoffman, S. I. and Strauss, S. (1985), 'The development of children's concepts of death', *Death Studies* 9, pp. 469–82.

Holden, G. W. (1983), 'Avoiding conflict: mothers as tacticians in the supermarkets', *Child Development* 54, pp. 233–40.

Holaday, B., La Montagne, L. and Marciel, J. (1994), 'Vygotsky's zone of proximal development: implications for nurse assistance of children's learning', *Issues in Comprehensive Pediatric Nursing* 17, pp. 15–27.

Holman, J., Braithwaite, V. and Hughson, B. (1984), 'Television and the preschool child: relating viewing habits to family life style, attitudes and children's adjustment', *Australian Journal of Early Childhood* 9, pp. 29–34.

Holmes, T. H. and Rahe, R. H. (1967), 'The Social Readjustment Rating Scale', *Journal of Psychosomatic Research* 11, pp. 213–18.

Holt, K. S. (1975), *Movement and Child Development*, Spastics International Medical Publications, New York.

Homer (1967 edn), *The Odyssey*, trans. V. Ried, Penguin, Harmondsworth.

Honig, A. S. (1986), 'Stress and coping in children: interpersonal family relationships', *Young Children*, July, pp. 47–59.

Honstead, C. (1968), 'The developmental theory of Jean Piaget', in J. L. Frost (ed.), *Early Childhood Education Rediscovered*, Holt, Rinehart and Winston, New York.

Hoorer-Dempsey, K. V., Bassler, O. C. and Burow, R. (1995), 'Parents' reported involvement in students' homework: strategies and practices', *Elementary School Journal* 95, pp. 435–50.

Horner, T. M. (1985), 'The psychic life of the young infant: review and critique of the psychoanalytic concepts of symbiosis and infantile omnipotence', *American Journal of Orthopsychiatry* 3, pp. 324–44.

Horner, T. M. (1988), 'Rapprochement in the psychic development of the toddler: a transactional perspective', *American Journal of Orthopsychiatry* 58, pp. 4–153.

Horney, K. (1937), *The Neurotic Personality of Our Time*, Norton, New York.

Horowitz, F. D. and Columbo, J. (1990), 'Future agendas and directions in infancy research', *Merrill-Palmer Quarterly* 36, pp. 173–8.

Howard, S., Dryden, J. and Johnson, B. (1999), 'Childhood resilience: review and critique of literature', *Oxford Review of Education* 25, pp. 307–23.

Howarth, K. (1987), 'Women and sport: issues of relevance to the female primary school teacher', *The British Journal of Physical Education* 18, pp. 269–70.

Howarth, M. (1989), 'Rediscovering the power of fairy tales', *Young Children*, November, pp. 58–65.

Howes, C. (1983), 'Patterns of friendship', *Child Development* 54, pp. 1041–53.

Howes, C. (1985), 'Sharing fantasy: social pretend play in toddlers', *Child Development* 53, pp. 105–13.

Howes, C. (1988), *Peer interaction of Young Children*, Monographs of Society of Research into Child Development 53, p. 1.

Howlin, D. (1980), 'Language', in M. Rutler (ed.), *Scientific Foundations of Developmental Psychology*, Heinemann, London.

Hudson, D. B., Elek, S. M. and Fleck, M. O. (2001), 'First time mothers' and fathers' transitions to parenthood: infant care, self efficacy, parenting satisfaction and infant sex', *Issues in Comprehensive Pediatric Nursing* 24, pp. 31–43.

Hug-Hellmuth, H. von (1965), 'The child's concept of death', *The Psychoanalytic Quarterly* 34, pp. 499–516.

Hughes, J. N. (1989), 'The child interview', *School Psychology Review* 18, pp. 247–59.

Hughs, C. B. and Page-Lieberman, J. (1989), 'Fathers experiencing a perinatal loss', Death Studies 13, pp. 537–56.

Hughs, J. R. (1984), 'Psychological effects of habitual aerobic exercise: a critical review', *Preventative Medicine* 13, pp. 66–78.

Hughs, P. and More A. J. (1997), *Aboriginal Ways of Learning and Learning Style*, Australian Association of Research Education Conference, Brisbane, 4 Dec.

Humphries, L., Wrobel, S., Wirgert, H. (1982), 'Anorexia nervosa', *American Family Physician* 26, pp. 199–204.

Hunt, J. McV. (1961), *Intelligence and Experience*, Ronald Press, New York.

Hyde, B. B. and McCown, D. E. (1986), 'Classical conditioning in neonatal intensive care nurseries', *Pediatric Nursing* 12, pp. 11–14.

Illingworth, R. S. (1987), *The Development of the Infant and Young Child*, Churchill Livingstone, Edinburgh.

Inhelder, B., (1975), 'Some aspects of Piaget's genetic approach to cognition', in J. Gants and H. J. Butcher (eds), *Developmental Psychology*, Penguin, Harmondsworth, UK.

Inhelder, B. and Piaget, J. (1958), *The Growth of Logical Thinking from Childhood to Adolescence*, Basic Books, New York.

Intergovernmental Committee on AIDS (1992), *A Report on HIV/AIDS Activities in Australia 1990–91*, Commonwealth Department of Health, Housing and Community Services, Canberra.

Irwin, C. (1987), 'Adolescent social behaviour and health', *New Directions for Child Development* 37, Jossey-Bass, San Francisco.

Irwin, C. E. and Millstein, S. G. (1986), 'Biopsychosocial correlates of risk-taking behaviours during adolescence', *Journal of Adolescent Health Care* 7, pp. 820–6.

Irwin, D. M. and Bushnell, M. M. (1980), *Observational Strategies for Child Study*, Holt, Rinehart and Winston, New York.

Irwin, M. (1984), 'Early onset of anorexia nervosa', *Southern Medical Journal* 77, pp. 611–14.

Irwin, R. R. (1996), 'Narrative competence and constructive developmental theory: a proposal for rewriting the Bildungsroman in the postmodern world', *Journal of Adult Development* 3, pp. 109–25.

Izard, C. E. (1971), *The Face of Emotion*, Appleton-Century-Crofts, New York.

Izard, C., Huebner, R., Risser, D., McGinnes, G. and Dougherty, L. (1980), 'The young infant's ability to produce discrete emotional expressions', *Developmental Psychology* 16, pp. 130–40.

James, A. L. and James, A. (2001), 'Childhood: toward a theory of continuity and change', *Annals of American Academy of Political Science* pp. 575–637.

James, A. L. and James, A. (2001), 'Tightening the net: children, community and control', *British Journal of Sociology* 52, pp. 211–28.

James, K., (1999), '"I feel really embarrassed in front of the guys." Adolescent girls and informal school basketball', *The ACHPHER Healthy Lifestyles Journal* 46, pp. 11–16.

James, W. (1890), *The Principles of Psychology*, Holt, Rinehart and Winston, New York.

James, W. (1910), *Psychology: the Briefer Course*, Holt, New York.

Jenkins, H. (1983), 'A life cycle framework in the treatment of underorganised families', *Journal of Family Therapy* 5, pp. 359–77.

Jenkins, H. (1988), 'Annotations: family therapy – developments in thinking and practice', *Journal of Child Psychology and Psychiatry* 31 (7), pp. 1015–26.

Jenkins, H. (1989), 'Precipitating crises in families: patterns which connect', *Journal of Family Therapy* 11, pp. 99–109.

Jenkins, J. M., Smith, M. A. and Graham, P. J. (1989), 'Coping with parental quarrels', *Journal of American Academy of Child and Adolescent Psychiatry* 28, pp. 182–9.

Jenkinson, J. (1991), 'The skill basis of psychological testing', *Psychological Test Bulletin* 4, pp. 5–12.

Jensen, A. R. (1969), 'How much can we boost IQ and scholastic achievement?', *Harvard Educational Review* 39, pp. 1–123.

Jensen, A. (1978), 'The current status of the IQ controversy', *Australian Psychologist* 2, pp. 7–27.

Jersild, A. T., Telford, C. W. and Sawrey, M. (1975), *Child Psychology*, 7th edn, Prentice-Hall, Englewood Cliffs, New Jersey.

Johnson, J. H., Sarason, I. G. (1978), 'Life stress, depression and anxiety: internal–external control as a moderator variable', *Journal of Psychosomatic Research* 22, pp. 205–8.

Johnson, M. (1988), 'Memories of mother', *New Scientist* 1600, February, pp. 60–2.

Johnston, G. (1964), *My Brother Jack*, Collins, Sydney.

Johnston, O., Crawford, J., Short, H., Smyth, T. R. and Moller, J. (1987), 'Poor coordination in 5 year olds: a screening test for use in schools', *Australian Paediatric Journal* 23, pp. 157–61.

Johnstone, M. (1984), 'Blending families in Australia: is the nuclear family changing?', *Australian Journal of Sex, Marriage and Family* 6, pp. 60–76.

Jones, K. L. and Smith, D. W. (1979), 'Recognition of the fetal alcohol syndrome in early infancy', *Lancet* 2, pp. 999–1001.

Jones, M. C. and Mussen, P. H. (1958), 'Self conceptions, motivations and interpersonal attitudes of early and late maturing boys', *Child Development* 29, pp. 491–501.

Jones, M. V. and Guidon, A. W. (1972), *Language Development: the Key to Learning*, Charles C. Thomas, New York.

Jordan, B. E., Radin, N. and Epstein, A. (1975), 'Paternal behaviour and intellectual functioning in pre-school boys and girls', *Developmental Psychology* 11, pp. 407–8.

Kagan, J. (1981), *The Second Year: the Emergence of Self Awareness*, Harvard University Press, Cambridge, Massachusetts.

Kagan, J., Kearsley, R. B. and Zelazo, P. R. (1978), *Infancy: Its Place in Human Development*, Harvard University Press, Cambridge, Massachusetts.

Kagan, S., Knight, G. and Martinez-Romero, S. (1982), 'Culture and the development of conflict resolution styles', *Journal of Cross Cultural Psychology* 13, pp. 43–58.

Kahle, J. B. (1987), 'Images of science: the physicist and the cowboy', in B. J. Fraser and G. J. Giddings (eds), *Gender Issues in Science Education*, Curtin University of Technology, Perth.

Kallman, F. and Sandler, G. (1949), 'Twin studies on senescence', *American Journal of Psychiatry* 106, pp. 29–36.

Kamin, L. J. (1981), 'Commentary', in S. Scarr (ed.), *IQ: Race, Social Class and Individual Differences. New Studies of Old Issues*, Lawrence Erlbaum, Hillsdale, New Jersey.

Kandel, E. R. (1985), 'Early experience, critical periods and developmental fine tuning of brain architecture', in E. R. Kandel and J. Schwarz (eds), *Principles of Neural Science*, Elsevier Sciences, New York.

Kane, B. (1979), 'Children's concept of death', *Journal of Genetic Psychology* 134, pp. 141–53.

Kapelis, L. (1983), 'The effects of video-taped modelling on young children's knowledge and attitudes about hospitals', *Australian Journal of Early Childhood* 8, pp. 32–6.

Kastenbaum, R. (1981), *Death, Society and Human Experience*, 2nd edn, Mosby, St Louis.

Kaye, K. (1982), *The Mental and Social Life of Babies*, University of Chicago Press, Chicago.

Kaye, K. (1985), 'Toward a developmental psychology of the family', in L. L'Abate (ed.), *Handbook of Family Psychology and Therapy*, Dow Jones-Irwin, Homewood, Illinois.

Kearins, J. (1976), 'Skills of desert Aboriginal children', in G. E. Keirney and D. W. McElwain (eds), *The Psychology of Aboriginal Australians*, Wiley, Sydney.

Keating, D. P. and Bobbitt, B. L. (1978), 'Individual and developmental differences in cognitive processing components of ability', *Child Development* 49, pp. 155–67.

Keating, P. (1980), 'Thinking processes in adolescence', in J. Adelson (ed.), *Handbook of Adolescent Psychology*, Wiley, New York.

Keefe, J. W. and Monk, J. S. (1986), *Learning Style Profile Examiner's Manual*, National Association of Secondary School Principals, Reston, Virginia.

Kelly, J. (2000), 'Children's adjustment in conflicted marriages and divorce: a decade review of research', *Journal of the American Academy of Child and Adolescent Psychiatry* 39, pp. 963–73.

Kelley, K. (1985), 'The effects of sexual and/or aggressive film exposure on helping, hostility and attitudes about the sexes', *Journal of Research in Personality* 19, pp. 472–83.

Kelly, S. J., Walsh, J. H. and Thompson, K. (1991), 'Birth outcomes, health problems and neglect with prenatal exposure to cocaine', *Pediatric Nursing* 17, pp. 130–6.

Keogh, J. G. (1965), *Motor Performance in Elementary School Children*, Monographs of Los Angeles California College of Education, University of California.

Kerlinger, F. (1973), *Foundations of Behavioural Research*, Holt, Rinehart and Winston, London.

Kessen, W. (1979), 'The American child and other cultural inventions', *American Psychologist* 34, pp. 815–82.

Kilmartin, C. (1988), 'Families – strong but diverse', *Family Matters* (Australian Institute of Family Studies Newsletter) 20.

King, A. J. C., Beazley, R. P., Warren, W. K., Hankins, C. A., Robertson, A. S. and Radford, J. L. (1989a), 'Highlights from the Canada youth and AIDS study', *Journal of School Health* 59, pp. 139–45.

King, K. A., Bradley, C. B., Daniels, K. L., Islam, R., and Prince, J. H. (1999), 'The depiction of exercise on prime time television', *Journal of Health Education* 30, pp. 137–40.

King, N. J., Ollendick, T. H. and Gullane, E. (1990), 'School-related fears of children and adolescents', *Australian Journal of Education* 34, pp. 99–112.

King, N. J., Ollier, K., Iacuone, R., Schuster, S., Bays, K., Gullone, E. and Ollendick, T.H. (1989), 'Child and adolescent fears: a cross-sectional Australian study using the revised-fear survey schedule for children', *Journal of Child Psychology and Psychiatry* 30, pp. 775–84.

Kinsbourne, M. (1980), 'Brain-based limitations on mind', in R. W. Rieber (ed.), *Mind and Body*, Academic Press, New York.

Klinzing, D. R. and Klinzing, D. G. (1977), 'Communicating with young children about hospitalisation', *Communication Education* 26, p. 308–13.

Kloth, S., Janssen, P., Kraalmaat, F. and Bruttey, G. J. (1998), 'Communicative styles of mothers interacting with their pre-school age children: a factor analytic study', *Journal of Child Language* 25, pp. 149–68.

Knafel, K, Brietmayer, B., Gallo, A. and Zoeller, L. (1996), 'Family response to childhood chronic illness: description of management styles', *Journal of Pediatric Nursing*, 11, pp. 315–26.

Knafel, K. and Deatrick, J. (1990), 'Family management style: concept, analysis and development', *Journal of Pediatric Nursing*, 5, pp. 4–14.

Knapp, P. (1981), 'School, cognition and the Aboriginal child', *Developing Education* 9, pp. 5–10.

Knoblauch, C. (1992), 'Perceptions of the future', *Youth Studies* 11, pp. 40–7.

Knobloch, H. and Pasamanick, B. (1974), *Gesell and Amatruda's Developmental Diagnosis: the Evaluation and Management of Normal and Abnormal Neuropsychologic Development in Infancy and Early Childhood*, Harper and Row, New York.

Knuckey, N. N. and Gubbay, S. S. (1983), 'Clumsy children: a prognostic study', *Australian Paediatric Journal* 19, pp. 9–13.

Kochanska, G., Foreman, D. R. and Coy, K. C. (2000), 'Implications of the mother–child relationship in infancy for socialisation in the second year of life'. *Infant Behaviour and Development* 22, pp. 249–65.

Koffka, K. (1925), *The Growth of Mind*, Harcourt Brace and World, New York.

Kohlberg, L. (1960), 'The development of children's orientations toward a moral order', *Vita Humana* 6, pp. 11–33.

Kohlberg, L. (1966), 'A cognitive-developmental analysis of children's sex role concepts and attitudes', in E. E. Maccoby (ed.), *The Development of Sex Differences*, C.A. Press, Stanford, California, pp. 82–173.

Kohlberg, L. (1971), 'From is to ought: how to commit the naturalistic fallacy and get away with it in the study of moral development', in T. Mischell (ed.), *Cognitive Development and Epistemology*, Academic Press, New York.

Köhler, W. (1927), *The Mentality of Apes*, Harcourt Brace and World, New York.

Kohn, A. (1991), 'Caring kids: the role of schools', *Phi Delta Kappan*, March, pp. 497–506.

Koocher, G.T. (1973), 'Childhood, death and cognitive development', *Developmental Psychology* 9, pp. 369–75.

Kopp, C. B. and Parmalee, A. H. (1979), 'Prenatal and perinatal influences on infant behaviour', in J. D. Osofsky, *Handbook of Infant Development*, Wiley, New York, pp. 29–76.

Kosky, R. (1987), 'Is suicide behaviour increasing among Australian youth?', *Medical Journal of Australia* 147, August, pp. 165–6.

Kostelnick, M. J., Whiren, A. P., Stein, L. C. (1986), 'Living with He-Man', *Young Children*, May, pp. 3–9.

Kozulin, A. (1984), *Psychology in Utopia: toward a Social History of Soviet Psychology*, The MIT Press, Cambridge, Massachusetts.

Kreppner, K., Paulsen, S. and Schuetze, Y. (1982), 'Infant and family development: from triads to tetrads', *Human Development* 25, pp. 373–91.

Kuipers-Holwerda, J. (1987), 'The cognitive development of low birth weight children', *Journal of Child Psychology and Psychiatry* 38, pp. 321–8.

Kurdek, L. A. (1981), 'An integrative perspective on children's divorce adjustment', *American Psychologist* 36, pp. 856–66.

Laflamme, L. and Eilert-Petersson, E. (1998), 'Injuries to preschool children in a home setting: patterns and related products', *Acta Paediatrics* 87, pp. 206–11.

Lamb, M. (1977), 'A re-examination of the infant's social world', *Human Development* 20, pp. 65–85.

Lamb, M. E. (1981), *The Role of the Father in Child Development*, 2nd edn, Wiley, New York.

Lamb, M. and Sutton-Smith, B. (1982), *Sibling Relationships: Their Nature and Significance across the Life Span*, Lawrence Erlbaum, Hillsdale, New Jersey.

Lancaster, P. L. (1989), 'Birth defects in Aborigines', *The Medical Journal of Australia* 151, pp. 241–2.

Lapouse, R. and Monk, M. (1953), 'Fears and worries in representative samples of children', *American Journal of Orthopsychiatry* 24, pp. 803–18.

Largo, M. H. and Stutzle, W. (1977), 'Longitudinal study of bowel and bladder control by day and night in the first six years of life: the role of potty training and the child's initiative', *Developmental Medicine and Child Neurology* 19, pp. 607–13.

Lawrance, L., Levy, S. R. and Rubinson, L. (1990), 'Self-efficacy and AIDS prevention for pregnant teens', *Journal of School Health* 60, pp. 19–23.

Lawson, D. E. (1992), 'Need for safeguarding the field of intelligence testing', *Journal of Educational Psychology* 84, pp. 131–4.

Leditschke, J. F. (1989), 'Surviving childhood', *Australian Child and Family Welfare* 30, pp. 25–6.

Lee, H. (1960), *To Kill a Mockingbird*, Heinemann, London.

Lee, J. A. (1974), 'The styles of loving', *Psychology Today*, October, pp. 44–50.

Lemlech, J. K. (1984), *Curriculum and Instructional Methods for the Elementary School*, Macmillan, New York.

Lennings, C. J. (1996), 'Adolescents at risk. Drug use and risk behaviour', *Youth Studies Australia* 2, pp. 29–36.

Lerner, R. M. and Galambos, N. L. (1998), 'Adolescent development: challenges and opportunities for research, programs and policies', *Annual Review of Psychology* 49, pp. 413–46.

Leung, C. (2001), 'The sociocultural and psychological adaptation of Chinese Migrant adolescents in Australia and Canada', *International Journal of Psychology*, 36, pp. 8–19.

Levin, G. R. (1973), *A Self-Directing Guide to the Study of Child Psychology*, Brooks/Cole Publications, Monterey.

Levine, M. D., Carey, W. B., Crocker, A. C. and Gross, R. T. (1983), *Developmental Behavioural Paediatrics*, W. B. Saunders, Philadelphia.

Levinson, D. (1978), *The Seasons of a Man's Life*, Ballantine Books, New York.

Lewis, C. S. (1954), *The Horse and His Boy*, Penguin Books, Harmondsworth.

Lewis, M. (1976), *Origins of Intelligence*, Plenum, New York.

Lewis, M. D. (2000), 'The promise of dynamic systems approaches for an integrated account of human development,' *Child Development*, 71, pp. 36–43.

Lewis, M. and Brookes-Gunn, J. (1979), *Social Cognition and the Acquisition of Self*, Plenum Press, New York.

Lieberman, S. (1982), 'Forging a marital bond', in A. Bentovim, G. Barnes and A. Cooklin (eds), *Family Therapy*, vol. 2, Academic Press, London.

Lindegard, B. (1956), *Body Build, Body Functions and Personality*, C. W. K. Gleerup, London.

Linz, D., Donnerstein, E. and Penrod, S. (1984), 'The effects of multiple exposures to filmed violence against women,' *Journal of Communication* 34, pp. 130–48.

Lippman, L. (1970, *To Achieve Our Country: Australia and the Aborigines*, Cheshire, Sydney.

Lipsett, L. P. (1983), 'Stress in infancy: towards Understanding the Origins of Coping Behaviour', in N. Garmezy and M. Potter (eds), *Stress, Coping and Development in Children*, McGraw-Hill, New York.

Lipsitz, J. S. (1979), 'Adolescent development: myths and realities', *Children Today* 27, pp. 4–10.

Locke, J. (1673), *Some Thoughts Concerning Education*, Cambridge University Press, Cambridge.

Lowrey, G. H. (1986), *Growth and Development of Children*, 8th edn, Medical Publications.

Lubetsky, M. J. (1989), 'The magic of fairy tales: psychodynamic and developmental perspectives', *Child Psychiatry and Human Development* 19, pp. 245–56.

McAllister, I., Makkai, T. and Jones, R. (1986), *Attitudes Toward Drugs and Drug Use in Australia*, Commonwealth Department of Health, Canberra.

McCabe, M. P. (1984), 'Toward a theory of adolescent dating', *Adolescence* 19, pp. 159–70.

McCall, R. B. (1977), 'Childhood IQs as predictors of adult educational and occupational status', *Science* 197, pp. 482–3.

McCall, R. B. (1990), 'Infancy research: individual differences', *Merrill-Palmer Quarterly* 36, pp. 141–56.

McCann, T. E. and Sheehan, P. W. (1985), 'Violence content in Australian television', *Australian Psychologist* 20, pp. 33–42.

McCartney, K. and Galanopoulos, G. (1988), 'A child care and attachment: a new frontier the second time around', *American Journal of Orthopsychiatry* 58, pp. 16–24.

McCubbin, H. I. and McCubbin, M. A. (1988), 'Typologies of resilient families: emerging roles of social class and ethnicity', *Family Relations* 37, pp. 247–54.

McCubbin, H., Thompson, A., Pirner, P. and McCubbin, M. (1988), *Family Types and Family Strengths: a Life Cycle and Ecological Perspective*, Burgess, Minneapolis.

MacDonald, D. (1989), 'Australian policy on mixed sex physical education', *British Journal of Physical Education* 20, pp. 129–31.

McDonald, P. (1983), 'Can the family survive?' *Australian Society*, December, pp. 3–8.

McDonald, P. (1988), 'Families in the future: the pursuit of personal autonomy', *Family Matters* 22, pp. 40–7.

McDonald, P. (1989), 'The second time around', *Family Matters* 24, pp. 28–9.

McDonald, P. (1990), 'The 1980s' social and economic change affecting families', *Family Matters* 26, pp. 13–18.

McElwain, D. W. (1969), 'Some aspects of the cognitive ability of Aboriginal children', in S. S. Dunn and C. M. Tatz (eds), *Aborigines and Education*, Sun Books, Melbourne, pp. 264–72.

MacFarlane, A. C. and Raphael, B. (1984), 'Ash Wednesday: the effects of a fire', *Australian and New Zealand Journal of Psychiatry* 18, pp. 341–51.

McGarrigle, J. and Donaldson, M. (1974), 'Conservation accidents', *Cognition* 3, pp. 341–50.

McGee, R. and Stanton, W. R. (1992), 'Sources of distress among New Zealand adolescents', *Journal of Child Psychology and Psychiatry* 33, pp. 999–1010.

McGhee, P. E. (1974), *Humor: its Origin and Development*, Freeman, San Francisco.

McGhee, P. E. (1976), 'Children's appreciation of humor: a test of the cognitive congruency principle', *Child Development* 47, pp. 420–6.

McGhee, P. E., (1979), *Humor: its Origin and Development*, Second edition, Freeman, San Francisco.

McGoldrick, M. (1989), 'Women and the family life cycle', in B. Carter and M. McGoldrick, *The Changing Family Life Cycle*, Allyn & Bacon, New York, chapter 2.

McGoldrick, M. and Carter, E. A. (1980), 'Forming a remarried family', in E. A. Carter and M. McGoldrick (eds), *The Family Life Cycle: a Framework for Family Therapy*, Gardner Press, New York.

McGoldrick, M. and Gerson, R. (1985), *Genograms in Family Assessment*, Norton, New York.

McGurk, H. (1975), *Growing and Changing: a Primer of Developmental Psychology*, Methuen, London.

McGurk, H. (ed.) (1978), *Issues in Childhood Social Development*, Methuen, London.

McInterney, D. M., Hinkley, J. and Dawson, M. (1998), 'Aboriginal, Anglo and immigrant students' motivational beliefs personal academic success: Are there cultural differences?' *Journal of Educational Psychology* 90, pp. 621–9.

McIntyre, M., Angle, C. and Stuempler, L. (1972), 'The concept of death in mid-western children and youth', *American Journal of Diseases of Children* 123, pp. 527–32.

McMurray, A. (1997), *Community Health and Wellness. A Sociological Approach*, Mosby, Sydney.

McTear, M. and Conti-Ramsden, G. (1992), *Pragmatic Disability in Children*, Wharr, London.

Maccoby E. E. (1980), *Social Development, Psychological Growth and the Parent–Child Relationship*, Harcourt Brace Jovanovich, New York.

Maccoby, E. E. and Jacklin, C. N. (1974), *The Psychology of Sex Differences*, Stanford University Press, Stanford, California.

Mackay, E. V., Beischer, N. A., Pepperell, R. J. and Wood, C. (1990), *Illustrated Textbook of Gynaecology*, 2nd edn, W. B. Saunders/Baillire Tindall, Sydney.

Madsen, M. C. and Shapira, A. (1970), 'Cooperative and competitive behaviour of urban Afro-American, Anglo-American, Mexican-American and Mexican village children', *Developmental Psychology* 3, pp. 16–20.

Mahler, M. (1961), 'Rapprochement sub-phase of the separation–individuation process', *Psychoanalytic Quarterly* 41, pp. 487–506.

Mahler, M. S., Pine, F. and Bergman, A. (1975), *The Psychological Birth of the Human Infant*, Basic Books, New York.

Main, M. (unpub.), Exploration, play and cognitive formation as related to mother–child attachment, unpublished PhD, John Hopkins University, 1973.

Major, C. (1980), 'Strategies for child accident prevention', *Australian Child and Family Welfare* 11, pp. 10–13.

Malatesta, C. Z., Culver, C., Tesmon, J. B. and Shephard, B. (1989), *The Development of Emotional Expression during the First Two Years of Life*, Monographs of the Society for Research in Child Development 54, pp. 1–2.

Malin, M. (1990), 'Why is life so hard for Aboriginal students in urban classrooms?' *The Aboriginal Child at School* 18, pp. 36–47.

Malina, R. (1982), 'Motor development in the early years', *The Young Child* 3, pp. 211–31.

Manheimer, D. E. and Mellinger, G. D. (1967), 'Personality characteristics of the child accident repeater', *Child Development* 38, pp. 491–513.

Manicas, P. and Secord, P. (1983), 'Implications for psychology of the new philosophy of science', *American Psychologist* 4, pp. 399–413.

Mann, L. (1985), 'Decision making', in N. T. Feather (ed.), *Australian Psychology: Review of Research*, Allen & Unwin, Sydney.

Mann, L., Radford, M. H. and Kanagawa, C. (1985), 'Cross-cultural differences in children's use of decision rules: a comparison between Japan and Australia', *Journal of Personality and Social Psychology* 49, pp. 1557–64.

Mann, L., Tan, C., Morgan, C. and Dixon, A. (1984), 'Developmental changes in applications of the majority rule in group decisions', *British Journal of Developmental Psychology* 2, pp. 275–81.

Maratsos, M. P. (1983), 'Nonegocentric communication abilities in preschool children', *Child Development* 44, pp. 697–700.

Marder, K., Harvey, J. and Russo, P. F. (1975), in J. Collins, (ed.), *Studies of the Australian Adolescent*, Cassell Australia, Sydney.

Marecki, M., Wooldridge, P., Thompson, J. and Lechner-Hyman, C. (1985), 'Early sibling attachment', *Journal of Obstetrics* 5, pp. 418–23.

Maresh, M. M. (1966), 'Changes in tissue widths during growth', *American Journal Disabled Children* 3, pp. 142–55.

Marsh, H. W. (1987), 'Masculinity, femininity and androgeny: their relations with multiple dimensions of self concept', *Multivariate Behavioural Research* 22, pp. 91–118.

Marsiglio, W., Hutchinson, S. and Cohen, M. (2000), 'Envisioning fatherhood: a social–psychological perspective of young men with kids', *Family Relations* 2000, pp. 133–42.

Martin, B. (1975), 'Parent–child relations', in F. Horowitz (ed.), *Review of Child Development Research*, University of Chicago Press, Chicago.

Maslow, A. H. (1954), *Motivation and Personality*, Harper and Row, New York.

Maslow, A. H. (1962), *Toward a Psychology of Being*, Van Nostrand, New York.

Maslow, A. (1971), *The Farthest Reaches of Human Nature*, Pelican, New York.

Masson, J. M. (1984), *The Assault on Truth: Freud's Suppression of the Seduction Theory*, New York: Farrar, Straus and Giroux.

Masten, A. S., Garmezy, N., Tellegren, A., Pellegrini, D. S., Larkin, K. and Larsen, A. (1988), 'Competence and stress in school children: the moderating effects of individual family qualities', *Journal of Child Psychology and Psychiatry* 6, pp. 745–64.

Matheny, A. P. (1980), 'Bayley's infant behaviour record: behavioural components and twin analyses', *Child Development* 51, pp. 1157–67.

Matheny, A. P. (1987), 'Psychological characteristics of childhood accidents', *Journal of Social Issues* 43, pp. 45–60.

Matheny, A. P., Wilson, R. S. and Dolan, A. B. (1976), 'Relations between twins in similarity of appearance and behavioural similarity: testing an assumption', *Behaviour Genetics* 6, pp. 343–51.

Mathur, S. R. and Rutherford, R. B. (1991), 'Peer mediated interventions promoting social skills of children and youth with behavioural disorders', *Education and Treatment of Children* 14, pp. 227–42.

Mattingly, C. and Hampton, K. (1988), *Survival in Our Own Land. 'Aboriginal' Experiences in 'South Australia' since 1836, a South Australian Jubilee Publication*, Hyde Park Press, Adelaide.

Maturana, H. R. and Varela, F. J. (1988), *The Tree of Knowledge: the Biological Roots of Human Understanding*, New Science Library, Boston.

Mead, M. (1970), *Culture and Committment*, Doubleday, Garden City, New York.

Meadows, S. (1986), *Understanding Child Development*, Hutchinson, London.

Medinnus, G. R. (1976), *Child Study and Observation Guide*, Wiley, New York.

Melhuish, E. C. (2000), 'The quest for quality experience continues', *International Journal of Behavioural Development*, 25, pp. 1–6.

Mijuskovic, B. (1986), 'Loneliness: counselling adolescents', *Adolescence* 21 (84), pp. 941–50.

Miles, T. R. (1957), 'Contributions to intelligence testing and the theory of intelligence', *British Journal of Educational Psychology* 27, pp. 153–65.

Miller, G. A. and Gildea, P. M. (1987), 'How children learn words', *Scientific American*, September, pp. 86–91.

Miller, P., Danaher, D. and Forbes, D. (1986), 'Sex-related strategies for coping with interpersonal conflict in children aged five to seven', *Developmental Psychology* 22, pp. 543–8.

Mills, J. L. and Graubard, B. I. (1987), 'Is moderate drinking during pregnancy associated with an increased risk for malformations?' *Paediatrics* 80, pp. 309–14.

Mills, M. and Melhaish, E. (1974), 'Recognitions of mother's voice in early infancy', *Nature* 252, p. 123.

Milne, A. A. (1984), *The House at Pooh Corner*, Magnet Books, London.

Miltich-Conway, E. and Gibbs, C. (1989), 'Young children in hospital – three years later … Does the theory match the practice?', *Australian Journal of Early Childhood* 14, pp. 23–28.

Minuchin, P. (1985), 'Families and individual development: provocations from the field of family therapy', *Child Development* 56, pp. 289–302.

Minuchin, S. (1974), *Families and Family Therapy*, Harvard University Press, Cambridge, Massachusetts.

Minuchin, S., Rosman, B. and Baker, L. (1978), *Psychosomatic Families: Anorexia Nervosa in Context*, Harvard University Press, Cambridge, Massachusetts.

Mischel, W. (1970), 'Sex typing and socialisation', in P. Mussen (ed.), *Carmichael's Manual of Child Psychology*, 3rd edn, Wiley, New York.

Mitchell, R. (1985), *Report of the Review of Services for Behaviourally Disordered Persons in South Australia*, Government Printer, Adelaide.

Monaghan, J., Robinson, J. and Dodge, J. (1979), 'The children's life events inventory', *Journal of Psychosomatic Research* 23, pp. 63–8.

Money, J. (1968), *Sex Errors of the Body: Dilemmas, Education and Counselling*, Johns Hopkins University Press, Baltimore.

Monk, S. (2001), 'Room to restart', *The Advertiser*, 24 July, p. 33.

Montessori, M. (1975), *The Child in the Family*, Pan Books, London.

Moon, C. and Wells, C. G. (1979), 'The influence of the home on learning to read', *Journal of Research in Reading* 2, pp. 53–62.

Moore, J. W., Jensen, B. and Hauck, W. E. (1990), 'Decision-making processes of youth', *Adolescence* 25, pp. 583–92.

Moshman, D. and Neimark, E. (1982), 'Four aspects of adolescent cognitive development', in T. Field, A. Huston, H. C. Quay, L. Troll and G. E. Finley (eds), *Review of Human Development*, Wiley, New York.

Mueller, E. and Lucas, J. (1975), 'A developmental analysis of peer interaction among toddlers', in M. Lewis and L. Rosenblum (eds), *Friendship and Peer Relations*, Wiley, New York, pp. 223–58.

Mukherjee, S. K. (1985), 'Juvenile delinquency: dimensions of the problem', in A. Borowski and J. M. Murray, *Juvenile Delinquency in Australia*, Methuen, Sydney, pp. 25–35.

Munro, C. (1987), 'White and the cybernetic therapies: news of a difference', *Australian and New Zealand Journal of Family Therapy* 8, pp. 183–92.

Munro, C. (1990), 'Implications for nursing of the human genome project', *Neonatal Network* 18, pp. 7–12.

Murphy, J. P. (1988), 'Best practices in interviewing', in A. Thomas and J. Grimes, *Best Practices in School Psychology*, National Association of School Psychology, Washington D.C.

Murray, C. and Thompson, F. (1985), 'The representation of authority: an adolescent viewpoint', *Journal of Adolescence* 8, pp. 217–19.

Murray-Harvey, R. and Slee, P. T. (1998), 'Family stress and school adjustment predictors across the school years', *Early Child Development and Care* 145, pp. 133–49.

Mussen, P. (1960), *Handbook of Research Methods in Child Development*, Wiley, New York.

Mussen, P. H., Conger, J. J. and Kagan, J. (1974), *Child Development and Personality*, Harper and Row, New York.

Muus, R.E. (1970), 'Adolescent development and the secular trend', *Adolescence* 5, pp. 267–84.

Myers, M. D., Rayner, H. A. and Epstein, L. H. (1998), 'Predictors of child psychological changes during family-based treatment for obesity', *Archives of Pediatric and Adolescent Medicine* 152, pp. 855–61.

Naeye, R. (1981), 'Influence of maternal cigarette smoking during pregnancy on fetal and childhood growth', *Obstetrics and Gynaecology* 57, pp. 18–21.

Nagy, M. H. (1948), 'The child's theories concerning death', *Journal of Genetic Psychology* 73, pp. 3–27.

National Population Council (1987), *What's Happening to the Australian Family?* Population Report 8.

Neal, B. (1989), 'Nocturnal enuresis in children', *Australian Family Physician*, August, pp. 978–83.

Neil, A. S. (1968), *Summerhill*, Penguin, Harmondsworth, UK.

Nelson, K. (1985), *Making Sense: the Acquisition of Shared Meaning*, Academic Press, New York.

Nelson, K. (1986), *Event Knowledge: Structure and Function in Development*, Academic Press, New York.

Nelson, W. D. (1985), *Helping Children Understand Death*, Australian Early Childhood Resource Booklets, Australian Early Childhood Association, Canberra.

Neugarten, B. (1968), *Middle Age and Aging*, University of Chicago Press, Chicago.

Neugarten, B. (1976), 'Adoption and the life-cycle', *The Counselling Psychologist* 6, p. 1.

Newacheck, P. W. and Taylor, W. R. (1992), 'Childhood chronic illnesses : prevalence, severity and impact', *American Journal of Public Health* 82, pp. 364–71.

Newman, P. R. (1982), 'The peer group', in W. B. Wolman and G.ÿStricker, *Handbook of Developmental Psychology*, Prentice-Hall, Engelwood Cliffs, New Jersey, pp. 526–36.

Newport, J. (1989), 'What can we do to help our young people resist the pressures to use and abuse drugs and alcohol?' *New Zealand Journal of Health, Physical Education and Recreation* 22, pp. 11–12.

Nicastro, E. A. and Whetsell, N. V. (1999), 'Children's fears', *Journal of Pediatric Nursing* 14, pp. 392–401.

Nichols, K. B., Cassel, J. and Kaplan, B. H. (1972), 'Psychosocial assets, life crises and prognosis of pregnancy', *American Journal of Epidemiology* 95, pp. 431–40.

Nichols, R. C. (1978), 'Heredity and environment: major findings from twin studies of ability, personality and interests', *Homo* 29, pp. 158–73.

Nicklin, L. and Sezak, P. (1988), 'What's the use of intelligence?' *The Bulletin*, June, pp. 40–9.

Nippold, M. A. (2000), 'Language developments during the adolescent years: aspects of pragmatics, syntax and semantics', *Topics in Language Disorders* 20, pp. 15–25.

Nixon, M. and Haron, F. (1987), 'Children's rights: what children think about them', *Australian Child and Family Welfare* 12, pp. 2–5.

Noller, P. and Callan, V. J. (1990), 'Adolescents' perceptions of the nature of their communication with their parents', *Journal of Youth and Adolescence* 19, pp. 349–62.

Noller, P. and Patton, W. (1990), 'Maintaining family relationships at adolescence', in P. C. L. Heaven and V. J. Callan (eds), *Adolescence: an Australian Perspective*, Harcourt Brace Jovanovich, Sydney, pp. 53–66.

Nowakowski, R. s. (1987), 'Basic concepts of C. N. S. development', *Child Development* 3, pp. 568–96.

Oakley, A. (1972), *Sex, Gender and Society*, Sun Books, Melbourne.

O'Brien, G. E. (1990), 'Youth unemployment and employment', in P. C. L. Heaven and V. J. Callan, *Adolescence: an Australian Perspective*, Harcourt Brace Jovanovich, Sydney, pp. 270–87.

Ochiltree, G. (1987), 'Adolescence and the family', *Australian Institute of Family Studies Newsletter* 10, August.

Ochiltree, G. (1990), *Children in Australian Families*, Longman Cheshire, Melbourne.

Ockleford, E. M., Vince, M. A., Layton, C. and Reader, M. R. (1988), 'Responses of neonates to parents' and others' voices', *Early Human Development* 18, pp. 27–36.

O'Connor, K., Mann, D. W. and Bardwick, J. M. (1978), 'Androgeny and self esteem in the upper middle-class: a replication of Spence', *Journal of Consulting and Clinical Psychology* 46, pp. 1168–9.

O'Connor, P. (1985), *Understanding Jung: Understanding Yourself*, Methuen, Sydney.

O'Connor, P. J. (1982), *An Analysis of Australian Child Accident Statistics*, Child Accident Prevention Foundation of Australia, Melbourne.

O'Connor, T. G., Caspi, A., DeFries, J. C. and Plomes, R. (2000), 'Are associations between parental divorce and children's adjustment genetically mediated? An adoption study', *Developmental Psychology* 36, pp. 429–37.

Oden, S. and Asher, S. R. (1977), 'Coaching children in social skills for friendship making', *Child Development* 48, pp. 495–500.

Oettinger, K. B. (1968), *Normal Adolescence*, Charles Scribner, New York.

Offer, D., Ostrov, E. and Howard, K. I. (1981), *The Adolescent: a Psychological Portrait*, Basic Books, New York.

O'Hara, M. W., Neunaber, D. O. and Zekoski, E. M. (1984), 'Prospective study of post-partum depression: prevalence, course and predictive factors', *Journal of Abnormal Psychology* 93, pp. 158–71.

Ollendick, T. H., Matson, J. L. and Helsel, W. J. (1985), 'Fears in children and adolescents: normative data', *Behaviour Research Therapy* 23, pp. 465–7.

Olson, D., McCubbin, H., Barnes, H., Larsen, A., Muxem, M. and Wilson, M. (1983), *Families: What Makes Them Work?* Sage, Beverly Hills, California.

Olweus, D. (1978), *Aggression in the Schools: Bullies and Whipping Boys*, Hemisphere (Wiley), Washington DC.

Olweus, D. (1984), 'Aggressors and their victims: bully at school', in N. Frude and H. Gault (eds), *Disruptive Behaviour in Schools*, Wiley, New York, pp. 57–76.

Olweus, D. (1989), 'Bully–victim problems among school children: basic facts and effects of a school based intervention programme', in K. Rubin and D. Pepler (eds), *The Development and Treatment of Childhood Aggression*, Lawrence Erlbaum, Hillsdale, New Jersey.

Oppenheimer, L. (1991), 'The self, the self-concept and self understanding: a review of "self-understanding in childhood and adolescence"', *Human Development* 34, pp. 113–20.

Osofsky, H. J. and Osofsky, J. D. (1980), 'Normal adaption to pregnancy and new parenthood', in P. M. Taylor (ed.), *Parent–Infant Relationships*, Grune and Stratton, New York.

Osofsky, J. D. and Osofsky, H. J. (1984), 'Psychological and developmental perspectives on expectant and new parenthood', in R. D. Parke, Review of Child *Development Research: the Family*, vol. 7, University of Chicago Press, Chicago.

Otto, R. (1989), 'Teacher stress', in P. Langford (ed.), *Educational Psychology: an Australian Perspective*, Longman Cheshire, Melbourne, pp. 343–63.

Overton, W. F.(1998), 'Developmental psychology: Philosophy, concepts and methodology' in W. Damon and R. M. Lerner (eds) *Handbook of Child Psychology*, 5th edn, John Wiley and Sons Inc., New York.

Owens, R. E. (1995), *Language Disorders: a Functional Approach to Assessment and Intervention*, 2nd edn, Allyn & Bacon, Needham Heights.

Oxhorn, H. (1986), *Human Labor and Birth*, Appleton-Century-Crofts, New York.

Pace-Owens, S. (1985), 'In-vitro fertilisation and embryo transfer', *Journal of Obstetric, Gynecologic and Neonatal Nursing*, November/December, pp. 44–8.

Paffenbarger, R. S. and Hyde, R. T. (1984), 'Exercise in the prevention of coronary heart disease', *Preventative Medicine* 13, pp. 3–22.

Page-Lieberman, J. and Hughes, C. (1990), 'How fathers perceive perinatal death', *Mother–Child Nursing* 15, pp. 320–3.

Paige, D. M. (1983), *Manual of Clinical Nutrition*, Nutrition Publications, Pleasantville, New Jersey.

Paintal, S. (1999), 'Banning corporal punishment of children', *Childhood Education*, 2, pp. 36–9.

Pangrazi, R. P. (2000), 'Promoting physical activity for youth', *ACHPER Healthy Lifestyles Journal* 47, pp. 18–21.

Panksepp, J. (1998), 'Attention deficit hyperactivity disorders, psychostimulants and intolerance of childhood playfulness: a tragedy in the making', *Current Directions in Psychological Science* 7, pp. 91–8.

Papini, D. R. and Sebby, R. A. (1988), 'Variations in conflictual family issues by adolescent pubertal status and family member', *Journal of Early Adolescence* 8, pp. 1–15.

Parke, R. and Wright, J. (2000), 'Through their eyes: an investigation into the physical activity needs and interests of young women', *The ACHPER Healthy Lifestyles Journal* 47, pp. 15–20.

Parke, R .D. (1979), 'Interaction designs', in R. B. Cairns (ed.), *The Analysis of Social Interactions: Methods, Issues and Illustrations*, Lawrence Erlbaum, New York.

Parke, R. D. (1981), *Fathers*, Fontana, New York.

Parke, R. D. (1989), 'Social development in infancy: a 25-year perspective', in H. W. Reese (ed.), *Advances in Child Development and Behaviour 21*, Academic Press, New York.

Parke, R. D., Berkowitz, L., Leyens, J. P., West, S. and Sebastian, R. (1977), 'The effects of movie violence on juvenile delinquents', in L. Berkowitz (ed.), *Advances in Experimental Social Psychology 10*, Academic Press, New York.

Partington, G., Godfrey, J. and Harrison, B. (1997), Perspectives on Retention of Aboriginal Students. Paper presented at Annual Conference of the Australian Association for Research in Education, Brisbane 3–4 December.

Patrick, J. (1982), 'Fetal breathing movements', *Clinical and Obstetrics Gynaecology* 25, pp. 787–803.

Patterson, D. (1987), 'The causes of Down syndrome', *Scientific American* 257, pp. 42–9.

Patton, W. and Noller, P. (1984), 'Unemployment and youth: a longitudinal study', *Australian Journal of Psychology* 36, pp. 399–413.

Pavlov, I. D. (1970), 'The discovery of the conditioned reflex', in W. H. Gantl, L. Pickenhain and C. H. Zwingmann (eds), *Pavlovian Approach to Psychopathology*, Pergamon Press, Oxford.

Pearn, J. H. (1985), 'Current controversies in child accident prevention: an analysis of some areas of dispute in the prevention of child trauma', *Australian and New Zealand Journal of Medicine*, pp. 782–7.

Peason, D., Rouse, H., Doswell, S., Ainsworth, C., Dawson, O., Simms, K., Edwards, L. and Falconbridge, J. (2000), 'Prevalence of imaginary companions in a normal child population', *Child: Care, Health and Development* 27, pp. 13–22.

Pederson, F. A. and Robson, K. S. (1969), 'Fathers' participation in infancy', *American Journal of Orthopsychiatry* 39, pp. 466–72.

Pellegrini, A. D. and Smith, P. K. (1998), 'Physical activity play: the nature and function of a neglected aspect of play', *Child Development* 69, pp. 577–98.

Pepler, D. M. and Craig, W. M. (1995), 'A peek behind the fence: Naturalistic observation of aggressive children with remote audiovisual recording', *Developmental Psychology* 1, pp. 103–26.

Perrin, E. C. and Gerrity, P. S. (1981), 'There's a demon in your belly: children's understanding of illness', *Paediatrics* 67, pp. 841–9.

Pesce, R. C. and Harding, C. G. (1986), 'Imaginary audience behaviour and its relationship to operational thought and social experience', *Journal of Early Adolescence* 6, pp. 83–94.

Peskin, H. and Livson, N. (1972), 'Pre- and post-pubertal personality and adult psychological functioning', *Seminars in Psychiatry* 4, pp. 343–53.

Petersen, A., Tobin-Richards, M. and Boxer, A. (1983), 'Puberty: its measurement and meaning', *Southern Journal Early Adolescence* 3, pp. 47–55.

Peterson, C. (unpub.), Cognitive and personality correlates of parent–adolescent conflict-resolution strategies, paper presented to I.S.S.B.D., Tokyo, 1987.

Peterson, C. and Bossio, L. M. (1991), *Health and Optimism*, Free Press, New York.

Petersen, C and Barrett, L. C. (1987), 'Explanatory style and academic performance among university freshmen', *Journal of Personality and Social Psychology* 53, pp. 603–7.

Peterson, C. C. (1990), 'Disagreement, negotiation and conflict resolution in families with adolescents', in P. C. L. Heaven and V. J. Callan, *Adolescence: an Australian Perspective*, Harcourt, Brace Jovanovich, Sydney.

Peterson, C. C. and Peterson, J. L. (1987), 'Australian students' ratings of the importance of AIDS relative to other community problems', *Australian Journal of Sex, Marriage and Family* 8, pp. 194–200.

Phillips, J. L. (1969), *The Origins of Intellect: Piaget's Theory*, W. H. Freeman, San Francisco.

Phillips, S. (1986), *Relations with Children: the Psychology of Human Development in a Changing World*, Kangaroo Press, Sydney.

Phillips, V. (1990), 'The Aboriginal and Islander student in the classroom', *The Aboriginal Child at School* 18, pp. 36–47.

Piaget, J. (1929), *The Child's Conception of the World*, Routledge and Kegan Paul, London.

Piaget, J. (1953), *The Origins of Intelligence in Children*, Routledge and Kegan Paul, London.

Piaget, J. (1954), *The Construction of Reality in the Child*, Routledge and Kegan Paul, London.

Piaget, J. (1965), *The Moral Judgement of the Child*, Free Press, New York.

Piaget, J. (1967), *Biology and Knowledge*, University of Chicago Press, Chicago.

Piaget, J. (1970), *Psychology and Epistemology: Towards a Theory of Knowledge*, translated by P. A. Wells, Allen Lane/Penguin, London.

Piaget, J. (1973), *The Child and Reality*, Viking Press, New York.

Piaget, J. (1976), *Judgement and Reasoning in the Child*, Littlefield Adams, Totona, New Jersey.

Piaget, J. and Inhelder, B. (1956), *The Child's Conception of Space*, Routledge and Kegan Paul, London.

Piaget, J. and Inhelder, B. (1969), *The Psychology of the Child*, Basic Books, New York.

Pinchbeck, I. and Hewitt, M. (1969), *Children in English Society*, vol. 1, Routledge and Kegan Paul, London.

Plas, J. M. (1986), *Systems Psychology in the Schools*, Pergamon Press, New York.

Plomin, R. and Daniels, D. (1987), 'Why are children in the same family so different from one another?' *Behavioural and Brain Sciences* 10, pp. 1–60.

Plomin, R. and De Fries, J. C. (1980), 'Genetics and intelligence: recent data', *Intelligence* 4, pp. 15–24.

Plomin, R. (2001), 'Genetics and behaviour', *The Psychologist* 14, pp. 134–9.

Poole, M. E. and Cooney, G. H. (1987), 'Orientations to the future: a comparison of adolescents in Australia and Singapore', *Journal of Youth and Adolescence* 16, pp. 129–51.

Poole, M. E. and Evans, C. T. (1988), 'The important things in life: group differences in adolescent concerns', *Australian Journal of Education* 32, pp. 203–22.

Poole, M. E. and Gelder, A. J. (1984), 'Family cohesiveness and adolescent autonomy in decision making', *Australian Journal of Sex, Marriage and Family* 5, pp. 65–75.

Pope, A. W., McHale, S. M. and Craighead, W. E. (1988), *Self Esteem Enhancement with Children and Adolescents*, Pergamon Press, New York.

Porter, L. (1995) *Student behaviour: Theory and practice for teachers*, Allen & Unwin, Sydney.

Prager, K., Malin, H. and Spiegler, D. (1984), 'Smoking and drinking behaviour before and during pregnancy of married mothers of live-born infants and stillborn infants', *Public Health Reports* 99, p. 117.

Prigogine, I. and Stengers, I. (1984), *Order Out of Chaos*, Flamingo, London.

Prior, M., Sanson, A., Smart, D. and Oberklaid, F. (2000), *Pathways from Infancy to Adolescence. Australian Temperament Project.* Institute of Family Studies.

Pryor-Brown, L. and Cowen, E. L. (1989), 'Stressful life events, support and children's school adjustment', *Journal of Clinical Child Psychology* 18, pp. 214–20.

Rae-Grant, N., Thomas, B. H., Offord, D. R. and Boyle, M. H. (1989), 'Risk protective factors and the prevalence of behavioural and emotional disorders in children and adolescents', *Journal of American Academy Child and Adolescent Psychiatry* 28, pp. 262–68.

Rappoport, R. (1963), 'Normal crises, family structure and mental health', *Family Process* 2, pp. 68–80.

Rappoport, R., Rappoport, N. and Strelitz, Z. (1977), *Fathers, Mothers and Others*, Routledge and Kegan Paul, London.

Raup, J. L. and Myers, J. E. (1989), 'The empty nest syndrome: myth or reality', *Journal of Counselling and Development* 68, pp. 180–3.

Raven, J. C. (1992), *Coloured Progressive Matrices*, Australian Council of Educational Research, Melbourne.

Reason, P. (1988) (ed.), *Human Inquiry in Action: Developments in New Paradigm Research*, Sage, London.

Reason, P. and Rowan, P. (1981), *Human Enquiry: a Source Book of New Paradigm Research*, Wiley, Chichester.

Reder, P. (1989), 'Freud's family', *British Journal of Psychiatry* 154, pp. 93–8.

Reed, S. C. (1963), *Counselling in Medical Genetics*, W. B. Saunders, Philadelphia.

Reed, T. and Brown, M. (2000), 'The expression of care in the rough and tumble play of boys', *Journal of Research in Childhood Education*, 15, pp. 104–12.

Reicher, S. and Emler, N. (1985), 'Delinquent behaviour and attitudes to formal authority', *British Journal of Social Psychology* 24, pp. 161–8.

Renouf, E. M. (1991), 'Always on your mind but not always on your hands: perspectives on parenting, particularly fatherhood', *Australian Journal of Marriage and Family* 12, pp. 39–45.

Rhea, D. J. (1998), 'Physical activity and body image of female adolescents', *Journal of Physical Education, Recreation and Dance* 5 pp. 27–31.

Rheingold, J. (1964), *The Fear of Being a Woman*, Grune and Stratton, New York.

Rice, M. H. and Howell, C. C. (2000), 'Measurement of physical activity, exercise and physical fitness in children: Issues and concerns', *Journal of Pediatric Nursing* 15, pp. 145–56.

Rich, A. and Kim, S. H. (1978), 'The three dimensional structure of transfer RNA', *Scientific American*, January, p. 52.

Richardson, R. (1990), *Child Maltreatment WELSTAT National Data Collection 1989–1990*, Parramatta.

Richardson, S., Dohrenwend, B. and Klein, D. (1965), *Interviewing: its Forms and Functions*, Basic Books, New York.

Richardson, T. (1980), 'Anorexia nervosa: an overview', *American Journal of Nursing* 80, p. 1470.

Richman, J. (1982), 'Men's experiences of pregnancy and childbirth', in L. McKee and M. O'Brien (eds), *The Father Figure*, Tavistock Publications, London, pp. 89–103.

Richman, N., Stevenson, J. and Graham, P. J. (1982), *Preschool to School: a Behavioural Study*, Academic Press, London.

Ridenour, M. V. (1978), 'Programs to optimise infant motor development', in M. V. Ridenour (ed.), *Motor development: Issues and Applications*, Princeton Book Co., Princeton.

Rifkin, J. (1998), 'The Sociology of the Gene', *Phi Delta Kappa* May, pp. 648–54.

Rigby, K. (1988a), 'Parental influence on attitudes toward institutional authority', *Journal of Genetic Psychology* 149, pp. 383–91.

Rigby, K. (1988b), 'Relationships among three concepts of authoritarianism among adolescent school children', *Journal of Social Psychology* 128, pp. 825–32.

Rigby, K. (1989), 'Gender, orientation to authority and delinquency among adolescents: a cross-cultural perspective', *Journal of Moral Education* 18, pp. 112–17.

Rigby, K. (1990), 'Youth and their attitudes towards institutional authorities', in P. C. L. Heaven and V. J. Callan, *Adolescence: an Australian Perspective*, Harcourt Brace Jovanovich, Sydney, pp. 26–50.

Rigby, K. and Densley, A. R. (1985), 'Religiosity and attitude to authority among adolescents', *Journal of Social Psychology* 125, pp. 723–8.

Rigby, K. and Dietz, B. (unpub.), Ramifications of disagreements between adolescents and their parents, unpublished paper, School of Social Studies, University of South Australia, 1991.

Rigby, K., Mak, A. and Slee, P. T. (1989), 'Orientation to authority, impulsiveness and self reported delinquency among Australian adolescents', *Personality and Individual Differences* 4, pp. 689–92.

Rigby, K., Metzer, J. C. and Dietz, B. (1990), 'Factors predisposing individuals to support nuclear disarmament: an international perspective', *Journal of Peace Research* 27, pp. 321–31.

Rigby, K. and Rump, E. E. (1981), 'Attitudes toward parents and institutional authorities during adolescence', *Journal of Psychology* 109, pp. 109–18.

Rigby, K., Schofield, P. and Slee, P. T. (1987), 'The similarity of attitudes to personal and impersonal types of authority among adolescent school children', *Journal of Adolescence* 10, pp. 241–53.

Rigby, K. and Slee, P. T. (1987), 'Eysenck's personality factors and orientation toward authority among school children', *Australian Journal of Psychology* 39, pp. 149–59.

Rigby, K. and Slee, P. T. (1991), 'Bullying among Australian school children: reported behaviour and attitudes towards victims', *Journal of Social Psychology* 131, pp. 615–27.

Rigby, K. and Slee, P. T. (1992), 'Dimensions of interpersonal relations among Australian children and implications for psychological wellbeing', *Journal of Social Psychology* 133, pp. 33–42.

Rinaldi, W. (2000), 'Pragmatic comprehension in secondary school-aged students with specific developmental language disorder', *International Journal of Language Communication Disorders*, 35, pp. 1–29.

Rindfuss, R. R. (1991), 'The young adult years: diversity, structural change and fertility', *Demography* 28, pp. 493–512.

Roberts, D., Gracey, M. and Spargo, R. M. (1988), 'Growth and morbidity in children in a remote Aboriginal community in north west Australia', *Medical Journal of Australia* 148, pp. 68–71.

Robinson, M. (1980), 'Systems theory for the beginning therapist', *Australian Journal of Family Therapy* 4, pp. 183–94.

Robinson, T. N., Wilde, M. L. L., Navracruz, L. C., Haydel, K. F. and Varady, A. (2000), 'Effects of reducing children's telivision and video game use on aggressive behaviour: A randomised controlled trial', *Archives of Pediatrics and Adolescent Medicine* 155, pp. 17–31.

Rochlin, G. (1967), 'How younger children view death and themselves', in E. A. Grollman (ed.), *Explaining Death to Children*, Beacon, Boston.

Roden, M. (1989), 'Covariates of divorce in Australia: an analysis using proportional hazards model', *Journal of the Australian Population Association* 6, p. 2.

Rodgers, B. (1996), 'Social and psychological wellbeing of children from divorced families: Australian research findings', *Australian Psychologist* 31, pp. 174–82.

Roiphe, A. R. (1970), *Up the Sandbox*, Simon and Schuster, New York.

Rolland, K., Farnill, D., Griffiths, R. (1997), 'Body figure perseptions and eating attitudes among Australian school children aged 8 to 12 years,' *International Journal of Eating Disorders*.

Root, A. and Powers, P. (1983), 'Anorexia nervosa presenting as growth retardation in adolescents', *Journal of Adolescent Health Care* 4, pp. 25–30.

Rosenthal, D. A. and Gold, R. (1989), 'A comparison of Vietnamese-Australian and Anglo-Australian mothers' beliefs about intellectual development', *International Journal of Psychology* 24, pp. 179–93.

Rosner, F. (1969), 'Haemophilia in the Talmud and rabbinic writings', *Annals Of Interactional Medicine* 70, pp. 833–7.

Ross, G. F. (1985), 'Styles of discipline: reported responses to a variety of child behaviours', *Australian Journal of Sex, Marriage and Family* 5, pp. 215–20.

Rossiter, J. (1979), 'TV advertising's general impact on children', *Australian Journal of Early Childhood* 4, pp. 30–1.

Rothman, S. (2001), 'School absence and student background factors: a multilevel analysis', *International Education Journal* 2, pp. 59–68.

Rousseau, J. J. (1914), *Emile on Education*, trans. B.Foxley, Basic Books, New York (first published 1762),

Routh, D. K., Schroeder, C. S. and O'Tuama, L. A. (1974), 'Development of activity level in children', *Developmental Psychology* 10, pp. 163–5.

Routh, D. K., Walton, M. D. and Padan-Belkin, E. (1978), 'Development of activity level in children revisted: effects of mother-presence', *Developmental Psychology* 14, pp. 571–5.

Rowling, J. K. (1999), *Harry Potter and the Philosopher's Stone*, Bloomsbury, London.

Rubin, Z. (1970), 'Measurement of romantic love', *Journal of Personality and Social Psychology* 2, pp. 265–73.

Rubin, Z. (1980), *Children's Friendship*, Fontana, London.

Russel, A. (2000), 'Sex differences in children's relationship learning' in R. Mills and S. Duck (eds), *The Developmental Psychology of Personal Relationships*, John Wiley and Sons, New York.

Russel, A., Aloa, V., Glover, A., Miller, H. and Palmer, G. (1998), 'Sex-based differences in parenting styles in a sample with preschool children', *Australian Journal of Psychology* 50, pp. 89–99.

Russel, A. and Russel, G. (1994), 'Co-parenting early school age children: an examination of mother–father interdependence within families', *Developmental Psychology* 30, pp. 757–70.

Russel, A. and Russel, G. (1992), 'Child effects in socialisation research: some conceptual and data analysis issues', *Social Development* 1, pp. 163–84.

Russel, A. and Saebel, J. (1997), 'Mother–son, mother–daughter, father–son, father–daughter: Are they distinct relationships?' *Developmental Review* 17, pp. 111–47.

Russell, B. (1974), *History of Western Philosophy*, George Allen & Unwin, London.

Russell, G. (1983), 'The father role and its relation to masculinity, femininity and androgyny', *Child Development* 49, pp. 1174–81.

Russell, G. and Wright, I. (1982), *The Changing Role of Fathers*, Australian Early Childhood Resource Booklets, Australian Early Childhood Association, Canberra.

Russell, M. T. and Russell, M. A. (1989), 'Temperamental accident occurrence in children: a pilot study', *Australian Journal of Advanced Nursing* 7, pp. 43–6.

Rutter, M. (1971), 'Parent–child separation: psychological effects on the children', *Journal of Child Psychology and Psychiatry* 12, pp. 233–60.

Rutter, M. (1979), 'Protective factors in children's responses to stress and disadvantage', in M. W. Kent and J. E. Rolf (eds), *Primary Prevention of Psychopathology, vol. 3: Social Competence in Children*, University of New England Press, Hanover, New Hampshire.

Rutter, M. (1983), 'Stress, coping and development: some issues and questions', in N. Garmezy and M. Rutter (eds), *Stress, Coping and Development in Children*, McGraw-Hill, New York.

Rutter, M. (1984), 'Resilient children', *Psychology Today*, March, pp. 57–65.

Rutter, M., Giller, H. and Hagell, A. (1998), *Antisocial Behaviour in Young People*, Cambridge University Press. Cambridge.

Sabatelli, R. M. and Anderson, S. A. (1991), 'Family system dynamics, peer relationships and adolescents' psychological adjustment', *Family Relations* 40, pp. 363–9.

Saint-Exupéry, A. de (1974), *The Little Prince*, William Heinemann, London.

Salinger, J. D. (1958), *The Catcher in the Rye*, Penguin, Harmondsworth.

Salmon, P. (1979), 'The role of the peer group', in J. C. Coleman, *The School Years: Current Issues in the Socialisation of Young People*, Methuen, London.

Sameroff, A. (1982), 'Development and dialect: the need for a systems approach', in W. Collins (ed.), *The Concept of Development: Minnesota Symposium on Child Development*, Lawrence Erlbaum, Hillsdale, New Jersey, vol. 15, pp. 83–103.

Sameroff, A. J. and Chandler, M. (1975), 'Reproductive risk and the continuum of caretaking causality', in F. Horowitz (ed.), *Review of Child Development Research*, vol. 4, Chicago University Press, Chicago, pp. 187–244.

Satir, V. (1964), *Conjoint Family Therapy: a Guide to Therapy and Technique*, Science and Behaviour Book, Palo Alto, California.

Scarr, S. (1985), 'Constructing psychology: making facts and fables for our times', *American Psychologist* 40, pp. 499–512.

Scarr, S. and Kidd, K. K. (1983), 'Developmental behaviour genetics', in M. M. Haith and J. J. Campos (eds), *Handbook of Child Psychology, vol. 2: Infancy and Developmental Psychobiology*, John Wiley, New York.

Scarr, S. and McCartney, K. (1983), 'How people make their own environments: a theory of genotype–environment effects', *Child Development* 54, pp. 424–35.

Scarr-Salapatek, S. (1975), 'Genetics and the development of intelligence', in F. D. Horowitz (ed.), *Review of Child Development Research*, University of Chicago Press, Chicago.

Schachter, S. and Singer, J. E. (1962), 'Cognitive, social and physiological determinants of emotional state', *Psychological Review* 69, pp. 379–99.

Schaffer, R. (1977), 'Mothering', in J. Bruner, M. Cole and B. Lloyd (eds), *The Developing Child*, Harvard University Press, Cambridge, Massachusetts.

Schanchere, K. (1990), 'Attachments between working mothers and their infants: the influence of family processes', *American Journal of Orthopsychiatry* 60, pp. 19–34.

Scheler, M. F. and Carver, C. S. (1992), 'Effects of optimism on psychological well-being: theoretical overview and empirical update', *Cognitive Therapy and Research* 16, pp. 201–28.

Schorsch, A. (1979), *Images of Childhood*, Mayflower Books, New York.

Schulz, T. R. (1998), 'A computational analysis of conservation', *Developmental Science* 1, pp. 103–26.

Schumacher, E. F. (1977), *A Guide for the Perplexed*, Abacus, London.

Schurch, P. and Hopson, E. (1989), *Exploring Diversity: Reflections Ten Years On*, Australian Early Childhood Resource Booklets, Australian Early Childhood Association, Canberra.

Schvaneveldt, J. D., Lindauer, S. L. K. and Young, M. H. (1990), 'Children's understanding of AIDS: a developmental viewpoint', *Family Relations* 39, pp. 330–5.

Schwebel, M. (1982), 'Effects of the nuclear threat on children and teenagers: implications for professionals', *American Journal of Orthopsychiatry* 52, pp. 608–18.

Scott, S., Jackson, S. and Buckett-Milburn, K. B. (1998), 'Swings and roundabouts: risk anxiety and the everyday watch of children', *Sociology* 32, pp. 689–706.

Scraton, P. (1997), (ed), *Childhood in Crisis*, UCL Press, London.

Sebald, H. (1989), 'Adolescents' peer orientations: changes in the support system during the past three decades', *Adolescence* 24, pp. 936–46.

Seligman, M. E. P. (1990), *Learned Optimism*, Pocket Book, New York.

Selman, R. (1976), 'Toward a structural analysis of developing interpersonal relations concepts: research with normal and disturbed pre-adolescent boys', in A. D. Pick (ed.), Minnesota Symposium on Child Psychology, Minneapolis University, Minneapolis.

Selverstone, R. (1989), 'Adolescent sexuality: developing self-esteem and mastering developmental tasks', *SIECUS Report* 18, pp. 1–4.

Selvini-Palazzoli, M., Cecchin, G., Prata, G. and Boscolo, L. (1978), *Paradox and Counter-Paradox*, Jason Aronson, New York.

Selwyn, N. and Bullon, K. (2000) 'Primary school children's use of ICT', *British Journal of Educational Technology* 31, pp. 321–33.

Senechal, M. (1997), 'The differential effect of storybook reading on preschoolers: acquisition of expressive and receptive vocabulary', *Journal of Child Language* 24, pp. 123–38.

Serafica, F. C. and Blyth, D. A. (1985), 'Continuities and changes in the study of friendship and peer groups during early adolescence', *Journal of Early Adolescence* 5, pp. 267–83.

Seyle, H. (1956), *The Stress of Life*, McGraw-Hill, New York.

Seyle, H. (1974), *Stress Without Distress*, J. B. Lippincott, Philadelphia.

Shanahan, M. J., Gulloway, F. J. and Hofer, S. M. (2000), 'Change and constancy in developmental contexts', *International Journal of Behavioural Development* 24, pp. 289–94.

Shantz, C. (1987), 'Conflicts between children', *Child Development* 58, pp. 283–305.

Shantz, D. (1986), 'Conflict, aggression and peer status: an observational study', *Child Development* 57, pp. 1322–32.

Shapiro, J. (1969), *Good Housekeeping Baby Book*, Ebury Press, London.

Shatz, M. and Gelman, R. (1973), 'The development of communication skills: modification in the speech of young children as a function of the listener', *Monographs of the Society for Research in Child Development* 38 (5), no. 152.

Shaughnessy, M. F. (1998), 'An interview with Rita Dunn about learning styles', *The Clearing House* 1, pp. 141–5.

Sheehy, G. (1976), *Passages: Predictable Crises of Adult Life*, Bantam Books, New York.

Sheldon, W. H. (1940), *The Varieties of Human Physique*, Harper, New York.

Shelley, J. D., Lindauer, S. and Young, M. H. (1990), 'Children's understanding of AIDS: a developmental viewpoint', *Family Relations*, July, pp. 330–5.

Sherefsky, P. M. and Yarrow, L. J. (1973), *Psychological Aspects of a First Pregnancy and Early Post Natal Adaption*, Raven Press, New York.

Shute, R. (1998), 'Peer relationships of children with chronic illnesses', in P. T. Slee and K. Rigby (eds) *Children's Peer Relations*, Routledge, London.

Sills, F. D. and Everett, P. W. (1953), 'The relationship of extreme somatotypes to performance in motor and strength tests', *Research Quarterly* 24, pp. 223–8.

Silverman, I. W. and Dubow, E. F. (1991), 'Looking ahead to parenthood: non parents' expectations of themselves and their future children', *Merrill-Palmer Quarterly* 37, pp. 231–50.

Simpson, E. L. (1974), 'Moral development research: a case study of cultural bias', *Human Development* 17, pp. 81–106.

Simpson, S. (2000), 'Dyslexia: a developmental language disorder', *Child, Health and Development* 27, pp. 13–22.

Sinclair, D. (1985), *Human Growth after Birth*, 4th edn, Oxford University Press, Oxford.

Singer, P., Kuhse, H. and Singer, C. (1983), 'The treatment of newborn infants with major handicaps: a survey of obstetricians and paediatricians in Victoria', *Medical Journal Australia* 2, pp. 274–8.

Sison, G. F. P. (1985), 'M*A*S*H*: an illustration of Kohlberg's stages of moral development', *Journal of Humanistic Psychology* 25, pp. 83–90.

Skiba, R. J. and Deno, S. L. (1991), 'Terminology and behaviour reduction: the case against "punishment"', *Exceptional Children* 1, pp. 298–312.

Skinner, B. F. (1948), *Walden Two*, Macmillan, New York.

Skinner, B. F. (1957), *Verbal Behaviour*, Appleton-Century-Crofts, New York.

Skinner, B. F. (1971), *Beyond Freedom and Dignity*, Jonathan Cape, New York.

Skinner, B. F. (1974), *About Behaviourism*, Knopf, New York.

Skinner, B. F. (1979), 'My experience with the baby-tender', *Psychology Today*, March, pp. 29–40.

Slee, P. T. (1983), 'Mother–infant vocal interaction as a function of emotional expression', *Early Child Development and Care* 11, pp. 33–45.

Slee, P. T. (1986a), 'The relation of temperament and other factors to children's adjustment to kindergarten', *Child Psychiatry and Human Development* 17, pp. 104–12.

Slee, P. T. (1986b), 'A study of children's adjustment to kindergarten', *Australian Journal of Early Childhood* 11, pp. 24–8.

Slee, P. T. (1987), *Child Observation Skills*, Croom Helm, Beckenham, Kent.

Slee, P. T. (1990), 'The nature of children's conflict resolution styles', *Children Australia* 15, pp. 10–11.

Slee, P. T. and Cross, D. G. (1988), 'Children's and adolescents' fears and the threat of nuclear war: an Australian study', *Australian Child and Family Welfare* 13, pp. 15–17.

Slee, P. T. and Cross, D. G. (1989), 'Living in the nuclear age: an Australian study of children's and adolescents' fears', *Child Psychiatry and Human Development* 4, pp. 28–34.

Slee, P. T. and Cross, D. G. (1990), 'A comparative study of mother and child characteristics in families of normal and behaviour problem children', *Australian Journal of Early Childhood* 15, pp. 36–41.

Slee, P. T., Owens, L. D., Flaherty, J. and Laybourne, A. (1997), 'Managing pupil behaviour', in L. Logan and J, Sachs (eds) *Meeting the Challenges of Primary Schooling in the 1990s*, Allen & Unwin, Sydney.

Slee, P. T. and Rigby, K. (1993), 'The relationship of Eysenck's personality factors and self esteem to bully–victim behaviour in Australian schools', *Journal of Personality and Individual Differences* 14, pp. 371–3.

Smith, P. K., Morita, Y., Yunger-tas, J., Olweus, D., Catalano, R. and Slee, P. (1999), (eds), *The Nature of Bullying: A Cross-National Perspective*, Routledge, London.

Smith, P.K. (ed.), *Violence in Schools: The Response from Europe*, Routledge, London.

Smyth, T. R., Johnston, O., Short, H. and Crawford, J. (1991), 'The South Australian motor screening test: an evaluation', *Australian Journal of Early Childhood* 16, pp. 33–7.

Sommerland, E. A. and Bellingham, W. P. (1972), 'Cooperation–competition: a comparison of Australian European and Aboriginal school children', *Journal of Cross-Cultural Psychology* 3, pp. 149–57.

Sontag, S. (1966), *The Benefactor*, Panther, New York.

Sorokin, Y. and Dierker, L. J. (1982), 'Fetal movement', *Clinical Obstetrics and Gynaecology* 25, pp. 719–34.

South Australian Child Protection Council (1989), *Reporting Child Abuse*, South Australian Child Protection Council.

Spender, D. (1989), *Invisible Women: the Schooling Scandal*, Women's Press, London.

Spitz, R. (1954), 'Unhappy and fatal outcomes of emotional deprivation and stress in infancy', in I. Galdstone (ed.), *Beyond the Germ Theory*, Health Education Council, London.

Spock, B. (1955), *Baby and Child Care*, Bodley Head, London.

Spock, B. (1979), *Baby and Child Care*, rev. edn, Bodley Head, London.

Sroufe, L. A. (1979), 'Socioemotional development', in J. D. Osofsky (ed.), *Handbook of Infant Development*, Wiley, New York.

Sroufe, L. A. (1983), 'Individual patterns of adaption from infancy to preschool', in M. Perlmutter (ed.), *Minnesota Symposium on Child Psychiatry*, vol. 16, Lawrence Erlbaum, Hillsdale, New Jersey.

Stacey, M., Dearden, R., Pill, R. and Robinson, D. (1970), *Hospitals, Children and their Families*, Routledge and Kegan Paul, London.

Stafford-Clark, D. (1971), *What Freud Really Said*, Penguin Books, Harmondsworth, UK.

Stamp, G. E., Williams, A. S., and Crowther, C. A. (1996), 'Predicting postnatal depression among pregnant women', *Birth* 23, pp. 218–23.

Stanislavski, C. (1948), *An Actor Prepares*, Theatre Art Books, New York.

Stern, D. N. (1977), *The First Relationship: Infant and Mother*, Fontana, London.

Sternberg, R. J. (1985), *Beyond IQ: a Triadic Theory of Human Intelligence*, Cambridge University Press, New York.

Sternberg, R. J. (1992), 'Ability tests, measurements and markets', *Journal of Educational Psychology* 84, pp. 134–41.

Sternberg, R. J. (2000), *Handbook of Intelligence*, Cambridge University Press, New York.

Sternberg, R. and Grigorenko, E. L. (1999), 'Myths in psychology and education regarding the gene-environment debate', *Teacher College Record* 100, pp. 537–53.

Stevens, G. and Gardner, S. (1982), *The Women of Psychology, vol. 2: Expansion and Refinement*, Schenkman, Cambridge, Massachusetts.

Stone, J., Smith, H. and Murphy, L. (1973), *The Competent Infant*, Basic Books, New York.

Storer, D. (1985), *Ethnic Family Values in Australia*, Prentice-Hall, Sydney.

Stott, D. H., McDermott, P. A, Green, L. F and Francis, J. M. (1988), *Learning Behaviours Scale and the Study of Children's Learning Behaviours: Research Education Manual*, The Psychological Corporation, San Antonio.

Strauss, E. (1966), *Phenomenological Psychology*, Tavistock Andover.

Sullivan, H. S. (1953), *The Interpersonal Theory of Psychiatry*, Norton, New York.

Svendson, M. (1934), 'Children's imaginary companions', *Archives of Neurological Psychiatry* 32, pp. 985–99.

Svyantek, D. J. and Brown, L. L. (2000), 'A complex systems approach to organisations', *Current Directions in Psychological Science* 9, pp. 69–74.

Swearingen, E. M. and Cohen, L. H. (1985), 'Measurement of adolescents' life events: the Junior High School Life Experiences Survey', *American Journal of Community Psychology* 13, pp. 69–85.

Sylva, K., Sammons, P., Melhuish, E. C., S-Blatchford, I. and Taggart, B. (1999), 'The effective provision of pre-school education project', *Technical paper 6*, London Institute of Education, DTEE.

Tamis-Lemonda, C. S., Bornstein, M. C., Kahana-Kalman, R., Baumwell, L., Cyphers, L. (1998), 'Predicting variation in the timing of language milestones in the second year: an events-history approach', *Journal of Child Language* 25, pp. 675–700.

Tanner, J. M. (1970), 'Physical growth', in P. H. Mussen (ed.), *Carmichael's Manual of Child Psychology*, 3rd edn, vol. 1, Wiley, New York.

Tanner, J. M. (1973), 'Trends towards earlier menarche in London, Oslo, Copenhagen, the Netherlands and Hungary', *Nature* 243, May, pp. 95–6.

Taylor, H. J. (1980), *The IQ Game: a Methodological Inquiry into the Heredity–Environment Controversy*, Rutgers University Press, New Brunswick.

Taylor, M. (1999), *Imaginary Companions and Children Who Create Them*. Oxford Universty Press, New York.

Taylor, T. and Toohey, K. (1998), 'Perspectives on sport: Voices of women from non-English speaking backgrounds', *ACHPER Healthy Lifestyles Journal*, 45, pp. 5–9.

Teo, T. (1997), 'Developmental psychology and the relevance of critical metatheoretical reflection', *Human Development* 40, pp. 195–210.

Teo, T. (1999), 'Functions of knowledge in psychology', *New Ideas in Psychology* 17, pp. 1–15.

'The HIV/AIDS epidemic: toward a New Zealand Strategy. A policy discussion paper', *New Zealand Journal of Health, Physical Education and Recreation* 22, pp. 9–12.

Thelen, E. (2000), 'Motor development as foundation and future of developmental psychology', *International Journal of Behavioural Development* 24, pp. 385–97.

Thelen, E. and Smith, L. B. (1994), *A Dynamic Systems Approach to the Development of Cognition and Action*, MIT Press, Cambridge MA.

Thomas, A. and Chess, S. (1977), *Temperament and Development*, Bruner Muzel Publications, New York.

Thomas, A., Chess, S. and Birch, H. G., (1969), *Temperament and Behaviour Disorders in Children*, New York University Press, New York.

Thomas, A., Chess, S., Birch, H. G., Hertzig, M. E. and Koin, S. (1963), *Behavioural Individuality in Early Childhood*, New York Universities, New York.

Thompson, R. A. (1990), 'Vulnerability in research: a developmental perspective on research risk', *Child Development* 61, pp. 1–16.

Thompson, R. A. and Nolan, C. A. (2001), 'Developmental science and the media', *American Psychologist*, pp. 5–15.

Thomson, N. (1990), 'A review of Aboriginal health status', in J. Reid and P. Trompf, *The Health of Aboriginal Australia*, Harcourt Brace Jovanovich, Sydney, pp. 37–79.

Thoreau, D. (1960), *Walden and Civil Disobedience*, A Signet Classic, New York.

Thorndike, R. L., Hagen, E. P. and Sattler, J. M. (1986), *Stanford-Binet Intelligence Test*, 4th edn, Riverside Publishing Company.

Tiggeman, M. and Dyer, G. (1995), 'Ideal body shape preferences and eating disorder scores in adolescent women', *Psychology and Health* 10, pp. 345–7.

Tizard, B. (1984), 'Problematic aspects of nuclear education', *Harvard Educational Review* 54, pp. 271–81.

Tizard, B. (1986), 'Can children face the future?', *New Society*, September, pp. 11–13.

Tolan, P. H. (1990) (ed.), *Multi-Systemic Structural–Strategic Interventions for Child and Adolescent Behavioural Problems*, Hawarth Press, New York.

Tolan, P. H., Cromwell, R. E. and Brasswell, M. (1986), 'Family therapy with delinquents', *Family Process* 25, pp. 619–50.

Tolan, P. H. and Mitchell, M. E. (1989), 'Families and the therapy of antisocial delinquent behaviour', in Tolan, P. H. (ed.), *Multi-Systemic Structural–Strategic Interventions for Child and Adolescent Behavioural Problems*, Hawarth Press, New York.

Tolman, E. C. (1932), *Purposive Behaviour in Animals and Man*, Appleton, New York.

Torgenson, A. M. and Kringlen, E. (1978), 'Genetic aspects of temperamental differences in infants: a study of same-sexed twins', *Journal American Academy Child Psychiatry* 17, pp. 433–44.

Tortora, G. J. and Anagnostakos, N. P. (1987), *Principles of Anatomy and Physiology*, Harper and Row, New York.

Townsend, M. A. R., McCracken, H. E. and Wilton, K. M. (1988), 'Popularity and intimacy as determinants of psychological well-being in adolescent friendships', *Journal of Early Adolescence* 8 (4), pp. 421–36.

Townsend, S. (1985), *The Secret Diary of Adrian Mole age 13¾*, Methuen, London.

Trevarthen, C. (1977), *Communication and Cooperation in Early Infancy: a Description of Primary Intersubjectivity*, Cambridge University Press, London.

Tripodi, T. (1981), 'The logic of research design', in R. M. Grinnel (ed.), *Social Work Research and Evaluation*, Peacock, Itasca, Illinois.

Trower, P., Bryant, B. and Argyle, M. (1978), *Social Skills and Mental Health*, Methuen, London.

Troy, M. and Sroufe, L.A. (1987), 'Victimisation among pre-schoolers: role of attachment relationship history', *American Academy Child and Adolescent Psychiatry* 26, pp. 166–72.

Turtle, A. M., Ford, B., Habgood, R., Grant, M., Bekiaris, J., Constantinou, C., Macek, M. and Polyzoidis, H. (1989), 'AIDS-related beliefs and behaviours of Australian university students', *Medical Journal of Australia* 150, pp. 371–5.

Valentine, G. (1996), 'Children should be seen and not heard? The roles of children in public space', *Urban Geography* 17, pp. 205–20.

Vance, A. L. A. and Luk, E. S. L. (2000), 'Attention deficit hyperactivity disorder: current progress and controversies', *Australian and New Zealand Journal of Psychiatry*, 34, pp. 719–30.

Vandell, D. L. (2000), 'Parents, peer groups and other socialising influences', *Developmental Psychology* 36, pp. 699–710.

Vandell, D. L. and Mueller, E. C. (1980), 'Peer play and friendships during the first two years', in H. C. Foot, A. J. Chapman and J. R. Smith (eds), *Friendship and Social Relations in Children*, Wiley, New York.

Van Der Veer, R. (1986), 'Vygotsky's developmental psychology', *Psychological Reports* 59, pp. 527–36.

Van Eflen, S. (1999), 'Students' motivational beliefs about personal academic success: Are there cultural differences?' *Journal of Educational Psychology* 90, pp. 621–9.

Van Geert, P. (2000), 'The dynamics of general developmental mechanisms: from Piaget and Vygotsky to dynamic systems models', *Current Directions in Psychological Science* 2, pp. 64–8.

Vernon, M. D. (1974), *The Psychology of Perception*, Penguin, Harmondsworth, UK.

Vescio, J. A., Taylor, T. and Toohey, K. (1999), 'An exploration of sports participation of girls from non-English speaking backgrounds', *ACHPER Healthy Lifestyles Journal*, 47, pp. 14–19.

Viadero, D. (1988), 'Corporal punishment', *Education Week* 1, pp. 38–9.

Viaro, M. (1985), 'Giochi interattiva familiari e terepia individuale', *Terapia Familiale* 19, pp. 85–93.

Viney, L. (1985), 'Editorial', *Australian Psychologist* 20, pp. 1–2.

Violato, C. and Wiley, A.J . (1990), 'Images of adolescence in English literature: the middle ages to the modern period', *Adolescence* 25, pp. 253–64.

Vygotsky, L. S. (1978), 'The pre-history of written language', in M. Cole, V. John-Steiner, S. Scribner and E. Souberman (eds), *Mind in Society: the Development of Higher Psychological Processes*, Harvard University Press, Cambridge, Massachusetts.

Vygotsky, L. S. (1984), 'Sobranie socinenjii', *Detskaja psichologija*, Pedagogika, Moscow.

Vygotsky, L. (1988), *Thought and Language*, The MIT Press, Cambridge, Massachusetts.

Vyuk, R. (1981), *Overview and Critique of Piaget's Genetic Epistemology, 1965–1980*, Academic Press, London.

Wachtel, E. F. (1990), 'The child as an individual: a resource for systemic change', *Journal of Strategic and Family Therapies* 9, pp. 50–8.

Waddington, C. H. (1957), *The Strategy of the Genes*, Unwin and Hyman, London.

Wadsworth, Y. (1987), *Do It Yourself Social Research*, Victorian Council of Social Service, Allen & Unwin, Sydney.

Wainwright, A. (unpub.), Children's Perceptions of and Affective Resources to Death, MEd thesis, University of New South Wales, 1980.

Wakely, A., Rivera, S. and Langer, J. (2000), 'Can young infants add and subtract?' *Child Development* 71, pp. 1525–4.

Walberg, H. (1984), 'Improving the productivity of America's schools', *Educational Leadership* 41, pp. 19–27.

Waldenstrom, U., Borg, I. M., Olsson, B., Skold, M. and Wall, S. (1996), 'The childbirth experience: A study of 295 new mothers', *Birth*, 23, pp. 142–7.

Walker, C. E. (1978), 'Toilet training, enuresis and encopresis', in P. R. Magrub (ed.), *Psychological Management of Pediatric Problems*, vol. 1, University Park Press, New York, pp. 129–89.

Wallerstein, J. S. and Kelly, J. B. (1980), *Surviving the Break-Up: How Children and Parents Cope with Divorce*, Basic Books, New York.

Wallon, P. and Baudoin, C. (1990), 'A new criterion in the assessment of the behaviour of the drawing child', *British Journal of Educational Psychology* 60, pp. 338–48.

Warton, P. W. (2000), 'Australian mothers' views about responsibility for homework in primary school', *Research in Education* 59, pp. 50–7.

Watson, J. B. (1930), *Behaviourism*, 2nd edn, Norton, New York.

Watson, J. B. and Rayner, R. (1920), 'Conditioned emotional reactions', *Journal Experimental Psychology* 3, pp. 1–14.

Watson, J. D. and Crick, F. H. (1953), 'Molecular structure of nucleic acids', *Nature* 171, pp. 737–8.

Watson, J. P., Elliott, S. A., Rug, A. J. and Brough, D. I. (1984), 'Psychiatric disorder in pregnancy and the first postnatal year', *British Journal of Psychiatry* 144, pp. 453–62.

Watts, B. H. (1982), 'Determination of school success', in M. K. Browne and L. E. Foster (eds), *Sociology of Australian Education: a Book of Readings*, 3rd edn, Macmillan, Melbourne.

Wearing, J. J. and James, D. (1985), 'The adolescent peer group re-visited in the 1990s', *Australian Journal of Sex, Marriage and Family* 6, pp. 143–53.

Webster-Stratton, C. (1983), 'Intervention approaches to conduct disorders in young children', *Nurse Practitioner* 8, pp. 23–4.

Webster-Stratton, C. (1989), 'The relationship of mental support, conflict and divorce to parent perceptions, behaviours and childhood conduct problems', *Journal of Marriage and the Family* 51, pp. 417–30.

Webster-Stratton, C., Kolpacoff, M. and Hollinsworth, T. (1988), 'Self administered videotape therapy for families with conduct problem children: comparison with two cost-effective treatments and a control group', *Journal of Consulting and Clinical Psychology* 56, pp. 558–66.

Wechsler, D. (1974), *Manual for the Wechsler Intelligence Scale for Children*, rev. edn, The Psychological Corporation, Harcourt Brace Jovanovich, San Antonio, Texas.

Wechsler, D., *The Wechsler Intelligence Scale for Children*, 3rd edn, The Psychological Corporation, Sydney, 1991.

Weininger, O. (1979), 'Young children's acceptance of dying and death', *Psychological Reports* 44, pp. 395–407.

Wekselman, K., Spiering, K., Hetteberg, C., Kenner, C., and Flandermeyer, A. (1995), 'Fetal alcohol syndrome from infancy through childhood: a review of the literature', *Journal of Pediatric Nursing* 10, pp. 296–303.

Wells, W. D. and Siegal, B. (1961), 'Stereotyped somatotypes', *Psychological Reports* 8, pp. 77–8.

Wenestam, C.-G. (1984), 'Qualitative age-related differences in the meaning of the word "death" to children', *Death Education* 8, pp. 333–47.

Werner, C. (1982), 'Developmental psychopathology: its nature and models', *Journal of Clinical Child Psychology* 3, pp. 192–201.

Werner, E. E. (1989), 'Children of the garden island', *Scientific American*, April, pp. 76–81.

Wertheimer, M. (1962), 'Psychomotor coordination of auditory-visual space at birth', *Science* 1961, p. 134.

Wertsch, J. and Youniss, J. (1987), 'Contextualising the investigator: the case of developmental psychology', *Human Development* 30, pp. 18–31.

Wetzel, S. K. (1982), 'Are we ignoring the needs of the women with spontaneous abortion?', *Maternal Care Nursing* 7, pp. 258–9.

White, M. (1983), 'Anorexia nervosa: a transgenerational system perspective', *Family Process* 22, pp. 255–73.

White, M. (1986), 'Negative explanation restraint and double description: a template for family therapy', *Family Process* 25, pp. 169–84.

White, M. and Epston, D. (1989), *Literate Means to Therapeutic Ends*, Dulwich Centre Publications, Adelaide.

Whitely, B. E. (1983), 'Sex-role orientation and self esteem: a critical meta-analytic review', *Journal of Personality and Society Psychology* 44, pp. 765–78.

Whitmire, K. A. (2000), 'Adolescence as a developmental phase', *Topics in Language Disorders* 20, pp. 1–12.

Wicks, J. (1987), *The Heart Foundation of Australia*, Australian Government Printer, Canberra.

Wilde, O. (1988), *The Selfish Giant*, Puffin Books, Harmondsworth, UK.

Wildermuth, N. L. (1990), 'Loneliness in adolescence: why it occurs and what to do about it', in P. C. L. Heaven and V. J. Callan, *Adolescence: an Australian Perspective*, Harcourt Brace Jovanovich, Sydney, pp. 255–70.

Wilks, J. and Callan, V. J. (1990), 'Adolescents and alcohol', in P. C. L. Heavan and V. J. Callan, *Adolescence: an Australian Perspective*, Harcourt Brace Jovanovich, Sydney, pp. 198–213.

Williams, A. (1989), 'Equal opportunities and primary school physical education', *British Journal of Physical Education* 20, pp. 177–9.

Williams, C. K. and Kamii, C. (1986), 'How do children learn by handling knowledge?', *Young Children*, November, pp. 23–6.

Williams, J. K. (1986), 'Genetic counseling in paediatric nursing care', *Paediatric Nursing* 12, pp. 287–90.

Williams, J. M. and Dunlop, L. C. (1999), 'Pubertal timing and self reported delinquency among male adolescence', *Journal of Adolescence* 22, pp. 157–71.

Williams, J. M. and Currie, C. (2000), 'Self esteem and physical development in early adolescence: pubertal timing and body image', *Journal of Early Adolescence* 20, 129–49.

Williams, L. R. T., McNaughton, D. M. and Mann, G. M. (1989), 'Personality and physique of female physical education students', *New Zealand Journal of Health, Physical Education and Recreation* 2, pp. 6–8.

Willingham, W. W. and Cole, N. S. (1997), *Gender and Fair Assessment*, Erlbaum, Hillsdale New Jersey.

Wilson, G. T. and Fairbairn, C. G. (1998), 'Treatments for eating disorders', in P. E. Nathan and J. M. Gorman (eds) *A Guide to Treatments that Work*, Oxford University Press, New York.

Windshuttle, K. (1979), *Unemployment*, Penguin, Ringwood.

Winnicott, D. W. (1964), *The Child, the Family and the Outside World*, Pelican, Harmondsworth.

Winnicott, D. W. (1971), *Playing and Reality*, Penguin, Harmondsworth.

Wishart, J. (1990), 'Cognitive factors related to user involvement with computer and their effects upon learning from an educational computer game', *Computers and Education*, 15, pp. 145–50.

Wohlwill, J. F. (1973), *The Study of Behavioural Development*, Academic Press, New York.

Wolfenstein, M. (1954), *Children's Humor: a Psychological Analysis*, Free Press, Glencoe, Illinois.

Wollett, A., White, D. and Lyon, L. (1982), 'Observations of fathers at birth', in N. Beail and J. McGuire (eds), *Fathers, Psychological Perspectives*, Junction Books, London.

Wollheim, R. (1974), *Freud: a Collection of Critical Essays*, Doubleday Anchor Books, USA.

Wood, A. (1988), 'King tiger and the roaring tummies: a novel way of helping young children and their families change', *Journal of Family Therapy* 10, pp. 49–63.

Wood, D. (1988), *How Children Think and Learn*, Basil Blackwell, Oxford.

Wood, D., Wood, H. A. and Middleton, D. J. (1978), 'An experimental evaluation of four face-to-face teaching strategies', *International Journal of Behavioural Development* 1, pp. 131–47.

Woodgate, R. and Kristjanson, L. J. (1996), '"Getting better from my hurts": toward a model of the young child's pain experience', *Journal of Pediatric Nursing* 11, pp. 233–42.

Woods, J. R. and Esposito, J. L. (eds) (1987), *Pregnancy Loss: Medical Therapeutics and Practical Considerations*, Williams and Wilkins, New York.

Wright, J. and Dewar, A. (1997), 'On pleasure and pain: Women speak out about physical activity', in G. Clarke and B. Humberstone (eds.) *Researching Women, Sport and Physical Education*, London, MacMillan, pp. 80–95.

Wright, J. D. and Pearl, L. (1995), 'Knowledge and experience of young people regarding drug misuse, 1969–94', *British Medical Journal* 309, pp. 309–10.

Wyness, M. (2000), *Contesting Childhood*, Falmer Press, London.

Yarrow, L. J., Rubenstein, J. L. and Pedersen, F. A. (1975), *Infant and Environment: Early Cognitive and Motivational Development*, Halsted, New York.

Yates, G. C. R. (1988), 'Classroom research into effective teaching', *Australian Journal of Remedial Education* 20, pp. 4–9.

Yates, G. C. R. and Yates, S. M. (1990), 'Teacher effectiveness research – towards describing user-friendly classroom instruction', *Educational Psychology* 10, pp. 225–38.

Yates, S. M., Yates, G. C. R. and Lippett, R. M. (1995), 'Explanatary style, ego orientation and primary school mathematics achievement', *Educational Psychology*, 15, pp. 23–34.

Yeaworth, R., York, J., Hussey, M., Ingle, M. and Goodwin, T. (1980), 'The development of an adolescent life change events scale', *Adolescence* 15, pp. 91–7.

Young, K. T. (1990), 'American conceptions of infant development from 1955 to 1984: what the experts are telling parents', *Child Development* 61, pp. 17–28.

Young, R. (1981), 'A study of teacher epistemologies', *Australian Journal of Education* 25, pp. 194–208.

Zigler, E., Levine, J. and Gould, L. (1967), 'Cognitive processes in the development of children's appreciation of humour', *Child Development* 37, pp. 507–18.

Zimmer, E. Z., Divon, M. Y., Vilensky, A., Sarna, Z., Peretz, B. A. and Paldi, E. (1982), 'Maternal exposure to music and fetal activity', *European Journal Obstetrics Gynaecological Reproductive Biology* 13, pp. 209–13.

Zion, A. B. (1988), 'Resources for infertile couples', *Journal of Obstetric, Gynecological and Neonatal Nursing*, July/August, pp. 255–8.

Zola, E. (1979 edn), *Germinal*, translated by L. Tancock, Penguin Books, Harmondsworth (first published 1885).

Zubrick, S. R., Silburn, S. R., Burton, P. and Blair, E. (2000), 'Mental health disorders in children and young people: scope, cause and prevention', *Australian and New Zealand Journal of Psychiatry* 34, pp. 570–8.

Zuckerman, B. S. and Frank, D. A. (1983), 'Infancy', in M. D. Levine, W. B. Carey, A. C. Crocker and R. T. Gross (eds), *Developmental Behavioural Paediatrics*, W. B. Saunders, New York, pp. 80–96.

INDEX

Page references followed by *fig* indicate a figure; page references followed by *tab* indicate a table.

STUDENT FEEDBACK FORM

Child, Adolescent and Family Development
By Phillip T. Slee

We have taken a great deal of care to ensure that this textbook is written, edited and published to the very highest standards. But there may be elements of the book that we could improve to make it better, so we value your feedback.

Please take the time to fill in this form and return it to us. You can either send us an email to info@cambridge.edu.au and address it 'To the Academic Marketing Department', or you can fax us on (03) 9676 9955.

---

1. Did you buy this book, or borrow it from a library?

2. Are you using the book as the main prescribed textbook for your course?

3. What is the name of the course for which you use this text?

4. At what type of institution are you studying?
   _____ university
   _____ college
   _____ TAFE
   _____ other (please specify)

5. Have you used most of the book in your course?

6. If not, how much of the book have you used?

7. What are the most useful parts of the book or CD for your course?

8. What elements of the book or CD do you like the best?

9. What elements of the book or CD do you not like?

10. Is the language used by the author easy to understand?

11. Have you any suggestions for improvement?

12. Will you keep this book for later reference, or do you think you will sell it?

Feel free to photocopy this page.

LaVergne, TN USA
12 July 2010

189124LV00003BA/1/P